ISBN: 9781290497565

Published by:
HardPress Publishing
8345 NW 66TH ST #2561
MIAMI FL 33166-2626

Email: info@hardpress.net
Web: http://www.hardpress.net

THE

LIFE AND ADVENTURES

OF

VALENTINE VOX

THE VENTRILOQUIST.

BY HENRY COCKTON,

AUTHOR OF

"GEORGE ST. GEORGE JULIAN, THE PRINCE."

WITH NUMEROUS ILLUSTRATIONS

By Phiz.

UNI ÆQUUS VIRTUTI.

PHILADELPHIA:

CAREY AND HART.

1841.

T. K. & P. G. COLLINS, Printers,
No. 1 Lodge Alley.

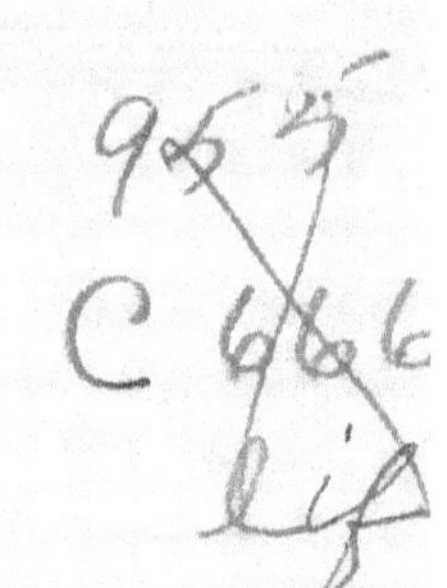

PREFACE.

"THE power of an accomplished Ventriloquist is well known to be unlimited. There is no scene in life in which that power is incapable of being developed: it gives its possessor a command over the actions, the feelings, the passions of men, while its efficacy in loading with ridicule every prejudice and every project of which the tendency is pernicious cannot fail to be perceived at a glance. The design of this work, although essentially humorous, is not, however, to excite peals of laughter alone: it has a far higher object in view, namely, that of removing social absurdities and abuses by means the most peculiarly attractive and pleasing."

This formed the prospectus of VALENTINE VOX; and that the design has been to a considerable extent satisfactorily carried out, the popularity which the work has acquired in the course of its publication in monthly parts may be held to be some proof.

There is, however, one monstrous system, the pernicious, the dreadful operation of which has been, if not vividly, truthfully portrayed—a system teeming with secret cruelties and horrors—I mean the system of private Lunatic Asylums—to which it will be needful for me here to refer, lest the scenes which have been described be considered too terrible either to occur in the present day, or to have indeed any foundation in fact. I will mention no particular case, I will allude to no particular asylum: I will go at once to the *system* under which men—sane men—can at any time be seized, gagged, manacled, and placed beyond the pale of the constitution, within the walls of an asylum, there to be incarcerated for life, with no society save that of poor idiots and raving maniacs, shut out for ever from the world as completely as if they were not in existence, without the power of communicating with a single friend, or of receiving from a single friend the slightest communication.

The Act by which Private Asylums are governed, viz: the 9 Geo. 4, cap. 41,—is intituled, *An Act to regulate the Care and Treatment of Insane Persons in England;* but were it called *An Act to facilitate the perpetual imprisonment of perfectly sane persons, with the view of promoting the unhallowed designs of the sordid and the malicious,* its effect would be better declared: for it is an Act, essentially an Act, for the promotion of such objects as those which avarice and malignity may, under certain circumstances, prompt, seeing that under it fathers may be incarcerated by sons, and sons by fathers: sisters by brothers, and brothers by sisters: children by parents: wives by husbands, and husbands by wives, when the object proposed is either adultery, the dishonest possession of property, the prevention of what are termed imprudent matches, or the foul gratification of revenge.

The personal liberty of no man is safe. Any one may in a moment be seized, manacled, and beaten into a state of insensibility, and carried away, without the power of appealing to any tribunal, without the most remote prospect of being able to let any friend know where he is. He is gone: completely lost to the world: those who were dear to him are led to believe that he is dead, and dead he is to society for ever. All that is required to authorize the perpetual imprisonment of a man under the Act is a certificate signed by two medical practitioners—who may be either physicians, surgeons, or apothecaries, they are not at all particular under the Act—or one will do, if two cannot at the time be conveniently procured, should any "special circumstance exist," and anything may be called a special circumstance—the signature of one apothecary—no matter how young, how inexperienced, or how ignorant he may be—is sufficient to consign either a man, woman, or child to a Lunatic Asylum for life.

During the progress of this work I have been apprehensive that my statements on this point might be deemed exaggerations; it is hence that I embrace this opportunity of showing that in illustrating this terrible subject, I have neither departed from facts nor exaggerated those facts in the smallest degree.

By the thirtieth section of the Act to which I have alluded, it is provided, "That every certificate upon which any order shall be given for the confinement of any person (not a parish patient) in a house kept for the reception of two or more insane persons, shall be signed by two medical practitioners, each of them being a physician, surgeon, or apothecary, who shall have separately visited and personally examined the patient to whom it relates; and such certificate shall state that such insane person is a proper person to be confined, and the day on which he or she shall have been so examined; and also the Christian and surname and place of abode of the person by whose direction or authority such person is examined, and the degree of relationship or other circumstance of connection between such person and the insane person; and the name, age, place of residence, former occupation, and the asylum, if any, in which such patient shall have been confined; and whether such person shall have been found lunatic or of unsound mind under a commission issued for that purpose by the Lord Chancellor, or Lord Keeper or Commissioner of the Great Seal intrusted as aforesaid; and every such certificate for the confinement of any person in a house licensed under this Act within the jurisdiction of the said visitors shall, if the same be not signed by two medical practitioners, state the special circumstances, if any, which shall have prevented the patient being separately visited by two medical practitioners; and any patient may be admitted into any such licensed house upon the certificate of one medical practitioner only, under the special circumstances aforesaid, provided such certificate shall be further signed by some other medical practitioner within seven days next after the admission of such patient into any such licensed house as aforesaid; and any person who shall, knowingly and with intention to deceive, sign any such certificate, untruly setting forth any such particulars required by this Act, shall be deemed guilty of a misdemeanour; nevertheless, if any special circumstance shall exist which may prevent the insertion of any of the particulars aforesaid, the same shall be specially stated in such certificate: provided always, that no physician, surgeon, or apothecary shall sign any certificate of admission to any house of reception for two or more insane persons, of which he is wholly or partly the proprietor, or the regular professional attendant; and any physician, surgeon, or apothecary, who shall sign or give any such certificate, without having visited and personally examined the individual to whom it relates, shall be deemed to be guilty of a misdemeanour."

What then is it necessary for a bad man to do whose object is to incarcerate any relative or friend whom he is anxious to put out of the way for ever? He has but to bribe a disreputable apothecary—and, unhappily, there are many in the profession who, for the fee of a guinea, have signed, and who are ready again to sign away the liberty of any man, pleading to their own consciences, perhaps, like Shakspeare's apothecary, that their poverty, and not their will, consents—he has but to bribe one of these men to certify that the victim is insane—or if he knows not one of these, he need but excite his victim, and call in any other medical man to see him, while in a state of excitement, and to declare as a "special circumstance," that he has just been attempting to commit suicide, or to do himself some grievous mischief, when the very energy with which he will deny the imputation, will tend to convince him who has been summoned expressly to see a madman, that he is mad—and when the certificate is signed, the proprietor of an asylum has but to be applied to, when keepers will be despatched to secure the victim, and the facility with which a second signature can be obtained in such a case is proverbial.

In Acts of Parliament penalties look very well, and appear *prima facie* to be very efficient: thus in this Act it seems to be a security against malpractices, that, "any person who shall knowingly, and with intention to deceive, sign any such certificate untruly setting forth any such particulars required by this Act, shall be deemed guilty of a misdemeanour;" but how is the guilt of such person to be proved? These things are done in secret; the victim is doomed, seized, hurried away, and confined, without having the power to offer a particle of proof or a moment's opportunity of appealing against this decision, which is rendered thereby final. But if even he should have such an opportunity—if by a miracle he should escape—how can he prove the misdemeanour? The medical man who possesses this monstrous power is licensed to act upon his judgment: he pleads that to the best of his judgment the man was insane: he is thereby protected. That license indemnifies him; his signature indemnifies the man who employed him, and that man's authority indemnifies the proprietor of the asylum in which the victim is confined: and this too in a country whose free institutions form its proudest boast—in England, the centre, the very heart of civilization.

Look at the position of the proprietor of a private Lunatic Asylum.

It is with him a pecuniary speculation. He may be an honourable man —he may be—but look at the temptations to dishonour with which the system is pregnant. His object is to obtain as many patients as he can, and to keep those patients as long as he can: his manifest duty is therefore diametrically opposed to his interest, and when it is so, experience proves it to be unsafe, to say the least of it, to give a man impunity, and trust to his honour. It is his duty, when he finds that a patient is sane, to restore him to society: his interest prompts him to keep that patient, because the sum which he receives, either weekly or quarterly, from the person at whose instance that patient has been confined, of course ceases to be paid on his being discharged. It is his duty, when the commissioners visit the asylum, to give every patient a fair opportunity of proving that he is of sound mind: his interest prompts him not only to misrepresent the actions of every sane patient, but to excite him by administering drugs or otherwise, in order that he may appear to the commissioners to be insane. So also is it his duty, when his patients are really insane, to do all in his power to cure them, while it is to his interest to keep them till death, by repudiating those means by which a cure might be effected. As far, therefore, as insane persons are concerned, the system of private asylums is pernicious, for interest will govern the actions of men in the aggregate; it will trample down duty, it will be in the ascendant; but looking at the operation of that system upon persons who are absolutely sane, it is monstrous that a power should exist which places every man in a position to be deprived of liberty for life, for the pure gratification of private avarice or revenge.

As far as regards the statement that men can be incarcerated for life without any friend or relative disposed to assist them having the slightest knowledge of where they are, it may be urged that on application being made to the commissioners such knowledge may be obtained; and so in ordinary cases it may; but when a man is missing, who ever dreams of applying to these commissioners? His friends in such a case are apt to suppose him to have committed suicide or to have been murdered: in scarcely one case out of a thousand would they suppose him to have been stolen from society and confined as a lunatic. But if even they do suspect this to be the case, what security does the Act afford against his perpetual imprisonment? What power does it impart to his friends to aid him? By the thirty-fourth section it is enacted, "That if any person shall apply to one of the commissioners, or any justice of the peace of the county in which any house of reception for two or more insane persons is situate, in order to be informed whether any particular person is confined in any of the said houses of reception for two or more insane persons, and the said commissioner or justice shall think it reasonable to permit such inquiry to be made, and shall sign an order directed to the clerk of the commissioners or clerk of the visitors for that purpose, the said clerk of the commissioners or clerk of the visitors is hereby required, upon the receipt of such order, to make search; and if it shall appear upon search that the person so inquired after is or has been confined in any of the said houses, the said clerk of the commissioners or clerk of the visitors shall immediately deliver to the person so applying, in writing, the name of the keeper in whose house the person so inquired after is or has been confined, the situation of such house, and a copy of the order and certificate upon which such person was received into such house, upon payment of the sum of seven shillings, and no more, for his trouble."

Well: he obtains this information—provided the asylum in which he is confined be within the jurisdiction of the commissioners, that is to say, within seven miles of London—he ascertains where his friend is, and what then can he do? He cannot see him, he cannot visit him: no man is permitted to enter an asylum save the commissioners and the persons by whose authority the inmates have been confined.

But assuming that he has the means at his command of rendering it "inexpedient," notwithstanding the certificate, for the vile party to detain his friend any longer in that asylum, what need that party do in order to make all sure? Why he need but remove him from the asylum within the jurisdiction of the commissioners to an asylum beyond the jurisdiction of the commissioners: that is to say, he need but send him to some country asylum, and if he send him there in another name, there is no power on earth to discover where he is.

In vain the victim may declare that the name in which he is entered is not his right name—that it is for instance Roberts, when he is entered as Jones—the very tenacity with which he adheres to his right name, will be held to be an additional proof of his delusion: he cannot be considered then otherwise than mad, and thus is he lost to the world for ever.

It must not be supposed, because cases of this kind are seldom brought to light, that they seldom occur: the secrecy in which everything connected with a Private Asylum is involved, renders frequent exposition of individual cases impossible; but if even they occurred less frequently than they do, the fact would not diminish the enormity of the system; it is enormous that in a country like this, it should be possible for a case of the kind to occur at all: but the facility with which it can be done is amazing.

In France, before the incarceration or *interdiction* of a person assumed to be of unsound mind can take place, there must be a *conseil de famille*, and subsequently the decree of a tribunal, before which—when three physicians appointed *by* the tribunal have examined the patient—he appears, and his acts of insanity are proved. And thus ought it to be in England. Instead of dragging a man to perpetual imprisonment, by virtue of the purchased signature of an apothecary, he ought, before he is permanently confined, to be publicly proved to be insane. It is in the last degree disgraceful to this country, that men can be for ever shut out from the world, and from all communication with the world, without having at least undergone some public examination.

With respect to the treatment experienced by patients in these Private Asylums, I need only refer to the published Reports of the various Committees of the House of Commons for proved cases of the most frightful cruelty; but as the cause of those who are afflicted or who are assumed to be afflicted with this the most dire calamity which can befall man, has never been made a party question, why of course, no step has been taken to put an end to such brutalities, and the system continues in full operation still. It is, however, to be hoped that philanthropy and faction may, with a view to the removal of this blot upon civilization, be conjoined, or that faction alone may take the matter in hand; for while faction, without the aid of philanthropy, can thunder forth its fierce denunciations, with amazing effect, philanthropy, I fear, unsupported by faction, has there but a still small voice.

I have been induced thus to dwell upon this terrible subject by the conviction of its being one of great importance; and if, in these hastily written pages, the dreadful system shall have been sufficiently illustrated to induce the legislature to take it into serious consideration, it must of necessity be the means of effecting a revision, and of thereby accomplishing one of the highest objects proposed by THE AUTHOR.

CONTENTS.

LIST OF ILLUSTRATIONS.

THE

LIFE AND ADVENTURES

OF

VALENTINE VOX,

THE VENTRILOQUIST.

CHAPTER I.

THE BIRTH AND EDUCATION OF VALENTINE, WITH THE PARENTAL PECULIARITIES AND PREMATURE DEATH OF HIS IMMEDIATE ANCESTOR.

In one of the most ancient and populous boroughs in the county of Suffolk, there resided a genius named Jonathan Vox, who, in order to make a fortune with rapidity, tried everything, but failed to succeed in anything, because he could stick long to nothing.

At the age of five-and-twenty, this gentleman, who was held to be a highly respectable Christian in consequence of his regular attendance at church twice every Sabbath day, became enamoured of the expectations of Miss Penelope Long, a young lady who had an uncle supposed to have made a mint of money somehow, and an aunt who was believed to have another mint somewhere.

To the best of Miss Penelope's belief, she had not another relative in the world, and as this belief was singularly enough imparted to Jonathan, he at once became inspired with the conviction that he could not conveniently do better than secure Miss Penelope, seeing that, if even he were not made wealthy at once, there was wealth in the family, which must at some period or other be his, as neither uncles nor aunts, though they live much too long for the convenience of many, are immortal.

Accordingly Jonathan embraced the very earliest opportunity of assailing Miss Penelope's heart, and this he managed to do with considerable comfort to himself, and with no inconsiderable satisfaction to the lady; for while on the one hand Jonathan had been cast in an insinuating mould, on the other, he and Penelope were of the self-same "order," a circumstance, which in a town where the eighteenpenny people cannot associate with the shilling individuals, without being regularly cut dead by the half-crowners, clearly renders the first advances in matters of this description peculiarly agreeable.

Jonathan, therefore, at once manfully commenced the attack with an original remark, having reference to the weather; but as he found this a somewhat barren topic, for a man cannot well keep on talking about the weather, and the weather only, for many hours in succession, he adroitly changed it to that of the eloquence of the minister of St. James's — a subject with which they were both of course perfectly conversant, and which lasted them, with sundry affectionate interpolations, until prudence compelled them to separate for the night.

The next evening, by appointment, the attack was renewed, and the thing was followed up with appropriate ardour for a period of fifteen years, Jonathan being naturally anxious to defer the consummation of his happiness as long as he possibly could, in expectation of an event which might cause both Penelope and himself to sport "the trappings and the suits of wo." At the expiration of this period, however, it having been delicately suggested by Penelope, that they had known each other long enough to know each other well, the day was fixed, and in the presènce of Uncle John and Aunt Eleanor, Jonathan and Penelope were united.

In less than twelve months from this period, Jonathan was generously presented with an interesting pledge of affection in the perfect similitude of a son. The presentation, of course, made his heart glad. He kissed his heir, sang to him, danced him on his knee, and would inevitably have killed him, but for the timely interposition of the nurse, who insisted upon taking the child away just as Jonathan was urging him to drink his pa's health in a glass of hot brandy-and-water.

Now Jonathan, as we have stated, could never, in pecuniary matters, get on, — a circumstance which was not attributable solely to his inability to adhere for any length of time to any one pursuit, but also to the fact that, with all his ardent love of independence — with all his eager anxiety to realize a rapid and a splendid fortune, he was exceedingly improvident, and had a really great contempt for all small sums of money. He was not a man capable of being prevailed upon exactly to ram a twenty-pound note down his gun if he wanted wadding, but he would lend twenty-pounds at any time, without the most remote prospect of its ever being returned, or accept a bill of exchange for that or any other amount without a chance of its being honoured by the drawer. This kept him perpetually poor. The more money he got, the more he thus got rid of: indeed he was always in debt, and that always in proportion to the amount of his income.

Uncle John knowing this to be one of the chief characteristics of Jonathan, and conceiving it to be high time to convince him of the propriety of acting with less improvidence in future, sought immediately after the christening of his heir, who at the instance of Aunt Eleanor, was named Valentine — to impress upon his mind the expediency of reforming. Of course Jonathan saw the force of the suggestion in a moment. He promised to reform; and he did reform. He was inexorable for a month. He would not lend a shilling; nor would he accept a bill to accommodate any man. He had a family, and in justice to that family he would not consent to do it. At the expiration of the month, however, his resolution vanished. He was induced by a friend to do that which he had often done before, but which he had promised Uncle John that he would never do again, and when the time came for honouring the instrument, neither he nor his friend could make up the amount, and the consequence was that he was immediately arrested.

Valentine was of course then too young to be actively engaged in promoting the release of the author of his being; but it is notwithstanding a fact, that he caused him to be released, seeing that through him, and through him alone, Uncle John paid the bill, and thus set him at liberty. This event had a salutary effect upon Jonathan. He had no more to do with those dangerous instruments. What he lent was lent in specie; he would not lend his name to any man after that.

Now, in obedience to nature's immutable law, Master Valentine gradually grew older; and when he had arrived at the age of nine years, he was placed by Uncle John under the care of the Reverend Henry Paul, a gentleman, who being unable with any great degree of comfort to support himself, a wife, and seven children upon the 50*l.* a-year which he derived from his curacy, took a limited number of pupils, that is to say, of course, as many as he could get, at twelve guineas per annum, and no extras.

The academy of Mr. Paul was in the immediate vicinity of Newmarket, and Mr. Paul himself was an extremely benevolent and virtuous man. He would shrink from even the semblance of a dishonourable action, and would, rather than be guilty of one, no matter how venial in the eye of the world it might be, live glorying in the rectitude of his conduct, on starvation's brink. His father had been an eminent merchant, and so successful in the early part of his career, that he had at one time realised a fortune of at least 200,000*l.* He did not, however, relinquish business. Determined to do all in his power for his son, who after having received a sound preparatory education, was sent to Cambridge; he continued to pursue his old course of amassing wealth with as much zeal and energy as if he had been labouring to procure the bare means of existence. The year, however, in which his son left Cambridge, was a disastrous year to him. A series of unsuccessful speculations completely ruined him. He not only lost every guinea he possessed, but was plunged into debt so deeply, that extrication was impossible. He therefore became a bankrupt, and in the room in which his creditors met for the first time, the consciousness of his position overpowered him, and he died of a broken heart.

Mr. Henry Paul was thus thrown at once upon the world without a shilling, and without a friend. He had neglected to make friends while at college, by being subservient to mere rank, with a view to patronage, and had therefore no prospect of promotion. For some considerable time he was literally starving; but he at length obtained a curacy, and soon after became enamoured of an accomplished young creature, who was a governess in the rector's family, and just as poor as himself, whom he married, and thus in a pecuniary point of view sealed the fate of both for ever.

From such a man Valentine need not have expected severity, albeit he had a lively apprehension of it at first. Mr. Paul regarded his pupils with the most considerate tenderness. Had they been his own children his treatment of them could not have been marked with more affection. His chief anxiety was to impart to them a knowledge of the right course, and a full appreciation of the advantages of which its pursuit is productive. His censure was embodied in his praise of others; his only punishment consisted in withholding reward.

When Valentine had been at this academy five years, during which time he had made very considerable progress, his father, while trying some nautical experiment in a narrow-bellied water-butt, pitched, to the unspeakable mortification of an extensive circle of friends, headlong to the bottom and was drowned.

This event was to Valentine a source of deep affliction as a natural matter of course; and he left school in consequence, nominally for a month, but in reality never to return, for after the solemn deposit of the remains of the departed in the family vault, the afflicted widow, as the only means of obtaining the slightest consolation, kept Valentine at home.

His grief, however, speedily vanished. He had everything he wished for—was petted and spoiled. Uncle John allowed the widow a respectable annuity, and the widow allowed Val to do just what he pleased. He was usually from home the greater part of the day, either shooting, hunting, fishing, driving, bathing, or cricketing, and as he soon became an adept at almost every active game, he invariably had some match or other on hand.

Thus matters went on for the space of four years, when a circumstance happened which influenced his conduct through life so materially, that had it not occurred, the probability is that his adventures would never have been published to the world.

CHAPTER II.

THE GENIUS AND CHARACTERISTIC HONOUR OF A GREAT MAGICIAN: VALENTINE INSPIRES THE SPIRIT OF HIS ART.

When the birth-place of Valentine was visited by Signor Antonio Hesperio de Bellamoniac, juggler extraordinary to the King of Naples, and teacher of the black art to Gwang Foo Twang, the Grand Emperor of China, it was announced that a wonderful exhibition of the noble science of legerdemain, of which the signor was for the nonce an Italian professor, would take place in a room at the back of the Bull, an inn celebrated for the extreme antiquity of its beer.

Now the Bull, in consequence of the peculiar celebrity it had acquired, was the nightly resort of a select number of townsmen, of whom the chief in the estimation of the company was a Mr. Timotheus Ironsides, the reporter and sub-editor of one of the journals—a gentleman whom the signor so delighted the evening previously to the wonderful exhibition, that he voluntarily promised to give him "a lift"—in consideration of which promise the signor gave him a *carte blanche* to send in as many friends as he pleased.

Well, the hour at which the performances were to take place arrived, and the signor saw with considerable dismay that he had embarked in a most atrocious speculation. There were not more than five-and-twenty patrons of art present, of whom seven only paid the admission fee; namely, the small charge of 3*d.* and therefore, as the gross receipts amounted to no more than 1*s.* 9*d.*, Signor Antonio Hesperio de Bellamoniac determined on starting the next morning for some place in which genius was more highly appreciated, and somewhat more liberally patronised.

On mentioning this, his fixed determination, after the performance, to Mr. Ironsides, that gentleman on the instant pointed out the extreme madness of the idea, explained to him that Wednesday was the grand market-day, that his paper was published on the Tuesday, that hundreds of farmers with their wives and daughters would then be in town, and that he was perfectly certain to have an audience crammed to the ceiling after the just and impartial criticism he intended to give. To this the signor listened with somewhere about half a smile, which was clearly indicative of the existence of a species of incredulity, which they who are in the habit of gulling others, invariably regard those who, as they imagine, are desirous of gulling them. He didn't see it exactly.

He had not the smallest doubt about its being all correct, and he knew that he was able to astonish them; but how were they to be caught? What sort of critique could be written to bring them? These were the questions which the signor regarded, and, very naturally, as of infinite importance.

"I'll show you," said Ironsides, "how we'll proceed: step here, and you shall judge for yourself."

They accordingly retired to a little back parlour, in which they remained somewhat more than two hours concocting a criticism on the evening's performance, which certainly was, according to the signor's own acknowledgment, "a regular flamer."

"Now," said the Signor, "can you get this in?"

"Certain," cried Ironsides, "my honour!"

"I don't doubt your honour," said the Signor; "but have you the power?"

"Beyond every species of doubt!" replied the journalist.

"Good," said the Signor — "good, very good: the justice of it pleases. Excellent good! Now I'll tell you what I'll do. That there's safe to draw 'em — there can't be two opinions about that. Vot say you, then: I'll hire the large concert room upon the Market Hill, and you shall go reg'lars in the profits."

"Agreed!" shouted Ironsides. "So certain am I that we shall have a good house, that I'll bear half the losses whatever they may be."

"That's precisely the game!" said the Signor — "I'm delighted! — *Have* you got such a thing as a crown? I 'spected some remittances this morning, which can't now be here before to-morrow."

"With pleasure!" cried Ironsides, and the money changed hands in an instant.

"I want to get some bills out," continued the Signor, "werry airly in the morning."

"Leave all that to me," observed Ironsides, "I'll undertake to do that. I'll have some flamers, my boy, struck off; aye, and posted before you are up."

"Good again!" cried the Signor. "You know more about them than I do. I'll leave it to you entirely — even as a child will I go by thy direction."

"You'll find no nonsense about me," observed Ironsides, rising and taking the Signor by the hand — "Good night."

"Be stirring with the lark, good Norfolk!" cried the Signor, as the journalist made his exit.

"Is this to go down to Mr. Ironsides?" anxiously inquired the landlord.

"Of course!" replied the Signor — "of course. Now a light!" In the space of three minutes Signor Antonio Hesperio de Bellamoniac—whose real name, it may perhaps be proper to observe, was John Tod — submitted to the embrace of Morpheus with all the Christian resignation at his command.

The next morning Mr. Ironsides wrote the placards, and had them printed and posted with so much expedition, that before twelve o'clock they illuminated the town.

The great magician beheld these flamers with delight, and when in the evening Ironsides, whose whole soul was centred in the spec, brought a paper down to show him the impartial critique, he applauded him even to the very echo that did, we have no doubt, applaud again. Everything was that night arranged. The room was swept, the chandelier polished, and the money-taker hired, while the cups, and the balls, and the thimbles, and the swords were placed in order to the infinite satisfaction, not only of Ironsides, but of Signor Antonio Hesperio de Bellamoniac himself.

In due course of time, the market morning arrived, and the town was, as usual, at an early hour, thronged. The Signor was in ecstacies, when he found so many gaily-dressed persons, whose countenances seemed to indicate that their possessors were perfectly ready to be duped, walking leisurely up and down the principal streets, with their mouths wide open, and ready to swallow anything. He therefore employed himself during the day in going round and round the town with the view of witnessing the avidity with which the contents of the placards were read, and took especial care *incog.* to impress upon each group a mysterious idea of the wonderful exhibition.

Well, seven o'clock came, and the Signor — sporting a pair of huge moustaches which he had purchased for this occasion expressly — wriggled his way through the crowd already assembled. The arrangements were admirable. Only one could pass in at a time, and there stood the magician, who drew a shilling from each person until the room was nearly filled, when, with an injunction to suffer no one to pass without paying, he surrendered his post to the responsible individual whom Ironsides had liberally engaged.

Now the Signor was what the world would call an exceedingly clever fellow. He knew that he was perfectly uneducated, and was conscious of the construction of his sentences being anything but strictly grammatical. To conceal this, therefore, on the one hand, and to inspire the audience with a belief of his being, what he represented himself to be, an Italian, on the other, he had recourse to a jargon of his own composition — an indiscriminate mixture of Cockney English and Yankee French — which never by any chance failed him, for when he happened to be "at home" he could make himself well understood, and when abroad, he had only to resort to his unknown tongue, to render himself as mysteriously unintelligible as possible.

At eight o'clock precisely the curtain went up and discovered the great magician enveloped in a horsecloth, which he had borrowed for the occasion of the ostler at the Bull, and which was meant to convey the idea of a robe. His appearance was singularly imposing, for he had tied on a long flowing beard, which, though black, had a peculiarly cabalistic and patriarchal effect, while his face — instead of being vulgarly daubed with vermilion — had been carefully rubbed over with whitening, to give him the aspect of one much addicted to study; and lines had been made with the edge of a burnt cork, with the view of indicating the furrows which that study had established.

As soon as the enthusiasm with which his appearance was hailed had subsided, the great magician, with due solemnity, stalked forward and addressed his audience briefly as follows:

"Ladi and Shenteelmongs, I have de honnare to say dis, dat I sall go troo warious parformong, and ven I sall svaller him sword town him troat, I vas give you vong speciment ob venter et loquer, dat am to say, speak in him pelly."

What was understood of this gave great satisfaction; but what was most applauded was that which was most unintelligible.

The performances then commenced, and the Signor went through a variety of old tricks very cleverly. But when he came to his ventriloquism, he completely astounded his audience, for never having heard anything like it before, they were in doubt as to whether there was not in him something superhuman. He then commenced playing the violin; and although he was an infamous fiddler, he managed to ravish his audience by producing a series of the most horrible sounds that ever assailed the ears of either man or beast, and thus terminated the wonderful performances of the evening.

Signor Antonio Hesperio de Bellamoniac's next care was, of course, to get the money which had been taken at the door during the performance, which added to the sum he himself had received, made the gross amount 23*l.* 15*s.* With this and his implements of jugglery — the whole of which were safely deposited in a small cotton handkerchief — he repaired to his quarters, where, of course, he was soon joined by his partner, the journalist.

"Oh! my dear sir!" exclaimed the Signor, as Ironsides entered, "I'm bound to you for hever."

"Don't mention it, my boy," cried the journalist. "You see I was right."

"That talented notice of yourn did the trick," observed the Signor, "that vos the game!"

"You have a pretty good haul," observed Ironsides.

"Hexcellent!" warmly exclaimed the Signor; "vords cannot hexpress my deep gratitude. Vot'll you take? I mean for to stand a good supper to-night, if I never stand another."

Accordingly supper was ordered and eaten, and brandy-and-water *ad libitum* drank, the whole of which was directed by the Signor to be put down to the general account, which was accordingly done upon Ironsides' sole responsibility.

"Now," said the Signor, when Ironsides had drank pretty freely, "shall we divide the receipts of this glorious night now, or in the morning?"

"As you please, my dear boy," said the journalist.

"Well, I want to get rid, you know, of some of it," said the Signor, "but perhaps arter hall it 'ud better be done in the morning?"

"Perhaps it had," hiccoughed the journalist.

"Vot time 'll you be down?" inquired the Signor.

"Any time you like," replied Ironsides.

"Shall we say twelve then?" observed the magician, "and by that time you'll be able to put down all you have paid for bills, and sutterer; and I shall insist upon your having a couple of guineas hextra for that critic of yourn in the paper."

"Not a copper," cried Ironsides.

"But I insist," said the Signor.

"So you may — but not a copper — not a cop —".

"Well I don't of course want to insult you. If you vont, vy there's a hend off the matter. — Come, drink."

But Ironsides could drink no more. He felt that he had already drank more than enough, and therefore left his friend and partner with the understanding that they were to meet the next morning at twelve.

The morning came and the journalist was as punctual as the sun; but Signor Antonio Hesperio de Bellamoniac was *non est inventus.* He had not been seen by any one connected with the Bull that morning. He had in short decamped with the money and his implements, without ever leaving so much as his card! Mr. Ironsides had therefore to pay for the concert-room, the flamers,

3*

the men, and the supper, with the collateral expenses incurred at the inn, which the Signor had honoured with his patronage — the whole of which he paid too in absolute silence, lest the facts of the case should become known, for he held it to be utterly inexpedient to be made the perpetual butt of the town.

CHAPTER III.

VALENTINE MAKES RAPID PROGRESS. HIS FIRST GRAND PUBLIC DISPLAY. STRIKING DEVELOPMENT OF POLITICAL INJUSTICE. A SANGUINARY LOCAL REBELLION SUBDUED.

Of all the magician's auditors on the great occasion to which we have alluded, Valentine was one of the most attentive, and that portion of the performances which struck him with the greatest force was the Signor's display of his power as a ventriloquist. Indeed, so deep an impression did it make upon his mind, that he firmly resolved to apply to the magician the following day with the view of ascertaining if it were possible for him to become a ventriloquist himself. Finding, however, that the Signor had so unceremoniously vanished from the town, he was left entirely to his own resources, and after trying with desperation for several days, he discovered, with equal astonishment and delight, that he in reality possessed the power of speaking with an abdominal intonation, and that zealous cultivation would cause that power to be fully developed.

He accordingly commenced a severe course of training. He rose early every morning and practised in the fields, and in doing so, frequently startled himself, for the power that was within him, not being quite under control, would occasionally send the sound in one place when he fully intended it to have been in another. The consciousness, however, of his possessing this extraordinary power urged him to persevere, and in less than six months it was entirely at his command.

He then began to astonish all whom he met. He would call an individual by name, and cause the sound to proceed apparently from the opposite side of the street. If ladies were walking before him he would instantly raise the dreaded cry of "mad dog!" and imitate the growlings of the animal in its paroxysms to perfection. If persons were passing an empty house, he would loudly cry "murder! — thieves!" when, if he could but persuade them to break open the door, he would lead them from room to room by imitations of convulsive sobs and dying groans, until the house had obtained the reputation of being haunted. It enabled him to be revenged upon all who had offended him; and so unscrupulous was he when he had such an object in view, that he absolutely on one occasion forbade the marriage of a young lady by whom he had been insulted, as he imagined, at a dance, by calling out in a female voice, when the minister had said, "If any of you know any just cause or impediment why these two persons should not be joined together in holy matrimony ye are now to declare it" — "I forbid that marriage."

"The person," said the minister on that occasion with due solemnity, "by whom this marriage is forbidden will be pleased to walk into the vestry."

The eyes of the congregation had immediate employment, but they twinkled and strained to no purpose. Of course no person appeared in the vestry; but the lady whose marriage had been forbidden, and whom cruel curiosity had prompted to be present, at once fainted, and was instantly carried away by the sexton.

Valentine's first grand display, however, in public, was at a meeting convened at the Guildhall, for the purpose of electing a fit and proper person to fill the vacancy occasioned by the lamentable death of Mr. Paving Commissioner Cobb. Party-feeling on that occasion ran high; and the hall at the appointed hour was crowded to excess by the friends of the candidates, who looked at each other as if the laws only prevented the perpetration of cannibalism on the spot.

As the mayor was about to open the important business of the day, with the expression of a lively hope that all parties would have a fair and impartial hearing, Valentine entered the hall, and having by virtue of perseverance, reached the steps of the rostrum from which the electors were to be addressed, prepared at once to commence operations.

The first speaker was Mr. Creedale, an extremely thin gentleman, with an elaborately-chisseled nose, who came forward on the liberal side to nominate Mr. Job Stone.

"Gentlemen!" said Mr. Creedale.

"Nonsense!" cried Valentine, in an assumed voice of course, which appeared to proceed from a remote part of the hall.

"Gentlemen!" repeated Mr. Creedale, with some additional emphasis.

"Pooh, pooh!" exclaimed Valentine, changing the tone.

"It may," said Mr. Creedale, "be nonsense, or it may be pooh, pooh! but, gentlemen, I address you as gentlemen, and beg that I may not be interrupted."

"O don't mind Tibbs; go on!" cried Valentine.

"Oh! Tibbs; indeed!" observed Mr. Creedale, with a contemptuous curl of the lip. "It's Mr. Tibbs, is it!"

"No! no!" cried the accused individual, who was a highly respectable grocer, and remarkable for his quiet and unassuming demeanour.

"I am surprised at Mr. Tibbs," said Mr. Creedale in continuation—"I have until now regarded him as an individual —"

"No, no!" again vociferated Tibbs, "It arn't me, I arn't spoke a synnable."

"If Mr. Tibbs," observed the mayor, "or if any other gentleman be desirous of addressing the meeting he will have an opportunity of doing so anon."

"Upon my honour!" exclaimed Tibbs, "I've —"

Here there were general cries of "Order, order! chair!" when Mr. Creedale continued:—

"Gentlemen; without adverting to any extraneous matter, it gives me unspeakable pleasure to propose —"

"A revolutionist!" growled Valentine in a heavy bass voice.

"That's me, I s'pose!" exultingly cried Tibbs, shaking his head and giving a most triumphant wink.

"I know whose voice that is," said Mr. Creedale, "That's the voice of the conservative bully. Yes, that's Mr. Brownrigg."

"What!" shouted Brownrigg, in a voice of indignant thunder.

"What?" echoed Mr. Creedale.

"Say it's me again," shouted Brownrigg, "just only so much as say it's me again."

"Mr. Brownrigg," observed the mayor, "will please to conduct himself *here* with propriety."

"What do you mean!" exclaimed Brownrigg. "Why fix upon me?"

"That is not the first time," observed Mr. Creedale, "that Mr. Brownrigg has been here with the view of blustering for the Conservatives; but it won't—"

"As true as life!" exclaimed Brownrigg, "I never opened my lips. If I did —"

Loud cries of "Order, order! Question! Chair, chair!" drowned the conclusion of the sentence, however interesting it might have been, and Mr. Creedale resumed:—

"As I was about to observe, gentlemen, when disgracefully interrupted, it gives me great pleasure to propose Mr. Stone as —"

"A Dickey!" screamed Valentine, assuming the shrill voice of a female—"Don't have him! he's a dickey!"*

Here the entire meeting cried "Shame!" and the candidate rose to repel the insinuation.

"Officers!" shouted the mayor, "instantly turn that depraved woman out!"

Hereupon a corps of corporate constables entered with their staves, and rushed to the spot from which the sound appeared to proceed; but no woman was discoverable.

"Whoop!" cried Valentine, throwing his voice to another part of the hall: and the officers rushed to that part with the most praiseworthy precipitation, legally assaulting every elector who stood in their way; but no sooner had they reached the spot proposed than "the depraved woman" appeared to be laughing outright in the very body of the meeting. Away went the constables, following the sound, and enraged beyond measure at their inability to catch her, when in an instant another "Whoop!" was heard to proceed from the spot they had just quitted. Back went the constables, knocking aside every man whom they came near, and thus creating a scene of indescribable confusion.

"Turn her out!" cried the mayor in loud tones of insulted dignity, "Turn her out!".

"Blarm me!" cried the fattest of the constables foaming with rage, "We can't find her!"

Again loud laughter was heard, in which at length the entire meeting joined on beholding the laudable ardour with which the constables kept up the chase.

"You abandoned creature!" cried the mayor, "why dont you leave the hall?"

"Let me alone! let me alone!" cried the 'creature,' "and I'll be quiet"—and immediately a scream was heard, succeeded by sounds indicative of the 'creature' being just on the point of fainting. The constables fancied that they were sure of her then, and therefore made another rush; but without more success. At length the mayor exclaimed, "Let her be: leave her to her own conscience," when the constables with the greatest reluctance withdrew, and comparative silence was restored.

Mr. Creedale then resumed:—"A weak invention of the enemy — [No, no! and loud cheers] — I repeat —"

"You're a fool!" cried Valentine in a singularly gruff tone, on which there were again loud cries of "Shame!" and "Order!"

"I'll commit the first man," cried the

* It will probably be necessary here to observe that in Suffolk a "dickey" is the short for an ass.

mayor with a swell of indignation, "who again interrupts these important proceedings, be *he* whomsoever he may."

"You can't old boy!" cried Valentine.

"Who, who is that?" said the mayor—"I demand to know instantly who it is that dares thus to —"

"Dares!" exclaimed Valentine.

"Dares! aye dares!" cried the mayor. "I'll give five pounds to any man who will point out to me that atrocious individual."

The electors at this moment stared at each other, and all appeared lost in amazement.

The mayor again rose, and assuming a more tranquil tone, said, "Really, gentlemen, this conduct is perfectly disgraceful. In the course of my experience I never met with anything even remotely comparable to —"

"Jonathan Sprawl," cried Valentine, "He is the man."

"If," said the mayor, "I thought that—but no, no, I am certain, Mr. Sprawl —"

"I assure you," said Jonathan, "interruption did not proceed from me, on my honour. He who says that it did, is a slanderer and no gentleman; and I tell him so openly to his teeth."

"I am satisfied," said the mayor, "quite satisfied, and therefore do trust that we shall now be permitted to proceed."

Mr. Creedale, who was still in possession of the chair, again resumed:—"I am not inclined," said he, "to indulge on this occasion in anything which may tend to create feelings of irritation; but I must be permitted to say that I am utterly astonished at the conduct of—"

"Mr. Maxill!" said Valentine, imitating the voice of Mr. Creedale the speaker.

"Demme!" cried Maxill, who was a short stumpy man, with a remarkably raw-beefy face, "I begs to rise to order. Demme! I claims the protection of the cheer, and if so be as Mr. Creedale means for to mean as it's me, why, demme, I repels the insiniwation —[Applause]—I repels the insiniwation, and means for to say this, that all I can say is —[Bravo Maxill]—all I can say is, demme, is this—"

"You're an ass!" cried Valentine, throwing his voice immediately behind Mr. Maxill, "hold your tongue!"

Within the sphere of the reader's observation, it has in all probability occurred, that a man, being in nautical phraseology, three sheets in the wind, and writhing under the lash of some real or imaginary insult, has made desperate efforts to reach an opponent through the barrier composed of mutual friends: if so, if the reader should ever have beheld an individual in that interesting position, foaming, and plunging, and blustering, and occasionally striking his dearest friend, in his efforts to get at the enemy, he is qualified to form some conception of the scene of which "little fatty Maxill" was the hero. He fancied that he had discovered the delinquent. Nothing could shake his faith in the assumed fact, that an individual named Abraham Bull, who happened to be standing at the time in his immediate vicinity, was the person by whom he had been insulted. He therefore sprang at him with all the ferocity at his command; but being checked by those around, who were conscious of Bull's perfect innocence, he, bent upon vengeance, continued kicking and bullying, and dealing out his blows right and left, with the most perfect indiscrimination, until the constables lifted him clean off his legs, and without any further ceremony rolled him into the street.

The mayor now fondly imagined that this would have the effect of restoring perfect order; he believed that after such an example as that, no individual, or body of individuals would dare to offer the slightest interruption to the proceedings of the day; and having expressed himself quietly to that effect, he bowed and waved his hand to Mr. Creedale.

That gentleman accordingly came forward once more, and said—"Gentlemen, it is with unspeakable ——"

"Blarney!" cried Valentine.

"Silence!" exclaimed the Mayor with a melodramatic stamp that shook the platform.

"The eye of England," said Mr. Creedale, "nay the eye of all Europe [Asia, Africa, and America, added Valentine] are upon you, and I can only say that anything more ——"

"Laughable," cried Valentine, assuming the voice of a respectable plumber who stood near him.

"Good heavens!" exclaimed the Mayor, "to what a depth of degradation have we dived! For the love of grace permit me to say that anything more disgraceful never came within the pale of my experience. Am I to be supported? (loud cries of yes, yes!) Then in the name of mighty reason, I call upon you loudly, boldly, emphatically, and that with all the energy of which I am capable to do so. ("We will, we will!" "Down with the tory myrmidons!" "Down with the rank revolutionary raff!" and loud cheers.)

At this stage of the proceedings the mayor quietly intimated to Mr. Creedale, that it would perhaps be, under the circumstances, expedient to cut it short; and Mr. Creedale having with half an eye perceived the propriety of that suggestion, concluded amidst general uproar, with the following most pointed remark : —

"Gentlemen, since you will not hear me speak, I shall beg at once to nominate my friend Mr. Stone, a man whose equal as a fit and proper person to be a Paving Commissioner is not to be found."

Hereupon, there were loud cheers from the liberal party, and hisses and groans from the tories, and when Mr. Leechamp rose to second the nomination, the cheering, and hissing, and groaning, were renewed.

Mr. Mac Ireling then came forward to propose Mr. Slabb, who had the whole of the conservative interest on his side; but the moment he appeared in front of the platform, Valentine cried, "Now for a signal retaliation ! now for our revenge ?"

"Gentlemen," said Mr. Mac Ireling.

"You'll not let a rank tory speak, if you are men !" exclaimed Valentine; and Mr. Mac Ireling was immediately assailed with a tremendous volley of groans from the liberals, who naturally believed that the conservatives had created the whole of the previous disturbance.

"Gentlemen ! — *Gentlemen !* — GENTLEMEN !" reiterated the mayor at intervals appropriately filled up with hissing, groaning, cheering, whistling, and yelling. "I demand to be heard. I insist — I insist upon silence. ('Order, order ! chair, chair !') In the name of all that's gracious let it not—let it not, oh ! let it not go forth to the world, that the men of this ancient and enlightened borough, in the nineteenth century, in the heart of the British empire ; in the centre, the very bull's-eye of civilisation, are slaves to passion, idiots, madmen, and fools. (loud cheers.) Am I a cipher ? (hear, hear !) On this instant would I dissolve this most outrageous meeting, were it not that I am determined to maintain inviolate the dignity of the office I have the honour to hold, and not to be intimidated, frightened, alarmed, or put down by mere clamour. (vehement cheering.) If we are to proceed, in the name of blind and impartial justice, of mighty and immortal reason, of invincible and sound constitutional common sense, in the name of all that is mighty, respectable, and just, let us do so."

This pointed and poetic appeal, delivered as it was, in tones of the most eloquent indignation, had the effect of inspiring the audience with awe, which induced something bearing the semblance of order to prevail.

Mr. Mac Ireling then again stepped forward, and said, "Gentlemen, I hope that my conduct has been of a character to command the esteem of ——"

"The Tories !" shouted Valentine.

"Heavens !" exclaimed the mayor, with his hands clenched, and raising his voice to the highest raging pitch — "by all that is powerful and pure, I'll commit that man who presumes again to utter a single syllable for the purpose of ——"

Valentine here sent into the body of the meeting an awfully melodramatic "Ha ! ha ! ha !" which appeared absolutely to electrify his worship, who loudly cried "Officers ! now do your duty !"

In vain those respectable functionaries, sweating with indignation, rushed to the middle of the hall, with the laudable view of arresting the delinquent. Loud laughter was still heard, but invariably behind them, whichever way they happened to turn. The perspiration poured down their cheeks, for their exertions were really terrific. They stamped, and puffed, and tore, and shook their fists, and looked eternal daggers at every man in their vicinity. The laughter was heard still ; and away they went again with fresh energy, inspired by his worship's reiterated cries of "Officers, now do your duty !" At length, fairly driven to desperation, and being in a state of the most excruciating mental agony, they resolved on seizing some one, and accordingly collared Mr. Lym, a highly reputable baker, whom they happily discovered in the atrocious act of smiling at the ridiculous character of their appearance. In vain Mr. Lym proclaimed his innocence ! — they had caught him in the act ! and hence proceeded to drag him towards the door with all possible violence. In the space of one minute Mr. Lym was divested of his top coat, under coat, waistcoat, and shirt ! — those articles of apparel having been torn completely off by the enraged functionaries in the due execution of their duty. Lym would have left the hall quietly enough, but the radicals would by no means suffer him to do so. They rushed to the rescue ; and on Valentine shouting out "Down with the republicans !" in one voice, and "Down with the tories !" in another, a general battle ensued, which was kept up on both sides with infinite spirit, while the mayor, duly mounted on the table, was engaged in denouncing the irregular proceedings with all the indignant energy at his command.

The voice of Valentine was now no longer needed. The electors were making amply sufficient noise without his aid. He therefore mounted the rostrum, partly for safety and partly with a view to the full enjoyment of the scene, and then for the first time discovered that instead of the combatants being divided into two grand political parties, as they ought to have been, they were levelling their blows with indiscriminate fury, regardless utterly of everything but the pleasure of conferring upon some one the honour of a hit. In one corner of the hall there was a dense mass of electors, of whom the majority were extremely corpulent, hugging and hanging on each other, like bees when they swarm, with such remarkable tenacity, that the entire body formed a most interesting exemplification of a perfectly dead lock. In another corner there were two lines of amateur gladiators, hitting out as hard as they could hit, but as they all, very discreetly, closed their eyes to preserve them, and went in head foremost, like bucks, their evolutions were not strictly scientific, although the hardest heads did the greatest amount of execution. In a third corner of the hall, there was a phalanx of individuals who formed a complete Gordian knot, and who contented themselves with elbowing and grinning at each other with most praiseworthy zeal; while in the fourth there were two distinct ranks of independent electors, one-half of whom were striving to protect their friends, by striking over the shoulders of those friends whom they kept with appropriate consideration in the front, to receive all the blows. The grand point of attraction, however, was in the centre. Here a circle of about two-and-twenty feet in diameter was strewed with quick bodies, horizontally twisting in and out—sometimes above the surface, and sometimes below—like so many eels in a tub, without even the possibility of any one of them achieving his perpendicular. They could *not* rise. The more desperate, the more abortive were their efforts to do so. They writhed, and kicked, and blustered, and rolled, but still preserved the true character of the scene, namely, that of a general sprawl.

While these really delightful proceedings were being conducted, certain well-intentioned persons, who had escaped, conceiving it to be the commencement of a sanguinary revolution, rushed with breathless haste to the Bull, which they knew to be the head-quarters of a troop of dragoons, then temporarily stationed in the town, and at once gave the alarm, that the rebellion might be nipped in the bud. Before the awful tale could be told twice, the trumpet sounded on the Market Hill, to horse! and in less than five minutes the entire troop, headed by a mounted magistrate, galloped to the scene of action.

On reaching the hall, the revolutionists were to the soldiers invisible. A tumultuous din was heard—a din which threatened to burst the casement; but nothing could be seen. The doors were fast. Not one of the rebels within knew how to open them; nor could they be conveniently opened from without. Mr. Alldread, the magistrate, however, in the king's name, commanded them to be instantly broken down, which command was obeyed with much alacrity by the alarmists. But here another difficulty presented itself; the rebels either would not, or could not come out! Mr. Alldread, therefore, determined to surmount every obstacle, in the king's name commanded the soldiers to gallop in. He was for checking the rebellion ere it got to a head! so certain was he, that if energetic measures were not promptly taken, the British empire would be crumbled into one chaotic mass of revolutionary ruin.

Now, for a troop of dragoons to gallop pell-mell into a densely crowded hall, was regarded, very naturally, by Captain Copeland, the officer in command, as somewhat of a novelty in military tactics; however, partly to humour the alarmed magistrate, and partly because he felt that the mere sight of the soldiers would be sufficient to put an end to all civil hostilities, he ordered his men to follow him with all possible care, and accordingly in they all went.

The eyes of the majority of the insurgents were at this crisis closed, and as those of the rest were fixed firmly upon their antagonists, the quiet entrance of the soldiers, except by a few near the door, was for a moment disregarded. Captain Copeland, however, ordered the trumpet to sound, and the trumpeter blew a shivering blast, so loud, that in an instant, as if by magic, hostilities ceased.

"Upon em!" loudly shouted Mr. Alldread; "char-r-r-ge!"

The gallant captain smiled; and his men had absolutely the cold-blooded audacity to wink at each other with gleeful significance.

"Heavens!" exclaimed Mr. Alldread, utterly astonished at the manifest indisposition of the soldiers to cut the rebels individually into mince-meat. "Why, what do you fear? In the king's name, again I command you to mow the traitors down!"

Captain Copeland, perceiving every eye fixed upon him, at once gracefully waved his bright sword until the point rested opposite the door, when the rebels, viewing this as an intimation that they would all be permitted to depart unscotched, rushed with all the alacrity at their command into the street, and in the space of five minutes the entire body of the hall was deserted.

A council of war was then held on the spot, at which the mayor was too exhausted to utter an audible sentence, but Mr. Alldread could not withhold the loud expression of his unspeakable surprise at Captain Copeland's peculiarly unconstitutional indisposition to promote the circulation of rank rebellious blood. It was, however, eventually decided that no further steps need be taken in the matter, and as the captain wished to spend a merry evening, he invited the mayor and every member of the corporation present to dine with him forthwith at the Bull. The invitation was accepted, and as they left the hall, certain straggling knots of rebels who were discussing the cause of the disturbance with great energy, took to their heels and ran to the various public houses they were in the habit of frequenting, each, of course, with the view of contending for the correctness of his own version of the origin of the fray. The soldiers smiled as they saw the rebels running; but, although Mr. Alldread insisted upon the propriety of the troop giving them chace, the party proceeded with due dignity to dinner, after which the bottle went round merrily till midnight, when the mayor and the rest of the members of the corporation, at the particular desire of Mr. Alldread, were conducted to the doors of their respective residences, under a most formidable military escort.

CHAPTER IV.

MATERNAL SOLICITUDE. GREAT-UNCLE JOHN IN CONVULSIONS. THE CHASTITY OF A MAIDEN IMPUGNED.

Nothing could exceed the delight with which Valentine contemplated the result of the first grand display of his latent power. He went home in ecstacies, and exercised his voice with so much violence, and imitated the contortions of the constables so grotesquely, that his affectionate parent absolutely believed him to be possessed of the same spirit as that which inhabited the swine. Again and again she implored him to explain to her what had occurred; but, inspired with the conviction that his power would lose a great portion of its value if its existence in him became known, he confined himself to a statement of the fact of his having been at the meeting and upset them all. The singular style, however, in which this statement was made, and the loud and irrepressible laughter by which it was accompanied, caused serious apprehensions on the part of Mrs. Vox that her Valentine had eaten of the insane root, and prompted her to go for advice to Uncle John, while Val was doing Justice to the cold remains of a fillet of veal and a knuckle of ham.

Now, for somewhat more than two-and-twenty years, without a day's intermission, Uncle John had reclined on three well-cushioned chairs, with a pipe in his mouth and a glass of remarkably stiff brandy-and-water by his side, from the time that the cloth was removed at two o'clock until five. From this position he never by any chance moved until old Hannah brought up the tea-tray, and it was in this position that Mrs. Vox found him.

"Well, Pen!" said Uncle John, as the poor lady entered, "come to see me — eh? There's a good girl."

Mrs. Vox approached the chair on which his head was reclining, and as she kissed his shining brow a tear dropped upon his nose.

"What's that!" cried Uncle John — "What's the matter, my girl! — what has happened? Come, come, sit you down and let's know all about it."

"Oh, Uncle!" said Mrs. Vox, "do, pray, see my Val."

"Why, what's the young dog been up to now?" cried Uncle John.

"Once for all," said Mrs. Vox, having taken a deep inspiration, "I believe that he's mad."

"Pooh, pooh, pooh — nonsense. child!" cried Uncle John, "Mad! Fiddledeedee, pooh, pooh, pooh — what has he been after?"

"I have told you before," said the afflicted lady, "what singular noises I have heard about the house when he is in it."

"I know, I know," interrupted Uncle John, "imagination, child, mere imagination — pooh, pooh, pooh — don't be superstitious."

"But to day," continued Mrs. Vox, sobbing—"to day, uncle, when he came home, not only did I hear dreadful noises all over the house, but he made up such horrible faces thathe frightened me out of my senses; and all I could get from him was, that he had done it — that he'd been to the meeting and had upset them all!"

"The meeting! What right has he to interfere with politics?" cried Uncle John, ringing the bell with unusual violence. "Surely there's plenty of politicians in the town without him! Upset 'em! — Here, Hannah," he continued as the old servant entered — "go, and tell that boy Valentine to come to me instantly. Bring him with you: don't come without him.

Upset 'em indeed! What right has a boy like that — he's not twenty yet — "

"No," interrupted Mrs. Vox, "he was only nineteen the 14th of last February —"

"What right has a lad like him to go to meetings? *I* never go to such places; that boy'll be ruined."

"But it isn't only that," said Mrs. Vox, "I shouldn't care, but I'm sure that he's touched: I'm quite certain the poor boy's possessed."

"Pooh, rubbish, child, rubbish!" observed Uncle John, "the boy's a splendid boy, a fine high-spirited boy. I'd not break his spirit for the world: — but he mustn't be spoiled — no, he mustn't be spoiled. If the devil *be* in him, why the devil shall come out of him: I'll not have him there; but we'll see, child — we'll see."

Uncle John then proceeded to refill his pipe, and having directed Mrs. Vox to mix a *leetle* more brandy-and-water, looked earnestly at the fire, and prepared for the attack.

"Well! young gentleman!" said he, knitting his brows and looking desperate.

Mrs. Vox turned quickly towards the door, and found that Uncle John was only rehearsing. Valentine, however, immediately after entered, and Uncle John commenced: —

"Well! young gentleman! Now, sir, what *does* all this mean?"

"All what, uncle?" quietly asked Valentine.

"All what, sir!" exclaimed Uncle John — "Why all this — this — *conduct*, sir! — that's what I mean."

"What conduct?" said Val, with perfect calmness.

"What conduct, sir!" cried Uncle John — "why, your conduct. Are you mad?"

"I hope not," said Valentine. "I am not aware that I am."

"Don't tell *me*, sir, that you are not aware of it!" shouted the old gentleman. "Here's your poor mother here fit to break her heart about your horrible noises. I'll have you put into the lunatic asylum, sir! You want a strait jacket! — but where have you been all day? — what have you been after?"

"I've been at the meeting," said Valentine.

"The meeting!" said Uncle John—"pray, what *business* had you at the meeting?"

"Come, uncle, don't be angry," said Valentine, smiling. "I'll tell you all about it: but you'll not be cross, will you?"

"Cross, sir!" exclaimed Uncle John. "I am not cross: I never am cross."

Valentine then drew a chair near the fire, and commenced an explanation of all that had occurred. At first he utterly astounded Uncle John, by the development of his power, and then proceeded with the relation of its effects upon the meeting. In ten minutes Uncle John had swallowed more smoke than he had done during the whole thirty years he had been a smoker. Seven several times did the brandy-and-water go the wrong way, and as he had a perfect knowledge of almost every man present at the hall, his imagination entered with so much spirit into the scene, and he laughed at the description of their movements so immoderately, that at length he could neither drink, smoke, nor sit, but paced the room holding his back and chest together — at intervals ejaculating "stop! stop! stop!" The more, however, Uncle John laughed, the more spirit did Valentine infuse into his tale, and at length in an absolute convulsion of mirth, the delighted old gentleman threw himself upon the sofa, and rolled to and fro like a butt in a groove.

"You young dog!" cried Uncle John, when he had recovered sufficient steadiness of breath to speak: "Don't you know, sir, it was wrong, very wrong thus to ——." Here he was seized with another fit of laughter, so loud and so painful, that for relief he moved his body first backwards and forwards, and then from side to side, while he literally mopped the perspiration from his face, which was as red as that of the sun, when, through a dark hazy atmosphere, he is seen to approach the horizon.

Nor did Mrs. Vox fail to enjoy the relation of the scene, for burying her face in her handkerchief, she was equally convulsed, although not quite so loud in the manifestation of her mirth.

"Hold your tongue, you young rascal!" was the command of Uncle John, whenever Valentine re-opened his lips to relate any incident that had previously escaped him. Valentine, however, was not to be silenced. So long as he found the old gentleman enjoyed it, so long did he keep up the fire, until at last Uncle John declaring solemnly that he could stand it no longer, commanded him to leave the room, which he did with the view of alarming old Hannah in the kitchen.

No sooner had Val made his exit from the parlour, than it occurred to Mrs. Vox, that if the thing became known to the authorities, the result might be anything but pleasing, and as Uncle John fell at once into her views, he began to think of the best mode of avoiding the discovery. At first he thought it sufficient to enjoin silence upon Valentine, but subsequently fancying that the "young dog" would deem the joke infinitely too good to be concealed, he thought that as he intended soon to send him to Mr. Goodman, an old friend of his who resided in London, the safest plan would be to start him off at once.

"But what am *I* to do?" inquired Mrs. Vox anxiously.

"Why, come and live with me," said Uncle John. "Now make no objections. He'll be well taken care of by Goodman, I know, or of course I wouldn't send him."

It was accordingly decided that he should start on the Wednesday morning, and when all the preliminaries had been arranged, Uncle John called Valentine just as he was charging old Hannah with having concealed a child, whose half stifled cries and convulsive sobs, in one of the large dresser-drawers, he had been imitating to perfection. Of course, on being called, Val left the surprised and indignant old maid in the kitchen, to prosecute her search; and after having had a few words with Great-Uncle John, on the subject of his journey, with the idea of which he was delighted, the little family separated for the night.

The whole of the morning of the following day, being Tuesday, was occupied by Valentine and Mrs. Vox in packing up, while Uncle John was engaged for several hours in the composition of a letter to Mr. Goodman; a document written with infinite care, and in a style of course peculiarly his own; and in the evening Valentine and his mother again visited the old gentleman, who employed himself till bed-time in giving Val instructions, having reference to his conduct in London.

CHAPTER V.

EXPLAINS HOW VALENTINE STARTED FOR LONDON; HOW ENTERTAINING TRAVELLING COMPANIONS CAN BE; HOW A VALIANT BLACKSMITH CAN BE A DEAD SHOT; HOW FIRM MAY BE THE FAITH OF A COACHMAN IN WITCHCRAFT; AND HOW IT IS POSSIBLE FOR A JOURNEY TO BE PROTRACTED.

There are probably no feelings at all comparable with those which are experienced by a sanguine country youth, on the eve of his first departure for London. His mind is all excitement. The single idea of visiting a place of which he has heard so much, and known so little, engenders thousands. Asleep or awake, his whole soul is set upon the journey, and were it necessary for him to rise at four in the morning, though he failed to go to sleep before two, he would be just as certain to wake in time to hear the clock strike four, as if the "warning" wire communicated with a galvanic battery sufficiently powerful to force him out of bed.

Valentine, after dreaming all night of the great city and its glories, rose some hours before his usual time, but not before Mrs. Vox, who had not slept at all, had re-ransacked every drawer and every box in the house, with the view of ascertaining if anything had been forgotten.

About an hour and a half before the time for starting arrived, in rushed Uncle John with a view of expressing his firm conviction, that if Valentine didn't look sharp the coach would certainly go without him, and of explaining, moreover, that the coachman, whom he knew, was like the eternal tide, seeing that he would wait for no man. Breakfast was therefore immediately prepared, during the preparation Uncle John compared watches, and having made them agree, compared them with the house-clock, and then sent the servant, and then went himself to ascertain if the house-clock agreed with the church. All this being eventually arranged to his entire satisfaction, down they sat to breakfast, with the watches of course upon the table. Valentine had no appetite. An egg however at length was seduced down his throat by the preliminary introduction of a piece of broiled ham, but even this was unconsciously swallowed, while with the coffee in his hand he was pacing the room. He could *not* keep his chair; nor could Mrs. Vox keep in hers, nor could Uncle John keep in his. They were all three in motion, but of course doing nothing, there being in reality nothing to do. A dozen times the girl was despatched to see if the horses were in, and after much feverish excitement it *was* at last announced that two females were standing by the side of three boxes in the gateway! That was sufficient. Off went the luggage in a wheelbarrow, on went Val's two upper coats, round went a large lambs-wool comforter, and down went a glass of raw brandy, and all in the space of thirty seconds. Mrs. Vox had been prohibited from seeing Valentine off; they therefore at once bade each other adieu, while Uncle John, standing at the door, was expressing his opinion that the coach would be gone; but no sooner had he succeeded in dragging Val away, than in spite of the prohibition, Mrs. Vox hurried on her bonnet and shawl, and started round the corner of the street, which she knew the coach would pass, for the purpose of catching a last glance of Valentine, and waving her hand.

"Now then, look alive there!" shouted the coachman from the booking-office door, as Uncle John and his charge approached. "Have yow got that are mare's shoe made comforble, Simon?"

"All right, sir," said Simon, and he went round to see if it were so, while the luggage was being secured.

"Jimp up, genelman!" cried the coachman, as he waddled from the office with his whip in one hand and his way-bill in the other; and the passengers accordingly proceeded to arrange themselves on the various parts of the coach — Valentine, by the particular desire of Uncle John, having deposited himself immediately behind the seat of the coachman.

"If you please," said the old lady, who had been standing with her daughter in the gateway for upwards of an hour; "will you be good enow please to take care of my darter?"

"All safe," said the coachman, untwisting the reins. "She shaunt take no harm. Is she going all the way?"

"Yes, sir," replied the old lady; "God bless her! she's got a place in Lunnun an I'm told."

"Hook on them ere two sack o' whoats there behind," cried the coachman, "I marnt go without 'em this time."

"God bless you, my dear! God bless you!" exclaimed the old lady, and the tears gushed from her eyes as she kissed her poor girl, whose heavy sobs choaked her utterance. "Heaven will protect you: I know it will, my child. You'll think of your poor old mother? There, cheer up, my dear — it's all for the best; I shall be very happy. You are all the world to me; but indeed I shall be very happy," and the tears burst forth in fresh streams, while she tried to reanimate the spirits of her child by affecting to smile.

"Now, all right there?" cried the coachman.

"Good bye, my dear," sobbed the old lady, almost heartbroken, kissing her child again as she stepped upon the ladder. "God bless you! do write to me soon, be sure you do — I only want to hear from you often. Take care of yourself. Here, my love," she added, taking a handkerchief from her neck, "tie this round your poor dear throat."

"No, mother, no," said the poor girl crying bitterly, "that's the only one you have left. I'll be plenty warm enough."

"Yes, do," said the old lady, "I'm sure you'll take cold."

"Hold hard!" cried the coachman as the horses were dancing, on the cloths being drawn from their loins. "Whit, whit!" and away they pranced, as merrily as if they had known that *their* load was nothing when compared with the load they had left behind them. Even old Uncle John, as he cried "Good bye, my dear boy," and waved his hand for the last time, felt the tears trickling fast down his cheeks.

"No, no room, marm!" said the coachman, shaking his head as he approached the corner of the street at which Mrs. Vox was standing.

Valentine's attention was thus directed to his mother, who was kissing her hand with considerable rapidity, when the salute was returned, and the coach passed on.

The fulness of Valentine's heart caused him for the first hour to be silent; but after that, the constant change of scene, and the pure bracing air had the effect of restoring his spirits, and he felt a very powerful inclination to sing. Just, however, as he was about to commence for his own amusement, the coach stopped to change horses, when Tooler, the coachman, of course got down, and as several of the passengers followed his example, Valentine got down too, and as they all went into the road-side house, and called for glasses of ale, why Valentine called for a glass like the rest, and drank it with equal enjoyment. In less than two minutes they started again, and Valentine, who then felt ready for anything, began to think seriously of the exercise of his power

"Whit, whit!" said Tooler, between a whisper and a whistle, as the fresh horses galloped up the hill.

"Stop! hoa!" cried Valentine, assuming a voice, the sound of which appeared to have travelled some distance.

"You have left one behind," observed a gentleman in black, who had secured the box-seat.

"O let un run a bit," said Tooler. "Whit! It'll give un a winder up this little hill, and teach un to be up in time in future. If we was to wait for every passenger as chooses to lag behind, we shouldn't git over the ground in a fortnit."

"Hoa! stop! stop! stop!" reiterated Valentine in the voice of a man pretty well out of breath.

Tooler, without deigning to look behind, retickled the haunches of his leaders and gleefully chuckled at the idea of *how* he was making a passenger sweat.

The voice was heard no more, and Tooler on reaching the top of the hill pulled up and looked round, but could see no man running.

"Where is he?" inquired Tooler.

"In the ditch!" replied Valentine, throwing his voice behind.

"In the ditch!" exclaimed Tooler. "Blarm me, whereabouts?"

"There," said Valentine.

"God bless my soul!" cried the gentleman in black, who was an exceedingly nervous village clergyman. "The poor person no doubt has fallen down in an absolute state of exhaustion. How very, very wrong of you, coachman, not to stop."

Tooler, apprehensive of some serious occurrence, got down with the view of dragging the exhausted passenger out of the ditch, but although he ran several hundred yards down the hill, no such person of course could be found.

"Who saw un?" shouted Tooler as he panted up the hill again.

"I saw nothing," said a passenger behind, "but a boy jumping over the hedge."

Tooler looked at his way-bill, counted the passengers, found them all right, and remounting the box, got the horses again into a gallop, in the perfect conviction that some villanous young scarecrow had raised the false alarm.

"Whit! blarm them 'ere boys!" said Tooler, "stead o' mindin their crows they are allus up to suffen. I only wish I had un here, I'd pay *on* to their blarmed bodies; if I wouldn't ——." At this interesting moment, and as if to give a practical illustration of what he would have done in that case, he gave the off-wheeler so telling a cut round the loins, that the animal without any ceremony kicked over the trace. Of course Tooler was compelled to pull up again immediately; and after having adjusted the trace, and asking the animal seriously what he meant, at the same time enforcing the question by giving him a blow on the bony part of his nose, he prepared to remount; but just as he had got his left foot upon the nave of the wheel, Valentine so admirably imitated the sharp snapping growl of a dog in the front boot, that Tooler started back as quickly as if he had been shot, while the gentleman in black dropped the reins and almost jumped into the road.

"Good gracious!" exclaimed the gentleman in black, trembling with great energy; "how wrong, how very horribly wrong of you, coachman, not to tell me that a dog had been placed beneath my feet."

"Blarm their carcases!" cried Tooler, "they never told *me* a dog was shoved there. Lay *down!* We'll soon have yow out there together!"

"Not for the world!" cried the gentleman in black, as Tooler approached the footboard in order to open it. "Not for the world! un-un-un-unless you le-le-let me get down first. I have no desire to pe-pe-perish of hydropho-phobia."

"Kip yar fut on the board then sir, please," said Tooler, "we'll soon have the varmint out o' that." So saying, he gathered up the reins, remounted the box, and started off the horses again at full gallop.

The gentleman in black then began to explain to Tooler how utterly inconceivable was the number of persons who had died of hydrophobia within an almost unspeakably short space of time, in the immediate vicinity of the residence of a friend of his in London; and just as he had got into the marrow of a most excruciating description of the intense mental and physical agony of which the disease in its worst stage was productive, both he and Tooler suddenly sprang back, with their feet in the air, and their heads between the knees of the passengers behind them, on Valentine giving a loud growling snap, more bitingly indicative of anger than before.

As Tooler had tightly hold of the reins when he made this involuntary spring, the horses stopped on the instant, and allowed him time to scramble up again without rendering the slow process dangerous.

"I cannot, I-I-I positively cannot," said the gentleman in black, who had been thrown again into a dreadful state of excitement. "I cannot sit here — my nerves cannot endure it; it's perfectly shocking."

"Blister their bowls!" exclaimed Tooler, whose first impulse was to drag the dog out of the boot at all hazards, but who, on seeing the horses waiting in the road a short distance a-head for the next stage, thought it better to wait till he had reached them. "I'll make un remember this the longest day o' thar blessed lives — blarm un! Phih'! I'll let un know when I get back, I warrant. I'll larn un to ——."

"Hoa, coachman! hoa! my hat's off!" cried Valentine, throwing his voice to the back of the coach.

"Well *may* I be phit!" said Tooler. "I'll make yow run back for't any how — phit!"

In less than a minute the coach drew up opposite the stable, when the gentleman in black at once proceeded to alight. Just, however, as his foot reached the plate of the roller bolt, another growl from Valentine frightened him backwards, when falling upon one of the old horse-keepers, he knocked him fairly down, and rolled over him heavily.

"Darng your cloomsy carkus!" cried the horse-keeper, gathering himself up, "carn't you git oof ar cooarch aroat knocking o' pipple darn?"

"I-I-I beg pardon," trembling, observed

the gentleman in black; "I hope I-I ——."

"Whoap-! pardon!" contemptuously echoed the horse-keeper as he limped towards the bars to unhook the leaders' traces.

"Now then, yow warmint, let's see who yow belong to," said Tooler, approaching the mouth of the boot; but just as he was in the act of raising the foot board, another angry snap made him close it again with the utmost rapidity.

"Lay down! blarm your body!" cried Tooler, shrinking back. "Here yow Jim, kim here, boi, and take this 'ere devil of a dog out o' that."

Jim approached, and the growling was louder than before, while the gentleman in black implored Jim to take care that the animal didn't get hold of his hand.

"Here yow Harry!" shouted Jim, "yare noot afeared o' doogs together — darng un *I* doont like un."

Accordingly Harry came, and then Sam, and then Bob, and then Bill, but as the dog could not be seen, and as the snarling continued, neither of them dared to put his hand in to drag the monster forth. Bob therefore ran off for Tom Titus the blacksmith, who was known to care for neither dog nor devil, and in less than two minutes Tom Titus arrived with about three feet and a half of rod iron red hot.

"Darng un!" cried Tom, "this 'ere 'll maake un *quit* together!"

"Dear me! my good man," said the gentleman in black, "don't use that unchristianlike implement! don't put the dumb thing to such horrible torture!"

"It don't siggerfy a button," cried Tooler, "I marnt go to stop here all day. Out o' that he must come."

Upon this Tom Titus introduced his professional weapon, and commenced poking about with considerable energy, while the snapping and growling increased with each poke.

"I'll tell you what it is," said Tom Titus, turning round and wiping the sweat off his brow with his naked arm, "this here cretur here's stark raavin mad."

"I knew that he was," cried the gentleman in black, getting into an empty wagon which stood without horses just out of the road; "I felt perfectly sure that he was rabid."

"He's a bull-terrier too," said Tom Titus, "I knows it by's growl. It's the worsest and dargdest to goo maad as is."

"Well what shall us do wi' th' warment?" said Tooler.

"Shoot him! shoot him!" cried the gentleman in black.

"O I've goot a blunderbuss, Bob!" said Tom Titus, "yow run for't together, it's top o' the forge."

Bob started at once, and Tom kept on the bar, while Tooler, Sam, Harry, and Bob held the heads of the horses.

"He's got un; all right!" cried Tom Titus, as Bob neared the coach with the weapon on his shoulder. "Yow'll be doon for in noo time," he added, as he felt with his rod to ascertain in which corner of the boot the bull-terrier lay.

"Is she loarded?" asked Bob, as he handed Tom Titus the instrument of death.

"Mind you make the shot come out at bottom," shouted Tooler.

"I hool," said Tom Titus, putting the weapon to his shoulder. "Noo the loord ha' marcy on yar sool, as joodge says sizes," and instantly let fly.

The horses of course plunged considerably, but still did no mischief; and before the smoke had evaporated, Valentine introduced into the boot a low melancholy howl, which convinced Tom Titus that the shot had taken effect.

"He's give oop the ghost; darng his carkus!" cried Tom, as he poked the dead body into the corner.

"Well, let's have a look at un," said Tooler, "let's see what the warment is like."

The gentleman in black at once leaped out of the wagon, and every one present drew near, when Tom, guided by the rod which he had kept upon the body, put his hand into the boots, and drew forth a fine hare that had been shattered by the shot all to pieces.

"He arnt a bull-tarrier," cried Bob.

"But that arnt he," said Tom Titus. "He's some'er aboot here as dead as a darng'd nail: I know he's a corpse."

"Are yow sure on't?" asked Tooler.

"There arnt any bairn dooor deader," cried Tom. "Here, I'll lug um out an show yar."

"No, no!" shouted Tooler, as Tom proceeded to pull out the luggage. "I marnt stay for that: I'm an hour behind now, blarm un! Jimp up, genelmen!"

Tom Titus and his companions, who wanted the bull-terrier as a trophy, entreated Tooler to allow them to have it, and having at length gained his consent, Tom proceeded to empty the boot. Every eye was, of course, directed to every thing drawn out, and when Tom made a solemn declaration that the boot was empty, they were all, at once, struck with amazement. Each looked at the other with astounding incredulity, and overhauled the luggage again and again.

"Do you mean to say," said Tooler, "that there arnt nuffin else in the boot?"

"Darnged a thing!" cried Tom Titus, "coom an look." And Tooler did look, and the gentleman in black looked, and Bob looked, and Harry looked, and Bill looked, and Sam looked, and all looked, but found the boot empty.

"Well, blarm me!"—cried Tooler—"But darng it all, he must be somewhere!"

"I'll taake my solum davy," said Bill, "that he *was* there."

"I seed um myself," exclaimed Bob, "wi my oarn oyes, an didn't loike the looks on um a bit."

"There cannot," said the gentleman in black, "be the smallest possible doubt about his having been there; but the question for our mature consideration is, where is he now?"

"I'll bet a pint," said Harry, "you blowed um away."

"Blowed um away, you fool!—how could I ha blowed um away?" said Tom Titus in tones of contempt.

"Why he *was* there," said Bob, "and he baint there noo, and he baint here naything, so you must ha blowed um out o't th' boot: sides look at the muzzle o' this ere blunderbust!"

"Well, of all the rummest goes as ever happened," said Tooler, thrusting his hands to the very bottom of his pockets—"this ere flogs 'em all into nuffin!"

"It is perfectly astounding!" exclaimed the gentleman in black, looking again into the boot, while the men stood and stared at each other with their mouths as wide open as human mouths could be.

"Well, in wi' em agin," cried Tooler. "In wi' em!—Blarm me if this here arnt a queer 'un to get over."

The luggage was accordingly replaced, and Tooler, on mounting the box, told the men to get a gallon of beer, when the gentleman in black generously gave them half-a-crown, and the horses started off, leaving Tom with his blunderbuss, Harry, Bill, Sam, and their companions, bewildered with the mystery which the whole day spent in the ale-house by no means enabled them to solve.

Valentine chuckled so desperately over the success of this scheme, that he dared not, for fear of being suspected, commence another for some considerable time. The absurd surmises of the puzzled Tooler, and the inferences of the gentleman in black, which were scarcely less ridiculous, kept him in a perpetual fever while they met the "down coach."

"You leave us here, of course?" observed the gentleman in black.

"Noo," said Tooler, "worse look, I'm agoin right through. I've made a 'rangement wi' Waddle, tother coachman. He wants to goo darn and I wants to goo up. It taint often I do goo to tarn, but whens'ever I do, suffin's sure to be the matter. I've got a 'pointment at seven to goo wi' moi gals to the play an noo you see, blarm it—phit! phit!—I'm a cupple o' hours behind."

"Hallo, my cherry bounce!" shouted Waddle, as he and Tooler pulled up. "What's the natur o'the game *now?* Here a matter o' *sixteen* mile out!"—Tooler shook his head thoughtfully. "A spill my old wegitable?—Anything broke?"—continued Waddle—"Any haccident?"

"*About* the rummest go," replied Tooler, "as yow ever had any notion on yet. But I marnt stop noo. I'll tell yow ool about it to-morrow—phit! phit!"

"Well, ta ta, my turnip!" observed Mr. Waddle, and away the coaches rattled in opposite directions, Tooler lashing his leaders with unparalleled severity.

Valentine, having regained full command over his muscles, and perceiving that Tooler's nerves were so perfectly unstrung, that the slightest thing would seriously annoy him, now began to indulge in his favourite imitations of a fretful child, upon the exactness of which he prided himself especially. He sobbed, and squalled, and coughed, and hooped, and strained, and held his breath, and then struggling convulsively with his voice again, with all the vehemence of which he was capable, while Tooler was whipping, and shuffling, and fretting himself into a fever of excitement.

"Blarm that 'ere child!" exclaimed Tooler looking round, "If yow'd keep that ere little un o' yourn quiet, marm, I'd thank yar." Valentine, however, still continued to persevere in his interesting imitations until Tooler, having worked himself up to such a pitch of excitement, that he could scarcely hold the reins, shouted angrily, "Marm! yow must keep that 'ere child o' yourn a leetle matter still. My horses carnt stand it: they carnt get along. Phit! Darng me, if it beant enow to drive a man mad!"

"I dare say it's after its teeth, poor thing!" observed the gentleman in black.

"It's teeath!" cried Tooler, "It ony wants the breast. *Jist* listen to it! Blarm my body."

"I *can't* keep it quiet!" cried Valentine, assuming the voice of a female. "It arnt o' no use: I must throw it away," and he immediately uttered a piercing shriek, and exclaimed, "The child, the *child!*—the child's off!"

Tooler, of course, stopped on the instant, and having given the reins to the gentleman in black, got down with the view of rescuing the infant from its perilous position, and of pointing out to its mother in terms of just indignation the extreme inhumanity of her conduct.

"Where is it, yow *baggage*;" cried Tooler, looking anxiously along the road.

"Ha yow drapped onythin cooarchman?" inquired a countryman, sitting behind.

"Drapped anythin?" angrily echoed Tooler. "Where, *where* is the child?"

"Woot choild?" inquired the countryman.

"Why that wumman's child as she jist throw'd away!" shouted Tooler.

"We arnt had noo choild here," said the countryman — a fact to which all who sat behind bore instant testimony.

"What!" exclaimed Tooler, "do yow mean to say? do yow mean to tell me you beant had a child there that's been cryin' the last hour, an' puttin' my horses into this ere darng'd sweat?"

"I tell yow," replied the countryman, "we arnt had no choild; we arnt seen nuffin like a choild here."

"Well, may I *be* darngd!" exclaimed Tooler, scratching his head very violently, and swinging his right arm with great force through the air. "This beats all as I ever *did* hear on afore. It doant siggerfy tawking," added he, on remounting the box; "the devil's aither an inside or an outside passenger. I've got 'un, to-day, sure enow." And Tooler drew out his way-bill with the view of ascertaining which was likely to be his Satanic Majesty *incog.*, while the gentleman in black, the three passengers who sat on the same seat with Valentine, and Valentine himself, were expressing to each other their utter astonishment at the extraordinary character of the occurrence, with great eloquence and warmth.

"That's it! — I have it!" said Tooler to himself as a countrywoman passed with a basket on her arm. "She said so — she said she would. Blarm her old body!"

It was easy to perceive that at that moment something had flitted across Tooler's mind, which had proved to him a source of fresh annoyance, for he appeared to be in a state of extreme agitation, and continued to be so, muttering short, and bitter sentences, scratching his head, striking the crown of his hat, and violently grinding his teeth, until he arrived at the end of the stage, when he ran into the stable with breathless haste, and returned before a second idea of his object could be conceived, with a box of tools in one hand and a horse-shoe in the other.

"Hold hard a bit, Bill," said he, kneeling upon the pole and nailing the horse-shoe to the foot-board. "There! now do your worst! Blarm yar carkus! I defy yar!" While horses were being put in, Tooler shook his head most triumphantly and smiled at the horse-shoe with intense satisfaction.

"What, in the name of goodness," said the gentleman in black, when Tooler had re-mounted, "have you nailed to the foot-board?"

"Hold hard! Phih! a horse-shoe!" cried Tooler; "The cooarch is bewitched, sir! — least ways it *was*; but I've cured it now — *that's* a settler!"

"Awful!" exclaimed the gentleman in black, with due solemnity. "How *can* you, coachman, entertain so impious a thought?"

"I know it!" said Tooler, "that wumman as we passed with a basket then brought it to my mind. She's, for all the world, like her."

"Like whom?" inquired the gentleman in black.

"Why, like the witch!" replied Tooler. "I'll tell yow ool about it. T'other day, when I wor comin' along the rooard, I seed this 'ere warmint a settin on the path, with a basket by her side. Young Harry, the nevy of our proprietor, was on the box wi' me, and so says he, Tooler, says he, I'll bet yow a crown bowl o' punch, yow doant hook that 'ere basket up here. Done, says I. It's a bet, says he, done. So I makes my whip ready, and jist as we come along side o'the warmint, I winds it round the handle of the basket, and, sartin enough, up it comes, when Harry catches it jist by the middle o'the handle, and I s'pose it mought ha' had in a cupple o'score of eggs, wi' the yolks of which, in course, we was smothered. Well, I pulls up at once, for I couldn't see my horses until I wiped some on it off; and while Harry and me was laughing at aich other, fit to split, up comes the old warment, and, praps, she didn't go it a good un! Well, as soon as I could get through the mess, to my pocket, I dropped her half-a-crown, and Harry dropped her another; but even this didn't satisfy the nasty old frump; she wanted them 'ere eggs, pitickler, it seemed, and no others would do; and she swore that I should rue the day I broke 'em. So says Harry; Do yow know who she is? Noo, says I, I carnt say as I do. Why, says he, that's the famous old witch! The devil it is, says I, and so it was; and this is the way she's been a sarvin' me out. But I've fixed her wi' the horse-shoe, there, darng her old carkus, she carnt do no more mischief now."

"Are you sure of that? Beware!" said Valentine, in an awfully hollow whisper, sufficiently loud only to reach Tooler's ear.

Tooler trembled for an instant; but his faith in the virtue of the horse-shoe being fixed, he soon regained his self-possession, and, giving his head a knowing devil-may-care twist, sat firmly in his seat, fully determined to take no heed of any thing that might threaten.

"Hoa! coarchman!" exclaimed one of the passengers at this moment; "only *look* at this wheel!"

Tooler sat like a statue. He did not deign to move a muscle.

"Coarchman! coarchman!" shouted the countryman who was sitting behind; "lookee how this off-wheel's a waddling!"

"Blarm un!" cried Tooler, "let un waddle! Phit! Phit!" and away went the horses down the hill; but in an instant Tooler saw the wheel whizzing a-head, at the rate of full thirty miles an hour.

"Lean all to the left!" shouted Tooler, and the passengers obeyed him, but he also pulled the horses to the left so violently that the coach coming in contact with the jutting bank, turned over and deposited him and the passengers upon a newly formed bed of manure.

Witchcraft was, in Tooler's view, again triumphant. His faith in the efficacy of horse-shoes vanished. He felt himself perfectly beaten, and, therefore, after having, with considerable difficulty, managed to get his insides out, he left his horses, coach, and luggage in the care of the persons who had fortunately witnessed the accident, and waddled with the fragments of the whip in his hand towards a road-side inn a few hundred yards distant. On reaching the house, of course, a thousand questions were asked in a breath: not one of them, however, did Tooler deign to answer. He threw himself carelessly into a large arm-chair, and, declaring that he would not drive that day another step, drank with infinite gusto, in a rummer of raw brandy, "Eternal perdition to the witch!"

CHAPTER VI.

PECULIAR LIBERALITY OF THE GENTLEMAN IN BLACK.—THE GREEN-EYED MONSTER PREVENTS THE PERFORMANCE OF A MOST DISINTERESTED ACT OF FRIENDSHIP.

UPON a man unused to profound thinking, profound thought has a peculiarly somniferous effect. No sooner does he get below the surface than he falls fast asleep, and although he dreams of his subject with unspeakable zeal, draws conclusions from his premises, solves collateral problems, establishes positions, and carries his designs into imaginary execution, his mind, when he awakes, leaps back over the interesting interregnum, and begins to toil again at the point from which it started.

Such had been the workings of Tooler's vivid imagination, and such was precisely his position when awakened by the arrival of the passengers at the Inn. Having proposed with great feeling, and drank with due sincerity, "Eternal perdition to the Witch," he fell at once into a train of deep thought which, as a natural consequence, induced deep sleep, in which he saw and held a visionary conversation with the hag whose unhallowed influence he was just on the point of overthrowing, when the passengers entered the well-warmed parlour in which he was snoring aloud.

"We've got un to roights," said John Brown, the landlord, who headed the group, "we've got un up again, *Sir!*" continued he in a much louder tone, shaking Tooler with what in any ordinary case might have been deemed most unnecessary violence.

Tooler unconsciously nodded an acknowledgment, and began to snore again just as loudly as before.

"Come coachman, come, *come* my good man," said the gentleman in black; but he could make no impression upon Tooler at all. At length, however, by virtue of bawling, tickling, and shaking, John Brown succeeded in causing him to open his eyes, which he at once commenced rubbing with great desperation.

"Now, Sir!" said John Brown, "It's all roight!"

"O—ah!" observed Tooler.

"We've got on the wheel, and all's ready," continued John Brown.

"Ah—yes—jis so—well," remarked Tooler at intervals, "anythin' brook?"

"Nothin; couldn't ha' split on a softerer place."

"Well, that's a blessing anyhow!" said Tooler. "Is the cooarch locked up safe?"

"Locked oop!" cried John Brown, "noo! she's standin' at the door here all ready to start."

"I shaunt stor another step this blessed night if I know it," said Tooler, taking his hat off and dashing it to the ground with the air of one whose mind, having been once made up, possessed the quality of being immutable.

"What!" exclaimed the gentleman in black,—"but, no, no; you are jesting."

In order to prove that nothing bearing even the semblance of a jest was intended, Tooler proceeded to pull off his shawl and box-coat, while the passengers exchanged looks of utter amazement.

"My good man," continued the gentleman in black, you surely do not mean to remain here? come, *come*, let us start."

"Here I am, and here I sticks," said Tooler firmly; and after shaking his head, he unbuttoned his boot-straps—a process which caused the antique tops, which were as large as a pair of moderate-sized chimney-pots, to fall upon his insteps *sans ceremonie*.

"I will not believe it," said the gentleman in black, "I cannot believe that you are serious; come, come, coachman, come!"

"It doant siggerfy tawkin' a button," cried Tooler, "we carn't get to Tarn noo to-night. 'Sides, if I was to break the wind of all my horses, I shouldn't be up afore twelve o'clock now, and what *is* the use o'that?"

"Yow'd be able to do it by ten," said John Brown.

"And what's the use o' ten?" inquired Tooler indignantly. "What's the use o' ten, when I ought to ha' bin in at six?"

"I am a man of few words," said the gentleman in black, "a man of very few words; and I beg you to understand that what I say I fully mean. I *must* be in London to-night, and therefore, if you are resolved on remaining here, I will post up to town, and make you or your proprietors bear the expense."

Having tremblingly delivered himself thus, the gentleman in black turned exceedingly white, and as he prepared to leave the room with the view of making certain necessary inquiries, Valentine, assuming his voice, ordered seven large glasses of brandy-and-water, and rump-steaks and onions for nine.

No sooner was this order given, than the whole of the domestic establishment of John Brown was in an uproar. Dan was sent out for the steaks; Mary was told to peel the onions; Roger was directed to wipe the bars of the gridiron, and Sally was ordered to make the fire clear with salt, while the hostess herself mixed the brandy-and-water, and scolded all about her with due bitterness and force.

While these preparations were making, the gentleman in black ascertained, to his unspeakable mortification, that there was not a single posting house within seven miles of the place. He, therefore, deemed it expedient to alter his tone, and having decided upon certain persuasive arguments, which he felt were too potent to fail, he returned to employ them as the hostess entered the parlour with the brandy-and-water on her best japanned tray.

"Now, coachman," said he, "my dear man, do consider the inconvenience of which this delay will be productive."

"It's o' no use," said Tooler, "it's o' no sort o' use. I carn't move from this ere blessed spot. It's unpossible. I arn't no more power over them are four horses than a babby. I *carn't* drive, and now yow've the long and the short on't."

"O! for that matter," cried Brown, "as I never am backard in coming forard to sarve a friend, I'll drive for yar."

"You're a *fool!*" observed the hostess, in an audible whisper, at the same time tugging with great violence at John Brown's coat-tails, and giving him certain significant sidelong glances of great import, as affecting his conjugal peace. John Brown, however, still persevered in expressing the pleasure he should derive from the performance of this act of disinterested friendship; for although he in general held the hints of his spouse in high respect, and understood that in this particular instance she was actuated by a desire to make the most of the party, one of whom had been so liberal in his orders at the commencement, he regarded it as being by no means improbable that Tooler would be in consequence discharged, and that *he* would be put upon the coach as his successor, which happened to be precisely what for several years he had been constantly on the look-out for.

"But do you think sariously," said Tooler, after a pause, "that yow'd be able to get up by twelve?"

"By *twelve!*" cried John Brown. "If I don't get in afore the clock strikes *ten*, I'll be bound to be pisoned. Ony jist say the word, and whiles the ladies and gentlemen is a having their snack, I'll be makin' myself a leetle matter tidy."

"Come, my good man; you'll agree to it, will you not—come?" said the gentleman in black, in a tone irresistibly persuasive.

"Well, well," said Tooler, with evident reluctance, "have it as yow like;" and he proceeded to button up his boot-tops again, while Mary was carefully laying the cloth.

The grand point being at length settled, John Brown left the room, and the hostess, assisted by her handmaids in clean white aprons, placed the rump-steaks and onions upon the table.

"*Now* if you please, sir," said the hostess,

bestowing one of her blandest smiles upon the gentleman in black, as she gracefully placed a chair for him at the head of the table. "Do'ee eat it while it's hot: there's some more inguns doin."

"Not any for me, I thank you," said that gentleman with great politeness. "I have not the smallest appetite, I'll take a glass of sherry and a biscuit."

"Oh! do'ee eat a leetle," urged the fascinating hostess. "It's done very beautiful. Look'ee!" added the tempter, as she took off the cover, and displayed a fine steak garnished with onions, the sight of which at once drew the rest of the passengers towards the table.

"Do have a bit with us sir, do!" cried the passengers in a chorus. "We shall not enjoy it half so much without you."

"Why not, my good people?" inquired the pastor.

"Cause," replied the hostess, "you was kind enow to order it!"

"*I*, my good woman!" exclaimed the astonished gentleman, peering over his spectacles with a look of amazement. "I ordered, I?"

"In course, sir, you did," replied the hostess, as the pleasing expression of her countenance vanished.

"Dear me! my good woman," rejoined the pastor, "you must have been dreaming."

"I 'peal to the gentlemen and ladies present," said the hostess, "whether you didn't order seven glasses o' brandy-and-water, and rump-steaks and inguns for nine."

"Oh that's right enough," said one of the passengers, "that wor the order ersackly, you doan't mean to go for to say as how it wasn't, sir, do yer?"

"Upon my honour, my good people," returned the pastor; "believe me, you were never more mistaken in your lives."

"Not a bit on't," observed Tooler, "I heerd yow myself."

"God bless my soul! Impossible! impossible!" cried the pastor, as he strove with great energy of mind to ascertain what sentence in the English language, bore the slightest resemblance in point of sound to "seven glasses of brandy-and-water, and rump-steaks and onions for nine."

"Well, whether or no," observed the hostess, "there's what was ordered, and I 'spects to be paid for it at all events."

"Come," said the farmer, who had occupied a seat at the back of the coach, "let's tackle it together, for I feel rayther peckish," and he and Valentine with two other passengers commenced; the rest modestly keeping aloof from the table, lest payment should be demanded of them respectively as a social matter of course.

"Yow may as well just have a mouthful as not," said the farmer, "sin' yow do mean to pay all the same!"

"Really," observed the gentleman in black, "I am unconscious of having made such an arrangement."

"Well, well," said Valentine, in his natural voice; "suppose we compromise the matter, as there appears to be some slight misunderstanding on the subject: you settle for the steaks, and I'll pay for the brandy-and-water."

"Well, coom, that's handsome!" cried the farmer, "and to show that I doon't want to shirk from my share, why I'll be a couple o' bottles o' wine,—coom, what say yow noo?"

"I cannot, under the circumstances, of course object to join you," replied the puzzled pastor; "but I must be permitted to say that those circumstances are in my judgment perfectly inexplicable: I never in any case like to be *positive*; I know that human nature is but human nature, and therefore cannot pretend to claim entire exemption from those weaknesses which form its distinguishing characteristics: I may be mistaken: I confess that I may; but I nevertheless hold it to be utterly impossible for any man to give such an order as that without knowing it."

"Oh! 'pon my loife," said the farmer, "it's a postyve fact."

"Of course I'll not presume to dispute it," returned the pastor, whose scepticism on the point still developed itself strongly. "All I can say is, that I am totally oblivious of the circumstances; but if I *did* give the order, I bow to your decision."

No sooner had this arrangement been completed, than the passengers who had before kept so modestly aloof, lost the whole of their interesting diffidence. They made themselves perfectly at home, and drew at once towards the table, at the head of which, of course, set the gentleman in black, who appeared to have borrowed, for that particular occasion, the well-trained appetite of an untamed elephant. As all social distinctions were, for the time being levelled, Tooler was invited to join them; but although he tried with zeal to compete with the rest, his gastronomic powers entirely deserted him. He ate scarcely any thing, albeit the dish before him was one which on ordinary occasions he especially favoured. He experienced, however, no difficulty in drinking. Of the wine and brandy-and-water he partook freely, with the view of drowning the unhallowed influence of the witch; but the more deeply he drank, the more strongly did he feel, that that influence was still in the ascendant.

As soon as John Brown found the party had ordered all the spirits and wine they were likely to order, he entered the room to announce the fact of his being ready, and to explain the expediency of an immediate start. The bill was consequently called for on the instant, when the amount was divided as per agreement, and paid, and the passengers prepared for the completion of their journey.

The moment, however, John entered the room, Valentine was led to suspect that he had some unfriendly design upon Tooler. He therefore watched him narrowly, and as his searching eye quickly discovered sufficient to confirm his suspicion, he resolved on thwarting the object of Mr. John Brown, by causing him to abandon his intention of performing the act of disinterested friendship proposed.

Accordingly, Valentine at once left the room, with the view of ascertaining what means were available; and as he saw the hostess standing with a butcher in the bar, whose conversation touched the toughness of a certain leg of mutton, he awaited in the passage the arrival of John Brown. He had scarcely, however, decided the course to be pursued, when John made his appearance whip in hand. Valentine saw that no time was to be lost, and therefore, assuming the voice of the hostess, whispered loud enough to reach John's ear: "Go now, my love, go; and return by-and-bye: you have nothing to fear: John will not be back to-night!"

"Indeed!" murmured John, starting back at the sound of an affectionate kiss with which Valentine concluded. "Indeed!" he repeated, and bit his lips violently and breathed with vehemence, as the group in the back ground pressed him towards the door, and thus forced him to see the pride of his heart and home in conversation with one who happened to be the identical butcher upon whom he had long looked with a peculiarly jealous eye.

Valentine now felt that he had struck the right chord, for the complexion of John turned as pale as it could turn — that is to say, it turned to a pale Prussian blue, as the nearest approach to whiteness of which it was capable, while his huge teeth rattled like a pair of castanets, and indeed his whole frame shook convulsively with passion pent up. Contrary, however, to the expectation of Valentine, John, after turning in the direction of the bar, his flashing eyes, which appeared to pierce the wooden partition with more facility than could a pair of the brightest gimblets, conjured up all his courage, and mounted the box. The start was a false one, for he dropped one of the reins and his whip at the same time. This, however, was soon remedied; but they had not proceeded far, before the attention of Tooler was drawn to the excited state of John's nerves.

"A'n't yow been havin' a drop o' suffin extra?" inquired Tooler, as they rolled from side to side.

"Not a drain!" replied John; and the coach gave another lunge. "But the fact of the matter's this," continued he, looking round to ascertain if they could be seen from his once happy home — "the fact is, I feels so uncommon poorly, that I'm afeered I shan't be able to go much furder arter all."

"Well give me the ribbons, then," said Tooler, who, feeling somewhat better, began to be ashamed of his inactive position. "I can manage, I des say. Do yow go back — I'm obleedged to yer, you know, all the same."

"Well, if you think you *can* drive," observed John.

"Why," interrupted Tooler, whose professional pride had been touched by that remark, "if I can't do it better than that, I can't do it at all!"

This was enough for John Brown. He pulled up on an instant; and after apologising for his inability to perform his promise, alighted, with the view of acquiring that knowledge which would most grieve his heart, and of disturbing the development of the assumed illicit loves of his amiable spouse and the cold-blooded butcher.

The moment, however, Tooler regained possession of the reins, the dreaded influence of the witch regained possession of his soul; but Valentine, who had removed to the vacant seat on the box, did all in his power to cheer him, and, as he firmly resolved to annoy him no more, he succeeded, after an infinite deal of persuasion, in inspiring him with the belief of its being an immutable ordinance of Nature, that the power of no witch should extend beyond the radius of forty miles.

CHAPTER VII.

INTRODUCES GREAT-UNCLE JOHN'S FRIEND AND HIS AFFECTIONATE RELATIVES, WITH A KNIGHT OF A NEW ORDER, TWO INVISIBLE BURGLARS, AND ONE MOST REMARKABLE SWEEP.

Mr. Grimwood Goodman, Great-Uncle John's friend, to whom Valentine had been consigned, was a gentleman possessed of some considerable wealth, derived chiefly from a series of successful speculations in sperm oil. He was remarkably thin — so thin, indeed, that his heart beat against his bare ribs with an energy which alone might have caused it to be discovered that that organ is more insensible to feeling than to sight. If, however, the heart of Goodman was — like the hearts of men in the aggregate — physically insensible, morally it was by far the most sensible of all the organs he possessed. A tear touched it acutely; a tale of distress at once caused it to open: indeed, sorrow in any shape had but to approach, to find itself surrounded by feelings of benevolence, which caused it to dry up its natural tears, and to shed those only of gratitude and joy.

In stature, Grimwood Goodman—although he boasted with pride of having stood full six feet without his shoes when a private in the Loyal Volunteers — was, at the time of which we write, about five feet eight. He would never allow that he had sunk so many inches; but he could not have been more, for he was able to walk under the six feet standard with his military cap on without moving a hair. He had never been married. His relatives — the only relatives of whom he happened to have any knowledge, to wit, a brother, a nephew, and their wives — had disinterestedly taken especial care of that, for in order that the idea of marrying might be effectually banished from his mind, he never visited them, nor did they ever visit him, without the occurrence of those interesting family broils with which the matrimonial state is occasionally enlivened. Not that his brother and nephew lived unhappily with those whom they had respectively pledged themselves to love and cherish: on the contrary, they enjoyed a greater share of domestic comfort than commonly falls to the lot of married men; but the arrangement between them was to appear to be steeped to the very lips in domestic misery whenever Grimwood happened to be present, with the view of deterring him from entering into that state of life to which certain maids and widows had modestly called him. And the scheme proved effectual. He trembled at the thought of embarking in a business, which they had led him to believe was extremely tempestuous at *best;* for what deterred him more than all, was the earnest anxiety which they manifested on all occasions to convince him that, although they snarled, and frowned, and growled, and wished each other dead, they in reality lived as happily together, if not more happily, than married people in general. He therefore having no sort of taste for the loving specimens of matrimonial felicity, which they so constantly placed before his eyes, kept aloof, resolved firmly to live a life of single blessedness unto the end.

Now, when these peculiarly affectionate creatures heard that Valentine was coming to London, they were thrown, perhaps naturally, into a feverish state of alarm; for, although they had never seen him, the accounts of "the young wretch" which had reached them, had been singularly flattering, and therefore they held him to be one who, by making a favourable impression on him in whom the whole of their expectations were concentrated, might "rob" them, as they termed it, of some portion of that wealth, for which, through the medium of Grimwood's death, they so ardently panted. They therefore lost no time in meeting, with the view of devising some scheme by which the loudest of their fears might be hushed, and as Mr. Walter Goodman had been deputed by his brother Grimwood to meet Valentine at the Inn, it was, after a long consultation, decided that he should represent himself to be Grimwood, secure Valentine in certain private lodgings, and eventually either procure for him a berth on board some man-of-war about to sail for a foreign station, or send him out as an adventurer to seek his fortune abroad.

Accordingly, Walter proceeded to the inn at the appointed time, while his hopeful son, Horace, prepared everything for Valentine's reception — it being arranged that the moment he arrived he should be hurried away, and that when he had reached his new residence, Grimwood should be informed that he had not arrived at all. Fortunately, however, for Valentine, the coach was so late, that Grimwood, having despatched the pressing business he had in hand, became seriously alarmed, and on going down himself to the inn, he insisted upon relieving brother Walter from all responsibility, and to the bitter mortification of that gentleman, waited in the coffee-room the arrival of the coach.

The design, however, of the affectionate family-party was not to be frustrated thus. No sooner had Grimwood determined on waiting himself than Walter started off to meet the coach, with the view of securing Valentine still; while Grimwood was seated in the coffee-room, drinking, without enjoyment, the pint of claret he had ordered, and mechanically reading the *Times*. Although his eyes were on the paper, his thoughts were on the coach, and he had just drank his last glass of wine, and began to marvel at the possibility of a man reading for hours without bringing his mind to bear upon any single sentence, when the clock struck ten.

"Waiter," said he to a sleek, round-faced person in pumps, "this is very extraordinary — is it not?"

"Why, sir," replied that interesting person, who being extremely fussy, and unable to speak without using his napkin, commenced wiping the bottom of Goodman's glass with great energy. "Why, sir, it is, sir, raythar, sir; but not werry neither, sir, cos the down coachman's comin' up, sir, today, and he's always extrornary late."

"I fear that some serious accident has occurred," observed Goodman.

"Oh, no fear of that, sir;" cried the fussy individual, who had commenced operations upon the bottom of the decanter; "it's all right enough, sir: old Tooler's rather slow, but werry sure — I never knowed him, however, to be quite so late as this, I must say."

Relieved somewhat by the fact of the delay not being deemed, under the circumstances *very* extraordinary, by the waiter, the old gentleman walked to the door of the inn — not exactly with the view of accelerating the arrival of the coach, but in order to speculate upon the probability of every vehicle that came in sight being the one for which he was so anxiously waiting. He had scarcely, however, taken his position on the threshold, when he saw brother Walter, followed by his hopeful son, Horace, bustling about the place in a state of feverish excitement, and inquiring again and again of the porters at the gate if they were perfectly certain that the coach had not arrived.

"Walter! Horace!" shouted Grimwood; and those gentlemen for the moment shrank back at the sound; but finding no means of escape, they approached, and after falteringly muttering something having reference to their astonishment, expressed their conviction that as the evening was cold, and as the coach might not come in till midnight, he had better go home and let one of them remain to take charge of Valentine when he arrived.

"I consider it very kind of you, Walter and Horace," said Grimwood, taking both by the hand, "to manifest so much anxiety about one in whom I take an interest — I shall not forget it. However, he cannot be long now; therefore, let us wait together, and have a glass of mulled wine."

Both Walter and Horace tried hard to be excused, but Grimwood resolved on securing them as firmly as if he had known the source from which all their anxiety sprang. They had scarcely, however, taken their seats in the coffee-room when the arrival of the coach was announced, and Grimwood instantly left his affectionate relatives in order to receive Valentine in the yard.

"It's all up!" said Walter, when Grimwood had left. "What a fool I was not to remain at the turnpike; but, Lord, I made sure that the infernal coach had passed."

"*I* couldn't imagine what the devil was the matter," cried Horace, "so I pelted down here like the devil to see."

"Well, it's of no use now," observed Walter; "we are completely done this time. But never fear, Horace," he continued, after a pause, "we shall be able to manage it yet," and both father and son became mute.

"Your name, I believe, is Valentine Vox?" said Mr. Goodman, addressing the youth who had just alighted.

"It is," returned Valentine.

"My name is Goodman — I am happy to see you. I hope that you met with no accident on the road?"

"Nothing of any very great importance," replied Valentine.

"Doant arks me any more questions," cried Tooler, as he strove to emerge from the group of inquiring horsekeepers and waiters, by whom he had been anxiously surrounded. "It's o' no use — blarm me if I arnt sick and tired o' the very thoughts on't. I have," continued he, addressing Goodman, "to thenk this young gentleman for gittin' up at all. If it hadn't ha' bin for he we shouldn't ha done it to-night, any how."

This remark had at once the effect of extorting five shillings from Valentine instead of half-a-crown, and of creating a very favourable first impression in the mind of Mr. Goodman, who having seen the luggage secure, presented Valentine to Walter and Horace, who received him with looks indicative of anything but delight.

"*Now*, my young friend," said Mr. Goodman, taking Valentine again by the hand and shaking it with much warmth, "I am so *glad* that you are safe; you are faint and cold — I know you are. Waiter! coffee for this gentleman; — what on earth could have detained you? But don't tell me now — you are fatigued."

"Not at all, I assure you," said Valentine, who felt himself perfectly at home with the old gentleman, although he viewed with an eye of suspicion the sinister looks of Walter and Horace.

"Come, take a glass of wine," said the warm-hearted Goodman, who felt as highly delighted with Valentine as if he had been his own son. "My dear boy!" he continued, pressing the hand of his protegé, and looking earnestly in his face. "God bless you!"

This was wormwood to Horace and his father. They could not conceal its effects, and therefore, after having addressed certain sneering observations to Valentine, who bowed without replying, they departed with the view of designing some villanous scheme which might induce the revival of those hopes which appeared to them to be on the point of being blasted for ever.

"Well, now," said the old gentlemen, when his relatives were gone, and Valentine appeared to be sufficiently refreshed, "come, tell me the cause of this extraordinary delay."

Valentine gazed upon him earnestly and smiled. He was at first almost afraid to explain the real cause; but the general expression of the old gentleman's countenance was so peculiarly fascinating, that it quickly inspired him with confidence: he felt that he might trust him with the secret of his power, which might moreover be to him a source of constant amusement, and therefore, after a little hesitation, confessed that the delay was attributable solely to him.

"But," said Goodman, "I understand that had it not been for you, the coach would not have reached London to-night."

"That is perfectly true," rejoined Valentine, "but it is also true that had it not been for me, it would have arrived here four hours at least before it did."

"Indeed!" exclaimed Goodman with an expression of astonishment; and Valentine hesitated again; but at length, feeling certain that the opinion he had formed of Goodman's character was correct, he proceeded to explain the whole of the circumstances described in the fifth and sixth chapters of this history — the relation of which caused the old gentleman to be so irrepressibly convulsed, that his contortions alone were sufficiently ridiculous to excite the mirth of all present, and at length the room rang with peals of sympathetic laughter.

"Now — now — my dear boy," observed Goodman, the very moment he had regained sufficient command over his muscles, "be sure that you tell this to no one. We shall have such amusement! But keep it, my boy, mind keep it a secret." And here he was seized with another fit of merriment in which the whole room again most ridiculously joined, while Valentine congratulated himself on the manner in which he had been received by his warm-hearted patron.

As soon as the frame of Grimwood Goodman became capable of assuming the semblance of tranquillity, he began to manifest impatience to witness the effect of that which appeared to him still to be almost impossible. He therefore strongly urged Valentine to give him a specimen on the spot, and as Valentine felt that he would be too much amazed for the moment to indulge in those loud bursts of laughter which might tend to create suspicion, he consented to do so at once.

"But, be careful, my dear boy, be careful," said Goodman.

"Oh! there is not the slightest danger of discovery.—Waiter!" said Valentine, throwing his voice into a box in which two extremely stout individuals were eating devilled kidneys.

"Yes, sir," cried the person in pumps, throwing his napkin under his arm, and approaching the box in question.

"Waiter!" said Valentine, assuming a voice which appeared to proceed from the box opposite.

"Yes, sir," repeated the waiter, turning round on ascertaining that that party had no orders.

"*Waiter!*" cried Valentine in precisely the same voice as at first.

"*Yes*, sir!" exclaimed the sleek functionary returning, "you call, sir?"

"No," said the gentlemen, "*we* did not call."

"WAITER!" shouted Valentine, throwing his voice to the other end of the room, to which end he of the pumps of course immediately pelted.

"Now, where is that bottle of port?" cried Valentine, bringing the voice about half way back.

"Beg pardon, sir, I'm sure, sir," said the waiter addressing the person from whom he imagined the sound had proceeded, "did you order a bottle of port, sir?"

"No," said the person addressed, "I'm drinking negus."

"WAITER!" shouted Valentine with all the force of which he was capable.

"YES, SIR!" cried the waiter with corresponding energy, and again he followed the sound, and continued to follow it until Valentine ceased, when the knight of the napkin, whose blood began to boil, approached the fire and poked it with all the power at his command.

"Jim!" cried Valentine, sending his voice up the chimney, while the waiter was taking his revenge — "get up higher: I'm roasting."

"Hush!" said Valentine, assuming the voice of "Jim," who appeared to be half-choked. "Hush! — don't speak so loud."

The waiter, who still grasped the instrument of his vengeance with one hand, raised the other to enjoin silence, and walked on tip-toe towards the bar, from which in an instant he returned with the landlord, the hostess, the barmaid, the boots, and in fact nearly the whole of the members of the establishment, who crept with the utmost care upon their toes towards the fire, when Valentine conducted the following interesting conversation between "Jim" and "Joe," in the chimney.

"It's flaming hot *here*, Jim, but there—that'll do. Did you ever in your born days see sich a fire?"

"Hold on a bit, Joe, our sweat 'll soon damp it."

"I wish he as poked it was in it."

"Oh that would'nt do at any price. His fat 'ud blaze to sich a hextent, it 'ud do us brown in no time."

The landlord approached. "So we've caught you at last then, you blackguards. Hollo!" cried he, peering up the chimney.

"Hush!" said the invisible Jim.

"Aye, *you* may say hush," said the host, "but you're trapped now, my tulips: come down, d'ye hear?"

The tulips did not condescend to reply.

"Here Jerry," continued the host, "run out for the policeman," and Jerry, of course, ran with all possible speed.

"You'd better come down there you wagabones," cried the landlord.

"Hexcuse us," said Jim, "you are werry perlite."

"If you don't, I'll blow you bang through the pot!" cried the landlord.

"You haven't enough powder," said the invisible Joe.

The policeman here entered, and bustling up to the grate, shouted "now, young fellows, come along, I wants you."

"*Do* you," said one of the young fellows.

"It's o' no use, you know," cried the policeman, who held his authority to be contemned, and his dignity insulted, by that tranquil remark. "You'd better come at once, you know, my rum uns."

"That's werry good advice, I des-say," said one of the rum uns, "only *we* doesn't think so."

"Why, it taint o' no use," urged the policeman, "you an't got a ha'porth o' chance. Here, give us hold of a stick or a broom," said he to the waiter, and the chambermaid ran to fetch one, when another policeman entered, to whom the first said, "Smith, go and stand by them ere chimley pots, will yer," and accordingly up Smith went with the boots.

"Now then," said the policeman, having got a long broom, "if you don't come down, my crickets, in course I shall make you, and that's all about it."

In reply to this acute observation, one of the "crickets" indulged in a contemptuous laugh, which so enraged the policeman, that he on the instant introduced the long broom up the chimney, and brought down of course a sufficient quantity of soot to fill an imperial bushel measure. This remarkable descension, being on his part wholly unexpected, caused him to spit and sneeze with considerable vehemence, while his face was sufficiently black to win the sympathies of any regular philanthropist going.

"Now then, you sirs!" shouted Smith from the top; "Do you mean to come up or go down? *Ony* say!"

As soon as the first fit of sneezing had subsided, the policeman below was just about to give vent to the indignation which swelled his official breast, when he was seized with another, which in its effects proved far more violent than the first.

"Good luck to you," said he on regaining the power to speak, "give us something to wash it down, or I shall choke. It 'll be all the worse for you, my kids, when I gets you. Do you mean to come down now? *that's* all about it. It's o' no use, you know, for in course we don't leave you. Once for all, do you mean to come down?"

"You are *werry* perlite," replied one of the kids, "but we'd much rayther not."

"Why then," said the constable in disguise, who as far as the making up of his face was concerned, appeared perfectly ready to murder *Othello* — "in course we must make you."

As this observation on the part of the policeman, was followed by another contemptuous laugh, that respectable functionary became so indignant that he entertained thoughts of achieving their annihilation by virtue of fire and smoke. While, however, he was considering whether a jury under the circumstances would bring it in justifiable homicide, manslaughter, or murder, it was suggested that as there lived in the neighbourhood an extremely humane and intellectual sweep, who had become particularly knock-kneed in the profession, and peculiarly alive to the hardships which the corrupt climbing system inflicted upon the sooty generation in general, had a machine which was patronized by the nobility and gentry, and which might in this instance have the effect of accelerating the process of ejectment. For this remarkable master

The Invisible Burglars about to be ejected.

P 42.

sweep, therefore, boots was despatched, while the policeman, bent upon a wicked waste of coals, endeavoured to persuade the invisibles to descend by making the fire blaze with a fury which a couple of young salamanders only could stand.

Nothing, however, bearing the similitude of blazes could bring the burglars down, and just as Valentine's guardian *pro. tem.* was declaring that he must either laugh loudly or burst, a stout stumpy man, who stood about five feet five, upon legs to which nothing stands recorded in the annals of legs, at all comparable in point of obliquity, was led in by boots, with the machine on his shoulder, and at once assumed the air of an individual conscious of the immaculate character of his motives, and of the general integrity of his professional reputation.

"I understand," said he, bowling with all the importance of which a master-sweep is comfortably capable towards the fire—"I understand that you have certain burglarious burglars up the flue. Well! as the integral integrity of this glorious and empirical empire demands that all sich dishonest thieves should be brought when caught to the barrier of judicial justice, ergo, that is for to say, consequently, therefore, they *must* descend down, and this 'll bring 'em! It was never known to fail," he added, drawing forth a huge bread-and-cheese knife to cut the cord which bound the machine together, "in any thing successfully attempted. It is patternised by the titled nobility, and clerical clergy in oly orders, besides the official officers of the loyal household, and the principal aristocratic members of the aristocracy in high life, and ought to be known in every particle of the globe and her colonies. It was ony t'other day as I was called in to hoperate upon the chimneys of one of our tip topmast dukes, a great agricultural proprietor of landed property, and a petickler friend of mine, wot had heered from some vagabone wot I holds werry properly in contemptuous contempt, that my machine had turned out a dead failure. 'So,' says he, when I'd done the job, 'Shufflebottom,' says he, you're a werry ill-used man, a hindiwidual wot's werry much respected uniwersally by all, and therefore, it's a werry great pitty that you should be sich a wictim of misrepresentation.' 'Why,' says I, 'my lord duke, you knows werry well as how I treats all sich wagabones with suitable contempt. But I'm obleeged to you, my lord duke, and I feels werry grateful as I allus does feel for any favour as is showed, and I allus likes to return it too, 'specially if them as shows it puts themselves you know werry much out of the way in the most friendliest spirit, and has their motives in consequence suspected."

"Well, come," said the host, interrupting this remarkable sweep, who displayed a disposition to go on for an hour, "let us see if we can get these rascals out of the flue."

Shufflebottom marvelled at this ungentlemanlike interruption, but after hurling a look of contempt at the illiterate landlord, he introduced the head of his machine into the chimney, and sent it up joint by joint. Of course, during its progress a considerable quantity of soot descended, but when the brush had reached the pot, the policeman above grasped it firmly, conceiving it to be the rough hair of one of the burglars, and pulled it completely out of Shufflebottom's hand.

"The blaggards is at top!" cried Shufflebottom loudly. "They've stole my machine!—go, go upon the roof!"

"Come with me," said the policeman, but as Shufflebottom had not sufficient courage for that, the policeman and boots went up together, with the view of rendering all necessary assistance. On reaching the roof, they of course discovered the cause of Shufflebottom's great alarm, and having sent his machine down the chimney again, descended with the view of deciding upon some other course. It was the conviction of the policeman above, that no burglars were in the chimney at all, for he himself had been nearly suffocated by simply looking from the top; but as this very natural idea was repudiated as monstrous by all below, Shufflebottom in the plentitude of his humanity, suggested that a sack should be tied tightly over the pot, in order that the invisible burglars might be stifled into an unconditional surrender. As this appeared to be decidedly the most effectual way of compelling them to descend, the policeman urged it strongly, and as the host did by no means object to its adoption, orders were given for the sack to be tied over at once.

This humane and ingenious operation had scarcely been performed, when the room was of course filled with smoke, and in less than three minutes, every soul had departed with the exception of the policeman and Shufflebottom the sweep, who soon deemed it expedient to crawl out on their hands and knees to avoid suffocation.

Valentine and his guardian, with several other gentlemen, repaired to the bar, when orders were given for the removal of the sack, and on its being decided, that when the smoke had evoporated, one policeman should remain in the room, and another on the roof of the house all night, a coach was ordered, and Goodman with his charge proceeded home irrepressibly delighted with the evening's entertainment.

CHAPTER VIII.

THE CONSULTATION OF AN INTERESTING FAMILY PARTY, AT WHICH IT IS DECIDED THAT SOMETHING MUST BE DONE.

"WELL, my love," exclaimed the affectionate Mrs. Goodman, as Walter and his son entered the room, in which she and Mrs. Horace had been anxiously waiting—"we have been in such a way you can't think, for Julia would have it you had failed."

"She was right," muttered Walter, sinking into a chair heavily.

"Right?" cried Mrs. Goodman. "What, have you not secured the young wretch? Horace! tell me?"

Horace shook his head.

"Ah!"—said the old lady, playfully patting the cheek of Walter, and giving him a series of matrimonial kisses—"he has not arrived."

"But he has," cried Horace, "and Uncle has got him!"

The old lady sank into her chair.

"Dear me!" said Mrs. Horace, who had derived a latent feeling of satisfaction from the circumstance of her having predicted a failure, "how could you have been so stupid?"

Horace explained, and the old lady wept, and Walter pulled his boots off with desperate violence.

"Then you did see the wretch?" said the old lady spitefully.

"Of course," returned Horace.

"What *sort* of a creature is he?" inquired the junior Mrs. Goodman.

"Why, I don't know," said Horace, "a sort of a rakish-looking scamp. What struck me more than all was his eye."

"Has he but one?" cried the old lady, somewhat revived.

"Not exactly," returned Horace, "he has two—"

"And they are odd ones?" interrupted the old lady, with confidence, which seemed to be teeming with pleasure.

"They are," replied Horace, "the oddest eyes that ever looked through a man: *such* piercers! They'd dart through the dome of St. Paul's or the earth, and see what was going on at our antipodes. *He'd* make the money fly!—he'd show the world how to spend it, if he ever had the chance.

The mere mention of money had the effect of arousing Walter from the lethargy into which he had fallen. He drew at once towards the table, and having placed his arms deliberately upon it, said firmly and emphatically, "*Something* must be done. I saw," continued he, after a pause, "the impression the young scamp had made upon Grimwood. I watched them both narrowly, and when I perceived the extreme warmth with which Grimwood grasped his hand, and looking earnestly in his face, said, 'My *dear* boy—God bless you!'—I could not but feel that the boy—the *dear* boy—stood a very fair chance of becoming his heir."

"Great Heaven forbid!" exclaimed Mrs. Goodman, senior, turning up the yellows of her bloodshot eyes, and throwing one of her arms round the delicate neck of the amiable Mrs. Goodman, junior, to express affection, while the other was raised as far above her head as possible, in order to express the highest pitch of surprise. "His heir! Good Gracious! What are his claims?—his pretensions? What is the relationship existing between them? What right has he to rob us of any portion of that which by every law of nature belongs to us alone?"

To this interesting string of interrogatories Walter replied simply by remarking, that none were ever robbed by right. "The question to be considered," said he, "does not apply to the natural right of the one: it has reference solely to the legal power of the other."

"But what a monstrous shame it is," said Mrs. Goodman, "that a man should have the power to leave his property to any but his relatives!"

"It is useless to talk about that," observed Walter. "He *has* the power, and that's sufficient. The question is, how is the exercise of that power to be in this case prevented?"

"But Uncle may not intend to do any thing of the kind," said the junior Mrs. Goodman.

"*May* not!" cried Walter. "He *may* not; but what if he should? What if he were to leave every shilling to this fellow: where then should we be? Why instead of living in affluence as we *ought* to live, we should be at once reduced to a state of destitution."

"Aye, that is the point, dear," said Mrs. Goodman, senior. "Just look at that! For my part I tremble to think on't."

"But do you think it likely," observed

the junior Mrs. Goodman, "that Uncle has the heart to behave so unkindly?"

"There's no telling, child," replied Walter. "If he happen to take a fancy to this boy, he may make him the inheritor of all; and if he should, my pitiful income from the stamp-office of 200*l.* a-year will be all that we shall have to exist upon; and that, when I go, will go too. I must, however, say, what I have said a thousand times, that if Horace had played his cards well, he might have been a greater favorite of Grimwood than he is."

"Why, what could I do with the old buck?" cried Horace, smoking a black cheroot with unequivocal desperation.

"Do!" replied Walter. "Why, you should have endeavored on all occasions to please him."

"Well I have," shouted Horace; "I have tried just as hard as any fellow could try, and he wouldn't be pleased. Haven't I asked him fifty times to go with me to the masquerade?—didn't I bite the best part of Bulhead's tail clean off when he had fast hold of the old boy's boot?—and when I pitched him into the water the day they rowed for the silver sculls, didn't I hook him out again like a Whitechapel needle? And yet I'm no favorite *because* I've not played my cards well!"

"You have not gone the right way to work," rejoined Walter.

"Why, what would he have," shouted Horace in a rage. "What's the use of blowing me up about it? If he wont't be pleased, how can I make him? I've done all I could, and if he don't like me, why he must do the other thing." And Horace, finding the cheroot during his speech had gone out, threw it indignantly into the fire, and proceeded to light another.

"Well, well," said the senior Mrs. Goodman, "it is useless to dwell upon that subject now. What's done can't be undone, and therefore we should turn our thoughts to what we have to do."

"*Something* must be done," repeated Walter, "and soon. The will is in our favor now. I know it: I have seen it.—How, then, are we to keep him from altering that will?"

"Yes, that is the question: that's just the very point," observed Mrs. Goodman senior. "It would be such a very dreadful thing, if, after having tried so hard all these years to secure it, we should be robbed of it, just as his constitution's breaking up.—I'm sure none could have taken more pains than we have: none could have taken more trouble to earn it. Heaven knows it has cost us a world of anxiety. We could not have watched him more closely than we have, if the sum had been fifty times as much as it is. That's impossible. He has been our thoughts by day, and our dreams by night. He has never been out of our heads, and therefore the idea of being robbed of it at last is quite shocking."

"Let's persuade the old boy," observed Horace, "that he can't expect to sleep very quiet when he's gone, unless he leaves the whole of his blunt to those who have the greatest right to it."

"Pooh!" said Walter contemptuously: "Grimwood's no fool!"

"Well, I'm sure," remarked the senior Mrs. Goodman, "that he ought to be made to feel that he cannot be so happy."

"Of course he ought," said Horace; "and that's just the way the old boy's to be walked over, too! Why, look at old Thingermybob there—what's his name?—Sniggers!—he had left nearly the whole of his dubs to build a jolly lot of alms-houses, for a crew of old women that didn't belong to him at all. Well, what did his son Harry do when he heard of it? Why, he no sooner found that he was to be pensioned off at so much a-month, that he sent old Fizgig there—Simpkinson—to talk about the old buffer's ghost, and the result was that Harry got it all?"

"Well, look at the late Mr. Lucas," said the senior Mrs. Goodmnn, in order to give an additional illustration of the position assumed: "*He* had very correctly left the whole of his property to his relatives; but no sooner did he connect himself with Cantall's congregation, than Cantall got hold of him, and worked up his feelings to a degree which induced him in the first place to build a new chapel, and a large house adjoining, and in the next, to will them, with the whole of his other property, to him who had thus poisoned his mind, and now, while the Cantalls are lolling in the lap of luxury, the relatives of Lucas are starving."

"To be sure," said Horace, lighting another very black cheroot. "And as the old boy's not always exactly wide awake, he's to be got over just in the same way. Only make him believe that if he should be guilty of so dirty and disreputable a swindle, his jolly old ghost will cut about in a most uncomfortable state of excitement from generation to generation, and we shall nail him dead as a herring."

"And you *think* that he wouldn't see through it?" said Walter, with a sneer.

"Not if the thing were managed properly," replied Horace. "It wouldn't of course do exactly for me to pitch the blarney, because I might come it a little too strong; but a fellow with a serious phiz, like old Neversweat—what's his name?—

5*

he who sits behind the black barnacles perched upon the stool next to yours—the fellow who *won't* die, you know, although, aware that you have been waiting about a couple of generations for his shoes."

"What, Coggle?" suggested Mrs. Goodman senior.

"Aye, that's the cove—Coggle: a venerable out-and-out old fool, now, like that, who never *had* above half a laugh in him, would be able to do the trick in no time."

"Pooh! nonsense!" cried Walter.

"Well, there could be no harm, you know," said Horace, "in trying it on!"

"I tell you," said Walter, "it is not to be done in that way."

"In what other way is it possible to do it?" inquired Horace.

Walter Goodman either could not or would not explain; but after supper this really interesting family party separated with the mutual understanding that SOMETHING MUST BE DONE.

CHAPTER IX.

VALENTINE'S VISIT TO THE HOUSE OF COMMONS.

NEITHER Walter nor Grimwood could sleep during the night, but oh! from what opposite causes! It were curious and interesting doubtless to inquire how many causes are capable of producing the same effect; but as the subject need not be long dwelt upon here, it will be perhaps quite sufficient to explain that while Walter was engaged in concocting certain intricate schemes of villany, Grimwood, delighted with the almost unbounded prospect of happiness which had opened before him, lay stretched in the unrestrained indulgence of those pleasing anticipations which sprang from the conception of innumerable scenes that crowded to tickle his vivid imagination.

Having wished for the morning all night, night avenged itself by introducing morning just as Grimwood had begun to wish morning at a distance. His head, however, continued to stick to its pillow with all the tenacity of the polypus until he heard the church clock strike *eleven*, when he rang for his water, and rolled out of bed.

Now Valentine, who had slept like a dormouse all night, and whose usual hour for rising had been *six*, could not understand this eleven o'clock business at all. He had been five hours awake, and was as hungry as a wolf; but as Grimwood's last injunction the previous night had been, "do not get up on any account until you are called," he felt bound to act in obedience to that injunction, and to await the call with all the Christian patience he could muster. For the first three hours he amused himself tolerably well by endeavoring to understand what the fellows had to dispose of, who kept continually bawling out, "Yar sto!" "Meyare mickrell!" "clo! clo!" "weep!" "ool ar rowin an ool ar' lowin!" and from nine o'clock till ten he listened attentively to the strains of a barrel organ, with a remarkably shrill whistling accompaniment; but when he heard the clock strike *eleven*, he fancied he might as well give the thing up. He had, however, no sooner turned upon his side to compose himself, if possible, for another night's rest, than he heard the knock of Grimwood, who had come to inquire if he would like to have breakfast in bed. The very knock was sufficient.—He felt himself free; and having answered the question in the negative, proceeded to dress with all possible speed.

His reception in the parlor was most ardent. The delighted old gentleman pressed his hand again and again, and during breakfast reviewed the occurrences of the previous evening with rapture.

"Well now, my dear boy," said he, when Valentine had satisfied his appetite, "what shall we do to-day?"

"I have but to write home," returned Valentine, "and then I am entirely at your disposal."

"You have never," said Goodman, "been in the Commons? of course you have not. Would you like to go?"

"Exceedingly," returned Valentine.

"Well, then, remember me at home; seal your letter; and we'll call upon a member who will take us to-day, I have no doubt."

Accordingly, an early dinner was ordered, and Valentine and his guardian proceeded without delay to the residence of a highly distinguished member of parliament.

Valentine's spirit had never been broken. His tongue had never learnt to assume the accents of a slave, nor had his soul been taught to shrink from the presence of a man, however high might be his station in society, or however severe and piercing might be his glance. He did, however, feel in some slight degree tremulous on entering the house of this eminent senator, of whom he had frequently heard, whose speeches he had frequently read, and whom he knew to have been distinguished for years in a place in which pretenders so soon find their level.

Conceive then his astónishment on being ushered into the sanctnm of this eminent personage, whose indefatigable exertions he had heard so many curse, when, instead of beholding in a magnificent library studded with richly bound volumes, a stately individual enveloped in a long flowing robe, with whose splendor the carpet alone might be comparable, he saw a stout common looking person in a singularly short jacket, whose tightness developed to perfection a tremendous swell *á posteriori*, perched upon a stool with his toes dangling down within half a dozen inches of a piece of old oil cloth, which as some sort of an apology for a carpet had been nailed to the floor.

At first, Valentine naturally imagined that the creature whom he beheld was the senator's butler, for he saw that he was anxiously casting up, what he felt *might* be the baker's account, and was just on the point of concluding, that if the consumption of the family were not immense, the baker gave very long credit, when the person in question said, "Seventy-nine—nine and carry seven, how are you?—nine—seven, how do?" And he cocked a stumpy pen into his mouth, and extending his inky hand, added, "Glad to see you: what can I do for you?"

"We want to go to the House to-night," said Goodman.

"Yes; will you call for me or meet me in the lobby?"

"We may as well meet you."

"I shall be down at a minute to four. Good day." And Goodman, who seemed to *expect* nothing more, dragged Valentine out of the studio, as the senator muttered in a sonorous wobble, "Seven: seven nine sixteen, twenty-four, thirty-one, forty, forty-six, fifty-two, sixty-seven, seventy-six, eighty, eighty-three," and was thus going on with amazing rapidity, when the door closed and shut in the sound.

"Is that the man?" said Valentine, when he had got fairly out.

"It is—the very man!" replied Goodman.

"Well, I shouldn't have supposed it possible," said Valentine, who had still in his mind's eye the singular jacket, and that which it set off to so much advantage.

"You will see him in a different character to-night," observed Goodman. "He has something important to effect, I can see by his manner."

Without being impressed with any elevated notions having reference to the style and address of a British senator, by the eminent specimen whom he had seen, Valentine was led by his guardian towards home, from which, after having had a somewhat hasty dinner, they proceeded at at once to the house.

It wanted precisely a quarter to four when Goodman and his charge passed Westminster Hall, and as the eminent statesman who was about to introduce them was certain to be neither a moment before nor a moment behind the time appointed, they continued to walk opposite the Abbey, endeavoring to discover in the countenances of the various members who approached the house, something indicative of extraordinary talent, until finding that they were within one minute of the time, they walked through a room, in which they saw two functionaries, who looked as if the mending of an additional pen would very seriously annoy them, and thence into a passage, in which were several hundred hooks, from each of which was suspended a piece of dirty pasteboard, on which the name of some honorable member was written.

They had scarcely reached the stairs at the end of this passage when the statesman whom they had seen in the morning arrived. He had exchanged his short jacket for a yellow waistcoat and a blue coat with gilt buttons; and having hurried them up, he went into a room in which sat a select committee, the members of which were immediately informed that the Speaker was at prayers. From this room they proceeded at once into the house, and when their guide had placed them upon an elevated seat near the entrance, they began to look round them.

"And is this the British House of Commons?" thought Valentine. "Can it be possible that these are our statesmen?"

Whatever surprise the dimensions of the house, or the mean appearance of its members, might tend to create, he felt that, as there could be no doubt about the matter, he might as well direct the whole of his attention to what was going forward.

In the first place, the Speaker cried "Order, order! order at the table! order, order!" and a mob of honorable members who had been standing round the table, immediately repaired to their seats. It was interesting to Valentine to behold the respect which the members paid the Speaker. When seated, they kept their hats on; but if they moved but a yard, they pulled them off, and replaced them the moment they were seated again; and if they passed from one side of the house to the other, they bowed to the chair as they passed, if they went over even but for an instant.

When a spare individual, who sported a court-dress, and whose only occupation appeared to be that of bowing profoundly, and carrying a mace which was nearly as large and as heavy as himself, had been trotting about for some time behind the bar, "Order, order!" was called again; and a certain bundle of parchment having been placed in the hand of the Speaker, he gave a brief, a very brief description of its title, and then observed, "This bill be read second time many's 'pinion say Aye cont' 'pinion s'no The Ayes have it—this bill be committed many's 'pinion say Aye cont 'pinion s'no the Ayes have it;" without the members saying either Aye or No—or attending, in fact, to the matter at all!

The speaker then called the name of an extremely spectral personage, who albeit the eldest son of a duke, looked as if he had lived all his life upon chips, and who shuffled up to the table, in remarkably short nankeen trousers, which scarcely reached that part of his leg at which Nature had intended to establish a calf. He had a petition to present, and in describing its character, displayed as much eloquence as Demosthenes ever could display, before he had recourse to the pebbles. "Laid upon the table," said the Speaker; and a stout red-faced man at once crushed it together, and threw it *under* the table, as a matter of course, when the noble earl by whom it had been presented returned to his seat, and having cocked upon his head an extremely small hat, put his left leg carefully over his right, with the air of a man conscious of having done all in his power to promote the peculiar objects the petitioners had in view.

"Sergeant!" cried the Speaker, when this job had been jobbed; and the individual in the court-dress bowed three times during his progress towards the table, when, taking up the mace which had been placed there, bowed three times during his backward retreat, and having said something to a couple of masters in chancery, who were the bearers of a couple of documents from the lords, he and they walked abreast to the bar, when they took *four* steps, and then bowed like a leash of Mandarins, then took four steps more, and again bowed, and then another couple of brace of steps, which brought them up to the table, at which they bowed again, when, after mumbling something having reference to something, and putting the documents down, they walked backwards four steps, and then bowed, then took four steps more, and bowed again, when, by way of a finish, they made four steps more, and having bowed, turned round, and rushed out of the house, laughing.

This proceeding appeared to Valentine to be supremely ridiculous, but what tended in some degree to neutralise his disgust was the fact, that not only were the masters in chancery afraid to walk backwards, without looking behind to see if anything happened to be standing in the way, but the person in full dress, whom Valentine ascertained to be the deputy-sergeant, was compelled to retreat, just as if he had been bandy from his birth, because he could not persuade his sword to keep from between his legs. Despite, therefore, every other feeling which this ceremony might naturally tend to create in one utterly incapable of perceiving its great national importance, Valentine could not repress a smile, and the moment he had arrived at the conclusion that neither a sergeant-at-arms, nor a deputy-sergeant, nor a master in chancery, could do the thing well without having served an apprenticeship to a rope-maker, "Order!" was again called; and then the name of a certain honorable member, who at once rose to direct the attention of the house to the continued existence of a certain abuse, with the bearings of which Valentine was not profoundly conversant.

The style of this honorable member was inflexible—his voice loud and sonorous. He had a certain provincial accent, which, to a refined ear, had a tendency to counteract the effect of whatever eloquence he might possess, and he assumed the tone of a man who had been accustomed to address myriads willing to hear and to applaud. He spoke frequently of the masses, of paper currency, of the markets, of specie, and commercial ruin, of imports and of exports, of America, France, Portugal, China and Spain; in short, he seemed resolved to leave no stone unturned in any quarter of the globe, which he conceived might tend to illustrate the position he had assumed.

It soon became manifest to Valentine, that whatever degree of importance might be attached to the opinions of this gentleman elsewhere, in that house they had no weight at all; for the few, the very few, who appeared to be attentive, were mingling their smiles with their sneers, while the rest were conversing and joking, and laughing, apparently unconscious of everything but that which had immediate reference to themselves. It was easy to perceive that this gentleman was capable of far more eloquence than that which he displayed; but the coldness of the members whom he addressed, appeared to chill his natural ardor, and he eventually resumed his seat without gaining a cheer.

This seemed to be a consummation that that had been devoutly wished, and no sooner had it arrived than the attention of the house was directed to one, who, albeit in person extremely small, appeared to be extremely great in the estimation of those who occupied one entire side of the house. He had risen with the view of showing that the arguments of the honorable member who had preceded him were entirely baseless and absurd; and although his tone and deportment were by no means commanding, while his eloquence sank to a great depth below mediocrity, his ahem-ing and a-ar-ing repntation was applauded with vehemence, by those who had failed to devote the slightest attention to the arguments to which the refutation applied.

When this small but important individual had concluded, a fine portly person whose hair was neither auburn nor absolutely red, and whose fort seemed to lie in the delivery of the bitterest sarcasms clothed in the sweetest tones, rose with what appeared to be a portfolio in his hand, for the purpose of impugning one particular branch of the policy pursued by the then existing government. He appeared to be regarded as an oracle, for the house when he rose was as silent as the grave. Every point that he made was cheered with rapture by those who sat on the same side of the house, and whenever he happened to place a strong emphasis upon the conclusion of any sentence in which no point was perceptible, he looked round with the view of making his friends understand that although they might not exactly see it, the sentence *did* contain a point, when they hailed it with enthusiasm accordingly.

The moment this political god had resumed his seat, amidst loud and protracted cheering, an honorable member whose countenance had been said to resemble an ugly portrait of Charles the First, and who appeared to hold razors in sovereign contempt, for he clearly had not used one for many a day, rose simply to observe that he agreed with every sentence that either had been said, might be said, or could be said, against the members of the existing cabinet, whom he held to be the vilest, the meanest, the shabbiest, and most atrocious political scoundrels with whom the British empire ever was or ever could be cursed. "I denounce them," said he with a cannibalistic scowl, which he had assumed with the view of imparting a most withering effect to the peroration of his philippic—"I denounce them as a gang of degraded political ruffians;—who, with a profligate and most unconstitutional suck, have drained the cup of degradation to the very dregs, and I shouldn't care so much as the ghost of a dump, if the whole crew were nailed to the walls of this house, and *stoned* to death with sacrificial brickbats to-morrow!"

To the astonishment of Valentine, this burst of indignation was productive of nothing but laughter, and before Mr. Goodman had time to explain that the house always laughed when that senator spoke, a statesman in miniature, knitting his brows, started up with almost as much velocity as if he had been sent like a shell from a mortar to scatter destruction around.

"That's a great gun," said Goodman; and Valentine thought so, for he at that moment heard a tremendous report, which he subsequently, however, ascertained to proceed from a box which adorned one corner of the table, and which the little man struck with the force of a young blacksmith, while he writhed and wriggled and tortured his poor little body into every conceivable attitude, precisely as if those who sat in his immediate vicinity, were out of pure wantonness pinching him behind. Even the reporters left off to indulge their amazement, for although his delivery revelled between a squeal and a shriek, his address was thickly studded with the most beautifully poetic images that ever developed the scope-and power of man's imagination. How the speeches of this little gentleman could be followed by the reporters, Valentine could not conceive. He knew that those speeches did appear, and having heard that the reports were most faithful, he was just on the point of concluding that the reporters must depend upon their memory, which he felt must be very extraordinary, seeing that they on one occasion gave a most faithful report of a speech which he only *intended* to deliver, when the shrieking stopped in an instant, like an alarum run down, and the general cheering became enthusiastic.

Before time had subdued this vehement applause, the honorable member by whom the miniature statesman had been preceded, rose obviously in a state of excitement, to inquire if a certain observation which had fallen from the little gentleman, and which appeared to have reference to buffoonery in general, was intended to apply personally to him. "If it were," said the honorable member, with a swell of indignation, "I hurl back the insinuation with scorn! I am not a man to be with impunity insulted by any dirty"—("order! order! chair! chair!")

"The good sense," observed the Speaker, "by which the conduct of the honorable member is so distinguished, will enable him to perceive that the course he is now pursuing is not strictly in order."

"I am willing," cried the honorable and indignant member, "to pay all due deference to the chair; but in the strongest terms the forms of the house will allow, will I denounce any vagabondising, *dirty*"—The extraordinary force with which he swung his arm round, in order to give full effect to the last word, caused the honorable member who had evidently dined, to fall heavily upon the heads of the members below him. This occurrence, of course, produced a loud burst of merriment, which had scarcely subsided, when Valentine, whose feelings of contempt had been aroused, cried "*Buffoon!*" assuming the voice of the mercurial statesman, who had made so exceedingly free with the box.

The members at this moment looked with astonishment at each other, for they did not expect that from *him*.

"I am sorry," said the speaker, in his blandest tone, without noticing the contentions of the member who had fallen—"I am sorry to be compelled to observe that such language is disorderly in the extreme."

The honorable member then rose to explain: "If, Sir," said he, "if it be imagined that *I* gave utterance to the offensive expression, which has called for that remark, I can assure you that it is altogether a mistake, for upon my honor I did not."

"I certainly did conceive," said the Speaker, "that the expression proceeded from the honorable member; but if ——"

"It did—it did!" shouted several honorable members.

"No, no!—it did not!" shouted several others, who were equally sure that it did.

"I have certainly no desire to interfere in this matter," said an honorable member who had a remarkable profile, and whose bushy hair was flowing luxuriantly down his back, "but I must say that I heard the honorable member distinctly make ——" Cries of "No, no!" from one side of the House, and loud cheers from the other, effectually drowned this honorable member's voice. Again he endeavored to make himself heard, and again, but was again and again interrupted, until at length he cried aloud in a voice of desperation, "You will not hear me now, but the time will come when you *shall* hear me! *Yes*, the time will come when you SHALL!"

"Sir," said an honorable and gallant member, who appeared to have been in the heat of some sanguinary battle, "if it did not proceed from the honorable member, I should like to know from whom it could proceed?—*Is* there in this house another member with such a voice?"

"Hear, hear!" exclaimed an honorable member, who prided himself upon his long top-boots and the bare-faced integrity of principle.

"Hear, hear, hear!" shouted another honorable member, whose small twinkling eyes imparted lustre to a remarkably full-blown countenance, of which the naturally good-humored expression was spoiled by some rather malicious feeling, which appeared to be in the ascendant.

"Is not the honorable and gallant member satisfied?" inquired the honorable member who had been accused. "Is not my word of honor sufficient?"

"Of course," replied the honorable and gallant member; "the forms of this house will not allow me to suppose it even possible for any honorable member to be guilty of a deliberate falsehood."

"Do you mean to impute deliberate falsehood to me?" shrieked the honorable member in question, who, as the reply was "I certainly heard it," attempted to rush from the house with what was supposed to be an extremely cold-blooded design, for the Speaker's attention was called immediately to the fact by an obviously important personage, who might in Greece have been mistaken for King Otho *incog.* "Does he mean to impute deliberate falsehood to me?" cried the honorable member again, as his friends were doing all in their power to exorcise the rampant little devil that was within him.

"The honorable and gallant member," observed the Speaker, "I am sure will perceive the necessity for doing that which the house has a right to demand." But the honorable and gallant gentleman stubbornly kept his seat. Member after member rose to beg of him to withdraw the offensive imputation; but his inflexibility was heroic! He knew, of course, that he should be compelled either at once to retract or to languish until he did in the custody of the sergeant, who, with that peculiar courtesy for which he had ever been distingushed, would have been but too happy to afford him every accommodation; but he felt that his reputation for courage might be perilled, unless he firmly held out till the last. The Speaker rose again and again to *demand*—in his peculiarly bland manner—the withdrawal of that expression which had given so much pain; but nothing *could* move, the honorable and gallant gentleman, until a personage with beautifully tinted cheeks proceeded to make a well understood motion, when he declared, what he could not before have declared, without involving his honor, that, in imputing deliberate falsehood to the honorable member, he meant nothing at all *personally* offensive, and here the matter ended.

An attempt was now made to recall the attention of honorable members to business; but as the majority of them manifested a strong disinclination to attend to any thing of the sort, Valentine, on being urged by Goodman, resolved upon releasing that majority from their legislative functions for the night.

Accordingly, just as a prosy individual, who had evidently placed a written speech in his hat, was trying to pick up the thread of the debate, Valentine, throwing his voice under one of the galleries, cried "Question!"

"Why, that *is* the question!" said the honorable member, who was compelled again to look at the speech in his hat.

"Let it be read by the clerk!" shouted Valentine.

"Order, order, order!" said the Speaker.

"Aye, give it to the clerk," cried two juvenile senators.

"Question! question!" and the cry on one side of the house becoming general, the hon. member indignantly resumed his seat.

At this moment two honorable members rose together, and the calls for both became general and loud. Both seemed extremely anxious to speak, and therefore neither felt disposed, for some time, to give way. At length, however, one of them yielded; but he had no sooner done so, than Valentine shouted out, "Down!" which shout found at least a hundred echoes, for in an instant nothing but "Down, down! down!" could be heard. The honorable gentleman, however, still stood firmly, and folded his arms with a look of defiance which seemed to enrage about fifty other honorable members who had previously been silent, but who now appeared to have caught a very sudden and severe cold, for they began to cough and sneeze with unspeakable violence.

No sooner had this coughing and sneezing been added to the loud shouts of "Down!" than several honorable gentlemen favored the company with a little howling; and then a little yelling was heard, and then admirable imitations of the languages peculiar to certain interesting zoological curiosities, and then mingling cries of "Order!" "Shame!" and "Bravo!" and then a very violent clapping of hands, and then loud and apparently hysterical laughter, until at length there arose a mass of hideous sounds, to which nothing could be comparable save those which might proceed from a den in which five hundred maniacs were battling with a corresponding number of very wild beasts.

Valentine had no idea that a storm could have been raised so soon; indeed, he never imagined that *such* a storm as that could have been raised there at all; but as it had been raised, he very quietly proceeded to analyse the body of sound by separating the various little interesting noises of which it was composed.

Upon one of the benches sat a couple of highly intellectual individuals who were naming the speaker for the next harmony by knocking him down for "a jolly good song," and behind them an honorable member was seriously engaged in whetting the ghost of a knife upon a spectral grindstone. A short distance from him sat a statesman promoting the prosperity of the country in general, and the interests of his constituents in particular, by buzzing through his teeth in imitation of that notorious hurdy-gurdy which won't *go* to more than one tune, and what that in its infancy might have been, it is utterly impossible to determine; for, having been played for so many years, it appears now to have been almost wholly worn away. A little farther on a profound politician was contending for the eternal nature of his principles by shouting "Quack! quack!" with an energetic feeling, which any duck in the universe might naturally have envied. By his side sat a senator resolved on upholding the dignity of the crown by playing what by a stretch of the imagination he had conceived to be a regular trombone, and immediately above him one who might have been a Premier in embryo, was drawing a lot of imaginary corks. Several aristocratic individuals under the gallery, who ought to have had "Ears pierced" painted over the doors of their respective residences, were whistling with the shrillness of gods, while a merry old boy who had several slips of paper stuck under the collar of his coat, was playing what he conceived for that particular occasion to be a Jew's harp, which, as a mere matter of justice it must be admitted, he managed with senatorial sublimity and tact. On one of the back benches sat a row of individuals, who being determined to support the Agricultural Interests by "a long pull, a strong pull, and a pull altogether," had imagined that they were hauling up an extremely heavy anchor, and as each had his arms round the waist of the victim immediately before him, they pulled each other backwards and forwards in a line, shouting out with great energy, "Yeo heave ho!"

The great point of attraction, however—

that which tended more than all to inspire Valentine with the conviction that he was then in the midst of the collective wisdom of the nation, inasmuch as those around him knew how to do everything—was a section of politicians who had formed themselves into a sort of a knot, and who not only seemed quite resolved to do all in their power to contribute to the harmony of the evening, but who absolutely did, to a sensible extent, succeed in swelling the general sound. One was striving to obtain justice for Ireland, by braying in the most natural manner possible; another was saving the country from revolution by squealing "A week, a week!" in humble imitation of a juvenile pig oppressed, a third was avenging the insults offered to the British flag by an extraordinary effort to crow like a cock; a fourth was sustaining the integrity of the empire by imparting an idea of the sound of a French horn; a fifth was supporting the Established Church by perpetually shouting, "Yoiks! Tallyho!" a sixth pledged to procure the abolition of military torture, was showing precisely how cat calls to cat; a seventh was endeavoring to put an end to the sanguinary civil war in Spain, by converting his own hat and that of a statesman who sat immediately before him into a couple of kettle-drums, which he certainly continued to beat with an energy that "nothing else could match;" an eighth who had been pledged to the abolition of the slave-trade was engaged in giving effect to a popular air; while a ninth was endeavoring to impress upon the house the necessity for an immediate extension of the suffrage by imparting to all around what he conceived to be a highly correct notion of the moral and physical effects of hydrophobia.

In vain the Speaker, during these irregular proceedings, tried to show that such conduct was not exactly consistent with the character of a deliberative assembly; in vain he strove to direct the attention of honorable members to the fact that the interests and the feelings of the country in general could not be thus really represented; he thundered forth "Order," and rose twenty times to enforce it in vain; his presence was unheeded, his authority contemned; and he therefore at length sank back in his chair to view the scene with mingled feelings of indignation and sorrow. Valentine felt for the old gentleman, for he appeared to be shedding tears; and being therefore determined to put an end to these proceedings if possible, he took advantage of a moment when the throats of those who composed the first assembly of gentlemen in the world displayed symptoms of exhaustion, and sent a most extraordinary cry of "Shame!" into one of the reflectors, which appeared for the moment to be under some supernatural influence, and which caused the majority of the senators below to look up with an expression of amazement.

As the noise became in consequence somewhat subdued, Valentine raised another sepulchral cry of "Shame," which was heard with far greater distinctness than the first, and which induced the identical old gentleman who had been playing the imaginary Jew's harp, and who was evidently indignant at this strange interruption, to rise with the view of directing attention to an extraordinary fact—one of which he appeared to have had no previous knowledge—namely, that of there being strangers in the gallery! The very moment this honorable gentleman rose, a loud burst of laughter drowned every other sound; for the whole house perceived that an humble petition had been cut into slips, and not only secured by the collar of his coat, but stuck firmly with wafers all over his back, reaching even below his expansive coat-tails. Of this the honorable member of course was unconscious; but as his object had been gained in so far as that the noise had been renewed, he very quietly sat down with the view of playing a few more popular and interesting tunes, with the instrument which he conceived he held tightly between his gums.

He was, however, soon interrupted again, for an honorable member who had made many ineffectual attempts to obtain a hearing, taking advantage of a temporary suppression of noise, rose to move an adjournment. The motion was followed by shouts of "No, no!" and a really extraordinary species of yelling; but as the honorable member declared that he was determined to take the sense of the house—to the utter astonishment of Valentine, who could not conceive where the sense could be found—the adjournment was agreed to without a division, and the immediate rush towards the door was tremendous.

As soon as the coast became sufficiently clear, Goodman and his charge left the house and proceeded homewards; but while the feeling which prevailed in the bosom of the former was that of unqualified delight, that which reigned in the breast of the latter was one of unmingled and boundless surprise.

CHAPTER X.

IN WHICH GOODMAN IS HONORED WITH A PECULIAR VISIT, AND SUBSEQUENTLY SEIZED IN THE MOST MYSTERIOUS MANNER POSSIBLE.

Without presuming to enter those peculiarly chaotic regions Geology might tempt the imagination to explore—without, indeed, going any farther back than the days of Adam and Eve—it may with safety be asserted—taking for a point that interesting period of our history when young Creation beat old Chaos hollow—that of all the destructive wars which have afflicted mankind, the War of Attachments has raged with the greatest constancy and fierceness. From the birth of the sun, moon and stars, to the deluge, from the deluge to the commencement of the Christian era, and from thence to the period of the publication of these adventures, the attachments have been savagely cutting each other's throats —scourging, smothering, and torturing each other in every conceivable variety of forms —in a word, all the evils with which man has been cursed are attributable solely to this War of the Attachments.

Now, in proportion as Goodman's attachment to Valentine increased, his attachment to his amiable relatives diminished; in fact, the one was very quietly smothering the other, when those relatives in turn formed certain new attachments which they conceived might promote the great object they had in view.

One heavenly morning, about twelve o'clock, when the leaves of the aspen were shivering in the breeze, when the cows were each moment expecting to be milked, and when, Valentine having been sent to the banker's, Goodman was reading in his library alone, the servant entered with a couple of highly glazed cards, which bore the following remarkable inscriptions —*Dr. Emanuel W. Bowlemout*, and Dr. Dionysius Dobb.

"Dr. Emanuel W. Bowlemout?—Bowlemout—Bowlemout," said Goodman, considering—"Dr. Dionysius Dobb?—Dobb? —Dobb?—I have not the slightest knowledge of these gentlemen. Ask them to walk in."

While the servant was seducing the two doctors out of the parlor, Goodman read the cards again and again, conceiving that their names might strike their full length portraits on his memory.

"Good morning, sir," profoundly observed a remarkably short and apoplectic individual, who appeared to have been afflicted with the dropsy from his youth.

"Good morning," said Goodman, waving his hand towards a couple of chairs, of which the doctors took possession.

"My name is Bowlemout," observed the dropsical person.—"My friend Dr. Dobb."

Goodman bowed and placed the cards upon the table.

"You are quite well, I hope?" said Dr. Emanuel W. Bowlemout.

"Perfectly," said Goodman; "thank God I never had a day's illness in my life."

Dr. Bowlemout looked at Dr. Dobb, who cocked his chin upon his stick, and eyed Goodman intently.

"May I," observed Goodman, after waiting in silence some considerable time —May I inquire the object of this visit?"

"Most certainly, my dear sir," replied Dr. Bowlemout, looking again at Dr. Dobb who still continued to sit like a statue in mourning for some dear friend—"It may, my dear sir, appear somewhat extraordinary that we should have called upon you thus without a previous introduction; but it is perhaps in these cases quite as well—quite." And Dr. Bowlemout looked once more at Dr. Dobb, who did condescend then to nod, by way of signifying that that observation had met his views precisely.

Goodman was still unable to imagine what the object of these gentlemen could be; but he ventured to suppose that he should know in good time, and therefore waited for its natural development with patience, while those gentlemen were viewing him with what he conceived to be an expression of pity.

"Do me the favor," at length said Dr. Bowlemout, placing his finger delicately upon Goodman's wrist, as his hand rested upon the table—"allow me."

"Gentlemen!" said Goodman firmly, withdrawing his hand, "You have honored me with a visit, and you have, I presume, some object in view; need I add that I consider it necessary for that object to be explained?"

"Why, my dear sir," replied Dr. Bowlemout, "the fact is, we have called at the request of certain intimate friends of yours, who fancy that you have not been looking quite so well of late—to ascertain the precise state of your general health."

"Indeed!" said Goodman smiling, "I ought to be exceedingly obliged to those friends. May I know to whom I am indebted for this extraordinary act of kindness?"

"Why that, my dear sir, is a matter of extreme delicacy," replied Bowlemout. "You will perceive that they are naturally apprehensive that they might be deemed too officious—too fond of parading their friendship."

"They," said Goodman, "who imagine that I should fail to appreciate this or any other act of kindness, can know me but imperfectly. There surely can be no serious objection to their names being mentioned?"

"I really," said Dr. Bowlemout, "do not feel justified in naming them."

"No, no, no!" gruffly exclaimed Dr. Dobb. "There is no necessity for that sort of thing."

"I can perceive no necessity for the other sort of thing," observed Goodman somewhat piqued at the roughness of Dr. Dobb. "This visit I trust did not originate in any idle curiosity?"

"Oh! not at all! not at all, my dear sir; not at all!" cried Dr. Bowlemout, "God bless me, no, not at all!"

"Then, gentlemen," said Goodman, "I am able to inform those exceedingly kind friends through you, that I am capable of forming a judgment on the state of my own health —"

"That's the point!—the very point!" interrupted Dr. Bowlemout, turning to Dr. Dobb, who gave several short nods.

"What's the point?" inquired Goodman.

"That men are *not* always able to form such a judgment," growled Dr. Dionysius Dobb. "You, for instance, may be afflicted with one of the most serious maladies that are incident to the human frame without being in the slightest degree conscious of the fact.—Have you heard by-the-bye from your friend the emperor lately?"

"I am perhaps," said Goodman after a pause—during which Dr. Bowlemout gave Dr. Dobb certain slight but mysterious winks—"I am perhaps bound to presume that your object is not to insult me?"

"Oh! dear me, no, not at all!" cried Dr. Bowlemout.

"I must say that that question appears to me to be extraordinary—indeed, the whole proceeding is of so strange a character, that I scarcely know even now what to make of it. Have you any thing more to say, gentlemen?"

"Why, there are," said Dr. Bowlemout, "two or three points upon which I should like to be informed. You are related, I believe, to the Royal Family?"

"Sir!" thundered Goodman, and his eyes flashed with all their wonted fire. "Old as I am, I am not a man to be insulted with impunity."

"Calm yourself; come, come, my dear sir, be cool!" said Dr. Bowlemout.

"Cool, sir!" cried Goodman; "do you take me for an idiot? Think you that I'll consent to be made the sport of fools? Who sent you? Were you in fact sent at all? If you were, why do you not, like *men* —"

"Mr. Valentine has returned," said the servant, who, after knocking for some time, had entered.—"He wishes to know, sir, if he may speak with you."

"Yes," said Goodman, "tell him I want him," and Valentine, who was then at the door, walked in.

"My dear boy," said Goodman, "I have been grossly insulted; I never was before so insulted as I have been by these two persons, of whom I have no sort of knowledge."

"We simply asked him," said Bowlemout, "if he were not related to the Royal Family?"

"And why ask so ridiculous a question?" said Valentine, with one of his peculiarly piercing glances.

"Because," replied Dr. Bowlemout, "we were informed that he claimed the British crown."

"And what if you were thus informed? What, if even he had such a claim, would it interfere with any claim of yours? What have you to do with the matter?—what is it to you?—Have you," added Valentine, addressing Goodman, "any desire to detain these *gentlemen?*"

"None whatever," replied Goodman; "on the contrary, I wish them gone."

"Then you will probably walk with me at once to the door," observed Valentine to the gentlemen in question, who still kept their seats.

"We came here, young man," said Dr. Bowlemout pompously, "to perform a public duty; and we shall *go* when we please."

"Then, if you do," rejoined Valentine, "you must *please* to go immediately."

"Why?" thundered Dr. Dionysius Dobb.

"Because, if you do not," replied Valentine, "I shall be compelled to make you go *before* you please."

At this moment a laughing duett of derision burst from Drs. Bowlemout and Dobb. They soon, however, found that they had made a slight mistake in their estimate of Valentine's character, for on the instant he seized Dr. Bowlemout by the collar, and without the smallest difficulty brought him to the ground. The moment Dr. Bowlemout was down, Dr. Dobb sprang at Valentine with the ferocity of a tiger, and Goodman sprang at him;

but before he had time to reach him, Valentine, who was then on one knee, caught hold of the legs of Dr. Dobb, and threw him cleverly over Dr. Bowlemout's back.

"Keep the fat one down!" shouted Valentine. "Don't let him stir! I'll come back for him in a moment." And he proceeded to drag Dr. Dobb to the door, which he opened, and having thrown him into the street, closed it again, and ran back for the other.

"Now, sir!" said Valentine to Dr. Bowlemout, who was panting for breath, and seemed nearly exhausted, "Do you wish to be thrown headlong after your friend, or will you walk?"

Of the two, Bowlemout decidedly preferred the latter mode of proceeding, and hastened at once to the door; but the moment he had reached the step in safety, he turned round, and scowling at Goodman, cried, with all the breath he appeared to have in his body, "*Oh!* you shall suffer for this!—*we'll* have our revenge!" and Valentine pushed him off the step and closed the door.

About half an hour after the departure of these gentlemen, Walter and Horace looked in to invite Goodman to meet a few friends at their house, in the evening.

To them he explained what had occurred, and they expressed their astonishment with extraordinary warmth. He also explained that he and Valentine were just about to start for Gravesend, at which they appeared to be equally surprised; and after having ascertained the precise time the boat started they hastily quitted the house.

CHAPTER XI.

THE MYSTERIOUS SEIZURE—A GENTLEMAN DROWNED IN IMAGINATION—FIRST APPEARANCE OF VALENTINE UPON THE STAGE OF THE ITALIAN OPERA.

When Goodman had adjusted the week's accumulation of papers, he and Valentine walked leisurely towards Cornhill, but as he had some little business to transact in the immediate vicinity of the Bank, he sent Valentine forward to amuse himself for half an hour, on the steam packet wharf.

Before the half hour had expired, Goodman had completed the business on hand, and as he felt that he might still be in time for the three o'clock boat, he walked rather briskly towards the quay from which it started. He had scarcely, however, turned into Fish-street-Hill, when two powerful looking fellows hastily crossed from the opposite side, and placed themselves immediately before him.

"Fine day, sir," said one of these persons in a singularly rough heavy tone.

"It is a fine day," observed Goodman, endeavoring to pass them, "a very fine day."

"You'd better have a ride along with us, sir," said the fellow, seizing Goodman's right arm.

"What do you mean, man!" cried Goodman, as he strove to wring his arm from the fellow's firm grasp.

"Why on'y that we're going to take a quiet country ride, and we wants you to obleedge us with your company, that's all;" and a coach, that had been waiting on the opposite side, drew up to the spot on the instant.

"In Heaven's name!" exclaimed Goodman, who had become much alarmed, "what *can* all this mean?" and again he made an effort to disengage his arm, but found it held as firmly as though it had been in a vice.

"Come, come, you know, be quiet; it an't o' no use, you know; none o' your tricks; it won't do," said the fellow.

"My good man," cried Goodman, "you are laboring under some strange mistake—indeed, *indeed* you are mistaken."

"Not a bit of it," growled the fellow, "not a ha'porth! your name's Goodman, an't it? Mr. Grimwood Goodman?"

"It certainly is, but —"

"Oh! it's all right! the fus cousin to the emperor of Chany, you know!—now if so be as you want to be treated like a genelman, you'll get in at once, without any more bones."

"But I will *not* get in!" exclaimed Goodman.

"Well," said the fellow, calmly, "there's not the least compulsion in life, you know —on'y you must."

"What,—what does it mean, sir?—where is your authority for this monstrous proceeding?"

"Oh, we have got lots of authority," cried the fellow; and his assistant proceeded to let down the steps, while the coachman held open the door.

"Help! help!" shouted Goodman as a

gentleman passed. "For Heaven's sake, save me from these ruffians!"

"What is all this about?" said the gentleman, approaching.

"It's all right, sir; all quite reg'lar," replied the fellow, first tapping his forehead, and then placing his thumb by the side of his nose, "you understand?"

"Poor fellow!" exclaimed the gentleman in accents of pity.

"My good sir, but hear me—pray hear me!" cried Goodman.

"Go quietly, there's a dear man," said the gentleman, evidently affected. "It is all for the best; these persons will not harm you, indeed they will not—come, come."

"Sir!" exclaimed Goodman—"Oh! hear me explain!—stay, stay but for an instant!—stay sir, if you are a Christian!" but the gentleman, who appeared to be in haste, sighed deeply while a tear stood in his eye, and passed on.

"Now are we to clap on a jacket or not!" cried the fellow, who began to be impatient.

"Good God!" exclaimed Goodman—"will no one assist me? Help! help! For the love of Heaven!—Help! help!" he repeated in tones the most piercing, while he struggled with all the strength at his command. He was, however, but as a child in the grasp of a giant; for the principal ruffian at once thrust him into the coach, in which Goodman, the benevoleut warm-hearted Goodman, sunk back and immediately fainted.

While this most extrordinary seizure was being made, Valentine was waiting with much impatience at the wharf. The packet by which they were to have started had left, and the latest, which had immediately after glided like a swan to the spot, was filling fast. It being Saturday, hundreds of persons, consisting chiefly of merchants, warehousemen, and clerks, whose families annually reside at Gravesend three weeks or a month, hastened down with the view of joining those families that night, and returning to buisness early on Monday morning. With these persons almost every seat upon deck was soon occupied. Some began to peruse the weekly journals, some to arrange the papers with which their pockets had been filled, while others, with their arms folded under their coat-tails, were thoughtfully watching the progress of the tide.

At length the men on board began to bustle about the deck, and the captain mounted one of the boxes by which the paddles were partially concealed and commenced giving orders about the adjustment of certain ropes. As every motion was now indicative of an immediate start, Valentine at once rushed on board, feeling certain that he must have missed Goodman in the crowd. He searched the deck and cabin, however, in vain; and as he looked with anxiety from the side of the vessel, to ascertain if Goodman were coming, the Captain gave his orders to let the boat go.

"But one moment!" cried Valentine, addressing the Captain. "I expect a friend here in an instant."

"Time's up, sir; can't stop," said the Captain. "Now, my lads, come, look alive!" and his people began to unfasten the ropes, whem Valentine leaping upon the barge to which the vessel had been secured, resolved on detaining her a few moments longer.

"Captain!" shouted Valentine, making his voice proceed apparently from a little wooden watch-box of an office, adorned with flaming red and blue placards.

"Hollo!" cried the Captain.

"You are wanted in the office!" shouted Valentine.

"Why, we're off!—who wants me?"

"One of the proprietors. Here! you must come!"

"Blow one of the proprietors!" growled the indignant Captain, *sotto voce*. "Here, old fast a bit: I wonder what's the matter now." And he jumped from the deck upon the landing barge, and proceeded towards the office, with a countenance expressive of anything but delight.

Valentine again looked most anxiously for Goodman, and just as he saw some one hastening towards the wharf whom he conceived might be him, the gallant Captain returned, and after knocking aside every man who stood in his way shouted, "Who was it said I was wanted? I should just like to know," he added, gruffly, on receiving no answer. "I'm blowed if I wouldn't pitch him right overboard bang!" and having scrambled to the top of the paddle-box, again gave the signal for starting.

Valentine, however, being determined to give Goodman a few minutes more, no sooner heard the well known signal given, than sending his voice under the stern of the vessel shouted—"Help! help! a boat, a boat! Help! help! help!"—so loudly, that in a moment the persons who were standing on the wharf joined in the cry simultaneously with the passengers on board. Down dashed the boat which had deen hawled up to the stern, with a force which must have killed any man out and out if one had happened to have been there; while other boats instantly came to the spot, and every available rope was in immediate requisition. The boats darted round and round the vessel, in vain, followed by the eyes of the passengers, who appeared to be in a state of great excitement, while the steam was hissing, panting, and snorting with as much angry violence as if it had been perfectly cognisant of the trick.

"Poor soul!" exclaimed a stout old gentleman, who stood upon the barge, "he has sunk, I fear, to rise no more!"

"Help! Here ,here, here!" shouted Valentine, and away the boats flew to the spot from which the sound appeared to proceed, while the passengers rushed from side to side with the most painful anxiety.

"Where, where are you?" cried one of the boatmen. "My good fellow—now, now! give another hail!—where are you?"

"Here!" cried Valentine.

"Starn! starn!" shouted the Captain in haste. "Look alive?" And away went the boats again astern. "Have you got him?" he inquired of the men; "have you got him?" But the reply was, "If we could but only see him we shouldn't care.

"Make haste," shouted Valentine.

"Where?" cried the Captain, "where, where, my poor fellow—where are you?"

"On the wheel," exclaimed Valentine, faintly.

"Hold on but a moment! now, now, my lads—now! to the wheel; now, hurrah!" cried the Captain, whose eyes at once sparkled with joy, for he felt that he should save the poor fellow at last.

"Move ahead!" cried Valentine, assuming the voice of a lad whom he had heard give the order before, and the wheels on the instant dashed violently round amidst a general shout of horror!

The wheels were stopt; the foam subsided; but the voice was heard no more. The passengers looked at each other aghast. The Captain stared at the boy and the boy stared at the Captain; but neither of them uttered a word—indeed for several minutes a deathlike silence prevailed, and the general conviction was, that the wheel had dashed down the unfortunate man, who had become too much exhausted to rise again to the surface.

Valentine again looked round for his guardian, but again was most grievously disappointed. The vessel was then half an hour behind time; and as he felt that it would be useless to detain her any longer, he made up his mind to let her go. The men in the boats were still watching the surface of the river intently; the Captain was explaining to the boy what he had done, and the boy was declaring to the sceptical Captain that the order to move ahead had not proceeded from him, while the passengers and the persons who stood upon the barge were relating to each other how the poor fellow struggled as they saw him in imagination go down; and descanting very freely upon all that was known of the characteristics peculiar to a watery grave.

The captain at length, feeling that nothing more could be done for the "poor fellow," again prepared to start, and Valentine, in order to relieve his mind, sent a loud shout of laughter immediately behind him. The effect was electrical. Nothing could exceed the astonishment displayed by the Captain. He turned sharply round, with a bosom swelling with indignation, in order to ascertain what manner of man he could be who thus had the cold blooded inhumanity to laugh at so awful a moment as that.

"It was only a joke!" said Valentine.

"A joke!" cried the Captain, indignantly "a joke!"

"Why, yes, I wasn't overboard at all!" shouted Valentine. "I only made believe!"

"Made believe!" cried the Captain, looking scornfully towards the quarter from which the sounds appeared to proceed. "Who is it that spoke? who only made believe? I'll give a crown out of my own pocket to know!—for that man, if he was even the king of England, should not remain aboard of my boat another instant. I'd make him go ashore, if I wouldn't—*who* was it?"

As the inhuman person in question refused to reply, and as the indignant captain found it impossible to discover the delinquent, he with evident reluctance again gave the signal for starting, when the vessel was released from her moorings, and glided majestically down with the tide.

The very moment the boat was out of sight, Valentine started to the residence of the citizen upon whom Goodman had called on his way to the wharf, and having there ascertained that he had left in great haste, he proceeded home fancying that something of importance might have occurred to induce his guardian to return. On hearing, however, that he had not returned, he concluded at once that he must have started by the first boat, unseen in the crowd, and after allowing the servant to bring up the tray with some cold beef and salad, he began to think how he should amuse himself until the morning, when he intended to follow by the earliest boat.

No sooner had he finished his meal and drank a couple of glasses of port, which had been left in the decanter, than Horace arrived in a state of great excitement, to inquire if within the last hour his father had been there? On being informed that he had not, his excitement increased, but on learning that Valentine had just returned alone, he smiled with intense satisfaction, and entered the parlor at once.

"Well, my young ancient!" cried Horace, "why, I thought you were off to the aristocratic regions of Gravesend!"

"I did start for that purpose," said Valentine, "but I unfortunately missed your uncle."

"Of course! Why you didn't expect any other thing, did you? It's just like the old undeniable. He and my governor in that little particular are just as much alike as two wheelbarrows. Only let 'em slip, and they go in-and-out, in-and-out, like a couple of crocodiles, and if you ever catch so much as a sight of 'em again, why you must have an eye like a Flanders brick. But I say, my little antediluvian, haven't you got a glass of wine to give a fellow? Where does old owe-nothing keep it?"

"Upon my word I don't know, but Ann will get us some, doubtless," replied Valentine, ringing the bell.

"Aye that's the very card," observed Horace, "for I'm about fit to drop." And he cocked his legs deliberately upon the table. "I say, my Seraphina," he continued as Ann entered the room, "here's a dreadful state of mind for a bottle to be in! come give it a belly full of something, old girl."

The order was confirmed by a nod from Valentine, and a bottle of port was brought up with the corkscrew, when Horace first pronounced Ann to be an out-and-outer, and then seizing the carving knife with which he cracked the shoulder of the bottle, very dexterously wrung its long neck off.

"Dear me, Mr. Horace!" exclaimed Ann, "how I wish you'd draw the corks, you do make such a mess."

"Bring us another glass, my old girl," said Horace, who, on its being brought, added, "now you'll know how much better it tastes in this way," and as Ann expressed a great disinclination to try it, he simply threw her down upon the sofa, when, having kissed her and forced her to swallow the wine, he laughed at her indignation, and allowed her to retire.

"It strikes me with just about the force of a sledge-hammer," said Horace, after having replenished his glass three times without relinquishing the bottle for a moment, "that you are neither more nor less than an out-and-out brick. Now what do you dream of doing with your body to-night?"

"I scarcely know," replied Valentine.

"Well then, I'll tell you what it is; just cock yourself comfortably under my care, and I'll show you a little of life."

"But I fancied," observed Valentine, "that you were going to have a party to-night."

"And so we are," returned Horace, "but you don't suppose that I'm such an out-and-out flat as to join them, do you? If uncle had been going, why I must then have stuck there of course, for he's such an excruciating old file, that he couldn't be happy without me; but as he'll not, you know, be there at all, don't suppose that I'm going to waste the evening with a parcel of jolly old dummies, some mumbling about the weather, some growling about the high price of bees'-wax, some whining about the anti-diminishable character of the national debt, and others showing how a jolly revolution might be averted by allowing pickled cabbage to be imported in the raw. A rubber's the very utmost to which they could be goaded, and then they're such wide awake warmint, you can't even so much as palm a card without being told of it, which happens to be the very thing I most hate. Why, then, should I join a crew of this particular kidney, unless indeed I wanted to cut the throat of time, or to commit an act of self-smotheration? It is true I shall have tea with them just for the wetness of the thing, and then of course I bolt; so if you like, you know, to place yourself under my care, I shall just put you up to a thing or two that isn't known to here and there one."

"Oh, I shall be most happy," observed Valentine.

"Well then, we'll finish this bottle, and stop just an hour at home, and then we'll run a regular trump to earth, who can take us where you never were before. But, remember, when I light my cheroot, and you see the old out-and-outers cocking up their jolly old noses, leave the room, and I'll be after you with all the alacrity of a bum."

Accordingly, the bottle was emptied, almost solely by Horace, and they proceeded to the house of his father, where they found half a dozen disagreeable old shrews whose husbands were expected to join them after tea.

"*Have* you seen your father, Horace?" inquired Mrs. Goodman.

"No," replied Horace, who winked at his dear and anxious mother, and drew her towards the window, where they kept up for some time a low conversational whisper.

"There he is," exclaimed Mrs. Horace Goodman.

"Not a bit of it, I know," said Horace, "that isn't the old buffer's knock."

"I know it is," observed Mrs. Goodman junior.

"I tell you it is not," cried Horace snappishly, "I think I ought to know. He'd never give such an out-and-out know-nothing tat-a-rat, rat-a-tat business as that. It's somebody that's just got over a soft single knock, and now doesn't know exactly when to leave off."

At this moment Walter entered as pale as a ghost, and, on catching the eye of Valentine, gave an involuntary shudder. He rallied, however, in an instant; but on extending his hand, Valentine found that it trembled violently.

As soon as Mrs. Goodman could conveniently manage it, she whispered, "Is it done?" and on receiving an intimation in the affirmative, she communicated the fact to Mrs. Horace Goodman, and it appeared to be highly satisfactory to both.

Tea was then brought up at once, and the whole party drew round the table; but it was easily perceptible by all, that Walter had on his mind something which bid defiance to tranquillity. When addressed on any subject he spoke with affected gaiety and smiled, but in an instant his brow again sank, and his features became sullen and rigid as before.

As Horace had described, it would have been dull work indeed, to spend the evening in the society of the persons there assembled. There was talking, it is true, a great quantity of talking, but not a single word was uttered in an hour, worth remembering a minute.

As soon, therefore, as this weary tea affair was over, Horace pulled out his case, and began to wet a cheroot by rolling it over his tongue with peculiar rapidity.

"You are not going to smoke," observed Mrs. Goodman junior.

"These ladies, I'm sure, will not mind it," said Horace.

"Oh! certainly not!" simultaneously exclaimed the majority of the ladies, at the same time bringing out their scent-bottles to prepare for the infliction.

"Mrs. Shrewell cannot bear it, I know," said the junior Mrs. Goodman.

"Oh, never mind me!" cried that amiable lady.

"If that's the case," said Horace, "why of course —"

"Dear me, no! by no means! I never allow Mr. Shrewell to smoke, but I don't at all mind it. On the contrary, I think it rather pleasant than not."

"Of course!"—exclaimed Horace, who well knew that the old lady would cough with sufficient violence to make her black in the face in five minutes. "Of course!" and after pulling out a peculiar description of lucifer, the nipping of which sent forth a villanous odor, he proceeded to ignite his cheroot.

This being the signal for starting, Valentine gladly left the room, and was instantly followed by Horace and his cheroot, to the unspeakable gratification of those amiable ladies of whom he was anything but ardently enamored.

"Now," said Horace, "let us be off," and accordingly he and Valentine started in the direction of the Haymarket, both highly pleased at having escaped.

"It strikes me," said Horace, on reaching Leicester-square, "that we shall just be in time for old Leatherlungs; and if so, you'll have a bit of a treat to begin with."

"Who's Leatherlungs?" inquired Valentine.

"That's only his professional name," replied Horace. "His real name is Growlaway. He's in the Opera chorus, and a regular trump he is too; this is the crib he patronises." And Valentine was dragged into a little dirty pot-house, and eventually reached a dark room at the back.

At first he was able to distinguish nothing, for in addition to the room being dark, it was densely filled with smoke, while a circular ventilator was rattling round and round at the rate of full thirty miles an hour. Horace, however, at once grasped the hand of a man who was smoking a remarkably long pipe, and when Valentine had been formally introduced to this gentleman, they all sat down cosily together.

"Well, what are you going to stand?" was the first question asked by Mr. Growlaway.

"Just whatever you like," replied Horace. "What have you been drinking?"

"Half and half," said Mr. Growlaway.

"That I can't stand," observed Horace. "Let's have some brandy-and-water," and the chorister's eyes sparkled, and he pulled away at his pipe with additional perseverance, until the brandy-and-water arrived, when he as nearly as possible swallowed the whole without taking his lips from the glass.

"We wan't to go behind the scenes," said Horace. "You can manage it for us, can't you?"

"Why," said Mr. Growlaway, "they're getting so nasty particular, one doesn't know how to act. You must take your chance, you know. Follow me right in. If you attempt to look round you are done, for they'll know in a moment you don't belong to the house."

"All right," said Horace.

"But had we not better pay at once?" inquired Valentine.

Horace smiled at his simplicity, and explained that no money was taken at the door they were to enter; and it having been eventually arranged that they should follow the steps of Mr. Growlaway, Valentine paid for the brandy-and-water out of a well filled purse, which Growlaway no sooner saw than he suddenly recollected that he was going to have a benefit on the following Monday evening, at the Bull's-eye and Rat-trap Tavern, at the same time pulling out a bnndle of tickets, five of which Valentine felt compelled to purchase, at the remarkably small charge of half a sovereign, and they then proceeded at once to the stage door of the Italian Opera.

Having passed the gate at the end of the hall, Mr. Growlaway intimated that all was quite safe, and they leisurely proceeded along a narrow dirty passage, which happened to be dimly illumined here and there with the remains of a narrow candle deliberately stinking in the socket of a tall tin lamp.

On arriving at the end of this passage they ascended a few stairs which led to a wide open space, in which certain painted people disguised as brigands, and peasants, and Spanish noblemen and Turks, were promenading. At the back sat a number of persons with their shirt-sleeves tucked up drinking porter, while above were suspended innumerable pulleys and ropes and ragged slips of painted canvass. On the left of this space stood what Valentine at first sight conceived to be a tall iron column, but which was in reality a round flight of cast iron steps, and the gaily dressed people who were perpetually ascending, imparted the idea of a regiment of butterflies running up a corkscrew.

"Now then," said Growlaway, darting up this singular flight of steps, and Horace and Valentine followed as fast as possible, and after twirling round until they were perfectly giddy, they turned into a little filthy room near the roof, in which about twenty individuals were dressing.

In this room Valentine at once seated himself upon the edge of an old chair with one arm and no bottom, which stood by the side of an ancient washing stand, the top of which was secured to the legs with what might in its infancy have been a towel, twisted tightly and ingeniously into the similitude of a rope, while in the hole stood a basin with about half a brim, which was occasionally supplied with water from a brown stone jug, which happened to have neither a handle nor a spout.

As soon as the giddiness occasioned by the twirling ascent had gone off, Valentine directed his attention to the proceedings of the professional gentlemen present, whose attitudes few could have failed to admire. One was endeavoring to perfect himself in the bass part of the opening chorus, by leaning over a book and singing the notes with infinite spirit, and certainly looked extremely cool and interesting, seeing that at that particular time he had nothing on but his shirt; another, in precisely the same costume with the exception of a pair of purple stockings, was engaged in making really desperate efforts to act; a third who had nearly completed his disguise, was splitting his habiliments in all directions, while striving to pull on a remarkable couple of buff cut-throat boots, which appeared to be *about* seven sizes too small; a fourth was jumping into a pair of pantaloons which might have been built for a twenty-stone Dutchman; a fifth who had dressed for a high-born Spaniard, and who looked like a journeyman tinker *incog.*, was adjusting the mantle of another noble person, who, in order that no time might be lost, was eating the remains of a cold pork-chop, which he had brought with bread and mustard in the crown of his hat.

In the middle of the room stood a table, round which several other professional gentlemen were engaged in giving the last tranquil touches to their formidable countenances, which really as a whole looked extremely picturesque. One was arching his eyebrows with a piece of burnt cork; another was bringing out his nose by drawing black zigzag lines on either side with a piece of smoked wire; another, being a peasant, was establishing upon his long upper lip an exact representation of a pair of military moustaches; another was laying on his cheeks with a rabbit's foot, a thick coat of red brickdust upon a waistcoat of pomatum; another was endeavoring to adjust a judge's wig, which had adorned the heads of a thousand professional gentlemen before him, while another was transforming a waggoner's hat into the perfect similitude of an Italian noble's, by carefully pinning the brim up in front, and making an additional hole in the crown for the reception of a long peacock's feather.

"Will you not dress and go on?" inquired Horace, when Valentine had feasted his eyes on this scene, "you will not get a view of the house unless you do."

"Oh, with all my heart!" replied Valentine, who seemed rather to like the idea than not.

"Of course!" observed Horace, throwing towards him a pair of yellow tights, which he had taken from a heap. "On with 'em and then you'll enjoy your noble self."

"But I'd rather not strip," said Valentine, approving the cut of the tights by no means.

"Well, tuck up your trowsers, and wind this affair round your calves"—said one who appeared to be the master of the ceremonies, throwing several yards of red and blue worsted binding, which was intended to convey to some distance a silken idea—"you can as well be a brigand as not."

Accordingly up went the trowsers above the knee, and round went the blue and red binding, when a jacket with spangles was selected and put on, and the man who had been fetching the professional gentlemen bread and cheese and half-and-half, politely offered to make up the face of the brigand.

As soon as this interesting operation had been performed, the overture commenced, and the call-boy came up to announce the important fact, conceiving probably that the whole of the professional gentlemen might suddenly have been seized with total deafness. Valentine just caught a glance of himself, and a beautiful brigand he fancied he looked! He then turned round to exhibit to Horace, but the chair in which Horace had been sitting, was at that moment occupied by "a malignant and a turban'd Turk," tying up his garters. He had no time to make farther scrutiny then, being pressed towards the door by the professional group; he therefore, conceiving that he should find his companion below, rushed down the iron stair-case with the stream, and having remained at the side until the curtain drew up, tucked a little plump peasant girl under his arm and gracefully made his *debut*.

It happened to be one of the grand nights of the season, and the house had an exceedingly brilliant effect. All the boxes were full, and while the people appeared to be dovetailed into the pit, the spacious gallery presented one mass of human beings, which reached from the rail to the ceiling.

As soon as he could see clearly over the foot-lights, which had in the first instance dazzled his eyes, Valentine felt that as he was there ostensibly with a view to the exercise of his talent, he might as well commence operations as not; and as he saw a small personage in one of the boxes on the second tier near the proscenium, applauding the *Prima Donna* with extraordinary vehemence, by shouting out, "bravo! bravissimo!" and clapping his hands most violently, with the obvious view of catching the eye of the lady, he thought that he would proceed to promote the views of that personage, at least so far as to render him an object of attraction.

Accordingly when the applause, which succeeded a really delightful scena, had subsided, he dexterously threw his voice into the identical box in which the lady-killing personage in question was seated, and exclaimed in tones of ecstacy, "Beautiful! ye gods! oh! excellent! never heard anything like it! encore! delicious, demme."

"Order! order!" cried at least a hundred voices on the instant.

"I tell you it is beautiful! demme! did you ever? bravissimo! encore, encore, encore!" exclaimed Valentine; and the small individual, whose voice he had assumed, sat twiddling his whiskers and grinning like an ape taking a bird's-eye view of the country from a descending parachute.

"Order! order!" again became the general cry, and every eye was directed towards the particular box in question.

"Demme!" continued Valentine, "don't I say that it's beautiful; and am I not perfectly in order? Did you ever hear any thing half so magnificent? She's a great creature—oh! she's a great creature, demme!"

"Silence!" exclaimed several highly indignant persons in the pit, "turn him out!"

"I repeat it," cried Valentine, "she is a great creature."

Loud shouts of "Order, order! silence! turn him out! drunk!" now proceeded from every part of the house, while the little ill-used gentleman, in a state of interesting unconsciousness, sat wondering why every glass in the house, both single and double barrelled, was so impertinently brought to bear upon him.

During the whole of this time the legitimate performances were stopped; and as the heroine of the opera had struck a certain position from which she could not possibly move before she had uttered a certain exclamation, and could not possibly give utterance to that exclamation before she had received a certain cue, she very quietly intimated the extreme propriety of dropping the curtain, which was accordingly done amid general uproar.

The very moment the curtain had fallen, the attention of the little individual was arrested by two persons who had been deputed to expostulate with him on the excessive inconvenience of the course which they naturally imagined he had been pursuing. To these persons he was heard to proclaim his perfect innocence with considerable earnestness and force, but they were seized with a fit of the most inflexible incredulity, and marvelled that he should so far disgrace the name he bore, as to descend to the utterance of so deliberate a falsehood as that of declaring that the interruption had not proceeded from him. Yet what could they do? They could have sworn, and would have sworn, that it had proceeded from him and him alone: yet here was a man, a highly distinguished patron of the opera, a nobleman! who declared that if they *had* thus sworn they would have committed an act of perjury! What could they do? Why they could do no more than they did—express a hope that the interruption might not be renewed, and retire.

As the little ill-used personage immediately after this became invisible to the audience, the uproar speedily subsided; and when the curtain again rose, the accomplished heroine was discovered in precisely the same attitude as that in which she had stood before it had fallen. The long-expected cue was then given, and then came the piercing exclamation, and then a loud burst of enthusiastic applause, during which the group of choristers marched off the stage, and as Valentine of course was compelled to march with them, the audience were left to the uninterrupted enjoyment of the recitative, the duetts and the trios that were to follow.

Now, when Valentine had ascertained that the ladies and gentlemen of the choir had two or three thousand bars' rest, he felt it to be his duty to keep them out of that mischief into which they were displaying a disposition to enter by glancing, and kissing, and squeezing, and whispering the softest possible nonsense to each other as they stood indiscriminately at the wings. Acting upon this amiable impulse, he looked anxiously round with the view of occupying their minds with something of a more virtuous tendency, for he at that moment felt more strongly than ever that it was absolutely incumbent upon every man to check the progress of indiscretion by all the means at his command.

Scarcely had he turned from these professional ladies and gentlemen, whose eyes appeared to be swimming in liquid naughtiness, when he saw about thirty old pieces of old scenery resting against the wall, and conceived that he could not conveniently promote the great cause of morality more than by setting the gentlemen to work to remove them.

With this extremely laudable object in view he therefore introduced behind the old scenery in question a shrill cry of "murder!" at which, of course, the ladies and gentlemen started and stared at each other in a really interesting state of amazement. The cry was repeated; and the ladies became alarmed, and crept to the panting bosoms of the gentlemen for protection. Again the cry was heard, and the excitement became more intense, but as the gentlemen, were equally affrighted with the ladies, and manifested no disposition to move, Valentine exclaimed in the voice of a female, "Release me! oh! help! get me out! remove the scenes! remove the scenes, or I faint!"

"Why don't you come here and lend a hand?" cried one of the carpenters who had been attracted to the spot, "don't you hear! haven't none of you got any bowels?"

This forcible appeal to the humanities had the effect of inducing the professional gentlemen to approach the old scenes in a body, when Valentine introduced a low melancholy moan which inspired them with the conviction that unless aid came speedily all would be over. They therefore at once set to work, regardless of the dust which lay upon each scene an inch thick, regardless of the splendor of their dresses, and of the dignity they had assumed, in fact, regardless of all but the removal of those frames which they naturally imagined were pressing the life out of some one.

"Stoop down!" cried the carpenter, when about half the scenes had been removed, "stoop down and creep out at the bottom."

"I cannot; I cannot! oh! do, do, remove them!" cried Valentine in the voice of one gasping for breath.

"Now bear a hand, gentlemen! bear a hand—quick!" cried the carpenter, and the nobles, and the brigands, and the pure unsophisticated peasantry, already completely covered with thick black dust, again set to work with unprecedented zeal, while the ladies, whose natural curiosity had subdued their alarm, were most anxiously peeping as each scene was removed to ascertain who on earth it could be, and expressing certain rather unequivocal suspicions, having reference to the purpose for which a lady had thus been induced to get behind.

As each scene increased both in weight and in size, the difficulty of removing them at length became extreme; but Valentine being resolved to keep them at it, stimulated them perpetually to renewed exertions by renewing his cries for instant succor. Every man who was not actually engaged upon the stage, was called upon loudly to assist; and as the necessary, or rather the required assistance was soon found to be incompatible with the progress of the opera, the lessee directed the curtain to be dropped, and went forward to state that a lamentable accident had unaccountably occurred, and to solicit the indulgence of the audience for a few moments, which the audience displayed a highly laudable disposition to concede.

All hands were now at work with unquestionable energy, and they rattled the old scenes about in a style in which they never had been rattled before. On the removal of each, a dense cloud of dust descended, but neither the nobles, the peasants, nor the brigands, were to be deterred from the performance of an act of pure humanity by any consideration of that kind. They worked away like colliers, and were nearly as black, while the perspiration gushed from every pore.

At length, by dint of almost super-human exertions, they got to the three last scenes, and as they appeared to be infinitely superior to the rest in point of weight, it was suggested that, instead of removing them bodily, it would answer every purpose if their bases were drawn from the wall. This excellent suggestion was acted upon at once, but Valentine would not cease to moan.

"Vill you not pe apel to come now out of it?" inquired the stage-manager, who was a Frenchman, and prided himself upon his ability to speak English with the purity and force of a native.

"Oh! no, no," cried Valentine faintly, "remove them—oh! do remove them all."

"Vale, vale; put you mosh pe ver pig if you vas non be apel to come avay now. Vat for you vas git pehind a tall?"

"Quick! oh quick!" cried Valentine; and another large scene was removed.

"Now giv to me you hand," said the stage-manager, kneeling, and extending his arm behind the two remaining scenes. "Now ten, now," he continued, "come, and I sall pull you out."

"I cannot reach it," said Valentine, "oh give me some water."

"Poor ting!" exclaimed the amiable stage-manager, "some vatare!" he shouted to the men who were standing by, and some water was immediately brought in a can which he placed behind the scenes, and pushed as far as he could reach.

As there were but two scenes now remaining, they were pulled further out from the wall; and as the moaning had ceased, and the general impression was that the female had fainted, a lanthorn was brought, with which the manager went behind, but in a moment fell over the can and extinguished the light. Another lanthorn, however, was instantly procured, and he then began to prosecute his search.

"Vhere vas you?" said he; "vere you you creep to, poor ting? Come to me! vere sall you pe got? *vere te tepple hap you creep?*" he continued in a most emphatic tone; and becoming somewhat alarmed on being able discover no one, he came out at once, and exclaimed with a shrug, "tere is nopotty in tere a tall!"

"What!" cried the carpenter, seizing the lanthorn, "I'll find somebody, I'll bet a crown," and in he rushed, but in an instant returned with the confirmation of the interesting fact upon his tongue.

"Well! have you got her out?" inquired the lessee, approaching.

"Non, che vas nevare in tere a tall!" replied the astounded stage-manager.

"Not what!" cried the lessee.

"Nopotty vas tere."

"Pooh! nonsense! she has fainted. Here give me a light," and in went the highly indignant lessee; "are you sure," he inquired, after having looked in vain, "that she did not glide out to escape detection?"

"Te tepple a pit!" replied the manager. "I hap von eye upon him hole all te time! che could not possible."

"You don't mean to suppose that you'll make me believe she was not there, do you?"

"It is ver extraordinaire, ver mosh rum, put tere vas noting ven I vas go in but te vatare which we place in ourselfs."

As the audience at this moment began to manifest impatience, the lessee, conceiving it to have been some favorite of the stage-manager whom he had allowed to escape, uttered several indignant exclamations, and ordered the legitimate performances to be immediately resumed. The principals engaged in the next scene were therefore summoned, and the curtain again rose despite the earnest entreaties of the chorus-master, who viewed the extremely dirty condition of those whom he led with a feeling of horror; for, independently of the dust which adhered firmly to their pomatum-covered countenances, streams of perspiration thickly coated with vermillion, had established themselves in all directions and looked like distant rivulets of veritable gore. The necessity for allowing these professional individuals time to beautify themselves, was therefore obvious to the meanest capacity; but the lessee was inflexible, and, as shortly after this the next chorus was called, on they went as they were.

The excitement which at this particular moment prevailed caused them naturally enough to strike up the wrong chorus—a circumstance which so highly incensed a fat ruby-nosed person who was prompting in a little covered pigeon-hole just above the foot-lights; that after shouting violently—"*Cedi il campo alla vendetta!—cedi il campo alla vendetta!*" he was about to pitch his book at the head of an individual who looked like a long-faced fiend who had just been scratched and pelted by a mob of young imps, when the band at once ceased operations. This remarkable little incident had singularly enough the effect of bringing the professional group to their recollection. They therefore commenced the right chorus at once, and after dashing clean through it in a style of which novelty was its only recommendation, the first act concluded amidst a volley of hisses, which five thousand serpents might have endeavored to emulate in vain.

Between the first and second acts the professional gentlemen were busily engaged in washing and repainting their faces, while the ladies were wondering who it was that had got behind the scenery, being all of them firmly convinced that it was one of the choir, and that she had glided from that equivocal position unseen. The stage-manager, however, with whom they were conversing, would not admit even the bare possibility of such an escape. "Tere vas put von vay," said he, "for to come out of te place, and I hat my eye upon him, and nopotty pass and so terefore it vas be te tepple it vas any potty a tall, and he vas knock me town ven I entare, and ten fly avay vit himself."

During the whole of the time the professional gentlemen were making themselves fit to be seen, Valentine was highly amused at their ridiculous and most improbable surmises. It was, however, at length carried unanimously, that whoever she was she really "no better than she should be," but how she escaped from behind was a mystery which they all declared their utter inability to solve.

The call-boy now entered to summon the choristers who descended, and the second act commenced. The audience were evidently piqued about something which might have been easily explained; but as the immediate object of Valentine was to restore them to perfect good humor, he directed his voice into the middle of the pit, and exclaimed in a half-suppressed tone, "mind your pockets."

No sooner had this simple exclamation been uttered, than a simultaneous movement on the part of the gentlemen proved how extremely anxious they were to profit by the advice which it conveyed; and while each was ascertaining if all he had brought with him were safe, he cast an eye of unwarrantable suspicion upon every individual in his immediate vicinity.

"Ladies! have a care!" shouted Valentine; and the rustling of silk dresses became really unexampled. "My watch!" he continued in the voice of a female, "you have got it! my watch! oh my dear little watch!"

At this interesting moment the entire pit rose, while the persons in the boxes looked with great anxiety, but to the perfect amazement of them all, they were utterly unable to discover the lady from whom the said dear little watch had been stolen.

"Officers! officers!" cried Valentine, assuming the same voice; and officers from various parts of the house rushed at once into the pit.

"I've got him!" continued Valentine.

"Where!" cried a gentleman armed with a staff.

"Here! officers! officers!" and those respectable functionaries followed the sound with considerable zeal and dexterity.

"You know that you have it! you know it too well! oh, give it me back and I'll let you escape."

"No! hold him!—hold him!" cried an officer, who rushed to the spot from which the sound had apparently proceeded, but having reached the point proposed, he was stung with disappointment. He could find neither a person who had stolen a watch, nor a person from whom any watch had been stolen. The people around him were staring at each other with astonishment, he could not obtain even the slightest information, and as the voice was heard no more, it was taken at once for granted, that the felony had been compromised.

With this conviction impressed deeply upon their minds, the people gradually resumed their seats, and when order was somewhat restored, another desperate attempt was made to proceed with the opera.

On the preliminary chord being struck by the gentlemen in the orchestra, who had just taken snuff all round with extraordinary violence—four of the principal *artistes* dashed forward in a rage to sing an affecting quartette. They commenced with an apparent contempt for the music, and proceeded in an extremely careless style, as if anxious to let the audience know that they didn't care whether they sang it or not. In order, therefore, that the house might be somewhat enlivened, Valentine, before the quartette was half finished, introduced a faithful echo into the omnibus-box; and as it was brought to bear upon some of the *Prima Donna's* brilliant passages, that lady gave a series of granite-piercing glances at the echo, and bounced off the stage with more fire than grace.

The progress of the opera was, therefore, again checked, and the audience became highly indignant. They called loudly and imperatively upon the lessee to appear, and when he did appear they would not permit him to speak. They saw him bowing with due humility, and trembling with due violence, but although they demanded an explanation of these irregular proceedings, they would by no means allow him to comply with that demand. As he bent his graceful body nearly double, and shrugged and grinned, and grunted, and placed his hand with great solemnity upon his heart, he seemed to be asking himself a series of highly important questions, and answering himself in the most unsatisfactery manner possible. At length, however, he ventured in an unrivalled attitude, to glide very cleverly off the stage, with the view of persuading the *Prima Donna* to re-appear. But he found that that lady was still inexorable. Nothing could induce her to yield. She declared that she would rather suffer death than go forward again then; and after having knocked one of her attendants fairly down, and pitched a looking-glass dexterously at the head of the other, she vented her indignation upon the unhappy lessee with extraordinary force and effect.

The noise in the body of the house still continued; for, as the lessee had anticipated, the audience viewed his departure as a mark of disrespect. He peeped through a hole in the curtain and trembled; then listened at the wings, and kicked a carpenter for sneezing; when, on being repeatedly called for in tones that were particularly unpleasing, he threw his hat at an innocent scene-shifter with unwarrantable violence, and went forward with the most profound humility again. His reappearance was hailed with a tremendous burst of anger, but he boldly maintained his ground until the lungs of the audience began to manifest unequivocal symptoms of exhaustion; when, getting as near the foot-lights as he comfortably could, he begged leave to announce, that in consequence of the sudden and severe indisposition of Madame Placidi, Madame Gratiani, with their kind permission, would have the honor of going through the remaining scenes.

On this proposition being put to the vote, it was impossible to decide whether the ayes or the noes had it; the lessee, however, assumed that his motion had been carried by an overwhelming majority, and left the stage in order to prevail upon Madame Gratiani, whom envy had placed upon the shelf—to go through the remainder of the opera. The lady at first expressed her unwillingness to do this, but when the lessee had portrayed the deep enthusiasm with which he stated the announcement of her name had been hailed, the glowing picture re-inspired her with hope, and she hastened to prepare for a triumph. Just, however, as Madame Gratiani was ready to go on, the astounding fact became known to Madame Placidi, who so suddenly recovered from her serious indisposition, that she insisted upon finishing the part herself. The lessee, as a sort of punishment, declared that as she would not, when she felt that it could not be done without her, she should not now she knew that it could; but this had no other effect, than that of making her the more desperate, and as the lessee had had many striking proofs of her amiable disposition, he eventually conceived it to be more discreet under the circumstances to yield. He, therefore, appeared before the audience again, to announce the extraordinary fact of Madame Placidi having happily recovered, and the performances were once more resumed.

Now, as the lessee had been unable to punish Madame Placidi, Valentine determined that, as a mere matter of justice, he would. He therefore, again gave breath to the interesting echo, which at length seemed to amuse the audience rather than not, but nothing could exceed in power, the rage of Madame Placidi. Whenever she came off the stage, no soul dared to approach her. She stamped and ground her teeth, and bit her lips, until they bled; and if, during her progress from the wings to her room, any little inanimate object—such for instance, as a brush or a banner—happened to stand in her way, she seized it at once, dashed it violently to the ground, and trampled upon it with ineffable scorn.

Under all these circumstances, therefore, the expediency of cutting the opera short, was suggested with great feeling by the bewildered stage-manager; and as this really excellent suggestion was approved in the proper quarter, the *finale* came before it was expected, but it certainly appeared by no means to be on that account the less welcome.

"Now," said the gentleman, who looked as if he might have been half an Italian and half a Turk, but whom Valentine eventually found to be Horace, "let us change our togs at once, and we shall be down before the ballet commences."

Accordingly, up he and Valentine ran, and after having hastily metamorphosed themselves into something bearing the semblance of respectable Christians, they descended the cast-iron column once more.

The stage now assumed a totally different aspect. The curtain was still down, and innumerable sylph-like forms, with dresses so short, and necks so white, and cheeks so rosy, and ankles so thin, were gaily flitting about in all directions. In the back ground a group of little fairies were reclining on a piece of deal board so painted as to convey the idea of a bank of wild roses, while on either side a row of angelic creatures were engaged in lifting up their legs to an extraordinary height—an operation which they repeated with so much perseverance, that Valentine positively blushed. He felt it to be impossible, however, for vice to reside in beings who looked so amiable, so pure! yet while he was willing to attribute these games, in which they seemed to take delight, to a buoyant, playful spirit; he nevertheless contended within himself, that they were games which ought strictly to be confined to the play-room. But then, oh! how beautiful they appeared! so innocent—oh! so happy!

"Get along, you beast!" cried one of them, addressing a very venerable looking gentleman, who had transferred the roseate hue of her cheeks to the palms of his white kid gloves. "I'll slap your face for you, you old fool!" observed the angel in continuation, and in driving past Valentine, she left a great portion of the snowy whiteness of her neck upon the sleeves of his coat, while the venerable old gentleman trying with all his might to look fascinating, continued to hobble after her with all the youthful agility he could assume. Valentine was amazed—"Is it possible that such an exclamation," thought he, "could have proceeded from so elegant a creature as that!" And he looked at his coat-sleeve again; but as he subsequently heard this identical angel call the venerable gentleman in question her dear, he fancied that he must have run against either a baker or a newly-whitewashed wall; but could by no means obliterate the impression, that although the old gentleman might be her grandpapa and very tiresome, moreover, and teasing, it was still extremely wrong of her to call him a beast.

Having taken a general survey of this interesting scene, he proceeded towards a group of aristocratic individuals—the majority of whom were about sixty years of age —near the curtain. They had formed themselves into a circle, and in the center a most beautiful girl was dancing apparently in a state of the most perfect unconsciousness of the presence of those by whom she was surrounded. Her hair was studded with flowers and golden combs, while her beautifully symmetrical neck was adorned with a row of sparkling diamonds secured to her bosom by almost invisible pieces of thread. Her dress was of the purest whiteness and most delicate texture, and as it scarcely descended twelve inches below her hips, it had the appearance of an open parasol, as she twirled round and round upon the point of her toe. While bounding, and pirouetting and cutting all sorts of graceful capers, the elderly gentlemen around her appeared to be lost in admiration; but there was in the countenances of them all an expression so *peculiar*, that Valentine was utterly unable to divine what description of feeling it portrayed.

"Well," said Horace, who had just escaped from one of the fairies, "what do you think of 'em, eh? Fine animals, a'n't they?"

"They are indeed elegant creatures," said Valentine; "but don't it strike you that they are somewhat indelicate?"

"Indelicate!" echoed Horace with a smile, "why you didn't expect to find much delicacy here?"

"But look!" exclaimed Valentine, pointing to a sylph whose left foot was on a level with the crown of her head; "now that appears to me to be highly improper.

Horace again smiled, and after a few more equally innocent observations, on the part of Valentine, exclaimed, "Why, what do you think these old venerables come here for? Don't you see how spicily they gloat over the scene? But look presently at those who have their families in the house. See what out-and-out jolly long faces they'll pull! Why by the time they get round to their wives and daughters, who are perhaps quite as beautiful as the creatures that are here, they will all look as moral as maggots."

At this moment a bell began to ring, when the stage was cleared, and up went the curtain. As Horace had predicted, the majority of the old gentlemen at once trotted off, and as Valentine had learned quite sufficient to convince him that virtue was not the distinguishing characteristic of those who remained, he felt that he might probably be conferring an essential benefit upon society by subjecting them to a grievous disappointment.

"Wait for me, love, in the hall!" said he, whispering in the ear of an ancient individual with the palsy, as a nymph glided past him to go upon the stage.

"Yes, yes, my little dear, yes I will," said the old gentleman, conceiving that the invitation had proceeded from the nymph; and he rubbed his hands rapturously, and pressed his withered lips, and sighed, and smiled, and looked as killing as he conveniently could.

"Oh, monstrous!" cried Valentine, throwing his voice behind the old gentleman; "for shame, sir, an old man like you!"

The palsied old gentleman turned round amazed; but being unable to ascertain whence the sound had proceeded, he inspired at that moment some feeling which induced him to move from the spot with all possible despatch.

In this labor of love Valentine was zealously engaged for the next half hour, and when he had made about fifty appointments, the whole of which were to be kept in the hall, he was urged by Horace to quit the scene, which he did without being by any means satisfied that its tendency was to promote the cause of virtue or to cultivate those feelings which bind man to man.

Horace now endeavored to prevail upon Valentine to accompany him to what he called his "club," a large house in the vicinity of the theatre, the door of which was partially open, and which appeared to be brilliantly illuminated; but as it was then twelve o'clock, and as he wished to rise early in the morning, he excused himself, and having called a coach, he left Horace to keep some appointment at the "club," and proceeded to the house of his guardian alone.

CHAPTER XII.

VALENTINE'S TRIP TO GRAVESEND.

With all their knowledge of the human heart, and of the springs of human actions, of the impulses, the promptings, and the guides of the soul, philosophers have never yet deigned to decide whether it be in reality natural for a perfectly unsophisticated youth to view the general conduct of our dashing metropolitan rips with contempt or emulation. Such a youth, if he be an observer at all, cannot fail to perceive in those rips the total absence of every virtuous or really honorable principle; he cannot fail to mark that they are selfish, heartless, brutal, and dead to every sense of common justice; and yet our grave men will not honor the world by deciding whether nature inspires him who perceives all this with the spirit of rivalry or that of disgust.

Now this is indeed a most extraordinary piece of business; but, without dwelling long upon a subject so profound—without stopping the current of these adventures to inquire whether the feelings which actuate those who delight in setting honor, virtue, justice, and decency at defiance, are attributable to property, blood, or education—it may be said with perfect safety, that Valentine, whether naturally or not, was impressed with no very high notions of Horace, with reference either to the strength of his head or to the soundness of his heart, for having watched his actions narrowly, and viewed the direct tendency of each, he had seen quite sufficient to convince him, that circumstances might make him a really great villain, but never could make him a really great man.

With this conviction deeply impressed upon his mind, he wound up his watch and went to sleep, and having dreamt of fairy land throughout the night, he rose unusually early, ate a most substantial breakfast, and started at once for the Steam Packet wharf.

It happened to be an extremely hot morning, and as the sun was making desperate efforts to send its bright rays through the vapors which mantled the earth, the sparrows, resolved to do business while they were able, were hopping about gaily from tile to tile, and from brick to brick, well knowing that when the mist had been dispelled, those tiles and those bricks would be too hot to hold them.

As he proceeded, the public vehicles were rattling over the stones with remarkable velocity, and while the horses were adorned with blue and yellow rosettes, with the view of enabling them to enjoy themselves with the knowledge of its being Sunday, each driver proudly sported his gayest clothes and the largest bunch of wall-flowers a penny could procure.

As Valentine drew near the wharf, crowds of persons were hastening in precisely the same direction: some with children in their arms, some with baskets of provisions in their hands, and others, who, although with neither children nor provisions, appeared just as happy as those who had both.

It was interesting to analyse the mass of individuals who crowded the deck of the vessel, for they indicated their social positions as plainly as if each had been stamped with a "distinctive die."

There stood the mechanic, the creases in whose coat told plainly not only that it was worn but once a week, but that infinite care had been taken to preserve the pristine beauty of the nap by keeping it folded in a trunk or drawer. There was, however, a strongly marked difference between the married and single mechanic; for while the former was calculating precisely how much the trip would cost, the latter, in the plenitude of his liberality, was priding himself upon the force with which he sent to perdition all idea of the expense. Nor was the distinction between the married and the single of this class developed by the gentlemen alone: the countenance of the married lady displayed an anxiety about her little household gods, and a strong disposition to show her authority as a wife by finding fault with every trifling thing that occurred, while the single lady had little thought indeed of home, and being resolved to appear highly delighted with every thing, laughed very merrily at anything or nothing. But the mode of wearing the shawl was alone sufficient to mark the distinction between them; for while the married lady would have hers spread upon her back in order that the whole of the pattern might be seen, the single lady carried hers gracefully upon her arm, with the only ostensible view of showing that she had such a thing as a shawl in her possession.

Aloof from these persons stood those who kept chandlers', butchers', and green-grocers' shops; and each gentleman belonging to this class prided himself especially upon having a handsome turn-out by his side in the shape of his "missis"—a lady who not only dresses herself, but superintends the adornment of her husband. He must wear his chain thus, and his shirt pin thus, and as she allows herself only, to tie his cravat, she has, of course, whatever knot she may happen to fancy. His hair must go so, and his waistcoat so—in a word, there is nothing in which she has not a hand, for although it may be true that she permits him to shave his own chin, he must be careful not to place his domestic peace in peril by spoiling the shape of his whiskers. With regard to the adornment of her own person, she exercises of course, her undoubted prerogative, by wearing precisely whatever she thinks proper. If she cannot procure a couple of red roses sufficiently large, she will establish a brace of becoming sunflowers between her cap and bonnet, the size of which latter affair is invariably immense; and she *will* have a long white veil and a plume of feathers, whether veils and feathers be worn by the aristocracy or not; and beyond all dispute when ladies in this sphere are dressed, they are dressed, for there never did appear in any rainbow a color that they have not got something about them to match. But even these with their husbands did not constitute in fact the *élite* of the vessel; there were very, very different beings on board;—the milliners, the shopmen, and the clerks!—but although the clerks and shopmen might be said to form one class of persons, the difference between even them was distinctly developed, for the clerks had pale faces and delicate hands, while the faces of the shopmen were full and their hands red as blood. There was moreover something in the expression of the eye, by which this distinction was marked. The eyes of the clerks were comparatively quiet and unassuming, but the shopmen had really very impudent eyes, and while they were lost in admiration of the ladies, the clerks appeared lost in admiration of themselves.

When the clock struck ten between five and six hundred individuals had managed to establish themselves upon the deck, and as the band, consisting of a harp, a violin, and a fife, began to play a highly popular tune, the boat started. Ginger beer and bottled stout were in immediate requisition, and while many of the unencumbered gentlemen were smoking their cigars, Valentine was learning the various orders that were giving by the Captain through the boy who stood just above the place in which the engine was working.

The vessel had not proceeded far, when, fancying that he could imitate the voice of the boy exactly, he determined to try the effect of the experiment; and as he had become quite *au fait* to the orders that were given, the very moment the boat had passed the shipping, he commenced with "Ease ar!"

"No, no: go on," said the Captain.

"Go on!" cried the boy.

"Ease ar!" shouted Valentine again.

"Who told you to ease her?" said the Captain to the boy.

"Stop ar!" cried Valentine, and the engine stopped at once.

"What are you about, sir!" shouted the Captain, "you'd better mind what you are after. Go on sir, and let's have no more of that nonsense."

"Go on!" cried the boy, who couldn't exactly understand it, although he looked round and scratched his head with great energy.

At this moment a wherry was seen just ahead waiting to put three passengers on board, and as the vessel approached her, the Captain raised his hand.

"Ease ar!" cried the boy who was watching that hand, and as it moved again, he added "stop ar!" when the steps were let down, and a man stood ready with a boat-hook secured by a rope, while the waterman was pulling away with all the strength he had in him.

"Go on!" cried Valentine, just as the boat had reached the side, and the vessel dashed away and left the wherry behind her.

"Stop her!" shouted the Captain very angrily; "what is the matter with you, sir, this morning?"

"Stop ar!" cried the innocent boy; and the waterman, who was very old and not very strong, pulled away again as hard as he could pull; but as he had to row against the tide, and had been left some considerable distance behind, it was a long time before he could manage to get up again, although he perspired very freely. He did, however, at length succeed in getting alongside; but just as he was reaching the steps again, Valentine cried, "Move her astarn!"—when, as the vessel went back very fast with the tide, she left the wherry some considerable distance ahead.

"Stop her! you scoundrel! go on! What d'ye mean, sir?" shouted the Captain indignantly.

"Stop ar!—Go on!" cried the boy, who could not make it out exactly even then—"ease ar!"—he cried again, as the captain waved his hand—"stop ar!"

"Go on!" cried Valentine, in precisely the same tone, and the vessel again left the wherry behind her.

As the Captain, at this interesting moment, threw his hat at the boy, and as the boy began to rub his head violently, as if it had struck him, the vessel proceeded so far before the order to "go on," had been counteracted, that the waterman, feeling that they were having a game with him, quietly gave the thing up.

Now the Captain was really a remarkable man, but the chief characteristics of his mind were even more remarkable than those of his body. He had been a most extraordinary swearer, but having imbibed a propensity for literature and art, a ten months' quiet indulgence in that propensity had made him altogether a different individual. Instead of going, like a man without a soul, every evening to a neighboring public house to smoke his pipe, and to have his stint—namely, seven four-pennyworths of hot gin and water, and he always knew when he had had that stint by the seven pewter spoons which he had placed in a row before him—he kept philosophically at home, with the view of obtaining a perfect mastery over the subjects of Theology, Geology, Phrenology, and Physiology, and as for *swearing!*—it will be necessary only to say this, that he had sworn that he would never swear again.

How then to express his feelings when irritated, became a difficulty which he had every day to surmount. He had not the least notion of bridling his passion; his object was simply to bridle his tongue; and as swearing—if use be indeed second nature—had clearly become natural to him, he was frequently in danger of bursting some very important blood-vessel, because he would not give vent to his rage in the language to which he had been so long accustomed. He would keep it pent up, and it was pent up while the steamer was dodging the wherry; but when he found that the waterman had ceased to ply his sculls, and that the opposition vessel would have the three passengers in consequence, his rage knew no bounds, "You beauty!" cried he to the boy at length, finding that he must either say something or burst. "Oh! bless your *pretty* eyes!—*You* understand me!"

"Ease ar!" cried Valentine.

"At it again!" exclaimed the Captain; "oh, you darling, you sweet pretty boy! Oh, I'll give you pepper! ony let me come down to you, that's all, you *duck*, and I'll give you the beautifullest towelling you ever enjoyed. Let her go, sir."

"Go on!" whined the boy. "It a'n't me; I can't help it."

"What! Say that again—ony say it—and if I don't make you spin round and round, like a lying young cockchafer, seize me. And the poor boy began to dig his knuckles in his eyes, and to whine a repetition of what was held to a falsehood.

"Ay, whine away, my dear!" cried the Captain, "whine away! If you don't hold that noise, I'll come down and give you a clout o' one side o' th' head that you *never* had afore!"

"Ease ar!" cried Valentine.

"What, won't you be quiet?"

"Stop ar!"

"What is it you mean, you young—*angel?* What is it you *mean?*" cried the Captain, as he stood in a sitting posture, with his hands upon his knees, "*do* you want a good welting? ony say, and you shall catch, my dear, the blessedest rope's-ending you ever had any notion on yet. Now I give you fair warning. If I have any more of this, if it's ever so little, I'll come down and give you the sweetest hiding that ever astonished your nerves! So ony look out, my dear! Take a friend's advice, and look out. Well!—are we to perceed?"

"Go on!" cried the boy; and he still worked away with his knuckles, and screwed up his features into the ugliest form they were capable of assuming.

"Oh you young beauty!—you know what I mean, cried the Captain, as he ground his great teeth and shook his fists at the innocent boy, whose eyes were by this time so swollen, that he could scarcely see out of them at all. "You stink for a good tanning, and I'll ease your mind, my dear—*if* I don't, may I be—saved! So now you know my sentiments." And having delivered himself loudly to this effect, he thrust his hands triumphantly into his breeches pockets, and directed the whole of his attention ahead.

His eye was, however, no sooner off the boy, than Valentine again cried "Ease ar! stop ar!" but long before the sound of the last "ar" had died away, the captain seized a rope about as thick as his wrist, and without giving utterance even to a word, jumped down upon the deck with a deep inspiration of the spirit of vengeance.

"Away boy! run!" cried Valentine, quickly; and the boy, who was anything but an idiot, darted, like lightning, among the passengers. The Captain, at starting, was close to his heels; but the boy shot ahead with such skill, and then dodged him round and round, and in out with so much tact and dexterity, that it soon became obvious that he had been chased in a manner not very dissimilar before.

"Lay hold of that boy," cried the Captain, "lay hold of him there!" but the passengers, who rather enjoyed the chase, refused to do any such thing. They, on the contrary, endeavored to shield the boy; and whenever they fancied that the Captain was gaining ground, although he would not have caught him in a fortnight, a dozen of the stoutest would—of course accidentally—place themselves quietly before him.

"Come here!" cried the Captain, panting for breath, "Will you mind what I say, sir? come here!" but the boy, who didn't seem to approve of that course, did discreetly refuse to accept the invitation, and the Captain was, in consequence, after him again.

At length Valentine raised a contemptuous laugh, and as it had in an instant at least a hundred echoes, the Captain's philosophy opened his eyes, and he saw the propriety of giving up the chase.

"Here, Robinson!" said he, "just give a look out here. Bless his *little* soul, he shall have a quilting yet," and after telling the gentlemen below to go on, he silently ascended the paddle-box again, and Robinson took the boy's place.

The vessel now proceeded without interruption, and as Valentine could not conveniently imitate Robinson's voice, until he had actually heard Robinson speak, he left for a time that particular spot, for the purpose of looking a little about him. The first person he encountered was a stoutly built black-whiskered gentleman, who was engaged in the destruction of a nice little book, by wantonly tearing out the leaves, and disposing of each for two shillings. The remarkable avidity with which these leaves were purchased, led Valentine naturally to believe that they contained some very valuable information. He, therefore, bought one of them at once, and having easily made himself master of its contents, cried—throwing his voice behind the destroyer—"Now, where are my seven?"

"Seven?" said the destroyer, "yes; three, five, seven," and seven of the leaves were torn out at one pull.

"Now then!" said Valentine, assuming the same voice.

"Here they are, sir, here they are," said the destroyer.

"Well, hand 'em over, will you?" cried Valentine.

"Here, sir; seven, sir? seven?" and the seven were offered to every man near him.

"Me and my missis vonts two," observed a gentleman who held his pocket open with one hand, and dived the other down to the bottom.

"Tip us a couple, old boy," said another, who sported a hat with a nine-inch brim.

"O ple sir, pa wants flee," said a very little lady with four ringlets hanging down behind rather thicker than her arm.

"Well! where are my seven?" cried Valentine again, assuming the same voice as before.

"None o' your larks yer know; cos it wont fit," said the angry destroyer without turning round.

"Then I'll just go ashore without paying at all," observed Valentine.

"Will yer?" said he who held the book with an ironical smile, at the same time looking full in the face of an individual who happened to be laughing at the moment. "Then praps you jist wont; for I'll jist keep a hextry look out. You call yourself a genelman, don't yer? So don't I;" and his blood began to boil, and his veins began to swell, and he tore some more leaves out with great indignation.

Valentine then at once proceeded to the "Saloon," but as he found only a few young ladies with their lovers indulging tenderly in sweet discourse, and sipping from time to time dead ginger beer, he left them to open their hearts to each other, and made his way into the "cabin." In this place the ladies and gentlemen seemed for the most part to have the same object in view, but were infinitely less sentimental in its pursuit. Bottled stout was apparently the favorite beverage, but some had a little gin-and-water on the top, and as most of the gentlemen were smoking, each appeared to be then in the full indulgence of the very purest sublunary pleasure, by holding a pipe in his right hand, and clasping the waist of his intended with the left.

Their conversation was by no means of a strictly private character. That which prevailed, touched the lowness of wages generally, and in order to demonstrate the cause of this remarkable state of things, an individual was creating an immense sensation, by showing the absolute necessity for the adoption of universal suffrage. The noise which proceeded from this highly accomplished orator, drowned the voices of all who wished to get a word in "edgeways," and if any one presumed to offer an opinion, which happened to be even in the slightest degree opposed to that which he had expressed, a volly of abuse, couched in terms neither elegant nor grammatical, was perfectly sure to assail him.

At length, Valentine, anxious to ascertain the extent to which he would go in support of his principles, took occasion to observe in a very gruff voice, as the orator was denouncing every man as a traitor, who hesitated to go what he termed "the ole og," with him—"We don't want uniwersal suffrage here."

"Ve don't *vont* huniwersle suffrage!" cried the orator. "Lor sen I may live!—not vont it? Vell strike me!—not vont huniwersle suff—Vell, may I be kicked to the middle o' next veek! Vy ve vont nothink helse! I am for hevery man bein alike vithout hextinction; and I means for to say this, that hevery man as isn't of the same sentiments, ought to be druv out o' society. *Not* vont huniwersle—Well may I—but stop, let's ave a little hargriment about that ere. Now then—Vy don't ve vont the suffrage to be huniwersle? That's the question!" and the orator winked and gave his head a most significant nod. "Vy don't ve vont the suffrage to be huniwersle?"

"Because," replied Valentine, throwing his voice to the other end of the cabin—"Because every fool like you would have it then to abuse."

That was sufficient. The orator laid down his pipe; took a deep draught of stout; pulled his coat off; tucked his shirt-sleeves above the elbows, and challenged the voice to a "kipple o' rounds—jist ony a kipple!"

In one moment the whole cabin was in an uproar. The ladies were respectfully begging their beloveds to abstain from all interference, while the orator's lady clung to his neck, and with tears in her eyes, implored him not to "bemean himself by dirtying his hands with any sich low-bred feller."

For some considerable time, the enraged orator was inexorable; but he was at length prevailed upon to put on his coat, when, although he vowed vengeance upon all who dared to differ with him in opinion, the minds of the ladies and their lovers were once more at ease.

There were, however, several married gentlemen here whose ladies were languishing on deck, and as Valentine thought this extremely unfair, he went up with a view to their immediate re-union.

"Do you know," said he, whispering, in an assumed voice of course, in the ear of a highly dressed dame, "do you know whom your husband is kissing in the cabin?" The lady looked round with an expression of amazement. "Do you know her?" he continued, and although quite unable to discover who had spoken, she started up at once and went to take a survey.

"Don't let your husband drink any more of that gin," said he to another with precisely the same result. "Do you suffer your husband to treat *every* girl he meets?" and thus he went on until he had sent nearly all the married ladies, whose husbands had absented themselves, into the cabin.

"Ease hor?" cried Robinson, in a rough heavy tone.

"That's the voice to imitate!" said Valentine to himself. "Now's the time for me to reinstate the boy," and as he saw a boat making towards the vessel ahead, he shouted with true Robinsonian energy, "Go on!"

"No, no!" cried the Captain, "no, no! you're as bad as the boy!"

"Ease hor!" shouted Robinson, "*I* didn't speak!"

"Go on!" cried Valentine, and round went the paddles again, for the engineer himself now began to be excited.

"Do you want to drive me mad!" cried the Captain.

"What d'yar mean?" shouted Robinson, "that wasn't me!"

"What! what!" exclaimed the Captain, "not you! Oh Robinson, Robinson! don't you know, Robinson, how very wrong it is for to tell a blessed falsity for to hide a fault?"

"I tell you it wasn't me then! If you don't like to believe me you may call out yourself!" and Robinson walked to the head of the vessel, and laying very violent hands upon a rope, dashed it desperately down upon the deck, when, having thus taken his measure of vengeance, he folded his arms, and seemed to feel a little better.

"Will you promise to behave yourself, boy, if I take you on again?" cried the Captain.

"Yes, sir," said the boy, as well as he could, considering that his mouth was at that moment full of bread and butter; when, watching the motion of the Captain's hand, he cried "ease ar!—stop ar!" for the boat was still approaching.

The boy now emptied his mouth as soon as possible, and wiped his lips clean with a handfull of oily tow, when Valentine, determined to let the little fellow recover the good opinion of the Captain by pursuing the proper course, proceeded to the side of the vessel.

In the boat, which drew near, sat an elderly gentleman, and an exceedingly elegant young person, who appeared to be his daughter. Valentine was struck with the extreme beauty of her countenance, and gazed on her intently. He felt that he had never beheld so beautiful a creature before; and the nearer she approached the side of the vessel—which was still, although the engine had been stopped, going gently, the more his rapture increased. Just, however, as the person who had the management of the hook caught the head of the boat, the old gentlemen rose from his seat, when the suddenness of the unexpected jerk which is invariably given at that moment, sent him back with so much violence, that he was plunged into the river in an instant.

"My father!" shrieked the lady, "my father!" and extending her arms, she fell breathless upon him.

"Save them!" shouted fifty of the passengers at once.

"Let the boat go!" cried the waterman, "let the boat go!" But the hand of the man who held the boat-hook was powerless, and as the bodies clasped together were floating with the tide, Valentine rushed to the stern of the vessel, and dashed at once into the stream. The force with which he plunged carried him down to a great depth, and his clothes became so weighty that they would scarcely allow him to rise, and when he did rise he found himself still some considerable distance from them; but he struck out gallantly, and reached them at the moment they were sinking to rise no more. The first thing he caught was the hair of the father, whose effort to seize the hand which held him was instantaneous; but Valentine dexterously evaded his grasp, and having caught the dress of the lady, whose arms were still twined round her father's neck, he held them up at arm's length, while the boats were approaching. The struggles of the old gentleman to seize Valentine now became desperate. His contortions were violent in the extreme. He dashed, and plunged, and struck at him like a maniac, and did at length succeed in winding his legs round the body of Valentine so firmly, that had it not been for the aid which arrived at the moment, they must inevitably have gone down together, for even when they had been dragged into the boat, the old gentleman would not relinquish his hold until they had managed to convince him of the fact, that he and his daughter were perfectly safe.

The vessel, which had been backing all the time with the tide, now arrived at the spot; and when the poor old gentleman had been assisted on board, Valentine took the young lady, who had fainted, in his arms, and having reached the deck, proceeded at once to the saloon, where every attention was paid to her and her father, with a view to their immediate restoration.

All being now perfectly secure, Valentine left the saloon for the cabin, and on his way a hundred hands were extended towards him by the passengers, who warmly exclaimed, "God bless you, my fine fellow! Nobly done! God bless you!" The ladies were deeply affected; and shed tears of joy as he passed, and would have dried his dripping clothes in their bosoms.

On reaching the cabin, he sent one of the men to the steward for a shirt and whatever other clothes he might happen to have, and while the steward was engaged in looking out a complete suit, he undressed, and after drying himself as well as he could without assistance, he got one of the passengers, who happened to be a master-blacksmith, to rub him down with a rough towel until his entire body became red as blood.

As soon as this glowing operation had been performed, he received a full suit from the hands of the steward. The first thing he put on was a rough-checked shirt, and then followed a pair of fine white lambswool hose which belonged to the amiable stewardess; he then drew on a pair of breeches, in which Daniel Lambert himself would not have felt at all uncomfortable, and then a pair of real smuggler's boots, which were indeed a decent fit, considering; then a waistcoat which had to be doubled over and over again at the back, but even then all the persuasion in the world couldn't make it come close, and when by way of a finishing touch, he got into the steward's striped jacket—the sleeves of which he tucked up about a quarter of a yard, in order to give his hands a breath of air—his *tout ensemble* was so complete, that a stranger might naturally have been led to infer, that if the clothes he then wore did fit him the day previous, he must have had a very bad night of it indeed.

However, thus attired he returned to the saloon, to see how those whom he had rescued were faring. He found the young lady recovering fast, and her father giving utterance to many fervent ejaculations; but the moment they were informed that he who had saved them was present, the old gentleman affectionately grasped one hand, while the lady seized the other and kissed it warmly.

"My brave young fellow! God bless you!" exclaimed the old gentleman, when, conceiving from his dress that he belonged to the vessel, he added, "Here, here is my card: call at my house, and I'll reward you; my brave young man, I'll reward you."

Valentine, perceiving his mistake, smiled, but took the card and spoke to the lady, who though extremely pale, looked more beautiful than before.

"Come, drink, my fine fellow! I like you!—you're a trump!" cried a jolly looking gentleman, in checked trousers, as he held out a glass of hot brandy-and-water. "You did it nobly—bravely! drink it up, my young hero, and then we'll have another. Up with it, my boy!—it'll keep all the cold out."

Of this fact, Valentine had not the smallest doubt, for he found it remarkably strong; but as he had drank with several persons before, he politely declined taking more than a sip.

The vessel now drew near Gravesend, and Valentine proceeded to take leave of her of whom he already felt too deeply enamored.

"You *will* call and see us, will you not?" said the lady as she pressed his hand and raised her eyes which looked like brilliants set in gold.

Valentine gazed on her beautiful face, and was silent.

"You will"—she continued—"you will promise to call? Papa will, I'm sure, be delighted to see you!—Why will you not promise?"

"I do," said Valentine, who, while listening to the music of her voice, had been perfectly unconscious of a reply being expected, "I do, I do promise; and when I assure you that nothing could impart so much pleasure"—He pressed her hand, but could say no more, for her eyes were again turned full upon him, and seemed to be beaming with gratitude and love.

"Come, take another sup!" cried the jolly looking gentleman, again approaching, "It strikes me you look raythier pale; and as for you not taking cold!—why my missis won't have it at no price."

"Not any more," said Valentine, who although he appreciated the warmth of his heart, at that moment wished him anywhere but there.

"The young lady perhaps, will have a drain?" continued the persevering pest. "Oh! have a little, Miss! It'll do your heart good. My missis is sure you'll be laid up if you don't, and whatever she says, why of course you know is gospel."

The lady, however, gracefully declined, and after many warm acknowledgments, on her part and on the part of the old gentleman her father, Valentine took leave of them, and went upon deck.

The Pier was now in sight, and the mind of the Captain had happily recovered its wonted tranquillity; but the boy, although he had endeavored to do his duty with the utmost zeal, was by no means sure that the Captain did not still intend to keep his promise with reference to the "quilting." It was true, the Captain spoke to him with perhaps a somewhat greater degree of kindness than he ever had spoken before; but this tended to increase the apprehension of the little fellow who having heard of the prelude to the crocodile's attack, at once fancied that this was but the prelude to an attack on the part of the Captain. He therefore most anxiously watched his every movement, and when the vessel had reached the pier, he trembled violently, for the Captain immediately descended from his post—an operation which he usually deferred until after the whole of the passengers had landed. Nothing could exceed the steadiness with which the boy kept his eye fixed upon him, and whenever he went within reach of a rope, he drew himself up for an immediate start. His fears were however vain; for the Captain's admiration of Valentine's conduct had effectually subdued every angry feeling, and as it became obvious that he had descended with the view of expressing that admiration, the boy began to feel a little comfortable again.

"I am delighted," cried the captain, taking Valentine by the hand, "I am perfectly delighted with your hero-like conduct in saving them two feller creturs. There's somethink wery like it in Ossian's Iliad—Ossian's?—of course, it is Ossian's—where a gentleman, I think it was Artaxerxes, but that I'm not sure of, dived down to the bottom of the Po to fetch up Peter the Great, who was washing his feet on the bank with Cassius, who was, you know, one of the Grecian gods.

"Ah, and did he succeed?" inquired Valentine, with apparent anxiety.

"I don't think it says," replied the Captain; "but at all events he never rose again."

"What a pity! Tut tut!—what a pity to be sure! Then, of course he couldn't inform the world whether he did or not?"

"By no means," observed the Captain, "and that you see's the mischief of history. No man was ever able to write his own life complete. He's certain to go off the hooks before he has finished it: that's the misfortune. It strikes me," he continued, looking earnestly at Valentine, "it strikes me, unless I am werry much mistaken, that you have the organ of courageousness powerfully deweloped. I should like to examine your head. That organ there, just above the eye there, seems to be werry full, and when that is combined to the one that is sittivated under the ear, it makes up courageousness perfect. But I was sure that you'd got it when you dived so beautiful. We find it in ducks werry strong."

"A phrenologist, I perceive."

"I take great delight in the science. I can tell a man's character to a hair. I've the whole of the organs at my finger's ends; now this, for instance ——"

"You've a fine sharp lad here," said Valentine, as the Captain was about to finger *his* organs, "he appears to be very attentive."

"Yes, he's all werry well," said the Captain, "but he an't got no soul. Besides, he don't know exactly how to behave himself sometimes. Did you see how he went on this morning?"

"Boys, you know, are but boys," observed Valentine, and the novelty of that remarkable observation, proceeding as it did, from so remarkable a man, had so striking an effect upon the Captain, that he at once consented to defer the promised "pepper," until the conduct of which he complained should be repeated.

"Now," said Valentine, "will you do me the favor to allow the boy to carry my wet clothes on shore?"

"By all manner of means in the world!" replied the Captain. "Here, boy! attend to this gentleman. Go and see after his things; and mind how you behave yourself, sir, d'ye hear?"

The boy obeyed with alacrity, and Valentine escaped from the Captain apparently with the view of surveying the pier. The passengers were still, as usual, crowding from the vessel. Had they gone in turn quietly they would all have got on shore much sooner, and with an infinitely greater degree of comfort to themselves; but they must crowd, and plunge, and show their teeth, and work away with their elbows, as each strove to get before the other. One lady was loudly lamenting over the fact of her bonnet being desperately crushed; another was endeavoring to recover her reticule, the strings of which she held, while the bag itself was fixed between the hips of two ladies who were going with the stream about five rows behind her, while another was looking particularly unamiable at a gentleman who was innocently digging his elbow into that particular cavity which is just beneath the ear.

"For goodness sake!" cried one, "don't squeedge." "Where are you drivin to?" shouted another. "I say, you sir!" cried a third, "jist take your fist out of the small of my back, good luck to you!" They still, however, crowded on, and displayed as much anxiety to quit the vessel as if she then had been in flames.

"Have you lost any thing, sir?" whispered Valentine in the ear of a tall gentleman, whose efforts to drive past his neighbors had been really very desperate.

The gentleman in an instant drew back, inspired with the horrid suspicion of having lost something, although it did not certainly appear that he had much to lose. In the first place, he felt in all his pockets at once, and then searched them again and again in detail; and then labored to recollect if he had brought anything from home, which he had not then about him; but even then, although he emptied his pockets and found all quite safe, he was anything but sure that he hadn't been plundered.

"Do you allow *that?*" said Valentine, throwing a whisper into the ear of an old lady, to whom nature, in consideration of her having but a single eye, had bounteously given a double chin.

"Mr. Jones!" cried the lady, who perceived two females by the side of Mr. Jones, "I'm ashamed of you. Keep back, sir; and let them gals pass."

"What's the matter, my dear?" said Mr. Jones.

"Don't dear me, sir! I saw you!" cried the lady; and Mr. Jones looked as if he at that moment felt that if he had never seen *her* it would have been a great comfort.

"Have you got your pass?" said Valentine, throwing his voice behind the person who was taking the tickets. "*I* want no pass," he added, assuming another voice, "I can always pass without."

"O! can yer?" cried the black whiskered gentleman, by whom those interesting little slips of paper had been sold. "Then I don't think you can. Jim! be a little hextry partickler there, will yer?" and he winked at Jim; and Jim winked at him as he stood in the gangway perfectly prepared to take his revenge out of the first man who attempted to pass without a ticket.

While the black-whiskered gentleman and Jim were thus occupied, Valentine went to the steward, who lent him a large hairy cap; and when his clothes had been carefully deposited by the amiable stewardess in a shawl, he, followed by the boy, took his leave of the philosophic Captain, and left the vessel, portraying the pleasurable effects of that astonishment, with which he fondly conceived poor Goodman would view the extraordinary character of his dress.

CHAPTER XIII.

IN WHICH VALENTINE IS INTRODUCED TO THREE NEW FRIENDS, WITH ONE OF WHOM HE PASSES A VERY PLEASANT NIGHT.

The surprise with which Valentine, on reaching the residence of Mr. Plumplee, ascertained that his guardian had not arrived, was as great as that with which he had intended to inspire Goodman, but of a character of course diametrically opposite. Nor, when the circumstances were explained, was that surprise felt by Valentine alone; Mr. Plumplee, and Mr. Jonas Beagle, an eccentric old gentleman, who murdered his time at Gravesend, with a view to the perfect restoration of his health, which had never, in fact, deserted him even for a day, felt and expressed a corresponding amount of astonishment, while Miss Madonna Plumplee, the virgin sister of Goodman's friend, begat at once to indulge in all sorts of conjectures having reference to the cause, for like most unaccountable occurrences, the scope which it afforded for the play of the imagination was unbounded.

"Who knows!" cried that amiable person, "he may have been run over and crushed to death, or a thousand things!—the drivers about London are so horribly reckless. I'm sure it was only the other day I was three quarters of an hour endeavoring to cross Fleet street;—and after all it was an absolute miracle I wasn't killed, for a dog-cart, with a dirty person sitting upon the edge, rattled down the street at such a dreadful rate that I thought, be run over I must! It is shameful such things are allowed. There sat the filthy creature deliberately smoking his pipe, and taking no sort of notice of the peril in which he was placing the lives and limbs of people, not even the slightest! He was, however, I am happy to say, properly punished, for no sooner had he passed me than the wheel, over which he had been sitting, bounced into the hole, when, happily, the entire concern upset, and he was instantly covered with cat's meat and mud."

"Oh! I don't expect that any serious accident has occurred," said Mr. Plumplee. "The report of such an occurrence would be certain to have reached home before this morning, for he never goes out without his card case; and his name and address are printed on his pocket-book, I know."

"But," suggested Miss Madonna, "he might have had his pockets previously picked, and then strangers, you know, would have no clue at all. London is such a place. I'm sure I was reading the other day, in one of the papers, of a gentleman who, having lost his handkerchief, went in to purchase a new one, ready hemmed, and he hadn't left the shop five minutes, before he lost that."

"And did he go in to buy another?" inquired Mr. Jonas Beagle.

"It didn't say; but such doings are positively dreadful," replied Miss Madonna. "I'm sure, I've said it a thousand times, and will maintain it—the police are of no sort of use. They are never at hand when people are being plundered."

"For my own part," said Mr. Jonas Beagle, "I think he has been kidnapped. The fact of his having been out all night, looks, I must say, remarkably suspicious. What business has a man to be out all night? None whatever, not the slightest; and I hold it to be, therefore, particularly shocking." And Mr. Jonas Beagle leered wickedly at Miss Madonna, while his little twinkling eyes seemed to indicate that in his judgment Goodman was not quite immaculate.

The attention of Mr. Plumplee and his amiable sister was now directed to Valentine's dress. A tailor in the vicinity was applied to at once, but as he had nothing likely to answer the purpose made up, the case was stated to a family next door, of which one of the younger branches politely sent in a complete suit, which fortunately happened to fit Valentine to a hair.

"Now then," said Mr. Beagle, "for a walk;" and as the conviction had obtained that it was useless to wait for Goodman, who might not arrive until the evening, Beagle, Plumplee, and Valentine left the house, and at once got into a stream of gay persons, who were heavily laden with children and provisions, and who appeared to have made a dead set at a windmill.

"Let's go to the Belly woo!" shouted one of these persons, who had one child on his arm and another on his back, while he dragged a third along by the hand.

"That's by fur the most delightfullest place," observed a lady, who appeared to be the mother of those interesting babes, and who carried a handkerchief, in which the shape of a dish was to all distinctly visible. "I prefers the Belly woo 'cause there we can set out at top and see the wessels so nice."

"The Belly woo!" cried Valentine. "What's the Belly woo?"

"The Bellevue, they mean, a little tavern on the hill," replied Mr. Jonas Beagle, who had no sooner imparted this interesting information, than he turned into what he called the Tivoli Gardens, which appeared to be the principal place of resort. On the right, as they entered, a marquee was fixed for the accommodation of those who preferred a cold dinner for a shilling to a hot one for eighteen pence; on the left stood a long wooden shed, or grand dining-room, established for the exclusive accommodation of the eighteen-penny people, round the door of which several polite gentlemen hovered, with a view of soliciting the pleasure of the company of all who looked as if they really had such a thing as one-and-nine-pence about them, while at the farther end were boxes for the convenience of those who had brought their own provisions; but as the public spirited proprietor of the establishment charged, according to the printed scale, something like three-pence for the loan of a table-cloth, two-pence for plates, three-half-pence for a knife and fork, a penny for pepper, the same for mustard, the same for vinegar, the same for salt, and for everything else extremely reasonable in proportion, these boxes were not very liberally patronised.

Having taken a survey of these gardens, they made for the hill, the summit of which they reached after an infinite deal of panting on the part of Mr. Plumplee and Mr. Jonas Beagle, and which certainly commanded a most extensive and delightful view of the surrounding country. Mr. Beagle's first task was to point out to Valentine the various features of the scene both rural and naval, and having developed in the performance of this task no inconsiderable amount of descriptive power, he led the way to a favorite spot under the brow of the hill to which he and Mr. Plumplee repaired daily for the purpose of unravelling whatever knotty point might happen to suggest itself at the moment. On reaching this spot they spread their handkerchiefs and took their seats, while below them groups of persons were sitting up to their lips in thick furze, and up to their hips in dusty sand, discussing internally the various viands with which they had been externally laden.

It was not long before a point of the knotty kind was started, and while Plumplee was engaged in refuting the extremely uncharitable position of Mr. Beagle, that practically the world's definition of friendship was that which prompts men to study the interests of others with a view to the promotion of their own, Valentine was occupied in watching the actions of one particular group that sat immediately below him. It was obviously a family circle, and in the centre stood a large beef-steak pie upon a sheet of the *Weekly Dispatch*, which had been spread with the view of conveying the idea of a table cloth, and of thereby imparting to the whole thing an unquestionable air of respectability. The crust of this pie was in proportion as thick as the thatch of a barn, while the little et-ceteras by which it was surrounded, bore a corresponding aspect of delicacy; and when all seemed prepared to commence operations, the cork of a well-washed blacking bottle was drawn, and the company, by way of grace before meat, had a glass of gin round. When this feat had been performed with really infinite gusto, the carver walked into the pie, and in the plenitude of his benevolence submitted to each man, woman, and child, an amount of matter which would certainly have taken any but a highly gifted stomach three days and three nights to digest. It was not, however, by any means long before every hand was empty again; far as the process of mastication seemed quite by the way, they no sooner got a mouthful fairly in than they rinsed it down their throats, as in duty bound, with porter. The purified blacking-bottle again went round, and its contents seemed to induce renewed gastronomic vigor: to each was submitted another lump of pie, and when that had been washed away precisely as before, the gentlemen began to unbutton their waistcoats, and the ladies to unhook their dresses behind, in order to enjoy another small glass of gin without any unpleasant sensation of satiety.

It now became clearly perceptible that their stomachs were about to assume certain aristocratic airs of pseudo-delicacy, for instead of being assisted to legitimate doses, they began to fish out the most tempting little bits they could find, until by virtue of each taking the piece which the others had rejected, the dish was eventually cleared with the exception of sundry little lumps of crust with which by way of a wind up the ladies proceeded to pelt the gentlemen, to the infinite satisfaction of all parties concerned.

This mutually interesting transaction had no sooner been closed, than one of the ladies, in order to cap the climax, produced a very small but a very unexpected bottle of brandy, of which each with great pleasure partook of a glass, for the purpose of keeping all down. This was evidently, however, intended as an apology for *Non Nobis*, for the moment the ceremony had been performed the gentlemen proceeded to light their pipes, while the ladies seemed determined that it should that day be known which was able to laugh the longest and the loudest.

By the time they had succeeded in torturing their muscles into the merriest possible shape, Mr. Plumplee and Mr. Jonas Beagle, had finished their argument according to an invariable custom of theirs, by each convincing himself that the other was wrong. Having thus brought this highly important affair to a happy issue, Mr. Plumplee applied to his watch, and after making an original remark, having reference to the rapid flight of time, they proceeded down the hill, passed a multitude of donkeys, which, while they bore their patronesses on their backs, were very delicately touched up behind by their owners; and reached home precisely at the very moment their presence became absolutely essential to the continuance of Miss Madonna's tranquillity of mind.

The first question asked was of course about Goodman, and as also of course Goodman had not arrived, they at once sat down to dinner, after which Beagle and Plumplee got into an argument touching the lamentable state of things in general, while Valentine and Miss Madonna were amusing themselves at the windows by making all sorts of deeply interesting remarks on the appearance of the persons who were constantly passing.

Towards evening, however, Valentine began to feel uneasy, and expressed a desire to return by the last boat; but Miss Madonna, whose word in that house had acquired the reputation of being law, very strenuously opposed it. It was by no means safe, she contended. The boats in the evening were crowded so densely, especially the last, that to escape being pushed over the side really amounted in her judgment almost to a miracle. Any attempt to refute an argument so potent as that would of course have been indicative of madness, and therefore it was decided that he should stop there all night.

Now there happened to be only four bedrooms in the house; the best of course was occupied by Miss Madonna, the second by Mr. Plumplee, the third by Mr. Beagle, and the fourth by the servant; but that in which Mr. Beagle slept was a double-bedded room, and Valentine had, therefore, to make his election between the spare bed and the sofa. Of course the former was preferred, and as the preference seemed highly satisfactory to Mr. Beagle himself, they passed the remainder of the evening very pleasantly together, and in due time retired.

Valentine, on having his bed pointed out to him, darted between the sheets in the space of a minute, for as Mr. Jonas Beagle facetiously observed, he had but to shake himself, and everything came off, when as he did not by any means feel drowsy at the time, he fancied that he might as well amuse his companion for an hour or so as not. He, therefore, turned the thing seriously over in his mind, while Mr. Beagle was quietly undressing, being anxious for that gentleman to extinguish the light before he commenced operations.

"Now for a beautiful night's rest," observed Mr. Jonas Beagle to himself as he put out the light with a tranquil mind, and turned in with a great degree of comfort.

"Mew!—mew!" cried Valentine softly, throwing his voice under the bed of Mr. Beagle.

"Hish!—curse that cat!" cried Mr. Beagle. "We must have you out at all events, my lady." And Mr. Beagle at once slipped out of bed, and having opened the door cried "hish!" again emphatically, and threw his breeches towards the spot as an additional inducement for the cat to "stand not on the order of her going," when, as Valentine repeated the cry, and made it appear to proceed from the stairs, Mr. Beagle thanked Heaven that she was gone, closed the door, and very carefully groped his way again into bed.

"Mew!—mew!—mew!" cried Valentine, just as Mr. Beagle had again comfortably composed himself.

"What? are you there still, madam?" inquired that gentleman in a highly sarcastic tone, "I thought you had been turned out, madam!—Do you hear this witch of a cat?" he continued, addressing Valentine with the view of conferring upon him the honorable office of Tyler for the time being; but Valentine replied with a deep heavy snore, and began to mew again with additional emphasis.

"Well, I don't have a treat every day, it is true; but if this isn't one, why I'm out in my reckoning that's all!" observed Mr. Jonas Beagle, slipping again out of bed. "I don't much like to handle you, my lady, but if I did, I'd of course give you physic!" and he "hished!" again with consummate violence, and continued to "hish!" until Valentine scratched the bed-post sharply, a feat which inspired Mr. Beagle with the conviction of its being the disturber of his peace in the act of decamping, when he threw his pillow very energetically towards the door, which he closed, and then returned to his bed in triumph. The moment, however, he had comfortably tucked himself up again he missed the pillow which he had converted into an instrument of vengeance, and as that was an article without which he couldn't even hope to go to sleep, he had of course to turn out again to fetch it.

"How many more times, I wonder, he observed to himself, "shall I have to get out of this blessed bed to-night? Exercise certainly is a comfort, and very conducive to health; but such exercise as this—why where have you got to!" he added, addressing the pillow, which, with all the sweeping action of his feet he was for some time unable to find—"Oh, here you are, sir, are you?" and he picked up the object of his search and gave it several very severe blows in the belly, when, having reinstated himself between the sheets, he exclaimed in a subdued tone, "Well, let's try again."

Now Mr. Jonas Beagle was a man who prided himself especially upon the evenness of his temper. His boast was that nothing could put him in a passion, and as he had had less than most of his contemporaries to vex him, he had certainly been able, in the absence of all cause for irritation, to preserve his equanimity. As a perfectly natural matter of course he invariably attributed the absence of such cause to the innate amiability of his disposition; and marvelled that men, men of sense and discernment, should so far forget what was justly expected of them as reasonable beings, as to suffer themselves to be tortured by excitement, inasmuch albeit as human nature and difficulties are inseparable, human nature is sufficiently potent not only to battle with those difficulties, but eventually to overcome them. If Mr. Jonas Beagle had had to contend against many of the "ills that flesh is heir to," he in all probability would have acted like the majority of his fellow-men; but as he had met with very few, and those few had not been of a very serious complexion, he could afford to be deeply philosophical on the subject, and felt himself competent, of course, to frame laws by which the tempers of men in the aggregate should be governed. He did, however, feel when he violently smote the pillow, that that little ebullition partook somewhat of the nature of passion, and had just commenced reproaching himself for having indulged in that little ebullition, when Valentine cried "Meyow!—pit!—Meyow!"

"Hallo!" exclaimed Mr. Jonas Beagle, "here again!"

"Mew!" cried Valentine in a somewhat higher key.

"What another come to contribute to the harmony of the evening!"

"Meyow!—meyow!" cried Valentine in a key still higher.

"Well, how many more of you?" inquired Mr. Beagle. "You'll be able to get up a concert by-and-bye;" and Valentine began to spit and swear with great felicity.

"Swear away, you beauties!" cried Mr. Jonas Beagle, as he listened to this volley of feline oaths; "I only wish that I was not so much afraid of you for your sakes! At it again? Well this is a blessing. Don't you hear those devils of cats!" he cried, anxious not to have all the fun to himself; but Valentine recommenced snoring very loudly. "Well, this is particularly pleasant," he continued as he sat up in bed. "Don't you hear! What a comfort it is to be able to sleep soundly!" which remarkable observation was doubtless provoked by the no less remarkable fact, that at that particular moment the spitting and swearing became more and more desperate. "What's to be done? he inquired very pointedly. What's to be done? my breeches are right in the midst of them all. I can't get out now: they'd tear the very flesh off my legs; and that fellow there sleeps like a top. Hallo! Do you mean to say you don't hear these cats, how they're going it?" Valentine certainly meant to say no such thing, for the whole of the time that he was not engaged in meyowing and spitting, he was diligently occupied in snoring, which had a very good effect, and served to fill up the intervals exceedingly well.

At length the patience of Mr. Jonas Beagle began to evaporate; for the hostile animals continued to battle apparently with great desperation. He, therefore, threw a pillow with great violence into the bed of his companion, and shouted so loudly, that Valentine, feeling that it would be deemed perfect nonsense for him to pretend to be asleep any longer, began to yawn very naturally, and then to cry out "Who's there?"

"'Tis I!" shouted Mr. Jonas Beagle. "Don't you hear these witches of cats?"

"Hish!" cried Valentine, "why there are two of them!"

"Two!" said Mr. Beagle, "more likely two-and-twenty! I've turned out a dozen myself. There's a swarm, a whole colony of them here, and I know no more how to strike a light than a fool."

"Oh, never mind," said Valentine: "let's go to sleep, they'll be quiet by and bye."

"It's all very fine to say, let's go to sleep, but who's to do it?" cried Beagle emphatically. "Curse the cats! I wish there wasn't a cat under heaven—I do, with all my soul! They're such spiteful vermin too when they happen to be put out, and there's one of them in a passion, I know by her spitting, confound her!—I wish from the bottom of my heart it was the very last spit she had in her."

Persecution of Beagle

P. 79.

While Mr. Jonas Beagle was indulging in these highly appropriate observations, Valentine was laboring with great energy in the production of the various bitter cries which are peculiarly characteristic of the feline race, and for a man who possessed but a very slight knowledge of the grammatical construction of the language of that race, it must in justice be said that he developed a degree of fluency which did him great credit. He purred, and mewed, and cried, and swore, and spit, until the perspiration oozed from every pore, and made the sheets as wet as if they had just been "damped for the mangle."

"Well, this is a remarkably nice position for a man to be placed in certainly," observed Mr. Beagle "Did you *ever* hear such wailing and gnashing of teeth? Are you never going to leave off, you *devils?*" he added, throwing the bolster with great violence under the bed, and therefore, as he fondly conceived, right amongst them. Instead, however, of striking the cats therewith he unhappily upset something which rolled with great velocity from one end of the room to the other, and made during its progress so singular a clatter, that he began to "tut! tut!" and to scratch his head audibly.

"Who's there?" demanded Plumplee in the passage below, for he slept in the room beneath, and the rolling of the article in question had alarmed him, "Who's there! d'ye hear! Speak! or I'll shoot you like a dog!" and on the instant the report of a pistol was heard, which in all probably had been fired with the view of convincing all whom it might concern that he had such a thing as a pistol in the house. "Who's there!" he again demanded: "You vagabonds, I'll be at you!" an intimation that may be held to have been extremely natural under the circumstances, not only because he had not even the slightest intention of of carrying so desperate a design into execution, but because he—in consequence of having supped off cucumbers and crabs, of which he happened to be particularly fond, seeing that as they didn't agree with him and invariably made him suffer, they partook of the nature of forbidden fruit—he had singularly enough been dreaming of being attacked by a party of burglars, and of having succeeded in frightening them away by holding out a precisely similar threat.

"Beagle!" he shouted, after waiting in vain for the street-door to bang.

"Here!" cried Beagle, "come up here! It's nothing: I'll explain! For Heaven's sake," he added, addressing Valentine, "open the door;" but Valentine was too much engaged to pay attention to any such request.

At this moment the footsteps of Plumplee were heard upon the stairs, and Mr. Beagle, who then began to feel somewhat better, cried, "Come in! my good friend, come in!"

"What on earth is the matter?" inquired Mr. Plumplee, as he entered the room pale as a ghost in his night-shirt, with a pistol in one hand and a lamp in the other.

"It's all right," said Beagle, "'twas I that made the noise. I've been besieged by a cohort of cats. They have been at it here making most healthful music under my bed for the last two hours, and in trying to make them hold their peace with the bolster, I upset that noisy affair, that's all."

"Cats!" cried Mr. Plumplee, "cats!—you ate a little too much cucumber, my friend!—that and the crabs were too heavy for your stomach!—you have been dreaming!—you've had the night mare! We haven't a cat in the house; I can't bear them."

"You are mistaken," rejoined Beagle, "they're about here in swarms. If I've turned *one* cat out this night, I'm sure that I've turned out twenty! I've in fact done nothing else since I came up! In and out, in and out! Upon my life, I think I can't have opened that blessed door less than a hundred and fifty times; and that young fellow there has been all the while fast as a church!"

"I tell you, my friend, you've been dreaming! We have never had a cat about the premises."

"Meyow—meyow!" cried Valentine quietly.

"Now have I been dreaming!" triumphantly exclaimed Mr. Beagle, "now have I had the night mare?"

"God bless my life!" cried Mr. Plumplee, jumping upon Mr. Beagle's bed, "they don't belong to me!"

"I don't know whom they belong to;" returned Mr. Beagle, "nor do I much care: I only know that there they *are!* If you'll just hook those breeches up here, I'll get out and half murder them! Only hook 'em this way!—I'll wring their precious necks off!"

"They're out of my reach," cried Plumplee. "Hish! hish!" Finding, however, that harsh terms had no good effect, he had recourse to the milder and more persuasive cry of "Pussy, pussy, pussy, pussy! tit, tit, tit!"

"Hish! you devils!" cried Mr. Jonas Beagle, who began to be really enraged!

"Titty, titty, titty, titty!—puss, puss, puss!" repeated Mr. Plumplee in the blandest and most seductive tones, as he held the pistol by the muzzle to break the back or to knock out the brains of the first unfortunate cat that made her appearance: but all this persuasion to come forth had no effect; they continued to be invisible, while the mewing proceeded in the most melancholy strain.

"What on earth are we to do?" inquired Plumplee, "I myself have a horror of cats."

"The same to me, and many of 'em!" observed Mr. Beagle, "Let's wake that young fellow, perhaps he don't mind them."

"Hollo!" cried Plumplee.

"Hul-lo!" shouted Beagle; but as neither could make any impression upon Valentine, and as both were afraid to get off the bed to shake him, they proceeded to roll up the blankets and sheets into balls and to pelt him with infinite zeal.

"Who's there? What's the matter?" cried Valentine at length, in the coolest tone imaginable, although his exertions had made him sweat like a tinker.

"For Heaven's sake, my dear young friend," said Mr. Plumplee, "do assist us in turning these cats out."

"Cats! Where are they? Hish!" cried Valentine.

"Oh, that's of no use whatever. I've tried the *hishing* business myself. All the hishing in the world won't do. They must be beaten out: you're not afraid of them, are you?"

"Afraid of them! afraid of a few cats!" exclaimed Valentine with the assumption of some considerable magnanimity, "Where are they?"

"Under my bed," replied Beagle, "*There's* a brave fellow! Break their blessed necks!" and Valentine leaped out of bed and after striking at the imaginary animals very furiously with the bolster, he hissed with great violence and scratched across the grain of the boards in humble imitation of those domestic creatures scampering out of a room, when he rushed to the door, and proceeded to make a very forlorn meyowing die gradually away at the bottom of the stairs.

"Thank Heaven! they are all gone at last!" cried Mr. Beagle, "we shall be able to get a little rest now, I suppose;" and after very minutely surveying every corner of the room in which it was possible for one of them to have lingered, he lighted his candle, bade Plumplee good night, and begged him to go immediately to Miss Madonna, who had been calling for an explanation very anxiously below.

As soon as Plumplee had departed, Valentine assisted Beagle to remake his bed; and when they had accomplished this highly important business with the skill and dexterity of a couple of thoroughbred chambermaids, the light was again extinguished, and Mr. Beagle very naturally made up his mind to have a six hours' sound and uninterrupted sleep. He had, however, scarcely closed his eyes when the mewing was renewed, and as he had not even the smallest disposition to "listen to the sounds so familiar to his ear," he started up at once and exclaimed, "I wish I may *die* if they're all out now! Here's one of them left!" added he, addressing Valentine, but Valentine having taken a deep inspiration answered only by respiring with a prolonged gargling sound. "He's off again by the living Jove!" continued Beagle. "I *never* heard of any one sleeping so soundly. Hollo! my good fellow! ho!—Fast as a four-year-old! Won't you be quiet, you *witch?* Are you determined not to let me have a wink of sleep to-night? She must be in the cupboard: I must have overlooked her; and yet I don't see how I could. Oh! keep the thing up, dear! Don't let me rest!" and he fumbled about for his box, and having taken a hearty pinch of snuff, began to turn the thing seriously over in his mind and to make a second person of himself, by way of having, under the circumstances, a companion with whom he could advise, and if necessary remonstrate.

"Well, what's to be done now?" inquired he of the second person thus established. "What's to be the next step, Jonas? It's of no use at all, you know! we can't go to sleep;—we may just as well try to get a kick at the moon!—nor must we again disturb—*Hish!* you——, Jonas! Jonas! keep your temper, my boy!—keep your temper! Don't let a contemptible cat put you out!" and Mr. Beagle took another pinch of snuff, from which he apparently derived a great degree of consolation. "What, at it again?" he continued, "I wish I had the wringing of your neck off, madam! You want to put me in a passion; but you won't! you can't do it! therefore, don't lay that flattering unction to your soul!—*Well*, Jonas: how are we to act? Shall we sit here all night, or take up our bed and walk, Jonas?—eh?"

Jonas was so struck with the expediency of the latter course, that he apparently urged its immediate adoption; for Mr. Beagle, in the first place, half-dressed himself in bed, and in the next, threw the counterpane, a blanket, and a sheet over his shoulder; when, tucking a pillow and a bolster under his arm, said, "We'll leave you to your own conscience, madam! Good night!" and left the room with the view of seeking repose upon the sofa.

Valentine was astonished at the coolness displayed by Mr. Beagle throughout the entire transaction; and after reproaching the spirit of mischief that was within him, and striving by way of a punishment, to disturb his own repose, and succeeded too as well as the monks of old did when they inflicted the scourge upon themselves—he proceeded to justify himself upon the ground that his object was to learn the true characters of men, and being perfectly satisfied with that justification, went soundly and solemnly to sleep.

In the morning, of course, nothing but tales of horror went down. Mr. Plumplee told his with the air of a man conscious of having been inspired with the spirit of valor; and Miss Madonna told hers with great feeling and effect; but when Beagle began to explain to them how *he* had been persecuted, they forgot their own troubles and laughed heartily at his, which was certainly, under the circumstances, extremely reprehensible, however natural philosophers may hold it to be for the risible faculties of men to be provoked by the little vexations which others endure.

But where, during the whole of this time, was poor Goodman?—While Valentine is on his way to town—for which he immediately after breakfast prepared to start—the next chapter will briefly explain.

CHAPTER XIV.

GOODMAN IS CONDUCTED TO HIS NEW RESIDENCE—THE LIBERTY OF THE SUBJECT ILLUSTRATED—THE COMMENCEMENT OF AN EXPOSITION OF A SYSTEM WHICH CANNOT BE GENERALLY KNOWN.

When Goodman, who had fainted on being thrust into the coach, had been restored to a state of consciousness, he found himself perfectly wet, for the ruffians, when they perceived all animation suspended, became apprehensive of having carried their violence too far, and, therefore, at once procured a bottle of water, with which they continued to sprinkle him, until he awakened to a sense of his position, when, grasping the arm of the fellow who sat beside him, and looking intently in his face, he cried, "Tell me, my good man, tell me the meaning of this monstrous outrage?"

"Oh, you'll know the meaning on't soon enough, don't be impatient," replied the fellow.

"But why have I thus been seized like a felon? What have I done? Whom have I injured? I am unconscious of having offended a single soul."

"Don't ask us any questions," replied the fellow. "We know nothing at all about it. We've got our orders, and that's enough."

"But tell me this," urged Goodman, "only this, to what place are you taking me now?"

"Oh, you'll know fast enough!—All in good time!—wait a little, and then an idea'll strike you."

"But surely you can have no serious objection to let me know that?" observed Goodman.

"O! tell the genelman," cried the ruffian who sat opposite. "He a'n't like some on 'em, you know. O! tell him! it can't make much odds you know now!"

"It taint reg'lar," cried the other; "I haven't no partickler objection, only it taint the thing. Howsever, I don't dislike him, 'cause he *is* a genelman, so I don't mind."

"Tell me, then," said Goodman, impatiently.

"Don't be in sich a hurry!" cried the fellow; "you patients always is in sich a sweat."

"Don't trifle with me, for Heaven's sake."

"There you go again!" cried the fellow, "there you go!—why can't you be cool? I don't *mind* telling you! we're going to take you where you're going to be taken care on."

"To a Lunatic Asylum?—Is it not so?" cried Goodman.

"You couldn't have guessed it much nearer if you'd tried every day for a month. But it's a werry nice place; werry private and genteel. None o' your public 'uns!—every thing slap and respectable!"

Goodman had heard much of private Lunatic Asylums: he had heard of the villanies practised therein—villanies, however, which he had conceived to be mere fictions, coined in the diseased imaginations of those who had been properly confined, for he had hitherto repudiated the idea of its being possible for such monstrous proceedings to to be tolerated in a country like this. Those acts of barbarity, however, which he had assumed to be fictions, at this moment flashed across his mind in the shape of realities, and prompted him to make a desperate effort to escape, for he felt quite convinced, that if once they secured him unknown to his friends, they in all probability would keep him there, lingering in tortures till the day of his death. He, therefore, in order that no suspicion might be excited, assumed an air of perfect calmness, and after having, as he imagined, sufficiently ingratiated himself with the ruffians by whom he had been seized, placed five sovereigns in the hand of him who appeared to be the principal, and explained to him that he would give him a cheque for a hundred more, if, instead of driving him to the so-called asylum, he would permit him to return.

"It's no go," said the fellow. "It can't be done. I wish it could. It's impossible. We're watched. The two doctors is behind with your ——" Here the fellow checked himself suddenly.

"With whom, my good friend, with whom?" inquired Goodman.

"Why—with—with the genelman as sent for the doctors," replied the fellow with considerable hesitation.

"And who is that?" said Goodman, anxiously. "Who is it? Tell me but that!"

"Why, that's against the law!" cried the fellow—"It's a secret! howsever, you'll know by and bye, I des say."

"Are they behind us now?" inquired Goodman, attempting to look out of the window.

"Yes, yes, they're acoming; sit down, sit down," said the fellow—and Goodman, whose object was to allay all suspicion, at once resumed his seat.

"Have we far to go now?" he inquired.

"Not far; we're just at hand; we shall be there in the matter o' ten minutes."

Goodman now saw that no time was to be lost, for he had made up his mind to make one desperate effort. He knew that if he once got fairly out of the coach, it would require an exceedingly swift man to overtake him, and, emboldened by that knowledge, he prepared for a spring.

"Another five minutes will do it," said one of the men, thrusting his head out of the window—a movement of which Goodman took instant advantage, and, making a desperate plunge, dashed clean through the opposite door.

"He's off, by —— Stop! coachman, stop!" shouted one of the fellows. "We shall never be able to catch him, for he has no flesh to carry." Nor would they have caught him, had it not most unfortunately happened that in plunging he sprained one of his ankles and fell.

The coach stopped on the instant, and the ruffians leaped out; and as Goodman was unable to use both feet with firmness, they easily overtook him, when one of them struck him a sledge-hammer blow upon the back of the neck, and felled him at once to the ground.

"Is this the way you serve us for all our kindness?" cried the fellow, as he kicked him most cruelly in the stomach. "Is this your gratitude?"

"Villains!" shouted Goodman, and the cowardly scoundrels kicked him more severely.

"Up with you!" cried one of them, "Sam! here, where are the ruffles?" and the fellow addressed instantly produced a pair of handcuffs, and begun to unlock them.

"I will not be manacled!" cried Goodman, seizing the handcuffs, and holding them up as a weapon of defence, "It is for my personal liberty I fight, and will peril my life to defend it. Although not mad, I am desperate now, and the blood of him who attempts again to seize me be on his own head!"

The fellows for the moment held back. Accustomed as they had been to deal with desperation, they for an instant appeared to be appalled. "Let me have justice!" continued Goodman, "If I am mad, let it be proved before the world! I will not be stolen from society thus!"

At this moment a coach drew up to the spot, towards which Goodman's eyes were directed with an expression of anxious hope, which the ruffians no sooner perceived, than they sprang at him, seized him by the throat, and kicked his legs from under him violently.

"Help!" shouted Goodman, as he saw the coach stop, "Help!—murder!"

"We'll help you!" cried a person alighting, "Oh! yes; *we'll* assist you with a vengeance!" cried another, who instantly followed, "We'll help you!"

Goodman remembered those voices well, and on turning to the quarter whence they came, every hope he had inspired was blasted by the sight of Doctors Bowlemout and Dobb.

"In with him!" cried Dobb, with a fiend-like smile.

"Your young bully is not here now!" shouted Bowlemout; and he and Dobb seized Goodman's legs, while the two keepers lifted his body and carried him towards the coach door.

Goodman, however, still struggled with all the strength at his command, and several times succeeded in thrusting the two doctors from him; and although they returned each time to the charge with renewed desperation, every effort to throw him into the coach proved abortive, which so enraged the two keepers, that after kicking him brutally in order to compel him to bend his legs, they again seized him violently by the throat with the view of making him insensible by partial strangulation. But all would not do. His struggles were still desperate. They could *not* get him in. They applied to the coachmen for aid; but in vain: they would render no assistance; they would not interfere.

"Tell him," at length cried Dobb, "that he *must* come! It's of no use; we shall never get him in; come, he *must!*" And as a man, who had till then kept concealed in the second coach, was being dragged forth by Bowlemout, Goodman shrieked, "Merciful God!—my brother!—Oh, Walter! Walter; dear Walter, save me! Save me from these murderous men!"

Walter approached; and Goodman struggled more violently than before, but instead of rescuing him from the hands of the ruffians, he assisted in throwing him into the coach like a dog!

The very moment he was in, the keepers followed, and the doctors followed them; when the former at once seized him by the collar and stuck their knuckles furiously into his throat; while the latter tied his legs and held them down.

"My brother!" cried Goodman—"my brother against me! God!—can it be?" and tears of agony rolled down his cheeks, and he sobbed like a child. "You need use no violence now," he continued. "My brother—my own brother! whom I have cherished, is my enemy: do with me as you please; I shall now make no further resistance!"

"No!" cried one of the ruffians, shaking him brutally, "we'll take care you don't! We've had enough of you for one bout, at all events. *We'll* take care we don't have any more of it." And the villain again thrust his knuckles into his throat, and continued to shake him like a fiend.

The coach stopped. The outer gates of an attractive and well built house opened to admit them, and closed again the moment they were in, when the fellow relaxing his hold, cried, "Now, you old scoundrel, consider yourself booked here for life. You are safe enough now! Give us as much of your nonsense as you dare!"

As soon as the door of the coach had been opened, the doctors alighted, and when the keepers had unbound Goodman's legs, they left him for a moment alone, still sobbing.

"Now, a'n't you coming out?" demanded one of them, at length; and poor Goodman, who felt quite exhausted, made an effort to alight, but before he had descended two steps, the heartless ruffian pulled him violently forward, and dashed him with his face downwards upon the rough gravel path.

"Come! up with you!" shouted the ruffian, kicking him over as he would a dead dog; when, as Goodman was utterly unable to rise, he proceeded to drag him along the ground, as the blood gushed in streams from his nose and ears.

"Act like men!" cried the coachman, who sickened at the sight. "If he *is* mad, damme don't treat him like a varmint!"

"Mind your own business," cried a black-looking scoundrel, who appeared to be the proprietor of this infamous den. "What's your fare?"

"Seven shillings!" indignantly shouted the coachman.

"Here it is. Now be off!—we want none of your insolence here."

"Lor send I may never have such another job as this!" cried the coachman on mounting his box. "If I'd ha' knowed it, you should ha' pulled me up five hundred times afore I'd ha' taken such a fare."—And he lashed his horses violently with a view of expressing his indignation, and gave the fellow who held open the gates an apparently accidental cut across the cheek, as he drove through.

Poor Goodman, as well as he was able, now looked for his unnatural brother, who, however, remained in the coach outside—but no sooner had he turned his head round, than he was dragged into a room, when, another flood of tears having somewhat relieved him, he said faintly to the person to whom a paper in which Bowlemout and Dobb had certified to his insanity, was delivered. "Are you, sir, the proprietor of this establishment?"

"I am!" said that person, with a scowl.

"Will you do me the favor then to show me your authority for my detention?"

"Hold your tongue, sir!"

"I merely wish—"

"Silence!" interrupted the scowling brute; "strip him, and put him to bed!" added he, addressing his myrmidons. "If he dares to show any of his devil's tricks here, why you know how to serve him."

Goodman was accordingly dragged into a narrow dark cell, stripped and thrown upon a pallet! when the ruffians, after swearing that they would come and knock his brains out if he made the slightest noise, locked him up for the night.

"Heaven's will be done!" exclaimed Goodman, on being left alone. "But, oh God! am I mad?—I must be—I feel that I must; for I thought and still think I saw my brother! that brother to whom I have never been unkind—whom I have cherished through life, with the most affectionate tenderness—whom I have sustained.—Oh! it cannot—impossible!—I am, I am *mad!* And yet—surely, this cannot be a dream? No!—no! I am awake *now!* GOD! what can it be? Not madness? I can remember every circumstance—can connect and review.—Those physicians! they spoke of my connection with an emperor! *I* never imagined myself to be thus connected! It must be a mistake. Yet who sent them? Walter? his motive?—immediate possession! It must have been! Oh! what a villanous system is this! what man is secure from being seized, confined, murdered? If I am not mad, I soon shall be!" And thus he proceeded until mental and physical agony induced absolute exhaustion.

CHAPTER XV.

VALENTINE VISITS THE BRITISH MUSEUM—IMPARTS BREATH TO MEMNON AND RAISES A VOICE FROM THE TOMB.

ON reaching the residence of Goodman, Valentine found the old servant in tears, and, as he became apprehensive of something of a very serious character having occurred, he walked immediately into the parlor, and desired her to follow him.—"Something has happened, Ann," said he with much earnestness, "tell me, what is it?"

Ann sobbed bitterly, but managed to observe, "I don't—know—what—I've done, sir—I thought—I—gave—good—satisfaction."

"What on earth is the matter?" cried Valentine impatiently.

"Master, sir's—given me—wa-arning."

"Oh—when did he return?"

"I haven't set eyes on him since Saturday, when he left with you, sir."

"Then how can he have given you warning?"

"He sent it by his brother," cried Ann. "Mr. Walter has been here and read a letter he'd just received from master, where he says he's going to be out of town for a time, and that I must look out for another place."

"And where is he now?"

"Mr. Walter says that mayn't be known."

"He read the letter to you?"

"Yes, all but where it came from, and—dear me, I'd almost forgot: he wished me to say, sir, that master's kind regards, and as he shouldn't p'rhaps come back for some weeks or a month, he thinks you'd better return to the country, and he'll send you another invitation by and bye."

"This is very extraordinary!" thought Valentine, "I'd no idea of his being even in the slightest degree involved.—When are you to leave, Ann?"

"To-night, sir."

"To-night!"

"Yes, sir, this blessed night! Mr. Walter has settled with me and paid me my month, and I'm to leave this night, sir!—would you believe it?"

"And who's to take charge of the house?"

"Mrs. Horace is coming this evening, and she and her husband are going to remain."

"Indeed! I must see Mr. Walter."

"Yes, do, sir. But won't you have nothing to take?—You'll come home to dinner, sir, wont you?"

"No, I shall dine out," said Valentine; and he left the house at once with the view of calling upon Walter. "Poor old gentleman!" he murmured, on his way, "He has been entering into some unsuccessful speculation. What an extraordinary passion is this love of wealth! An old man like that now, having plenty, to risk probably all that he possessed with a view of gaining more than he could possibly enjoy! How is it that men are never satisfied with that which they have?" Before he had framed a satisfactory answer to this question he reached the door of Walter's residence.

"Mr. Goodman is not at home sir," said the servant, in answer to Valentine's inquiry.

"Nor Mrs. Goodman?"

"No, sir; they went out with Mr. and Mrs. Horace, and I don't expect them home before night?"

"Valentine perceived in a moment by the unsteady eye and the hesitating speech of the girl that what she had stated was not exactly correct. He did not, however, press the matter farther, but left his card, and bade her say that he would call in the evening.

"Now what shall I do with myself?" thought Valentine, as he walked very leisurely from the house. "I wish that I knew a little more about London. However, I must, I suppose, be content to take my chance." And he continued to walk, without knowing or caring much where. He had not, however, proceeded any very great distance before he came to an old-fashioned red brick building, on either side of the gates of which a sentinel was walking, with a view to the uninterrupted circulation of his blood.

"What place is this?" he inquired of one of these national guardians.

"Brish Museum," returned the sentinel, marvelling at his ignorance, and walking away as stiffly as if he had that morning swallowed his ramrod by mistake.

"The British Museum!" said Valentine, without thanking the soldier for his extraordinary politeness! "The very place I want to see!" And he entered the courtyard at once, and after looking with a curious eye at a creature in a long wooden wig, and at a canoe of great antiquity, which appeared to have been constructed by some ingenious wild gentlemen out of the bark of a tree, he reached the hall, when, after having purchased a catalogue of one individual, and delivered his stick to another, he passed a well stuffed rhinoceros that had evidently known what it was to have a bullet or two in his body, and proceeded up stairs, at the top of which stood a few very gigantic giraffes, with necks sufficiently long to have enabled them to dine without the slightest inconvenience in an attic, while standing outside the street door.

Having surveyed these lofty creatures, he passed through the rooms in which the specimens of various animals were so numerous that a student in Natural History might spend the full term of his natural life without acquiring a perfect knowledge of their respective characteristics! These, however, did not appear to the majority of the visitors to be the most attractive animals in this vast collection. The chief attraction seemed to be centred in the visitors themselves, and from the number of nods of recognition, and meetings by appointment which came under the immediate cognisance of Valentine, he was naturally led to infer that this national establishment was a national place of assignation. He never had lavished upon him at any one time so many really wicked glances. The widows were desperately intent upon something; they appeared to be especially on the *qui vive*, and as his eyes met theirs at every turn, he jumped at once to the conclusion that if they were really virtuous they were really not very discreet, and after taking a good steady look at a lobster, that was pinned very closely to the wainscot, he proceeded to the Gallery of Antiquities below.

This place he found remarkably cool and pleasant. He surveyed, without the slightest interruption, a legion of little gods which appeared to have been barbarously mutilated in their infancy; and then turned his attention to a number of young artists, who had obviously inspired the conviction that they were on the high road to immortal fame.

One was sketching a goddess without a nose: another was portraying a ram-headed lady; a third was engaged upon a striking colossal fist; a fourth was drawing the fragment of some hero, who appeared to have lost the greater part of himself in some desperate battle; a fifth was depicting an excellent woman, who had not only lost her head and one of her shoulders, but out of whose arm a large piece appeared to have been bitten, and who was represented kneeling behind a tablet well covered with exceedingly interesting hieroglyphics; while a sixth was engaged upon three very bandy little deities, who looked as if they might have accomplished great things in their time.

Having inaudibly awarded to these artists all the praise which appeared to be due to them respectively, Valentine passed on until he came to a figure of which a number of persons appeared to be at that moment lost in admiration. This figure was placed upon a huge block of stone, and although its face was by far the most pleasing of them all, one side of its head had been chopped off, apparently with some heavy implement, while the left arm and shoulder with the whole of the body below the third rib had been blown clean away.

On referring to his catalogue, Valentine found this to be the bust of young Memnon, and as certain elderly gentlemen who formed part of the group were conversing on the subject of oracles in general, he listened with considerable attention to their discourse, and found them to be exceedingly communicative men.

"There is nothing," said one of the elderly persons, "that can have so great a tendency to prove the rapid progress of the human intellect as an oracle. If any man of the present age were capable of even dreaming that a mere mass of stone had the power to speak, he would be set down at once as a natural fool; yet to what an extent did the priests and false prophets, the eugastrimandi of the Greeks, the magicians, the soothsayers, and sorcerers of Rome impose, in the remote ages, upon the superstitious multitude!"

"Surely," thought Valentine, "those prophets and priests knew nothing of ventriloquism!"

"They were artful cards doubtless," observed a tall thin person, who wore a singularly small pair of spectacles; "but how did they manage it? that puzzles me. By what means were they able to carry on their games?"

"It is utterly impossible to say," replied the elderly gentleman who had started the subject. "It is reported, you know, of the famous Kireber, that, in order to undeceive the credulous people, and to account for certain strange things relating to the celebrated Delphic Oracle, he fixed a tube in his bed-chamber, so that when persons came to his garden gate, he could hear them if they but whispered, and by means of this tube he asked questions and gave answers, and that he afterwards removed it to his museum and fixed it in a figure, so that it seemed to be animated, and distinct sounds apparently issued from its mouth, for he clearly supposed that the pagan priests by using such tubes, used to make the superstitious believe that the idol itself returned answers to their questions. And there can be no doubt that it was done by some trickery on the part of the priests, who, when they found their power waning, sought to sustain it by the performance of miracles of this kind."

"Was this *Memnon* a vocal god?" inquired the tall thin gentleman.

"Of course he was! and one of the very greatest."

"He appears to have been a big one, but I can see no tube, nor any place into which a tube could possibly have been inserted."

"It was not done with tubes!" said Valentine to himself. "In those days I should have made an excellent miracle-monger; I may as well try the effect now;" when, placing himself in a favorable position, "Fools," he cried, in a deep sepulchral tone, making his voice proceed apparently from the thick lips of Memnon, "Think ye that Memnon was *never* inspired?"

The group at once shrank back appalled; some felt quite faint for the moment, as they stared at the statue and trembled, while the rest looked amazed at each other, but neither of them ventured to utter a word.

"Be off!" shouted Valentine through Memnon. "If they hadn't left my legs behind in Egypt, I'd jump down and kick you out of the place!"

"Wonderful!" involuntarily exclaimed the old gentleman, who had been so severe upon the pious men of old.

"Wonderful!" cried Valentine, contemptuously; "convince thyself! Test my prophetic soul! test it! Would'st thou know thy destiny? Speak!"

"Ye-yes!" cried the stout old gentleman, who evidently prided himself upon his courage. "Who's afraid?"

"Tip then!" cried Memnon. "Tip! I never did duty without it, and I shan't commence now!"

The astonished group again stared wildly at each other. "Did you see his lips move?" inquired one. "I thought that I did!" replied another; "I fancied I saw them move."

"Fool!" exclaimed Memnon; "dost thou wish to insult me? Think'st thou, idiot, the inspired Memnon would condescend to wag his sacred lips like a grovelling mortal?"

At this moment an individual who had a remarkably red face, and whose breath told a tale about his having indulged recently in hot rum-and-water, approached, and when the assumed fact of Memnon having spoken had been communicated to him, he laughed very heartily as a matter of course.

"You will not believe it?—Speak to him and be convinced," urged the stout old gentleman seriously.

"Speak to him?" cried he with the florid face; "speak to him?—Well, my old trump, how's your mother?"

"Irreverent wretch!" exclaimed Memnon indignantly; "know thyself and drink less rum!"

"Hollo!" cried the gentleman with the highly colored countenance. "Hul-lo!" and he closed one eye in order to have a good stare at the statue with the other, while his mouth was as wide open as a mouth of that size could conveniently be strained.

"Are ye satisfied?" cried Memnon. "Learn to respect what ye cannot comprehend. I want repose. D'ye hear? Be off; and disturb me no more!" And Valentine viewed with silent pleasure the astonishment depicted in the countenances of the group while engaged in conversing on the marvellous nature of that which they imagined they had witnessed.

Having heard these amazed individuals declare, that although they might meet during their progress through life with many staunch unbelievers, nothing on earth would ever be able to shake their faith in the assumed fact that the oracle had absolutely spoken, Valentine proceeded to survey the Elgin marbles, and derived much amusement from a couple of highly-gifted connoisseurs, who were loudly and learnedly descanting on their peculiar excellencies.

"Well, Jones," said one of these gentlemen, "What do you think of them—eh?"

"Think of 'em!" contemptuously cried Jones, thrusting his hand into his ample coat pockets. "I wouldn't give two-pence for the lot."

"You don't know the value of them surely?"

"I don't if they're worth more money. Did you ever in all your born days see such rubbish? Why I wouldn't pick 'em up in the street! I wouldn't own 'em! If they belonged to me I'd pitch the whole biling into the Thames."

"But look, my dear fellow—take this for example—just look at the symmetry —"

"Symmetry! What's the good of that? He aint got no head and not above half a body. Where are his legs gone to?—look at that arm there chopped all to smash at the elbow! Symmetry! come, that's good, Why I've got a group of goddesses at home that I gave fifteen pence for, that would, in point of symmetry, beat the whole biling into fits!"

"But take them as fragments."

"That's precisely what I do take 'em as! I can't take 'em as any thing else!—and pretty fragments they are!"

"But their age, my dear fellow!"

"Now, don't tell me! Just look at this woman here! Send I may live!—why there aint above a quarter on her left!"

"But you must look at the parts that are remaining!"

"And so I just do! There's nothing *else* to look at! It won't do, you know, at least, it won't do for me!—*However* they can gammon the people to believe that there's any thing fine in such rubbish as this, puts me out altogether. There isn't one of 'em perfect, nor any thing like it. That fellow there's the best of the bunch, and they've smashed off the biggest part of *his* corporation!—to have a post mortal examination I *s'pose!* Of all the rum rotten trash that *ever* was scraped together this queer lot bangs all!—Come!" he added, seizing the arm of his friend and dragging him from the room; "let's go and look at something a leetle worth while."

Valentine derived so much pleasure from the learned observations of this individual and the John-Bull-ish, solemn, self-satisfied air with which those observations were made, that he left the Elgin marbles to follow him and his friend, with the view of still farther indulging his taste for the sublime.

"This is a pretty good sized coffin," observed Mr. Jones approaching a ponderous granite sepulchre, the lid of which was held up by a strong wooden frame that the whole of the interior might be viewed. "It would hold a couple of dozen dead bodies well packed! The water couldn't get in very well here I say, could it? And as to the worms!—they might try till they ground their teeth down to the level of their old gums before they'd be able to nibble their way through. This is just the sort of coffin that I should like to have now—only it would cost so much to carry it to the grave. It would take twenty men, and even then they'd make a muddle of it. Here's another of them," he added as he crossed to the opposite side, "they appear to be fellows."

Now as the lid of this happened to be down, and as it was perfectly obvious that Mr. Jones had entered the Museum expressly in order to be astonished; it recurred at once to Valentine, that it *would* be a pity to allow him to depart disappointed. He, therefore, while apparently admiring with others an exceedingly broad Egyptian pedestal, introduced a quiet groan into the sepulchre, as Jones was engaged in pointing out to his friend the ridiculous character of certain heiroglyphics.

"Hush! hush!" cried that gentleman, starting back suddenly and seizing the arm of his friend. "*Hush!* didn't you hear?"

"I thought I heard something," observed his friend whispering.

"Hush! hush-sh! Listen!" and Valentine sent in another small groan.

"Send I may live!—'tis a man!" exclaimed Jones.

"Impossible!" cried his friend. "Why, do you know the age of this thing?"

"I don't care a dump about the age! If it is in its fifty millionth year it don't matter a button: there's something alive in it now—listen again!" and the violence of his action drew several persons round, of course anxious to ascertain what had caused so much excitement.

Now Valentine happened to be by no means conversant with the language of the Egyptians, and as he conceived that it might spoil the whole thing if he ventured to speak, he confined himself simply to the introduction of a long drowsy yawn which he presumed to have been well understood in all ages and climes. Before he had finished yawning, however, Jones again started up, and addressing an individual who was sleeping in a chair with a long white wand in his hand, cried, "Here! he's been buried alive! —He's just awoke!—do you hear?"

The individual with the wand opened his eyes, and scratched his head and approached crying, "What's the matter?—what's all this—eh?"

"Why here's somebody been buried alive here," said Jones.

"Pooh! nonsense!—are you mad?" cried the person with the wand assuming some considerable amount of official dignity.

"I don't care a straw what you say," returned Jones, "I know that there's some one in there!—did you never hear of a man being buried in a trance?"

"Why you must be insane!" cried the functionary. "That tomb has been empty ever since before you and your grandmothers and grandfathers before you were born!"

"I don't care a button how long it has been empty! I'll bet fifty pounds that there's some one in now!"

"I certainly myself heard something," observed a gentleman who had been attracted with others to the spot.

"Oh nonsense!"—cried the official—"Why it was only cleaned out the other day!"

"But satisfy yourself!" exclaimed Jones, really wondering at the stubborn cool-blooded incredulity of the man.

"I am—I am satisfied!" cried the official; but another yawn which Valentine dexterously introduced at the moment, caused him to start back amazed. Down went his wand, and away he flew, in order to proclaim as well as he could the fact to his brother officers; who, inferring from the highly excited state of his nerves that something was the matter, returned with him at once, with the view of rendering whatever assistance the case might demand.

The very moment, however, that the case was explained, they treated the thing with an air of derision. They all laughed as heartily as men could laugh, and in a manner well calculated to be serviceable to them in a physical point of view—inasmuch as it gave them great pain, as they had not had a really good laugh for an age.

"Why, Simpkins," cried one, "upon my soul, I didn't think you'd been so soft!" But Mr. Simpkins by no means regarded it as so excellent a joke as they appeared to imagine, He took an altogether different view of the matter, for although he felt perfectly sure that the tomb did not contain an Egyptian, as he had seen it but a few days previously open and empty, he was not quite so sure that the workmen in closing the lid had not shut in some poor devoted laborer, whom they had either forgotten or cared not to release. He, therefore, heeded not their derision; but being an extremely humane man kept his ear very closely to the tomb, while they were laughing and joking with glee by his side.

"For Heaven's sake!" at length he exclaimed, "be silent for a moment!" But they would not be silent: they continued to laugh very loudly and very wantonly, until Jones and several others made an earnest appeal to their humanities, begging them to hold their peace, but for an instant, in order that they themselves might be convinced that the sounds were not the offspring of mere imagination.

"Well, let's give these very silly people a chance!" cried one of the men who had been so strongly moved to laughter. "Let us listen to the cries and groans of this mummy. Now hush!—hush!" And several of those who had been thus enjoined to silence commenced groaning very furiously—a feat which not only excited another peal of laughter, but inspired Mr. Jones with much real indignation. "Inhuman wretches!" he exclaimed, "assist me in raising the lid of this tomb, I tell you there's some one inside; I know it; I'm sure of it; I'll bet any one of you fifty younds of it!" And Mr. Jones produced a pocketbook containing a roll of notes, which astonished the official eyes of the functionaries around him and caused them respectfully to open their ears. The effect was electric. Their countenances dropped in a moment. A more powerful argument could not have been adduced, for they began to believe at once that there must be something in it, and, hence, to pay all due attention.

Finding that the general impression was that he whom they imagined to be in the tomb, was not an Egyptian, but a laborer, Valentine concluded that as a laborer must of course mean an Irishman, he couldn't go very far wrong if he gave them a spice of the brogue.

"Och!—what the blazes will I do thin!" he cried, "be me sowl I'm clane didd althegidher entirely—murther!"

"Now, what d'ye think of it!" cried Simpkins, triumphantly.

"Somebody's there, sure enough;" said one of those who had previously treated the whole thing with contempt. "But how could he get in?"

"Never mind a dump," cried Jones, "how he got in; let's try to get him out."

"Dirthy wather to ye, lit me thin have a brith of air—I'll be shmudher'd complate wid th' want of it—och!"

"But a moment, my good fellow—now—now give a lift!" And Mr. Jones and the whole of the officials put the palms of their hands to the lid of the tomb, which however defied all their strength.

"Run—run, for the workmen!" cried Simpkins, "bring them at once, or the man will be a corpse!" and two wand-bearers started off immediately for the men who were engaged in a different part of the museum.

"What a lucky thing it was that I happened to hear him!" observed Mr. Jones. "If I hadn't, the chances are that he'd never have come out alive. It was the merest miracle in nature I heard him groan."

"Why," said Simpkins, "he must have been in five days—the thing hasn't been opened since Wednesday."

"Five days!" exclaimed several of the visitors, in a breath, as a violent thrill of horror ran through them. "Five days!" and they made up their minds to see a skeleton.

"Shall nobody thrag me out of this?" cried Valentine. "Will I be shmudher'd at last?"

"Wait a moment, my good fellow, wait but a moment!" cried Jones putting his lips to the lid of the tomb.

"In a moment I'm didd widout doubt. I fale dhreadful. Arrah thin you devils! Is it thin at yer aise ye'd be afther shtanthing whin yer say a boy murther'd to dith! Take the top off complate, or be the sowl that's inside o'me—"

"Don't be impatient!" cried Jones—"You must not be impatient."

"It's *impatient* yer mane? Opin the top then, bad luck t'yer, opin the top! Aint it just like a baste I've been thrated sure?—Opin the top!"

At this moment the workmen arrived with their tools, and after some slight delay—during which the imaginary Irishman was engaged in calling out very fiercely—they succeeded in introducing a lever. This was no sooner done than Valentine perceiving that the game was nearly up, cried, "It's all complately over wid me now. I'm quite murthered—I'm gone—I'm at pace!"—and turned round with a view to the full enjoyment of the scene.

The visitors were in a state of the most painful anxiety; the wand-bearers felt scarcely able to breathe; while the workmen perspired with infinite freedom, for the weight of the lid was immense. They did, however, eventually succeed in raising it sufficiently to enable them to examine the interior, and this was no sooner accomplished than a dozen simultaneously looked in, very naturally expecting to behold a fellow-creature lying prostrate at the bottom.

"Where is he!" cried one. "I can't see him!" cried another. "Not here!" cried a third—"the thing's empty!"

"Oh nonsense!" shouted several of the visitors who were behind.

"Well you'd better come and find him," said those who had looked, giving way to the incredulous creatures who had not.

"Where can he be got to?" inquired Mr. Jones.

"He was never there at all!" cried the very official who had previously laughed the very heartiest of the lot. "It's precisely what I said! The idea of a man being in! How could he have got there?"

"Do you mean to say," observed Jones, "that you don't think a man was in this thing at all?"

"I do!" replied the official very firmly.

"Then *I* mean to say you know nothing about it! The go is a rum go certainly, a very rum go; but isn't a man to believe his own ears? I heard him myself! Didn't you, sir?—and you?" As several of the visitors bore testimony to the fact of having heard some voice proceed from the tomb, Jones continued, "Of course! We all heard it! One may be deceived, or two may be deceived, or even three may be deceived, but, send I may live, we can't all be deceived?"

"Well where is he now?—where is he?"

"That's jist the very pint that I can't make out: it's in fact the only pint to be considered."

And the point was considered—very deeply considered—but the consideration yielded nothing bearing even the semblance of a conjecture! They could not conceive how a man could have escaped, nor could they believe that no man had been there. They examined the tomb minutely again and again, but failed to find even so much as a crack to give weight to any opinion having reference to the exit of any thing like a human being. They still, however, tried very hard—very, very hard indeed—to reconcile the fact of their having heard the voice of a man, with the fact of no man being there; and as Valentine's appetite began to be somewhat troublesome, he left them engaged in unravelling that mystery which he perfectly well knew they were unable to solve.

CHAPTER XVI.

THE SALE OF GOODMAN'S PROPERTY BY WALTER, AND THE EXTRAORDINARY STOPPAGE THEREOF BY VALENTINE.

HAVING dined at the first decent tavern he came to, Valentine started for poor Goodman's house; but as he found it locked up and entirely deserted, he proceeded at once to the residence of Walter, with the view of ascertaining, if possible, the cause of this unusually sudden change.

On reaching the house, he found the servant at the door, and in answer to his numerous inquiries, the girl told an interesting tale about how Mr. Goodman, her master, had been out all the day with her mistress: how Mr. and Mrs. Horace had been out all day with them; how they were all out together on some pressing business, then, and how she didn't expect they would be home before midnight.

"I'll leave a note for your master," said Valentine; "I suppose I shall find a pen and ink in the parlor?"

"Oh," said the girl, placing herself hurriedly before him, "Missis has locked up the parlor, sir; she always does when she goes out for any time."

"Has she locked up the drawing-room too?" inquired Valentine.

"Yes, sir—there's a tavern over the way, sir: if you'll write a note there, sir, if you please, I'll be sure to give it master, directly he comes home."

At this moment Walter, of course quite unconscious of the door being open, rushed out of the parlor in his morning gown and slippers, and was about to proceed up stairs, when he caught a glance of Valentine in the passage.

"Oh! how do you do?" he cried, making an extremely awkward attempt to conceal the confusion into which he had been thrown. "Happy to see you!—very happy to see you!—walk in," and he gave a most withering look at the girl, although it was clearly by no means her fault.

On entering the parlor Valentine found the whole family engaged in the perusal of a mass of papers with which the table had been strewed; and although they received him with much affected pleasure, he perceived in a moment that he was an unwelcome guest.

"So the old buffer's bolted and left you in the lurch," observed Horace, trying to conceal the iron safe which belonged to Goodman. "It's just like the old out-and-outer."

"I hope nothing serious has occurred," observed Valentine.

"Oh, not a ha'porth of it!—*serious!*—no chance of that!" returned Horace. "But you know he's such a jolly old rum un there's no such thing as holding him any how."

"I feared," said Valentine, "that he had entered into some unsuccessful speculation, and had thus become involved."

"Speculation!" cried Horace, "well, come, that's rich! Why, did you ever suppose that a regular old know-nothing out-and-out cove of his kidney had half enough pluck to ——"

"My dear Horace, how you do talk!" interrupted Mrs. Goodman, "when you know that he has been speculating ——"

"Oh! ah! exactly!" said Horace, who had evidently forgotten his part.

"The fact is," said Walter, "he has been dabbling a little, aud that has rendered it inexpedient for him to be seen for a week or two—you understand?" Valentine nodded, for he did understand what they wished him to understand; but no more. There is something behind, thought he. These hesitating speeches and secret looks mean *something*.

"And what do you think of doing, my trump?" said Walter, as Valentine was steadily watching their actions. "Do you mean to remain here in this little village, or do you mean to cut back?"

"Why the thing is so sudden, I've not at present made up my mind. Of course I shall eventually return."

"My brother," observed Walter, "in his letter to me, states that he should advise you to return at once, and that when everything is settled he shall again be most happy to see you."

"Had he written to *me* to that effect," said Valentine, "I should doubtless have acted at once upon his advice; but as he has not—and I cannot but think it most extraordinary that he has not—I feel justified in looking to my own feelings for a guide."

"We ought, I'm sure, to make a thousand apologies," observed Mrs. Goodman; as she pinned three pieces of parchment together, and marked them; "but I hope that the next time you favor us with a visit we shall not be so deeply engaged."

"Where do you think of holding out until you cut it?" inquired Horace.

"I hardly know yet," replied Valentine.

"I'm sorry," said Mrs. Goodman, "that we have not a bed to offer you; but we shall be truly happy to see you whenever you will favor us with a call."

"My boxes," said Valentine, "I suppose that if I send for them to-morrow, I can have them?"

"Most certainly, my dear sir," replied Walter, "I'll see that they are safely delivered myself."

"Well, ta, ta, my tulip, if you *will* go," cried Horace: "Take care of yourself, and let's know where you are, you know!"

Valentine promised to do so, and after taking leave of the ladies was attended to the door by Walter, who displayed an extraordinary degree of politeness; and left the house deeply inspired with the conviction that something was exceedingly wrong.

As he wandered down the street reviewing steadily all that he had seen, it occurred to him that in a window immediately opposite the house in which he and poor Goodman had resided, he had noticed a card on which was printed "APARTMENTS FOR A SINGLE GENTLEMAN;" and as he strongly suspected foul play, and felt that by engaging those apartments he should be able to watch the movements of Walter and his family unseen, he went at once to the house—came to terms with the widow by whom it was kept, and after stating the fact of his having lived opposite—a fact which appeared to be perfectly well known—took immediate possession.

He had not been seated long at his window, which commanded of course a full view of Goodman's house, when he saw Walter, Horace, his wife and her servant, with two workmen, enter. The moment they were in, the door closed, and soon after the workmen were seen in the drawing-room and then at the windows above, where they appeared to be receiving instructions from Walter, with reference to the removal of certain fixtures, and shortly afterwards quitted the house with him, leaving in charge of it Horace and his wife.

As the evening drew on, the shutters were closed, and all seemed secured for the night, when Valentine, who had had but little sleep the night previously in consequence of having persecuted Beagle with the cats, had a very early supper and retired.

In the morning the whole family were at work long before he was up, and throughout the entire day they were busily engaged with clerks, carpenters, and porters with green aprons, examining, tying up and lotting the furniture. Valentine watched their actions narrowly, and towards the evening slipped out, took a coach, and called himself for his boxes, without apparently noticing the confusion that prevailed; and after driving right away that they might not know where he resided, came back to his lodgings unseen.

That night about ten a cart came to the door, and when a number of baskets which evidently contained plate, china and glass, had been deposited with care it drove off, when Valentine watched it to the house of Walter, saw it emptied, and returned.

Nothing more was removed that night, but early the following morning three large vans were loaded with great facility. Walter appeared to be extremely anxious for them to start, and when they did start, Valentine followed and saw their contents deposited at the rooms of an auctioneer. He then knew of course that they were to be sold off at once, and as he saw by the papers that a sale of household furniture was to take place the following day at those rooms, he resolved to be there, in order to fathom the thing, if possible, to the bottom.

Accordingly at twelve the next day he started off, and having arrived at the entrance, on either side of which were exhibited a variety of catalogues and placards—he proceeded up a long narrow passage, and then ascended a small flight of steps, which led immediately into the Sale Room.

In the centre of this room stood a circular table, round which certain children of Israel were seated with a view of securing all bargains to themselves, while behind them stood small mobs of people of the same persuasion, conversing on the expediency of giving certain sums for certain lots, and of out-bidding any Christian person who might have a desire to purchase those "lots worth the money."

The moment Valentine entered, he looked round for Walter and his amiable family, whom, in a short time, he saw in a state of great consternation, which had evidently been induced by his unexpected presence. He seemed, however, to take no notice of them; but apparently directed the whole of his attention to the actions of those who by constantly attending these Sale Rooms raise fortunes upon Fortunes' ruins.

Before he had concluded the minute survey he had commenced, a tall white-faced personage entered the room, and having jumped upon the circular table, shut himself quietly in a juvenile pulpit, made a sort of speech touching the matter in hand, stuck an eye-glass very dexterously between his cheek bone and his brow, and brought forth his professional hammer. He was a remarkably short-sighted person, and had to bring his head down within an inch of the catalogue in order to ascertain the exact number of the first lot; and when this had been accomplished to his entire satisfaction, he very delicately scratched his head, every whitey-brown hair upon which seemed to be too independent to stand on any but its own bottom, when after having slightly rubbed his nose, which, albeit, it was hooked like the majority of the noses present, was yet of a totally different caste, inasmuch as in his case the hook was inverted; he coughed twice with spirit, gave several a-hems! and then boldly commenced operations.

The first lot was put up and knocked down without the slightest interruption from Valentine, for although he had made up his mind to stop the sale, he was compelled of course to wait until he had ascertained precisely how the thing was conducted; but when the second lot came—which happened to be poor Goodman's writing desk, worth about forty or fifty shillings—he felt himself sufficiently *au fait* to begin.

"A pound," said a Jew-looking gentleman.

"One pound is bid," said the auctioneer.

"Thirty shillings," cried Valentine, in an assumed voice of course.

"Thirty shillings; a splendid rose-wood writing desk, secret drawers complete for thirty shillings."

"Two pounds," cried Valentine in a different voice.

"Two pounds bid — *going* for two pounds!"

"Five," said an Israelite.

"Five—two five—for two pounds five"—when as this was the highest legitimate offer, Valentine's voices had it all their own way—"*Going* for two five!"

"Two pounds ten," cried Valentine.

"Two ten—two pounds ten—Any advance on two ten?"

"Three pounds."

"Three bid; three pounds—"

"Ten."

"Thank you—three ten! This elegant writing desk going for three ten."

"Four pounds."

"Four pounds bid; four pound. Any advance on four *pound*."

"Four pounds ten."

"Four ten in two places; four ten. This most valuable writing desk going for four ten."

"Fifteen."

"Four fifteen—four fifteen—*going* for four fifteen!"

"Five pounds."

"Five pounds bid: no advance on five pound?"

"Five pounds ten."

"Five ten—for five ten—going for five pounds ten! I'm sure the value of it cannot be generally known. Any advance on five ten?"

"Six pounds."

"Six pounds—this is really a most valuable desk—six pound—going for only six pound."

"Ten."

"Six ten—six pound—*going* for six ten."

"Seven bid—seven pounds—any advance on seven pounds—*going* for seven!"—and down went the hammer.

The Israelites marvelled exceedingly, and began to reproach themselves for not bidding higher; feeling perfectly certain that in one of the drawers either notes, gold, or diamonds were secreted.

"What name for this writing-desk?" inquired the auctioneer.

"Goodman!" cried Valentine, assuming Goodman's voice, at which Walter and his family started up amazed, and trembled violently as they looked round the room in the full expectation of seeing Goodman himself.

The clerk went to the spot from which the voice appeared to proceed, but no purchaser could be found.

"Who purchased this writing-desk?" demanded the auctioneer; but no answer was returned.

"Putsh te pargain up againsh," cried an Israelitish gentleman, "tatch te fairesht vay ma tear, tatsh te fairesht vay!" and it was put up again, and as the Jews bid higher under the impression that it contained something valuable, Valentine easily ran it up again to seven pounds, when the auctioneer, whose sight was not sufficiently strong to enable him to see who had bid, stopped to inquire the name of the bidder, "Who bid seven pounds?" said he.

"Goodman!" cried Valentine.

"Cootmansh againsh!" cried a Jew, "Arl for Cootmansh!"

The clerk looked again for the purchaser, while the violence with which Walter and his family trembled had the effect of confirming the suspicion of foul play which Valentine had so deeply inspired. Had they murdered poor Goodman, thought he, they could not be more alarmed at the sound of his voice; and the idea of their having murdered him absolutely seemed to be under the circumstances extremely reasonable.

"This is very extraordinary," observed the auctioneer, when he found that no purchaser came forward. "If there be any persons here who have come with the view of creating confusion they had better leave before they are turned out!—our time cannot be wasted in this way. Put the desk aside;" he added, addressing the porter, "and let's have the next lot. The next lot, gentlemen, is an elegant silver gilt tea service, milk jug, and finely-chased basin, complete. What shall we say for this elegant service?"

From thirty shillings the Jews ran it up to four pounds, and from four pounds Valentine ran it up to ten, when of course, on its being knocked down, no purchaser was discoverable.

"What's the meaning of this?" demanded the auctioneer, indignantly. "Who is the purchaser of this lot?"

"GOODMAN!" cried Valentine, and Mrs. Walter uttered a loud shriek and fainted.

"Cot plesh ma hart! Cootmansh?—veresh Cootmansh? Nothing put Cootmansh!" and the whole of the Israelites looked round amazed as Mrs. Walter was borne insensible from the room.

Under any other circumstances Valentine would have rushed to her assistance, but the impression that she must have been a party to the execution of some dark design upon Goodman caused him to regard whatever pain he might have inflicted as a measure of retributive justice. Indeed, so perfectly convinced did he feel that the absence of Goodman had been induced with a view to the promotion of some villanous object, that he absolutely saw with delight Walter struggling with those feelings which his conscience had created.

"This is very extraordinary," observed the auctioneer. "If this course be pursued, it will be utterly impossible to go on with the sale."

"Veresh Cootmansh!" cried a Jew. "Vat ish he? Letsh know vat he ish, ma tear!—tatsh te propersh vay ma tear to shettle arl tish."

"Will Mr. Goodman step forward?" said the auctioneer; and at that moment Walter being unable to stand, fell into the arms of Horace, who, with the assistance of a broker, carried him into an adjoining room.

"Te shentilmansh fainted arl avay," cried an Israelite. "Vatsh to pe tun wit tish lotsh?"

"Put it aside," said the bewildered auctioneer. "The next is a pier glass with richly carved frame. What shall we say for this lot?"

The Jews bid with their accustomod liberality, and then Valentine commenced, and when the thing had been knocked down for five times its value, the name of the purchaser was called for again, and the reply was again, "*Goodman.*"

"Shtill Cootmansh!—arl Cootmansh!—he'll puy ush arl upsh," cried a Jew, whose bright sally was received with a loud burst of Israelitish merriment.

"It's of no use going on thus," said the auctioneer, warmly. "I must ascertain the meaning of this," and he bounced out of his pulpit and proceeded to the room into which the trembling, conscience-stricken Walter had been carried. During the whole of the time he was there, the Jews were laughing and joking with infinite glee. One of them, seizing the greasy hat of another, called out, "Mishter Cootmansh ma tear!—vill you pid for tish lotsh?" This produced another loud burst of laughter which lasted till the auctioneer returned.

"Well, gentlemen, let us proceed;" said he, on remounting his pulpit, and the next lot was brought by the porter and put up, and bid for with precisely the same result, when the auctioneer really began to exhibit strong symptoms of pent-up rage.

At length Valentine cried in a loud commanding voice, which apparently proceeded from the other end of the room. "Who authorised this sale?"

"Mr. Goodman," replied the Auctioneer.

"Cootmansh againsh! Vell, shtrike ma!" exclaimed all the tribe, in a breath.

"He has no authority," cried Valentine. "The goods are not his."

"Vell vatsh tat mattersh ma tear?" said several of the Israelites looking towards the spot from which the voice had apparently proceeded. "Te shentelmansh reshponshible ve sphosh if he shtole 'em!"

"Will that gentleman accompany me into the other room?" said the auctioneer, who was really a respectable man, and who had inferred from the highly excited state of Walter's feelings that something was wrong. "Will he be kind enough to follow me?" he added, going again towards the room in which Walter was still trembling.

No one followed, but in he went, and the Jews became more and more lively. They still called for Goodman to bid for the various articles which they held in their hands. "Vill you puy ma stockingsh, Mishter Cootmansh?" cried one of them. "Vat vill you pid for ma shirtsh?" cried another. "Heresh a coot pair of beautiful pootsh," cried a third, as he forced the legs of his neighbor upon the table, and displayed a pair of bluchers *rather* dropsical and airy, while a fourth cried, "Shelp ma! I'll shell ma own shelf to Mishter Cootmansh!"

The auctioneer returned, and having mounted his desk, said, "Gentlemen, I'm sorry to inform you that this sale cannot proceed." This announcement was met with a burst of much Israelitish murmuring. "I am sorry," he continued, "as sorry as any of you can be, but I will not be a party to any thing wrong.—(Cries of.

"Vy notsh? You're intemnified, I shposh?")—No indemnity, gentlemen, will do for me, unless I am satisfied that all is correct." An observation which was treated with marked contempt by the Israelites generally. "I, therefore, gentlemen, will not detain you any longer, and can only express my sorrow that I have taken up so much of your valuable time."

The countenances of the tribe at this moment developed much dark indignation, and by degrees their murmurings swelled into a loud Jewish yell, which seemed to threaten extensive destruction. The fact of its being suspected that all was not right, appeared to possess the sharpest sting, for they looked at the loss of what they thereby might have gained. In vain the auctioneer endeavored to calm them. They would not be pacified. "I'll preak arl te cootsh in te plash!" cried one. "Vatsh you mean by making foolsh of us?" shouted another. "Vy don't you go on wit te sale?" cried a third; and the auctioneer perceiving their rage likely to increase, left the room, followed by the indignant sons of Israel, who hooted, yelled, and pushed him about, until he had locked himself securely in an office below, when Valentine, who had then no desire to see Walter, or any part of his family, quitted the place with the angry Jewish stream.

CHAPTER XVII.

VALENTINE VISITS GUILDHALL—BECOMES ACQUAINTED WITH THOSE ANCIENT AND RESPECTABLE WARRIORS, GOG AND MAGOG, TO WHOM HE IMPARTS SPEECH PRO TEM., AND THEN PROCEEDS TO DISCUSS MATTERS OF PERSONAL IMPORTANCE WITH THE ELOQUENT MEMBERS OF THE COURT OF COMMON COUNCIL.

WHAT a thimble-rig is human life!—the thimbles being the emblems of fate: the peas the types of its slippery chances. How mortals gamble at this rig even from the cradle to the grave! They fix intently on a pea and see it covered; they watch its windings, firmly convinced of its being there, or there; they back that firm conviction with a stake; and when they lose they lavish curses on their adverse stars; but should they win, how pleasantly they swindle themselves into the belief of the fact being attributable solely to their own most extraordinary acuteness!—they cannot tolerate the slightest reference to the power by which the thimbles move—that power which holds the pea at pleasure to place it where it will. A moment's reflection will enable all well-disposed persons to perceive that this juggle, which has been so vehemently denounced, really comprehends all human actions, and that its invention—if an invention it may be called—instead of being dated from Alfred the Great, may be traced clearly back, without any mistake, to "the good old days of Adam and Eve."

Now in this most remarkable "rig" Valentine began to take an extremely active part. He congratulated himself very naturally upon the skill with which he found out the Furniture pea; but there yet was a pea which he had to discover, and that pea was Goodman. His energies were therefore directed to the task of ascertaining under what earthly thimble poor Goodman could be found.

Bent upon this subject, he on the morning after the day of the intended sale by auction, started for the city for the purpose of consulting with Mr. St. Ledger, the merchant upon whom Goodman had called on his way to the steam-packet wharf. The Royal Exchange clock, as he passed, struck twelve, and the chimes were playing merrily the favorite tune of "See the conquering hero comes!" as he entered the office of Mr. St. Ledger, and found that gentleman not only at home, but disengaged.

"I have called," observed Valentine, after the usual brief ceremonies had been performed, "to solicit your advice in a matter which to me appears very extraordinary."

"Well, my young friend, what is it?" inquired Mr. St. Ledger. "You may command my best judgment; but why not solicit the advice of friend Goodman?"

"It is precisely because I cannot find him," returned Valentine.

"What! have you not seen him since you called upon me before?—did you not find him at home?"

"He has not been at home since; and I therefore wish to know by what means I can ascertain where he is to be found."

"Upon my word I can't guess. Have you been to his brother?"

"I have; and he says that in consequence of some unsuccessful speculation he is at present compelled to keep out of the way."

"Indeed!" exclaimed Mr. St. Ledger, as

he pulled down a thick heavy book, and referred to a certain page with some apparent anxiety. "It's very, very singular," he continued, having closed the book with an air of satisfaction, that *I* should have known nothing about it. Speculation!—Oh! Spanish of course. Very foolish! I could have told him all about it; but if men will act without advice in matters of this kind, they must of course take the consequences. Don't, however, disturb yourself about it. It will all come round right by and bye, I dare say. Foolish man!—foolish man!"

"But is it not very extraordinary that —"

"God bless my life, not at all! I know fifty in the same predicament, and in another week—mark my words—we shall hear of fifty more. I know it; I'm sure of it; I'd stake my existence upon it. I saw how it was going from the first."

"But the whole of his furniture —"

"My dear young friend," interrupted Mr. St. Ledger, "when you are older you'll know more;" and having made this remarkable observation, he placed his hand firmly upon Valentine's shoulder, and in a lower tone added, "Don't say a single syllable about it to any soul. You may injure his credit materially. He may be involved in other matters, you know, and if he be, men will pounce upon him like tigers as they invariably do, when there happens to be anything like a screw a little loose."

"But I fancied that he was a man of some considerable property."

"And so he is; but men don't let their property sleep. Few men are able to pay all demands at an hour's notice. You have heard of a run upon the Bank?—Same thing —same thing. Foolish man! He'd no business to do anything of the sort; but make no stir, no noise, no inquiries; not a word on the subject to any single soul if you dont't wish to injure his credit."

Valentine had certainly no wish to do that, and as he found that he could get nothing more from Mr. St. Ledger, who treated the whole thing as a business-like matter of course, he left the office considerably relieved; albeit when he reflected upon the extraordinary conduct of Walter in the sale-room as he imitated Goodman's voice, he still felt that there was something at the bottom of the affair which had not entered into Mr. St. Ledger's purely commercial calculations. He therefore resolved to keep an eye upon the family, and just as he had made up his mind to be silent for a time, he crossed a well-built business-like street, at the bottom of which stood an old-fashioned edifice, whose front was adorned with a couple of rampant and highly respectable looking griffins which seemed to be grinning with remarkable energy at an overgrown cauliflower cap which stood between them, and digging their claws into a poor devoted heart which already contained a dagger, and which, with the griffins, surmounted the motto of "*Domine Dirige Nos.*"

As the gates of this remarkable edifice stood open, and as persons were walking in and out with great freedom of step, he at once passed the portal, and introduced himself into a fair-sized hall with a flag-stone floor, two apologies for galleries, four groups of sculpture upon rather lofty pedestals, and a queerly stained window at each end. As Valentine entered, the place seemed to wear a vacant hungry aspect, but on turning to the western extremity, he perceived a rather interesting couple of full-blown gentlemen on guard, and concluded, that if they had been trained in that hall, it was clearly no place for the genius of starvation. As these two gigantic gentlemen seemed to form the chief attraction, Valentine approached them with a view to a more minute survey. The first that he examined sported a pair of white trousers, which he had outgrown considerably, and he stood in his shirt sleeves quite ready for action. His breast was adorned with a broad crimson scarf, and in his right hand he held a long pole, from the top of which hung a ball studded with interesting spikes, invented obviously to puzzle the brains of all with whom they might come in immediate contact. This personage looked down very mournfully, albeit his countenance was very much flushed, and his brows were adorned with a painted wooden circlet, which conveyed to the imaginative the idea of a wreath of laurels. The other was a bolder looking fellow altogether, but even he looked as if he had not for some time been quite comfortable in his mind. He wore a green tunic, held a shield in one hand, and a spear in the other, while his sword belt and sandals were so painted, as to impart a correct notion of sapphires, rubies, and pearls.

Just as Valentine had concluded his survey of these warriors, two pale thin diminutive individuals approached. They were Spitalfields weavers, and had been conducted to that quarter of the world to receive a magisterial admonition for hunting an old cow, which, by an extraordinary stretch of the caoutchouc imagination, they had conceived to be a raving mad bull.

"Sen I may live, Bill! · My hi, vot a vunner!" exclaimed one of these interesting young gentlemen. "Jist on'y twig his shanks! Vy it'd take seven yards and a arf o' thrums on'y to make that 'ere cove a pair o' garters!"

"Vich is Gog and vich is Magog?" inquired his companion, who was an emblem of simplicity in his way.

"Vy him in the smalls to be sure!" replied the other, "an they both on em cuts avay to dinner ven they 'ears that 'ere clock strike vun."

"Vorker!" observed his companion, as with a knowing wink he pointed to his left shoulder. "Tell that to the moreens."

"Vel on'y jist vait till they 'ears it, an' then you'll be conwinced," said the other with a chuckle. "Them 'ere's the on'y two vich Jack the Giant-killer couldn't vop"—an observation which induced his companion to gaze upon the long-bearded giant with mingled admiration and amazement.

"*Well!* exclaimed Valentine, imparting a deeply indignant tone to the great Gog; "What are you staring at—*eh?*"

The greener individual grasped the arm of his guide, and as *he* was at the moment in the act of shrinking back himself, the additional impetus knocked him fairly down, and his friend fell heavily upon him.

"Away!" cried Gog, through the immediate instrumentality of Valentine. "How dare you insult my friend!" exclaimed Magog, through precisely the same medium; "Retreat!" and the two little terror-stricken weavers scrambled up with all imaginable alacrity, and rushed towards the portal. The moment they had reached it, a personage, evidently high in office, enveloped in a robe trimmed tastily with fur and embellished with an immense gold chain, preceded by a military individual, with a Marshal's hat in one hand and a staff in the other; and a graver looking person, who carried a remarkably long sword, happened to be proceeding, with unequivocal solemnity, into the hall, from the gaily emblazoned carriage, from which he had just alighted. Against those who composed this truly dignified procession, the little weavers ran, most certainly without premeditation, and almost unconsciously, but with so much force, that in an instant the personage, adorned with the chain, was on the ground, with the two little weavers struggling desperately upon him. The grave bearer of the long sword, and the military-looking individual, at once dropped their dignity and rushed to his assistance, while several minor officials tried to secure the little weavers, who managed, however, to bob through their hands like a couple of small silver eels, and succeeded eventually in darting right away.

The affectionate concern manifested by those around towards the personage who had been so unceremoniously placed in a horizontal position was excessive. Their apprehensions for the safety of his person as a whole, and for the perfect integrity of each particular limb, were unspeakable. They could not by any process make up their minds to believe, that he was unhurt: they were perfectly certain that he had been in the receipt of some serious injury; and it was not until he had earnestly reiterated his assurance that all was quite right, that the procession moved slowly and solemnly across the hall, and then up a flight of steps into a long narrow passage.

"To what place does that lead?" inquired Valentine, of a person who was standing very thoughtfully with his thumbs stuck firmly in the arm-holes of his waistcoat.

"Which? That? Oh, to all sorts of offices, and rooms, and courts, and places," replied that thoughtful person.

"Indeed!" observed Valentine, gratefully acknowledging the extremely explicit character of the information; "Is there any thing of importance going forward?"

"Why, I s'pose," said the communicative creature, "they're agoing for to hold a Court of Alderman perhaps, I shouldn't wonder, or something of that sort no doubt, but I don't exactly know;" and he walked towards the statue of the great Lord Chatham.

In Valentine's mind the idea of an alderman was associated with all that is fat. Steaming spectres of barons of beef, venison, turtle, ox-tail, and mulligatawny flitted vividly across his imagination the very moment he heard the sound of the name. He expected to see them all with glorious countenances, adorned, of course, with rich purple pimples, and noses resembling fine bunches of grapes, without double chins, immense backs, and bellies immeasurable, extending, in fact, so far forward as to render it impossible for any one of them to catch even a glimpse of his toes, which, as a natural matter of course, he conceived must be gouty. He had, from his earliest infancy, been led to believe, by every print which had even the smallest pretensions to a faithful portrayal of aldermanic characteristics, that no kind of men could in reality be aldermen, unless they were beefy-faced, broad individuals, whose most capacious paunches imparted to them the power of gorging, and stowing away quantities of matter altogether unexampled. He, therefore, at once made up his mind to see twenty-four natural curiosities, exclusive of the Lord Mayor, whom, of course, he imagined to be the fattest and the jolliest of the lot, and hence proceeded up the passage, placed a coin into the open hand of a person in a blue stuff gown, and requested to be shown at once into the Court.

"It ain't a Court of Aldermen to-day," said that person.

"Well, what is it then?"

"It's a Court of Common Council."

"Indeed! who presides?"

"Vy, the Lord Mayor in course!"

"Oh, that will do," said Valentine, and into the chamber he went; but as he saw a small thin-faced personage in the chair—the very personage, in fact, whom he had seen knocked down by the little weavers—he felt perfectly sure that there must be some mistake! He, therefore, came out at once, and addressing the individual in the gown, said, "I wanted to go into the *other* court!"

"Vot other court?"

"Why, the Court of Common Council!"

"Vell! that is the Court of Common Council!"

"Indeed," observed Valentine, with an expression of incredulity; "when will the Lord Mayor arrive?"

"The Lord Mayor *has* arrived! That's him in the cheer."

Valentine looked at the fellow as if he meant to pin him to the wall. "Do you mean to tell me," said he, "that that little man is the real Lord Mayor?"

"In course he's the real un, *and* nothink else," replied the man. "Don't you see his goold chain, and the sword of jistice afore him?"

"Well," thought Valentine, "this is extraordinary." "Has he been ill?" he inquired.

"Hill? no; vot made you think of that 'ere?"

"Simply because he seems to be wasted almost wholly away."

"Oh, he never was bigger," replied the man. "He was always the same size since I know'd him, and a good size too."

Valentine again felt amazed. "Is it possible," thought he, "that a person so small can be the Lord Mayor of London! Why, he is only the ghost of a Lord Mayor!—the mere skeleton of one! If the whole of the aldermen at the present day are any thing *like* the same size, what a strangely degenerate race they must be!"

With such reflections as these he re-entered the court, which was really an unique and a well-arranged place, not certainly quite so large, but far more elegantly fitted up than the present House of Commons.—At the extremity sat the president, who, in spite of the unjustifiable incredulity of Valentine was the real Lord Mayor, while on either side of the chamber, compact rows of civic senators were arranged on remarkably well-stuffed benches, and they all looked extremely nice and comfortable, except when they ventured to rise. Valentine could not help smiling at the change which the mere act of rising induced in the countenances of the honorable members generally. When sitting they appeared to be perfectly at ease, confidence glowed upon their cheeks, and they looked as fierce as Bengal tigers whenever the development of fierceness was deemed essential to the safe conveyance of an idea of opposition to any sentiment advanced; but when they rose they became as pale as spectres crossed in love, and each trembled with more energy than a Neapolitan greyhound with a cold. There were, however, two or three honorable exceptions who laid about them, right and left, with extraordinary force and effect, as men who are great among little ones will, more especially when the whole of our glorious institutions are about to crumble into sanguinary dust, and revolution stares us full in the face without moving a muscle.

Valentine had no desire to interrupt business. He, therefore, waited with patience until all the important questions of the day had been duly considered, when he felt that he might as well enliven the honorable members, of whom the majority—as was indeed under the circumstances extremely natural—manifested a strong inclination to sleep.

Accordingly, as a prosy individual was proceeding to explain how essential to the security of the city's health it was that a certain Augean stable, which formed a short arm of the Thames, should be purified; Valentine ventured to cry, "enough!" making his voice proceed apparently from the other end of the court.

"My Lord Mayor," said the honorable member, who was then on his legs; "it may, my Lord Mayor, be 'enough' for the honorable members opposite. Every thing in nature is 'enough' for them. They would have things remain as they are.—They would have, my Lord Mayor, they would have every thing stagnant. They would have, not a huge heap of physical filth alone, but one chaotic *mass* of moral muck, that nature might wallow in reeking corruption. They would have, my Lord Mayor, the city covered with intellectual chickweed, spreading its contagious influence from Temple Bar to Aldgate pump!"—a highly poetical observation, which was loudly cheered by the honorable members on the eloquent gentleman's side, of whom several cried *sotto voce*, "Walk into him!—give it him home!—sarve him out!"—

"They would have," continued the speaker, "they would have, my Lord Mayor—"

"Sit down!" cried Valentine.

"Oh! of course! doubtless;" resumed the interrupted individual, in a highly sarcastic tone. "They would like me, my Lord Mayor, to—"

"Stick to the question!" cried Valentine.

"The question," observed the speaker, "is the very thing to which I do stick? It is solely in consequence of my sticking to the question that makes me—"

"An idiot!" cried Valentine. "Down! Don't expose yourself."

"Order! order! order!" shouted several honorable members; while several others chuckled at the prospect of a somewhat lively scene.

"Will the honorable member who was pleased to make that observation stand forth like a man?" cried the eloqnent speaker very loudly, and with no inconsiderable wrath.

Valentine inquired the name of an honorable member who happened to be asleep in one corner of the court, and having ascertained his name to be Snobson, proceeded, in various voices, to call upon Mr. Snobson for a prompt and unconditional apology. The name of Snobson was loudly reiterated by honorable members, who felt sure that Snobson was the man, and that he was then feigning asleep for the sole purpose of avoiding detection.

At length the calls for Snobson became so loud, that that gentleman awoke, and after rubbing his eyes with some considerable energy, begged naturally enough to know why he was called upon, seeing that he had no motion whatever to bring before the court. His innocence, however, was felt to be assumed, and it was held that such an assumption ought not to protect him. They therefore called still more energetically, "Snobson! Snobson!" accompanying that call, with the demand for a most ample apology.

Mr. Snobson felt confused. He was a stout stumpy person, but still he felt confused. He looked pale and red alternately for some few minutes, when his complexion settled down into a yellowish blue; and as the demand for an apology was reiterated with increased zeal, he at length said, with all due solemnity and point:—"My Lord Mayor, I can't say as I exactly understand the true natur of this 'ere business; but all I've got to say is, that all I can say is this 'ere, wiz: that if I've done any body any how wrong, I am willing in course to make it right; for there's no indiwidual in this 'ere court more readier to apologise for the same."

"Apology! apology!" shouted several honorable members.

"Vot for? Vot have I done? Tell me that?" cried Mr. Snobson, who really began to get warm upon the subject.

"If the honorable member," observed the Mayor, with much precision and dignity, "made use of the expressions attributed to the honorable member, I am sure that the honorable member will perceive the necessity which exists for its immediate withdrawal."

Here the demand for an apology were loudly reiterated by those who were anxious to fix upon some one, it mattered not whom a single straw, so long as he happened to be a political opponent, for party feeling at that period ran high, and as every question brought before the court was made a pnrely party question, that which had immediate reference to Mr. Snobson was regarded as an exception by no means.

"My Lord Mayor," said the honorable accused calmly, after a pause, during which he had been looking about him as if he had lost some dear friend. "Ven I know the percise natur of the acquisation, I'll perceed for to rebut the same, *and* not afore."

"It wont do, Master Snobson! it wont *do*, my boy!" cried Valentine in a sonorous wobbling voice, whose tones singularly enough resembled those of an honorable member who appeared to be deriving much amusement from the manifest confusion of the accused.

The Lord Mayor, as soon as he had recovered from the state of amazement into which he had been thrown by the anti-senatorial style of that wobbling address to Mr. Snobson, rose steadily and solemnly, and looking with due severity of aspect full in the face of the honorable member whose voice had been so unjustifiably assumed, said:—"I really am sory to be compelled to make any remark touching the conduct of any honorable member, but I have a great public duty to perform, which duty I certainly should not perform, were I not to say that honorable members should remember that they are *where they are!*"

The tail of this stinging rebuke was so pointed, that it appeared to pierce the soul of the honorable member for whom the whole of its poignancy was designed, for he instantly rose, and placing his hand with much solemnity upon his heart, said:—"My Lord Mayor. Hif it be imagined it was me, it's a hutter mishapprehension, 'cause it wasn't!"

"Why you know that it was!" shouted Valentine, throwing his voice just behind the honorable member, who on the instant turned round with the velocity of a whipping-top, and scrutinized the countenance of every member in his vicinity, with the view of ascertaining who had uttered those words!

"Really," said the Mayor, "these proceedings are most irregular;" and the justice of that observation was duly appreciated by all, save Valentine, who, with the most reprehensible temerity, exclaimed, "Mind your own business!" and that to the Lord Mayor!

"Mind my own business!" cried his Lordship, utterly shocked at the monstrous character of that injunction. "Mind my own business!" he repeated in a still more intensely solemn tone; and he looked round amazed, and held his breath to give his bosom an opportunity of swelling with indignation, and then turned to the Recorder, and said, "Did you ever?" to which the Recorder replied, "No, I never."

"Shame! Shame!" shouted several honorable members the very moment they had recovered the power to shout.

"Mind my own business!" cried his lordship for the third time, and Valentinr, regardless of the official dignity of the first magistrate of the first city in the world, absolutely cried again, "Yes! mind your own business!"

A thrill of horror ran clean through the court. Every member appeared to be paralysed. However cold-blooded, however atrocious, however unequivocally vile that observation might have struck them as being, it was one to which they were unable to conceive a sufficient answer. Several of them made desperate efforts to rise, with the view of protesting against and denouncing its spirit, but every faculty, physical as well as moral, appeared to have forsaken them, and death-like silence for some time prevailed.

At length his lordship, reccollecting what was due to himself as a Mayor and as a man, broke the spell which had bound him, and said "I demand an explanation!"

"An explanation?" said Valentine.

"Aye! an explanation!" cried his lordship with great magnanimity. "I have been told by some honorable member to mind my own business. I am, I beg to say, I am minding my own business. I beg the honorable member to understand that it *is* my own business; and I beg to inform him farther, that so long as I have the honor to occupy this chair, the respect which is due to the office I have the honor to hold shall be *enforced.*"

At this moment Valentine had the audacity to make three distinct bursts of laughter apparently proceed from three different quarters.

"I wish," continued his lordship, tugging desperately at his official habiliments; "I wish honorable members distinctly to understand that I am not to be insulted. The dignity—"

"Dignity!" interrupted Valentine, in a tone of bitter mockery, which, under any circumstances, would have been extremely culpable. "Dignity!"

"I repeat it!" cried his lordship with considerable warmth. "The *dignity* of the office to which I have been elected shall descend from me untarnished!"

Before the cheering which this majestic observation elicited had completely died away, an honorable member, whose portly person and crimson face met Valentine's views of what an alderman *ought* to be, rose for the purpose of moving a direct vote of censure; but no sooner had he explained the object for which he had risen, than Valentine shouted, "Upon whom?" and in a moment there were loud cries of "Name! name! name!" which seemed to puzzle the honorable member exceedingly. "I am not," said he at length, after having held a conference with those around him, "in possession of the honorable member's name, but probably some other honorable member will inform me."

Valentine had unfortunately heard but one honorable member's name mentioned, and therefore had no hesitation in calling out "Snobson!"

"No, no!" cried that honorable member, starting up and appealing energetically to many other honorable members who bore instant testimony to the fact of his being innocent.

"As far as I am personally concerned," observed his lordship, who had been struggling to regain his apparent equanimity, "I should take no farther notice of the insulting expression, but, I feel it to be my duty as chief magistrate."

"You a chief magistrate!" cried Valentine, who had really a great contempt for the size of his lordship, albeit he held the office in very high respect. "You are joking!"

"Joking!" cried his lordship with an expression of horror.

"Do you think that you are fit now to be a chief magistaate?" said Valentine, "Why you don't weigh above nine stone two!"

An honorable member knitting his brows and looking remarkably fierce, rose to move that the offensive expressions be taken down; and "Mind your own business."—"You a chief magistrate!"—"Do you think that you are fit now to be a chief magistrate?"—and "Why, you don't weigh above nine stone two"—were taken down accordingly.

"Now," said the honorable gentleman, "I will not, my Lord Mayor, look for precedents with the view of ascertaining how to act in this case, for as conduct like that which we have witnessed is altogether unprecedented, no precedent for such conduct can be found; but I mean to say this, my Lord Mayor, that nothing more utterly disgraceful, more desperately atrocious, more palpably irregular, or more altogether out of the way, ever occurred in this or any other court, either in this or in any other country, laying claim to the highest point in the scale of civilisation; and all I can say, my Lord Mayor, is this, that such conduct reflects the very lowest aud most abominable pitch of shame upon the honorable member—I care not who he is—for he has not the common manliness to avow like a man the detestable atterance of language on the one hand so monstrously vile, my Lord Mayor, and so rash and extremely leatherheaded on the other!"

This burst of indignant eloquence was hailed with loud cheers, and as the general impression was that the offending party never could stand such a broadside as that, honorable members looked round with considerable anxiety for the rising of the delinquent. For several seconds the suspense was profound, when, as the offender by no means came forth, due contempt was inspired for the character of such a man, and an alderman rose with the most perfect self-possession for the purpose of expressing his sentiments on the subject.

It was evident at a glance, that this worthy individual was one of the most brilliant of the sparkling wits with which civic society is so abundantly studded. He appeared to be perfectly at home. and after smiling a most interesting, if not a most fascinating smile, observed:—"Really this appears to be a very queer business; but that branch of the business which seems the most queer, is that which refers to your lordship's weight. The honorable member complains that your lordship don't weigh more than nine stone two, and his estimate appears to be, as far as it goes, as nearly correct as possible; but he contends that your lordship is not a fit and proper person to be a chief magistrate, *because* you don't weigh more than nine stone two! Why what in the name of all that's rational would he have a chief magistrate weigh? Would he like to have every Lord Mayor a huge mountain of flesh—a human porpoise? Would he have him elected by weight with the standard fixed at twenty or five-and-twenty stone?"

"He ought certainly to have a little flesh upon his bones," cried Valentine, throwing his voice behind the speaker.

"Flesh!" cried the worthy and eloquent alderman, wheeling sharply round, "A little flesh! Upon my word this is very extraordinary. An error has been engendered in the minds of the ignorant—an error which has descended in fact, from generation to generation with the most hereditary regularity, until it has partaken of the character of an heir loom—that aldermen possess all the external characteristics of gluttons in consequence of their assumed unconquerable inclination to feed to satiety, when, in point of fact, aldermen, instead of being gorgers, and crammers, and stowers away of immense masses of food, are decidedly the most abstemious body of men in existence. I know—nay, we all know, that aldermen, like bishops, are, to please the morbid taste of the vulgar, represented as persons with red bloated cheeks, mulberry noses, and immense corporations, although the great majority of them are extremely narrow-bellied, with no more inclination to obesity than drummers; but when I hear an honorable member of this court, who must know all the aldermen personally, contend that a man is unfit to fill the office of chief magistrate because he don't weigh above nine stone two, I must say, that in the annals of *queer* affairs, a queerer don't stand upon record."

This novel and eloquent speech did not appear to give general satisfaction. It is true, the worthy aldermen present—of whom there were several—held their savory breath, and tried desperately to make their abdominal drums look genteel, and endeavored—with a virtuous view doubtless—to swallow the belief that they really were very abstemious men; but the commoners, who had been in the habit of looking forward with delight to the grand periodical feasts, keenly felt that if such an inhospitable, hungry idea as that of abstemiousness being held to be one of the civic virtues, were to obtain, the glowing members of the corporation would be frozen into whole-hog tee-totallers, and the Mansion-house itself would be metamorphosed, eventually, into a shivering temperance den. That so revolting a state of things ought by no means to be promoted, they were perfectly and naturally convinced: they, therefore, felt it incumbent upon them as citizens, to repudiate the notion with sovereign contempt, and, as Valentine perceived the expression of this feeling to be almost universal, he raised a loud laugh at the conclusion of the worthy alderman's oration, which was promptly responded to in tones of bitter irony.

"It's hall werry well for the court to be merry," said an honorable member, when the laughter had subsided; "but touching the hinsult! vot about that?—the indignity showered upon the cheer!—that's vot I mean for to contend should be noticed."

"Vot a hanimal!" said Valentine, "exasperating the *h*, and contemning the correct pernounciation of the wowell."

"Such language," cried his lordship indignantly, "cannot be tolerated."

"Why don't you then make him speak better?" cried Valentine, which was certainly, under the circumstances, extremely reprehensible.

"Order!" exclaimed the Lord Mayor, "I will not sit here to be thus insulted!"

"Shame! shame!" shouted several honorable members simultaneously, while his lordship conferred with the recorder.

"It's perfectly disgraceful!" cried several others, but the majority were smiling as if they enjoyed it.

"I do not," said his lordship, having taken the opinion of his legal adviser, "by any means envy the feelings of those honorable members whose conduct this day has been so highly discreditable, but I do hope and trust that they will reflect upon the course they have adopted, and as I find it impossible to recall due attention to business, I have only to add, that this court is adjourned."

His lordship then rose, and as the honorable members were forming themselves into groups, with the view of expressing their private opinions on the subject, Valentine left them to revel in conjecture, and quietly quitted Guildhall.

CHAPTER XVIII.

SHOWS WHAT A CONSCIENCE GOODMAN'S BROTHER HAD.

It has been said that some men have no conscience; but if such men there be, they must be dead men; and as dead men have been said to be no men at all, the two positions form a problem, of which the solution is not easy. It seems plain enough—yet who knows?—that a man without a conscience must be be without a soul; and were the existence of such an animal recorded in natural history, the thing would be at once as clear as crystal; but as we have no record of any such thing, the fair inference is, that the first grand position has yet to be established. Be this, however, just as it may, it is perfectly certain that Walter had a conscience; and one, too, which belonged emphatically to the working class of consciences—a conscience which delighted in the cultivation of moral thorns, which pricked and stung him day and night with much point and effect. His brother's form was perpetually in his "mind's eye;" his brother's voice as perpetually rang in his imagination's ear: nature's sweet restorer was conquered and kicked about by nature's grim disturber, and a very fine time of it he had upon the whole. Nor were the minds of his amiable family much more at ease; forasmuch as they had no precise knowledge as to the whereabout of Goodman, they were induced by the horrible state of Walter's nerves to apprehend that he had either murdered him, or caused him to be murdered, but dreaded that only in consequence of such an event being calculated to bring down upon him the vengeance of the law.

"It's of no use," observed Mrs. Walter, a few evenings after the furniture had been sold by private contract; "It isn't of the slightest earthly use, you know, attempting to go on in this way. I must have a separate bed. I really cannot sleep with you—I cannot indeed; for you talk, and groan, and sigh, and throw your arms about, and *kick!*—I'm sure my legs are nothing but one mass of bruises; and *as* for the clothes!—if I pull them on once during the night, I have to pull them on at least fifty times. I can't endure it—I really cannot if you go on in this way, and so it don't signify talking!"

"It's very unpleasant!" observed Mrs. Horace, sympathetically.

"Unpleasant, my dear!—it's really dreadful! I wonder, I'm sure, that I don't catch my death. There was only last night—you know how tired I was?—well, I hadn't been asleep five minutes when he turned on his right side, and off they all went!—blankets, sheet, counterpane—every thing in the world; although I pinned them, as I thought securely to the palliasse, and tucked them well in before I got into bed."

"That's just for all the world like my Horace, when he comes home a little bit tipsy."

"Of course!" cried Horace. "What is it I don't do?"

"Why you know you do every thing that's disagreeable, then; you turn about and snore, and—"

"Now you have said it! *I* snore!—come that's good—you won't beat that to-night! I never snore; I'd scorn the action! If I were ever to catch myself at it, I'd get up and cut my own throat. I detest it—I can't snore."

"My goodness, Horace!"

"I never do it, I tell you!—Surely I ought to know!"

"But how can you know when you're asleep!"

"Do you mean to tell me that you'll make me believe that if I were to snore away, and grunt like a jolly old hog in distress, I shouldn't wake myself?"

"Well," said Mrs. Walter, "I don't know, I'm sure, who it was; but when you slept in the next room to us, I know one of you used to make a horrible noise."

"Why, of course!—that was Poll!" observed Horace, "*she's* a regular out-and-out snorter."

"Why, good gracious, Horace!"

"Well, you know that you are! It's of no use denying it. Before I got used to it I couldn't get a wink while you were cutting away in that dreadful state of mind; but, like every thing else, it has become so natural that I look for it, and can't close my eyes till you begin."

"Well, your father never snores," said Mrs. Walter, "I must say that; but he does kick most cruelly."

"Well! some more grog!" growled Walter, whose obsequious manners had been changed into those of a bear, and whose countenance developed a fixed and sullen gloom.

"Don't drink any more, there's a love!" said Mrs. Walter, "you've had five very strong glasses already."

"What if I've had five-and-fifty! I don't care a dump: I want more!"

"Well, it must be a very, very little, and that very weak."

"Here, push it this way!—I'll mix for myself. You scarcely take the rawness off the water." And he did mix, but scarcely took the rawness off the brandy; and having mixed, and swallowed the greater part of the mixture, his muscles appeared to be a little relaxed, and he made a very lamentable effort to sing

"Mynheer Van Dunk, who never got drunk,
Sipped brandy and water gaily;
He quenched his thirst with two quarts of the first,
To a pint of the latter daily,
To a pint of the latter, daily."

"The governor's getting mops and brooms," whispered Horace to his amiable spouse; "he's going it! I shouldn't at all wonder if he opens, by-and-bye, like a porcupine. I say," he continued, addressing his venerable father, "won't you have a cheroot? Here's an out-and-outer here!" and he picked out the blackest and strongest he could find, which Walter took, and began to smoke desperately.

"Try him now," whispered the senior Mrs. Goodman.

"Well, how do you like it?"

"Not at all: it's particularly nasty," replied Walter, "but any thing to drive the blue devils away.

'Begone dull care! I pr'ythee begone from me!'

I say, old girl! let's have a bowl of punch!

'If any pain or care remain,
Let's drown it in a bo—o—owl.'

Who cares? who cares, eh? Give us a kiss, old girl! Why don't you sing? Come, let's have a song all round!"

"The thing was well managed," said Horace, "after all, eh?—wasn't it?"

"No! not at all! it wasn't well managed! —he saw me;—it wasn't well managed!"

"I wonder how he liked it."

"Ask him!" cried Walter, directing his eyes to a vacant part of the room. "There! ask him!—there he is!"

"Where?" shouted Horace, as he, his wife, and mother turned to the spot to which Walter still pointed.

"Why, there! Are you blind?—He has been standing up there for the last hour!"

"Good gracious! how you frighten me!" exclaimed Mrs. Goodman, "you make my very blood run cold. It's just the way you went on last night. You would have it that he was standing at the foot of the bed."

"And so he was!—but who cares?" and he nodded to the space to which he had pointed, and emptied the glass. "Well, why don't you sing?—Here! mix some grog."

"I say, where have you stowed him?" inquired Horace.

"Don't I tell you he's there!"

"Oh, nonsense! but where did you take him to?"

Walter pushed the candles aside, and having closed one eye to make the other more powerful and steady, looked earnestly at Horace; and said, "Don't ask me any questions, and then you'll not have to tell lies.—Now, where's this brandy-and-water? —The treacherous crew! They'd no right to let him out! They promised they wouldn't, so long as I kept up my payments; yet there he is now!" and he covered his eyes with his hand, and sank back in the chair, in which, yielding to the combined influences of brandy and tobacco, he soon fell asleep.

"He has dropped off," said Horace, "don't wake him. I never before saw him above half so far gone."

"But how strange!" said Mrs. Goodman, "is it not? There is, however, one consolation; I think he hasn't rushed into extremes."

"No! that's pretty certain," said Horace, "I thought he had at first. But where can he have stowed him? That puzzles me above a bit. He couldn't have cocked him into a workhouse; nor could he well have fixed him in prison. It certainly is about the rummest thing I ever heard of."

"Probably," suggested Mrs. Goodman, "he has sent him abroad!"

"Not a bit of it!" cried Horace, "he's somewhere near at hand. Besides, you know, he isn't a fool. He wouldn't be kept there—hush!" he added sharply, for Walter at the moment gave a strong convulsive start.

"That's the way he goes on throughout the night," gently whispered Mrs. Goodman, "hush, listen!—he's dreaming!"

"There are a kind of men so loose of soul,
That in their sleep will mutter their affairs;"

and one of this "kind" was Walter.

"Now do your worst!" cried he, folding his arms with an air of defiance. "Do your worst!—I am safe!—The certificate!—that was the authority.—Well, I know it! what of that?—And so you were!—you were mad!--No! not at all!—Why for your safety!—Look to those who certified.—Not a word!—Do it!—I'm ready to defend myself!--Cool! very cool—Never! don't believe it." Having uttered these sentences, as if in answer to a series of interrogatories, he curled his lip proudly; but in tossing his head, he struck it against the back of the chair with so much force, that he awoke on the instant, and started up, exclaiming, "Oh, you shall pay dearly for that!—that blow shall be your last! Now!"

"Walter!" exclaimed Mrs. Goodman, who, with the assistance of Horace, sustained him. "Walter! awake!"

"Did you not see him strike me?"

"No! no! he is not here."

"How can you tell me that? why there he stands now?—Am I not to believe my own eyes? Have you all turned against me? Curse you all! Why do you hold me?—I'll strangle him!—Why do you hold me?" and he stared again wildly, and pointed to the imaginary form of him whom he had injured. "Let me go!" he continued struggling with additional violence; "Am I to be pinioned here, while he thus triumphs over me?"

"Come, come!" said Horace, "fight it out another time. I'll bet ten to one you can beat him; but let's have a clear stage, you know, and no favor."

"My dear, dear Walter, wake up," said Mrs. Goodman, "it is nothing but a dream. Indeed, indeed, he is not here, love! he is not, indeed!"

"No, he isn't here now; you have let him escape!"

"Of course, he has cut it," said Horace. "Never mind; take it out of him to-morrow. He has got no bottom, you know; he never had. Come, governor, come!" and as Walter had sunk into their arms in a state of exhaustion, they quietly carried him up to bed.

"The murder's out now," said Horace, returning to the parlor. "He has put the old boy into some private madhouse: there can't be two opinions about it. I see it all now."

"Good gracious me, impossible!" exclaimed Mrs. Goodman. "Why, he is not mad!"

"Oh! that makes no sort of odds at all!" rejoined Horace.

"But surely they would not take him in unless he were?"

"Wouldn't they! What does it matter to *them* whether a man's mad or not, so long as he's paid for? I could shove the old governor there to-morrow if I chose; and he could do the same for me. It don't matter a straw who it is. They've only to send for a couple of jolly mad-doctors, the majority of whom are to be bought for half a sovereign, and they'll sign away like rattle-snakes."

"What! without knowing whether the man's insane or not?"

"Without knowing!—what is it to them? They are called in to certify;—they are paid to certify;—they therefore do certify, and pocket the coin."

"You perfectly astonish me!" exclaimed Mrs. Goodman.

"That's good!—Astonish *you!*—Why one-half the world would be astonished to learn how the thing is arranged by these medical snobs."

"But they examine them of course?"

"Not a bit of it! They will occasionally certify without even seeing the 'patient;' and if they do take the trouble to visit him, they question him, and harass him, and put him into a most uncomfortable state of excitement, in order that they may satisfy their beautiful consciences that he is in reality insane."

"But isn't that very wrong?"

"Why it's very convenient. Of course, if we come to the rights of the thing, it is clear that no man should be confined in any one of these dens, until his case had been fully, and publicly investigated. But then, you see, that wouldn't answer! They would never be able to get a sane man out of the way, however rich he might be, if that system were adopted."

"But how do they manage it?" inquired Mrs. Goodman.

"Why, suppose, now, I wanted to lock up the governor. Well, I have only to write to the proprietor of one of these private bastiles to this effect:—

"Sir:—I beg you will send me two blank forms of order and certificate to-morrow morning, together with two stout keepers, for a very violent patient who is dangerous, and whom I desire to commit to your care, and if you will send also two doctors to certify, it will save a deal of trouble, and much oblige."

"Well, at the time appointed, in walk the doctors, who bore the old govenor with a series of out-and-out questions, until they excite him to such a pitch of glory, that he threatens, very naturally, to kick them out of the house; and he no sooner reaches this point of the compass, than they call in a couple of coal-heaving keepers, who clap a strait jacket, or a pair of handcuffs upon him, without any ceremony, and bundle him off, with the certificate signed, to the bastile to which they belong."

"And would you be justified in doing this by law?"

"Law! What should I care about law? Law has little to do with private lunatic asylums. Once in, the poor devils are booked for the whole distance: it must be, indeed, an extraordinary occurrence which enables them ever to get out. There they are, and there they stick, so long as the payments are kept up; and when they die, why what does it matter where or how they are buried? If they are murdered, it's just the same thing: no inquest is held upon the body. The coroner has no power there—not a bit of it—nothing of the sort."

"This really appears to me," said Mrs. Goodman, "to be very dreadful; but of course they are well treated?"

"Oh! of course!" returned Horace ironically; "of course! they have every comfort in life, and all its luxuries. The proprietor is paid for each so much a-year; and of course he don't want to make anything out of them! He is generally a mild, out-and-out nice man—a man whose humanities are conspicuously developed—and he spends all the money he receives, no doubt, in administering to their several necessities, and becomes at once so fond of them, that he never parts with one if he can possibly help it, while the payments continue to be regular: nay, his attachments are so extremely strong, that if one of his patients should die or escape, he regards it as a very, very serious loss indeed."

At this moment the cry of "Murder!" was heard from above, and that cry was succeeded by a heavy crashing fall. Mrs. Goodman gave a shrill scream and fainted; and Horace rushed into the bed-room of Walter, whom he found lying prostrate upon the floor. On being raised, he was perfectly insensible, and it was some considerable time before animation could be restored; and when it was, his delirium continued wild and powerful. Horace, therefore, consented to sit up all night; and having sent his wife and mother to bed, got a bottle of brandy and a box of cheroots, and then dropped into a large easy chair with appropriate resignation.

CHAPTER XIX.

THE WIDOW'S VICTIM.

As Valentine sat in his own room alone the evening on which the conscience of Walter had developed itself to his amiable family, wondering what had become of the card which had been given to him by the father of the lovely creature, whom he rescued from "Old Father Thames," the servant of the widow with whom he lodged knocked gently at the door, and having entered, said, "O, if you ple, sir, missceses compliments, and says she hopes you'll excuse the liberty, but she has a little party to-night, and she will be so happy if you'll join 'em, as she's sure it must be lonesome to be here alone."

"Yonr mistress is very polite," said Valentine, "I'll do myself the pleasure—Oh, have you seen a small glazed card about the room?"

"No, I haven't, sir—least ways, not to my knowledge, but if I should see"—

"I have it!" said Valentine. "My compliments to your mistress; I'll be down in five minutes."

Although it may probably be inferred from Valentine's exclamation, "I have it!" that he had it, he had it not; but simply recollected at the moment that he had left it in the pocket of the steward's striped-jacket, which had been lent to him to go on shore at Gravesend. He knew not the name of the steward, nor did he know the name of the vessel to which he belonged, but then —which was certainly the next best thing— he knew the name of the wharf from which she started. He, therefore, at once made up his mind to go down to that particular wharf the next morning, with a view to the recovery of the card, and proceeded to join his fair landlady's party in the parlor.

Now of all the speculations whose fruits have a tendency to confer immortal honor upon the learned, there is probably not one so directly, so eminently calculated to send a man down to posterity, as that which has reference to the origin of personal names. That there are so many Smiths, may be easily accounted for, seeing that there *are* so many Smiths—namely, white Smiths, black Smiths, silver Smiths, gold Smiths, lock Smiths, coach Smiths, gun Smiths, and so on, whose descendants have assumed the pure name, although clearly the son of the first Mr. Smith should have called himself Smithson; the son of Mr. Smithson, Smithsonson; and the son of Mr. Smithsonson, Smithsonsonson; or, for shortness, Smithsonsonsgrandson. This, however, might have been very fairly objected to, on the ground that such a course, however proper, would, in a few generations, draw the names of the descendants of the original Smith to a somewhat inconvenient length. But how the thousands, nay, the millions of names which are to be met with in civilised society, were originally got hold of by our ancestors respectively, is a question which opens a very wide field for antiquarian research—a field whose cultivation would doubtless confer upon mankind, in the aggregate, benefits incalculable. They who might enter this glorious field might meet with a few proper names of a very queer character; they might, indeed, be for a time, in some slight degree, gloriously puzzled; but there could be no doubt of their eventual success if they boldly and resolutely proceeded upon the just and eternal principle, that every effect must have a cause.

This profound vein of reflection has been opened by the fact that Valentine's landlady possessed the name of Smugman. That she got it from her late lamented husband is manifest, but how did the *original* Smugman obtain it? The solution of this mystery is not, however, absolutely essential to the progress of these adventures, and therefore it may as well at once be observed, that Mrs. Smugman had been languishing in a weary state of widowhood for nearly twelve months, and that, however, ardently she might have loved the name of Smugman at one time, she then had an equally ardent desire to change it. Her husband had been in the navy, and from the Admiralty she received, in consequence, seventy pounds per annum, to which, in conformity with the general practice, she was entitled so long, but only so long, as she remained a widow—a practice whose tendency is far more immoral than the wise men by whom it was established, conceived; for, as the annuitants cannot legally marry without sacrificing their respective annuities, the temptation to marry illegally is sometimes too strong to be resisted by those who do not in reality prize virtue as it ought to be prized, above all other sublunary blessings.

That such considerations, however, entered not into the head of Mrs. Smugman, all are bound to believe, for, independently, of her being strictly virtuous, she had her eye upon two most respectable bachelors—namely, Mr. Foxglove, a quiet bank clerk, and Mr. Crankey, a money-making grocer, the latter of whom she did *rather* prefer, but in consequence solely of his wealth being calculated to cause the match on her part to obtain the direct sanction of prudence.

The gentleman upon whom this preference was bestowed was a sour-looking, porcupine-headed person, whose smiles were so forced, that they gave pain to all who beheld them; yet the widow was conversing with him very affectionately when Valentine entered the room. A variety of greetings and fussy introductions to the ladies and gentlemen, who were engaged in the purely commercial game of speculation, were immediately consequent on his *entrée*, for the fair widow really felt honored by his presence, and scarcely knew how to lionize him enough.

It soon became manifest, however, to Valentine, that Crankey by no means approved of these attentions; that he looked dark and dreadful, and scowled very furiously, both at the widow and at him; and as he subsequently made himself particularly disagreeable, indulging occasionally in certain very pointed insinuations having reference to the impropriety of such attentions to young men in general, Valentine resolved on punishing Mr. Crankey for his bear-like behavior.

"What a sour old crab, to be sure," said he, making his voice apparently proceed from the speculation table. "I can't say I admire the taste of Mrs. Smugman."

"Indeed!" muttered Crankey, knitting his black bushy brows, and looking round the table in question, with the view of ascertaining who it was that had spoken. "My presence," he added, addressing Mrs. Smugman, "doesn't appear to be very agreeable to some of your *friends!*"

"Oh nonsense!" observed Mrs. Smugman. "It's nothing but a silly remark. There's no meaning in it: nonsense!"

"You should not invite persons to meet *me*, Mrs. Smugman, who are capable of making silly remarks with no meaning in them."

The widow bit her lips, but said nothing. Mr. Crankey, however, was by no means disposed to be silent, for he enlarged rather eloquently upon the fact of his not having come there that evening to be insulted.

"Did you ever!" cried Valentine, throwing his voice in the same direction. "The fellow's a bear!"

"Gentlemen," said the widow, approaching the table as a burst of surprise had been induced, by the fact of a lady having turned up the ace after selling the king for fivepence-half-penny, "I really must beg of you not to indulge in unpleasant observations."

The whole of the speculators stared at the widow, with an expression of amazement. "You must remember," continued that lady, "that Mr. Crankey is my friend, as you are all my friends, and I should not like to hear an unpleasant observation applied to any one of you."

"Mr. Crankey, I'm sure, must be mistaken," observed one of the gentlemen at the table, "I have heard no such observation made."

"But I have!" growled Crankey.

"Well, all I can say is that *I* have heard nothing of the sort," returned the gentleman.

"Nor have I," cried the whole of the speculators in a breath, which was literally the fact, for they had all been too busy turning up prematurely and estimating the value of the best card turned in proportion to the wealth of the pool, to pay attention to anything else.

Mr. Crankey was not satisfied; but the speculators were, that Mr. Crankey had been mistaken, and the merry game proceeded.

Valentine had by this time understood the precise terms upon which Mr. Crankey and the widow were, and very naturally felt that the sooner such a match were completely broken off, the better it would be for the lady; and although he clearly recognised the right of that lady to choose and to judge for herself, he resolved that she should become that evening acquainted with Mr. Crankey's disposition, of which she really appeared to be totally ignorant.

"Come," said the widow, after a very awful pause, during which Crankey looked as black as a thunder-cloud just on the point of bursting; "what say you to a rubber?"

"Any thing you like, ma'am," said Crankey, "I am ready for *any thing!*" and he hurled at the speculation table a dark look of defiance.

"Well come, you'll cut in, will you not?" observed the widow, addressing Valentine, whom she honored with one of her sweetest smiles, which appeared to make Crankey's blood boil.

Valentine expressed his willingness to join them, and when they had cut, he had Crankey for a partner, and their opponents were Wrightman and Foxglove, who really were very quiet gentlemanly men.

By the desperate character of his play, it very soon became manifest that Crankey's whole soul was in arms, and he devoted so much attention to the noise which proceeded from the speculation table—applying almost every observation to himself—that in playing the very first hand he revoked. The fact was duly noticed by Mr. Foxglove, who at once enforced the penalty.

"Then you mean to play the *strict* game?" said Crankey, with much earnestness.

"Of course, my dear sir, we play the game!"

"Very well. As you please. It makes no odds to me: not a bit," said Mr. Crankey, shuffling the cards with unequivocal desperation. "Now, sir!—It's my deal."

"Oh, he can't play!" whispered Valentine, throwing his voice behind Mr. Crankey as he dealt. Mr. Crankey looked round, and albeit, he simply said, "*Can't* he!" the consequence was a misdeal.

"Who the devil can deal cards or play, or do any thing with such interruptions as these?" exclaimed Crankey.

"What interruptions?" inquired Mr. Foxglove.

"Why these ungentlemanly observations, these whisperings and titterings while a man is dealing."

"I heard no observations," said Mr. Foxglove.

"But I did, sir!—I am not deaf, sir, if other people are!"

"I told you he couldn't play," cried Valentine, throwing his voice among the speculating people.

Crankey rose and gnashed his teeth with

considerable violence, and grasped the back of his chair with great energy and firmness, and after having taken a comprehensive view of the speculating group, cried, "Indeed! If he can't he'll play *you* any day in the week for what you like. It makes no odds to me; from a crown to ten pound!" and he jingled what money he had in his pocket, with the view of imparting the conviction that he was a man of some considerable pecuniary substance.

The entire party looked at Mr. Crankey with an expression of wonder, but as no one accepted the challenge, he hurled a look of contempt upon the speculators in the aggregate, and eventually resumed his seat.

The game was then continued, but Mr. Crankey was so excited that he was unable to recollect a single card that had been played. His opponents were making almost every trick, and the game looked particularly desperate, when as Wrightman was considering which card he should next lead, Valentine made it appear that Mr. Foxglove softly whispered "diamonds," which happened to be trumps, and accordingly Wrightman conceiving that his partner had a hand which would carry all before it—a diamond was led.

"Oh! that's it, is it?" cried Crankey sarcastically, throwing up his cards. "I knew it was something of that. *I* thought we were playing the game!"

"And so we are," said Mr. Foxglove, "are we not?"

"Do you call intimations, sir, playing the game?"

"What do you mean?" said Mr. Foxglove.

"Why this is what I mean, sir—that you had no right to tell your partner to lead trumps, sir! that's what I mean!"

"*I* tell my partner to lead trumps!—I deny it, sir, flatly deny it," and the denial was so palpably barefaced in the eyes of Mr. Crankey, that he was at the moment too utterly astounded to reply.

"You are making yourself very disagreeable," continued Mr. Foxglove. "I will not descend to argue the point, but in order to prove that I did *not* call for trumps, there are my cards, sir, I have not a *single* trump in my hand," and the cards were duly placed upon the table.

"*I* have all the trumps," said Valentine, exhibiting no less than seven, which would of necessity have carried the game; but that game was of course claimed by Mr. Foxglove, in consequence of Crankey having thrown up his hand.

"You are satisfied, I hope," said Mr. Foxglove. "I *presume* that you are satisfied. Come, if we are to play the game, for Heaven's sake, sir, let us play it pleasantly. I hate to have any dispute."

"And so do I, sir; but if I didn't hear it—"

"You must have been mistaken," interrupted the widow, who began to be really ashamed of his conduct, and to recognise the justice of Mr. Foxglove's observations, very much to the satisfaction of that gentleman.

"I tell you I heard diamonds called, Mrs. Smugman!" cried Crankey, with a look which seemed to chill the widow's blood. "Isn't a man to believe his own ears?"

"Then it must have been mentioned at the speculation table."

"I don't know where it was mentioned, ma'am, nor do I care; I only know it *was* mentioned, and that's enough for me."

"Well," said Valentine, "shall we have another game?"

"Oh, with all my heart!" said Mr. Foxglove.

"We'll see them once more, Mr. Crankey?" said Valentine, and as that gentleman doggedly consented, the cards were again dealt.

Mr. Crankey made the first three tricks, but just as he was about to lead off for the fourth, Valentine throwing his voice immediately behind him, whispered "hearts."

"I'm obliged to you; but I play my own game. I want no advice, no instruction," said Crankey, turning round with a most unamiable scowl, of course expecting to find some gentleman at his elbow, but as he could see no one standing on the right, he twirled round to the left, and as he couldn't find any one near him at all, he led spades in the spirit of opposition. His hand happened to be a good one; and as it enabled him to score seven points, he took a deep sip of brandy and water, with a huge pinch of snuff as an obligato accompaniment, and began in reality to feel a little better.

"I wish to goodness he would go," said Valentine, assuming the voice of a female.

"*Do* you?" cried Crankey, inspiring at that moment a fresh stock of indignation. "If you do, madam, why I shall stop all the longer!" and he honored the speculators indiscriminately with a purely sardonic smile, and waved his hand very gracefully, and bowed with great politeness, and then, with a look of supreme contempt, turned round to examine his cards.

"What a comical wretch!" said Valentine, assuming a totally different voice.

"A wretch, sir! a comical wretch!" cried Crankey, starting upon his legs. "What do you mean by a wretch?"

"For goodness sake what *is* the matter?" cried the widow.

"The matter, ma'am?—this is the matter! I did not come here to be insulted, ma'am, grossly insulted!"

"Who has insulted you—who—who is it?"

"Who is it, ma'am? Why it's one of your *friends*, that's who it is!"

"But which of them?"

"What do I care!" cried Crankey, and he turned from the widow and dropped upon his chair, with a force which most powerfully tested the stability of its bottom.

Had young love himself been lingering in the heart of the widow, in order to advocate Crankey's cause at that moment, his retreat would have been perfectly certain; but as it was—as the widow preferred Mr. Crankey to Mr. Foxglove only in consequence of his being a little more wealthy, she simply acknowledged his politeness by a bow, and took no farther notice of the matter.

"What's trumps?" cried Crankey. "If people think that *I'm* to be insulted, they're mistaken—I can tell 'em—as mistaken as ever they were in their lives!"

"Oh indeed!" said Valentine.

"Yes! indeed!" cried the victim, turning again to the speculation table; "why I could buy up the whole kit, if that's what you mean!"

"There's the knave to beat," said Valentine in his natural voice.

"I see there's the knave to beat," cried Crankey, dashing down the queen with extraordinary force.

"Well, well," said Valentine calmly, "don't be angry with me."

"Who the devil, sir, can help being angry? Curse me, if it ain't enough to turn the very sweetest disposition into verdigris. But *I* won't stand it! They've got the wrong man—the wrong man, sir, I can tell 'em!"

At this moment a burst of merriment proceeded from the speculation table, and Mr. Crankey immediately started up again, and commenced an active scrutiny, but as he found all, save one, laughing heartily at the fact of that one having given sevenpence-halfpenny for the queen, when he had both the ace and the king in his own hand, Mr. Crankey again resumed his seat, muttering something which sounded not much like a blessing.

"Your play, sir," observed Mr. Foxglove.

"I know it," cried Crankey, who could not then bear to be spoken to.

"Hearts," whispered Valentine, assuming the voice of Mr. Foxglove, and the ace of hearts was led by Mr. Foxglove's partner; which Crankey no sooner perceived, than he started up again, dashed the cards very violently upon the table, and, having hurled upon those around him a withering look of scorn, placed his arms most majestically beneath his coat tails, and bounced out of the room.

His departure was hailed with satisfaction by all; and the remainder of the evening was spent most agreeably. The speculators played until twelve, then had supper, and then sang some very sweet songs; and Mr. Foxglove, who was really a very decent fellow, had that night the high satisfaction of hearing the amiable widow acknowledge that *he* was the absolute master of her heart.

CHAPTER XX.

CONTAINS A BIRD'S-EYE VIEW OF GOODMAN'S UNENVIABLE POSITION.

Although it may be very profoundly contended, that use is second nature, and that afflictions, however poignant, lose their virtue in time;—although theorists, in illustration, may bring forth the fact of a man having been sentenced to sleep upon spikes so long that, when compulsion had ceased, he still stuck to his spikes when he wanted to sleep, as a matter of comfort;—it seems to be abundantly clear that there are certain states of existence which, however much used to them men may become, shut out all prospect of reconciliation.

Goodman was an universal-happiness man. He delighted in contending that happiness was equally diffused; but from the moment of his incarceration in Dr. Holdem's den, his views on that subject had gradually changed. It may appear at first sight extraordinary that a man of fixed principles like Goodman should have been so inconsistent; but lest his inconsistency should be deemed reprehensible, it will be perfectly proper to describe the exact process by which the change in his opinions on this matter had been wrought.

It was about eight o'clock on the morning after the seizure, that a fellow unlocking the door of the cell in which Goodman had spent a most horrible night, shouted, "Now then! up with you! d'ye hear?"

Goodman, at the moment, involuntarily shrank from the scowl of this ruffian. He however soon recovered his self possession and attempted to rise, but found every limb so stiff and sore, that he sank back groaning with agony.

"Now then! Come, none of that rubbish! It won't do here!"

"My good man," said Goodman, "pray, pray don't be harsh. I am too ill—I really am too ill to rise."

"We'll see about that," cried the ruffian, catching hold of the edge of the mattrass, and with a sudden jerk flinging poor Goodman upon the floor. "Come, tumble up with you! I'm not going to stay here all day!"

Goodman made another desperate effort to rise; but the pain which accompanied that effort, at once caused him again to sink back.

"Oh! I'm not going to stand all this here, you know!" shouted the fellow, as he seized him by the throat and dragged him up.

"If I am to be murdered," cried Goodman, "be merciful; kill me at once;—don't! pray don't torture me thus!"

"Do what!" cried the ruffian, clenching his fist, and grinding his huge teeth desperately; "Give me any more of it—say another word, and I'll show you what's what in about half a minute."

Goodman, finding that he was completely in the ruffian's power, was silent; and having managed, in a state more dead than alive, to draw on his clothes, was dragged into a room in which a number of persons were sitting at breakfast.

As he entered, a chorus of sighs burst at once from the group, and they gazed upon his countenance with an expression of sorrow. A person of gentlemanly exterior rose, placed a chair for him at the table, and then sat beside him, and having pressed him with much delicacy to partake of the refreshment provided, which consisted of lumps of bread and butter and weak tea, he endeavored to cheer him, and did at length succeed in making him feel that he should have at least one consolation, namely, that of his society.

"Now then!—come into the garden!" shouted a fellow, when the lumps of bread and butter had vanished; and the patients —as they were called, but the prisoners as they were—rose, and walked away mournfully: Goodman alone lingered.

"Now then! are you going?" cried the ruffian.

"I'm really too ill," said Goodman faintly, "to walk."

"Oh, rubbish!—be off!—Now then start!"

"I wish to write a letter!"

"Be off into the garden, I tell you! Do you hear what I say?"

"Yes, yes!—but—can I see the proprietor?"

"Don't bother me!—Come, start!—there, that's all about it!"

On his way to the garden he met Dr. Holdem, whom he ventured to address.

"I know nothing," said he, "of your regulations; but, pray do not suffer your servants to treat me so brutally!"

"Brutally!" cried the doctor; "My servants treat you brutally!—pooh, pooh! it's all your delusion!"

"No, sir!" said Goodman emphatically; "it is not a delusion. I am, sir,"—

"Hullo! hullo! none of your insolence!" interrupted Dr. Holdem—"Be off!"—And one of his myrmidons seized him by the collar and dragged him away.

On reaching the place which was dignified with the appellation of a garden, in which there were about a dozen withering plants, poor Goodman was joined by Mr. Whitely, the gentleman who at breakfast had so kindly addressed him. From him he learned the rules of this dreadful place; and received advice with reference to the mode in which he might escape much ill-treatment. He advised him to make no complaint—to bear whatever indignities might be heaped upon him in silence, and to hope for the means of eventually escaping."

"Escaping!" cried Goodman, "why, can I not write to my friends?"

"No, that is not allowed."

"Not allowed?—you have visiting magistrates?"

"The commissioners visit us occasionally. They are compelled to come four times a-year, but that is frequently at intervals of five or six months."

"Well, when they do come, and I appeal to them, they will, of course, see that I am not mad?"

"Ah! that was my impression. There was my hope; but the first time they came, the keeper gave me a certain drug, and then goaded me into a state of excitement, which, when I was examined, made me appear to be insane, and that impression has never been removed."

"God bless me!" said Goodman; "but there are *some* insane persons in this wretched place?"

"There are some; but very, very few," replied Mr. Whitely.

"That is one, I presume?" said Goodman, pointing to a melancholy creature, who was hand-cuffed and chained to a log.

"He is no more insane, sir, than I am," said Whitely; "but having, about twelve months ago, made an effort to escape, he has been handcuffed and chained day and night ever since."

At this moment one of the keepers approached, and with a single blow, knocked down a man for throwing a stone over the wall. The poor fellow took no notice of this outrage, but rose to avoid being kicked, and walked away.

"What a monstrous proceeding!" cried Goodman indignantly.

"Nothing," said Whitely, "is too monstrous to be perpetrated here. But silence! —he's coming this way."

"So you'll go and tell the doctor you're ill-used, will you?" cried the ruffian—with whom the doctor had expostulated, fearing that as Goodman was exceedingly weak, too much cruelty would deprive him of life, and thereby deprive the establishment of a certain sum per annum.—"You'll tell him I hurt you again—eh?—will you?" he continued, grasping Goodman by the throat, and shaking him with violence—"I treat you brutally, do I?—Brutally!—brutally!—brutally!"

At each repetition of the word "brutally" he kicked him with all the force at his command, and then left him to fall upon the ground in a state of exhaustion.

While this atrocious outrage was being committed, many of the inmates came to the spot. Whitely's blood boiled, but he dared not interfere; and several of the other sane victims felt equally indignant but equally powerless. A religious enthusiast looked up to Heaven as he pointed to the ruffian's brutal exercise of his power, while two poor idiots dangled their hands, and appeared to be utterly lost in amazement.

The moment the fellow had left the spot, shouting, "There! now tell the doctor again!" Mr. Whitely lifted Goodman from the ground, and endeavored to console him. He begged of him not to mention the occurrence to Dr. Holdem, as the ruffian would be certain to have his revenge, and labored to impress upon his mind the inutility as well as the danger of complaining. Goodman sobbed bitterly, and big scalding tears chased each other down his cheeks as he acknowledged the kindness of his friend.

At one o'clock they were all ordered in to partake of a miserable dinner, and immediately afterwards turned again into the yard. At five, being tea-time, the same degrading ceremonies were performed; and at eight they were all locked up for the night. There was the same round of wretchedness, day after day, without the slightest employment or amusement of any description. Not a letter could be written: not a book could be procured: nothing calculated to mitigate their misery for a single moment was permitted, from the time they rose in the morning till they were driven, like cattle, into their cells, there to linger for twelve weary hours in darkness, torturing their minds by reflecting on the monstrous inhumanity of those to whom nature had prompted them to look for affection.

CHAPTER XXI.

THE EQUALRIGHTITES' MIGHTY DEMONSTRATION.

Why are not all men socially equal? Are they not born with equal rights? Have they not sprung from one common parent, and have they not, therefore, a right to share equally every comfort the world can afford? If nature herself be perfection, does it not follow that that which is not in accordance with nature must be in proportion imperfect? Why, of course! And hence, as a state of civilisation is diametrically opposed to a state of nature, civilisation is palpably the most imperfect scheme that ever afflicted the world. Nature prescribes no social inequality!—yet some men are wealthy, while others are poor; and those who toil zealously, day by day, are absolutely, in a social point of view, worse off than those who are not forced to labor at all!

With a view to the correction of this monstrous state of things, an appropriately organized body of patriots had a mighty demonstration on Clerkenwell-green, the very day on which Valentine learnt with much pain that, by some young gentleman—acting upon the same eternal principle of equal right—the steward's striped jacket had been stolen.

As he strolled towards the place which

had once been an actual Green, doubtless, but which was a Green only nominally then, he was not in the happiest spirits; for although he had previously thought little of the card, or of the lady whose name that card bore, he now began to be unspeakably anxious about the one, and to feel himself desperately in love with the other. On perceiving, however, the mighty masses assembled, he forgot for the moment both, and pushed through the crowd towards a waggon which had been drawn to the spot by an animal, looking about the ribs really wretched, but still, as he then had his nose-bag on, he kept nodding his perfect approbation of the arrangements, as far as they went. In the waggon—or to write with more propriety—upon the hustings, stood a dense mass of partriots, sweating with indignation, and panting to inspire the mighty masses with a perfect appreciation of the blessings which would, of necessity, flow from a system of social equality; nay, so intense was the anxiety of the patriots present to advocate boldly their dear country's cause, that when the waggon was full of them, literally crammed, many very patriotically hung on behind, which clearly proved to the sovereign people, that there was absolutely nothing which those patriots would not endure, to carry out that essentially glorious down-with-every-thing-no-nothing principle, of which they professed to be so ardently enamored.

When the time had arrived for the commencement of the highly important proceedings of the day, it was most inconsistently felt by some of the leaders, that they ought to have a chairman; but an eminent patriot no sooner stepped forward for the purpose of nominating a highly distinguished Flamer, than certain whole-hog-equalrightites contended that all of them possessed an equal right to be in the chair; and that therefore no one had a right to be placed above another. This was clearly very appropriate, and very consistent with the eternal equalrightite principle; but as it was suggested that they might, without compromising that principle, so far yield to the grossly corrupt prescriptions of civilisation, the mighty masses at once recognised the Flamer as their president, and hailed him, as he pulled off his hat to address them, with three very vehement cheers.

"My Fellow Countrymen!" said he, conceiving doubtless that to address them as "Gentlemen" would be rather too much of a joke to tell well—"This indeed is a glorious sight! When I behold the sovereign people pouring down like a mighty torrent which sweeps all before it, and which nothing can stem—when I behold the glorious masses with agony groaning beneath the iron hoof of oligarchical tyranny and crushed to the very earth by a monstrous accumulation of bitter wrongs—when I behold *you*, my countrymen, rushing here to burst your degrading chains asunder, and to shout with one universal voice—'WE WILL BE FREE!'—my heart throbs with delight, my eyes sparkle with gladness, my soul seems inspired, and my bosom swells with joy [*immense cheering!*] What are you, my countrymen—what are you?—*Slaves!* base, abject, spiritless SLAVES!—Slaves, in the eyes of the world, of the vilest description: Slaves, with the power to be free! Arise!—Shake off that apathy which acts upon your energies like an incubus. Down with the tyrants by whom you are oppressed. Arm!—arm to the very teeth [*vehement applause!*] Follow the glorious example of your brave fellow countrymen in the North! Join them in the Holy Month. Strike!—and run for gold! Convert all your notes into specie!—let *that* be the first grand step towards the universal paralysation! Be resolute! Be firm! Act like men who know their rights and will maintain them! The hour is at hand! *Hurl* the base tyrants into universal chaos!"—

"We will! We will!" cried the mighty masses holding up and brandishing a forest of knives which glittered picturesquely in the sun.

Valentine no sooner saw this display than he drew out *his* knife—the blade of which was full an inch and a half long—with a view to his own safety, by making it appear to those around that he was ready to go the whole hog, and feeling that he was bound as a loyal subject to put an end to these proceedings if possible at once, shouted "Soldiers! soldiers!" throwing his voice just behind the chairman—and the mighty masses buried their knives in their breeches' pockets, and looked round eagerly for the appearance of the troops.

"The soldiers!" cried the chairman, having satisfied himself that none were near. "The soldiers are our friends! And if even they were not, why—why need we care for the soldiers? But I know that they are ready to join us to a man! Let but the Holy Month—"

"The Holy what?" cried Valentine.

The chairman contemptuously turned to the quarter from which the voice appeared to proceed, but scorning the ignorant character of the question, disdained to make any reply. "I say let but the Holy Month," he continued, "be commenced, and you will see the soldiers"—

"Mowing you down like grass!" cried Valentine.

"No, no! Let them try it on!" shouted the mighty masses, again brandishing their clasp knives and yelling like furies.

"We have, my fellow-countrymen, traitors in the camp!" cried the chairman. "We are surrounded by spies from the Treasury; but let the degraded hirelings go back to the tyrants whom they serve, and tell them from us, that we not only bid them defiance, but hold them in sovereign contempt!"

This burst of courageous indignation was followed by three dreadful groans for the spies; and when the Treasury tyrants, by whom they were employed, had been similarly honored, the chairman introduced a Mr. Coweel for the purpose of proposing the first resolution.

"Feller-kuntrymen! I'm a hopperative!" shouted Mr. Coweel who was a powerful man, but very dirty; "I'm for down with all taxes, all pensions, all sinnycures, and all other speeches off rotten corruption.—I'm hallso for down with the church! Why should we have a holly-garkle harmy of fat bishops? Why should we pay 'em a matter o' nineteen million o' money a-year to support their kids and konkybines—eh? What is the good on 'em? Why, I'd —"

"Down! down!" cried Valentine, assuming the chairman's voice.

"What d'yar mean by down?" said Mr. Coweel to the chairman.

The chairman bowed to Mr. Coweel, and assured him that he had not spoken.

"Well, I thought," said Mr. Coweel, "the hobserwation was rayther too hunconstitutional for you; but as I was a sayin the holly-garkle bishops —"

"Get down, you fool!" cried Valentine, throwing his voice behind the speaker.

"What d'yar mean?" cried Mr. Coweel, "I'll down with *you* in just about no time, my cove, if yer any ways nasty. What! d'yer think I care for you? P'r'aps you'd like to take it out on me, 'cos if yer would, yer know, why ony say so, that's hall!" and Mr. Coweel looked daggers at every patriot whom he at that moment caught in the act of smiling, and having signified his ability to "lick seventy dozen on 'em, jist like a sack, one down and tother come on," he returned, at the suggestion of the patriotic chairman, to the episcopal business he wished to explain. "Well!" said he, again addressing the mighty masses, "I'm for down with all hunconstitutional —"

"Silence, you idiot! I'll kick you out of the waggon!" shouted Valentine with all the power of which he was capable.

"What!" cried Mr. Coweel, turning round with due promptitude—"what'll yer do?—kick me out o' the waggon? How many on yer, eh? I should werry much like to give *you* a quilting any how!—kick me out!—try it on!—kick me out o' the waggon!"

At this interesting moment a patriot, who was panting to address the sovereign people, and who was standing about six feet from Mr. Coweel, had the temerity, in the plenitude of his impatience, to cry, "either go on, or cut it!"

"Oh ho!" exclaimed Mr. Coweel, "I've found you out, have I, my tulip? It's you that'll kick me out o' the waggon then, is it?" and Mr. Coweel aimed a blow at the tulip, but missed him by about two feet and a half. This miss did not, by any means, impart satisfaction to Mr. Coweel. He was anxious to hit conviction into the mind of the tulip that he was not the sort of man to be kicked out of a waggon. He, therefore, struck out again very forcibly and freely, but every blow aimed, fell more or less short. This seemed to enrage him. He looked very fierce. His elbows were sharp, and he used them: he dug them with so much decision and point, and, moreover, to such an extraordinary depth into the backs and the stomachs of those who stood near him, that really his struggles to get at the tulip became so particularly unpleasant to the patriots who were standing in his immediate vicinity, that, feeling it to be a duty incumbent upon them—a duty which they owed, not only to themselves as individuals, but to society at large—they pinioned his arms, caught hold of his legs, and pitched him among the mighty masses below.

A loud shout burst from the sovereign people!—a shout which was echoed by Hick's Hall, and reverberated clean through the house of correction. The masses, albeit they clearly perceived that the principle upon which Coweel had been pitched from the waggon was that of purely physical force, could not at the moment precisely comprehend the great fundamental principle upon which that physical force had been developed. They fancied at first that he was one of the spies; but when he mounted the nave of the near hind-wheel, and—after having dealt out his blows with really desperate energy, and that with the most absolute indiscrimination—addressed the mighty masses as Britons and as men, denouncing this unconstitutional act of tyranny, and calling upon them, as they valued their liberties, to aid him in turning the waggon upside down—they held him to be a man who simply sought the redress of wrongs, and hence felt themselves bound, by every just and eternal principle by which their

their souls were guided, to assist him in pitching the vehicle over.

Just, however, as those who were nearest to the hustings were proceeding with due promptitude to carry this design into actual execution, a loud and warlike shout of "THE PEELERS! THE PEELERS!" burst upon their patriotic ears, and induced them to defer *their* labor of love; while mighty sections of the sovereign people rushed with due magnanimity from the scene, rolling over those masses which had fallen before them, and forming themselves, in turn, stumbling blocks to those of whom *they* had courageously taken the precedence.

"The Peelers!" thought Valentine—"the Peelers!—what manner of men are the *Peelers*, that their presence should generate so much alarm in the minds of the Sovereign People?"

His conjectures, however, having reference to the probability of their being either hideous monsters, or gigantic fiends, were very speedily put an end to by the approach of six policemen, who marched with due solemnity of step towards the hustings; and as they approached, those sections of the mighty masses who still kept their ground, were as quiet as lambs.

It at once became abundantly manifest, that those six Peelers had arrived with some object in view; and before the Sovereign People had time even to guess what that object might be, one of the Peelers very coolly deprived the horse of his nose-bag; another just as coolly returned the bit to his mouth; and a third, with equal coolness, got hold of the reins, when a fourth, who was certainly not quite so cool, did, by virtue of the application of a short round truncheon, persuade the passive animal to move on.

At starting, the horse had so tremendous a load, that, in order to draw it all, he was compelled to put out all the physical force he had in him, but the patriots displayed so much alacrity in leaping out among the Sovereign People, who were roaring with laughter, that before, long before it had reached Mutton-hill, the mighty masses beheld the vehicle perfectly empty.

Valentine was lost in admiration of the tact, and tranquillity of spirit displayed by the Peelers. It is true they met with no opposition;—it is true that they had only to lead the horse off to compel the patriots either to leap out of the wagon, or to have a ride *gratis* to the Green-yard; but the cool, the dispassionate, the business-like manner in which they conducted the whole thing, struck Valentine as being admirable in the extreme.

The vehicle, on reaching Mutton-hill, was lost to view; and as Valentine turned to ascertain what the mighty masses contemplated next, he met the full gaze of a person who looked like a decent master blacksmith, and who, addressing him, said, "Are *you* an Equalrightite?"

"I certainly profess to have at least an equal right," replied Valentine, "to ask you that question."

"You have a knife about your person, have you not?"

"I have," said Valentine, "What then?"

"You had it open in the crowd near the hustings."

"Well! and what is that to *you?*"

The individual, who was a Peeler *incog.*, at once beckoned to his undisguised comrades, who came to the spot, collared Valentine firmly, and proceeded to drag him away.

The mighty masses had their eyes upon those Peelers, whom they viewed as their natural enemies. They had previously suspected that they were anxious to capture some one, and as there were but two of them then, they felt, of course, bound by every principle they professed, to oppose with firmness whatever tyrannical movement they might make. When, therefore, they saw in the seizure of Valentine the liberty of the subject contemned, they raised a shout of indignation and rushed boldly to the rescue. The Peelers saw in a moment—and it really is astonishing how quickly those fellows do see—that the sovereign people meant something. They, therefore, pulled out their truncheons and grasped the collar of Valentine with more firmness still; but in spite of these palpable signs of determination, the mighty masses rushed like a torrent upon them and tried to persuade them, by knocking them down, to relinquish their tyrannous hold. The Peelers were firm. Although down, they held on. They were resolute men, and would not be defeated. They applied their short truncheons, with consummate force, to the ankles and shins of the sovereign people, and that too, with so much *effect*, that they again rose up like giants refreshed, with Valentine still in their grasp. The mighty masses once more rushed upon them, and the Peelers once more shook them off by the prompt application of their tyrannous truncheons to the sacred hats of the sovereign people, and to the sacred heads of those whose hats were at their Uncle's. It was in vain that Valentine begged of them to desist. They wouldn't hear of it! No!—they returned to the charge, caught hold of his legs, and felt victory sure!

"Let go!"—shouted Valentine indignantly. "You *asses*, let go!"—which, however ungrateful, was perfectly natural under the circumstances, seeing that between the sovereign people and the Peelers, he was really being torn limb from limb.

The mighty masses were, however, too near the consummation of their hopes to attend to this burst of ingratitude. They wanted him away, and would have him!—if it were only to defeat their natural enemies. They therefore gave another loud "Hurrah!"—and in a moment—in the twinkling of an eye!—when Valentine thought that his arms and legs were all off together—they got him away from the Peelers!

A loud shout of triumph rent the air as they held up their trophy aloft; and having given three cheers for the sovereign people, and three gorgonian groans for the Peelers, they converted their high and mighty shoulders into a species of triumphal car, upon which they paraded him round the scene of action until they were ready to drop; when he broke away from them, jumped into a coach, and happily made his escape.

CHAPTER XXII.

IN WHICH HORACE SETS TO WITH THE GHOST OF GOODMAN, AND WALTER BURNS THE SPECTRE OUT.

"Come, come! I say, governor! come!" exclaimed Horace, about the middle of the third night of his sitting up with his venerable father, whose delirium continued to be active and strong; "this *won't* do, you know—flesh and blood can't stand it."

"Hush!" cried Walter, raising his hand as he fixed his glazed eyes on vacancy; "there!" he continued in a thrilling whisper—"there!—there again! Turn him out! turn him out!"

There are times at which even the most thoughtless, the most reckless are struck with a feeling of awe; when the blood seems to chill, and the heart seems to faint, and all physical power appears to be gone—when the soul is startled and the cheeks are blanched, and each function appears to be under the influence of some indescribable paralysis. Oh! it is, questionless, one of the most strikingly beautiful feelings of which human nature is susceptible, and this feeling crawled over Horace, as he exclaimed, "Pooh! it *won't* fit, you know! it's all out-and-out stuff."

Unconscious of having inspired this amiable sentiment, unconscious of the character of his affectionate son's reply, Walter grasped his arm firmly, and pointing to the spectre, cried "Now! get behind him! there! seize him by the throat!"

"I say, I say, governor!" exclaimed Horace, shaking his parent with more force than feeling, "can't I *any* how drive into your stupid head, that there's nobody here but ourselves? Just listen to reason; do you mean to tell me that you'll make me believe that you think that if he were really here I couldn't see him? Is it likely? Is it like anything likely? Pooh! rubbish, I tell you! Shut your eyes, there's a trump, and go to sleep."

"I will have him out!" cried Walter fiercely, "out! out!"

"Well, well, then I'll turn him out; come if that's all." And Horace opened the door, and addressing the apparition, said, "Now, old boy! just toddle off, will you? you're not wanted here; come, cut it!" and he walked round the room, and lavished upon the apparition a series of kicks, which, in a spectral sense were extremely severe, and after grasping him firmly in imagination by the incorporeal collar, he gave him a spiritual impetus behind, and closed the door with an air of the most absolute triumph.

His venerable father was not to be deceived, however, thus; the pantomine of Horace was really very excellent—he managed the thing with consummate ability, nay, with "artistical" skill; but the phantom was still in the mind's eye of Walter; to him it appeared to have been untouched! and therefore, when Horace returned to the bedside to receive that applause which the development of genius ought ever to ensure he was utterly astonished to find, not only that his exertions had not been appreciated, but that Walter still glared at the spectre as before.

"Come, I say, he's off now!" exclaimed Horace; "I've given him a little dose at all events, *if* I haven't broken his jolly old neck. He wont come back here in a hurry. I say! didn't you see how he bolted! I should think he's had enough of it for one night any how, eh? shouldn't you?"

Walter took no notice of these appropriate observations. He made no reply. He appeared not to know that a word had been uttered. His spiritual enemy was there! and his eyes were still wildly fixed upon him. "I will have him out!" he exclaimed, after a pause, "he shall not be here."

"He is not here," cried Horace, seizing the arms of his father; "I wish I could drive a little sense into your head. I say, governor! why, don't you know me?"

Walter turned his eyes for an instant, and then again glared at the spectre; I'll not have him here!." he cried, "out he shall go! If you will not do it, I will," and he made another effort to rise, but Horace held him down; he struggled, and Horace struggled with him, until he was struck with an idea that the self-same power which caused him to imagine some one there, might cause him also to imagine that he had driven him away, when, in order to give him every possible chance, he very quietly relinquished his hold.

Walter was no sooner free than he darted towards the space to which he had pointed, and made a really desperate effort to clutch the phantom, which, however, appeared to retreat, for he chased it round and round with great swiftness and zeal, until he became so exhausted that Horace lifted him again into bed, exclaiming, "Come, come, it's no sort of use; you can't grab him!"

"But I will!" cried Walter, again struggling to rise.

"No, no! I'll tackle him! stay where you are. I must," he continued in an under tone, "swindle the old boy somehow," and he pulled off his coat, and threw himself at once into a gladiatorial attitude, and after having very scientifically squared at the apparition for some considerable time, he struck out with great force and precision, and continued to strike right and left until he found that he had struck his arms pretty well out of their sockets, when, precisely as if the enemy had been regularly vanquished, he put it to him whether he had had quite enough, and then, without farther ceremony, threw up the sash, and "made him believe" to pitch him out of the window.

All this was, however, good energy thrown away; for while he was laboring to inspire the belief that he was breaking the neck of the spectre, that spectre, in Walter's imagination, was still in the self-same position as before. Horace was amazed, when, on closing the window, he found his father staring as wildly as ever. "It's of *no* use," said he to himself, in despair, as he mixed another glass of warm brandy-and-water, and pulled out another cheroot; "I may just as well drop it—he's not to be done. Come, I say," he continued, addressing his father, "it's all stuff, you know! shut your eyes, and then he'll start; he won't move a peg till you do."

Walter now lay perfectly motionless.—His last effort seemed to have exhausted him completely; and as he continued to lie, without uttering a word, Horace fondly conceived that he should have an hour's peace, and therefore threw himself back in the easy chair, and very soon became extremely interested in the report of a fight between Simon the Tough un and Konky Brown.

Now, those who have had the intense satisfaction of sitting up with a delirious person all night will recollect, that between three and four in the morning, the mind reverts with peculiar pleasure to a cup of strong coffee and a muffin. If the patient then under your special protection be at that hour silent, the silence which reigns over the chamber is awful, and nothing in nature, save coffee with a muffin, seems calculated either to occupy the mind or to arouse the dormant energies of the body.—This hour—this dreary, solemn hour had arrived, when Horace perceiving that his father's eyes were closed, stole softly from the chamber, and proceeded to the kitchen, where the coffee was on the hob, and the muffins were on the table, with everything essential to a comfortable breakfast.

The very moment, however, Horace left the room, his father, who had cunningly watched every movement, and had only pretended to be asleep, leaped at once from the bed with the full determination to turn out the phantom by which he had been haunted. He first tried to clutch it—then lost it for a time—then stared about wildly—then saw it again, and then chased it round the room, until he fancied that he had driven it beneath the bed, when he caught up the candle, set fire to the clothes, and in an instant the bed was in a blaze.

"Now!" he cried, "Now will you go? Ha! ha! ha! ha! I can't get you *out!* Ha! ha! ha! ha! ha! ha!"

Horace heard the loud hysterical laugh, and darted up stairs in a moment. Dense volumes of smoke issued forth as he burst in the door. He could not advance!—the whole room was in flames!

"Father!" he cried, "Father! fly to the door! save yourself! save yourself! Father!"

The laughter was heard still; but the next moment it died away and Walter fell.

"Fire! fire! fire!" cried Horace, and his cries were immediately answered by screams from above. He rushed into the street, and there raised the alarm, and the neighborhood resounded with cries of "fire! fire!"

The police were immediately on the spot; and several laborers who were going to work came at once to their assistance.

"My father! My father's in the room!" shouted Horace. "For God's sake save him—save my father!" and he darted up stairs with the view of rescuing his mother and his wife. His wife had fainted, and his mother was too terror-stricken even to move. "Help! help!" he shouted, "Here!" and a laborer rushed in a moment to his aid and seized the mother, as Horace caught his fainting wife in his arms, when both were in safety borne into the street.

The fire was now raging fiercely. The flames were bursting forth in all directions. The rafters had caught, and the crackling was awful.

"Who's in the house now?" shouted one of the laborers.

"My father! my father!" cried Horace, returning.

"Where's the girl?—where's the servant?" demanded a policeman.

"Up stairs!" replied Horace, by whom she had been forgotten, and away went the policeman; but the girl could not be found.

"Father! father!" he again shouted, and at that moment a deep thrilling groan reached his ear. "To the door!—to the door!"

Crash went the windows, and a stream of water poured into the room in which Walter was writhing in agony. No one could enter. That room was one sheet of vivid fire, and the flames, as the water rushed in at the window, were driven with violence hissing towards the door.

Another groan was heard. It appeared to proceed from a spot near the wainscot. Horace instantly tore down the bannister, with part of which he dashed in the pannel. An angry stream of fire burst like lightning through the orifice, but there lay Walter!

"He is here!" cried Horace, seizing him eagerly and dragging him into the passage. "He is *not* dead! Help!"

Assistance was at hand; and Walter was borne at once into the street; but presented so frightful a spectacle, that a shutter was procured, upon which he was placed and carried to the house of the nearest surgeon.

The engines now arrived from all quarters, and began to play gallantly upon the flames, which were bursting through the bricks, and streaming in liquid curls from every window. Horace, notwithstanding, rushed again into the house. His object was to secure his father's papers. He reached the room which contained them, and burst in the door!—another step would have precipitated him at once into a gulf of hissing fire. The floor of the room had fallen in, and the flames were ascending in forked streams from below. The spectacle struck him with horror. He stood for a moment paralysed. A crash was heard behind him! The stairs—the stairs up which he came had given way. All retreat was cut off. The flames were gathering round and like hideous monsters ready to devour him. What was to be done? One hope—one poor forlorn hope—urged him forward! he dashed through the crackling blazing passage, reached the stairs, and darted up, with the fire following fiercely at his heels. By a miracle he gained the attic. The window was open. He leaped upon the parapet, and there, turning his eyes to the opening heavens which reflected the flames, he clasped his hands and with fervor thanked God!

A falling beam beneath him warned him from the spot; and he crept on his hands and knees, along the roof until his blood chilled on touching a human face! It was that of the servant, who, having escaped through the window, had fainted. He shrank back for the moment, appalled; but on recovering himself he placed the poor girl upon his back, and proceeded over the roofs of the adjoining houses until he reached a stack of chimneys which impeded his further progress.

Here he put his burden down, and turned to the ruins from which he had escaped, and for the first time felt the dreadful effects of the fiery ordeal through which he had passed. He was frightfully scorched. His hair had been singed completely off his head, and the clothes that remained on him were reduced to mere tinder. He cried aloud for help, but he could not be heard: he could see the mob below—but he could not be seen. The engines were playing, and the shouts of those who worked them would have drowned the most dreadful clap of thunder.

"Look out!" shouted fifty of the firemen in a breath; and a rush was made to the opposite side. The next moment a tremendous crash was heard. The roof had fallen in; and the clouds of smoke and dust which ascended with a roar were succeeded by a shower of blazing laths and sparks which threatened destruction to all around. The effect was terrific. The sky itself seemed to be one sheet of fire descending to mantle the earth.

Another shout burst forth: Horace was perceived!—every object being now distinctly visible. An escape-ladder was raised, and a fireman ascended. "*Here!*" he cried addressing the startled Horace, who had just caught a glimpse of his head, "Get into this canvass! Now don't be afraid."

Horace carried the poor fainting girl to the parapet, and wished her to be taken down first.

"Give me the girl," continued the fireman. "There! Now you get in, but mind don't go fast." And Horace got into the canvass tube, and gradually slipped to the bottom.

On coming out of this tube he was literally naked, for during the descent, his clothes, which were but tinder, had been rubbed completely off. A blanket, however, was immediately thrown around him, and he was carried at once with the girl to the surgeon's.

By this time the house was completely gutted, and the engines were playing only on the hot party walls that the fire might not reach the houses adjoining. This effect was produced: those houses were saved; and in a short time although the engines still kept playing, nothing but smoke could be seen.

CHAPTER XXIII.

VALENTINE ATTENDS A PHRENOLOGICAL LECTURE, AND INSPIRES A MURDERER'S SKULL WITH INDIGNATION.

What a beautiful science is that of Phrenology! In the whole range of sciences where is there one which is either so useful or so ornamental? Fortune-telling is a fool to it. It stands with consummate boldness upon the very pinnacle of fatality. To the predestinarian it is a source of great comfort: to all who desire to take themselves entirely out of their own hands—to get rid of that sort of responsibility which is sometimes extremely inconvenient—it is really a positive blessing. When this delightful science shall have made its way home to the hearts of mankind universally, as it must, what a lovely scheme of life will be opened before us!—what a charming state of society will be based upon the ruins of our present dreadful system of civilisation! Then, and not till then, will mankind be quite happy! Then will perfect liberty obtain. Then will men see the sand-blindness of their ancestors, and sweep away like chaff the dreadful injustice which forms the very essence of punishment. Then will it be seen that law and liberty are inimical—a thing which has but to be seen for our statute books to be converted into one monstrous cinder and placed upon a pedestal as an everlasting relic of excruciating tyranny. It will then be acknowledged that men are but men—that they are by no means accountable for their actions—that they do thus or thus simply because they have been predestined to do thus or thus—and that therefore they cannot be censured or punished with justice. It will then seem amazing that punishments should have been countenanced—amazing that men should have been made by their fellow-men to suffer for actions over which they clearly had no control—nay, actions which they were, in fact, bound to perform!—for, why, it will be argued, do men commit murders? Why do they perpetrate rapes and pick pockets? Why—clearly because they can't help it! And what line of argument can be shorter? And as for its soundness!—why that will of course be perceived at a glance.

It is lamentable—absolutely lamentable—to think that this extremely blessed state of society stands no sort of chance of being established before the next generation; and we, who endure the atrocities of the present cramped-up scheme, may with infinite reason envy the sweet feelings, the delightful sensations, the charming state of mind, which the establishment of a phrenologically social system must of necessity induce. There are of course some unhappy individuals in existence sufficiently ill-conditioned to contend that phrenology *never can* bring about this unspeakably glorious state of things; and really none can wonder at it!—none can wonder that the cool contemplation of such a delightful state of society should confirm the incredulity of the naturally incredulous—but that it will, when carried out to its legitimate length, be productive of all those extraordinary blessings, reflection—disinterested reflection—will render abundantly clear. It is all very well and very natural for lawyers, physicians, and such kinds of people to uphold the present system, inasmuch as it is by that system they thrive. They perfectly well know that if a system were established upon these two bold and eternal principles—first, that "Whatever is, is right," and secondly, that "They who are born to be hanged can never be drowned;" their respective occupations would be gone! seeing that nature would then be allowed to take the entire thing into her own ample hands.

But there are also "phrenologists sufficiently weak to maintain that there own immortal science is by no means designed to accomplish the great objects to which reference has been had. These, however, are not pure phrenologists. They take an extremely rotten view of the thing, and are much to be pitied. The professors of a science ought never to under-rate the advantages of the science of which they are professors. It isn't right; such a course has a direct and natural tendency to bring the thing eventually into contempt. If nature has implanted in our skulls certain organs containing the germs of certain passions, whose internal working not only produce an external development, but force us to act as they direct or in obedience to their will, we have clearly no right to the reputation of being responsible creatures, and we have but to believe that we possess no such right, to recognise the injustice involved in all punishments, and thus to lay the foundation of that sweet social system which cannot be thought of without pure delight.

Now with the view of inspiring a due appreciation of the blessings with which this delightful science teems, a distinguished professor was about to deliver a highly interesting lecture as Valentine passed an institution to which his attention had been directed by a crowd pouring in.

Valentine happened to be dull that evening; for while he could obtain no tidings of Goodman, he saw no probability of finding out the residence of her of whom he felt more than ever enamored. He therefore, with an hour's amusement for his object, applied for a ticket, and having obtained one, entered a well constructed room, in which there were seats raised one above the other, and capable of accommodating about four hundred persons; while on the rostrum stood a table, upon which were placed several peculiarly formed skulls, the nominal relics of some of the greatest scoundrels, fools, philanthropists, and statesmen, that ever had existence. The place was crowded, and when the appointed time had passed without the appearance of the professor, the audience began to manifest that respectable sort of impatience which develops itself in a gentle timid tapping of sticks and umbrellas. The amount of intelligence displayed by the audience was truly striking; and as Valentine was able at a glance to perceive who were really phrenologists, and who really were not, by the mode in which their hair was arranged—for the phrenologists wore theirs entirely off their foreheads, in order that every bump which could be seen might be seen, while the anti-individuals suffered theirs to hang roughly, or, if it would curl, to curl accordingly upon their latent brows—he became extremely interested in speculating upon the extent to which the advocates of the science would be, at once, prepared to go. He had not, however, speculated long when a movement was made upon the rostrum—a movement which was palpably indicative of something. Every eye was of course directed most anxiously towards the door; and when the professor, who formed part of a solemn procession entered, the applause was exceedingly liberal and loud. The members of the committee then seated themselves at a most respectful distance on either side, and when the professor had recovered his self-possession, he coughed slightly, gave several peculiar ahems! and then in sweet silvery tones said:—"Ladies and Gentlemen: In speaking of the science of phrenology the first consideration which suggests itself is, whether the external development of man's propensities and passions be the cause or the effect of those propensities and passions. Now, in order that I may illustrate clearly that such development is the effect, not the cause, I propose to direct your attention to the peculiar organization of the heads of certain well known characters, whose skulls I have here. Now," continued the learned professor, taking up a very singularly formed skull in both hands and looking at it very intently—"this is the head of Tim Thornhill, the murderer."

"The what?" cried Valentine, dexterously pitching his voice into the skull.

The startled professor dropped it on the instant; and as it rolled with peculiar indignation upon the rostrum, the audience simultaneously burst into a convulsive roar of laughter.

The professor at first did not laugh. By no means; he looked amazed, turned pale, very pale, and slightly trembled, as he stared at the rolling skull. But when he had sufficiently recovered himself, to know that all were laughing around him, he certainly made a lamentable effort to join them. And this gave him courage, for he proceeded to pick up the object of his amazement; but no sooner had he got his hand upon it again, than Valentine, cried, "A murderer?" in a tone of great solemnity.

The professor again started back; but the laughter of the audience was neither so loud nor so general as before, seeing that many had been struck with the idea that there was something supernatural about it.

"This is strange, very strange—extraordinary!" said the professor, with great intensity of feeling—"very, very extraordinary!"

"A murderer!" repeated Valentine, in a deeply reproachful tone, which of course seemed to proceed from the relic of Tim Thornhill.

The audience laughed no more. They did not even smile. They looked at each other with an expression of wonder, and felt that the skull was under some ghostly influence, while the learned professor, albeit by no means prone to superstition, was utterly lost in amazement.

"Is it possible," thought he, "that this skull can be inhabited by the spirit of Tim Thornhill? Is it possible that that spirit can have spoken?" He was not prepared to say that it was impossible, and the assumption of its not being impossible generated the consideration of its probability, which, added to the evidence of his own ears, at length reduced the thing to a certainty, or something very like it. And this seemed to be the conclusion at which the members of the committee had arrived, for they looked extremely grave and altogether at a loss to give expression to their feelings on the subject.

"Ladies and Gentlemen," said the professor, after a very awful pause, during which it happened to strike him that he ought to say something. "I scarcely know how to address you. This occurrence is of so extraordinary a character, that I really don't know what to think. With a view to the promotion of science—"—

"Ha!--ha!—ha!" cried Valentine, in a O smithian tone, and at melo-dramatic intervals, throwing his voice behind the professor, who started, but dared not look round--"Ha—ha!--ha!" he repeated, making the voice appear to proceed from a much greater distance; and while the chairman, the professor, and the gentlemen of the committee had scarcely the power to breathe, the skulls on the table seemed to enjoy the thing exceedingly; for they really, in the imagination of all present, appeared to be grinning more decidedly than ever.

There is nothing in nature which startles men more than a noise for which they cannot account. However strongly strung may be their nerves: however slight may be the sound which they hear, if they cannot account for that sound, it at once chills their blood, and in spite of them sets their imagination on the rack. If the voice which apparently proceeded from that skull had reached the ear of a man when alone, the effect would have been infinitely more striking; inasmuch as, if pious, he would have looked for that protection for which we all think of looking when no other aid is near; while, if impious, he, with the greatest possible promptitude, would have exclaimed, "why, the devil's in the skull," and run away. As in this case, however, there were nearly four hundred intellectual persons present, they stuck to each other for protection, and during the awful silence which for some time prevailed, the more reflecting began to to reason themselves over the shock thus:—"Why what have we to fear? We never injured Tim Thornhill. He might have been a very ill-used man: but we never ill-used him: he might have been innocent of the crime for which he suffered, but we did not cause him to suffer. His spirit therefore cannot be angry with us, unless indeed it be a very unreasonable spirit. What then have we to fear?"

By virtue of this profound course of reasoning many recovered their self-possession, and as Valentine remained silent to enjoy the effect he had produced, he had time to reflect upon that moral weakness of which we are peculiarly the victims.

"It is probable, thought he, "that there are in this assembly many strong-minded men—men whom nothing on earth tangible could appal, who would fight like lions undismayed, and who have courage to endure the most intense physical torture without a groan: yet see how the slightest sound alarms them!—they can stand unmoved while the mighty thunder roars; yet let them hear but a whisper for which they cannot account, and their blood runs cold and their hearts sink within them."

There are, however, some individuals in the world, who, as soon as the shock has subsided, begin to ridicule that which alarmed them, and one of these happened to be the chairman of the committee. He had been startled by the sounds perhaps more than any other man present; but when he could hear it no longer, he no longer feared it; and therefore commenced laughing at and pinching those gentlemen who sat near him, and tried to bring the whole affair into contempt. This course of proceeding was not, however, relished by those gentlemen much; for although they very naturally shrank back when he pinched them, they preserved a solemnity of aspect, which was, under the circumstances, highly correct. He then approacheed the professor, and labored to convince him that it was "after all, nothing," and did certainly succeed in relaxing the rigidity of that gentleman's features.

"Pick up the skull!" cried Valentine, who was anxious to see what he would do with it; and the chairman adjusted his cravat, looked magnanimous, and picked up the skull! Valentine was silent, the professor was silent, and the audience were silent, while the chairman held the skull in his hand, and examined it minutely. He felt that his courage had excited admiration, and was by this feeling prompted to show off a little more. He therefore turned the skull over again and again, and after placing its grinning jaws to his ear very boldly, he tossed it up as if it had been a mere ball, and caught it again with considerable skill.

This had the effect of restoring the audience to something bearing the semblance of good humor. A smile seemed to be anxious to develope itself upon their features, and although it was more than half suppressed, the valiant chairman grew bolder and bolder, and being determined to throw contempt upon their fears, he rolled the skull from one point to another, put his fingers between its huge teeth, and really treated it altogether with unparalleled indignity.

"What is the matter with you, eh?" said he, playfully patting the skull; "what ails you? Are you not well, Mr. Thornhill? Dear me, I'm exceedingly sorry you've been so disturbed."

The audience now began to laugh heartily again, and to believe what they had wished all along to believe, that they had been very grossly mistaken. But just as they were about to feel ashamed of themselves for having suffered the sounds which they had heard to alarm them, the chairman rattled the skull of Tim Thornhill against that of an eminent philanthropist so violently, that Valentine, in a deep hollow tone, which appeared to proceed from behind the committee, who were joking with great freedom and spirit, cried "forbear!"

The effect was electric. The members of the committee were on their legs in an instant; the chairman dropped the skull, and stood trembling with due energy; the professor turned pale, opened his mouth, and held his breath, while the audience were, if possible, more amazed than before. "Bless me!" cried one, "what on earth can it mean!" "Good heavens!" cried another, "it must be a spirit." "The place is haunted," cried a third. "Let's go!" said a fourth; and "let's go," had at once about fifty female echoes.

There was a rush towards the door. The whole of the ladies departed, and none remained behind but really strong-minded men, who had been induced to do so in consequence of Valentine having shouted "surely two hundred of us are a match for one ghost!"

This however was an excessively wicked observation. It was felt to be so generally, although it had the effect of inducing them to stop; for however impious might be the notion, that a ghost, if it felt disposed to tackle them, could not beat them all into fits, they felt that it was probable that one might appear, and that in the society of two hundred men, they should rather like to see it. They therefore looked for its appearance with considerable anxiety, while the members of the committee were expressing their amazement in decidedly cabalistic terms.

"What's to be done, gentlemen?" at length said the professor; "what is to be done?"

Those gentlemen raised their eyes to the ceiling, and shook their heads solemnly. The chairman looked very mysterious. He shuffled and fidgetted and pursed his thick lips, and scratched his head violently—in fact his appearance altogether was nothing at all like what it was when he playfully patted the skull of Tim Thornhill.

At length one of his colleagues—a scraggy individual, whose nose was quite blue and as round as a ball—rose to observe that he had always maintained through thick and thin, right and left, that every effect must have a regular legitimate cause; that although it would sometimes occur that when the cause was absent the effect would be present, it might not be so in that particular instance—and that he would therefore suggest that if the sounds which they had heard did proceed from that skull, it was perfectly probable that if the skull were removed, the sounds would go quietly with it.

This was hailed as an excellent suggestion. They all marvelled how they could have been so stupid as not to have thought of it before. They felt that of course it was likely—that nothing in fact could be in reality more likely than that the removal of the skull would have precisely that result: they were certain that it would; they were never so certain of any thing in their lives—but the question was, who would remove it? The professor did not appear anxious to do so: the chairman did not seem to like the job at all: the gentleman by whom the suggestion had been made thought naturally enough that he had done his share towards it, and his colleagues as naturally imagined that by urging the expediency of acting upon that suggestion, they had done quite as much as they could under the circumstances be reasonably expected to do.

At length the chairman was struck very forcibly with a bright and novel thought. The porter was in the hall? He *might* have heard something about the extraordinary occurrence from those who had departed, but it was held to be very unlikely, seeing that he was not only an Irishman, but a very sound sleeper. The porter was therefore sent for at once, and he came. He seemed rather confused as he bowed most respectfully, first to the professor, and secondly to the chairman, thirdly to the gentlemen of the committee, and fourthly to the audience, for as it was clearly his

A new feature in Phrenology

first appearance on any stage, he felt very awkward, and looked very droll.

"Murphy," said the chairman, "pick up that skull, and take it into the hall."

"It's the skull yer mane, sorr? Yes, sorr?" said Murphy; and he opened his shoulders precisely as if he had been about to remove some remarkably heavy weight, but he had no sooner got it fairly up, than Valentine, sending his voice very cleverly into it, cried, "Beware!"

"*Murther!*" cried Murphy, dropped the skull, and raising his hands with his fingers stretched as widely as possible apart. He appeared not to have sufficient breath to give utterance to another word, but standing in that attitude with his mouth wide open, he stared at the skull with an expression of horror.

"Well, sir? well?" said the chairman after a pause. "What's the matter? Take it up, sir, this moment."

Murphy stared at the chairman, then at the professor, then at the audience, and then at the skull. He had no wish to be disobedient, although he feared to obey. He therefore kicked the skull a little; then shrank from it a little; then examined it a little; and then kicked it again.

"Do you hear, sir?" shouted the chairman.

"Ye-*es*, sorr!" cried Murphy, who trembled with great freedom. "It's alive, sorr! —taint didd!"

"Nonsense!" cried the chairman, "away with it at once!"

"What the divil will I do," said Murphy, whining in a most melancholy tone.

"Do you hear me, sir? Take it below instantly."

Murphy again approached it; then rubbed himself all over; then tucked up his sleeves to gain time, and then touched it again with his foot, while he shook his head doubtfully, and eyed it with great fierceness.

"Now then!" cried the chairman, and Murphy again stooped, and then put out his hand within a yard of the skull, and drew near to it gradually inch by inch; but the moment he was about to place his hand again upon it, Valentine again cried, "Beware!"

"*Och!*" cried Murphy, striking an attitude of terror, in which, with his eyes fixed firmly upon the skull, he shrank to the very back of the rostrum.

The chairman and the professor here held a consultation, of which the result was an announcement that the lecture must be of necessity postponed. "What we have this night heard," said the professor, "is so mysterious—so strange, that I really cannot trust myself to speak on the subject. It is, however, a mystery which I trust we shall be able to solve by—"

"Bury me," interrupted Valentine, "Let me rest in peace, and seek to know no more."

The professor did not finish the speech he had commenced; but bowing to the audience, he left the stage, followed by the chairman and the gentlemen of the committee. Murphy could not of course take the precedence of any one of them: he therefore, with his eyes still fixed upon the skull, backed out as closely to the last man as possible, but before he had made his exit an idea seemed to strike him—and that too with horror—that when all had departed, he was the man who would have to extinguish the lights!

CHAPTER XXIV.

BRINGS THE READER BACK TO GOODMAN, WHO BOLDLY CONCEIVES A PARTICULAR PLAN, THE EXECUTION OF WHICH IS UNAVOIDABLY POSTPONED.

Although Goodman strongly felt that the parties to the conspiracy of which he was the victim would not escape eventual punishment, little did he think that retribution had already descended upon the head of his unnatural brother. Walter, he thought, might be living in luxury; having obtained possession of all, he might be squandering it away, or existing apparently at ease, but he envied him not; he, on the contrary, pitied him sincerely; he felt that his outraged conscience would afflict him with mental torture, but he of course had no conception that he was at that time writhing in the most intense physical agony.

There is a spirit—let us disguise its effects, or labor to repudiate its power as we may—which prompts us to cherish a feeling of gratification when they who have deeply injured us suffer those pangs which sooner or later bad actions induce. The entertainment of this feeling may indeed be attributed to want of charity; but as it forms one of the chief characteristics of the human heart, it must be at the same time deemed perfectly natural, and as we are not divine, it may with safety be asserted that no mere man ever existed on earth, to whom retributive justice upon those who had deeply injured him failed to impart secret pleasure.

Goodman was never vindictive; few indeed could boast of being actuated so slightly by the spirit of revenge: he labored to forgive his enemies; he would have forgiven Walter—freely, heartily would he have forgiven him; still when he reflected upon the misery which springs from the wounded conscience, when he reflected that his brother must absolutely hate himself for doing that which he had done, the reflection imparted that amount of gratification which made him feel that, after all, he was the happier man.

This feeling enabled him to bear up with firmness against all those indignities and brutalities to which he was then subjected: in fact he became in a short time comparatively reconciled, and he and his friend Whitely, who was his constant associate, resolved to make the best of their position, by amusing themselves as much as the bitter circumstances would allow.

Goodman very often thought of Valentine, whom he had introduced by name to his friend Whitely, and they frequently occupied their minds all day in conceiving the various scenes he had the power to produce. This was indeed to them a source of great enjoyment. They bound each other down to imagine and to describe scenes alternately, and for hours and hours they forgot their cares, and laughed as heartily as if they had been free.

Their laughter, however, struck them very often as sounding strangely, mingling as it did with the screams of a female who was shut up alone within four brick walls at the bottom of the garden. Goodman had frequently expressed a desire to see this poor lost creature; and Whitely, who was in favor with one of the keepers, succeeded, after much solicitation, in persuading the fellow to take him and Goodman into one of the upper rooms, which directly overlooked the den in which she was confined.

From the harsh screams and bitter imprecations which proceeded from this den, Goodman was led to imagine that its inmate was an old withered, wretched looking creature, whose intemperance had reduced her to a raving maniac, and whose former life had been spent among the vilest and most degraded. Conceive then, his astonishment, when, instead of a miserable, wasted, haggard being, he beheld a fair girl, whose skin was as pure as alabaster, and whose hair hung luxuriantly down her back in flaxen ringlets, running round, shouting, screaming, and uttering the most dreadful imprecations that ever proceeded from the lips of the most vicious of her sex.

"God!" exclaimed Goodman, "what a sight is this!"

"Horrible!" said his friend, "most horrible!"

"Poor dear girl! my heart bleeds for her. Has she no friends?"

"Relatives she has," replied Whitely, "or she would not be here."

"But she is insane?"

"Doubtless; but is that the way to cure insanity? Is it fit that a young creature like that—not yet arrived at womanhood, scarcely eighteen, should be buried within four walls, and not suffered to see a single soul save the wretch who casts her food into her den during the day, and chains her down to her pallet at night? Is that the way, I ask, to effect a cure? Is it not, on the contrary, directly calculated to increase the disease? But she has not been sent here to be cured; poor girl! Eternal shame on her unnatural relatives!—their only object is to keep her confined."

"But suppose," suggested Goodman, "that having done all in their power, they found her incurable?"

"Her age," replied Whitely, "forbids the supposition. The malady with which she is afflicted could not have developed itself until she had arrived at the age of fifteen or sixteen, and she is not eighteen yet. The idea of their having done all in their power to cure her is, therefore, absurd. If they had wished to have her cured, they would not have sent her here. It is monstrous that the lovely young creature, in the bloom of youth and beauty, should be subjected, under any conceivable circumstances, to such horrble treatment as this."

"Hear how wildly she calls upon the skies," said Goodman, "as if she expected aid from there."

"From there, and from there only, poor girl! will aid ever come to her."

"Well, you two! have you seen enough on her?" cried the keeper, on re-entering the room in which he had left them for a moment, as a special mark of favor.

"Thank you, Johnson," said Whitely, who knew how to manage the ruffian.—"How long has this poor girl been with you?"

"Oh, a matter of two year. That there place was built for her. Nice place for a small party, ain't it?—capital patient, though—pays more than any on 'em—mopusses comes in reg'lar as clock-work."

"And has she been always as violent as she is now?"

"No, she wasn't at first; but she soon found her voice.—I say, ain't she got a throat?—Can't she come it when she likes?—and that's in course always, for she never sleeps, she don't.—That's the rummest go. I don't suppose she's had above a dozen winks the last twelvemonth. She's night and day, night and day, eternally howling."

"That is her bed-room, I suppose," said Whitely, pointing to the upper part of the den, for the place was constructed like a pig-sty, one part being roofed, and the other quite open.

"Yes, that's where she—sleeps, I was going to say—but it's where she don't sleep—ony where she's chained down."

"The character of her disease," observed Whitely, "I suppose, is very dreadful?"

"No, there ain't much the matter with her. She only wants a husband; but as she ain't much chance of meeting one here, why she ain't much chance of leaving us yet awhile."

At this moment the poor girl saw them at the window, and her shrieks were truly awful. She raved, and spat at them, and flew round the den, and endeavored to clutch them, and folded her arms as if she had one of them in her embrace, and then shricked again horribly.

"Come," cried the keeper, "come, come along down; you've seen quite enough on her now;" and he led the way back into the garden.

During the whole of that day the two friends spoke of nothing but the appalling spectacle they had witnessed, and when the time for being driven into their cells had arrived, they retired with hearts full of sorrow.

In the morning, however, Goodman was a different man. His spirits were buoyant, if not, indeed, gay; and as he shook the hand of his friend with more than usual ardor, he smiled with intense satisfaction. Whitely was delighted with his altered appearance. He felt that he must have heard some good news, and being well assured that *his* liberation would be the prelude to his own, he manifested the utmost anxiety during the whole of the time they were at breakfast.

On reaching the garden, Goodman again smiled; when Whitely grasped his hand, and looking intently at him, said, "My dear friend! you have heard—something?"

"No," said Goodman, still however smiling—"No."

"Heard nothing?" cried Whitely whose hopes at once vanished. "Then why do you smile?"

"Because I have thought of something," replied Goodman, "which may perhaps answer our purpose as well."

"Indeed!" cried Whitely, whose hopes again revived. "What is it?"

"I can of course confide in you, and will therefore explain. I have arranged it all in my own mind. I have been nearly the whole of the night bringing the plan to bear. We cannot fail. We are perfectly certain to be successful."

"Well, what is it? what is it?" cried Whitely with great impatience.

"I conceived a scheme last night," said Goodman, "which has but to be carried into execution, for our freedom to be at once secured."

"I see—I see," said Whitely shaking his head, "an escape. Ah, my friend, don't believe it to be possible."

"But I do," said Goodman, "I cannot but believe it to be possible. In the first place, how many of these fellows—these keepers are there here?"

"Six," replied Whitely, "with the man at the gate."

"Six; very well. How many patients or prisoners are there who are perfectly sane?"

"Thirty, perhaps; but say twenty-five."

"Well, say that there are but twenty. I am an old man, still I have some strength; you are much younger, and have more strength than I, and many whom I could point out have much more than you. Now is it not disgraceful that twenty or five-and-twenty strong hearty fellows should suffer themselves to be kept in so dreadful a place as this by half a dozen tyrannous scoundrels, whom, if it were necessary, they could strangle in five minutes! Is it not, I ask, monstrous, that we, who have health and strength and justice on our side, should permit half a dozen degraded myrmidons, hired to sustain one of the most frightful systems with which men were ever yet cursed, to tyrannize over and trample upon us, to chain us down like felons, and to kick us like brutes, when by simply displaying the strength which we possess, we might at once obtain our liberty?"

Mr. Whitley shook his head, and slightly smiled, and then sighed; but he made no reply.

"I admit," continued Goodman, "that, man to man, they would be more than a match for us—that we could not compete with them at all; but twenty-five to six—that is, more than four to one!—Upon my life, I do think that the fact of our being here reflects disgrace upon us as men. There would not be the smallest necessity for hurting those persons. God forbid that I should injure any man however cruelly he may have injured me; but what, my friend—what if we were to go in a body to the gates, and to tell them firmly and resolutely to refuse us egress at their peril? Is it to be supposed that they would make more than the mere show of resistance, or that if they even were to resist us, we could not at once overcome them? Does it not, I ask, strike you as being dreadful, that five-and-twenty men, who have been stolen from society as we have been stolen, should continue to suffer these brutal indignities, should be kept here like convicts by a handful of wretches whom we have the power to crush?"

"It does," said Whitely, "it does seem dreadful."

"Then why do we continue to endure it?"

"Because—simply because we cannot help ourselves, my friend."

"But why can we not? What is there to prevent our escape in a body, and that too at once?"

"Do you think," observed Whitely, with great calmness, "that you and I now could thrash the six keepers, were we to set to work manfully, and put out our strength?"

"Alone? certainly not. I have already said that man to man they would be more than a match for us; but twenty-five to six! consider that."

"I have, my friend, considered it, calmly considered it, and have arrived at this conclusion, that if we cannot thrash the six keepers ourselves, your scheme, is, under the circumstances, utterly impracticable?"

"But why is it impracticable?"

"Because," replied Whitely, "we should have to depend solely upon ourselves; we could not calculate upon having the slightest assistance. Our poor fellow-prisoners have been here so long, that their minds have become enervated; they have not the strength—the moral courage to join us. I readily grant, that if all, or even a third of them were staunch, we might, by taking these myrmidons by surprise, effect our object; but their spirits are broken; they have lost all energy; they could not be depended upon for a moment; they have no heart, no resolution. Were we to propose the thing to them, no matter with what eloquence and force they would shrink from the attempt; they would not dare to join us; they would at once agree with you, that our imprisonment under the circumstance, reflects disgrace upon us as men, and that, if an attempt were made, success would be almost certain; but they would look at the consequences of a *failure*, and that would be sufficient to deter them from acting; for they know by sad experience, that albeit they are assumed to be unconscious of their actions, they are punished for those actions in spite of that assumption, and that the punishment which would inevitably follow the failure of an attempt like that which you have suggested would be dreadful. I myself thought of the same plan the day I came here, and felt as certain as you now feel, that it might with ease be carried into immediate execution; but when I had sounded several of those whom I had fancied were likely to join me, I found their minds so enfeebled, their spirits so low, that if even I had succeeded in goading them on to an attempt, they would in all probability have deserted me at the very moment when energy and resolution were most essential to success. They have not the courage, my friend—depend upon it they have not the courage. Every man, sir, in an enterprise of that kind, would act like a child."

Goodman was silent, but by no means convinced of the impracticability of this scheme. He still felt sure that it might be carried into effect, for "what," thought he, "if the minds of these persons are enervated, is it impossible for their energies to be aroused?" As, however, precipitation was in a matter of this kind to be condemned, the subject was for that time dropped; but he still resolved to make every effort in his power to inspire his companions with spirit sufficient to join him and Whitely in effecting their escape.

CHAPTER XXV.

VALENTINE VISITS THE VICTUALLER'S FANCY FAIR.

In the Coffee Room of the tavern at which Valentine occasionally dined he saw, a few days after his display among the phrenologists, a placard, which was headed, "The Licensed Victuallers' Asylum," and which announced that a Fancy Fair and a Fete Champetre were about to take place under most distinguished patronage.

"The Licensed Victuallers' Asylum!" thought Valentine, who had been taught to associate Licensed Victuallers with all that is selfish, grasping, and gross; is it possible that they can have erected an asylum—that they can have been prevailed upon to sustain the unfortunate, the aged, and the infirm! And yet why should they not?"

He stuck at this question. He couldn't answer it. He couldn't tell why they should not be benevolent; and being anxious to study the character of every class of men with whom he came in contact, he invited a remarkably corpulent, good-natured looking old fellow, who he felt could be nothing but the landlord, to have a glass of wine.

"What is the nature of this asylum?" said Valentine, when the old boy had squatted himself down, which he did without a second invitation, and began to pant fiercely, blowing out his cheeks at every pant, as if, conscious of the remarkably precious nature of breath, he wished to retain it in his mouth as long as possible.

"Why, sir," said the landlord whose name was Broadsides, "that, sir,'s the Witlers' 'Sylum, 'stablished by Witlers, and a capital 'sylum it is, sir, too."

"No doubt," observed Valentine, "but what are its objects?"

"Why of course, sir, to perwide a good home for old broken down Witlers, and a werry good home it perwides. We take care of their children, too, poor things! We've a school for 'em fit for any nobleman in the land. You should see 'em, God bless 'em, how happy they are. It's a blessing to look at 'em, that it is, a blessing."

"You are going to have a Fancy Fair, I perceive?"

"Of course, sir! We always do, annally, and an out-and-out thing it is too. You'd be pleased, if you never was there. If you've nothing better to do, I'd adwise you to go. It's a treat sir. I love it, the object is so good."

Valentine was delighted with the feeling tones in which the old gentleman spoke, more especially when he alluded to the children; for tears stood in his eyes, as he said, "Poor things! God bless 'em!" which, without the slightest effort to conceal them, he mopped up mechanically with his thick Belcher handkerchief, and seemed to blow away with considerably more freedom.

"There is much of the pure spirit of benevolence in this man's composition," thought Valentine, "rough as he is; and if he be in reality a fair sample of the lot, they are indeed a very good set of fellows."

"Say you'll go?" cried Broadsides, slapping the thigh of Valentine, as if he had known him for years.

"Well, I will!" cried Valentine, rubbing his thigh, and smiling.

"Then I'll tell you what it is. I rayther like you; I think you're a good sort, and I'm not often out of my reckoning; if you'll go I'll drive you down, and give you as good a glass of wine as can be got when we get there."

"You must leave the wine to me in that case," said Valentine; "but I hope that I shall not be depriving any part of your family of a seat?"

"By no means in life! My Missus and the girls goes the second day, 'cause you know, business must be attended to; so, of course, I shall be glad to have your company down."

It was settled. The morning came, and Valentine went to the house of Mr. Broadsides, who shook him by the hand with the warmth of a friend; introduced him to his wife and two daughters, and after having what he termed a "leetle snack" in the bar, the gig was brought to the door, and they started.

The very moment they were off, the old boy began to talk. He, in the first place, gave the pedigree of his horse, explained how many miles an hour he had done, how many miles an hour he was able to do then, and how about twenty years ago, when he was younger, he trotted from London to Brighton within the six hours, and that, without sweating a hair. He then spoke of the peculiarly good qualities of Mrs. Broadsides, as a woman of business; he explained that she was "an extrornary good wife, and an excellent mother," but that she had a "particular nasty temper," and that *that* was all he had to complain of. He then touched upon the virtues of his daughters, whom he described as "the best girls any where—none could be better, let them come from where they might;" he showed very clearly what treasures they would be to those who might have the good fortune to marry them; and after having dwelt upon their peculiar characteristics for some considerable time with great eloquence and pride, they reached a road-side inn, at which he put up his horse, and then waddled by the side of Valentine down a lane, which led at once to the Asylum.

A scene of gaiety presented itself the moment they reached the gate; and after passing the marquee, in which toys of every description were set out for sale, they entered the building, which was really very extensive, and reflected great credit upon the Victuallers as a body.

Broadsides was recognised at once by a number of jolly-looking persons, who wore their hats on one side, and their hands in their pockets, and never took them out, except indeed for the purpose of greeting their friends. After an infinite deal of nodding, and slapping, and squeezing through the passage, Valentine and Broadsides proceeded up stairs to the board-room, round which the names of the donors and the amounts of the donations were emblazoned in letters of gold.

"That," said Broadsides, pointing to a well-executed portrait which hung at one end of the room, "that, of course is the founder of the institution."

Valentine could not resist the temptation; he therefore threw his voice into the picture, and said, "How are you? how do?"

Broadsides started; and the expression of his countenance was singularly droll. "Didn't you hear?" he cried, seizing the arm of Valentine, who replied that he heard something.

"Something!" he continued. "It's the picture!" and he began to blow away with great energy.

"Don't be alarmed! don't be alarmed!" said Valentine, again throwing his voice towards the portrait, and the founder seemed to smile as Broadsides nodded, but in a way that seemed to indicate that he didn't understand it all.

"I say, Bowles! Bowles!" cried Mr. Broadsides, seizing the arm of a friend who had just entered. "I say, here; look at that pictur!—I just heered it speak!"

"Heered it what?" cried Mr. Bowles, with a smile of incredulity.

"Speak!" returned Broadsides, and Mr. Bowles laughed very heartily.

"As true as I'm here, it's a fact; I heered him, as plain as I ever did when he was alive!"

"Why what *are* you talking about, you jolly old fool?" said Mr. Bowles. "Have you been having a drain already this morning? What have you got into your stupid old head?"

"I don't care a farden about what you say. I tell you I heered the pictur speak as plain as flesh and blood!"

"But how could it?"

"I don't know how it could; I only know that it did, and that's enough for me."

Bowles slapped Mr. Broadsides on the back, and told him in friendly terms, that he was an out-and-out old ass; and moreover observed, that he should see him again, he supposed, by and bye.

"Well, this is sartny *about* the rummest go," said Mr. Broadsides, when Bowles had left the room, "that mortal man ever heerd tell on."

"By no means," said Valentine, through the medium of the founder; "did you never hear of a spirited portrait?"

The idea of a spirited portrait appeared to strike a light into the soul of Mr. Broadsides. He *had* heard of a spirited portrait, and felt that he never knew, till then, to what species the term legitimately applied. He fancied, however, that he saw it then clearly; and, although he did not exactly tremble, he felt very queer.

"Did you know him?" inquired Valentine, who feigned great amazement.

"Know him!" replied Broadsides. "Him and me were buzzum friends! Many's the bottle of wine we've had together!"

"Well, then, you've no reason to fear him."

"Fear him!" cried Broadsides, he wouldn't hurt a hair of my head. It isn't that—it's only the rumness of the thing, you see, that gets over me." And Mr. Broadsides sat down, and gazed upon the portrait, until he fancied that he could see the benevolent founder's lips curl and his eyes sparkle, as they were wont, when the original received an unusually large order.

"Well, shall we see what they are doing below?" said Valentine.

"Yes—yes!" replied Mr. Broadsides, whose eyes were still fixed on the portrait. "Yes: the only thing, you see, that puzzles me is, that it isn't his voice;" a fact which was certainly by no means extraordinary, seeing that Valentine had never, of course, heard the founder speak. "But I suppose," continued Broadsides, "that spirits don't speak in the same tones as regular flesh and blood."

"Good day," observed Valentine, throwing his voice again towards the portrait.

"God bless you! Good day," said Mr. Broadsides, who after taking another long gaze, caught hold of the arm of Valentine and waddled from the room.

Now when Broadsides had got about half way down stairs, it struck him again as being very extraordinary. He therefore stopped short; and after blowing out his cheeks to the fullest extent, and looking with considerable earnestness at Valentine, said, "Well, this is out of all doubt the most singularest thing I ever met with in all my born days," and having delivered himself of this remarkable sentiment, he and Valentine slowly descended.

On reaching the end of the passage which led through the building, Valentine found that, although the Fancy Fair was confined to the front of the Asylum, the chief attraction was behind; for a spacious lawn opened before them, which was literally crowded with gaily dressed persons, promenading with great propriety, and looking very happy; while at the bottom of the lawn there were several well constructed marquees, which were uniformly pitched, and had a striking effect.

"Well, now, this exceeds my expectations," said Valentine, waving his hand towards the scene which so brilliantly opened before him.

"Yes," observed Broadsides, "yes, yes; very pretty, very pretty; but that pictur—I can't get that out of my head; that gets over me above a bit."

"Oh never mind the picture," said Valentine. "What are they doing here?" and he dragged Mr. Broadsides, who looked very solemn, towards one of the marquees, before which a crowd of persons were standing. In this place there was a very great variety of toys, but the attraction was an affair which was termed "the wheel of fortune," out of which, by paying the small charge of one shilling, any lady or gentleman was entitled to draw a slip of paper, the number emblazoned upon which referred to some valuable little article in stock. An interesting child about seven years old turned the wheel, and when a bluff individual—who kept continually recommending the ladies and gentlemen present to "try their luck, for as they was all prizes and no blanks at all, they couldn't do nothing but win"—had looked at the papers drawn, he called the numbers, and another individual with a list in his hand named the articles to which the numbers respectively applied, which articles were delivered to the individuals who had had the extraordinary good fortune to gain them.

When Valentine had ascertained how this business was managed, he could not be silent; he felt himself bound to play some of his highly reprehensible tricks. He therefore imitated the voice of the bluff individual, to such perfection, and called so continually certain numbers which had never been drawn, that at length that individual became extremely angry with the other individual, who kept as continually naming little articles which had not been won.

"Now then," said the former, "twenty-two."

"No, twenty-seven," cried Valentine, assuming his voice.

"Twenty-seven," said the person who held the paper. "Twenty-seven—."

"Twenty-two!" cried the bluff individual. "Mind what you're about."

"But you said twenty-*seven*," said his assistant, who didn't at all like to be spoken to thus before company.

"I say that I said twenty-two, sir," shouted the bluff individual, looking particularly black.

"Twenty-two," said his assistant, "is a shaving brush," which article was at once handed over to the lady by whom it had been so appropriately won.

Valentine perceived that if he went on in this way he should probably destroy that good understanding which had previously existed between these two persons, and as he had no desire to do that, especially as one of them clearly felt compelled to put up with the blustering insolence of the other, he took the arm of Mr. Broadsides, who still kept harping upon the "pictur" and walked to the principal marquee.

"Oh, ho!" cried Valentine on entering, "all who drink here will not go home sober to-night!" which, although it was unheeded by Mr. Broadsides, was certainly a very natural exclamation, inasmuch as the marquee in question was lined with flaming pink-and-white festooned glazed cambric, which had so exceedingly dazzling an effect, that a single pint of wine drank there would have excited a man as much as a couple of bottles would, drank in a quiet-colored room.

"Come," said Mr. Broadsides, "now let's have a little bit of summut to eat here. Here, waiter! Now, what have you got!" and an ugly little rascal, who was the counterpart of Fieschi, and who personated the character of a waiter for that particular occasion, replied, "Fowls, sir, ham, sir, fowls and ham, roast beef, ham and beef, sir, tongue and roast duck."

Fowl and ham were ordered for two, and part of a leg with part of a wing were eventually placed upon the table.

"What d'ye mean by bringing us these two mites!" cried Mr. Broadsides, indignantly digging his fork into one of them with the view of inspecting its dimensions more closely.

"Fowl and ham for two, sir, you ordered," said the waiter.

"D'ye call this fowl and ham for two? Bring us a whole un, and plenty of ham, not two tiny dabs like them!"

Fieschi looked if possible more ugly than before, as he took away the dish, the contents of which looked, after having been disturbed, by no means calculated to impart satisfaction to any man's stomach. He soon however returned with what was by courtesy termed a whole fowl, particularly small and very skinny. But such as it was, Broadsides pushed it towards Valentine for the purpose of dissection, and Valentine not being a family man, thought the shortest way of carving up the animal would be to cut at once right across the breast bone, and thus to divide the thing equally; but he had no sooner made the first cut, which effectually severed the body in twain, than Broadsides cried, "Send I may live! What *are* you at? Here, give us hold"—and called upon Fieschi to bring him a skewer. Fieschi accordingly produced a skewer which he said he had "drawed from a buttick o' beef," with which Mr. Broadsides stuck the fowl again together, and then proceeded to cut it up very scientifically into a number of pieces—which Valentine fancied unnecessarily small, as it would be all the same in the long run which was about to take place in the course of five minutes—Mr. Broadsides observing, as he dexterously took out the small bones which young ladies in farm houses pull to ascertain whose fate it is first to be married, that he had been "head cook in the principalist tavern in London, and never in all his experience seed a chicken attempted to be carved in sich a fashion as that." He contended that half the beauty of it was in the carving, while Valentine thought it all consisted in the eating; but as the experience of Broadsides enabled him to get the better of the argument, he felt satisfied, and called for a bottle of wine.

"Have you got a bottle now," said he, "at all fit to drink?"

"Capital wine, sir?" replied Fieschi.

"Well, bring us some of the decentest you have, d'ye hear?"—and a bottle of sherry was accordingly brought, which Broadsides no sooner tasted, than he began at once to spit, and to blow, and to make up such a very extraordinary face, that Fieschi imagined that he had by mistake brought forward a bottle of vinegar.

"Do you call this wine?" cried Broadsides, spitting and blowing still with remarkable energy.

"Beg pardon," replied Fieschi, putting the cork to his nose, "it smells like wine, sir."

"Smells like wine," echoed Broadsides, contemptuously. "It has naything the smell nor the taste of wine. It's enough to give an elephant the deliberate tremens. Give my compliments to your master, and tell him that may name's Broadsides, and if he can't send me a little better bottle of wine than that, he'd better set to work at once and drink it himself. Here, leave this now as it's opened, and go fetch something a little matter fit to go into a christian's stomach.—Did you ever taste such wine?" he continued, addressing Valentine, who thought it very fair wine, and said so; but Broadsides declared that "if he ever brought up such a bottle of wine as that to any customer of his, he'd go and cut his throat."

The name of Broadsides appeared to have a great effect upon the master of Fieschi, for he not only sent a bottle of wine of which Broadsides approved, but ordered Fieschi to bring the other bottle away! This act of liberality had in return a great effect upon Broadsides, who praised the last bottle before he had tasted it, and told Fieschi to let the other remain. Fieschi, however, respectfully insisted upon obeying his master's order, and Broadsides in return insisted upon Fieschi's master coming to take a glass with him as soon as he had a moment to spare.

"Now, this is very decent, considering," said he, "but lor! it ain't no more like what's in my cellar—but then, lor, how can you expect it!"

By this time Valentine had demolished his share of the chicken, and had even commenced the process of flaying the back bone, when another was produced, which Mr. Broadsides instructed him how to carve properly; and he eventually did it to the entire satisfaction of that gentleman, who declared that, after that, he "would be fit to cut up anything in the world, at any table in life."

Now, when Valentine and Broadsides had finished their meal, Mr. Bowles came into the marquee with three remarkably red-faced friends, to whom Broadsides, although he knew them well—was introduced as "the man wot heard the picture speak."

"I just did," said Broadsides, "and no mistake!" Upon which Mr. Bowles and his red-faced friends began to laugh very heartily and very loudly. "I don't care a dump," he continued, "about what you think, or what you say. If I didn't hear it speak, why I never heered nothing."

"You always was a rum 'un," observed Mr. Bowles.

"I don't care for that," returned Broadsides. "Come, I'll tell you what I do now, I'll bet you a rump and dozen I heard it now, come!"

This favorite and highly approved method of settling an argument, seemed for a moment to stagger Mr. Bowles, for he felt that he could not prove that Mr. Broadsides didn't hear it, and that if the onus of proof even rested with Broadsides, he had the evidence of his own ears at least, to bring forward, while he himself could produce no evidence at all; thinking, however, subsequently that the affirmative could not be proved, he said, "Done," and Valentine throwing his voice behind Mr. Bowles cried, "You've lost."

"How lost?" shouted Mr. Bowles, turning sharply round. "Who says I have lost?" His red-faced friends stared at each other, but neither of them spoke. "Who says I have lost?" he again inquired. "Who's to prove it?"

"I," cried Valentine, sending his voice above. "I!—the spirit of Hodgson!"

"Now, will you believe me?" cried Broadsides, triumphantly, "Now am I a stupid old ass?"

Mr. Bowles looked amazed, and so did the red-faced friends of Mr. Bowles. They stared, first at each other, and then round the marquee, and after Mr. Bowles had expressed his decided conviction that the thing was "onaccountably rum," he and his friends at once sat down, and having thrust their hands to the very bottom of their breeches pockets, began to look particularly solemn.

"Isn't it queer?" said Mr. Broadsides, who was the first to break silence.

"Queer!" replied Bowles—"Here, give us some wine, and don't say a word more about it." And Mr. Bowles helped himself, and then pushed the bottle round, and when his friends had filled their glasses, they said with due solemnity, "Here's luck," and the wine was out of sight in an instant.

Another bottle was ordered; and when Fieschi had produced it, Mr. Broadsides begged leave to propose as a toast, "The immortal memory of the Founder," which, of course, was duly honored in silence.

A pause ensued. They were all deep in thought; they were turning the circumstance over in their minds, and were, apparently, just about coming to the conclusion that the sounds were imaginary after all, when Valentine, throwing his voice into the folds of the pink-aud-white cambric, said in tones of appropriate solemnity, "Gentlemen, I rise to thank you for the honor you have conferred upon me, and beg, in return, to drink all your good healths."

Mr. Broadsides, Mr. Bowles, and his red-faced friends, held their breath. They stared at the cambric with an expression of astonishment, but for some moments neither of them uttered a word. At length, Mr. Bowles broke silence. "Well, said he, "this beats all my acquaintance. I'm not going to stop here, and that's all about it."

The friends of Mr. Bowles seemed to like this idea; and as Broadsides did not appear to be by any means opposed to such a proceeding, the bottle was emptied, and when the amount of what was termed the "damage," had been paid, the whole party left the marquee.

On reaching the lawn again, where they began to breathe with infinitely more freedom, the firing of cannon was heard, and several persons in the crowd exclaimed, "the children! the children!" Again and again the cannon were fired, and the visitors rushed to the sides of the lawn, round which the poor children were to pass. The band by which they were preceded drew nearer and nearer, and all hearts seemed gay, although the eyes of the old people glistened with tears.

At length a policeman marched out of the passage which led through the asylum. He was followed by the band; then came a double row of octogenarian pensioners, whose appearance was calculated at once to upset all the tea-total doctrines in the world, at least, as far as those doctrines have reference to longevity: then came the gentlemen of the board, with their blue rosettes and smiling faces: then came the children, and then the schoolmaster! whose head, albeit remarkably large, and attached to a body weighing, at least sixteen stone, seemed inclined to repudiate the idea of its being impossible to find out perpetual motion. Thus formed, the procession marched round the ample lawn, and the children appeared to impart great delight to the bosoms of their benevolent patrons.

"I don't know how it is," said Mr. Broadsides, when they had passed, "but them children there always makes me feel, I don't know how;" and a couple of big tears, as he spoke, dropt into his white waistcoat-pockets.

"I say, Broadsides," said Bowles, who at the moment approached with his red-faced friends, "what fools we all are!"

"What about?" said Mr. Broadsides.

"Why about that there voice, there," replied Mr. Bowles. "I see it all now. Why mightn't it have come from some vagabone at the top?" and Mr. Bowles gave Mr. Broadsides a dig in the ribs, and laughed again loudly, and his red-faced friends joined in full chorus.

Mr. Broadsides dropped his head on his left shoulder, thoughtfully; but after a time an idea seemed to strike him, and he exclaimed, "so it might! some wagabone *might* have been a top o' the tent; but how could he get in the *pictur?*"

This, in return, seemed to puzzle Mr. Bowles: but after scratching his head for some considerable time, he cried, "well! I don't care;—I won't believe in any of your supernatteral nonsense. I say there must have been some blaggard outside. Will you make me believe that a ghost could return thanks in that there way? Ain't it out of all reason? Come, let's go and see where the vagabone could have stood." And he dragged Mr. Broadsides to the back of the marquee, when Valentine, fancying that if he remained with them the wine would go round perhaps a little too fast, left the spot, and proceeded to another marquee, in which the whole of the provisions were dispensed.

The person who presided over this large establishment was a man whom nothing seemed to please. He cut about among the bottles in such a dreadful state of mind, freely sweating, and loudly swearing that every body robbed him, and laboring apparently under the horrible apprehension that he was working very hard to make himself a ruined mau. The good which he did himself was, indeed, very trifling; but he jumped from one end of the tent to the other with the velocity of a grasshopper, pushing aside all who happened to come in his way—scolding some for putting too much spirit in the grog, and others, for not putting in enough—declared that one hadn't paid him for a bottle of stout, and that another wished to swindle him out of a plate of boiled beef—in short, he seemed to be, on the whole, a most unhappy individual, although a decidedly good-looking man.

"Well, old boy," said Valentine, throwing his voice behind this remarkable person; "and how do you get on?"

"On!" cried that person, "good luck to you, don't say a word to me now, whoever you are. I shall go raving mad;—every body's robbing me; every body's at it; I don't believe I've got a single honest man about me."

"Do you see," cried Valentine, "how your wine's going under the tent there?"

"Under the tent!" cried the busy person, "where? Here, Tomkins! Smith! Lucas! run behind, and knock down those vagabonds, *dy'e hear!* Behind there! behind!" and away went three waiters. "I *thought*," he continued, "that the wine went somewhere. I've lost a couple of dozen, at least; and nobody 'll look out, nobody 'll assist me, although I am surrounded by plundering thieves; nobody 'll move hand or foot; I must do all myself."

"*There's* nobody behind!" cried Lucas, returning; and Tomkins, and Smith bore testimony to the fact.

"I tell you they've been forking out the wine! but you're all in a gang. I expect to see you all, by and by, as drunk as devils. If I've lost one bottle, I've lost five dozen. But let 'em come again—only let them try it on! *I'll* keep my eye upon 'em—I'll sarve them out, the warmint!" and he placed an empty bottle near a hole in the canvass, and a carving-knife upon a hamper beside it, with the view of having a cut at the very next hand that happened to be clandestinely introduced.

Valentine feeling that it would be cruel to tease this unhappy man under the circumstances any longer, left the spot, and proceeded across the lawn with the view of inspecting the female visitors, of whom all were well dressed, and some very beautiful, but none in his judgment one-half so beautiful as the fair unknown whom he had saved to lose, he feared, for ever. There was in the crowd one who, with soft sleepy eyes, which when opened were brilliant and full, bore some slight resemblance to his idol; but even she was not comparable to her of whom he felt so much enamored, for while her features were irregular, and her figure inelegant, her voice, which he heard as he passed, contrasted harshly with those sweet silvery tones which he so well remembered.

His ear, was, however, at this moment assailed with a different species of music, for the band commenced the overture to *Der Frieschutz*, with the wild unearthly phrases of which he had before felt enchanted. He had scarcely, however, reached the lawn in front of the Asylum, on which the band was stationed, when he was startled by a remarkably heavy slap on the shoulder, which on turning round he found to proceed from Mr. Broadsides, who had evidently been taking more wine, and who exclaimed, "Well, old fellow, why, where have you been poking to? We've been running all over the place to find you. Come, let's see what's agoing forrard here;" and taking the arm of Valentine, he at once led the way into the booth termed the "Ladies' Bazaar," in which all sorts of toys were exposed for sale, and the avenue was crowded, but they nevertheless stopped to inspect every stall.

"Will you buy me a work-box, please, Mr. Broadsides," said Valentine, assuming a female voice, which appeared to proceed from a very gaily dressed little lady who stood just beside him.

Mr. Broadsides chucked the little lady under the chin, and said, "Certainly, my little dear, which would you like?"

"*Sir!*" cried the little lady, tossing her head proudly, and turning away with a look of indignation.

Broadsides blew out his cheeks with an energy which threatened to crack them, and after giving a puff which nearly amounted to a whistle, he tossed his head in humble imitation of the little lady, and turned round to Bowles.

"Hullo!" said that gentleman, "Can't let the girls alone, eh? still up to your old tricks? I shall tell Mrs. Broadsides."

Now, although Mr. Bowles had no intention whatever of carrying this threat into actual execution, the bare mention of that lady's name caused Broadsides to blow with more energy than before. "Why," said he, "didn't you hear the cretur ask me to buy her a work-box?"

"It's all very fine," replied Bowles, "but it won't do, old boy, it won't do."

"Well, if she didn't, I'm blessed!" rejoined Broadsides, "and that's all about it."

Mr. Bowles, however, still very stoutly maintained that if she had, she would never have bounced off in that way, and as that was an argument over which Mr. Broadsides could not very comfortably get, he seized Valentine's arm and pressed back through the crowd.

"Well," said he, on returning to the lawn, "how do you find yourself now?"

"Why," replied Valentine, "particularly thirsty, can't we have some tea?"

"Tea is a thing I never do drink," said Broadsides; "but if you'd like to have some I'll tell you what we'll do; we'll give one of the old women a turn, you know, instead of going down to that there tent."

Valentine, of course, was quite willing to do so; and as the charitable suggestion was applauded by Mr. Bowles and the only red-faced friend he had with him, they went into one of the little rooms in the Asylum, and after Broadsides had warmly kissed its occupant, who was remarkably old, but remarkably clean, he at once ordered tea for half a dozen.

"There are but four of us," observed Mr. Bowles, as the delighted old lady left the room to make the necessary preparations.

Oh! never mind," said Broadsides, "it'll be all the better, you know, for the old woman. She don't have a turn every day. You wouldn't believe it," he continued, "but that old cretur, there, when I first knew her, kept one of the best houses of business in London!"

"Is she a widder?" inquired Mr. Bowles.

"Now she is, but she wasn't then; old Sam was alive at that time."

"And when he died I suppose things went to rack and ruin?"

"Oh, that occurred before he went home. He was the steadiest man any where, the first seven years he was in business, and made a mint o'money; but when he lost his daughter, a beautiful girl, just for all the world like my Betsy, he all at once turned out a regular Lushington, and everything of course went sixes and sevens. He always made it a pint of getting drunk before breakfast, and ruination in one way of course, brought on ruination in another, until he was obliged for to go all to smash. Poor Sam died very soon after that time you see, because he couldn't eat. It don't matter what a man drinks, so long as he can eat, but when he can't eat, he ought to leave off drinking till he can. That's my sentiments."

"There's a good deal in that," said Mr. Bowles, "a good deal."

"Well, dame," said Broadsides, as the widow re-entered the room; "why you are looking younger and younger every day. It's many years now since you and me first met."

"Ah!" said the poor old lady, with a sigh, "I've gone through a world of trouble sin' then; but, God be praised for all his goodness, I'm as happy now as the days are long."

"That's right, my old girl," said Mr. Broadsides, "that's right! I say now, can't you get us a bottle of decent port anywhere about here?"

"I dares to say I can," replied the old lady, and she put on her bonnet, and having received a sovereign, trotted out.

Mr. Bowles now began to roast Mr. Broadsides about the little indignant lady and the work-box; but that gentleman turned the tables on Mr. Bowles by reminding him, that when he lived at Brixton, and was at a party at Kennington, he insisted upon seeing a young lady home, not knowing where she lived; and when the favor was granted, he had to walk with her, at twelve o'clock at night, into Red Cow Lane, near Stepney Green.

"Is that a fact?" inquired the red-faced friend of Mr. Bowles.

"Oh that's true enough," replied Bowles, "and all I could do, I couldn't get her to ride."

Hereupon Mr. Broadsides and Valentine, and the red-faced gentleman indulged in loud laughter, and Mr. Bowles very heartily joined them, and when the old lady entered with the wine, she laughed too; but the sight of the bottle subdued Mr. Broadsides, who in an instant began to uncork it. "Keep the change, old girl, till I call for it," said he, and the old lady said that he was a very good man, and hoped that God would bless him, and that his family might prosper.

Valentine had to make tea; and Mr. Broadsides sat at another little table over his wine, which he drank very fast and very mechanically, for his thoughts were on the mysterious occurrences of the day. Valentine, however, would not let him rest, for taking advantage of an unusually silent moment, he introduced under the table at which he was sitting, an exact imitation of the squeaking of a rat.

"Hallo!" cried Broadsides, starting up in a moment, and seizing the poker, and in doing so, knocking down the shovel and tongs; "only let me come across you."

"What's the matter with you *now?*" exclaimed Mr. Bowles.

"Shet the door, shet the door!" cried Broadsides to the widow, who had entered, on hearing the rattling of the irons. "Here's a rat—a rat!" and the old lady dropped upon a chair and wound her clothes in an instant round her legs as tightly as possible, while Broadsides was anxiously removing every article of furniture in the room, and searching in every corner with the poker in his hand.

"Lor' bless us!" cried the widow, "I didn't know there was a rat in the place," and another squeak was heard, upon which Mr. Broadsides jumped upon a chair with all the alacrity at his command, which was not very considerable, and looked very fierce.

The laughter of Mr. Bowles and his red-faced friend at that moment was particularly hearty, for they were not afraid of rats! but Mr. Broadsides was, and so was the old-lady, who continued to sit in an interesting heap.

"Only let me ccme across him!" cried Broadsides again, and doubtless had a rat at that moment appeared, it would have stood a very fair chance of giving up the ghost, for Mr. Broadsides shook the poker with great desperation, and looked altogether extremely ferocious.

"Come down from that chair, do, you jolly old fool," cried Mr. Bowles; "as true as life, I shall bust!" and another roar of laughter proceeded from him and his friend, in which Valentine could not help joining. Indeed he laughed so heartly, that all alarm subsided, for as he couldn't *squeak* for laughing, Broadsides eventually descended from the chair.

"They're nasty things are rats," said he, "particular nasty things. I can't abear 'em," and he began to give an account of the ferocious characteristics of those little animals, describing the different species and the different parts at which each of those different species took it into their heads to fly; and while he was drawing the line between the grey rat and the black rat, the old lady still holding her clothes down very tightly, managed to rush, with great presence of mind, from the room.

Mr. Bowles and his friend, however, continued to laugh, and as the squeaking had ceased, Mr. Broadsides laughed too, while Valentine, who then had a stitch in his side, slipped away in a dreadful state of muscular excitement.

The very moment he got out of the place, he met one of the red-faced friends of Mr. Bowles, walking between two gaudily dressed ladies, one of whom was remarkably short and fat, while the other was remarkable only for her decided skeletonian characteristics. To these ladies Valentine was formally introduced; the short fat lady, as the wife of the red-faced gentleman, and the tall thin lady, as Miss Amelia Spinks.

"We are going to have a dance," said the red-faced gentleman, "will you join us?"

"With pleasure," replied Valentine, looking into the little laughing eyes of the short fat lady, who mechanically drew her arm from that of her husband, and Valentine as mechanically offered her his.

Thus paired, though by no means matched, they proceeded across the lawn, and having reached the dancing booth, they paid the admission fee, and entered.

The place was dreadfully hot, as were indeed all who were in it, for they not only danced with all their souls, and with all their strength, but, in consequence of the place being so crowded, they bumped up against each other's bustles at every turn, while the professional gentlemen in a sort of box were scraping and blowing away, like North Britons.

Valentine solicited the hand of the short far lady for the next set.

"Oh dear," said that lady, "I'm so werry horkard; but is it to be a country dance?"

Valentine hoped not, from his soul, under the circumstances, and was gratified to learn that country dances were there repudiated, as vulgar. He, however, ascertained that they were going to have a Spanish dance, which certainly was the next best thing; and, having communicated that interesting fact to the lady in question, he prevailed upon her eventually to stand up.

The gentlemen now clapped their hands with due energy, with the view of intimating to the musicians, who were sweating like bullocks, that they were perfectly prepared to start off, and after a time those professional individuals did consent to sound the note of preparation.

Now in order that all might be in motion together, every third couple were expected to lead off, and as Valentine and his partner happened to form a third couple, they of course changed sides, and the dance commenced.

"I do hope," said she, when they had got to the bottom, "that we shall have to go all the way down again, it is beautiful." But unfortunately for her the music ceased the next moment, and the dance was at an end. And then, oh! how she did run on! Nothing was ever half so lovely, one quarter so nice, or one hundred and fiftieth part so delightful as that Spanish dance. She was sure thero never was such an elegant dancer in this world as Valentine, and she did sincerely hope to have the pleasure of, seeing him often at "the Mountain and Mutton Chops."

And Valentine was very happy; and the red-faced gentleman was very happy; and they were all very happy, and laughed very merrily, and perspired very freely.

"Come," said the red-faced gentleman, holding forth a glass of hot brandy-and-water. "Drink, sir: I'm happy to know you as the friend of Mr. Broadsides, and you're worthy of being the friend, sir, of any man—drink!"

Valentine sipped. He fancied that hot brandy-and-water would not be exactly the thing after the work he had had to perform, and therefore went for some ices and sundry bottles of lemonade for himself and the ladies, who, during his absence, were lost in admiration of his pleasing companionable qualities, which certainly were very conspicuous.

The next dance was called—the Caledonians! "Now," thought Valentine, "I am in for it beautifully."

"I shall have you again for a partner," said he, "of course?"

"Oh, dear me, yes, I shall be so happy," cried the little fat lady, starting up, "but you must teach me, you know; and then I don't mind." Nor did she. Had it been a minuet or even a hornpipe, it would have not been of the slightest possible importance to her then, so long indeed as Valentine consented to instruct her.

The music commenced. "Hands across, back again to places," cried a person who officiated as master of the ceremonies in a a voice so peculiar that Valentine fancied that he might as well imitate it as not. The first figure was accomplished; and the little fat lady who would not stir an inch without being led by Valentine, went through it very well; but just as they were commencing the second, Valentine assuming the voice of the M. C. cried, "*L'été!*" and those who happened to hear him, began to do *L'été* in defiance of the master of the ceremonies, who shouted, "no, no! Caledonians!—not the first set!"

The error, after some slight confusion, was rectified, and they went on advancing, and retiring very properly; but when they arrived at the "promenade" Valentine cried, "*chassez croisez!*" and those who obeyed, met those who were promenading with great euergy of mind, well knowing that they were right, and so violent was the contact, that in a moment at least fifty couples were on the ground! The promenaders had the worst of it decidedly, for they galloped round at such a rapid rate, that when one couple fell in a set, the others rolled over them, as a purely natural matter of course. The confusion for a time was unparalleled, and the laughter which succeeded amounted to a roar, but Valentine gallantly saved his little partner; for, suspecting what was about to occur, he seized her by the waist, and he drew her at once into the centre, where he stood viewing the tumult he had thas reprehensibly induced with feelings of intense satisfaction.

Of course the fallen parties were not long before they scrambled up again, and when they had risen, the brushing on the part of the gentlemen, and the blushing on the part of the ladies, were altogether unexampled, while the musicians, whose eyes were firmly fixed upon the notes, worked away as if nothing had happened, until they had completed the tune.

"Why did you call *chassez croisez?*" shouted several of the gentlemen, in tones of reproach. "We were all right enough until you interfered."

The master of the ceremonies assured those gentlemen, individually and collectively, that he did not call out "*chassez-croisez*" at all, and that somebody else did.

Valentine now thought that it would be a pity to disturb the clear current of their enjoyment again. He, therefore, permitted them, without interruption, to go through the various figures prescribed, and made the fat little lady perform so much to her own satisfaction, and that of her husband—who appeared to be exceedingly fond of his little wife—that at the conclusion, their pleasure knew no bounds.

Every dance after that, she stood up for, and she and her husband appeared to be so grateful to Valentine, and made him feel so conscious that the highest possible pleasure is involved in the act of imparting pleasure to others, that he really felt happy in giving her instructions, although she did work him most cruelly. Indeed, so much did he enjoy himself, that he continued in the booth until the band struck up the national anthem, whem finding that it was past ten o'clock, he took his leave. and went to look after Broadsides.

That gentleman, he ascertained, after having searched for him in all directions but the right one, had started ten minutes before with Mr. Bowles. He therefore immediately left the gay scene, and having found that every vehicle about the place had been previously engaged, he set off on foot towards town. He had not proceeded far, however, before he arrived at a spot, on one side of which was an open field, and on the other a row of houses, which stood back some distance from the road. All was silent, and dark: it appeared so especially to him, having just left the glitter and noise of the fair. He, however, walked on pretty briskly; but just as he had reached the termination of this field, two fellows stood immediately before him. He could see them but indistinctly, but he heard them with remarkable distinctness cry, "stand! your money, or your life!"

"Oh, oh!" muttered Valentine, "that's the game, is it!" and he drew himself back with the view of striking out with freedom, but the fellows, as if conscious of his object, seized him in an instant, and one of them holding to his head something, he couldn't tell whether it was the muzzle of a pistol, or the end of a bludgeon, nor did he much care, cried "out with it! quick!—and your watch!"

Valentine did *not* like to part with his watch; nor was he very anxious to part with his money: he, therefore, finding the rascals particularly impatient, and by no means disposed to wait until he had consulted a friend—shouted, throwing his voice behind him "here they are!—here are the scoundrels!—secure them!"

The fellows, on the instant, relinquished their hold, and turned round with unspeakable velocity; and just as the last man was darting away, Valentine presented him with a *souvenir*, in perfect similitude of a kick, and proceeded towards home without further molestation.

CHAPTER XXVI.

IN WHICH VALENTINE VISITS THE LONDON DOCKS, AND MOST REPREHENSIBLY INDUCES A WICKED WASTE OF WINE.

As a matter of christian courtesy, Valentine called upon Broadsides the following morning, and found that gentleman undergoing the connubial operation of having his ears pierced painfully by the amiable Mrs. Broadsides, in consequence of his having returned from the Fancy Fair, in her judgment, a little too affectionate and merry. The very moment, however, Valentine passed the bar-window, Broadsides felt somewhat relieved, seeing that, strange as it may appear, he had been waiting all the morning for the entrance of some friend, whose presence might cause his lady's tongue to sound sowewhat less harshly. He, therefore, on the instant started up, and having grasped the hand of Valentine, observed that he really was a very pretty fellow, for running away the previous evening; and, having made this truly remarkable observation, he caused him at once to sit down in the bar, and slapped his thigh with all the force of which he was capable, and wished, very particularly, to know how he felt himself then.

"Why, he's not like somebody I know," observed the highly sarcastic Mrs. Broadsides, volunteering an answer to the question proposed. "He can go out and have a day's pleasure without making a beast of himself, and that's more than some people can do." And she looked very spitefully at Mr. Broadsides, and bottled some bitters, and, having driven the cork against the edge of the bar very violently, began to darn up an extraordinary hole in Mr. Broadsides' speckled worsted stockings.

"Why," said Valentine, addressing Mr. Broadsides, "you were all right when you came home, were you not?"

"Right, sir!" cried the lady, "he never is right. Go where he may, and when he may, he always comes home like a beast. It's wonderful to me—it really is wonderful, that men can't go out without drinking and swilling, and guttling to such an extent, as to make themselves stupid. What pleasure—what comfort—what enjoyment can there be in it? That's what I want to know! *We* can go out, and be pleasant and happy, and come home without getting tipsy: but you!—there, if I wouldn't have every man who gets in that state, kept on brown bread and water for a month I'm not here! What, if I were to go out, and come home like you, reeling!"

"Oh, that would be a werry different thing," observed Broadsides.

"Not at all! Don't tell me! We have just as much right to get tipsy as you have. It's just as bad for one as for the other, and no worse. If a woman gets tipsy, she's everything that's dreadful. Oh! nothing's too bad for her: it's then the fore-runner of all sorts of wickedness. But a man!—he has only to get sober again, and nothing more is said or thought about the matter. I say, that like many other things, it's as bad for the man as for the woman, only the mischief of it is, it isn't thought so, that's all."

During the rapid delivery of these interesting observations, Mr. Broadsides was scratching his whiskers, and fidgeting, and winking, and nodding towards the door, with the view to inspiring Valentine with the conviction, that by leaving the bar, their mutual comfort would, in all probability, be very materially enhanced. It was some time, however, before he was able to make these peculiarly cabalistic signs understood; but he was at length successful, and Valentine; acting upon the natural suggestion, directed a pint of wine to be sent into the coffee-room, and invited Mr. Broadsides to join him.

"You had better stay here," said the lady, addressing Valentine, "I don't allow every one to be in the bar, but I don't mind you; and it *shall* be more comfortable here than in that cold room: it has just been scoured out and is still very damp."

Valentine apparently felt flattered. *He* had not the smallest objection to remain; but Broadsides most certainly had, and this was no sooner perceived by his lady, than she inquired, with bitter earnestness, whether he had any particular wish to have another fit of the gout? This affectionate interrogatory settled the business. They remained in the bar, and Valentine, with appropriate solemnity, inquired if Broadsides were really very bad when he returned.

"As sober as a judge, sir!" replied that gentleman.

"Good gracious!" exclaimed the lady, as Broadsides left the bar to look after a boiled chicken. "How can you say that, when you know that you were as tipsy as tipsy could be?"

"Well," cried Valentine, throwing his voice immediately behind Mrs. Broadsides, "that's a good one."

"The lady, on the instant, wheeled round, expecting, of course, to see some person there; but, as this expectation was by no means realised, she felt, in some slight degree, alarmed, and looked very mysterious, and then turned to Valentine, of whom she inquired if he had heard that extraordinary remark.

Valentine, who seemed to be reading most intently, took no apparent notice of this natural question, but added, with his eyes still fixed upon the paper—"I intended it for you. It could reach no farther. Why, I ask, are you a scold?"

The tones in which this observation was made, bore, in the judgment of Mrs. Broadsides, some resemblance to those of the voice of the waiter, who happened to be standing a short distance from the bar, counting his money again and again, scratching his head with great violence, and endeavoring to recollect whether two very hungry individuals, who had consumed nine chops and six kidneys the previous night had, in reality paid him or not.

"What's that you say, sir?" inquired the lady, with a sharpness which quite confused all his calculations.

"Me, mum!" cried the waiter, turning round with great velocity, "*I* did'nt speak, mum."

"You did speak! I heard you, sir! Let me have no more of your impertinence, I beg."

The waiter felt confused. He couldn't understand it! He twisted his napkin and swung it under his arm with great energy of mind; but he could not unravel the mystery at all. He did, however, eventually venture to observe that, upon his soul, he had never opened his lips.

"How dare you," cried the lady, "tell me that wicked falsehood, when I heard you as plain as ————"

"No! you heard me, mum!" cried Valentine, throwing his voice with reprehensible dexterity into the mouth of the waiter.

"Don't I say so!" continued the lady, "I know it was you, and yet you have the impudence to tell me to my face, that upon your soul you didn't open your lips!"

"No more I did! 'twasn't me!" cried the waiter, whose blood really began to bubble up.

"If it wasn't you, who was it then, sir? That is what *I* want to know!" cried the lady; but the waiter couldn't tell her. He looked extremely puzzled, and so did his mistress, who at length began to believe that it couldn't have been him, and while, with their mouths wide open, they were giving each other a lingering look, which plainly signified that it must have been some one; Valentine who seemed to be still intent upon the paper, cried in a deep hollow voice, which appeared to recede gradually—"Farewell! treat him better.—He's kind to you: be kind to him!"

Now, whether the tender conscience of the lady was pierced by these pointed remarks: whether she felt it impossible to treat Broadsides better, or was anxious to keep him in a blissful state of ignorance of better treatment, having thus been enjoined, a liberal and highly enlightened public will in all probability be able to guess, on being informed that not a syllable having reference to the mystery was breathed when Mr. Broadsides returned to the bar. It was, however, easy to perceive that an impression had been made upon the mind of the lady, for albeit she appeared to be thoughtful and gloomy, her tone was considerably changed, when in reply to Mr. Broadsides' inquiry, as to whether she intended to go with the girls to the fair, she said—"Well, dear, I don't much care if I do."

"That's right, my good girl!" exclaimed Broadsides, absolutely electrified. "I love the old woman when she's pleasant and happy!" and he rewarded her at once with a smacking kiss, which might have been heard in the midst of a storm.

"But," said the lady, "how long shall you be gone?"

"Oh, not above a couple of hours: but don't wait for me; run away now and make yourself tidy, and go off at once. I'll make it all right before I leave.—I'm going down to the docks," he continued, addressing Valentine. "You never were there I suppose? What say you? you may just as well run down with me."

Valentine consented; Mrs. Broadsides left the bar; and the waiter, who had evidently not got quite over it, brought in the tray.

"That's the best wife in the world," observed Broadsides, "that of mine. It is true, there ain't none on us perfect, but if she could but get over that temper of hern, sir, she'd be perfection, and not a ha'porth less."

"But you were of course tipsy last evening?" said Valentine.

"Why as to the matter of that, perhaps I was, you see. a little bit sprung,—I don't deny it; I might have been a small matter so, but, lor? that makes no odds in the least. I've been married now two-and-twenty year, and I don't suppose that during that period of time I ever came home drunk, or sober, without being, according to the old woman's reckoning, a beast. But lor! practice makes perfect, and use is second natur. She has done it so long, that she has brought the thing at last to such perfection, that I railly shouldn't feel myself quite at home without it. But she's a werry good sort: and you know there's always something; and the best thing a man can do, is not to look at either the dark or the bright side alone, but to mix 'em up together, and see then what sort of a color they produce. They say that white is the union of all colors, and depend upon it woman is the same. They're in the lump, the union of all that's good and bad; yet the mixtur you see is so particular pretty, that we can't get on at all without loving 'em, no how."

Valentine agreed with this practical philosophy, and in due course of time, which was not inconsiderable, Mrs. Broadsides descended full-dressed—not indeed in an aristocratic sense, for in that sense the term "full-dressed" may signify, when interpreted, the state of being nearly half naked; but in a really legitimate sense full-dressed, swelled out to an enormous extent at every point; and as she was an extrémely stout lady, and rather tall for her age, which fluctuated at that interesting period of her existence, between forty-five and sixty, her *tout ensemble* was particularly fascinating—a fact of which she appeared to be by no means unconscious. She sported, on the occasion, a lilac satin dress, with four full twelve-inch flounces, which were delicately edged with crimson fringe, a yellow velvet shawl, striped with crimson, to match the fringe of the flounces, and trimmed with bright emerald bullion; a pink-and-blue bonnet of extraordinary dimensions, with a bouquet of variegated artificials on one side, and a white ostrich plume tipped with scarlet on the other; and a long white veil, sweetly flowered all over, and so arranged as to form a sort of festooned curtain, which hung about six inches over the front. Nor will it be improper to speak of the jewellery, with which certain points of her person were adorned, for she had on a pair of really Brobdignagian ear-drops studded with Lilliputian spangles, an elegant mother o'pearl necklace with a cross attached in front; a massive gold chain, which hung completely over her shoulders, and which communicated with an immense gold chronometer on one side of her waist, and on the other to an extraordinary bunch of about a dozen seals of all sorts and sizes; an eye-glass attached to a chain made of hair, which enabled it to hang down in front quite as low as her knees; an average of three rings on each particular finger of each particular hand, and a scent bottle adorned with a chased gold top, which peeped for a breath of air just out of her heaving bosom. Thus equipped, she had a small glass of brandy-and-water warm, and when the two young ladies had pronounced themselves ready, Valentine submitted a glass of wine to each, and then handed them elegantly into a decent hackney coach, the driver of which had engaged to take them there and bring them back for twelve shillings and two drops of something to drink.

"Now," said Mr. Broadsides, the moment they had started "we'll be off," and after having given certain instructions to his servants, he and Valentine walked to the stand, and got into a low sedan-chair sort of a cab, which, as Broadsides very justly observed, might have been kicked into very little bits if the horse had felt disposed to be handy with his hind legs. They sat, however, in the most perfect safety, for they happened to be behind one of those poor devoted animals which have not more than half a kick in them, albeit in the space of half an hour he brought them to the entrance of the London Docks.

"Well, here we are," said Broadsides, as they passed through the gates, at which certain official individuals were looking with peculiar suspicion at every person who passed out. "Them are the sarchers which sarch all the laborers afore they go home, which I don't like the principle of, 'cause it is treating them all just as if they was thieves."

"And I suppose by that means they are kept honest?" observed Valentine.

"Why I des-say it keeps a good many from stealing; but that's altogether a different thing you know from keeping 'em honest. Honesty's honesty all over the world. If a man has the inclination to steal, he ain't a ha'porth the honester 'cause he can't do it. That's my sentiments."

"I suppose that, notwithstanding, there is a great deal of smuggling going forward!"

"I believe you! The men does a pretty goodish bit in that way; but the women are by far the most reglarest devils, 'cause, you see, them at the gate can't so easily detect 'em. They wind long bladders, filled with spirits, round their bodies to such an extent you'd be surprised. But they can't smug quite so much away at a time now, 'cause in consequence you see of the alteration of the fashion. But when the balloon sleeves and werry large bustles were in wogue, they could manage to walk away gallons at a time."

"Indeed!" said Valentine, "but how?"

"Why, you see, independent of the bladders which they wound werry comfortably round 'em, they could stow away nearly half a gallon in each sleeve, for as them sort of sleeves required something to make 'em stand out, they werry natterally fancied that they might just as well have the bulgers blown out with rum and brandy as with air, so all they had to do was to strap their little water-proofs carefully round their arms, and their sleeves look as fashionable as life; and then, as for their bustles, why that you know, of course, was werry easily managed, for they had but to tie their big bulgers with different compartments round their waists, and they could stow away a gallon of stuff any hour in the day, and then walk through the gates with it hanging on behind, just as natteral as clock-work."

Valentine smiled; but Broadsides laughed so loudly at the idea, that his progress was for a very considerable time impeded. He did, however, after having blown out his cheeks with great vehemence to check the current of his mirth, succeed in regaining the power to waddle onwards. "There," said he, stopping at the window of one of the little shops which are let to certain merchants who deal in ship's stores, and directing the attention of Valentine to a row of little canisters, labelled "Roast Beef," "Beef and Vegetables," &c., "That there's the stuff to make your hair curl! That's the sort of tackle to take out on a long woyage! There's a pound on it smashed into about a square inch. Of course the merest mite on it will fill a man's belly. He can't starve any how, so long as he's got a quarter of an inch of that in him. But come, we must keep on moving, you know, or we sha'nt get half over the business today."

"Are those empty?" inquired Valentine pointing to several hundred casks which were lying to the left of the entrance.

"Empty! Full of wine, sir—full, sir, every man jack on 'em. But lor! that's nothing to what you'll see below. Why they've got in the wault about a hundred thousand pipes; and the rent, if we awerage 'em at five and twenty shillings a-year apiece, will be something like a hundred and twenty-five thousand pounds, while the walue, if we take 'em all round at five and forty pound a pipe, will be nearly five million of money!—five millions, sir! What do you think of that?"

Valentine thought it enormous, and said so; and Broadsides expressed his opinion, that England could never be conquered, so long as she possessed such an immense stock of wine. "What," said he, "has made the British nation so glorious? What has made our generals and admirals so wictorious? Wine, sir, wine, and nothing but wine! Wine, sir!—as sound as a nut. That's my sentiments;" and the eloquence with which those sentiments were delivered, threw him into such a state of perspiration, that he stood at the entrance of the vault for some considerable time with his hat off, in order to wipe himself dry.

"Lights!" shouted a man, as they eventually descended; and two very oily individuals fired the wicks of two circular lamps, which were stuck upon sticks above two feet long; one of which it was the custom to give to each person to carry in his hand round the vault. Broadsides then drew forth some papers, and having arranged them to his own satisfaction and that of the clerk in attendance, a cooper was called, who conducted them at once into the far-famed place which contained, according to Broadsides, a hundred thousand pipes of of the essence of Great Britain's glory.

Valentine was for some time unable to see any thing distinctly, but the lamps, which were stationed in various parts of the vault, and which burned very dull and very red; but Broadsides who had long been accustomed to the place, was not nearly so much affected by the gloom. "I say," said he, holding up the lamp he had in his hand, "only look at the fungus!" and Valentine saw, suspended from the arches, huge masses of cobweb, which had the appearance of fine black wool. Some of these cobwebs were hanging in festoons from point to point, about as thick as a man's leg, while others hung in bunches about the size of a man's body, and formed altogether an extraordinary mass of matter, which certain learned members of the British Association would do well to examine with appropriate minuteness, with the praiseworthy view of reporting thereon at the next merry meeting.

"How much of this rail is there down in the wault?" inquired Broadsides, of the cooper, as he pointed to the iron plates which were planted along the middle of each avenue, for the purpose of rolling the casks with facility.

"Nine-and-twenty mile," replied the cooper.

"Twenty-nine miles!" cried Valentine in amazement.

"Nine-and-twenty mile, sir; and I'll be bound to say there ain't a foot over or under. Here we shall find them," he continued on reaching the arch under which were some of the wines that Mr. Broadsides wished to taste; and while the cooper was looking for the particular casks, Broadsides called the attention of Valentine to one of the ventilators. "There's a glorious battle!" said he; "did you ever behold such a shindy? It's the foul air fighting with the fresh. One you see wants to come in, and the other one wants to get out; neither on 'em seems inclined to wait for the other, and thus they go on continally at it in that state of mind, you see, world without end."

"This is No. 1," said the cooper, at this moment bringing an ale-glass full of wine.

Broadsides took the glass by its foot, and held it up to the light, and then shook it a little, and spilt about half, and then smelt it, and turned up his nose, and then tasted it, and spurted it out again, and having made up an extraordinary face, he proceeded to blow out his cheeks to an extent which made it appear that he might at that time have had in his mouth a remarkable couple of overgrown codlings. "That won't do at no price," said he, after a time, "just walk into Six," and a glass of No. 6, was accordingly drawn, and when he had shaken it and smelt it, and tasted it as before, he pronounced the whole lot to be "pison."

"I suppose," observed Valentine, while Broadsides was occupied in bringing his mouth into shape, "that you frequently make persons tipsy down here?"

"They frequently make theirselves tipsy," replied the cooper, "when they come down to look and not to buy, you know—to swill and not to taste. There was yesterday, for instance, three young bloods came in with an order to taste five and twenty quarter casks, and sure enough they did taste 'em. They made me tap every cask, and swallowed every glass that I drawed, and when I'd gone right clean through 'em, they tried to overpersuade me to begin the lot again at the beginning. Now, there ain't above four of these 'ere to a pint, so they couldn't have taken in less than three bottles a-piece. I warned 'em of the consequence, for I saw they knew nothing at all about it, but the fact was, they came for a swill, and a swill they most certainly had. They didn't, however, feel it any great deal down here, but pre-haps they didn't when they got out! I knew how it'd be, so I went up the steps just to watch them, and lor! directly they smelt the fresh air, and saw the light of the blessed heaven, they all began to reel just like so many devils. I thought that bang into the dock go they must, and if they'd only seen the water, in of course they would have soused, for they ran right bust against everything they tried to avoid."

"Then persons don't feel it much while they are down here?" observed Valentine.

"No," replied the cooper, "very seldom unless they happen to have had a glass of ale before they come down, and then they just do if they drink at all any ways freely. The other day, now, a lushington of this kind came in with two others, and I attended 'em; and when they had tasted, and tasted, and tasted until I thought they'd all drop down dead drunk together, this gent slipped away, and his friends very natterly fancied that, finding his stomach a little out of order, he'd started off home, and as I couldn't see him no where about, why I natterly fancied so too; but the next morning just as I went into No. 5, north, for a sample, who should I see, but this identical indiwidual sitting in the sawdust with his head upon a pipe as comfortable as a biddy, and snoring away like a trooper. I woke him of course, and he got up as fresh as a daisy; but in order to avoid all row, you see, I made him keep behind till a party came in, and he slipped out with them without any body knowing a bit about the matter."

"I presume you don't drink much yourselves?" observed Valentine.

"Why, that, you see, depends upon circumstances. The old hands don't: the smell's enough for them; but the new and werry green uns are contini*ly* sucking like infants. It's a long time before sich as them can be weaned. It was only the Saturday night before last, that one of this sort got locked down. We didn't know a word about the matter, and the vault wasn't of course going to be opened again before Monday; but he got pretty sober in the course of Sunday morning, and after having spent a few happy hours at the grating, he gave wiew holler to one of the outside watchmen, who sent for the key, and got him out very quietly. But it cured him. I don't believe he has had so much as a suck since then."

"Well, come," said Broadsides, "now I am here, let's see how my extra-particular get's on."

This happened to be under the opposite arch, and while the cooper was in it with Broadsides, Valentine, who was looking very intently at some cobwebs, perceived a tall dark figure march past him in a manner which struck him as being extremely mysterious. He was angry, very angry with himself for being startled, although he couldn't help it; and after having reproached himself severely in consequence, he walked to the opposite arch. "A tall person passed just now," said he to the cooper. "Who was it?"

"One of the watchmen. They walk in and out in the dark to see that no indiwidual pays twice. There's lots on 'em about. You'll see him again by'n bye."

"Very well," thought Valentine, "if I do, I'll startle *him*," and while the cooper was broaching the extra-particular, he looked round the vault with an anxious eye.

"Now then," said Broadsides, handing him a glass, "just tell me now what you think of that."

Valentine tasted, and found it so splendid, that he almost unconsciously finished the glass.

"That's something like, ain't it? That's what I call wine! It's as sound as a nut. Let's have another glass," and another glass was drawn, and while Broadsides was smelling it, and shaking it, and spilling it, and tasting it, and spurting it over the saw dust, and making it go through all sorts of manœuvres, the watchman passed again.

"*Hush!*" cried Valentine throwing his voice among the casks, which were near him. "He's here!"

The watchman stood perfectly still. He would scarcely allow himself to breathe. He was a man who reflected upon the imaginary rehearsal of his actions—an extremely cautious man, and his name was Job Scroggins. Instead therefore of rushing like a fool to the spot, he, with admirable tact, held up his hand to enjoin silence, and tried with great optical energy to pierce the extremely dense gloom of the vault. This he found to be impracticable. All was dark, pitch-dark, in the direction from which the voice appeared to proceed. Nothing could be distinguished. Twenty men might have been drinking there unperceived. Scroggins therefore having formed his plan of attack, said in a delicate whisper to the cooper, "If you stand here, we shall nab 'em," and crept very stealthily round to the opposite side of the arch.

Now this was precisely what Valentine wanted. He wished but to excite the suspicion of the watchman that persons were having a clandestine treat, to enable him to keep up the game. Job Scroggins had therefore no sooner got round than Valentine sent a faint whisper very near him, the purport of which was that Harry was a fool not to get behind the casks.

"*Hallo!*" shouted Scroggins in a voice of thunder, on hearing the faint expression of that affectionate sentiment.

"Get behind! get behind!" cried Valentine, "we shall be caught!"

"Hallo!" again shouted Job Scroggins with all the energy at his command. "What are you about there? D'ye hear!"

"Hush!" said Valentine, "hush! not a word."

"I hear you, my rum 'uns! Come out of that, will you! Here, Jones!"

"Hallo!" shouted Jones. "What d'ye want?"

"Come here!" cried Scroggins. "Here, quick!—No. 9!—We'll nab you, my lushingtons!—we'll find you out!" and he tore away a stout piece of scantling, while Broadsides handed the glass of wine to Valentine, and tucked up his sleeves to assist in the caption.

"Now then," cried Jones, who had been engaged in the *fortification* of two pipes of port, and whose nose glowed with ineffectual fire. "What's the row?"

"Here's a lot of fellows here," replied Scroggins, "swilling away at the wine like devils."

"*Where?*" cried the fiery-nosed cooper with extraordinary fierceness.

"Here!" shouted Scroggins. "Lights! lights!"

"What's the matter? Hallo!" cried two voices in the distance.

"Here! Nine! Lights! lights!" reiterated Scroggins, who appeared to be in a dreadful state of excitement just then.

"All safe now. Lie still," said Valentine throwing his voice behind a lot of quarter casks which stood to the left of Job Scroggins.

"Ah, you're safe enough!" exclaimed Job, in a tone of bitter irony. "Pray don't alarm your blessed selves! you're quite safe—to be nabbed in less than no time. Now then there look alive—now, quick!" he continued, as two additional coopers approached the spot with lights. "If you get away now, my fine fellows, why, may I *be* blowed. There, you go behind there, and you stand here, and you keep a sharp look out there. Now then, if they escape, we'll forgive 'em!"

Having stationed the coopers with lamps in their hands at various parts of the arch, Job Scroggins stole gently between two distinct rows of pipes, and Valentine, wishing to render all the assistance in his power, preceded him. Just, however, as he reached the darkest part of the arch, he cried, in an assumed voice of course, "Let's drown him," and threw the glass of wine he held in his hand over his head so dexterously, that the whole of it went into the face of Mr. Scroggins, who was looking about behind in a state of anxiety the most intense.

"Here they are! Here are the thieves!" shouted Scroggins, wiping his wine-washed face with the sleeve of his coat. "Look out there!—look out!" and he rushed past Valentine with great indignation, and peered with considerable fierceness of aspect into every cavity sufficiently large to admit the tail of a consumptive rat.

"Hush!" cried Valentine, sending his voice right a-head; and away went Scroggins to the spot from which the whisper appeared to proceed, while the coopers were looking about with great eagerness, expecting every moment to see the thieves rise.

"Quiet, Harry! quiet! They'll catch us," whispered Valentine.

"Catch you!" cried Scroggins, "to be sure we shall!" And he poked his stick with infinite violence between the casks, and rattled it about with consummate desperation, and *looked!*—as the lamp was beneath his wine-stained face, it imparted so ghastly a hue to his features, that really he looked like a fiend.

"Ha! ha! ha! ha!" cried Valentine, merrily sending his voice right under the arch adjoining.

Away went Job Scroggins backed up by the coopers, who struck their shins cleverly against the corner casks, and stumbled over the scantling, one after the other with infinite presence of mind.

"Away, away!" shouted Valentine, throwing his voice towards the spot they had just left; and Job Scroggins rushed back with the coopers at his tail, of whom the whole were inspired with the spirit of vengeance.

"Stand there!" shouted Scroggins, "they must pass that way!" and he poked his thick stick between the casks again desperately, and flourished it about with unparalleled zeal.

"It's all up with us, Harry: we're blocked right in," whispered Valentine despairingly. "Forgive us!" he added in a different voice, as if Harry had really become very much alarmed—"forgive us! we'll do so no more: have mercy!"

Mercy! If there be in the English language one word which tends more than another to soften a truly British heart, that word is beyond question, mercy. There is magic in the sound of that soft soothing word. A true Englishman's sympathies swell when it is breathed, and his anger is strangled by that string of benevolence, which he winds with pride round his compassionate heart. Tears of blood, flow they never so freely, are not more effectual in cutting the throat of vengeance, than the magical sound of this beautiful word, for the moment it strikes on the drum of the ear, the spirit of Atë is kicked from the soul, and benevolence rises great, glorious and free in loveliness, even surpassing itself. About this it is clear there can't be two opinions; and hence, none can marvel, that when the word reached the soft sensitive ear of the true-hearted Scroggins, he should have exclaimed with all the fervor of which he was capable:—"mercy! *mercy?*—You don't have a squeak!"

"Come out!" he continued; "you guzzling vagabones!—mercy indeed!—with a hook!"

"We have not drank a great deal," said Valentine imploringly. "We haven't indeed. You shall have it all back if you will but forgive us."

Scroggins smiled a sardonic smile.

"This is how the wine goes," said Mr. Broadsides.

"And then we get's blowed up sky-high for the 'ficiency," added the fiery-nosed cooper.

"Now then! are you coming out or not?" shouted Scroggins.

Valentine sent forth a laugh of defiance, which caused the heaving bosom of Scroggins to swell with the essence of wrath. He might have been somewhat subdued by humility although that was not extremely probable then—still he *might* by such means have been softened; but when he reflected on the monstrous idea of being defied! he couldn't stand it! he wouldn't stand it! He flew to the spot from which the laugh had apparently proceeded, and struck the surrounding casks with peculiar indignation.

"Will you come out or not," he exclaimed, "before I do you a mischief?"

"No." shouted Valentine.

"Then take the sconsequence," cried Scroggins, who looked at that moment remarkably fierce. "Now then," he continued, addressing the coopers, "we'll give 'em no quarter: we'll have no more parley: we'll drag 'em out now, neck and eels!"

Previously, however, to the effectual accomplishment of this extremely laudable object, it was obviously and absolutely necessary to find them—a remarkable fact, which struck Scroggins and the coopers with such consummate force, that they set to work at once, with the view of effecting this highly important preliminary, and displayed an amount of zeal, which really did them great credit.

"They're somewhere about here, I know," observed the fiery-nosed cooper.

"Oh, we shall find 'em! we'll have 'em!" cried Scroggins; "and when we do catch 'em, they'll know it!"

The highly sarcastic tone in which these words were uttered, was clearly indicative of something very desperate; and as the coopers, who were beginning to get very impatient, were running round the arch with unparalleled energy, Valentine, unperceived, threw the glass he had had in his hand upon a pile of pipes under the gloomy arch opposite, and immediately cried: "there's a fool! now we can't get another drop."

"Here they are!" shouted Scroggins, on hearing the crash. "Now then, boys! hurrah! we shall nail 'em!"

This soul stirring speech put the coopers on their mettle, and they rushed towards the arch with unprecedented spirit; but before they reached the spot in which the broken glass was lying, Valentine—who did not exactly comprehend the precise meaning of the words: "now we'll nail 'em," albeit he fancied, that if poor unhappy persons had really been there, they would have stood a fair chance of being mercilessly hammered—cried "now let us start: we can get no more wine!"

"Stop there, you vagabones!" cried Scroggins, vehemently, thinking to frighten them out of their wits. "We are cocksure to catch you, you know! You may just as well give up at once!"

They had now reached the spot in which the glass lay smashed into a really extraordinary number of little pieces. "Here we have hocklar demonstration," he continued: "here's where the vagabones was."

"Stoop down," whispered Valentine.

"Come *out!*" cried Scroggins. "It's o' no use you know; we see you!" An observation which, how laudable soever its object might have been, involved a highly reprehensible falsehood.

"Now then!—crawl gently," whispered Valentine.—"Come on!"

Scroggins leaped over the pipes in an instant, and looked round and round with an expression of surprise.

"Have you got 'em?" inquired the fiery-nosed cooper.

"Got 'em!" echoed Scroggins, "I ony just wish I had, for their sakes. I 'stablish a trifle or two in their mem'ries to sarve 'em for life. I'll warrant they wouldn't forget it a one while."

Valentine now sent a slight laugh so very near the legs of Mr. Scroggins, that that gentleman spun round with the velocity of a cockchafer, and felt very angry indeed with himself when he reflected that the "Lushingtons" still were at large. "Where can they be crept to?" he cried, in amazement. "They're not a yard from me, and yet—why where the ——"

"There's no room for two men to hide their bodies here," observed the fiery-nosed cooper.

"They must be particular small," said Mr. Broadsides.

"They must be particular *active*," said Scroggins; and Valentine sent another laugh very near him.

Job Scroggins looked savage—undoubtedly savage! He shook his red head with extreme desperation, and ground his great teeth with maniacal zeal. "Where can they be hid?" he exclaimed, with great emphasis. "Blister 'em! Where can the scoundrels be got to?"

He paused for a reply, and fixed his eyes upon his companions, and his companions fixed their eyes upon him, while Broadsides scratched his head with his right hand, and rubbed his chin very mysteriously with his left.

At this interesting moment an intelligent cooper, who had theretofore searched without uttering a syllable, ventured to offer a rational suggestion, the purport of which was, that they certainly must be somewhere.

"Somewhere!" cried Scroggins, very angrily: "We know they must be somewhere; but where is that somewhere? That's the grand pint!"

The intelligent cooper, who offered this suggestion, was silent, for he saw that Mr. Scroggins looked ready to eat him: and Scroggins was a big man, and had an excessively carnivorous aspect. Silence was, therefore, a species of wisdom, which the little intelligent cooper displayed, and the search was resumed with increased perseverance.

But Valentine himself now became somewhat puzzled. He scarcely knew how to proceed. He was anxious to send the invisible "Lushingtons" off with *eclat*, but the question was, how could he get them away? While, therefore, the watchman and the coopers were hunting about in all directions, poking their sticks into every kind of cavity, asking themselves all sorts of queer questions, and answering themselves in all sorts of queer ways, he was quietly conceiving a design to carry into immediate execution, with the view of thickening the mystery in which they were involved. He had not, however, to puzzle himself long, for, being blessed with an exceedingly vivid imagination, he had but to give it full swing for a time, and a host of ideas would dart across his brain with about the velocity of lightning; and, although it occasionally happened that they rushed in so wildly, and upset each other so wantonly, and caused so much confusion, that he was really compelled, in self-defence, to kick them all out together; in this particular instance they entered in the most orderly manner possible, and after playing at leap-frog clean down each other's throats, the most powerful remained, having swallowed all the rest; and that Valentine seized by the collar at once, with the view of making it perform that particular office for which it had been created. This was, however, a desperate idea, it being no other than that of introducing his voice into one of the pipes of wine, is order to see how Job Scroggins and his companions would act; but Valentine, resolved not to repudiate it in consequence of its desperate character, held it firmly, and just as the energetic Job, after running round and round with great fierceness of aspect, and vowing the most extraordinary species of vengeance, had paused to regain a little breath, and to wipe the perspiration from his face, with the cuff of his bob-tailed coat, he pitched his voice dexterously into an extremely old cask and cried, "Wasn't it lucky we found this one empty eh?"

Job Scroggins stared; and so did old Broadsides, and so did the fiery-nosed cooper; and they drew near the cask from which the sound had apparently proceeded, and listened again with an expression of amazement.

"Keep in the head," whispered Valentine, very audibly.

"They're here!" shouted Scroggins, snatching an adze from the fiery-nosed cooper. "Look out!—now they're nailed!" and without a single moment's reflection, without considering whether the cask were full or empty, without even giving the slightest notice to those who were with him, he smashed in the head of the pipe, and the wine, of course rushed out in torrents.

"You fool!" cried the fiery-nosed cooper, as the stream dashed the lamps from their hands, and extinguished the lights.

"Held! help'" shouted Scroggins.

"Silence, you *ass!* hold your tongue!" cried the fiery-nosed cooper. "Hoist the cask up on end!—Now!—Stick to it!—Now!—All together!—Hurrah!"

In an instant the thing was accomplished, for Valentine who was really very sorry for what had happened, put forth with the rest all the strength at his command.

"Now, don't make a noise," said the fiery-nosed cooper; "get a light from the lamp, there—quick!" And Scroggins, who was then in a dreadful state of mind, groped his way at once out of the arch, while the rest were, of course, in total darkness, and up to their ankles in wine. It was not, however, long before Scroggins returned, and when he did, the very first question asked was—"What cask is it?"

"All right:—all right!" said the fiery-nosed cooper, after having examined it minutely. "It's one of them old uns that's been here so long."

"What one of them three!" cried his comrade. "Well that's werry lucky as far as it goes. It'll never be cleared. It was only t'other day I was saying that I'd bet any money the warrants was lost."

"Come, that's most fortunate," thought Valentine.

"But what are we to do?" cried the greatly alarmed Scroggins. "How are we to hide it?—There's such a rare lot on it spilt!"

"Now don't make no noise," said his fiery-nosed friend: "I'll cooper it up, and you get all the sawdust you can—now be handy! It's an awful puddle surely; but the sawdust 'll soon suck it up." And he began to repair the cask, while the rest were engaged in scraping sawdust together and mixing it up with the wine, and then throwing it, when it became perfectly saturated, under the scantling to dry.

By dint of great labor—for all, including Broadsides, who puffed away frightfully, assisted—in the space of twenty minutes the pool became pretty well absorbed; and as the fiery-nosed cooper had by that time completed his job, the pipe was carefully placed upon the scantling again, and when more fresh sawdust had been strewn over the spot, the place looked so much as if

The head driven in to look after the voice.

P.142

nothing had happened, that it might even then have been passed unnoticed.

"Well," cried Scroggins, "it's well it isn't no worse; but if I'd ony ha' caught them 'ere warmint, whoever they are, if I wouldn't have sarved 'em out, blister 'em, blow me!"

"But did you ever hear of such a fool," observed the fiery-nosed cooper, "to smash in the head of a pipe, when he knew we hadn't got an empty cask in the place?"

"Why, you see," said Mr. Scroggins, in extenuation, "I did n't then give it a thought. It was a mad go; I know it—a werry mad go; but, you see, I was so savage, that I did n't know rayly what I did; and I fancied I heered the two wagabones inside."

"And so did I," said his fiery-nosed friend; "but then I know'd it couldn't be."

"They must ha' been *behind* that 'ere pipe," continued Scroggins, "I'm sartain they must, and I *ony* just wish I'd ha' caught 'em, that's all; if I wouldn't ha' given 'em pepper!—may I never set eyes on my babbies again!"

During this extremely interesting colloquy, Broadsides and Valentine were industriously occupied in wiping their sticky hands and faces, and making themselves sufficiently decent to pass without exciting special notice. They found this, however, a difficult job, for the wine had spurted over them freely; but when they had carefully turned down their collars, and buttoned their coats so closely up to their chins that scarcely a particle of their deeply-stained shirts could be perceived, it was unanimously decided that they might venture.

"But you want to taste the other pipe of port, sir, don't you?" observed the cooper.

"The stink of them lamps," replied Broadsides, "has spylt my taste for a fortnit: besides, I don't care a bit about it; I only came to taste, what I wouldn't have at no price, them six pipes of pison."

The business being therefore at an end, the fiery-nosed cooper polished Valentine's boots with his apron, when Broadsides gave the men half-a-crown to drink his health, and he and Valentine—who gave them half-a-sovereign—were ushered very respectfully out of the vault, and after passing the gates without exciting more than ordinary attention, got into a cab, and rode home.

CHAPTER XXVII.

VALENTINE BECOMES ACQUAINTED WITH A FRIGHTFUL CALAMITY, AND HAS A HEART-RENDING INTERVIEW ON THE SUBJECT WITH HORACE.

There is a remarkable bit of sublimity—a powerful, pale, universal reflector, which is sometimes above us, and sometimes below us, and sometimes on a line precisely parallel with us—a reflector of which the composition is unknown, but which is ycleped by our sublunary philosophers—a moon. That this moon will be ever cut up into stars, may rationally, notwithstanding the idea originated with our own immortal Shakspeare, be doubted; but there can be no doubt that as it derives its pale lustre from the sun, so mankind in the aggregate derive their lustre from money; and albeit the connection between the moon and money may not at a glance be perceived, except, indeed, by superficial men of genius, and philosophers steeped to the very lips in learned mud, that there is a connection between them will be acknowledged by all, when they reflect upon the fact of the moon being silver by prescription.

Now, money is said to be the devil; and if it be, it is beyond all dispute an extremely pleasant devil, and one of which men are so ardently enamored, that they absolutely worship it as if it were a god. No matter of what material this money may be composed—no matter whether it consists of precious metals, precious stones, or precious little bits of paper, for every convertible representative of money is equally precious, its accumulation and distribution in reality constitute the principal business of men's lives. Some despise it for a time; they never despise it long: they soon suffer for the indulgence in that bad passion. Others will do anything, however dishonorable, to obtain it. If a man has money, he's all right; if he has none, he is all wrong. It matters not what hermits and monks may say, if an honest man be poor, his fellow-men despise him; while a wealthy villain, in the world's estimation, is a highly respectable member of society, and hence the penealty on poverty is greater than that which is attached to any absolute crime. Nor is this all, as the saying is; nothing like all. It's astonishing the spirit of independence the possession of money inspires, and equally astonishing are the dejection and humility which the non-possession of it induces. If a man has no money, his mind is ill at ease; he cannot feel comfortable any how—it amounts to an absolute physical impossibility for him to hold up his head like a man who has lots. He can't do it! It's of no use to physic him with philosophy! All the philosophy in the world is insufficient to cure his pecuniary disease. He can't understand your philosophy then, and he won't understand. He knows better. He knows that he has *got no money!*—a species of knowledge which affects alike body and soul. And yet, notwithstanding money is so valuable—so precious, that its absence teems with misery and humiliation; notwithstanding it is so dear, so highly prized when it is wanted, that we will risk even our lives to obtain it, how thoughtlessly we waste it! how freely we squander it away, when it is gained, as if its possession inspired the belief, that we should never want another five-pound note so long as we had the ability to breathe! Beyond all dispute—for there cannot exist two opinions on the subject—in this little matter a man is an ass.

Now, all this is very profound, but Valentine really knew nothing about it. He only knew this, that in a pecuniary sense he was getting remarkably short, and that it became absolutely necessary to write to Uncle John for a fresh supply. A blessed position for a man to be placed in is that, in which he has but to say, "I want so much," and so much is sent as a matter of course. This was precisely the position of Valentine; but before he wrote home, he was anxious to see the Goodmans, in order to ascertain if they could, or would, give him any farther information with respect to his benevolent old friend.

Accordingly, on the morning of the day on which he intended to write to Uncle John, he set off for the residence of Walter, and was certainly somewhat startled on being unable to discover the house in which he had lived. On arriving at the spot where the house had stood, he could see but the foundation, and a few burnt beams; but on making inquiries at a shop in the vicinity, he not only ascertained what had happened from a person who gave him a really heart-rending account of the occurrence, but was informed that Walter and his family were at that time lodging in a house directly opposite. Thither of course he immediately went, and having sent up his card, paced the parlor into which he had been shown with considerable anxiety; for, possessing a heart in which the kindliest feelings of our nature had been implanted, he deeply sympathised with those of whose dreadful sufferings so frightful a picture had been drawn. He had not, however, dwelt upon the calamity long, when a person dashed into the room, and exclaimed, "Hallo, my young trump! don't you know me?"

Valentine in a moment knew the voice to be that of Horace; but his person he certainly would not have known. "Good God!" said he, grasping his hand, "is it possible?"

"It just is," cried Horace, "and no mistake about it. *Don't* I look a beauty, eh? Did you ever see such a Guy? But thank Heaven for all things," he continued, pulling off a large wig, and displaying his head, the black skin of which had just began to peel. "It's a comfort no doubt, if you can but just look at the thing in the right light."

"And how is your father?" inquired Valentine.

"Why," replied Horace with great solemnity of aspect, "he's as much like a jolly old cinder as possible. He's frizzled all up into one lump of coke. *I'm* rummy enough, but lor! *he's* out and out! There's no mistake at all about him."

"But he's out of all danger, I hope?"

"Oh! yes; he's getting on like a brick. I thought he was booked though at one time, for of all the unhappy looking bits of black crackling!—did you ever happen to see a smoked pig? Because if you ever did, you have seen something like him.—You wouldn't believe him to be flesh and blood. You wouldn't know him in fact from a jolly old piece of burnt cork. He stood it, however, throughout, like a trump, and I'll back him after this against any regular salamander going."

"And the ladies, how are they?"

"Why, they're only tollolish. You know what women are. They don't like the look of the governor at all, and certainly he don't look particularly fresh."

"Well," said Valentine, rising, "I'm really very sorry for what has occurred, and if you think that I can be of service to you in any way, I hope you will command me. I'll not detain you now."

"I wish you would, old boy," said Horace, with much earnestness. "You'd be doing me a very great favor. The fact is, our out-and-out old fool of a doctor won't let me have more than one glass of wine a day, which of course is particularly rotten, more especially now I'm getting all right again. But the old fool won't listen to reason; nor will the two women, who are of course on his side, and who keep the blessed wine locked up, just as if body and soul could be kept on decent terms with each other, by that nasty lush which he expects me to swallow by the pailful. Upon my soul, that little wretch of a boy, to whom he gives about two pence a month to carry out all his poison, is everlastingly at the door with his basket *full* of some infernal tincture of filth. I've kicked him right bang into the road three times; but he still comes, and comes. I'll half murder him some day."

"But of course it does you good?"

"Is it rational to suppose it? Is it any thing like rational to entertain the idea, that such hog-wash as that can do any fellow good? It's the nastiest muck that ever was concocted to disorder the bowels of a Christian. Do you happen to know what assafœtida is? Because, if you do, you know what sort of physic I swill, for they shove a lot of that into every blessed bottle. I'm certain it's that: there can be no mistake, I should know it a mile off; that, and the stuff they sell to poison the bugs, constitute 'the mixture as before,' and an extremely pleasant mixture it is, if you can but get it down. Now, I want you, therefore, to do me this kindness; if you'll stop —if it be only for a quarter of an hour, I shall take it as an especial mark of friendship, for I can gammon them out of some wine for you, and that's the only way in which I can see my way clear to get a glass for myself; for of course I can't stir out of the house with this jolly old smoke-dried countenance, tattooed and scored like the nob of a Chocktaw Chief. It's worse, ten to one worse, than having the small-pox. The measles are a fool to it; and as for the itch!—there, you may believe me or not, as you like, but if all the infernal tribes of wasps, bugs, musquitoes, fleas, and every other kind of vermin in nature were marching about me in everlasting legions, they couldn't produce an itch like it. I'll defy them to do it! and yet that old donkey that scours me out, has the face to tell me that I ought not to scratch it! I'm regularly drowned about seven times a day, in what *he* christens lotion—the nastiest, greasiest, slipperiest muck that ever made a tom-cat sick. It does me no good; it only makes me itch more, as I tell the old fool, who however takes no sort of notice at all of what *I* say, as if I didn't know about my own feelings best! If I seriously expostulate with him, he only laughs and directs them to 'rub it in; rub it in! Oh! never mind; rub it in!' And they do rub it in like devils. But don't go just yet, there's a trump," he added, and rushed from the room quite delighted with the idea of having an additional glass of wine.

"What an extraordinary creature!" thought Valentine, on being left alone. "How dreadfully he must suffer; and yet how his spirits sustain him. Most men, if in *his* present state, would be lying in bed, increasing by dwelling upon their agony, and groaning as if groans alone were capable of effecting a cure."

"All right! all right!" cried Horace, bouncing into the room, "I've done the trick. I've gammoned them both, that you've been walking a very long distance, and feel most particularly faint. So it's to come down directly. They wouldn't trust me with it, though; I suppose they fancied that I should walk into the decanter on the stairs. But no matter—come in!—Now I look upon this as very friendly."

The servant at this moment entered with the wine, and Horace observed that there was no mistake about her.

"If you please, sir," said the girl, addressing Valentine, "Missises compliments, and she'd take it as a particular favor, if you wouldn't allow Mr. Horace to have more than half a glass.".

"Why you out-and-out, know nothing, wretch! what d'ye mean?" cried Horace. "Is this your gratitude? Didn't I carry you over the tiles? Be off!—I hate the sight of you!" and he pulled off his wig and threw it at her with great energy, as she darted like lightning from the room. "You see!" he continued, as he picked up his wig, "this is just the way they serve me day after day. If I hadn't the temper of an angel, they'd drive me into fits. But come! —May we never want nothing."

Having earnestly delivered this beautiful sentiment, and emptied his glass, he smacked his lips with really infinite gusto, and replenished.

"*Bring* me a bottle of wine, there's a trump!" said he. "*Do*, if you have any charity in you. You haven't an idea what a favor I should esteem it. It's the handsomest present you could possibly make me. You *could* call to-morrow, you know, and bring it snugly in your pocket. But don't let them see it, if you do, I'm done. It would be to me the highest treat in nature. Success to you, old boy!" he continued, again emptying his glass. "You don't *know* how happy I am to see you!"

"Well, now," said Valentine "how did this dreadful calamity occur?"

"Why, you see," replied Horace, "the old governor was a little bit thick in the clear, and they fancied that somebody ought to sit up with him. Of course, I saw in a twinkling, who that somebody must be; I knew that, being a pleasant job, I was to have it; and I wasn't at all out of my reckoning. I did have it, naturally; I had it for three blessed nights, and as I went to bed immediately after breakfast, I snoozed very soundly till supper time came. Well, you see, on the third night the governor was unbearable, for what must he do but take it into his jolly old sconce, that Uncle Grim was in the room! It's a fact upon my soul! He would have it that he was standing at the foot of the bed, and nothing could drive it out of him. I tried all I *knew* to swindle the old ass into the belief that I had pitched him neck and crop out of the window; but no; he wouldn't have it; he fancied he saw him there still; and after cutting away like a jolly old lunatic for two or three hours, he dropped off as I thought to sleep. Well! as soon as I saw his eyes closed right and tight, I left the room to get a cup of hot coffee, which I knew was all regular in the kitchen, and I *suppose* that as soon as my blessed back was turned, the old ass jumped out and set fire to the bed-clothes, for on running up again, which I did like a wheelbarrow, I found the room in flames, and him laughing like a fool fit to split. I called to him again and again, but he took no notice; I put it to him whether he didn't think he was a donkey, but he made no reply; I couldn't drag him out; I couldn't get at him; I couldn't even get into the room, and it was not until the whole house was one flake of fire and he was as black as an old tin pot, that I was able, by smashing in the panel of the wainscot, to lug him into the passage, and thence out of the house. I ran up again after that, to lay my fist upon a little lot of documents; but lor! the room was full of blazes, and to add to the comfort of my position, I wish I may die if the jolly old stairs didn't fall the very moment I wished to descend. Well, up to the attic I flew, and out upon the tiles I bounced like a ball. It was there, that I met with that girl whom you saw—who certainly did startle me a little above a bit—and there we were forced to remain, till one of the firemen—who was a trump every inch of him—came to our assistance. Well! having caught hold of the girl, with about the same coolness, as if there had been nothing the matter, he cocked me into a sort of a long cotton stocking, and down I slipped gradually from the parapet to the ground. But the friction!—Oh don't mention it! My skin was like the crackling of a roast leg of pork overdone; and as for my poor toggery! —the fire had made it so particularly rotten, that I came out as naked as a new-born devil. I didn't however feel much more then; but in the morning, when the excitement had gone a little off, perhaps I didn't! Talk of Fox's Book of Martyrs! I'll bet ten to one there wasn't a martyr among them that suffered a tithe of what I did. It made me so *savage!* But don't let us talk *any* more about it. Every evil is pregnant with good; the offspring of this is the fact of its being over, and that is an absolute blessing."

Valentine listened to all this with the utmost attention; but that which struck him with greater force than all the rest, was the fact of Walter having endeavored to burn the apparition of his brother out of the room. "What could possibly have induced him," thought he, "to have recourse to such an expedient? One would have thought that the notion of his brother being present, instead of exciting angry feelings, would have been calculated to comfort and console him. But every thing tends to confirm my belief of his being the victim of some foul play."

There was a pause; but it was not of long duration, for Horace again replenished his glass, and gave as a toast: "the knock-kneed quaker."

"Have you seen or heard any thing of your uncle?" inquired Valentine with considerable earnestness.

Horace looked at him intently, as if he wished to read the motive which prompted the question, and then answered, "No, I can't say that I have; I believe that he is all right somewhere, but where I don't know, nor does any one else but the governor."

"Then," thought Valentine, "when the governor is convalescent, since his imagination is so susceptible of apparently supernatural influences, I'll wring the secret from him by apparently supernatural means."

"What, are you off?" cried Horace as Valentine rose.

"I have letters to write, which will take me some time."

"Well, if you must go, you know, why you must: but mind, don't forget me, there's a charitable soul. You've no idea what a relief this glass or two of wine has been to me to-day. If you can't bring a bottle, you know, bring a pint. That thief of a doctor, I know, wants to rattle my life out, with his nasty messes; therefore, don't forget to bring me some, there's a good fellow."

Valentine promised that he would not, and after wishing him well over it, and requesting to be remembered up-stairs, he left the house, with the view of writing forthwith to Uncle John.

CHAPTER XXVIII.

THE MASQUERADE AT VAUXHALL.

Moralists declaim against masquerades; they contend that they are things which ought not to be countenanced; they will not hear a syllable advanced in their favor, although it is manifest that they who denounce them, are extremely inconsistent, if they fail to denounce the whole world, inasmuch, as the world is one grand masquerade, and all who live in it are maskers: from the king to the mendicant, all are masked and their actions form neither more nor less than one grand social system of mummery. Deception is the primary object of all, and there is nothing they seek to disguise more than that. What man can tell what another man is? He may guess; he may make up his mind that he is this or that; but he is able to discover his true character no more, than he is able to discover the seat of the soul; for while each assumes a character he wishes to sustain, all strive to appear to be that which they are not.

Masquerades are therefore the types of the world, and are, with the world, to be applauded or censured equally. Each is a miniature world of itself, in which goodness, vice, folly, and knavery mix with the most absolute indiscrimination, aud whether our view be comprehensive or limited, we see that the object of all is disguise.

Independently, however, of this high consideration, masquerades are an exceedingly pleasant species of entertainment, and the only wonder is, that in private life they are not to greater extent upheld. When men say, that vice invariably attends them, they say but that which is applicable to all entertainments; but if they be properly conducted a more really delightful kind of amusement can scarcely be conceived.

Now Valentine had heard much about masquerades, but of course, as they are confined to the metropolis, he had never been at one. Having an anxious desire, however, to witness the scene, he embraced an opportunity which a "carnival" at Vauxhall afforded, and having purchased on the evening appointed a ticket, and a very extraordinary nose, which he placed in his hat, that it might not be spoiled, started off in high spirits alone.

It was a beautiful evening, and as the moon shone brightly and the air was refreshing, he made up his mind to walk at least half the distance; but he had not proceeded far, before his attention was attracted towards a really magnificent-looking creature in a splendid Grecian dress, who was holding a conversation with a dirty-looking cabman. Valentine thought the association odd, but as he heard, in reply to the cabman's remark, "It's a hateenpenny fare"—the Grecian beauty say, "I have but a shilling," the mystery was solved in a moment.

"I can lend you some silver," said Valentine, "how much do you want?"

"I—feel obliged," said the Grecian beauty who seemed greatly confused, "I want but sixpence."

Valentine placed half-a-crown in her hand, and walked on until he came to the coach-stand, at Kennington Cross, when fancying he had walked far enough, he jumped into a cab, and was whirled to Vauxhall in the space of five minutes.

There was a crowd round the entrance, consisting of about a thousand persons, who had assembled for the purpose of catching a glance of the maskers; and as Valentine had seen, at the bottom of the bills, an announcement to the effect, that no person would be admitted without a mask, he fancied it proper to put on his nose before he alighted from the cab.

"Oh! oh! there's a conk! there's a smeller! Oh! oh!" exclaimed about fifty voices in chorus.

Valentine felt flattered by these notes of admiration, and having bowed to the crowd passed in.

Now when their Royal Highnesses Rieza Koolee Meerza, Najaf Koolee Meerza, and Saymoor Meerza, of Persia, were in London, they went to Vauxhall on an ordinary night, and this is their description of the place and its glories:—"In the evening we visited a large garden, beautifully lighted up, and the fireworks we saw here made us forget all others that we had already seen. A garden, a heaven; large, adorned with roses of different colors in every direction, the water was running on the beautiful green, pictures were drawn on every wall. Here and there were young moonly-faces selling refreshments. There were burning in this place about two millions of lights, each giving a different color; the lanterns and lights are so arranged as to make poetry, in such a manner that they have no end. On every side there appeared the moon and the sun, with the planets, each moving in its orbit; and in every, there were about 10,000 Frank moons, walking and gazing about, where the roses and their tribes were admiring their beautiful cheeks. Each was taken by the hand; such a company in such a place says to the soul, 'Behold thy paradise!'"

Now, however absurd this description may seem—however ridiculous it may in reality be, it portrays the feelings with which Valentine was inspired, when the brilliant scene opened before him. He felt absolutely enchanted, and gazed upon the spectacle in a state of amazement the most intense. He beheld the appareutly interminable festoons of variegated lamps, and heard the merry shouts, and the martial music in the distance. His whole soul was inspired, and he felt that peculiarly thrilling sensation which modern philosophers so beautifully describe, when they say of a mortal, that "he don't know exactly whether he is standing on his head or his heels." He pulled off his nose, but that made no difference: he was still completely lost in admiration; and when he did at length manage to find himself again, he saw around him groups of gaily dressed creatures, who appeared to have come from all quarters of the globe, with the view of imparting life and spirit to the scene. Greeks, Germans, Chinese, Russians, Dutchmen, Turks, Persians, Italians, apes, bears, sylphs, wild Indians, and devils, were the most distinguished foreigners present; while the most distinguished natives were, beadles, clowns, pantaloons, soldiers, sailors, sweeps, jugglers, barristers, knights, jockeys, beef-eaters, firemen, nuns, footmen, widows, harlequins, ballad-singers, romps and old maids. The Persian princes saw the "full moons" in petticoats only; Valentine but beheld a great variety of them in trowsers, and after having reviewed them for some considerable time, his astonishment somewhat subsided; he began to feel himself again, and replaced his nose, and having got into the middle of a stream of mortals and immortals, who were following the sound of a bell, he soon found himself within a really elegant little theatre, in which a poor man was mouthing what were termed "imitations" of some of the most popular actors of the day.

Valentine listened to the commencement of this pitiful buisness with an expression of contempt. He felt it to be a dreadful waste of time which ought not, on such an occasion, to be tolerated; and, therefore, throwing his voice just behind the poor creature, said solemnly in the notorious jumping wobble of the particular actor whom the man was pretending to imitate, "Sir-r-r, do you-er expect me to endure-er this insult?"

The fellow turned round very sharply in the full expectation of seeing his prototype behind him; and although he was in this little particular disappointed, the confusion into which the idea of his being there had thrown him, made him look so exceedingly droll, that the audience began to laugh very naturally and very merrily.

"Enough! enough!" shouted Valentine, and the shout had at least a hundred echoes, which had the effect of confusing the poor man still more; and although he tried desperately hard to recover his self-possession, every faithful imitation he attempted drew forth such ludicrous expressions of ridicule, that he eventually shuffled off the stage with a look of scorn which was highly theatrical, appropriate, and telling.

The audience, however, remained to see some other dreadful buisness—a fact which Valentine held to be, under the circumstances, monstrous. He therefore rushed from the theatre with the laudable view of hunting up the individual who had the management of the bell, and having happily found him with the instrument under his arm, he made up his mind to get hold of it somehow.

"*Well*, old fellow," said he, sitting down in one of the boxes, "Do you ever drink brandy-and-water?"

"Always, sir, when I can get it," replied the witty bellman.

"Well," said Valentine, throwing down a shilling, "then run and get a glass and bring it hot."

The unsuspecting individual placed his bell upon the table, and trotted off at once with an expression of pleasure the most profound, which happened to be precisely what Valentine wanted, for he immediately laid hold of the noisy instrument in question and taking it with him into one of the dark walks near the back of the theatre, commenced ringing away with unparalleled fury. This suited his views to a hair. The effect was instantaneous throughout the gardens: all were in motion—a living stream issued from the theatre—in fact, from all quarters the rush towards the spot in which he rang the bell so furiously was sufficiently tremendous to realize his fondest anticipations. He beheld with delight the mighty torrent coming towards him in the full expectation of seeing something very grand; but as they approached, he slipped away through the shrubbery which led to another walk equally dark, where holding the bell in both hands, he began to ring again with all the energy in his nature. Back went the crowd thinking naturally enough that they had taken the wrong direction, and as Valentine kept ringing as if he wished to raise the dead, their curiosity was excited to an extraordinary pitch, and they increased their speed in proportion. The stream turned the corner; and down the walk it rushed, when Valentine, perceiving a somewhat short cut into the middle of the gardens, walked very deliberately in that direction, deriving at the same time considerable amusement from the fact of the people still rushing down the walk, of course wondering what on earth was to be seen. By the time this particular walk became full, he had reached the open space in the centre of the gardens, and having jumped upon one of the tables which stood just behind the grand orchestra, he recommenced ringing as furiously as before. The crowd for a moment hesitated, as if they really doubted the evidence of their own ears; but having satisfied themselves as to the quarter from which the sound of the bell proceeded, they rushed back at once, and there Valentine stood, still ringing away with all the force at his command. He did not attempt to move an inch from the spot, nor did he mean to move until he had drawn them all round him, which he had no sooner accomplished, than, perceiving the hoax, they simultaneously burst into one roar of laughter.

Determined to keep up the spirit of the thing, he now began to issue a formal proclamation; but the crowd were so convulsed, and made so deafening a noise, that his own voice was drowned in the general clamor.

"Hurrah! now my lads!" shouted the leader of a press-gang—"Now, then! bear a hand!" and a dozen stout fellows, whom he led, raised the table upon which the Herald Valentine was standing, with the praiseworthy intention of bearing him in triumph round the gardens.

Any thing but that would have met his views precisely; but it did so happen that he *had* been borne in triumph before!—the equalrightites had borne him in triumph round Clerkenwell Green—a fact of which he had so lively a recollection, that, he seized the very earliest opportunity of leaping from the table; when, pulling off his nose, that he might not be recognised, he mixed with the crowd, who seemed to enjoy the thing exceedingly.

His first object now was to restore the bell to the individual who had the really legitimate management thereof, and having accomplished this to the entire satisfaction of that individual, he proceeded very leisurely towards the spot in which Neptune was represented sitting majestically in his shell drawn by fiery looking steeds, out of whose extended nostrils issued streams of living water. This group looked extremely picturesque, and while it was being admired by Valentine, a little fellow dressed as a school boy with a hoop in his hand, approached with a child who had a skipping rope tied round her waist.

"That, my little dear," said the school-boy, "is Neptune the god of the sea," and the tones in which this information was conveyed, had the effect of even startling Valentine, who thought it a most extraordinary voice to proceed from a boy; and yet he was dressed in every particular like a boy, and had on an exceedingly juvenile mask.

"It's very pretty, isn't it?" observed the little girl. "But what does it mean?" The school boy began to explain to her Neptune's transformations and their object; but Valentine no sooner perceived his design, than throwing his voice towards Neptune, he exclaimed, "Wretch!—Forbear!"

The boy trembled, and dropped his hoop, and then fumbled about his pockets, and eventually drew out a pair of gold spectacles; but the moment he lifted up his juvenile mask to put them on, the child shrieked and ran away, for he displayed the shrivelled face of a decrepit old man, who really appeared to be an octogenarian.

Valentine naturally felt disgusted, and drew a little aside; when, as he took no apparent notice of what had occurred, the boy pulled off his cap, and exhibited a little head perfectly bald, and having lifted his juvenile mask up higher in order to see through his spectacles with greater distinctness, he examined the group with an expression of amazement.

"Shame!" cried Valentine, sending his voice in the same direction, "You wretched, wretched old man! Are my actions fit to be explained to a child?"

The "boy" trembled again violently, and while looking and shuffling about in a state of great alarm, he placed his foot upon the edge of the hoop that had fallen, and as it rose on the instant it came in contact with his shin with so much force that he absolutely groaned with the pain it occasioned.

"Away!" cried Valentine, through Neptune, "Reform! ere it be too late!" and the "boy" hobbled away as fast as his feeble legs could carry him towards a spot in which the lights were most brilliant. Here he got into one of the boxes to look at his old shin, and while he was rubbing away with great energy, and cursing both Neptune and the hoop very profoundly, Valentine entered the same box and sat down unperceived.

"Have you hurt yourself much, my little fellow?" said he at length. "Oh! never mind, my man. It will soon be well! Don't cry! Let me rub it with a little cold brandy-and-water. Here, waiter! some brandy-and-water, cold—quick!"

The very moment, however, the "boy" became conscious of Valentine's presence, he left off both rubbing and cursing, and limped with considerable dexterity into the next box.

"That poor little boy has hurt his leg," said Valentine, on the brandy-and-water being produced. "Just see what you can do for him will you?" and he and the waiter proceeded at once to the box in which the little boy was rubbing his shin, still in great apparent agony. "Here, my little man," he continued, "let the waiter rub some of this in for you, there's a good boy. I'm sure you must have injured yourself very much."

The good little boy left off rubbing again, and having muttered something which sounded very much like a naughty exclamation, he limped across the gardens with his dear little hoop.

"You'll excuse me, sir," said the waiter, who had been laboring very laudably to suppress a fit of laughter, "but how werry green you are, sir! Why that little boy's a hold man!"

"I know it," said Valentine, "I was anxious to make him ashamed of himself, that was all."

"Ah!" exclaimed the waiter, shaking his head very piously, "you'd never do that, sir; he's too far gone. He's a lord, sir, and nothing can shame him. He's always here after the werry little gals, and the leetler they are, sir, the better he likes 'em."

As Valentine made no farther observation, the waiter of course left him, and he continued in the box until the fireworks were announced, when he proceeded at once to the gallery, in order to have an uninterrupted view.

"Oh! oh! oh!" exclaimed at least a hundred voices, as the first splendid rocket ascended with a roar; but, albeit these ironical exclamations were perpetually uttered, they failed to divert the attention of Valentine, who really thought the whole exhibition magnificent. He had never witnessed any thing at all comparable in point of grandeur, and hence the only thing which failed to delight him, was the fact of the last device shooting itself away.

The very moment the fireworks were over, there was a fresh importation of noise. A mob of sweeps, and a legion of recruits were introduced, and the clamor they raised was decidedly terrific. The sweeps had apparently been boiled for the occasion, and then very delicately tinted with soot; while the recruits were preceded by the "merry fife and drum," which had an effect so enlivening, that Valentine almost unconsciously marched with them, until he came in front of a place which was called the grand pavilion, and which commanded a view of the greater portion of the gardens.

"That's a delightful place to sit in," thought Valentine, "I may as well go up at once;" and accordingly into the pavilion he went, and found it thronged with very droll-looking creatures, apparently full of life and spirit.

Having seated himself in one of the boxes in front, so as to have a full view of the scene, he again took off his really extraordinary nose to look round him with more perfect freedom. Immediately beneath him, some remarkable characters were having a quadrille, and this had a very curious effect, inasmuch as all distinctions appeared to be levelled. A dustman was dancing with a Persian princess; a wild red Indian with a nun; a learned judge with a nut-brown gipsy; and a sweep in his May-day habiliments with a sylph; while the style in which each of them moved, was so strikingly characteristic, that they appeared to have studied to make the scene as grotesquely ludicrous as possible.

"Most potent, grave, and reverend signors," said a scraggy creature, stalking into the pavilion, in the character of Othello, with a remarkably short pipe in his mouth, "that I have ta'en away this old cock's daughter —." He was about to proceed, but as he had placed his heavy hand upon the head of a very fiery old gentleman, he received in an instant a glass of champagne in his sooty countenance—an insult which the "valiant Moor," put in his pipe, and stalked out with appropriate solemnity to smoke it.

"What did you order, sir?" inquired one of the waiters addressing Valentine.

"Nothing: what have you to eat?"

"Ham and chicken, sir, roast —"

"That will do: let me have it as soon as possible," said Valentine, who in the excitement had altogether forgotten his stomach, which now began to hint at the fact of its being empty.

He had scarcely, however, time to reflect upon this circumstance, before the dishes were placed before him, and having ordered some wine, he commenced a very pleasing operation, to which the gay scene imparted an additional zest.

As the place in which he sat was so conspicuous that those who passed the pavilion could scarcely fail to see him, it was not long before he was recognised by the identical Grecian beauty, whom he had seen in conversation with the cabman, and who entered the pavilion at once.

"I have to thank you," said she, removing her mask, "for your kindness to me this evening. It is more than I could have expected from a perfect stranger."

"Oh, the cab!" said Valentine, recollecting the circumstance, don't name it. You have been here of course ever since?"

"I have," she replied; "I have been looking in vain for a person whom I fully expected to see."

"You must feel very faint?" observed Valentine, "sit down and have some supper."

"I'm extremely obliged, but—I fear I shall be intruding."

"Not at all! not in the least! sit down." And she did so, but with evident timidity.

"There is," thought Valentine, "in the midst of this scene at least one heavy heart—a heart probably susceptible of all the most amiable feelings of our nature, yet blasted by the consciousness of guilt." And he gazed with a feeling of pity upon the beautiful creature before him, and as he gazed, he perceived the tears trickling down her cheeks, which she appeared to be most anxious to conceal.

Fancying that his steady look had somewhat embarrassed her, he assumed an air of gaiety—although he did not at that moment feel gay—and began to direct her attention to the most grotesque creatures that came within view. He could not, however, extort from her a smile. She appeared to feel grateful, exceedingly grateful, for all the attentions shown, but her features were as rigid as marble. She ate but little, and was silent, except indeed when it became necessary for her to answer the direct questions of Valentine.

"You are not in good spirits this evening?" he observed, after having for some considerable time tried to divert her.

"I never am," she replied faintly; "I have not been for many, very many dreadful months."

There was something irresistibly touching in the heart-broken tones in which these words were uttered; but as Valentine was anxious not to increase the pain she evidently endured, he at once waived the subject, and tried again to cheer her.

"Is *that* the earl?" inquired a person who sat behind Valentine, pointing to a small sallow consumptive-looking creature, who was leaning against the side of the pavilion, as if he had not the power to stand without support.

The Grecian beauty started, and appeared much confused.

"Why do you tremble?" inquired Valentine.

"'Tis he," she replied, "he who has been the cause of all my affliction." And the tears again sprang into her eyes, and she sobbed, while endeavoring to conceal them.

Valentine turned towards the earl, and looked at him with an expression of contempt.

"But for him," continued the miserable girl, "I should still have been virtuous—still pure."

"Is it possible?" said Valentine, "that a wretched-looking creature like that could have robbed *you* of virtue?"

"It was his title," she replied, "it was that by which I was fascinated—not by his person."

"But how came you first to know him?" inquired Valentine. "Come, come, tell me all;" and having at length succeeded in somewhat subduing her emotion, he prevailed upon her to explain to him, briefly, the circumstances out of which her affliction arose.

"My poor father," said she, "is a clergyman residing nearly a hundred miles from London, and the disgrace which I have brought upon him, afflicts me more, far more than all besides. By him, about six months since, I was taken to our election ball. The earl was there; I danced with him; he paid me marked attention throughout the evening, and called the following day, and on becoming acquainted with the circumstances of my father, who had then an exceedingly limited income, he exerted his influence in his favor, and the result was, my father's preferment. I was grateful—we were all, of course, exceedingly grateful to him for this act of kindness, and he became a constant visitor; but his object—although, alas! it was not then perceived—was my ruin, and that he eventually accomplished. I eloped and came with him to London, where he engaged a house for me, and was for a few short weeks most attentive and kind, but after that his visits gradually became less and less frequent, until at length he deserted me entirely."

"And is your father aware of your present position?"

"He is not; I have not dared to write to him."

"Do you think that he would not receive you again, if you were to explain to him how you are situated, and that you are anxious to return?"

"I fear not: I much fear that he would not; but having heard that the earl would be here to-night, I borrowed this dress, which is like one he gave me, and came expressly in order to prevail upon him, if possible, to give me a sum sufficient to enable me to return to my poor disgraced father, that I may throw myself in penitence at his feet, and on my knees implore forgiveness."

"How much do you require for that purpose?" said Valentine, whom the relation of these circumstances had touched most acutely.

"I could manage it with even thirty shillings," she replied, "even that would enable me to return."

Valentine instantly drew out his purse. He had but two sovereigns and some silver. He gave her the two sovereigns, and urged her not to speak to the earl, but to go home at once and prepare for her journey.

The poor girl appeared to be overwhelmed with gratitude. She a thousand times thanked him with eloquence and warmth, and having blessed him and kissed his hand fervently, left the pavilion unseen by the earl.

Valentine now tried to shake off the feeling which the tale of this beautiful girl had inspired. He replaced his nose, walked again round the gardens, went to look at the hermit, and astonished the persons who were standing around, by sending his voice into the moon-lit cell, and making the old anchorite apparently repeat certain passages in Byron's *Corsair.*

Still he felt somewhat dull, and returned towards the theatre, and as he found that the maskers were dancing there merrily, he joined them at once, and having engaged an active partner, in the similitude of a little female midshipman, he became again one of the gayest of the gay.

Having enjoyed himself exceedingly for about an hour here, his ears were suddenly assailed by a series of extraordinary shrieks which apparently proceeded from the pavilion, and as several of the females rushed in to inform their friends that "Slashing Soph" was having a glorious set to with a broom girl, he ran with the stream which at once issued forth, towards the spot.

In front of the pavilion a crowd had assembled: a ring was formed, and the spectators stood a dozen deep. He could still hear the shrieks, mixed with loud exclamations of "Cut away, Soph!—Pitch into her, Broomy!" and so on, but could not obtain even a glimpse of the belligerent powers.

"I will see who she is!" shrieked a female in the centre.

"That voice!" thought Valentine, "that voice!" He instantly elbowed his way through the crowd, and beheld in "Slashing Soph" the Grecian beauty!

He rushed to her at once and drew her back; but she desperately resisted every effort to hold her.

"Let me alone!" she exclaimed, "I can lick her!—I'll murder her!—Let me alone!"

"Foolish girl! I will not!" cried Valentine firmly; but he had no sooner uttered the words, than she turned round and struck him in the face with considerable violence.

He indignantly relinquished his hold, and she no sooner found herself free, than she sprang at the broom-girl, who was backed by a dustman, and tore her cap and mask in an instant to tatters. The broom-girl, although a much more formidable-looking person, stood no chance whatever with her, for she stood up firmly, and struck fairly out right and left, like a man; and while she did so, indulged in the most horrible language that ever proceeded from human lips.

Valentine was so utterly disgusted, that he pressed at once out of the ring, and on approaching a female in the character of a nun, he inquired if she knew the Grecian beauty.

"Know her!" exclaimed the nun, "what, Slashing Soph!—who don't? Why, I've known her ever since she wasn't higher than six-pen'orth of ha'pence. We were brought up together—only she happened to have a better education than me, and that has made her the most artful card that ever walked on two legs."

"But her parents are respectable, are they not?" said Valentine.

"Her father was, no doubt," replied the nun, "for her mother made him pay pretty handsomely for her. Why, she's the daughter of old mother Maxwell, don't you know?"

Most certainly Valentine knew nothing of the sort: he knew, well knew, that he had been duped, and that was all he did know about the matter. "But what was the cause of this battle?" he inquired.

"Why, you see," replied the nun, "about an hour ago, Soph got together a few of the girls, and stood champagne all round, and then brandy-and-water. She had just been playing modest, she said, to a sensitive young fool, whom she wheedled out of a couple of sovereigns, to enable her to return to her father, and she laughed so heartily as she explained to them how she did it, and drank so freely, that when she had spent all she had, she became so quarrelsome—as she always is when she has been drinking—that she pitched into the very first girl she could lay hold of, who happened to be this poor Broomy, as harmless a creature as ever lived."

"But he who gave her the money must have been a fool indeed!" observed Valentine, by no means expecting a reply very flattering to himself.

"Why, I don't know so much about

that," said the nun, "when she makes a dead set at a man, she never leaves him until she has accomplished her object. He is down to every move on the board, who is able to get over Soph."

At this moment another fight commenced. The dustman, who had backed the broom-girl, becoming excessively indignant at what he considered an unwarrantable interference on the part of an ape, thought proper to strike that gentleman, who at once returned the blow with full interest thereon, and at it they went with appropriate desperation. The ape being by far the more active of the two, had decidedly the best of the battle, a fact which so enraged a very singular looking Scotchman, that, determined to take his revenge out of some one, he began to hammer away at a tall thin military individual, who was conversing with a lady in a Turkish dress, and this a sailor regarded as so strikingly unfair, that he rushed upon the Scotchman, and beat him most cruelly. This in return had the effect of arousing the pugnacity of many others, and in a short time the battle became general. Nor was it confined to this particular spot, for as a gentleman in the character of Punch, while leaning over the front of the pavilion, had amused himself by pouring a quantity of wine into the mouth of a mask which its owner had raised expressly for the purpose of kissing a flower-girl, the individual thus operated upon, was so indignant at the outrage, that he rushed up at once with the laudable view of deliberately pummelling Punch in the pavilion, which he did so unmercifully, that, as some cried "shame!" and others, cried "bravo!" two parties were immediately formed, and the fight became general there.

From the pavilion, the battle gradually spread over the gardens, and a series of running fights were kept up with great spirit. The peaceably disposed shrieked with fear, and ran about in all directions with desperate energy. Some sought refuge in the theatre, but even that soon became a gladiatorial arena, while others rushed into the bar, near the entrance, and the rattling of punch bowls and glasses became awful. Boxes were broken down, and benches were pulled up, trees were shorn of their branches, and tables were smashed—in short, every thing which could be made available as a weapon, was with the utmost avidity seized by the more desperate, while at the extreme end of the gardens, the more rational were engaged in the interesting occupation of pulling down the variegated lamps, and pitching them dexterously at each other, which had a very good effect, inasmuch as each lamp contained a quantity of oil, with which those whom they struck were profusely anointed, and contrasted very amusingly with the furious onslaught made by those, who appeared to feel that they were bound by some just and eternal principle to do all the serious mischief in their power.

Valentine wisely kept aloof from all this. He saw the combatants dealing out desperate blows with the most perfect indiscrimination, and had no disposition whatever to join them, for their weapons were employed, in some instances, with frightful effect. The men were shouting and swearing, while the women were screaming; some were struggling on the ground, while others were trampling over them; some were climbing into the pavilion, while others were leaping from it upon the heads of those below; in fact, they fought so fiercely, and yelled with so much fury, that had a corresponding number of maniacs been let loose, they could neither have made more noise, nor have battled with more desperation.

The police did all in their power to quell the riot, but were incapable of accomplishing much; their authority was utterly contemned, for their numerical strength was but small. They did, however, eventually, by dint of great exertions, succeed in getting hold of the Grecian beauty, whom they dragged out of the gardens, with the view of locking her up; when Valentine—who by no means regretted this proceeding, and who had seen quite enough of the madmen who were battling, they knew not why nor with whom—left them, while they were still very desperately at it, with just sufficient money in his purse to carry him home, and no more.

CHAPTER XXIX.

IN WHICH VALENTINE HAS THE PLEASURE OF MEETING TWO PERSONS IN WHOM HE TAKES GREAT INTEREST, AND WHOM HE ACCOMPANIES TO A WAX-WORK EXHIBITION.

"It is!" exclaimed Valentine, one calm delightful evening, as he turned into Grosvenor-square. "It must be the dear, sweet girl whom I rescued!" And this was unquestionably, under the circumstances, an exceedingly natural exclamation; for he at that moment met a most elegant creature, whose glance, as she passed him, appeared to pierce his soul.

He stopped on the instant; and breathed extremely hard. His blood thrilled through his veins: he heard his heart beat violently, and felt altogether particularly odd.

"I am sure," he continued, "quite sure!—and—and—why what an idiot I am!" and he began to be really very angry with himself for entertaining a feeling so essentially queer; still he had not the power to shake it off. "Val! Val!" he exclaimed, addressing himself in the second person singular, "What, what are you about? Do you mean to remain standing here like a statue?" The person thus addressed, appeared to repudiate the idea; for he instantly commenced an irregular rush towards the object of his adoration.

With what graceful dignity she moved!—with what elegant ease did she hang on the arm of him who, as a natural matter of course, was her father! Her air was, in the bright imagination of Valentine, that of a sylph, or of an angel!—there was poetry even in the folds of her train as it swept the ground clean at each fairy-like step.

He approached her! and experienced that peculiar heart-sinking sensation in a greater degree than before. He passed!—and felt that he had never in the whole course of his life walked so awkwardly. He could scarcely walk at all! and as for keeping on the same row of flags! that became at once an absolute impossibility. And then, where were his hands? His right was sometimes in his breast; then it wandered to the arm-hole of his waistcoat—then up to his stock—and then into his coat pocket—while his left was, if possible, more restless still. He could not tell exactly how it was, but he had never found his hands at all troublesome before. He drew off his gloves, and then drew them on, and in doing so, split one of them clean across the back. Well, then, that wouldn't do: he pulled it off again, and carried it in his hand; and after fidgetting forward in this most undignified fashion for a very considerable distance, he made a dead set at some celestial body which his vivid imagination had established in the heavens for that particular occasion, and stopped with the view of making a few profound astronomical observations thereon, until the beautiful creature came up. This he held to be an admirable *ruse*, and therefore looked—and looked—and felt so *droll!*—She was a long time coming!—a very long time. He must have shot a-head very fast!—He became quite impatient—he ventured to look back; and found to his horror that she had vanished! Which house could they have entered? It must have been one of them! Did they reside there! It was then too late for them to be making flying calls! Well! what was to be done? Was he to remain there till midnight, or, to give a look up in the morning? He stood still, and turned the thing over in his mind, and eventually arrived at the conclusion, that it would be, under the circumstances, best for him to walk up and down for an hour or so then, when, if they did not come out, the probability would be, that they did reside there, in which case he would simply have to come every morning until he saw her, which he argued must, in the natural course of things, be very soon. The instant, however, he had arrived at this remarkable conclusion, a most extraordinary idea struck him! They might have turned down the street he had just passed over!—They might!—He flew to the corner of that particular street, and there they were walking very leisurely in the distance.

"Well of all the stupid idiots," thought he, "—but no matter. I pass them no more until I see them safely housed." And he followed them straight; and walked much more steadily, and felt himself very considerably better. "And have I discovered you at last?" he exclaimed as he viewed the graceful creature before him with a feeling which amounted to ecstasy. His heart told him that he had; and he began to consider how he should act when he had succeeded in tracing them home, and continued to be occupied with this important consideration until he saw them step into a house, near which stood a long line of public and private carriages. He hurried forward and reached the spot. It was not a private house. "Some concert," thought he, "and I am not dressed. Well, have I not time to run home?" He looked round for a cab; but before he called one, he inquired of a person who was standing at the entrance, what place it was.

"The Wax-work Exhibition, sir," replied that person.

"Excellent!" thought Valentine; "nothing could have been better;" and he passed through the hall and ascended the stairs, and having given some money, he scarcely knew what, to a little old lady who sat on the left, he proceeded at once into a fine lofty room, in which a variety of life-like figures were arranged in strikingly picturesque groups; while from the ceiling were suspended innumerable lamps, which imparted an additional lustre to the scene, which, on the whole, looked extremely imposing.

Without, however, giving more than a cursory glance at these figures, he walked round the room, and, of course, soon found himself immediately opposite the fair one, for a sight of whose beautiful features, he had so long, and so ardently panted. Her veil was down; and as she held it in her hand, it was fluted, of course, treble, and it was, moreover, one of those tiresome thick veils which ought not, in any christian country, to be tolerated. He could not see her face. Her eyes he could perceive, and they appeared to sparkle brilliantly, but that was not enough: he wished to see her entire face, and that he could not do. Well! how was he to act? He looked at her father again and again, and he certainly appeared to be a different man; but then, men will look different under different circumstances, and he had to consider that when he saw him before, he had just been rescued from the muddiest part of the Thames. His altered appearance was therefore held to be no proof at all of his not being the same individual. But that was of very little moment. The object of Valentine was to see the fine features of her—and his panting heart told him in language the most intelligible that it was her—of whom he was so deeply enamored; yet those features continued to be concealed by this villanous veil.

"Patience, Val, patience," he whispered to himself; "she may presently raise it." And she might have done so; but as he perceived no symptoms of the fond hope involved in that act being realized, he felt himself bound by every principle of love and manhood to have recourse to some quiet manœuvre. But what could he do? He considered for a moment. An idea flashed across his brain. They were examining every figure minutely: they would not suffer one to escape notice. Well, could he not himself represent a wax figure, and thereby attract their especial attention? It was then the only thing he could think of: he determined to do it, and being thus determined, he placed himself firmly by the side of a life-like representation of some diabolical person at which he appeared to be looking most intently.

He had scarcely been standing in this position a moment when a company of ladies drew near, and gazed upon him with an expression of wonder. "Bless me," said one, "Did you ever see anything so perfectly natural?" "Why it seems absolutely to breathe," said another. "Well I declare," said a third, in a somewhat merry mood, "I don't know what they will bring things to next, but I suppose they will be brought by and bye to such perfection that we shall be having for husbands wax men, by mistake."

Valentine felt that it would do, and therefore kept his position, while the ladies were first looking about him to see if he were ticketed, and then referring to their catalogues respectively, in order to ascertain what distinguished individual he could be; but as he soon became anxious for *them* to depart, he turned his eyes full upon them, when they shrank back almost as much alarmed as if he had absolutely risen from the tomb. He could not avoid smiling at the astonishment displayed, and as the smile had the effect of destroying the illusion, the amazed ones, after indulging in a few highly appropriate exclamations of surprise, *sotto voce*, passed on. The very moment they had left him he perceived the approach of her whose attention he was anxious to attract and therefore stood as before like a statue.

"That's *very* good!—excellent indeed! Is it not?" observed the father of the lady, waving his hand towards Valentine. "Who is it?"

The lady referred to her book, and Valentine stood with a firmness which really, under the circumstances, did him great credit. Being unable to find anything like a description of him in the catalogue, she again raised her eyes, and looked earnestly at him, and as she found it impossible to see him with sufficient distinctness, she lifted her veil! In an instant Valentine turned his eyes upon her, and beheld—*not* her in whom all his hopes were concentered! no, nothing at all like her! It was a lady with dark, piercing eyes, it is true, but with a face thickly studded with scarlet carbuncles.

"You did it excellently well, sir," observed the old gentleman, smiling, and tapping him playfully on the shoulder: "Upon my life I imagined you to be a real figure."

Valentine of course felt flattered—highly

flattered; but was really so enraged that he would scarcely be civil. He did, however, manage to force up about half a smile, of a particularly wretched *caste*, and walked at once to the other end of the room. He had never before met with so serious a disappointment, and he felt so exceedingly vexed, that he could with pleasure have quarrelled with any man breathing. He threw himself carelessly upon one of the seats, and looked upon all around him as if they had been really his natural enemies. He several times called himself a fool most emphatically, and twisted, and fidgetted, and knocked himself about—very naturally, it is true, for he was then extremely wretched—but certainly with most unwarrantable violence. He felt that he wanted something, either to do or to drink, he neither knew nor cared which, albeit at that moment he could have drunk a pint of wine off with infinite gusto. Wine, however, could not be had there; but, as he saw a very decent old fellow in spectacles sitting beside him, and looking about very quietly with a little black box in his hand; he felt that perhaps a pinch of snuff, if it gave him no comfort, might somewhat revive him; and, therefore, addressing this spectacled person said, "Will you oblige me?"

The old boy appeared not to hear him. He continued to move his head right and left, and to turn his eyes about in all directions, but neither uttered a syllable nor offered the box. Valentine, therefore, fancying that he must be either deaf or lost in a maze of admiration, said, raising his voice, "May I trouble you?"

The old fellow still looked about him, but positively took no more notice of the request than if it had never been made! Of course Valentine thought this extraordinary conduct, and began to be very angry with the cross old bear; but just as he was about to expostulate with him—to ask him what it was he really meant—for he was just in the humor to consider himself insulted—he heard a half-suppressed tittering, which he found to proceed from two merry little ladies behind him, when in an instant his eyes were opened, and he saw at once that *wax* was the *materiel* with which the old boy had been built.

"Well, this is extraordinary!" thought Valentine, whom the incident restored to good humor; and he smiled at the deception —indeed he as nearly as possible laughed—and on looking round, saw many very pleasant people who were laughing both at him and with him.

"Thart's a dead tak in, zir, thatt there be," observed a ruddy-faced person, who was dressed like a farmer; "I thowt mysel it wor flash and blud, darng me if I didn't;" and he grinned very desperately, and crammed a great portion of his handkerchief into his mouth, feeling, probably, that, although he had a very sweet laugh when it had its full natural swing, it *might* not be altogether decent to allow it to break loose there.

"It is very amusing," said Valentine, addressing this person; and he absolutely felt it to be, so, and that feeling prompted him to walk round the room with the view of examining the rest of the figures, which he did with that species of pleasure which is at once very natural and very remarkable; for although curiosity may be generally acknowledged to be a feeling, of which the indulgence is essential to the pleasurable existence of us all, there is probably nothing in which that feeling is so strikingly manifested as in the peculiar gratification which we derive from a sight of the most famous, and most infamous men of the age. Whether they, who step out of the ordinary track, be philanthropists, murderers, warriors, or villains, we are anxious to see what sort of men they are, and if that be impossible—if we cannot see them *in propriâ personâ*—why the next best thing in public estimation, is to see their portraits—being public lions, or objects of public curiosity—and as wax models are a species of portraiture which is by far the most striking, and which approaches the nearest to nature, the gratification they impart, if they be perfect, is greater than that which is derived from representations on canvass. Nothing can give so correct an idea of the features and figures of men as wax models: every shade, every line, every little peculiarity, may be so portrayed as to make it appear that the originals are living and breathing before you. It is impossible to take a portrait on canvass for life; but a perfect wax model may be taken for a living man; and hence, if the most exact imitation of nature be the perfection of art, the art of wax-modelling, as far as portraiture is concerned, may be held to be by far the most perfect.

This is, however, by no means established; nor is it absolutely essential to the progress of this history that it should be; for if all the legitimate orthodox artists in the universe were to form themselves into one grand corporation, with the view of upsetting it *in toto*, it would not interfere with the indisputable fact, that Valentine was pleased with the whole exhibition, and fancied that as *he* had taken one of the figures for life, he ought, in justice to himself, to extend the deception, in order to witness its effect upon others.

Now this singular fancy had no sooner been conceived, than he observed at the upper part of the room a little ancient individual, who was obviously, in his own estimation, a decided Narcissus. His hair was powdered, and his coat was powdered too: a white cravat sustained a very highly glazed collar, which appeared to entertain the design of sawing off both his ears; and while his waistcoat was white, and his hat was white, he sported white cords, and white tops to his boots, and carried in one hand a pair of white gloves, and a scented white handkerchief gracefully in the other. Valentine of course became highly amused with the bearing and dress of this respectable individual, whose politeness was so excessive, that when persons approached in an opposite direction, he would bow and slip aside to allow them to pass—an operation which he had to perform about ten times per minute. He nevertheless looked at every figure most intently, and as Valentine almost unconsciously drew near, it struck him that he might, perhaps, for a moment inspire the belief that there were fewer inanimate objects in the room than there really were. Accordingly, just as the ancient Narcissus was about to examine the representation of an elderly gentleman standing alone, Valentine, throwing his voice towards that elderly gentleman, exclaimed, "Ah! glad to see you!—how do?"

Narcissus gazed very curiously, and bowed very profoundly, and then with a sweet smile, observed, "Upon my honor, you have the advantage of me—really—I beg pardon—but positively I" —

"What! have you forgotten me quite?" said Valentine.

"Why where have I had the pleasure of meeting—tut!—bless my life and heart, how stupid to be sure!—I know those features; and yet, for the life of me, I cannot call to mind" —

"*Do* you mean to say," observed Valentine, "that you don't remember me?"

Narcissus dropped his head upon his shoulder, and tried with all the energy of mind he possessed to recollect where he had met that gentleman before. "Why I know you," said he, "as well as possible; and yet, do you think that I can call to my recollection?—bless my life and soul, what a memory I have!—Now this is really very extraordinary. But wait—wait a bit," he continued, raising his hand to enjoin silence; —"At Brighton?—Why to be sure!—Mr. Pringle. My dear friend, how are you? I hope I have the pleasure" —

Narcissus paused—and very properly; for albeit he held out his hand with the view of grasping that of Pringle with affectionate warmth, Mr. Pringle by no means displayed a corresponding amount of affection. Narcissus looked utterly amazed! He was perfectly unconscious of having offended Mr. Pringle; and therefore felt quite at a loss to account for that gentleman's coldness. He could not at all understand it. He felt that an immediate explanation was due, and was just on the point of *demanding* such explanation with appropriate firmness and force, when a remarkable idea flashed at once across his mind, of which the substance was, that Pringle was not the man he took him for—that he was, in a word, a man of wax! He therefore pulled up his fiery indignation, and examined the figure before him more minutely, and having eventually satisfied himself on the particular point at issue, he took off his hat and exclaimed, "Well! I never!" And the fact of his having indulged in this extraordinary exclamation was, under the peculiar circumstances of the case, an extremely natural fact; and here the matter would have ended, but for the mystery!—he had distinctly heard a voice! His eyes might have been, and evidently had been, deceived: he was fully prepared to admit that; but he certainly was not prepared to admit that his ears had been deceived at the same time. And yet, whence could the voice have proceeded? The thing was inanimate! It could not have proceeded from that: it was impossible; and yet he had heard it. He examined it again from head to foot very minutely, and drew his hand across his chin very lightly, and very thoughtfully; but he *could not* get over it, and Valentine, leaving him lost in conjecture, adjourned to a seat in the centre of the room.

Now on the left of this seat there was a figure which he had not seen before, but which was nominally an exact representation of the beautiful Madame St. Amaranthe, of whom the wretch, Robespierre, became enamored, and whom he eventually destroyed for being sufficiently virtuous to reject his addresses. This figure was lying at full length on a couch; and it certainly did look as much as possible like a lovely little creature asleep. It was perfectly evident that the sympathies of those who stood around were very strongly excited, and as they were descanting very freely upon the character of the sanguinary monster of whom Madame Saint Amaranthe was the victim, Valentine threw a series of well-directed sobs beneath the veil with which the figure was covered, when in an instant the persons who were standing around simultaneously shrank back appalled.

"My goodness!" cried a remarkably stout matron, "if it isn't alive, I'm not here!"

"Gracious, ma!" exclaimed one of her interesting daughters, "How excessively ridiculous!"

"Don't tell me, child," rejoined the affectionate matron, "when I heard the poor dear sobbing, fit to break her heart."

Valentine here introduced a short cough and after that a long yawn, which, seeing that the arm of the figure was placed above the head, had a strikingly natural effect.

"There, there! I knew it was alive! I said so!" continued the old lady, who being disposed to render all the assistance in her power was about to remove the veil.

"You reely mustn't touch, mam, if you please," said a girl who was stationed near the couch, and who began to explain to an individual in her immediate vicinity how extraordinary a thing it was, that notwithstanding there was an announcement on almost every figure to the effect that visitors were not to touch, touch they would, and nothing in nature could keep them from touching.

"Depend upon it, dear," said the matron, in a whisper, it's all an imposition; it's alive, dear, and that's the very reason why we musn't touch, to see whether it is or is not."

"This acute observation, on the part of the old lady, induced her exemplary daughter, who was dressed with extraordinary gaiety, to toss her head proudly, and to curl her lip contemptuously, and to exclaim very pointedly, "Dear me, ma! how excessively vulgar to be sure!"

"You may say what you please," rejoined the matron, "but I know what I know," and having made this highly appropriate and self-satisfactory observation, she looked at Madame St. Amaranthe very earnestly again.

"Where are you pushing?" cried Valentine, assuming the shrill voice of a scolding woman, and throwing it towards the figure of a little old lady, in a black silk cloak which stood at the foot of the couch.

"You are very polite, I must say," observed a rough individual, turning very sharply round; "where did *you* go to school? You'd better have the whole room to yourself, marm! Well I'm sure!—what next!" and he looked very fiercely, and felt very indignant, until he discovered his mistake, when he laughed very heartily, and the people around, of course, joined him very freely.

At this moment, however, the two persons who had been the immediate cause of Valentine's visit to the exhibition walked past, and the sight of them plunged him into misery again. He felt wretched, particularly wretched. His dearest hopes had been dashed from the eminence to which they had been raised, and that eminence was so high that they appeared to have reached the very depths of despair. "Am I never to see her again," thought he, "never?" He rose and left the room; and as he proceeded towards home, two lines of a song which he had heard in infancy suggested themselves, and which ran somehow thus:—

"Shall I never again hear her voice
Nor see her loved form any more?"

And the peculiarly interesting interrogatory involved was so appropriate, that he involuntarily hummed the poetical reply, namely:

"No, no, no, I shall never see her more!
No, no, no, I shall never see her more!
No! no! no! I shall *never* see her more!"

CHAPTER XXX.

GOODMAN MATURES HIS PLAN OF ESCAPE. THE COMMISSIONERS ARRIVE. HE PREPARES TO CONVINCE THEM OF HIS ABSOLUTE SANITY, AND IS GOADED ON TO MADNESS. HE RECOVERS; AND, HAVING REORGANISED HIS FORCES, RESOLUTELY MAKES THE ATTACK.

Notwithstanding Whitely labored to inspire his friend with the conviction that the design he had conceived would be impracticable, Goodman, who saw no other prospect before him than that of perpetual imprisonment if that design were not carried into actual execution, had been busily occupied, maturing his scheme every day since that on which the important subject was broached. He sounded all in whom he felt that confidence might be placed, and with pleasure found all whom he sounded willing to join. Still Whitely felt doubtful of success. He saw twenty men, of whom the majority were young and muscular, prepared to make a simultaneous effort to regain that liberty of which they had been with really cruel injustice deprived; yet, although there were but five or six keepers to be conquered, he believed that the minds of the twenty had become so enfeebled, that their spirits had been, by brutal treatment, so broken, and their native resolution so completely subverted, that however delighted with the project they might be, however anxious they might seem to carry it into effect, when the moment for action arrived, they would shrink back dismayed, and thus secure to the six ruffians a signal triumph.

The process of organization, notwithstanding, went on—the day was fixed; but in proportion as Goodman became more resolute and sanguine of success, his friend Whitely became more feverish and fearful.

The day arrived; and on the morning of that day, they ascertained that two of the keepers out of the six were to be absent, in all probability with the view of seizing another victim.

"Now," exclaimed Goodman, on hearing this news, "we are safe! Nothing could have been more fortunate. Everything, my friend, is in our favor. There will now be but four of these men to overcome, and, if taken by surprise, there may be but one. What, therefore, think you now? Why if even the hearts of two-thirds of our companions were to sink, success would be certain."

Whitely shook his head mournfully and sighed, and slightly trembled.

"My dear, dear friend," continued Goodman, "be firm. Upon my life, I doubt your resolution more than that of any man to whom I have spoken on the subject. Consider the monstrous character of our position. Consider how we have been kidnapped—stolen from society; consider also, that unless we do make our escape thus, imprisonment for life is inevitable."

"I do," returned Whitely, "I do consider all; but I cannot avoid looking at the consequences of a failure."

"A failure!" exclaimed Goodman; "It is madness to think of it. Think of success, my dear friend, not of failure. Suppose we admit the possibility, or even the probability of failure; what then? Is not the chance of regaining our liberty worth all the risk? Are we, or are we not to make the attempt? If we are, why then, perish the thought of a failure! Why should we think of it? What was ever achieved by entertaining the thought? What would have been our national character if the consequences of failure had preyed upon our souls? We have been, as a nation, invariably successful, because we have invariably felt sure of success, even under the most adverse circumstances. Had it not been for that, we should have been in the world's estimation a nation of cowards. Why speak of a failure, then, now? In a case like this, which entirely depends upon individual firmness and resolution, we must succeed, if we believe we shall succeed; but we cannot succeed if we fear that we shall fail. Come! come! be a man. Think of twenty opposed to four; and the cause of that twenty indisputably just: think of this, and feel ashamed to dream even of a failure. If we be but firm, our freedom will be achieved: I feel perfectly certain of that. All depends upon us. We are to lead, and have therefore the power within ourselves to inspire our companions with the courage of lions, or to cause them to cringe like spaniels again. *Shall* we not make the attempt?"

"We will!" cried Whitely, with unusual firmness, grasping the hand of Goodman as he spoke, "We will!—come what may, the attempt shall be made."

Goodman was delighted. He felt far more sanguine than ever. He went round to his companions, spoke to them cautiously one by one, lest suspicion should be excited, and found them all impatient to commence the attack. Twilight, however, was considered the fittest period for the commencement of operations. Goodman was then to give the signal by drawing forth a sheet which he had cut into strips, with which the principal keeper was to be bound, when, having obtained the keys, they were to rush to the door which led to the residence of the proprietor of the asylum, and which they had but to pass to be free. This was well understood by them all, and all were anxious for the day to wear away; but just as they were about to be summoned to what, by an extraordinary stretch of the imagination, was conceived to be a dinner, it was announced that the commissioners had unexpectedly arrived, when, of course a general rush was made by the servants of the establishment, with the view of getting things in order for the mockery of an inspection about to take place.

"Now," said Whitely, the moment he heard of their arrival, "as far as you are concerned, this attempt need not be made. The commissioners were not expected: the keepers have therefore no time to excite you; and as you are the only 'patient' whom they have not yet seen, you are perfectly sure to be called before them. Be firm; be composed: for Heaven's sake, my friend, say nothing which may develop the smallest degree of excitement. Appeal to their judgment. Be calm—quite calm. The keepers may wish you to take a glass of wine before you enter the drawing-room: if they should, be sure that it is drugged; be quite sure!—on no account touch it. Remember, my friend, the way in which they excited me, and thus made it appear that I was really insane, which the commissioners believe to this day. Therefore do not touch anything before you see them, as you value your liberty."

This caution was received with gratitude by Goodman, who felt sure that he should be able to convince the commissioners that he was a perfectly sane man, and therefore at once began to think of the best mode of commencing his appeal; but while he was thus engaged in the full conviction of success, the proprietor was occupied in giving instructions to his head-keeper; for he also felt certain that Goodman—whose mildness and perfect self-possession he had had ample opportunities of witnessing—would, if fair play were allowed, succeed in establishing his perfect sanity; and he did not forget that, in such an event, he should, of course, lose one of the most profitable patients he had.

Accordingly, Goodman had scarcely time to decide on the commencement of his address, before the head-keeper entered the garden, and addressing him, shouted, "Now then—here—*you!*—This way here, you're wanted!"

"Success! success!" exclaimed Whitely; "Be calm! God bless you! My dear friend, God bless you!" And as the friends shook hands, the tear which stood in Whitely's eye portrayed the feelings of his heart with far more eloquence than words.

"Now then!" shouted the keeper, "how much longer are you going for to make me keep waiting here, hay?"

Goodman joined him at once with the utmost firmness. He felt that all depended upon his tranquil bearing then, and hence determined not to notice any indignity that might be offered. Instead, however, of being introduced to the commissioners, who were appropriately taking wine in the drawing-room, the keeper led him to the cell in which he slept, and in which he found another keeper loaded with an armfull of chains.

"Now then," cried the principal ruffian, "come, strip! and look alive."

"Am I not to see the commissioners?" inquired Goodman, calmly.

"And no mistake, you are. They're a coming here directly. So you'd better look sharp!"

"Pray," said Goodman, humbly, yet earnestly, "allow me to see them as I am."

"Strip, I say, and be quick! d'ye hear me? come! I'm not going to stand all thish 'ere dilly dallying. Sam! here, just lug off his coat." And the fellow threw the chains upon the ground, and tore the coat off accordingly.

"My good men, pray tell me your object in ——"

"Silence!" interrupted the ruffian. "Hold your mouth, or I'll make yer!"

The very moment the coat was off, they slipped on a strait waistcoat, and then threw him down upon the bed; and while one of them was fastening an iron collar round his neck, and locking the chain attached to a stanchion, the other was engaged in pulling off his shoes and stockings, and chaining his legs firmly to the bottom of the bed.

Goodman remained silent. "Let them do what they please," thought he, "I shall still have the power to speak to the commissioners. Let them load me with chains, I must not be excited."

The sleeves of the strait waistcoat, were now tied to the bedstead, on either side; his bare feet were chained securely; he was unable to move hand or foot, he had not even the power to raise his head.

"Now," said the principal ruffian, addressing his assistant, "Do you go down, and let me know when they're a-coming."

The fellow obeyed, and the moment he had done so, the keeper deliberately drew a feather from his breast, and having straightened it, and looked at it with an air of the most intense satisfaction, knelt down at the foot of the bed.

"What, in heaven's name," thought Goodman, "is about to take place? My good man," he exclaimed, in a state of great alarm, "what, what are you going to do with me?"

Scarcely had the last word been uttered when the miscreant began to tickle the soles of his victim's feet!

"Oh! *oh!*" exclaimed Goodman; "Oh! Do not! Pray do not! *Oh!*—God! I cannot endure it! Mercy! Murder! Murder! Murder!" and he struggled and shrieked, and the more he shrieked and struggled the more quickly was the feather applied. The blood rushed to his head. He strained horribly. The torture was exquisite. His cries might have pierced the heart even of a fiend, yet that wretch still kept up the dreadful process. "My God! My God!" exclaimed Goodman, "What agony!"

These were the last words he consciously uttered, for his veins began to swell, and his face became black, and his eyes appeared to be in the act of starting from their sockets. The room shook with his convulsions. He raved with maniacal fury! In a word, he had been goaded to madness.

"They are here! they are here!" cried the assistant, rushing into the room.

"All right; I've done the trick," said the miscreant, concealing the feather, and throwing a blanket over the feet of his victim.

The commissioners entered! Goodman was a maniac!—laughing and raving, alternately—torturing his features into shapes the most hideous—writhing with frightful energy to get loose, and screaming horribly.

"Here is the poor man," observed the humane proprietor, with an expression of the purest sympathy; "Poor gentleman! Really, it is enough to make one's heart bleed to see him."

"Dreadful!" cried one of the commissioners.

"Dreadful, indeed!" exclaimed another.

"Poor fellow! Is he often thus?" inquired a third.

"Not very often so out-and-out bad, sir," replied the brutal keeper; "only about twice a week; and he's much to be pitied: there ain't a patient I pities more than him." And he winked at the proprietor, and the proprietor winked at him, as the commissioners drew near to the bedside, while poor Goodman was shouting, "Villains! Murderers! Fiends!" He was mad!—raving mad! The commissioners were satisfied. Accustomed as they had been to such scenes, this struck them with horror, and they prepared to leave the room.

"It's shocking when they are so," observed the christian proprietor, "truly shocking. Take care of him, Johnson; treat him tenderly, poor man!"

"I will, sir, depend on't," replied the keeper; and the commissioners quitted the scene, much affected.

The very moment they had left, the miscreant burst into a loud roar of laughter, and congratulated himself on the success of his brutal experiment. He had tried it before frequently; and although one of his victims had died under the dreadful operation, while another had been struck with paralysis, and a third had been reduced to a state of idiotcy, in which he continued till death, it had occasionally so far failed as to induce almost immediate exhaustion, which had been found not to answer the proposed end so well. In this case, however, he had been perfectly successful, and therefore, after having remained in the room until the commissioners had quitted the asylum, he left his raving victim with a fiend-like smile to receive the applause of his infamous master.

Poor Goodman's dreadful paroxysm lasted without a moment's intermission for more than six hours; and when consciousness returned, his exhaustion was so absolute, that he instantly sank into a deep heavy sleep—a sleep, indeed, so profound, that although the two keepers divested him of the chains, the strait waistcoat, and the iron collar, and even completely undressed him, he did not awake.

About twelve o'clock, however, that night, he was aroused by a series of desperate pinches, and, on opening his eyes, he perceived the proprietor—who had become apprehensive of losing a patient for whom he was so liberally paid—standing over him.

"Wa-ater!" he gasped, after a violent effort to uncleave his tongue from the roof of his mouth; and the proprietor gave him a cordial, which in a short time considerably revived him.

"How horribly!—oh! how horribly have I been used!" said Goodman, faintly, as soon as he had recovered the power to speak. "I hope *you* did not authorise this dreadful treatment?" he continued, as the feverish tears rolled upon the pillow on either side as he lay.

"Dreadful treatment!" exclaimed the proprietor, with an expression of utter amazement. "*What* dreadful treatment?"

Goodman briefly, but warmly explained.

"Pooh! It's all your delusion," exclaimed the proprietor "It's all your *delusion!*"

"Delusion!" echoed Goodman in a mournful tone. "That man, that desperately wicked man well knows that it is no delusion. May God in his mercy forgive him!" he continued; and again the tears gushed from his eyes; his heart was full, and he sobbed bitterly.

"Johnson!" said the proprietor in an angry tone, "Have you been ill-using this patient?"

"Me, sir! Me ill-use patients! I never ill-uses 'em: on the contrayry, I always treats 'em in the kindestest manner. How ever patients can get up sich 'bom'nable lies, puts me out altogether: but then they know nothink, you know, when they're that way. The commissioners seed that there warn't no mistake."

"The commissioners!" cried Goodman, "Then they *have* been here. They have seen me, in all probability, raving. They are satisfied that I am mad! Oh, villany! —Monstrous villany!"

"Come, come! none of that! none of that!" cried the proprietor; "compose yourself, and don't run away with such fancies. I tell you, it's all your delusion, and nothing but delusion: go to sleep: go to sleep." And thus he left him.

"Now," said the ruffian, when his master had left, "do you want any other little thing afore I go; cos if you do, you don't have it. I ill-uses you, do I? Never mind. I'll sarve you out for that, one of these here odd days, mark my words; now, you mind if I don't!" And he slammed the door of the cell, and having locked it securely, poor Goodman was left to his reflections for the night.

For one entire week he never quitted his cell; which, independently of the acute physical pain he endured was, of itself, a dreadful species of torture, for neither a book nor a paper of any description was he allowed; not a soul was he permitted either to speak to or to see, with the single exception of that savage ruffian, the very sight of whom induced an involuntary shudder.

Meanwhile, his companions in misfortune were marvelling what had become of him. The keepers would, of course, give them no information. They could not hear of his being still in the asylum, nor could they hear of his having obtained his liberty; but when four or five days had elapsed, the impression became general that, having succeeded in convincing the commissioners of his sanity, he had been quietly suffered to depart.

At the expiration of the week, however, he again appeared amongst them, and the feelings which were excited by his re-appearance, were those of mingled pleasure and regret. As far as they were concerned, they were delighted to see him; for the goodness of his heart, which was at all times conspicuous, had won their affections; but as far as regarded himself, they beheld him with sorrow.

Their gladness was, however, soon permitted to preponderate; for although he was feverish and physically weak, his strength of mind had been unimpaired by the monstrous outrage to which he had been subjected, and being, if possible, more firmly determined than before, to effect an escape, they viewed him as their liberator, and placed implicit confidence in his judgment and resolution. He aroused their enthusiasm by an explanation of what had occurred, and they looked upon success as a matter of course. There was, however, one whose enthusiasm he could not excite, and that was Whitely—the horrible consequences of a failure having again taken possession of his soul.

"My friend," said that gentleman, when Goodman had labored to warm him again with his eloquence, "let us now trust entirely to Providence. He never deserts those who put their whole trust in Him."

"I believe it," said Goodman, "I firmly, religiously believe it: I do trust in Providence, and have implicit confidence in His goodness: it is hence that I believe that our enterprise will be successful, being, as it is, indisputably based upon justice; but be assured that it never was intended that a man should trust in Providence and be inactive—that he should suffer those faculties with which he has been endowed, to lie dormant, looking to Providence for the accomplishment of that which Providence has given him the power to achieve."

"If we believe," rejoined Whitely, "that He who works the universe, guides even the worm; that He permits the varied ills of human life, and forms the varied moulds in which the minds of men are cast, and that in His judgments He is merciful and just: how can we believe that He will ever desert those who put their whole trust and confidence in Him? We have suffered; we suffer still; but did suffering increase in power with its age, we must have been goaded to death or to madness; but even in our position, we see that pain and pleasure cannot be divorced, for there is no wound which can be inflicted, at which we do not feel the God of Nature administering, at least, the balm of hope. Man never despairs. He cannot do so wholly. He looks to Him with confidence, even in the last extremity. In Him, therefore, let us confide. Let us look to Him for aid. Let us hope!—still hope!—and be resigned."

"My friend," said Goodman, solemnly, "the presence of resignation in such a case as this of necessity supposes the absence of hope. When liberty is wounded, men *will* hope; they mourn, and mourn, and call her virtues up, and pant and pray for her recovery—the slightest change reanimates their souls while they believe that she yet may be restored: it is when she becomes to us dead, when we are sure that she is gone, never, never to return, that hope gives place to resignation. I feel, with you, that they who firmly confide in Him will not do so in vain; but that feeling by no means prompts the conviction, that all human exertion is therefore unnecessary, or that all such exertion, of necessity, amounts to opposition to His will. We look to Him for aid; but is it, therefore, our duty to lie dormant? That, indeed, would be illustrating with a vengeance the apathetic faith of the fabled waggoner, who called for the aid of Jupiter. We must put our *own* shoulders to the wheel, my friend. *Aide toi, et le ciel t'aidera.*"

It by no means required all this to convince Mr. Whitely of the fact, that trusting in Providence did not suppose it to be the duty of man to remain inactive; but being anxious to induce Goodman to forego his design, he had recourse to every thing bearing even the semblance of an argument which might tend to subvert his resolution. Finding, however, that this was impossible, he again declared his readiness to join him, and promised to think no more of a failure, but to act with the resolute firmness of a man of feeling perfectly sure of success.

Accordingly, the next day was fixed upon as the one on which the attempt should be made, about twilight; and Goodman, by calling into action all the eloquence at his command, succeeded in inspiring his companions with so much courage, that they were to a man as determined as himself.

The morning came; and on being turned into the garden, they all seemed to have the impression, that it was for the last time. They breathed more freely, and stepped more lightly, and smiled at each other with an air of satisfaction the most absolute. The day appeared to wear away but slowly, for they held as little communication as possible with each other lest the keepers should have their suspicion aroused.

Twilight approached! and all, save Goodman and Whitely, who remained firm as rocks, were in a state of the most feverish excitement.

Their lips were pale, and their hearts beat violently. They walked round and round, and to and fro, with hurried steps, tugging at the sleeves of their coats, trying the firmness of the muscles of their arms, and grinding their teeth with apparent desperation. They could not control the development of their feelings. "Be firm!" whispered Goodman to each as they passed him, "be firm!" and each replied with a look of resolution.

"*Now*," said Goodman, addressing Whitely, as the ruffian who had tortured him entered the garden. "The time is come! Every eye is upon us. See! all are prepared. They will rush to our aid in an instant. Not a man will keep back; not one of them—I know it! Now, all is understood. The very moment we have him down, we bind him; when, having obtained possession of his keys, we rush to that door which leads into the house, and we are free, my friend—free! *Once* commence, we must, of course, break through all opposition."

The friends shook hands. "I am ready," said Whitely. The keeper approached, with his hands in his pockets, whistling snatches of popular tunes. Every eye was fixed on Goodman. The keeper passed! and Goodman, in an instant, drew the cord from his breast, and having thrown it over the head of the ruffian, brought him heavily to the ground.

"Now!" cried Whitely, "*Now!*" and his companions rushed like lightning to the spot. "Help! Murder!" shouted the keeper, struggling desperately, and dragging down several of his assailants.

"Stop his mouth," cried Goodman, "bind his legs! Now his arms! The keys! the keys!" he shouted, holding them up, and his companions gave a deafening cheer.

Such a cheer had never before been heard within those walls. The poor insane people appeared perfectly electrified, and began to laugh and shout, and to perform the most extraordinary antics, dancing, capering, and rolling about the garden in a state of ecstatic delight.

Two keepers rushed out! The insane people ran into a corner; but Goodman's companions were firm. "Down with them!" cried Whitely, and the keepers were dashed to the ground on the instant. Another appeared! "Offer no opposition!" shouted Goodman, "stand aside!" But the fellow at once sprang at him and seized him by the throat, which Whitely no sooner perceived, than with one well-aimed blow he struck the ruffian to the earth; and another shout, louder than the first re-inspired them.

"To the door!" cried Goodman, "to the door!—Follow me!"—and they darted through the asylum to the door which communicated with the residence of the proprietor.

At that door, a gigantic keeper armed with a bludgeon, stood waiting to receive them. "Stand back!" he cried, "*stand!* I'll dash the brains out of the first man that dares to come near me!"

Goodman sprang at him on the instant, and the uplifted bludgeon descended upon the head of Whitely with so much force, that it brought him to the ground.

"Villain!" cried Goodman, seizing the instrument, which he eventually wrenched from the ruffian's grasp.

"Go on!" shouted Whitely, "I am not hurt; go on!—Now!—the keys!"

They were lost!—"No matter!" cried Goodman, and he dashed in the door at one blow with the bludgeon.

"Hurrah!" again shouted the prisoners. Another door had to be passed. The proprietor on hearing the shouts, had darted to that door, which he opened the very moment it was about to be dashed down.

"Stand aside!" cried Goodman; "stop us at your peril!" and he and Whitely sprang through the house and were free!

None followed. "Let us go back," cried Goodman, "to their assistance."

"Not for your *life!*"—exclaimed Whitely, "come on!"

On they went.—Still none followed;—not one!—The very instant they had passed, the proprietor, with desperate energy forced to the door and locked the spring! In vain the prisoners dashed up against it. It defied all their efforts. They could not make it yield. They eventually succeeded in kicking in the weakest portion of the lower panel, but at the moment three of the keepers, armed with pitchforks, came round, and, by striking at the legs of the patients through the aperture, lamed all who stood within their reach.

"Back! back!" they shouted, "back!—if you value your souls;" and having stuck their forks into the flesh of the patients until they retreated in despair, they threw open the door, rushed upon them with savage desperation, and in less than ten minutes they were in a state of the most absolute insensibility, handcuffed and chained!

"Where's Johnson? Where's Johnson?" cried the proprietor, when this had been accomplished. "Where's Johnson?"

He was still in the garden, where he lay bound and bellowing with rage, while half a dozen idiots were dangling their hands and dancing round and round him with infinite glee.

His brother ruffians now heard him. He was instantly released, and, on being informed of the escape of Goodman and Whitely, he and the giant rushed into the stable, twisted the halters into the mouths of two horses, and, taking a rope with them, gallopped off at once without either saddle or bridle towards town.

The two friends had got some considerable distance, when, being exhausted, they crept behind a hedge. They heard the horses tearing along the road, and saw the keepers urging them forward with looks of desperation. They approached; and the two friends would scarcely allow themselves to breathe. They passed!—at full gallop. "Bravo!" said Whitely; "now, now we are secure. Now let us be off."

"No, no!" cried Goodman; "not yet, not yet: they are not out of sight."

"Be guided by me," rejoined Whitely; "I know every inch of the road. Let us once get across this field, and we shall be far more safe than we are here. Come, come! there's not a moment to be lost."

Goodman yielded: they started off, and the keepers saw them in an instant.

"Quick, quick! we are perceived!" cried Whitely.

The keepers turned; leaped their horses over the hedge, and were in the field before Goodman had got half across it.

"Come on!" shouted Whitely; "Come on!"

"They must catch us," cried Goodman; "let us stop to take breath, and meet them firmly man to man."

"Come on! come on!" reiterated Whitely.

"Turn!" shouted Goodman, "we shall be exhausted: we shall not be able to cope with them. Turn!"

Whitely did turn. "Be resolute," he cried; "give me the stick: I am stronger than you."

The next moment the keepers were on the spot. "As you value your lives," exclaimed Whitely, "keep off!"

The keepers alighted with an expression of contempt, and at once rushed upon them. Whitely aimed a desperate blow at the head of Johnson, and struck him to the ground, and, at the same instant, Goodman was felled by the giant.

"Fly and save yourself! Fly!" shouted Goodman, as the giant knelt upon him.

"Never!" cried Whitely, "until you are free." And he rushed upon the gigantic ruffian, who caught him as he rushed, and held them both down together.

"Now, now!" cried the giant, "bring the ropes!—bring the ropes!"

Johnson rose and shook his head. Whitely's blow had confused him. He did, however, manage to stagger up to the spot, and the giant, while kneeling upon Goodman's neck, bound Whitely hand and foot.

"Now for the horses! Bring the horses!—here!" shouted the giant. Johnson staggered towards them and fell.

Goodman could not be bound. They had no more rope left. To secure him, the giant, therefore, gave him a blow upon the head which stunned him, and ran for the horses himself. He soon brought them to the spot; and threw Whitely across the back of one of them just as he would have thrown a sack of oats; and, having placed Johnson behind, he threw Goodman in the same way across the back of the other and mounted himself; and thus the two friends were carried back to the asylum as nearly as possible dead.

CHAPTER XXXI.

UNCLE JOHN ANNOUNCES HIS INTENTION OF RUNNING UP TO TOWN, AND VALENTINE VISITS A WEALTHY INDIVIDUAL, TO WHOM HE FAILS TO IMPART MUCH PLEASURE.

On the morning of the day on which the occurrences recorded in the preceding chapter took place, Valentine received a long-expected letter from Uncle John, which ran as follows:—

"My Dear Boy:—I wish to know what it is you mean, sir, by wanting more money? Have you any idea how much you have had? Does it happen to *strike* you that you are living at a ruinous rate? I dare say that you have been at some expense in endeavoring to discover friend Goodman; and you are a good boy, no doubt, for your pains, poor fellow! But do you think that I am made of money, eh? I shall send you no more, sir!—not another shilling. It puzzles me however you get rid of so much. When I was your age, a hundred a-year would have enabled me to live like a prince; and here you have been living away at the rate of four! What do you mean, sir? Do you think that I pick money up in the street? An extravagant dog! Why, you'd beggar the bank of England, and so your mother says, and I perfectly agree with her; and she insists upon your keeping an account of every shilling you spend, and how you spend it, that we may know that you spend it properly. No doubt you get sadly imposed upon, and living in London is very expensive I dare say; but these extravagances must be checked, and they ought to be checked; your mother says that they ought to be checked; and I am exactly of her way of thinking. Mark my words, sir, extravagance is the root of all evil; and I therefore don't feel myself justified in encouraging you in any thing of the sort, by supplying you with the means of being extravagant. But don't return. I'll not allow you to come back until you have found Goodman. I am quite of your opinion that there has been some foul play. I'll be bound to say that it is so; but I'm not at all satisfied with your exertions in the matter. Do you suppose that if I were in London I should not have discovered him long before this? You don't go the right way to work about the business. I'm sure you don't. You can't. And now I come to think of it, I'll run up to London myself. I'll soon find him out. It is all very well to look, and look; but it is always my plan to go to the fountain head at once. You will see me some day, about the week after next. I don't exactly know which day; but, as you have nothing much to do, you can be at the inn, where the coach arrives, every evening till you see me.

"Your poor mother has not been so well the last two or three days. She caught cold the other evening coming from the Beeches. I knew she would, because she always does; and I said so, but she wouldn't believe me, and now she finds out her mistake. She sends her dearest love, which is more than you deserve, and accept the same from,

"My dear boy,
"Your most affectionate Uncle,
"John Long."

"P.S.—I have said, that I'll not send you up another shilling, and I'll not break my word; but, if you should—mark! if you *should*—want any money, before you see me, you can go to Mr. Fledger; you know his address, and as there is a balance between us of sixty pounds or so in my favor, you may get him to give you five pounds, if you like, but on no account draw more than twenty—mind that.

"Expect to see me about next Wednesday se'nnight. Be sure, my dear boy, that you meet me at the coach. God bless you.—J. L."

The portion of this affectionate epistle which gave the greatest pleasure to Valentine was the announcement of Uncle John's intention to visit London. He knew that, whatever might be said about extravagance in the body of the letter, there would be something in a pecuniary point of view rather pleasing in the postscript; but he did not expect that the old gentleman could ever have been prevailed upon to come up to town. It was precisely what Valentine wanted him to do, and he was therefore delighted with the announcement; and having ascertained from the widow, Smugman, that she would, with much pleasure, and moreover could, with great convenience and comfort, provide the accommodation required, he began to think of Fledger, who resided at Bermondsey, and of whom he was to receive *not more* than twenty pounds.

Valentine had frequently heard of Mr. Fledger. He had heard of his being the owner of an immense number of houses, and consequently a man of considerable wealth. He knew that Uncle John became acquainted with the existence of such an individual through a friend to whom he had sold some property in Essex, of which Fledger became subsequently possessed, in consideration of his paying to Uncle John the balance of the purchase-money due, and this was all that he knew of Mr. Fledger.

He had however heard, in addition to this, that there was no chance of catching that gentleman at home until the evening, and having accordingly waited until the evening drew near, he started off, with his heart and purse equally light.

It struck him, however, as he passed down Regent street, that the distance to Bermondsey was rather too great for him to walk; and being anxious on that particular occasion to act upon the most approved principle of economy, he decided upon patronising an omnibus as far as the Elephant and Castle. He, therefore, hailed the very first that came up, and jumped in; but, before he could reach a vacant seat, the conductor, who perceived at that moment an opposition omnibus approaching, slammed the door, when, as the horses, knowing the signal, at once started off, he was forcibly thrown backwards upon the knees of the passengers, who permitted him to slip very quietly upon the straw.

This was pleasant. He thought it very pleasant; especially as the people at that interesting moment began to laugh very loudly and very merrily. He scrambled up, however, by no means disconcerted, and having at length reached a seat, he waited patiently until the burst of merriment had subsided, when being determined to take his revenge out of the conductor, he shouted, "Ho!" throwing his voice towards that person, who was perched upon a board by the side of the door, where, with one of his arms hooked in a strap, and the other raised high in the air, he perpetually bawled, "Cas-*all!* El'phant Cas-*all!* Cas-*all!*"

"*Ho!*" shouted Valentine, louder than before.

"Hold hard!" cried the conductor, and the vehicle stopped. Of course no one attempted to move. "Look alive, sir, please," he continued, as the opposition omnibus passed him. "Any lady or gentle want to get out?"

"The Circus!" cried Valentine, in an assumed voice, of course.

"The Cirkiss! Why couldn't yer say so?" observed the conductor, and he slammed the door to with additional violence.

It thus became clear, that this course of proceeding was one of which he did not exactly approve. He, notwithstanding, cried, "Hold hard," on reaching the Circus, and descended from his perch to reopen the door. "Now then, sir! The Cirkiss!" he continued, "what genelman wants to get down at the Cirkiss?"

To this natural question no answer was returned, a fact which struck the conductor as being most extraordinary! he didn't know exactly what to make of it! he couldn't understand it at all!

"You will not forget to put me down at the Athenæum Club," observed an elderly gentleman who sat near the door.

"The Athneem!—you said the Cirkiss just now! I wish people could know their own minds!" cried the conductor, who was not perhaps the mildest individual in existence, and who had possibly been prompted to make that observation by the fact, that at that particular instant, *another* opposition omnibus passed him.

"It was not I," observed the elderly gentleman, who evidently prided himself upon the strikingly grammatical construction of his sentences. "It was not I who said the Circus: it was the gentleman whom you previously addressed."

Long before this highly appropriate speech, short as it was, had been brought to a conclusion, the conductor had closed the door, and the horses had started off again; while the passengers were looking very earnestly at each other, with the laudable view of ascertaining who it was that had signified a wish to alight at the Circus.

They were utterly unable, however, to get at the fact which at that particular period of time interested them so deeply. They had their suspicions; and the object of those suspicions was a cadaverous looking person, with black wiry whiskers, who appeared to be fast asleep at the farther end of the vehicle; but that, of course, according to the general impression, was a feint.

"Now," said the conductor, as he opened the door on arriving at the corner of Waterloo-place, "p'raps this ere 'll suit yer?"

"It is here that I wished to alight," replied the Athenæum gentleman emphatically.

"Well, come, that's a blessing any how," rejoined the conductor, who was by no means an ill-tempered man, but occasionally very sarcastic.

"*What* is that you say, sir?" cried the Athenæum gentleman, whom the conductor's ironical observation had failed to propitiate.

"Why, only that it's a comfort you're suited at last."

"I beg," said the gentleman of the Athenæum, handing over his sixpence, "that you will not be impertinent, or I shall be under the disagreeable necessity of taking your number."

This roused the indignation of the conductor, who very promptly, and very loudly cried, "Take it! D'yer want to stop the buss a million o' times, while all the other busses is cuttin past us?"

The gentleman of the Athenæum looked perfectly amazed, and was about to give expression to his sentiments on the subject; but before he had time to commence, the conductor having intimated that *that* wouldn't agree with his complaint, banged the door, hopped with infinite alacrity upon his perch, and renewed his "Cas-*all!* El'phant, Cas-*all!* Cas-*all!*"—and continued thus to shout until they stopped at Charing Cross.

In front of the house before which the "buss" stopped, stood a person enveloped in a peculiarly constructed great coat, a small pocket on one side of which had been made for the reception of a watch, upon the face of which he gazed, on the average, about twenty times per minute. He held a paper in his hand, and a pen in his mouth, and appeared to have been established in that particular spot for the express purpose of proving to all whom it might concern, that time would fly away, despite his efforts to keep it.

"You're behind Bill again, Bob, and Joe too, this time," observed that individual, addressing the conductor.

"Behind Bill and Joe!" cried the conductor, "and no wonder, nayther. An old file has been a havin' a game with me a comin' along, makin me pull up at one place to tell me he wanted for to stop at another. I should ony just like to 've had a fair kick at him; that's all the harm I wish *him.* I'll warrant he wouldn't be able to sit in *my* buss a one while with any degree of comfort," and having delivered himself thus, he proceeded into the house with the view of drowning his cares in a pint of porter.

After remaining in this spot for about three minutes—during which time the passengers had been engaged in the expression of the most conflicting opinions, having reference immediately to the subject which had so much confused them—the individual with the watch cried, "All right!" and the conductor resumed his professional position.

"Downing-street, please," said Valentine, assuming the voice of a female.

"Yes, marm," said the conductor, who appeared to have got over it a little; but the passengers looked round and round with great curiosity. They had not perceived the lips of either of the ladies move; but that was attributed to the fact of its being dusk. At all events, the suspicion which attached to the individual who sported the wiry whiskers, was not, in this particular instance, strengthened, and the omnibus went on until it arrived at the corner of that street, the offices in which are considered so extremely eligible.

The door was opened. The conductor stood holding it in his hand. "Now, marm!" said he, when he found that no one offered to alight. "Downing-street, marm, if you please!—Is this 'ere *another* game?"

"Please bring a lamp to find a purse in the straw," said Valentine.

"Well, this is pleasant!" observed the conductor, "we shall get the buss along by and by, p'raps, no doubt! I wish people ud just keep their pusses in their pockets. I aint got no lamps"—which was a fact; although one of which Valentine had no previous knowledge.

"I don't care!" said he, "I'll not get out without my money."

"Then you must go a little further till we gets to the shops," cried the conductor; who, after having shouted "All right!" began to mutter away desperately, and to give indications of something being, in *his* view, decidedly "all wrong."

Having turned the corner of Bridge-street, he politely procured a lantern, and, on opening the door, cried, "Now, then, where's this puss?"

"Here," said Valentine, throwing his voice to the extreme end of the vehicle, and the conductor thence proceeded, treading, of course accidentally, but not very lightly, upon the toes of the passengers during his progress, when having at length arrived at the spot, he knelt down and searched with great perseverance among the straw.

"I can't see it no where about. It isn't here, marm!" said he, raising his eyes to the lady at whose feet he had been so diligently prosecuting the search. "Are you sartin you dropped it?"

"It does not belong to me," replied the lady addressed.

"Then it's yours?" inquired the conductor, of the lady who sat opposite.

"Oh! dear me, no; it's not mine!"

"Well, there's no other lady in the buss!" cried the conductor, "it must belong to one on yer, any how! Who does it belong to, ony say? Who told me to pull up at Downing Street?"

"Not I," said one of the ladies. "Nor did I," said the other.

"Well, then, what d'yer mean!" cried the conductor. "This here's a nice game, and no *mistake!*" And he looked very fierce, and grumbled very naturally; and as another opposition buss passed as he retired, he gave it as his opinion, that in this, his extremity, it was enough to drive a man to make a hole in the water.

"What's in the wind now, Bob!" shouted the driver.

"What's in the wind!" echoed Bob. "I've a nice load this journey, and no mistake about it. They're only havin' a lark."

"A lark!" exclaimed the driver. "We can't stop for larks!" and with great impartiality he lashed both his horses, apparently that one might not laugh at the other, and they flew over the bridge as if unable to forget it.

"Marsh Gate!" cried Valentine, "Stop at the Marsh Gate!"

The conductor descended from his eminence to the steps beneath the door, and having introduced his head into the omnibus, in which he saw his "nice load" in a convulsion of laughter, said, with a drollery of expression which was of itself irresistible, "Now, is this another game, or ain't it, ony say? Does any body want to get out at the Mash Gate?"

"Did I not say the Marsh Gate!" replied Valentine, assuming a tone which seemed to be indicative of some slight degree of anger.

"Oh! very well, sir, very well! I only asked! There ain't much harm in that, I *suppose!*"

They reached the gate in question, and the omnibus stopped. "Mash Gate!" cried the conductor, "Now then, sir, Mash Gate! —What another dodge!" he continued, on perceiving that no one attempted to move; "Oh! It's all very fine, but I don't stop no more, you know, for nobody: that's all about it!—All *right!*"

The conductor kept his word. He would *not* stop. Valentine tried him in vain. An individual was anxious to get out at the Obelisk; but although this was perfectly legitimate, he could make no impression at all upon the conductor, who amused himself by quietly informing that individual that he would take him right on to the Elephant and Castle, without any extra charge; and having reached his destination, he inquired very deliberately if they were perfectly satisfied with their evening's entertainment, and, moreover, wished particularly to know if they were going to return that same night, because, as he explained, if they were, he would *rather*—if it made no difference at all to them—that they patronised some other "buss."

This sally had the effect of inducing him to believe, that he really had the best of it after all, and as Valentine was by no means anxious to diminish the pleasure with which this belief very evidently teemed, he passed through the merry group of passengers, who continued to laugh with extraordinary zeal, and proceeded along the New Kent Road, until he arrived at an inn, ycleped the Bricklayers' Arms.

Not being well acquainted with the locality of the place, he entered a shop to make the necessary inquiries; and on being informed that he was to take the first turning to the left, and the second to the right, and then to keep straight on till he got to the top, he went down a street which led to the bottom of the Grange Road, and which appeared to be a spot to which the whole of the laboring poor of the metropolis had sent all their children to play. He had never before beheld such a dense mob of infants. They were running about in legions, shouting, laughing, crying, fighting, pelting each other with mud, tumbling into the gutter, and scraping the filth off their habiliments with oyster shells and sticks. Some of the young gentlemen, larger than the rest, had, with bits of ragged packthread, harnessed others, whom they were driving in the imaginary similitude of teams of prancing horses: some were valiantly tucking up their sleeves, and giving expression to their anxiety that certain other young gentlemen, by whom they had been assaulted, would only just hit them again; some were squatting near the base of a highly popular piece of architecture, while others whom they had chosen as the most eloquent members of the corporation they had formed, were importuning every passenger for a slight contribution, and begging of him earnestly to "remember the grotto." By far the most striking and apparently pleasureable species of amusement, however, was the perpetual shaking of two bits of slate or broken crockery, which by being placed ingeniously between the fingers did, by dint of zealous exertion, produce a rattling which might in the dark ages have been taken for the soul-stirring music of the Spanish castanets; but, beyond all dispute, the great majority of the young ladies and gentlemen were bawling, and running, and rolling about, without any specific object, apparently, in view, save that of promoting the circulation of their blood. Valentine had never in the course of his life seen so many little children together. He could scarcely get along for them! really it was like walking through a flock of sheep.

He did, however, succeed eventually in wading through the swarm; and having reached a certain point, which appeared to be their boundary, he had nothing to do but to walk on and snift, for the air appeared to have a scent different from that of any air he had ever before inhaled—a remarkable fact which he was inclined to attribute to the children, but which was in reality attributable to the tan.

On arriving at the top of the Grange Road, he inquired for the residence of Mr. Fledger, and was directed to a dirty, old dilapidated house, which stood fifty feet from the road, and which appeared to have been erected in a hole. The gate was split in divers directions, and the rails which once adorned it were crumbling deliberately away. Nearly the whole of the windows were broken—the apertures being filled up with old rags—while the tiles, the majority of which had already fallen off, appeared to threaten to split the heads of all who had the boldness to venture beneath them.

As everything, therefore, indicated penury and want, it was but natural for Valentine to suppose that this could not be the residence of the wealthy Mr. Fledger, and hence, on perceiving a little shop almost immediately opposite, he crossed the road at once to inquire again.

"Can you tell me," said he, addressing a person behind the counter, "where Mr. Fledger lives?"

"Fledger! over the way, sir," replied that person.

"I mean *the* Mr. Fledger," said Valentine, emphatically, "the rich Mr. Fledger."

"Well, that's it; you can't make a mistake," replied the man. "There is only one Fledger in Bermondsey."

"Oh, indeed!—ah, thank you," said Valentine, who began to be extremely apprehensive about the sum of twenty pounds, which he thought it most unreasonable to expect that he should ever get there; and it must be conceded, that appearances were decidedly in favor of the irrational character of such expectation. Across the road, however, he went, and having opened the gate of which the timber was particularly rotten, while the hinges were remarkably rusty, he walked over the space in front of the house very firmly, and knocked at the door very boldly.

"Who's there?" demanded the cracked voice of a female, after a pause.

"Is Mr. Fledger within?" inquired Valentine.

"Yes; what do you want?" cried the female.

"I want," replied Valentine, "to see Mr. Fledger."

The mild tones in which this appropriate information was conveyed seemed to allay the suspicions of the female inside, for after drawing a few bolts, and removing a few bars, and turning a few keys with very great apparent difficulty, she opened the door as far as the chain would allow it to be opened; and having taken a survey through the aperture thus established, she made certain inquiries which had immediate reference to the business in hand.

"I wish to see Mr. Fledger," repeated Valentine, "my business is with him."

"Well, so I suppose," returned the female, somewhat piqued, and having again examined him minutely, and being eventually satisfied that there was nothing very desperate in his appearance, she closed the door, for the purpose of unhooking the chain, and Valentine was admitted into a most filthy passage, where he remained in the dark, until the woman had taken in his name and that of his uncle.

"Well," thought he, "this is rather a black beginning, but there *may* be something a little more lively inside."

"You may come in!" shouted the miserable looking woman, as she returned with her rushlight; and Valentine was accordingly ushered, with the smallest possible ceremony, into a truly wretched den, which appeared to be the kitchen, parlor, bedchamber, scullery, and all.

"Sit down," said Mr. Fledger, whose features bore some slight resemblance to those of a respectable fiend, newly whitewashed. "Well, what is your business?"

"I have received," replied Valentine, "a letter, in which my uncle states, that on applying to you I shall receive twenty pounds."

"Ah," said Fledger, pursing his lips, "I have no authority for paying you that sum. I can't do it without an order."

"Will not this be a sufficient authority?" said Valentine, producing the letter, and pointing to the postscript.

Fledger coolly drew his spectacles from his forehead, and cocked them upon his nose.

"*Five* pounds," said he, having read the important postscript.

"Or not more than twenty," added Valentine. "Twenty is the sum that I want."

"Ah; but this you know isn't an order. It should have been an order to me to pay the bearer, and so on."

"But will not my acknowledgment do as well?"

"No. How do I know that you are the person to whom this letter is addressed?"

"Do you take me for a swindler?" exclaimed Valentine, fiercely. "Do you think that I should make application for this money, if I were not the person to whom this letter is addressed?"

"I cannot tell;" was the laconic reply.

"You cannot tell!" echoed Valentine, whose blood began to boil. "Do I look like a swindler?"

Fledger opened the drawer of the table

at which he sat, and after searching for some considerable time, produced a coin, which he breathed upon, and rubbed very deliberately: he then drew forth another from his pocket, and having placed them before Valentine, said, "Did you ever see two coins look more like each other?"

"That has nothing to do with me!" cried Valentine, very angrily; "I came to you on business."

"I see that you are too hot to answer this question. I will answer it for you. They seem to have been struck from the self-same die—to be equally valuable. To all appearance they are precisely alike; and yet one is a counterfeit! Sir, I took that for an honest shilling: I was deceived. What follows? Why, that if I take you for an honest man, I may be equally deceived. As nothing looks so much like a bad coin as a good one, so no man looks so much like an honorable man as an accomplished villain. Were it not for the resemblance they bear to each other, villany could never, to any great extent, succeed."

Valentine felt that he was correct in this particular, and therefore became more subdued.

"How then am I to know," continued Fledger, "that you are an honest man—that you are really the person you represent yourself to be?"

"The possession of this letter, I should think, would be sufficient—"

"Not at all! not at all! You may have stolen that letter—mark me well!" he continued, on perceiving that Valentine was again getting up in his stirrups, "I say you *may* have stolen it! How am I to tell that you have not?"

Valentine indignantly crushed the letter into his pocket, and rose.

"Don't be rash!—don't be rash, young man!—don't be rash! I am an older, a much older man than you. *I* have lived long enough to know that no one can thrive in this world, who does not look upon and deal with every man as a rogue, until he has proved him to be an honest man. I don't mean to say that I believe you are one; but I do mean to say, I can't tell that you are not."

"Then, of course, you refuse," said Valentine, with impatience, "to let me have this money?"

"I did not say that. I am disposed to believe, in this instance, that all is straightforward and correct. It is a risk, it is true; but I am inclined, notwithstanding, to run that risk—at least I should have been inclined, but that it happens that I have no money by me just now."

"Had you told me that at first," said Valentine, "you might have saved yourself all this trouble; and he again rose, and looked very angrily at Mr. Fledger.

"Do you particularly want the money?" inquired that gentleman.

"Of course I do, or I should not have come here."

"Well, if you want it particularly now, you can *draw* upon me if you like for three months."

"*Draw* upon you!" said Valentine, who was ignorant of the meaning in this case, of that popular term—"Draw upon you?"

"Aye; I've no objection to give you my bill for the amount."

"And of what use would that be to me?"

"Of what use! Why certainly of no other use than this—that you could get it cashed immediately."

"Where?" inquired Valentine. "Who would do it?"

"I don't know whether you are aware of it, young gentleman, but my bill is as good as a bank note, sir! Any man in the habit of doing bills, will do mine."

"But I know of no man who is in the habit of *doing* bills."

"Well, in that case I tell you what I'll do: I have got, I think, as nearly as possible, twenty pounds in the house, which I must of necessity pay away to-morrow; but as I am anxious to do the utmost in my power to oblige your uncle—and I suppose that by obliging you, I shall be also obliging him,—draw the bill for twenty pounds, deduct the discount, and I will give you the money now. It strikes me very forcibly that a friend of mine will be able to get it done for me in the morning."

"Well," thought Valentine, "this is certainly better," and according to dictation he drew the bill. "Now," said he, "what am I to deduct for discount?"

"Oh, the usual business: fifteen per cent.," replied Fledger.

Valentine knew nothing about the "usual business," but he deducted fifteen per cent. which reduced the amount to nineteen pounds five.

"But you have only deducted fifteen per cent. *per annum*," said Fledger.

"I know it. Is not that correct?"

"No; fifteen per cent. upon the amount; that is to say, a shilling in the pound, per month."

"Why that's sixty per cent.!" returned Valentine; "I have then to receive, instead of twenty pounds, only seventeen?"

"Exactly!" replied Fledger, "with a villanous grin, "deducting two-and-sixpence for the stamp, and a penny which they always charge for profit. I see you understand it."

"But I don't understand. I think it most exorbitant."

"And so it is," rejoined Fledger, "so it is most exorbitant; but these people always are most exorbitant, always. The question amounts simply to this: will it be worth your while to pay them for the accommodation?"

"I had no idea that I should have all this difficulty about the matter, and I am sure that my uncle had not. I fancied the money was due."

"I know it's due," replied Fledger; "I don't dispute that. But then, what's to be done? You want the money, and I have not got it; and a man without money can't pay! The question therefore is, will it answer your purpose better to give a shilling in the pound, per month, for it now, or to wait until I *can* pay, which will be in the course of three months, I've no doubt."

Valentine could not wait three months, that was clear: he therefore consented to take off the sixty *per cent.*; when Fledger, delighted at having made so good a bargain, proceeded to a cupboard, and brought forth an iron-bound box, which he placed very carefully upon the table.

Of course Valentine knew not that this man had been a notorious money lender himself—that he had ruined more persons by discounting bills, than any other man alive—that he had obtained the whole of his houses by insisting upon holding the titles as collateral security for dishonored acceptances, and by goading the acceptors by renewals, extortion, and legal expenses, either to commit suicide, or to surrender all claim to those titles—and that he had then become an abject, miserable miser, and had given up the recognised game of extortion, in consequence solely of his having become so distrustful, that he had not sufficient courage left to risk even a shilling. Of all this, Valentine was utterly ignorant; but there was something in the creature's countenance when he brought out the box which inspired him at once with the conviction that he was, in reality, an usurious wretch; and therefore richly deserved to be frightened at least.

Well, he opened the box, and placed the back of it towards Valentine, who could tell in an instant by the sound, as the sovereigns were carefully extracted one by one, that the box was as nearly as possible full, and that, therefore, in stating that he had but twenty pounds in the house, the wretch had told him an abominable falsehood, with the view of swindling him out of the sixty per cent. He therefore felt that, as a matter of justice, he ought to be punished; and having imbibed this feeling, which was not, under the circumstances, highly reprehensible, he cried, throwing his voice into the passage, just as ten of the sovereigns had been counted, "In this room!—now the door!"

The effect upon the miser was electric. He instantly leaped up, as if he had received a pistol-shot in his heart; and in doing so, upset the ricketty table. Down went the box, and away flew the sovereigns!—five hundred, at least, were rolling in all directions upon the floor. This was somewhat more than was anticipated by Valentine, who smiled; but the miser stood aghast!—trembling with the utmost violence, and rolling his eyes from the door to the gold, and from the gold to the door, while his sister, who was not quite so utterly lost, seized the broom as the miserable girl whom they nominally kept, and who displayed far more courage than either of them, peeped through the keyhole of the door.

In this position they remained for some considerable time, as if utterly unable to move hand or foot. Valentine, however, at length broke silence by inquiring if he should assist in gathering up the gold.

"No, no, no!" cried the paralysed wretch, whom the question at once restored to a state of consciousness, and he placed his skinny hand upon the shoulder of Valentine, as if in order to compel him to remain in his seat. He then flew to the cupboard, and bringing forth a brace of pistols, thrust them hurriedly into the hands of Valentine, and implored him to shoot through the heart of the very first man that entered, when, sinking upon the ground, he commenced at once picking up the gold with unparalleled zeal and dexterity.

His sister still kept near the door, her fears prompting her to fancy that she heard strange breathings, divers delicate whisperings, and an infinite variety of footsteps outside; while Valentine quietly amused himself with watching the grasping exertions of the wretch upon the ground, who still trembled as energetically as if he had been seized with a violent fit of the ague.

At length he completed his task. The whole of the sovereigns—at least all he could find—were restored to the box, which he locked, and placed securely in a hole up the chimney, when, dropping into a chair by the side of Valentine, apparently half dead, he inquired what was best to be done.

"Be silent!" said Valentine, "let us first see what *they* mean to do. I am perfectly prepared to receive them."

"I thank you! I thank you! I know that you are brave!—very brave!" cried the miser, "you'll be a match for them—I know you'll be a match for them. *Hark;*—didn't you hear?"

"No, no!" replied Valentine very firmly, and looking very valiant, "I think the noise alarmed them. It strikes me they are gone. If not, why let them come!—they will meet with a warm reception."

The unflinching firmness exhibited by Valentine gradually inspired the wretched trio with courage. The females withdrew from the door, the table was raised, the miser resumed his old position, and Valentine began in an ironical strain to congratulate him on the sudden acquisition of so much wealth.

It is astonishing how much easier men find it to do evil than to bear to be told of the evil they have done; and it is equally astonishiug that men who can utter a series of straight-forward falsehoods, without a blush, find it difficult to endure the painful process of conviction. Even this wretched miser, dead as he was apparently to every feeling which actuates the human heart, save that of avarice, shrank from the gaze of Valentine—whom he could browbeat before—when he found that that gaze was intended to convey to his sordid soul the impression, that the falsehood of which he had been guilty was now too apparent to deceive.

"Well!" said Valentine, when the limbs of the wretch had in some degree resumed their accustomed tranquillity; "since it seems that you have a little more money in the house than you expected, you will be able to give me the twenty pounds in full?"

"No no," said the miser, "at least, not now, not now—we'll talk about it: give a look up in the morning."

"Why, that," said Valentine, "will be very inconvenient."

"I cannot help it. I'm sorry for it, but cannot help it. I would not touch that box again now for the world."

"Why you have nothing to fear," rejoined Valentine, who now felt *determined* to have the money; "I will still keep strict guard."

"I don't care," said the miser, "it's safe where it is. It shall not come out of that place to-night, if I know it."

"Indeed," thought Valentine, "we'll very soon see about that." And he rose from his seat, saying, "well then, I suppose that I must call upon you in the morning."

"If you please," said the miser; "yes, do."

"Have you got it?" inquired Valentine throwing his voice very dexterously into the chimney.

"I'm ruined! I'm ruined!" cried the miser. "I'm ruined!" and he darted, like lightning, across the room; and having found the box, of course, where he had placed it, he drew it forth, and hugged it fondly to his heart, shouting, "thieves! fire! murder! thieves! thieves!"

His sister at this moment followed his example, "thieves! thieves!" she cried, opening the window which overlooked a field; but as the room was at the back of the house, and they dared not go in front, the wind carried their voices from the road, and they gradually died away, unheard.

"Where are the pistols!" shouted Valentine. They were lying upon the table. He seized one in an instant, and having cocked it with an air of invincible valor, let fly up the chimney.

Of course nothing but soot descended; but it did the chimney good, for it was previously choked as nearly as possible up to the pot: it therefore cured that completely, and this was all the good it could do; but the bravery involved in the act so excited the admiration of the miser, that he *almost* relinquished the box to embrace him.

"Do you think that there *could* have been any one there?" inquired Valentine, very mysteriously.

"I heard a voice!" cried the miser, "I'm sure I heard a voice! Didn't you?" he continued, addressing his sister.

"Of course I did!" replied that respectable female, with infinite promptitude and spirit; "Do you think that I'm deaf? It's my belief there's a man in there now."

"If there be, he's a dead man," said Valentine, "if the pistol I discharged contained a ball."

"Oh yes! oh yes!" cried the miser; "oh yes! and a capital ball it was too. It's a pity it was fired off for nothing."

"It *is* a pity, when you come to think of it," said Valentine.

"That powder too: powder costs a *deal* of money; its very expensive—very."

"Well," said Valentine, apparently in the act of departing—an act which he had really no intention to perform, without having the sum of twenty pounds in his pocket —"I suppose that I can be of no more service now?"

"Stay, stay!" cried the miser. "Pray do not go yet., Stay a quarter of an hour longer; but a quarter of an hour!"

"I really cannot," returned Valentine, "if I'm to come up here again in the morning."

"Well—stay!—I'll give it you now—I'll give it you now. Only stop."

Of *course* Valentine stopped! He had not the least intention of going, until he had gained possession of that which he came for. He therefore sat down again, without a second invitation, and displayed a very laudable anxiety to come to the point at once. "You mean, of course," said he, "to pay me now in full."

"Well, well; but you must take me off discount."

"What, sixty per cent!" exclaimed Valentine.

"No—no!" said the miser; I'll be satisfied with ten. You must take me off ten?"

"As the money is *due*, I don't feel myself justified in consenting even to that. But perhaps," he added, rising again, "I had better look up in the morning."

"No—no," said the miser, still dreadfully alarmed; "I'll not trouble you; no, I'll not trouble you. But really you must take me off five! It's a regular thing, you know, quite—quite a regular thing."

"Well, you'd better settle that with my Uncle, when you see him. He understands more about the business than I do."

"Well, well; I suppose I must.—Hush!" he exclaimed, and, having listened most attentively for several seconds, he opened the box.

All was silent. He would not suffer one of the sovereigns to click against another. He drew them out one by one, very carefully and very reluctantly; and, having counted them over again and again, locked his box and said:—"There, there are twenty."

Valentine had been in the habit of counting money only when he paid it away; but in this particular instance he felt that, as a matter of common justice to himself, he ought to adopt the same plan when he received it. He therefore did count it: he counted it twice as the sovereigns were lying on the table, and the result was a natural result, under the circumstances, seeing that there were but nineteen.

"There's one short," said he, eyeing the miserable dog: "only one."

"Dear me, I thought I counted twenty, I'm sure!" cried the wretch, with a villanous smirk, and he counted them again and again, for the show of the thing, and then added, "Why there *are* but nineteen! How singular!"

"Very!" said Valentine, sarcastically, "*Very!*" and he looked at the wretch as he reluctantly drew forth the twentieth, with an expression which seemed to confuse him a little. He nevertheless counted them over again, being firmly determined not to suffer him to reap, even from sleight-of-hand villany, the smallest advantage; and having satisfied himself as to the correctness of the sum, he surveyed the wretched group with a feeling of disgust.

There sat the miser, whose soul seemed to have sunk beneath the weight of his iniquities, trembling and groaning under the lively apprehension of losing that which, to him, was intrinsically valueless, seeing that, with the means of procuring all the luxuries, he denied himself even the common necessaries of life; and while his sister, the very type of sordid wretchedness, sat, with her elbows upon her knees, and her chin upon her hands, in a chair, the ragged horse-hair of which, that once formed its plump bottom, hanging down to the floor, the poor girl, whom fate had doomed to live beneath the same roof, lay miserably huddled up in one corner of the room, starving, absolutely starving in the midst of wealth!

Valentine sickened at the sight, and therefore put on his hat.

"Must you go?" said the miser.

"I must," replied Valentine.

"Well, well!" said the miser, seizing the pistol that was loaded, "do carry this for me till you get to the door. My hand trembles. I'm sure I can't take a true aim."

Valentine carried the pistol accordingly, and after an infinite deal of listening, they reached the outer door, which was no sooner opened than he fired the pistol off, which so alarmed the trembling wretch, that he closed the door instantly, shutting his unsuspected tormentor outside.

"What shall I do with the pistol?" thought Valentine.

He had not to think long. He dashed it at once through the window, and departed; while the feelings with which the inmates were inspired by the rattling of the glass, were questionless very lively, but not very gay.

CHAPTER XXXII.

THE FIRST CONCERT GIVEN BY THE NATIVE TALENT ASSOCIATION.

Valentine had from childhood been extremely fond of music. He was unable to play upon any instrument; he knew nothing of the technicalities of the science, nor had he the slightest wish to know. The enchanting effects were sufficient for him; he cared not to study the minutiæ of the cause. Having had, however; an ardent desire at one period to become acquainted with musical men, that desire had been gratified to no inconsiderable extent, and he for some time enjoyed their society, being delighted with their apparent simplicity of soul; but the charm which their companionship primarily imparted was quickly broken, when their prevailing characteristics were laid open to his view. He found them reckless, gay, improvident, polite, but not one was he able to point to as being a really virtuous man. He was aware of course that virtue in classes was difficult to be found, but although in every other class he had perceived it shining brightly in the actions of individuals, he had never had the pleasure to meet a professionally musical man, whose private character would bear even a superficial investigation. As men they were indolent and dishonorable; as husbands they were faithless; as fathers they were heartless; as friends they were envious and insincere.

Valentine had in all probability been unfortunate in his introductions to these musical people, seeing, that doubtless he might have been introduced to some who were really good men; but having been in a position to analyse the characters of many from the highest to the lowest in the profession, it was but natural for him to infer from the result of his experience, that however kind, generous, and amiable they might appear, they were all at heart equally hollow.

This consideration, however, by no means subdued the ardor of his passion for music, and he was anxious to do all in his power to promote its cause, by the cultivation of a musical taste among the people, it being, to him at least, manifest, that nothing could have a more powerful tendency to soften their tone, to counteract their bad passions, or to induce that refinement in popular pleasures which is so absolutely essential to a high state of civilisation. It is true, that when this was placed in juxtaposition with the view which he entertained of the private characters of professionally musical men, they at first appeared inimical; but when he looked at the mode of life so peculiar to those creatures, when he saw the temptations to vice and dishonor with which they were perpetually assailed, and perceived that if their minds were not indeed too weak to make any resistance to those temptations, they exhibited no inclination to resist them; when he found that every thing bearing even the semblance of domestic happiness was their abhorrence, and that all they had to talk about, or cared to talk about, or even seemed to have the ability to talk about, was music mixed up with intrigue, he very soon became convinced that their characters were not formed by music, but in spite of its softening influence, by their pernicious communication with those by whom vice and dishonor in every shape are applauded.

Now, it happened, that at this particular period of our history, a great outcry was raised about what was then yclept NATIVE TALENT. The court was denounced; the aristocracy was denounced; the whole country was denounced because native talent failed to be patronised with commensurate liberality. Cargoes of foreign artistes were imported from time to time, and exported with wreaths of laurel and purses crammed with British gold, to the great discouragement of native talent. At the Royal Concerts none but foreigners were engaged; at the soirées of the nobility none but foreigners were engaged, while every theatre in which foreigners were not engaged was empty: in fact, native talent appeared to be in such a dreadful state, that they who possessed the real and recognised ability to snatch it from contempt, crossed the Atlantic—it being well understood that the Americans upheld native talent, which was certainly much to their credit—while our citizens gloried in being jammed in the pit, or stewed to rags in the gallery of the Opera, to hear that which they could by no means understand, with the view of having it in their power to speak with enthusiasm of the brilliancy of the prima donna, and the surpassing richness of the primo buffo, and to explain how the adored—*You know wochee poke afar;* and how deeply they were enamored of *Dye pitch her my balsam core.*

Such being the lamentable state of the case then, certain highly influential and remarkably staunch, musical individuals, entertaining an extremely laudable anxiety to rescue native talent from the impending doom of extinction, conceived the idea of establishing a Native Talent Association, with the view of getting up a series of native talent concerts, at which nothing of course but native talent should be developed; and having perfected their project, they proceeded to carry it at once into execution, in order to prove that, although foreign talent might then be the rage, native talent was of an infinitely superior caste, and, therefore, ought to be more liberally patronised by a truly enlightened British public.

Accordingly, the first of the series was announced, and Valentine having purchased a ticket, attended. The room was crowded. He at first saw no prospect at all of obtaining a seat; but having secured one at length near the orchestra, he commenced a perusal of the programme which had been given to him at the door. It began with a prospectus, and that prospectus read well; very well;—it promised much, it is true; but it promised no more than might with ease have been performed. He was therefore delighted with the prospectus; but how great was his astonishment, when, on looking below he found that nothing but German and Italian pieces were to be sung! "Is this," thought he, "intended to develope native talent! Why, at best, it can be but the native talent of imitation! Here we have a selection of Italian and German music to be sung by English singers, after the fashion of the Italians and the Germans and that with the view of inspiring an appreciation of native talent!" He of course, and very naturally, felt that this ought not to be; and as he wished most sincerely to promote the cause which its more active advocates, doubtless with the best possible intentions, had labored with so much zeal to injure, he felt himself bound, as one who possessed the power to warn them with effect against the course they were pursuing, to impress upon their minds that the act of imitating the singing of foreigners, however excellent that imitation might be, developed native talent no more than the act of imitating the language of foreigners, and that instead of inducing a higher appreciation of native talent, its tendency was to depreciate it, seeing that it raised foreign talent in public estimation.

This to Valentine appeared to be indisputable; and while he was endeavoring to decide upon the course, which, under the circumstances, he ought to pursue, the band commenced the overture to *Zauberflote*, and certainly went through it very well. The audience applauded vehemently, and demanded an encore, which was of course extremely grateful to the feelings of the performers in the aggregate; and while they were taking snuff with due gusto and effect, the conductor very quietly winked at the leader, who as quietly winked at the conductor in return.

Having inquired of a polite old gentleman who sat in his immediate vicinity, Valentine ascertained that the projector of the scheme was the identical individual who on this occasion wielded the baton, and as he felt that he was, therefore, the man whom he ought to address, he fixed his eyes very intently upon him.

Now the visage of this individual was extremely long, and strongly marked, and pale in proportion. His hair was black; and while it was parted in front with the utmost nicety, it hung in wild ringlets upon his shoulders. He had on an undeniable black satin stock, figured delicately with very little lilies, and studded with three remarkably suspicious-looking Brobdignagian brilliants. An eye-glass attached to a piece of black ribbon was stuck with consummate ingenuity between his left cheek bone and brow: and a gold colored chain of surpassing circumference was really very tastefully arranged over a white satin vest. His coat was of course a full dress coat, an indigo blue coat, with black velvet collar, silk facings, and figured silk buttons, and while his left hand was adorned with a delicate French white kid glove, the taper fingers of his right were embellished with a variety of rings, which he positively felt himself bound to display as much as possible.

Valentine could not avoid smiling as he inspected this elegant, fantastic, and really fascinating creature; but as the overture was now again brought to a conclusion amidst thunders of applause, he was on the *qui vive*. A rattling Italian buffo song stood first upon the list, and as he perceived a professional genius stepping forward to do execution on the same, he very naturally conceived that it was then the time for action.

Well! the symphony commenced; and as the professional gentleman whose uvula appeared to be down, was a-heming with unprecedented violence, Valentine throwing his voice behind the exquisite conductor, who was then at the piano-forte, ran up and down the scale in such a singularly unprofessional fashion, that all eyes were directed towards the spot in an instant.

"Hist! hist!" hissed the conductor, looking very sharply round, "Hish! *hish!*" But Valentine kept on—changing the key for the express accommodation of each particular roulade—with a perseverance, which under any other circumstances certainly would have been highly reprehensible.

The conductor became indignant, and cried "hish! *hish!*" with greater vehemence than before. It seemed perfectly clear to him, that there was some one very near him in a truly provoking state of inebriety. But who was it? He could not tell. He took the glass from his eye, for as he could see better without it, he thought it highly probable that that might have theretofore prevented the discovery upon which he had set his soul. But no, he saw the instrumental people looking with amazement at each other, and the bosoms of the vocalists swelling with scorn; but he could see nothing more: nothing more. He tried back: he recommenced the brilliant symphony, and the stout vocal genius, who felt much confused, for he could not at all understand it, again plucked up his courage and his collar to begin, when Valentine introduced a very admirable imitation of the French-horn. In an instant every eye was upon the French-horn players, who were zealously engaged in amputating their instruments, with the laudable view of pouring out the concentered perspiration, which the performance of the overture had induced. It could not have been them. That was clear. The conductor *looked* at them!—No: their instruments were in bits. This was held to be most extraordinary; but Valentine did not stop to wonder much at it, but proceeded to give excellent imitations of a variety of little instruments until the conductor became so enraged, that he started from his seat, and looked round with an expression of indignation, the most powerful his strongly marked features could portray.

The harmony produced by Valentine ceased, and all was silent. The audience were amazed, they were utterly unable to make it out; but as anon they begun to hiss with unequivocal zeal, the conductor, who looked as if he couldn't really stand it much longer, bounced down upon his stool, and struck the chord with an energy altogether unparalleled in musical annals.

The vocal genius became nervous. The truth flashed across his mind, that in this world men have not the choice of their own positions. He would clearly not have chosen that in which he then stood, for it certainly was a most unpleasant position. He slightly trembled: Valentine saw that he trembled, and pitied him—nay he was eventually so far melted as to suffer him to go through his *Largo Factotum.*

The style, however, in which he accomplished this song was particularly droll. It was abundantly manifest that the genius did not know the meaning of a word he had to utter, and equally manifest was it that he didn't want to know: all he cared a single straw about, was an imitation of the voice and gestures of the particular primo buffo, whom at the opera he had heard sing the piece with great applause, and as the gestures which he labored to imitate were remarkably extravagant, the whole exhibition was a caricature of the most gross and ridiculous caste.

This Valentine held to be monstrous, and felt it to be incumbent upon him to express his extreme dissatisfaction, when the features of the genius—who during the applause had smiled blandly as he bowed—underwent a most extraordinary change as he retired.

"Native talent!" cried Valentine, throwing his voice into the middle of the room, "Is this the development of native talent?"

The conductor stared wildly, and so did the whole of the gentlemen in the orchestra; but although two or three individuals cried "silence!" in a very authoritative tone, the majority of the audience were so powerfully struck with the novelty of the question, that they glanced at the programme, and looked at each other very mysteriously, and really began to consider it an extremely proper question, and one which ought therefore to be answered.

"English music! English music!" again shouted Valentine, and the audience now responded to the shout with loud cheers, which caused the conductor to shrug his shoulders and pass his taper fingers through his curls, and to open his eyes very widely, and to look altogether remarkably odd. He, however, said nothing; but began to play the symphony of an Italian *scena,* as Valentine repeated his demand for English music, the propriety of which was acknowledged by the audience again.

Several gentlemen who were stationed near the orchestra, and who appeared to be members of the native talent committee, now conferred with the conductor, who after the conference came forward and said with due emphasis, "Ladies and gentlemen: if there be any person in the room at all dissatisfied with the performances, his money will be returned on application being made at the doors."

This was fair, very fair: nothing in fact could have been fairer, but this was not at all what Valentine desired: he wished to make them understand that mere imitations of the Italians could not tend to the development of native talent, and therefore cried "No: the money is not what we want: we simply want English music!" and as this was again hailed with loud cheers, the conductor again conferred with the gentlemen of the committee, and during the conference, Valentine was occupied in assuming various voices, and sending them in various parts of the room expressive of an anxiety to open the eyes of those gentlemen, that they might clearly see the course which they ought to pursue; and eventually their eyes became opened: they appeared to be enlightened on the subject as if by magic!—but what was to be done?—the singing people had studied those pieces for the occasion, and although they had questionless the ability to sing others, it was held to be unsafe for the experiment, without notice, to be tried. They therefore pretended to be still completely blind to the propriety of the suggestion, a course which Valentine held to be remarkably stupid, inasmuch as they had but to announce that the error would in future be rectified, and the concert might have gone on without any further interruption; but as it was, as the committee were still stubborn, and as the conductor, who didn't like it, as the selection had been left to him—began to look extremely big, and to shake his head angrily, and to purse his lips contemptuously, and to frown and pitch the music about the orchestra, and knock down the stands in the fulness of his rank official pride, of course Valentine felt determined to bring him to his senses, and therefore again loudly demanded a display of native talent.

"Ladies and gentlemen!" said the conductor, stepping again in front of the orchestra, after indulging in an additional series of really unbecoming airs—"If any rival society has employed noisy persons to interrupt the performances of the evening—"

"No, no!" shouted Valentine, "no, no! We are simply anxious to promote the cultivation of native talent!" And as loud cheers followed this appropriate explanation, the conductor felt it to be a duty incumbent upon him to be signally savage, and he retired to the piano forte, and struck a variety of chords with unprofessional violence; and after amusing himself in this way for several seconds, he commanded a female to come forward in order to sing the next *scena*. The lady did not much approve of the tone which the conductor had assumed in this particular instance, but she nevertheless glided very gracefully forward with a dirty piece of music in one hand, and in the other a lace-edged handkerchief pinched precisely in the middle; but she had no sooner reached the front rail of the orchestra, than Valentine introduced a highly correct imitation of the trombone.

This the conductor very naturally conceived to be dreadful, and he therefore began to perspire with rage. He thought it quite enough—and so it was quite enough—that the audience was against him; but the idea of his own instrumental performers having joined in the opposition made his blood bubble up! He therefore instantly turned towards the professional individuals who performed on the delicate instrument in question, and discovered them in the very act of enjoying a quiet pinch of snuff together in the utmost amity. The trombone nevertheless did apparently continue to sound. This he thought more extraordinary still! He couldn't tell, he didn't know, what to make of it at all. It was clearly not the men whom he had suspected, and yet—well: the trombone ceased, but at that particular moment another most unpleasant sound broke upon his ear! The majority of the audience were roaring with laughter!—and that too at him! This he held to be extremely inconsistent with the character of a British audience, and he consequently felt quite confused.

"Go on! Go on!" exclaimed several voices in the distance; but albeit these highly appropriate exclamations were benevolently intended for his especial solace, they in reality did not console him at all.

The professional lady whose plume waved proudly about a foot and a half above her forehead, now became extremely fidgetty, and felt very awkward and very warm, and was about to retreat, when the conductor struck a chord with unexampled desperation.

"Retire!" said Valentine, throwing a whisper just behind the fair artiste; and the lady, to whom the whisper appeared to be most welcome, bowed and blushed, and retired accordingly.

"Madam!" cried the conductor, as she passed him, "remain."

"You requested me to retire," said the lady.

"No such thing! No such thing, madam. *No* such thing!" But the lady, who felt much confused, without appearing to notice these hasty observations, passed on.

The conductor now imagined—and perhaps it was but rational for him to imagine—that it was a regularly planned thing—that all in the room had conspired against his peace. He therefore bounced up again with the view of conferring with the committee, who saw plainly that a very wrong course had been pursued; but then he didn't see it, and couldn't see it, and wouldn't see it! The committee, however, at length insisted upon his expressing their sentiments on the subject, when he accordingly, but with infinite reluctance, came forward and said:—"Ladies and gentlemen: it appears to be the opinion of the committee of management, that the fact of English artists singing nothing but foreign music, tends rather to create a morbid taste for such music, and to enhance it in the estimation of the public, than to promote the cultivation of native talent, which is of course their chief aim. I am, therefore, ladies and gentlemen, directed to state that as this appears to be also your impression, ladies and gentlemen, if you will be kind enough to permit the performances chosen for this evening to proceed, as we are not exactly prepared on so short a notice to change them, especial care, ladies and gentlemen, will be taken, that in future, at these concerts, English music alone shall be sung."

The audience cheered this announcement. It was all they required, and as Valentine wished for nothing more, the performances proceeded without the slightest additional interruption; although every piece tended to convince him and them more and more that the view he had taken of the subject was correct, inasmuch as if it even were admitted that those pieces were well sung, it must also be admitted that the Italians sang them better, which alone had the effect of inspiring the conviction of *their* superiority, instead of a due appreciation of that style in which the English excel.

Valentine was therefore quite satisfied. He felt that he had inflicted some pain by the confusion he had created; but he also felt that he had thus succeeded in accomplishing an excellent object; namely, that of promoting the cultivation of native talent, by inducing Englishmen, instead of imitating, and thereby enhancing the value of foreign singers, to leave foreign talent to itself.

CHAPTER XXXIII.

IN WHICH WALTER AND HIS AMIABLE FAMILY HAVE A HIGHLY CHARACTERISTIC CONVERSATION ON THE SUBJECT OF GOODMAN'S RELEASE.

Although Walter had been gradually recovering from the effects of the fire, he was still extremely weak, and continued to be occupied night and day by Nature, whose efforts to restore him to his pristine complexion were accompanied by a certain cutaneous excitement which he held to be particularly disagreeable. His appearance at this time was indeed very singular: the skin on one side of his face being black, while on the other it was as sanguine and shiny as that of a fair-haired boy. This rendered it natural, perhaps, for him to amuse himself by prematurely peeling off the dead skin by inches, in order to re-establish a facial uniformity. This was not, however, the most interesting part of his active occupation: by no means. While under the regimen originally prescribed by the physician, his mind was comparatively at ease; but no sooner was he permitted to take somewhat more generous food, and a glass or two of wine every day, with a view to the restoration of his physical strength, than this vivid imagination began to revel again in the creation of the most extraordinary phantasms which failed not to afford him perpetual entertainment. Nor were the minds of his amiable family at this time unoccupied: their nights were spent in dreaming, and their days in relating those dreams to each other, for the purpose of ascertaining and establishing the most approved interpretation thereof. The house of Walter was therefore a very busy house; but the business of its inmates was unhappily not of a character calculated to increase their joy. On the contrary, their spirits were dreadfully depressed: even those of the volatile Horace—albeit he still retained his vulgarity—sank several degrees below par; for while confinement did not meet his views, three somewhat severe attacks of fever, induced by his going out too early, and drinking too freely, had convinced him that such confinement, how unpleasing soever it might be, was absolutely essential to his perfect restoration.

Of course every member of the family was now acquainted with the manner in which Walter had disposed of poor Goodman, and the female portion failed not to ascribe the whole of their recent misfortunes to that.

"I am sure," said Mrs. Horace, one evening when the family, for the first time since the accident, were having tea in the parlor, "I am perfectly sure that we shall never have a moment's peace of mind until uncle is released from confinement."

"I am quite of your opinion, dear," observed Mrs. Goodman, "for we really have had nothing but misfortune and misery since; and I am fully persuaded by the truly frightful dreams I have had of late, that we can expect no comfort, no happiness, no peace, so long as he remains where he is."

"Then I deserve all I've got, I suppose! —You regard it as a species of retributive justice," cried Walter with a scowl.

"No, no, my love! I did not say that."

"Didn't say it! I know you didn't say it; but you mean it nevertheless."

"All I mean to say is this," rejoined his wife with unusual firmness, "that the horrible dreams I have had of late convince me that until he is released, we shall have nothing but misfortune; and it really is very dreadful that he should be thus imprisoned, you know, when you come to think of it."

"The only question at issue," said Horace, "is this—will the old boy's release tend to improve our position? That's the only point now to be considered. Never mind about dreams, because they are all rubbish, and may be produced by pickled salmon or stewed cheese; let us look at the thing as it stands, thus:—what will be the effect of his release upon us?"

"Why this!" replied Walter, "we shall be at once reduced to a state of absolute beggary."

"Well, in that case, you know," rejoined Horace, "there can't be two rational opinions about the conclusion at which we ought, as reasonable beings, to arrive."

"Well, I'm sure," said Mrs. Horace, "that for my part I had rather be poor and happy, than live in such continual misery as this."

"Poor and happy!" cried Horace, "It's all very fine. I might say the same thing: *I* might say, oh, I'd much rather live poor and happy: O yes!—but who's to do it? Had we been reared with the heavy hand of poverty upon us, we should probably not be much startled by her slaps, because a thing, you know, is nothing when you are used to it; but fancy yourself now in a state of destitution! I know that I should be walking into the jugular, or perpetrating some other sanguinary business; while you would be flying off the Monument, or pitching head first over Westminster bridge; and then how would you bring it in?—not, 'poor and happy!'"

"But I'd work the very flesh off my bones, rather than continue to live as we do now."

"Work the flesh off your bones!" echoed Horace contemptuously. "How could you get it to do; and if you did get it, how could you do it? and what do you fancy you are fit for? I might say that I'd work the very flesh off my bones; but who'd employ me! That's the point; and then what could I do? While thousands upon thousands, who are capable of performing the various jolly little offices of life are unemployed, how can I, who know nothing at all about anything, hope to walk over their heads? I know better, you know; it's all stuff."

"It certainly would, I must confess," said Mrs. Goodman, "be a very dreadful thing to be reduced; but do you really think we should be so utterly destitute?"

"Nobody can doubt it for a moment," replied Horace; "for what resource have we? What have we got to fly to? The governor has given up his berth, which I have said all along he ought not to have done; and then what are my prospects? I have no profession!—we have nothing to look to."

"But don't you really think," said Mrs. Goodman, addressing her husband, "that we might manage it so as to set him free, and yet be as well off at least as we were?"

"How absurdly you talk!" replied Walter. "Why any one would think you were an idiot! What on earth have I to hope for from him? Suppose, for a moment, that I were to release him; what would be the consequence? He knows that I placed him where he is; the house in which he lived of course is clean gone, and I have sold all his furniture. Well! he comes out. I am the first man to whom he applies. He cannot proceed criminally against me, because the certificate of the doctors had the effect of taking from me the whole of the responsibility of the seizure; but he demands the restitution of his property, and how is it possible for me to meet that demand? A great portion of that property is not now in my possession; he has, therefore, but to bring an action against me, and my ruin is complete. But let us take the most favorable view of the case. Suppose he insists only on the restoration of his papers. They are restored; and he, as a matter of course, instantly discards us. What then are we to do? I have no property, no income. We must starve. Any assistance from him were altogether out of the question. He would have, of course, nothing whatever to do with us. How should we act in that case? We could not act at all; we should go to the dogs."

"Of course!" cried Horace. "And that's the very bottom of it. We can't be such fools as to believe that he wouldn't at once cut us dead. He might not, as the governor says, proceed you know legally, but—blister this itching!"—he added rubbing his back against the chair very violently, and making up a very extraordinary face. "I shall rub all the flesh off my bones: I know I shall; and now the old governor's at it!—Well, what was I saying?—Come, come! I must rub if you do. If it were not for you, I shouldn't do it at all. You put me in mind of it. Come, I say, governor! Give it up, come! I cannot think of anything while you keep rubbing away thus." And really the process of itching is a very extraordinary process. It amounts to a contagion. Mankind itch by virtue of sympathy; and it is highly probable that most living philosophers have observed that the power of sympathy is extremely comprehensive; but whether the profound observations of those philosophers have extended to this interesting particular or not, it is nevertheless true, that of this most extraordinary power men are absolute slaves.

"But do you not think now," observed Mrs. Goodman, "that if you were to acknowledge that you have acted very wrong, and were to throw yourself as it were at once upon his generosity, that—"

"Pooh!" exclaimed Horace. "Generosity! Fancy the governor throwing himself upon any thing like the old boy's generosity! How would he have to go to work? I'll just tell you, and then you'll know how it would sound:—'My brother'—he would have to say, pulling the longest possible phiz, 'my dear brother, I cocked you into a madhouse, in order of course to swindle you out of your property. You are not mad, my brother; you never were mad—I know that remarkably well; but notwithstanding into the lunatic den you were thrust, as indeed you are in all probability aware. Now, I really am sorry, particularly sorry; I have sold the house, sold the whole of the furniture, pocketed the pecuniary chips they produced, and as a matter of course, spent those chips liberally. My conscience, however, told me that I had done extremely wrong, and that I ought to release you. I acted upon the suggestions of that unhappy wretch of a conscience, and released you accordingly; and now, my dear brother, having acknowledged my error, I throw myself upon your generosity.' Now I know the old boy pretty well: I know him to be occasionally rather of the warmest; but leaving what *he* would be likely to do for a moment out of the question, I'll just explain to you how *I* should act in a case of the kind myself:—In the first place, then, I should secure all the papers, and having secured them, I should say, 'Now I tell you what it is: you're my brother—more's the pity—but as you are my brother why I don't want to ruin your prospects in life; but if you don't leave the room before I can lift up my foot, I'll do my best to kick you into the autumn of next year; and if ever I catch you near my house again, I shall consider it my duty on purely public grounds, to hunt you at once from society.' 'But I throw myself upon your generosity!' you would exclaim, 'I am sorry for what I have done, dear brother: I cannot say more!' 'Be off!' I should cry with certain highly appropriate epithets, 'and never, by any chance, let me see you again!' That I should hold, without any disguise, to be about the most generous act of my life."

"You are right; you are right," said Walter, "quite right. No, no, no; it won't do. I am sorry, and that's a fact, sincerely sorry I went so far; but I cannot now retreat: he must remain where he is."

"As a natural matter of course!" cried Horace. "It would never do now. Let him be. The old boy, I've no doubt, is as happy as a Hottentot, and what can he want more? The idea of his being locked up there as an old lunatic is rather of the ratherest, certainly; but he'll soon get over that. And then they shouldn't have such laws. Blister the laws! they make it positively dangerous for a man to be safe. Therefore, henceforth, lay all the blame upon the laws, and let him remain. I don't suppose —I can't suppose he wants for any comfort: I dare say they treat him as a friend of the family: at all events we must not bring upon ourselves an uncomfortable load of starvation, that's clear."

"Well, I cannot but feel," said Mrs. Goodman, "that we shall never be happy again—that we shall never have anything but misery and ill luck."

"And what sort of luck would that be which reduced us to a state of destitution?" rejoined Horace. "It strikes me that such luck would be extremely rotten: it would not, at all events, be particularly brilliant; and as for your miseries! compare them with the miseries with which abject poverty teems, and then say no more about it. We of course have no practical knowledge of those miseries; but it occurs to me that they must be unpleasant in the extreme. It is true that if we were thus reduced, the old governor, by trotting out daily with a broom, might manage to pick up a few odd coppers; and it is also true that, by driving a cab, I might possibly obtain enough to buy bread and cheese; but when I take into calm consideration all the rotten ramifications of the business, I really don't think that it would answer our purpose so well."

"No, no, no!" cried Walter, "it will not bear a thought. Come what may, he must remain where he is."

And to this opinion, all of them eventually subscribed; for, although their dreadful dreams were recounted, and interpreted according to the best book of fate, when the miseries which they had to endure then, were fairly weighed with those which Goodman's release would entail, it was found that the former at once kicked the beam, and were therefore, of course, to be preferred.

CHAPTER XXXIV.

UNCLE JOHN ARRIVES IN TOWN, AND WITH VALENTINE ATTENDS THE CIVIC PAGEANT AND FEAST.

On the evening appointed for Uncle John's arrival, Valentine went to the inn, and the very first man whom he recognised there was the waiter who had exhibited so laudable an anxiety to expel the invisible burglars. Of this person he inquired how they eventually acted on that remarkable occasion; and from him he ascertained that it was generally deemed the most extraordinary thing in nature, inasmuch as, notwithstanding one policeman paraded the leads, while another was stationed at the coffee-room door throughout the night, those burglarious individuals could not be captured. "In the morning," continued the waiter, "we all thought they were still in the chimbley, you know, and to tell you the truth, you know, I had a hidea that, having been smothered in smoke, we should have found 'em a couple of corpses, you know; so what did we do, but we sent for a chimbley sweeper's boy, who went up for to see into the merits of the case; but no, not a bit of it!—they were not there—they were nowhere! However they managed to cut away, you know, as they must have done some how or another, is a mystery which can't be exploded."

Valentine smiled at the recollection of the scene; but as the waiter was about to give additional particulars, the coach rattled into the yard. There sat Uncle John upon the box by the side of Tooler, and Valentine, without waiting for him to alight, at once leaped upon the wheel and grasped his hand.

Uncle John was for a moment unable to speak. His heart was far too full of joy; and as he pressed the hand of his nephew with the warmth of affection, his eyes swam in tears.

"I am so pleased to see you!" said Valentine.

"My boy!—my boy!" cried the affectionate old gentleman, gazing upon him as well as he could through his tears with an expression of ecstasy—"God bless you! God bless you!—Why how you have grown!" he continued after a pause. "Your poor mother would scarcely believe her own eyes!"

"She is well, I hope?"

"Oh, yes: quite well!—quite well!"—and while he answered, he continued to gaze upon his "boy" in the fulness of affectionate pride. He was then so happy that it singularly enough did not occur to him that he was still on the box: nor would it in all probability have occurred to him for the next half hour, had not Tooler addressed him on the subject of his luggage.

"Well," said Valentine, when his uncle had alighted, "what sort of a journey have you had?"

"You young dog, sir!" exclaimed Uncle John, "I never had such a journey! My life has been in jeopardy all the way. I have as nearly as possible fallen off that box twenty times! How dare you serve a man as you served poor old Tooler the day you came up, sir? He has told me all about it. I know that it was you! He has kept me for the last forty miles in one continual roar. The idea!—and then for him to fancy"—here he again began to laugh with so much energy and spirit, that it was with difficulty he managed to point out his ancient portmanteau and trunk. This feat was, however, eventually accomplished, and the coachman came up ostensibly with the view of expressing his most anxious solicitude, having reference to its being all right.

"Well, Tooler," said Valentine, "how is the witch?"

"Oh!—Ah!—Yow were the young genelman as were wi' me sir. How d'ye due? We were puty nigh makin a muddle on't that time, sir, warn't we?—the baggage!"

"Have you seen her of late?"

"Oh blarm her no, not very lately; nor don't seems to want. She out to be swum, sir!—that ud cule her!"

"Get away, you young dog!" said Uncle John, as he placed a half-crown in Tooler's hand; when as Valentine smiled, and as Uncle John laughed, Tooler stared precisely as if he was unable to tell the meaning of it exactly, while Valentine who had no disposition to enlighten him on the subject, directed one of the porters to call a coach, into which he and his uncle got with the luggage without any unnecessary delay.

On arriving at Valentine's lodgings, they found that everything required had been duly prepared by the attentive little widow; the fire was blazing brightly; the tea was quite ready, and a ham which had been cooked for that particular occasion, stood prominently forward embellished with an infinite variety of devices which had been cut out of carrots and turnips with surpassing ingenuity, and truly artistical taste. Uncle John looked carefully round the room, and having expressed himself satisfied with the whole of the arrangements, drew the sofa near the fire, and sat deliberately down with the air of a man having no other object in view than that of making himself quite at home.

After tea, Valentine presented him with a meerschaum, which he had purchased expressly for that occasion, and which Uncle John examined and appeared to prize more highly than any other thing in his possession. But before he commenced smoking, he insisted that Valentine should enter into a compact of a serious character, the spirit of which was, that the conversation should be confined that evening to the extraordinary case of Goodman, for as he had already laughed enough for one day, he contended that he could not endure the relation of any reprehensible tricks. This was accordingly understood and agreed to, and on the subject of Goodman's absence, they therefore conversed. Uncle John felt quite sure that he should be able to find him, being determined as he explained, to go at once to head-quarters, and with this conviction strongly impressed upon his mind, he eventually retired for the night.

Now it happened that on the following morning he had occasion to go into the city, and it also happened that that very morning was the morning of the 8th of November. For the city, therefore, immediately after breakfast, he and Valentine started, and on reaching Cheapside, they heard Bow church bells ringing very merrily and firing very fiercely, and hence naturally imagined that some civic business of importance was about to take place. They had not proceeded far before they heard a lively flourish of trumpets, and saw a long line of private carriages approaching, some of which were extremely gay, preceded by certain official individuals on horseback, having under their immediate surveillance a little legion of constables, of whom the majority were zealously occupied in striking the noses of horses attached to vulgar vehicles with their staves, and commanding their drivers, in a duly authoritative tone, to get out of the way down the back streets at once, if they wished to avoid the consequences of their official displeasure.

Of course Valentine inquired into the meaning of all this, and was informed that the newly elected lord mayor was about to be sworn into office: he also ascertained that none were admitted into the Guildhall to witness the solemn ceremony, but those who had orders. "I should like to be present exceedingly," said he, "but then where are these orders to be procured?"

"Probably," suggested Uncle John, "we shall be able to get them of Clarkson, upon whom we are now about to call."

To Clakson's they therefore hastened, and after the business in hand had been transacted, Mr. Clarkson sent out for an order at once.

"But you should go to the Lord Mayor's dinner," said that gentleman, when the messenger had departed. "That indeed would be a treat if you never were there."

"Is it possible," said Uncle John, "for any but members of the corporation to be admitted without a special invitation?"

"Oh dear me, yes! You have but to procure a ticket of an alderman, or one of the common-council."

"It unfortunately happens, that I have not the honor to be acquainted with any one of those gentlemen," rejoined Uncle John; "but could I not purchase two, for me and my nephew, by applying at head quarters?"

"They are not to be purchased there."

"I'd give ten pounds for two of them to any man with pleasure."

"In that case," observed Mr. Clarkson, "you have only to put an advertisement to that effect into one of the morning papers, to be gratified. The common-councilmen frequently dispose of them in that way. But, now I come to think of it, it strikes me that there is a chance of my being able to get them without any such expense. It is certainly rather late; but I'll try—I'll do my utmost. Leave your address. I think that I may almost venture to promise."

"My dear sir!" cried Uncle John, "you can't conceive how much obliged to you I should feel. Why, it would be to us the highest treat in nature! Val, write the address."

This was accomplished of course with great alacrity, and the messenger having returned with the order, Uncle John again explained how highly he should esteem the promised favor, and proceeded with Valentine at once to Guildhall, descanting with due eloquence on the politeness of Mr. Clarkson.

On reaching the entrance, they found it surrounded by a number of constables, who were watching, with apparently intense interest, certain groups of rather suspicious-looking young gentlemen, who wore their hats over their eyes, that the back of their heads might be sufficiently well aired, and one tastefully inverted curl immediately over each temple. Without entering, however, into the spirit of the interest thus created, Uncle John submitted the order to a person in attendance, and they proceeded at once into the body of the Hall, which then assumed an appearance very different from that which distinguished it when Valentine imparted apparently speech to the civic giants. On this occasion, a great variety of banners, shields, and other insignia were displayed with appropriate taste in all directions; and while on the left a number of workmen were engaged, some in making all the noise they deemed essential to the manufacture of tables and forms, and others on taking the mock men in armor out of blankets, with the view of placing them in the various niches of the Hall; on the right stood between three and four hundred persons, who were occupied in looking, with great apparent curiosity, at about fifty solemn individuals, in gowns trimmed with fur, who were sitting with appropriate grace and gravity on either side of an open space, at the upper end of which stood a large arm chair, behind an ancient and dirty little table.

"Who are those gentlemen?" inquired Valentine, of a person who stood near him.

"The common-councilmen," replied that person; "they are waiting for the Lord Mayor and aldermen, who are now in the council chamber up them there steps."

At this interesting moment, sundry high official personages ran down those steps, and after bustling backwarks and forwards, and looking very mysterious, ran up them again with great presence of mind. This proceeding appeared to be indicative of something, for it instantly caused many others to bustle, with equal dexterity and tact, and, doubtless, with an equally high object in view.

At length an extremely important personage made his appearance, and every eye was in an instant directed to the steps down which he had majestically glided. The noise of the workmen ceased—a procession approached. A death-like silence pervaded the hall: the suspense was truly awful. The style in which the mighty individuals who composed this procession stepped out, was inconceivably grand! Solemnity was the chief characteristic of each look—importance was perched upon each ample brow. Their air was noble! They seemed to feel the weight of their respective responsibilities, albeit they bore them with dignity and ease. Some were adorned with violet gowns, richly embellished with massive chains of virgin gold; but although some had gowns without any such embellishment, and others had no gowns at all, all who formed the procession looked equally immense, and equally resolved to inspire spectators with awe.

Well! on arriving at that part of the Hall, in which the grave common-councilmen were sitting in all their glory, the civic king, who was about to abdicate, proceeded majestically to the chair. He really appeared to know that it was for the last time, but he nevertheless kept up his spirits, and absolutely smiled upon all around with surpassing grace, although it was, beyond dispute, an extremely trying moment.

It may have been in all probability observed, that when mortals do any thing for the last time—conscious of its being for the last time—they feel it; but who that hath not been a Lord Mayor himself, can appreciate the feelings which rack a lord mayor on his resigning *in toto*, that which had for years been placed upon the pinnacle of his ambition? It was suggested, some few years ago, that it was hard that the Mayor should lose his title with his office; and it is hard, very hard, particularly hard!—the title ought to be retained. To be addressed as "my lord," for twelve calendar months, and as "sir" for ever after, is monstrous! But this matter will be seen in the right light by-and-bye, and posterity will hold the age in which we now live, to be one of the dark ones in consequence. However, be this as it may, there is one thing quite clear, and that is this—that the Lord Mayor, in this instance, sat for the last time in the state chair, with truly admirable resignation, and that the Lord Mayor elect, who was a much stouter man, sat beside him.

Such, therefore, being the state of the case then, an individual, who was at that time yclept the common crier, walked solemnly in front of the state chair, and made an extremely profound reverence, with the mace upon his shoulder. He then took three very graceful steps, and made another low reverence, and then three steps more, when, having made another reverence of a character still more profound, he ingeniously made the mace stand upright before the table. On this highly appropriate piece of unspeakable solemnity, being accomplished to the entire satisfaction of all concerned, a grave personage, who rejoiced in the extraordinary title of Town Clerk, marched in front of the state chair, and after taking nine well-measured steps, halting three times, of course, to make three very distinctly marked reverences which were quite as low as those that had been made by the Town Crier—he happily arrived at the table, when the Lord Mayor elect most majesticaly rose with a view to the reception of the oaths.

Those oaths were administered; and when the Lord Mayor elect had placed his signature in a journal expressly provided for that purpose, the old Lord Mayor left the chair, and after solemnly approaching the new Lord Mayor and taking him affectionately by the hand, he smiled a peculiarly gracious smile, said an encouraging something, handed him, with unexampled elegance to that seat which he had for twelve months occupied with honor to himself and advantage to the city, and sat beside him amidst a loud clapping of hands, which was at once very solemn and very enthusiastic. The worthy aldermen then rose with all the dignity at their command, for the purpose of congratulating the new civic king, and shaking hands with his lordship individually, and warmly, and when this had been gracefully and satisfactorily accomplished, the Chamberlain—a person, on the subject of whose solemnity of aspect two rational opinions could not be entertained, stood in front of the new Lord Mayor and made a reverence, and having measured the distance with his eye, took *four* steps—in consequence of his steps being shorter, although his legs were longer than those of the common crier and the town clerk, who, in three steps got over the same space of ground—and made another low reverence; and then he took four steps more, and having made a third reverence, equally profound, he presented the late Lord Mayor with a sceptre, and the late Lord Mayor having nothing then to do with it, handed it over to the new Lord Mayor, when the new Lord Mayor returned it to the Chamberlain, who placed it upon the table and made a fourth low reverence, and took four steps backwards to make a fifth low reverence, and then four steps more to make a sixth low reverence, when he held out his hand for the seal, and having advanced and retired in like manner, taking the same number of steps, and making the same number of reverences, he gracefully held forth his hand for the purse, with which the same solemn ceremony was performed, with this addition, that the new Lord Mayor did shake the purse with the view of ascertaining what was in it—a proceeding which shocked the grave personages present, who obviously held it to be a species of levity which was, under the awful circumstances of the case, reprehensible in the extreme.

This feeling, however, lasted but for a moment, and the Chamberlain had no sooner finished his task, which he appeared to hold in high admiration, than the junior clerk advanced in the self-same fashion, but with somewhat less grace than the Chamberlain had displayed, and having taken the sceptre, seal, and purse from the table, retired, stepping backwards as a matter of course, and making six profound reverences altogether, when another individual bearing a sword, which seemed to be within an inch or two as long as himself, advanced and presented it to the late Lord Mayor, who presented it to the new Lord Mayor, who returned it to the individual who had submitted it to their notice, and who retired with it backwards, having made the prescribed number of reverences with a tact which the junior clerk must have envied.

This was all very solemn and very interesting; but Uncle John could not appreciate its importance! "What," said he in a whisper, "what in the name of reason is the use of it? What does it all mean?"

Valentine was not then prepared to explain either its use or its connection with the name of reason, but he suggested that the probability was that it meant something, and hinted at the possibility of those reverences being absolutely essential to the preservation of the city's charter. It struck him, however, at the same time forcibly that a sufficient number of reverences had not been made, for he remembered that at the House of Commons they made eighteen bows—that is to say three to every four steps—whereas here they had made but six, which amounted to a clear taking off of two-thirds of the solemnity.

Thus, however, this part of the ceremony was accomplished, and the late Lord Mayor, when the bearer of the sword had retired, rose again to shake hands with the new Lord Mayor, when the aldermen rose for the same solemn purpose, then the whole of the common councilmen, and then the great officers of the various companies, and then all the rest of the functionaries attached to the corporation: in fine, his lordship was shaken by the hand by about three hundred individuals, and as they all shook as if they were anxious to shake his hand off, his lordship, immediately after the operation, very carefully placed his right hand in his bosom with a view to the eventual restoration of his wrist, when the whole of the ceremony being thus completed, he and the late Lord Mayor, preceded by the officers, and followed by the aldermen, left the hall in the same solemn style as that in which they had entered.

Uncle John, however, still thought the whole of the ceremony—with the exception of the process of administering the oaths—most absurd. He did not approve of it: he could not approve of it: he held it to be the most foolishly ridiculous piece of mummery he had ever beheld; but Valentine suggested that men should not denounce or even deem that absurd, the utility and meaning of which they could not understand. "In those reverences," said he, "for example, there may be more, much more than meets the eye. Upon them the rights and privileges of the citizens may for aught we know entirely depend. But independently of this, it is abundantly clear that in denouncing these proceedings as mere foolery, we denounce by implication as fools, all by whom these proceedings are upheld, and we must not allow it to escape us, that we are now in the very first city in the world, the most enlightened spot upon the face of the globe, the very centre of civilisation. We therefore ought not to suppose it to be likely that these ceremonies, however ridiculous they may appear, would be upheld if there were not something in them of a solemn and useful character."

Uncle John was by no means convinced of the soundness of this argument which he fancied at the time had been seriously adduced. He felt still that the ceremony was foolish, and although he would not go so far as to say that those grave and enlightened looking personages whom he had seen were really fools, he contended that they ought to repudiate those absurdities as things which were utterly beneath them.

"But," said Valentine, although he quite agreed with Uncle John, "if we even admit that these ceremonies are in the abstract absurd, are we sure that it is not expedient to uphold them? Authority must not be stripped of its trappings; and as the world still consents to be deceived by ornament, the universality of the deception forbids the supposition of its maintenance being utterly vain."

"There is certainly a little more in that," said Uncle John, "and I suppose we should find it the same at head-quarters; but I must say that in this case the thing has been carried a little beyond bounds, for instead of those ceremonies having the effect of inspiring the people with awe, they have a tendency only to excite their contempt; and so that question's settled." And as Valentine permitted it to be thus settled, they at once left the hall; but as Uncle John on reaching Cheapside, would stop to inspect, minutely, the contents of almost every shop-window, their progress was indeed but slow. They did, however, eventually arrive at St. Paul's Church Yard, and as they perceived, on passing the north door of the Cathedral, that it was about half open, Uncle John expressed an anxious wish to enter the noble edifice, and having ascended the steps, they saw the door-keeper just inside, with a piece of cold meat on a thick slice of bread in one hand, and a clasp knife of really assassinating dimensions in the other.

"Can we be admitted?" inquired Valentine of this person.

17

"Tuppence each!" said the fellow, as he unhooked the chain which held the door.

"Two-pence each!" cried Uncle John, with an expression of indignation. "What do you mean, sir? Here is my card, I demand admittance!"

"It's tuppence each!" repeated the door-keeper emphatically; and Valentine drew out his purse.

"By no means!" said Uncle John, restraining him, "by no means. It is not the money but the principle at which I look. It is a monstrous principle—a principle that I never will encourage; it being neither more nor less than that of converting the House of God into a twopenny exhibition. It is perfectly disgraceful," he continued, addressing the door-keeper. "Your conduct shall be known, sir, at head-quarters!"

The fellow replaced the chain, laughed, and took another mouthful of bread and meat, as Uncle John descended the steps with Valentine, descanting with due eloquence upon the monstrous character of this truly impious species of extortion.

They now proceeded home, where they found that Mr. Clarkson had already sent the tickets, with a most polite note, in which he strongly recommended them to see the procession. This they thought extremely kind. Uncle John at once declared that he should never forget it, and a very considerable portion of the evening was in consequence occupied with a discussion, the object of which was to decide which had the preponderance in the world—good or evil.

In the morning, immediately after breakfast, they started for Guildhall, and London seemed to have poured the whole of her artizans into the city. It was then, and had been for the three preceding centuries at least, a grand day for the sight-seers of the metropolis. The streets through which the glorious pageant had to pass, were densely thronged with men, women, and children, splashed up to their very necks, while the windows of the houses on either side were filled with gaily dressed persons, who amused themselves by making the most pleasing observations upon those who were moving below them in the mud.

The nearer they got to Guildhall, the more dense the crowd became, but as Uncle John insisted upon going to "head-quarters," they turned into King Street, and tried with desperation to thread the mortal labyrinth there established. Uncle John was, however, very soon out of breath, for he met with all sorts of obstructions; and as those obstructions increased, and were likely to increase as he proceeded, he wisely resolved upon seeking some spot, in which he might stand comparatively free from annoyance.

"What a shame it is, that women should bring children in arms," said he, on hearing a female, who had an infant at her breast, scolding two men for "squeedging her babby." On looking round, however, he saw that by far the greater portion of the women were similarly circumstanced, and hence, assuming that the fact might have some direct, or indirect, connection with the privileges peculiar to the city, he said no more on the subject; but passed on at once to a place, in which they felt the mighty pageant might be viewed without any serious pressure.

"The sight must, I should say, be magnificent to draw such a multitude together," observed Valentine.

"Magnificent!" exclaimed Uncle John, "I have always understood it to be the most gorgeous affair the imagination of man can conceive! But we shall see. I don't pretend to understand the utility of it exactly; but I expect it will be splendid. We shall see."

The crowd now increased about the spot in which they stood, aud all were naturally anxious to get in front. "Vill you be so obleeging as to let my little boy stand afore you, if you please," said a woman addressing Uncle John.

"By all means, my good woman," and he immediately made way for the little boy; but the moment the space was opened, the good woman herself, duly followed by a knot of tall coal-heaving creatures, rushed in, and thus placed Uncle John in a position in which he could not see at all. He, therefore, made an observation, of which the purport was, that such a proceeding was by no means polite: and the coal-heavers heard this remarkable observation; and it struck them as being so novel and so good, that they enjoyed it exceedingly, and laughed very loudly.

Valentine, therefore, drew Uncle John to another choice spot, in which they waited with due patience for some considerable time, making other observations of an equally remarkable *caste*, and being occasionally enlivened by sundry loud cries of "Here they come!"

At length they saw a mighty rush, and heard the trembling trumpets sound! The effect was electric! The crowd was seized with an universal thrill! The glorious pageant was on the move! The band approached!—the drums rolled!—the earth seemed in convulsions!

An immense individual on horseback now darted about, spurring his proud steed so hard that already had he fretted him into such a dreadful state of perspiration, that his neck, back, and haunches were covered with white steaming foam.

"That's a fool! said Uncle John, as this person galloped backwards and forwards with the view of making himself as conspicuous as possible. "He ought to blush. That horse is not his own; or if it be, it's the first he ever had, and he hasn't had it long. He seems to me to be quite new in office: hence he thus frets and stews that poor animal in order to show his official assiduity."

"It's essential to the progress of the pageant, no doubt," observed Valentine.—"Depend upon it, the procession couldn't get along without him. Behold with what elegance he bows!—and see those respectable coal-heavers there, how gracefully, with a nod of recognition, they wave their lily hands. He has, doubtless, the honor of being extremely intimate with those gentlemen."—And away the great officer galloped again, as Uncle John boldly declared it to be his unbought and unbiassed opinion that the animal *must* very soon drop down dead.

A mounted military band now passed playing fiercely; then came a mighty host of distinguished individuals in blue and yellow caps, and pink calico gowns, most appropriately headed by an extremely dirty streamer, the arms magnificently emblazoned upon which might, in ancient times, in all probability, have been sensible to sight. The first of these warlike creatures groaned beneath the weight of a mighty scaffold-pole, of which the circumference at its base was about twenty inches, and to which were attached three other long poles, borne by three other creatures for the purpose of keeping the mighty one steady; but despite all their efforts—which were really very desperate, and very laudable—every slight gust of wind which caught the glorious streamer, made them stagger like warriors in the last stage of lively intoxication.

"What do they make those poor men carry such an enormous thing as that for?" inquired Uncle John.

"Doubtless," replied Valentine, "with a view to the maintenance of the peculiar rights and privileges of the city."—And other hosts passed with other long streamers, looking equally ancient and equally glorious; and after a line of glass-coaches—the drivers of which were adorned with cockades of extraordinary dimensions—there came a mighty warrior clad in complete steel, with a countenance which, while it expressed true nobility of soul, was embellished with whitening, burnt cork, and vermilion. He was mounted, of course, on a warlike charger, which appeared to be endeavoring to understand the precise meaning of a piece of steel which had been strapped in front of his head, with the view of imparting to him the semblance of an unicorn; but the warrior himself really looked very fierce, very noble, and very uncomfortable.

"What is that fellow for?" inquired Uncle John, with really reprehensible irreverence.

"In all probability," replied Valentine, "to *fight* for the peculiar rights and privileges of the city."

"To fight!—and there's another in brass! Do they look like fighting men? A cane would be sufficient to unhorse them, and what would they have it in their power to do then?"

This was clearly a very ungracious observation, for the noble warriors tried to look as desperate as possible as they passed, with the yeomen of the guard—with remarkably low crowned hats, and equally remarkably high plaited frills—on either side.

The late Lord Mayor followed, leaning back in his carriage, and looking very grave and very gloomy. His chief object was to conceal himself from the crowd as much as possible, and this is acknowledged universally to be a development of sound discretion. *Late* Lord Mayors are seldom popular with the mob. In the performance of their high functions, they are called upon to punish so many, that were they to make themselves at all conspicuous, they would be sure to be popularly recognised, and recognitions of that kind are at all times, and on both sides extremely disagreeable.

The *late* Lord Mayor, therefore, passed in solemn silence, without apparently wishing to provoke any unpleasant recollections, and was followed by six individuals who sported very highly polished pumps, and very delicate French-white silk stockings, and who, as they walked on the tips of their toes, appeared to be in a dreadful state of mind, although the tact and dexterity with which they all hopped from stone to stone, were truly amazing. They took no sort of notice of the admiration they inspired; and as for raising their eyes from the mud!—they wouldn't have looked at their own mothers. Their whole souls seemed centered in the one great and glorious object of avoiding the innumerable little puddles in the road, and to this all their moral and physical energies were exclusively devoted, while they bore unbrellas—expecting rain as a purely natural matter of course—with the view of imparting to all around, the conviction, that a smart shower only was required to render their happiness complete.

On that great occasion, however, this was denied them. They, nevertheless, passed on in peace, and were immediately followed by the chief object of attraction,

THE RIGHT HONORABLE THE LORD MAYOR!

There sat his Right Honorable Lordship, in that extremely unique and notorious machine, yclept by the vulgar the "civic state carriage," scarcely knowing what to make of it, and looking as fascinating, and bowing as grotesquely as possible, while two important personages sat looking out of the windows, apparently with the view of exciting loud laughter, their prominent characteristics being really so droll.

"Hooray!" exclaimed a mob of very dirty individuals on the left of Uncle John. "Hooray!" His Right Honorable Lordship smiled graciously, and bowed with excessive dignity, and looked very happy, and very healthy. The sight was glorious! —but as this machine wound up the pageant, it had no sooner passed than Uncle John began to swell with indignation. "Is it—*can* it be possible?" he exclaimed, "that this trumpery, pitiful, gingerbread business, should have induced so many thousands of persons to leave their homes to be knocked about, insulted, and covered with mud! Why, it is beyond dispute, the most vile and contemptible piece of mummery I ever witnessed. Is this, forsooth, your most enlightened city in the world? What is the object of it—what does it all mean? As true as I'm alive it's the most paltry, the most absurd, unmeaning, tin-pot piece of foolery, the most ridiculous, disgraceful—I've been robbed!" he continued, thrusting his hand into his pockets. "I've been plundered!—they've stolen my handkerchief."

"Nothing else?" inquired Valentine.

Uncle John felt in the whole of his pockets at once, and then searched them seriatim, and then said: "No—no—nothing else. But then what could I expect? If the object were to draw together multitudes of thieves, it were utterly impossible to conceive a better plan. Nothing in life could be more directly calculated to give the pickpocketting scoundrels full swing. It is fit for nothing else in the world. The authorities, and those who uphold or even fail to denounce it, ought to blush."

"But how can you conceive it to be possible," urged Valentine, "for the dignity of the city to be upheld without it?"

"The dignity of the city!" echoed Uncle John contemptuously, "Don't tell me that the dignity of the city can be upheld by such an atrocious and trumpery mockery as this. It is an absolute disgrace to the city. It tends to bring every thing bearing the semblance of dignity into contempt. It is amazing, that the people at head-quarters should sanction so childish an exhibition. There is not a spark of reason in it—nothing to save it from ridicule, or to qualify contempt. It is pardonable certainly under the circumstances that *we* came; but if it were possible for any man living to prevail upon me to witness such a display of tomfoolery twice, I should never forgive myself—never! If they must go to Westminster, let them go like men—but come along my boy, come along."

"But you'll go and see the pageant on the water?" said Valentine.

"*I* see the pageant on the water!" exclaimed Uncle John, "No, no; I've had enough of it, more than enough;" and having called the first coach that came in sight, they at once proceeded home.

Valentine was highly amused at the indignation displayed by Uncle John. He regarded it as a sort of compensation for the disappointment he had experienced, and he could not disguise from himself that he had been disappointed, for instead of the procession being magnificent, as he certainly expected it would have been, he held it to be a most senseless affair, and wondered quite as much as Uncle John, how the grave authorities of the City of London could uphold a species of mummery so wretched.

"Well!" said Uncle John, on reaching home, "we will go at all events and see the end of this business; but if the banquet be conducted in a smilar style, I shall set down the great corporation of London at once as a great corporation of fools." And having thus expressed his sentiments on the subject, he began to bustle about, and continued to be particularly busy until the time for starting had arrived, when they sent for a coach, and set off for Guildhall, with no very magnificent anticipations.

On entering the hall, Uncle John was, however, so struck with the dazzling splendor of the scene, that Valentine could scarcely get him along. "Well," said he, "this is indeed very brilliant. It makes up for all. They could produce nothing better than this at head-quarters."

Valentine assented at once to this opinion, but urged him again to proceed, and after an immense deal of pulling and persuasion, he succeeded in seating him at one of the tables, when he explained that he was at that moment perfectly happy.

This was pleasant; and when the ceremony of receiving the distinguished guests had been duly accomplished, the tables began to crack beneath the weight of immense tureens: and when grace had been said with due solemnity and force, the guests commenced operations in the twinkling of an eye.

Uncle John, however, at first felt quite nervous. The scene had so excited him, that it was not until he had been challenged by several gentlemen, with extraordinary politeness and grace, that he was able to enjoy himself at all. The wine, however, very soon braced up his nerves by placing him on somewhat better terms with himself, and he began to feel perfectly at home, and succeeded in eating an excellent dinner, and freely expressed his sentiments on the chief characteristics of the banquet, and conversed with much eloquence and warmth with several exceedingly communicative persons, who politely pointed out the most distinguished of the guests—an operation in the performauce of which, most men experience peculiar pleasure.

Well! in due time the Lord Mayor commenced the list of toasts, and the speeches, cheers, and glees which succeeded were so enlivening and appropriate, that they seemed to impart universal delight.

But it happened that at that particular period of British history, the Ministers of the Crown were extremely unpopular with the party to which their immediate official predecessors belonged—a fact which is of so striking and extraordinary a character, that it becomes highly correct to record it in these adventures. They were remarkably unpopular with that particular party; but as it was usual on such occasions for the Ministers of the Crown to be invited, all who happened at the time to be in London, notwithstanding their extreme unpopularity, came, and moreover the health of those Ministers of the Crown, was placed on the list of toasts.

Now Valentine knew something of the power of party spirit. He knew that principle and honor were perpetually sacrificed at its shrine. In the town in which he was born, he had witnessed it rising upon the ruins of friendship and affection; and had found it in the metropolis to be equally powerful, and equally pernicious. The little experience he had had of its effects, had hence inspired him with the conviction of its being alone sufficiently powerful to subvert almost every generous feeling by which men are actuated; but he wondered if it were possible for its developement to be induced there, where so many of the first men of the age—men distinguished for wealth, probity, and wisdom—had assembled, and where joy and good fellowship seemed to be in the ascendant.

He looked round: they all appeared happy. The dark passions were subdued. Envy, hatred, malice, and all uncharitableness seemed, for the time being, by common consent, to be extinguished. They had assembled for no party purpose; but with a view to the cultivation of those feelings which impart a zest to life, and which bind man to man. Every heart seemed open—every hand seemed ready to give and to receive the warm pressure of friendship. It appeared to be a moment peculiarly adapted for the reconciliation of friends who had become enemies, their hearts seemed so ardent—their feelings so pure.

Notwithstanding all this, however, Valentine determined, for his own satisfaction, on trying the experiment. He inclined to the opinion, that the slightest manifestation of party-spirit would, at such a time, be treated as so great an indignity, that it would instantly be drowned in enthusiastic cheers, in which men of all parties would readily join; but in order to test the soundness of this opinion he resolved, nevertheless, when the time came, to manifest some *slight* disapprobation, just sufficient to make it understood, and no more.

Accordingly, when in due course the Lord Mayor rose with the view of proposing the health of the Ministers, Valentine, the very moment their names were announced, sent a sound along the table, which amounted to no more than a murmuring buzz. In an instant the demon of party arose! That sound, slight as it was, was hailed as the signal for confusion. Every countenance changed as if by magic. They of the Ministerial party applauded with unparalleled vehemence; while they of the opposition hissed and groaned like tortured fiends.

The Lord Mayor knit his brows and pursed his lips, and looked very indignant. His exertions to restore order were desperate but ineffectual. In vain he denounced it as an irregular proceeding. Innumerable were his efforts to convince them of its being one of which he did not, and could not, and ought not to approve. The opposition would not hear him. The party tocsin had been sounded, and it proved the knell of peace. They who a moment before seemed so happy and so joyous, were now in fierce contention, their bosoms swelling with party spite.

At length, however, the action of the Mayor was so extremely energetic, that it produced an effect which enabled him to make a few additional observations, which were really very just and very much to the purpose; but the moment the Premier rose with his colleagues, with a view to the simple acknowledgment of the toast, the frantic sounds which assailed them were comparable only with those which Valentine had heard in the House of Commons. Had the Ministers been fiends, the opposition could not have expressed a greater amount of indignation: had they been gods, the ministerialists could not with greater enthusiasm have cheered them.

They nevertheless still kept their ground and that with just as much calmness as if they had been used to it. The Premier slightly smiled at his colleagues, and his colleagues smiled slightly at him. This seemed to enrage the opposition still more; but the louder they manifested their sentiments on the subject, the louder were the sentiments of the Ministerialists expressed. The Lord Mayor again rose, and the opposition seemed to groan even at him, when Uncle John deeming that most atrocious, started up and cried "shame!" with an expression of indignation which nothing else could match.

Valentine, however, immediately drew him down, and begged of him earnestly not to interfere; but Uncle John could not endure it. "The ingrates!" he cried, "thus to groan at head-quarters after having been swelled out as they have been, and that with all the delicacies of life! It's really monstrous!"

"It is, it is, I know it is," said Valentine, "but don't interfere."

Uncle John shook his head very fiercely; he was very indignant; and the Lord Mayor said something which could not be heard; but which appeared to be generally understood to be very severe, for it had the effect of somewhat subduing the most noisy; but the moment the Premier opened his lips to address them, the opposition recommenced operations, and the conflict between them and the ministerialists became far more desperate than ever.

"Silence! You *wretches!*" exclaimed Uncle John.

"Uncle! Uncle!" cried Valentine, pulling him down, "they'll take you for one of the opposition!"

"Let them!" returned Uncle John. "Let them take me for one of the opposition; I am one of the opposition; but I'd scorn to oppose men in this cowardly way."

The Lord Mayor again rose, and with most indignant emphasis said, "really;"—but as this was all the opposition suffered him to say, he at once resumed his seat with a look very strongly indicative of anger.

It became quite impossible now for Uncle

John to remain quiet. He kept fidgetting about, grinding his teeth, and biting his lips, and exclaiming as he clenched his fists, "oh! I should like to be at some of them dearly!" He put it to those around him, whether it were not most disgraceful, and their affirmative replies made him infinitely worse. Had they wisely dissented, they might have calmed him at least in so far as to induce him to argue the point, but as the case stood, Valentine found it impossible to restrain him.

"If," said the Premier, with really admirable coolness and self-possession, taking advantage of a temporary lull: "If the gentlemen will only be silent for *one* moment—" No!—They would not be for one moment silent: they recommenced groaning like furies, and this of course again induced thunders of applause.

"Where are these groaners?" thought Valentine. He could hear them distinctly enough, but couldn't see them. "Are they all Ventriloquists?"

His attention was at this particular moment directed to an elderly individual whose mouth was apparently closed. He watched him narrowly. He was straining at something. His face was remarkably red, and while his eyes appeared to be in the act of starting from their sockets, he was obviously perspiring with infinite freedom. Could he be a groaner? He was! He was then hard at work: no man could have been more zealous although he kept his eyes fixed with surpassing firmness upon the table as if watching the evolutions of some very minute natural curiosity, and apparently noticing no other thing.

"Shame!" cried Valentine, throwing his voice dexterously behind this indefatigable person, who turned sharply round, being duly apprehensive of detection, but as, contrary to his lively anticipations, he saw no one there, he very wisely returned to his interesting task, which really seemed to afford him unspeakable pleasure.

"I see you," said Valentine, throwing his voice again just behind the individual in question, and again he looked round with an expression of intense interest; but as of course he could see no one near him, he appeared to regard it as by far the most astonishing circumstance that ever occurred to him during the whole course of his life. "I see you!" repeated Valentine, which was really the fact: he saw him in a state of amazement the most remarkable he ever beheld. The individual seemed not to know at all what to make of it. He felt that surely he could not be mistaken, that surely he had heard some one speak, and that surely he was at that moment under no direct or indirect supernatural influence!—and yet, where was the man who had addressed him? This was a mystery which he had by no means the ability to solve, but it had the effect of inducing him to be silent, although the groaning in other quarters was as fierce as before.

The opposition, however, were not alone to be blamed. The ministerialists themselves were highly culpable. Had they left the groaning people to pursue that great course, which appeared to inspire them with so much delight, unmolested; had they been content with giving, at the commencement, three glorious rounds of enthusiastic cheers, and then leaving the groaners to themselves, the confusion might thus have been avoided. But this they would not do. They would have a battle. They seemed to be prompted by some eternal, and essentially cabalistic principle, to beat them. They *would* make more noise: and they did make more noise: they made ten times more noise than the groaners. It was they who would not let the Premier speak: it was they who drowned the voice of the Lord Mayor. The groaners could never have stopped the speeches themselves, and of this, the ministerialists appeared to be conscious, for they lent them throughout their most powerful aid.

It is a fact, which may in all probability be held to be extraordinary, that the slightest sound of disapprobation, if persevered in, is sufficient to create in an assembly, however honorable and enlightened, universal confusion; but there is yet another fact, which is not perhaps of quite so extraordinary a character, but which is this—that constant straining, to state it shortly, will in fulness of time produce exhaustion; and the moment a practical illustration of that fact was in this particular instance afforded, the Lord Mayor, who was a manly and rather a handsome individual, again rose, and said very properly, and very energetically, "that he and the sheriffs had not been treated as they expected."

"Of course not!" exclaimed Uncle John, who very seriously thought, that as every thing had been provided in a style the most delicate, and the most sumptuous, from the two hundred and fifty tureens of real turtle to the several hundred thousand plates of pippins, such treatment was monstrous in the extreme.

The Lord Mayor said no more: he resumed his seat with dignity, but still with an expression of noble indignation, and that expression was hailed with loud cheers; but the moment the Premier—who with his colleagues still manfully maintained his position—re-opened his lips, the opposition, who felt themselves bound to produce the next harmony, favored the company with a little more groaning. The ministerialists again knew their cue, and they again set to work as one man, and did really succeed in the production of the greatest amount of noise that ever issued from a corresponding number of human throats. Nor were they content with vocal music. By no means. They beat the tables with all the energy of young drummers, while Uncle John was striking that at which he was sitting with the force of a Cyclops.

The glasses danced with peculiar animation, and shook out the wine that was in them that they might do it with all possible effect; and while the pippins seemed to fancy, that they had been magically metamorphosed into marbles, the dishes they had deserted rattled after them fiercely, with the apparent view of convincing them that such was not the fact.

The Lord Mayor now appeared to be somewhat more tranquil. It seemed to have struck him with peculiar force, that it was perfectly useless to manifest anger. There the belligerents were: some were hissing, some were groaning, some were shouting, and some were laughing, while others were indignantly fidgetting about and explaining what they thought of the matter on the whole. It was impossible therefore for his lordship to do any good by being angry. He could not by such means quell the riot. He seemed to feel this forcibly, and hence, quite conscious of having done all he had the power to do, he very wisely made up his mind that it was a duty incumbent upon him as a magistrate, as a mayor, and as a man, to endure it all with the most perfect resignation.

The Premier stood like a smiling statue. He was anxious to have it distinctly understood, that if they conceived him to be the man to sit down, before he had said what he had to say, they were dreadfully mistaken. He, therefore, stood as firmly as a rock, and continued thus to stand, until the majority of those who were engaged in the conflict, displayed unequivocal symptoms of exhaustion, when taking advantage of that interesting moment, he managed to say something, which appeared to have some slight reference to the army and navy, and resumed his seat boldly and instantaneously, amidst an unexampled burst, composed of hisses, cheers, and groans.

This, however, in a very few minutes subsided, and the glorious conflict was over. The opposition party prided themselves on having produced it, and the ministerialists, with equal pride, felt that they had had the best of it on the whole. The Lord Mayor expressed his sentiments on the subject to those around him, and those around him expressed theirs, with due eloquence and point: in fact, every man present—not excluding the professional individuals in the orchestra—was on this subject warmly contributing to the universal buzz, which for a long time pervaded the Hall.

Valentine really was very much annoyed at having tried the experiment. He contended within himself, that he ought to have known that party spirit was sure to develop itself, whenever an opportunity arose; it mattered not, whether it were in the senate, the banqueting hall, or the church. He was, therefore, by no means content: for although he was perfectly conscious, that they who had permitted themselves to be so powerfully influenced by party feelings at such a time, and on such an occasion, ought to blush; he felt, nevertheless, that he had awakened those feelings; that—although it had all been accomplished by a murmur—he had converted a joyous happy scene into one of malicious confusion.

The mischief, however, had been done, and as he thought that it was, therefore, extremely impolitic to vex himself any more about the matter then, he turned, with the view of diverting the current of his thoughts to some more agreeable subject, and found Uncle John fast asleep! He had been beating the table with so much energy, and shouting—order! silence! and shame!—with such extraordinary zeal, that he had become quite exhausted; and there he sat with folded arms, his soul sealed to the consciousness of care, and his lips pouting perfect contentment, while, as he nodded, nature gave him an occasional jerk, with the sublime view of keeping him up.

"Uncle!" said Valentine, shaking the sleeper, who murmured and nodded, and went to sleep again. "Uncle!" he continued, "Do you know where you are?"

The sleeper was unable, at that precise moment, to tell whether he really did or not, but he opened his eyes in order to satisfy himself on the subject, and then said:—"Why, bless me! I'd no idea that I was asleep! not the slightest! I hope no one noticed it? Dear me! it's highly incorrect; very wrong—very wrong. But I'm all right now—as wide awake as I was in the morning. Well! they have settled it I see: you have had no more disturbance?"

"No," replied Valentine; "but look at the people: how dull they all are! The Lord Mayor has been laboring very hard to restore them to good humor, but without any sensible effect. They have made up their minds now not to be pleased." And this really appeared to be the case. They seemed to be dissatisfied with every thing. Toasts were proposed, and speeches were made; but neither speeches nor toasts could re-inspire them.

Of course the Lord Mayor could not, under these circumstances, feel very happy. He did all of which he was capable with a view to the restoration of those harmonious feelings which existed before the disturbance commenced; but as he failed in this—signally failed—he left the chair as soon as he could with due regard to his dignity, and, before twelve o'clock, every guest had departed.

The matter was, however, by no means allowed to rest here. The effects of the disturbance were terrific!—it induced a paper war of the most desperate character—a war which raged with really unparalleled fierceness for weeks. The opposition journals hailed it as a glorious and indisputable proof of the surpassing unpopularity of those Ministers whom they had with extraordinary acuteness discovered to be totally unfit to rule the destinies of this mighty empire.

"How," they exclaimed, "can those atrocious, and disgusting political anthropophagi dare to drag on their disreputable, dirty, and degraded official existence after this unexampled—this mighty demonstration of universal scorn? It is an insult to the whole British nation!—a gross, comprehensive, unmitigated insult!—an insult which cannot, and shall not be endured! What can be in reality more contemptibly atrocious than the conduct of men who have the brazen audacity—the unblushing impudence—to pretend to rule a deeply reflecting people who cannot regard them but with loathing and disgust? Can any thing reflect more disgrace upon a mighty and highly enlightened nation, than the existence of men as ministers, so utterly contemptible, so justly abhorred? How, then, with any show of decency, can they for a moment retain office after such an universal burst of popular execration? Yet are they in office still! Conscious of the whole country being against them;—conscious of being the laughing-stock of Europe;—conscious—they cannot but be conscious—of being despised aad contemned by all the intelligence, all the wisdom, all the wealth, respectability, and virtue of this great nation; these abhorrent, these imbecile, shabby, contemptible, political jugglers still cling, with the tenacity of polypi, to power, that they may dip their unhallowed fingers into the public purse to enrich themselves and their execrable satellites! Englishmen! will you suffer this humiliating state of things any longer to exist? Britons! are you prepared to become the slaves—the vile, crawling, abject slaves—of that detestable clique, of which the members now bid you defiance? If there be a single drop of the patriotic blood of your forefathers thrilling through your veins, you will arise, and, with one universal and simultaneous burst of indignation, denounce these degraded political reptiles—as they were denounced at Guildhall—and hurl them at once from that position in which they now have the impudence to stand!"

While the opposition journalists were engaged in the manufacture of these highly appropriate philippics, they on the ministerial side were contending with extraordinary force and ingenuity, that the disturbance in question, instead of being as pretended, a striking proof of the unpopularity of the ministers, in reality proved that they never were so popular, seeing that whereas it all originated with a disappointed alderman who had under his immediate surveillance just forty individuals, about twenty years of age, from whom the whole of the groaning proceeded, it would not have been worth any disappointed alderman's while to have organised those groaning individuals, if the popularity of the ministers had been on the wane, or if it had not in fact been increasing.

And this was held to be an extremely strong argument—one which absolutely carried conviction on the face of it; and as the opposition journalists, in their presumptuous efforts tó answer it, tried desperately to shake it to its base, it was again and again repeated with additional tropes, and hereupon the fierce journalists fell foul of each other.

The ministerialists commenced the attack; they undertook to prove, with mathematical precision, that they of the opposition were blackguards; and the opposition journalists being equally chivalrous, assumed to themselves the province of reducing to a dead certainty, that they on the ministerial side were natural fools. And strange to say, they both eventually succeeded to their own most entire satisfaction, but—which is still more strange—they were utterly unable to obtain acknowledgments of success from each other!—hence, at the happy termination ef the struggle, they ostensibly held the same views on the subject as those which they held when the struggle began.

It is a duty, however, which the historian owes as well to himself as to the public, to state that these amiable and truly ferocious journalists in all their contentions for the one grand point were sincere. They who were on the opposition side of the question, did most sincerely think that the statesmen who were at that particular period in office, ought not to retain it—that they ought to make way for the statesmen whom they had supplanted, and who—with a species of patriotism not often to be met with, but as admirable as it is rare—were absolutely ready again to take upon themselves the cares of office, and thus to sacrifice, to an extent altogether unknown, their private comforts and conveniences to the public good: they did most sincerely feel that this glorious opportunity was one which ought not to be lost—that the country owed those patriots a debt of gratitude amounting to something very considerable, for offering without the slightest solicitation, to come forward at that truly awful crisis, to snatch the British empire from the jaws of destruction, and thereby to save those institutions which were crumbling into one undistinguishable mass of revolutionary dust. And equally sincere were the ministerial journalists, when they declared it to be their decided opinion that the ministers ought by no means to resign—that the government of the country could not by possibility be confided to men of whose principles and general conduct they could so highly approve—that they were just the very men whom the people should support through thick and thin as the only men capable of meeting the exigencies peculiar to that period—and that they could have no manner of confidence in those who then formed the corrupt and purely factious opposition. Hence they labored night and day to inspire the people with a due appreciation of the importance of sustaining the ministers, as the only chance left of averting a most sanguinary revolution, and hence they were indefatigable in their efforts to disseminate the belief that every act of the ministers developed surpassing soundness of judgment, and perfectly unexampled intellectual vigor—while every act of the opposition displayed an extreme narrowness of soul and a dearth of judgment really pitiable.

The sincerity of those journalists being then so conspicuous and extensive, it can scarcely be deemed marvellous, that the contest on that occasion should have been so extremely desperate as it was; but that which in all probability will, in the present day, appear more extraordinary than all, is the fact, that notwithstanding the choicest epithets were culled on both sides, with due care, and applied with due ferocity, the contest failed to affect in any way the stability of the government, for while the zealous exertions of the opposition did weaken it by no means, it derived from those of the ministerialists no additional strength; and the result of the glorious war was, that while on the one hand, the ministers were recommended never again to accept an invitation to the grand civic feast; on the other, it was boldly and powerfully urged, that as ministers they surely never would.

From this struggle Valentine certainly did derive much amusement, and when he had explained to Uncle John, that the whole affair originated with his own slight murmuring buzz, that gentleman—albeit he very properly condemned the thing at first—viewed the progress of the battle with feelings of delight. Morning after morning, and evening after evening did he study the various modes of attack and defence, but although he laughed heartily and constantly at the arguments based upon arguments that were themselves based upon nothing, the contest failed to increase his admiration of that uncompromising zeal, which forms so peculiarly the characteristic of the fourth estate of the realm.

CHAPTER XXXV.

VALENTINE RECOVERS THE HIGHLY VALUED CARD, AND PROCEEDS WITH UNCLE JOHN TO THE EXHIBITION OT FAT CATTLE.

Albeit Uncle John had come to London expressly to go at once to head-quarters, with a view to the discovery of Goodman; he was in town more than a month before he managed to find time to take even the preliminary step. He had formed highly laudable resolutions every evening, with a species of regularity which was really of itself truly striking; but every morning with precisely corresponding regularity there had arisen fresh temptations sufficiently powerful to set those highly laudable resolutions at defiance. "I never saw such a place as this London," he would observe; "upon my life I don't appear to have time to do a thing: I keep going on and on in a perpetual state of fever, driving here, there, and everywhere, racing and chasing, and bobbing in and out, and really seem to do nothing after all. I can't understand it. It's a mystery to me. The place seems to have been designed expressly to worry men to death." And it really is an absolute fact that he did feel occasionally very much confused—nay it would sometimes happen that a temporary derangement of his intellects would develope itself —and hence it will not be deemed in the long run extraordinary that every day after dinner he should fall fast asleep with his highly-prized meerschaum in his mouth.

Now as it is not very generally known, it cannot be very incorrect to observe that Uncle John was one of those remarkable men who invariably make a dead stop in the street when they have anything striking to communicate, to look at, or to learn.—This practice at first annoyed Valentine exceedingly, for although his uncle never stopped dead in the road, but flew over every crossing with as much of the facility of a greyhound as he comfortably could, whether carriages were or were not within view; he would frequently do so in the midst of a mortal stream, when they who happened to be behind could not avoid running forcibly against him. Sometimes a butcher's boy would poke his hat off with his tray, and then a heavily laden porter would send him staggering a dozen yards or so, and then a carpenter shouting politely "by'r leave," would cut a piece out of his coat with the end of a saw, which invariably disdains to be wholly smothered in a basket; but even these natural results failed to cure him of the practice: he would adhere to it in spite of them; but certainly the most remarkable stop he ever made was precisely at the bottom of Holborn Hill.

"Now there's a place!" said he on that memorable occasion. "Did you ever?—How people can breathe in such holes puzzles me! Let's go and have a look at them; come; I dare say the poor creatures are all fit to drop; pale, emaciated, spiritless, and wretched. Shall we go?"

"Oh! with all my heart," said Valentine; and they entered the hole which bore the semblance of a great commercial alley, the ancient houses on either side of which seemed as if they had been striving for a century at least to lean against their neighbors opposite for support, and had still a trembling hope of accomplishing that object before their tottering frames had quite crumbled into dust. Instead of being spiritless and wretched, however, the inhabitants were all life and jollity—laughing, singing, joking, and chatting as gaily as if they had been in the Elysian fields. Some were vending old shoes, some fried fish, and some tenth or eleventh-hand garments; but the real aristocracy of the place were those who exhibited an infinite variety of handkerchiefs pinned upon sticks, and so arranged that each windowless shop formed a most attractive picture. Into these shops from time to time sundry young gentlemen darted, and taking off their hats as became them, produced from the interior in some cases three, and in some half-a-dozen bandannas which they seemed to have been fortunate enough to pick up in the street just before.

"Can't I sell you one to-day?" said a black-eyed Jewess, whose tightly twisted ringlets, like well tarred cords, lashed her bosom. "I should like to deal with you," she continued, addressing Uncle John with a perfectly heart-winning smile.

"They don't appear to me to be new," observed that really unsophisticated gentleman.

The Jewess turned her black eyes full upon him, and seemed in an instant to have read the whole history of the man. "I think we can do a little business together," she observed. "Just step inside here.—There's no harm done, you know: I have something particular to show you."

"Uncle John looked at Valentine as if he did not understand it exactly; but as Valentine who did understand it but smiled, Uncle John at once followed the fascinating Jewess, who proceeded at once to a drawer, and producing a bundle, said, "Now I've something here that'll do your eyes a world of good to look at."

The bundle was opened, and the first thing which struck Uncle John was the handkerchief he lost in Cheapside while looking at the Lord Mayor's pageant.—"Why," said he, "what's this? Why that's mine!"

"That's what every gentleman says when he sees a hankecher at all like his'n," replied the Jewess.

"But how did you come by it?" inquired Uncle John.

"Oh, I took it in the regular way of business, of course."

"But it's mine," exclaimed Uncle John.

"Now what a mistake that is when its mine," said the Jewess. "But how do you know it ever did belong to you? Do you think they never make two hankechers alike?"

"*I'll* soon convince you: mine are all marked," said Uncle John; and while he looked at each corner with very great minuteness, the Jewess smiled, and eventually asked him if he were satisfied.

"No, I am not," said he; "I am not by any means. Although I can't find the mark, I still believe it to be mine." And as he looked round, it absolutely struck him that the whole of those handkerchiefs which then met his view had been stolen!—an extraordinary idea, which at that moment made him so indignant, that he prepared to leave the shop.

"But come, we can deal for all that," said the Jewess. "Here take it for three-and-six, and say you've got a good bargain."

"What, compound a felony!" exclaimed Uncle John.

"Well, here take it for three," said the Jewess, "and I shan't get a ha'penny by you."

Uncle John looked remarkably fierce, and said very severely, "It's my firm belief that these things you have here were not honestly come by," and having pointedly delivered himself to this effect, he turned his back upon the Jewess, who was laughing very loudly, and quitted the shop. "It is really my opinion," he continued, addressing Valentine, "that the whole of those things have been stolen."

"Why, of course. That is well understood."

"Indeed!" cried Uncle John, and as he stopped short to wonder that things which were well understood to have been stolen, should be unblushingly exposed in open day, the attention of Valentine was fixed upon a jacket which hung at an old clothes shop opposite. "It must be the same," thought he, "surely!—but then there's no chance of the card being in it."

"Any things in ma vay to-day?" said a Jew who had been watching his countenance. "Any things to puy or to shell?"

"Let me look at that jacket," said Valentine.

"What are you about?" cried Uncle John.

"I merely wish to see that jacket."

"What, are you going to set up on your own account, Val, as a barber?"

Uncle John smiled and felt much amused; but Valentine smiled not at all: he took the jacket with great eagerness from the hands of the Jew, and searched the pockets. They were empty! His hopes were again blasted. He searched them again, and again; and at length found—a hole! He revived. The card might have worked its way through it. He extended his search zealously between the striped material and the lining, and eventually in the corner he felt something closely doubled up. He drew it forth; it *was* the card of him whom he had rescued!—the father of her in whom his dearest hopes had been centred. He saw the name of Raven distinctly: he could also make out the greater part of the address. At that moment how pure was his happiness! He felt so delighted, so joyous! Uncle John looked amazed, and the Jew, whose first impression was that the card was at the very least a fifty pound note, looked quite as much amazed at Uncle John.

"What is the price of this jacket?" inquired Valentine.

"Vy," said the Jew, "it shan't be tear at a crown. The card sheems to pe vorth arl the moneesh."

"I want but the card," said Valentine, giving the sum demanded. "I'll make you a present of the jacket."

"Nothing elsh in ma vay?" said the Jew who felt very much dissatisfied with himself for having asked so small a sum.

"No, nothing," replied Valentine. "Nothing," and he hurried his uncle out of the lane as soon as possible.

"Now what's all this—what's all this business?" demanded Uncle John, having made a dead stop at the corner.

"I am happy," cried Valentine, "perfectly happy," and he entered at once into a minute explanation of the circumstances connected with the much valued card.

"Well, and what do you want to see the girl again for?" inquired Uncle John. "You can do nothing more for her now."

"But she wished me to call," observed Valentine; "and so did her father, and therefore I must, as a matter of mere courtesy."

"Courtesy! Fiddlesticks!" rejoined Uncle John. "It's my opinion that you'd not be so anxious about the business if it were but a matter of mere courtesy. Did you ever see the girl before?"

"No, never!"

"Then its my firm belief that you had better not see her again. You'll only make a fool of yourself. I don't at all like these romantic affairs—they never come to any good. It was all very well for you to save a fellow-creature. I admire your spirit and your motive; but, take my advice, and don't go."

"But she is so sweet a girl," observed Valentine.

"Sweet! pooh! so they are all: I never heard of a girl being saved who was not. Besides, how do you know who she is, or what she is? that's the point."

"I don't know—of course I can't tell. I am hence the more anxious to ascertain."

"Well, I know how it will be—I see it all plain enough. But you can't go to-day, that's quite clear."

"But, why can I not?"

"What! have you forgotten that this is the last day of the cattle show? I wouldn't miss that for fifty pounds."

"But it surely is not necessary for me to go with you?"

"Not necessary! How do you think it possible for me to find my way about in this wilderness alone? Besides, I may be run over. A thousand things may occur. How can you or I, or any body tell what may happen!"

Of course Valentine could not pretend to any knowledge of what might occur; but he nevertheless wished the fat cattle were drowned in the Dead Sea. He, had, however, one great consolation—he had recovered the card; and as they rode towards the place at which the cattle were exhibited, he felt twenty times to ascertain if it were secure, and eventually determined to wait, with all the patience at his command, till the following morning.

"Now," said Uncle John, on arriving at the place of exhibition, "I expect to have a treat, Val—a glorious treat!" and having entered, they found the place crowded with all sorts of people, from the nobleman down to the butcher's boy without a hat.

To the pigs on the left Uncle John first directed his attention. He was a great judge of pigs, and there lay the poor animals, grunting and snoring, and panting, and squeaking, while the connoisseurs around were engaged in the pleasing occupation of slapping their haunches and pinching and twisting their tails, with the ostensible view of ascertaining how much noise it was possible for them to make. They had, of course, been made so fat that their ability to stand was out of the question altogether; yet, although they were all in the finest state of corpulency, they looked as uncomfortable as pigs could look by any conceivable possibility.

"Now, there's a pig for you!" observed Uncle John, as he pointed to a black lump of flesh, which appeared to be particularly unhappy. "That pig weighs—now, what shall I say?—it weighs above fifty score!"

"You're wrong!" cried Valentine, throwing his voice towards the head of the pig; "I'll bet you a bottle of wine I don't weigh above forty!"

Uncle John pursed his lips and knit his brows, and then looked at the pig's head in a very straightforward manner, and then cocked his hat on one side, and scratched his head with great freedom, and felt altogether in a confused state of mind, until he turned towards Valentine, who happened to be smiling, when he saw in the twinkling of an eye what it was, and cried, lifting his stick, "You young dog! there! if I didn't think that pig spoke, I'm not here!" and Uncle John roared with laughter. "What a fool!" he continued. "The idea of a pig offering to bet a bottle of wine he didn't weigh forty score!" and again Uncle John burst out very merrily, until at length, screwing his countenance to a very solemn pitch, he gravely added, "But he weighs fifty score for all that."

Well, they now left the pigs, and went at once to the other side, where the first class oxen were arranged, with backs as broad as those of full-sized elephants, and withal so remarkably flat, that had they happened to have rolled upon those backs, they would have stood no more chance of getting up again, without mortal aid, than a turtle, on being placed in a corresponding predicament. And they appeared to be perfectly cognisant of this, for whenever nature called upon the beasts to lie down, they obeyed her call as cautiously as Christians.

"What is the use," inquired Valentine, "of fattening these creatures up to such an extent?"

"The use!" cried Uncle John—"the use! Why, the use of it is to see how fat they can be made."

"But what is the use of seeing how fat they can be made?"

"Why, of course, to ascertain which kind of cattle will fatten, and which kind will not."

"Is that the only good accomplished?"

"The only good!" exclaimed Uncle John. "Is not that good enough? What would be the use of throwing away a lot of fodder upon cattle that won't fatten at all?"

"There is," said Valentine, as gravely as possible, "a society in this wilderness, as you are pleased to term it, for the prevention of cruelty to animals. Now the officers of that society, I think, ought to take special cognisance of this exhibition, for in my view there cannot be a species of cruelty more refined than that of fattening animals up to a state in which they are compelled to gasp at least a hundred and twenty times per minute. Just notice those poor distressed creatures, how they pant! Can any man believe that they are not in great pain? Suppose, for instance, that you and I were in the power of graziers who felt disposed to experimentalise upon us; what a sweet state of mind we should be in, if they succeeded in making us in proportion as fat as those beasts."

"The grazier who could succeed, Val, in making you fat, would deserve a gold medal, thickly studded with precious stones. But we are men, and they are beasts; that makes all the difference. The cases are therefore by no means analogous."

Valentine did not suppose that they were; but he conceived that Uncle John might have been brought to explain more distinctly why beasts were thus fattened to an extent which rendered their existence a burden, and hence, following the example of

False Alarm at the Cattle Show

Uncle John with the pig, adhered firmly to his first position, that the Society for the Prevention of Cruelty to Animals were bound to interfere.

Now it really was interesting to observe how the farmers and the butchers felt the various popular parts of the animals as they stood; but more interesting still was it to notice how the far more fashionably-dressed individuals, having stolen a few lessons from the butchers and the farmers, felt precisely the same parts of those animals, and looked quite as learned as the butchers and the farmers themselves. One individual, an external pink of the purest water, made himself particularly conspicuous in this way; first performing the operation of nipping the animals, and then giving his judgment upon each to two ladies, who were of his party, with infinite eloquence and point. Valentine was highly amused by this exquisite pretender: he felt his proceedings to be ridiculous in the extreme, and therefore watched him very narrowly until he reached the ox which had gained the first prize, and which he began to feel, of course, with consummate dexterity.

"Now, *don't* pinch!" cried Valentine, throwing his voice towards the mouth of the ox, which, as if to complete the illusion, at that moment turned its head round, "it's of *no* use!—you *don't* understand it!"

The exquisite started back greatly confused, while the ladies were excessively alarmed at the announcement.

"Well, dang my boottons!" cried a countryman, "if ever I heered tell o' the like o' that!"

"It is very extraordinary," suggested the exquisite.

"Strornary! I never come across such a thing afore in all my boorn days. That's woot he goot the prize for, dang me, I shoodn't wonder, I'll be bound to say—no doot."

Uncle John could keep silent no longer. He burst into a roar, which so powerfully convulsed him, that he felt himself bound to hold on by the tail of the next ox.

This seemed to awaken the suspicions of the pink. He could not, it is true, understand it exactly; but he was satisfied that the animal had spoken by no means. His courage therefore returned, and being positively brave, he placed his hand upon the animal again.

"Don't! there's a good fellow!—pray don't!" said Valentine, throwing his voice as before. "You've no idea how sore I am round about the tail."

And this doubtless was precisely what the animal would have said, if it could in reality have spoken; for as he had been at the exhibition some days, his most popular points, that is, being interpreted, those points which true judges invariably assail, must have been extremely tender; but whether these were the words which the animal would in such an event have uttered, or not, it is perfectly certain that they had the effect not only of inducing the exquisite to withdraw his hand on the instant, but of inspiring those around him with wonder.

"Here, Bill!" cried a butcher, addressing his friend, "p'raps this *aint* a rum start! sen I may live if this hox carn't talk reg'lar."

"Do vot?" cried the gentleman to whom this important communication had been addressed.

"Vy, talk like a brick, and as reg'lar as a Christian."

"Yes—over!" said his friend, with an expression of incredulity.

"But I tell yer I heered him—so there carn't be no mistake."

"Vot! do you mean to go for to think that you'll gammon me into that ere?"

"Vell arks these ere genelmen!—don't believe me arout you like!—they all heered him." And the butcher proceeded to accumulate such collateral evidence as he felt must establish the thing to the entire satisfaction of his incredulous friend; but as Uncle John still roared with laughter, and kept holding on by the tail of the next ox with such unexampled firmness that the animal must have felt that the design was to pull out that ornament by the root, it was deemed right by Valentine—just as the butcher was eloquently entering into the details of the affair—to leave the interesting group to solve that which of course was regarded as a mystery by all.

It was, however, by no means the work of a moment to release the ox's tail from the grasp of Uncle John. The poor animal stood the tugging with really exemplary patience; and being too fat to kick, looked round simply, as if anxious for a brief explanation of the circumstances connected therewith; but he clearly must have felt that if an assault of such a character had been made before he was fattened, the assailant would have had his reward.

By dint of great exertion on the part of Valentine, however, Uncle John was eventually severed from the tail; but before they had reached the place in which the sixth and seventh classes were exhibited, loud cries of "A bull! a bull! a bull broke loose!" were heard, and an awful rush was made towards the pigs. Some terror-stricken gentlemen leaped with due agility upon the broad flat backs of the cattle, others mounted the frames near the horns of the beasts, which those beasts were by no means inclined to submit to, and hence used the weapons with which nature had provided them, with no inconsiderable force and effect; but by far the greater portion of the alarmed connoisseurs rushed with all discreet haste towards the entrance with countenances strongly expressive of the most lively apprehensions, while the females were screaming, and the male alarmists shouting "A pole axe!—a pole axe there!—let him be killed!"

As soon as the place from which the terrorists had so unceremoniously decamped became clear, Uncle John, who had slipped with surpassing dexterity behind an ox, followed Valentine in, and beyond all dispute there was a short-horned heifer endeavoring with all the zeal and ingenuity of which she was capable to slip the halter over her head, having evidently been pinched until her popular points had become so sore that she had made up her mind to endure it no longer. Two laborers however most bravely approached and effectually frustrated her ladyship's design—a striking fact which was duly and promptly announced, and as the alarmists were returning with appropriate caution, Uncle John ascertained that it was time for him to start, when he and Valentine left the exhibition highly pleased with the varied entertainment it had afforded.

CHAPTER XXXVI.

THE MUTUAL RECOGNITION AND THE INTERVIEW—THE POLITE INVITATION, AND THE DINNER.

It may, as a general thing, be stated that men spend their most miserable hours in bed, when they are anxious to go to sleep and cannot. They turn and turn, and with every turn thoughts of a most uncomfortable character are engendered; yet although they pray heartily and fervently for the morning, their heads really seem to be sealed to their pillows, when that which they prayed for arrives. Such, however, was not the case with Valentine. It is true he turned over and over continually throughout the night, but his thoughts were of the most pleasing character, being of her whom he felt that he loved: it is also true that he wished for the morning, but when it arrived instead of finding him apparently sealed to the pillow, it found him knocking violently at Uncle John's door, and exerting all the powers of suasion at his command to induce him to get up at once. He really marvelled that men should lie in bed so long. It was then eight o'clock, and although his own time had been heretofore nine, it then struck him as extraordinary that it had not been seven, and having eventually extorted a promise from Uncle John that he would rise on the instant, he returned to his own room to dress.

Now, it has been said that all is vanity; and if vanity be thus contradistinguished from pride, that whereas pride prompts us to esteem ourselves highly, vanity stimulates us to win the esteem of others—it is quite clear that vanity is not a bad passion, but on the contrary one which ought fondly to be cherished. But it has also been said, and that too by an ancient philosopher, that man is too proud to be vain, and if he be, it is abundantly manifest that vanity is not quite so general a thing; but assuming this to be wrong, that is to say, assuming that men are in reality vain, and that vain men are in the abstract essentially wicked, it still appears to be quite consistent with reason to contend that if there be a time at which the development of vanity is venial, it is that at which men are about to see those whom they love, and by whom they therefore hope to be loved in return. They are then the most anxious to win the esteem of others; and if this be the true definition of vanity, it follows that Valentine himself was most vain on the memorable morning in question. He was never so long dressing before. He was indeed so extremely particular that he even astonished himself; but eventually, conceiving that Uncle John must be out of patience, he gave a last long lingering look at the glass, and went down into the parlor. Uncle John was not there. He too must have been more than usually particular that morning, for in general he was dressed and down in less than five minutes. Well, Valentine waited: he waited ten minutes, and thought that sufficiently horrible; but when he had waited a quarter of an hour, he darted at once up to Uncle John's room, and knocked as if the house had been in flames.

"Aye, aye," cried Uncle John, whom the knocking had awakened from a dream which had reference to some astonishing turnips which he had seen at the show the day before, and immediately after he had said, "Aye, aye," he gave a very, very long cosey yawn.

"What, are you not up yet?" cried Valentine.

Uncle John instantly rolled out of bed, and cried, "Up! yes, of course!" which, of course, was the fact. "I'll be down in five minutes," he added with truly remarkable presence of mind, and within the five minutes he was down.

"What a time you have been!" observed Valentine, seating himself at the table.

"I've been dreaming," returned Uncle John, "of those turnips. I thought that you undertook to swallow one six and thirty inches in circumference whole."

"And did I do it?"

"To the utter astonishment of all beholders it slipped clean down like a pill."

"It must have appeared that I possessed a most extraordinary swallow; but do you think of going out this morning at all?"

"Why no, my boy, really I don't think I can. This racing about day after day knocks me up altogether."

"Then I'll return as soon as possible. I shall not be gone long."

"Gone? Why, where are you going?"

"To call on those persons I named to you yesterday. Don't you remember?"

Uncle John it was clear had forgotten all about it; but he now recollected the circumstance, and shook his head gravely. "I know," said he, "that if I endeavor to persuade you to keep away from that girl, you will be the more anxious to go; that is perfectly clear. I shall therefore say no more about it. You are at liberty to go, sir, but remember, if you associate yourself with any creature who can be picked up on board a steam-packet, I disown you—at once, sir, I disown you."

"Uncle!" said Valentine, in a tone of remonstrance, "can you suppose—"

"I'll hear nothing more about it," interrupted Uncle John; "I see clearly how it will be. You'll make a fool of yourself, sir!—but go by all means, and if you are not back in less than two hours, I shall go out without you. I can't live in this hole of London without a little exercise; no man can do it. Therefore, two hours, mark! I'll not wait another moment."

It will hence be perceived that Uncle John was rather angry; but he, notwithstanding, shook hands with Valentine, and explained before he left that, as he had great confidence in his judgment and discretion, he felt sure that he would commit no act of folly that would shake it.

The concluding observation he deemed highly politic. "Suspicion," thought he, "is the parent of the thing we suspect; but let any one feel that full confidence is reposed in him, and he will think and think a long time before he betrays it."

Without hearing another discouraging word, therefore, Valentine started for Bryanstone-square, but on his way felt as if within the hour he should know if the germ of his life's happiness would strike root or wither. He had never before conceived it to be possible for the slightest imperfection to characterise her in whom his hopes were concentered. His impression had been that he had but to see her again to be happy. Uncle John had placed his thoughts in a doubting direction: yet where the grounds were that could justify doubt, really Valentine could not conceive. "If she be not," thought he, "what I feel that she is, why—why then must I strive to forget her: but I'll not do her the injustice to suppose that she is not. I feel convinced that I am not mistaken." And with this conviction firmly impressed upon his mind, he reached the house.

It was a *large* one! rather awfully large: he could not help feeling that he should have liked it somewhat better, had it been a little smaller!—he had had no idea of its being such a size! It could not be the right one! He must have made a mistake, either in the name of the square, or in the number! He passed it, and drew forth the card. No!—all was correct! "Surely," thought he, "this must be the *same* card? And he really began to feel not quite sure even of that; but, in order to put an end to all doubt on the subject, he went to the door and knocked boldly—albeit, there was something in the sound of the knocker a *little* too aristocratic.

"Mr. Raven," said he, when the door had been opened, in a tone more than usually decided and severe.

"Not at home, sir," replied the servant, whose livery was of the gayest description.

"What time is he usually at home?" inquired Valentine, drawing forth his card-case.

"About this time, sir, generally," said the servant. "He is seldom out before one or two."

Valentine having left his card, thereupon turned from the door; but his eye was at the moment attracted by one who had darted to the window, and who recognised him instantly! What was to be done? The recognition was mutual; yet ought he—she bowed to him!—that was sufficient: he returned: the door had not been closed; but before he had time to say a syllable to the servant, an angel, in the perfect similitude of her whom he had saved, seized his hand, and led him into the room.

"I am so glad to see you!" she exclaimed. "Indeed I scarcely can tell how delighted I am!"—and she led him to a seat, and sat very, very near him; and they gazed upon each other, and looked very pale, and felt really very awkward and stupid.

Valentine could not get over it at all!—but he had always been a fool in the presence of ladies. He would have met Satan himself, in the shape of a man, without a nerve being fluttered; but if one of his majesty's most minute imps had appeared in the semblance of a woman, that imp would *in limine* have beaten him hollow.

It will not, therefore, by any means be deemed very extraordinary, that the lady, in this instance, should have been the first to recover: in fact, the recovery of Valentine was rather remote, when she exclaimed, "Oh, how I *do* wish that papa would return! He would, indeed, be so happy to see you. He has been talking about you every day since; and we did so wonder you had not called—there he is!" she continued, starting up, as a knock came to the door. And it really was a most undeniable knock. It was like the commencement of the overture to *Semiramide*. She therefore could not by any possible chance have been mistaken. It seemed, too, as if the servant knew something of the tune; for the last bar had scarcely been executed, when he flew across the hall, with an apparently just and well-grounded apprehension of an immediate encore.

Valentine now heard the voice of authority, which was also the voice of Mr. Raven; and as his daughter glided gracefully to meet him in the hall, he cried, "Well, Louise!—anything turned up fresh?"

"This is the gentleman, papa, who preserved us," said Louise, as he entered the room.

"Ah! my brave fellow!" exclaimed Mr. Raven. "How are you? Glad to see you —very glad—right glad!—God bless you! —But why have you not been before?"

Valentine—whom the presence of Mr. Raven had relieved from all embarrassment —now explained all the circumstances connected with the card; and as he dwelt with considerable emphasis and eloquence upon his anxiety to regain it, and the pleasure its recovery had induced, Louise watched his countenance with the earnestness of love; and every word, every tone, sank deep into her heart.

"God bless you!—God bless you!" exclaimed Mr. Raven, and something like a tear stood in his eye as he spoke; and he shook the hand of Valentine again very warmly, as he added, "You don't know—you can't know—how *anxious* we have been to see you! But come, come!—you'll dine with us to-day, as a matter of course?"

"I should be happy—most happy—but my uncle is in town," observed Valentine.

"Well, bring your uncle with you of course!" said Mr. Raven. "Give my compliments, and tell him I shall be happy to see him to take pot-luck. I'll send my carriage for him at five."

"Pot-luck!" thought Valentine—"that's very extraordinary." He had heard of pot-luck before, certainly; but never in immediate connection with a carriage. However, he fancied that all this would tend to astonish the nerves of Uncle John; and therefore having acknowledged the politeness of Mr. Raven, he rose and took leave, as the bell rang a peal that would have inspired a whole village with spirit.

"Well, what think you now, Val?—What think you now?" said he, addressing himself in the second person singular, the moment he had left the house. "She is indeed very beautiful—very! But what sort of people can they be? She is elegant in her manners—very ladylike indeed—but her father is clearly not very refined; and yet what a superb style they live in! He must be some one of importance—yet I cannot remember to have heard the name associated with distinction!" He was puzzled—greatly puzzled. He conceived that Mr. Raven had scarcely the manners of a gentleman, and certainly not those of an aristocrat! Still he found it hard to associate vulgarity with the style in which he lived. What he had been, or what he could be, therefore, Valentine was unable to conceive. It was a mystery altogether; and one in which he continued to be so mentally involved, that he had reached home before he even thought that he was near.

"Well, my boy," said Uncle John, who as Valentine entered was sitting with his heels upon the mantel-piece; "well, have you seen her?"

"I have," replied Valentine.

"Ah! she's a lovely girl, isn't she? fascinating, interesting, beautiful! eh?"

"She is indeed!"

"Of course!" cried Uncle John, "I could have sworn it! She is all that is graceful and elegant, highly, very highly accomplished, with a German or perhaps a Grecian nose, and a remarkable couple of beautiful black eyes of course blazing away like brilliants. That's the girl! Is she a milliner?"

"No, she lives with her father."

"Is her father a cobbler, or does he keep a snuff-shop?"

"I can't make out at all what he is. I am unable to imagine what he can be."

"He lives by his wits, perhaps; a gambler, or something of that sort?"

"No, I don't think he is," said Valentine carelessly.

"Don't *think* he is! Pray, did you see him?"

"Oh, yes; he has invited you and me to go and take pot-luck with him."

"Pot-luck!" said Uncle John; "I expect it would indeed be pot-luck, and very poor pot-luck too. What is he going to have, Val, pickled pork and cabbage?"

"I don't at all know what he'll give us; but of course you'll go?"

"Go—I go? Decidedly not."

"But his carriage will be here for you at five."

"His what!" cried Uncle John; "his carriage!" The idea struck him as being so amusing and so good, that he laughed very heartily; he really could not help it. "What sort of a carriage is it, Val?" he inquired, "what sort of a carriage, my boy?"

"Upon my life," replied Valentine, "I don't know what *color* it is, never having seen it; but if it corresponds at all with the liveries, and I dare say it does, it's a dasher!"

Uncle John looked at Valentine earnestly. He thought there was something in it—certainly he did go so far as to think that; but then he really could not go one single step farther. "Now," said he, "*is* this one of your jokes? Because if it is, you had better tell me, that I may know how to act. Is it, or is it not, a joke?"

"Upon my honor," said Valentine, "no." And to the utter astonishment of Uncle John, he explained all the circumstances just as they occurred.

"Why, what an extraordinary piece of business to be sure!" said Uncle John, with an expression of amusement. "But I'll go!—oh! I'll go! although I'm sure to make a fool of myself. I'm sure of it! *I* know nothing of aristocratic etiquette, which changes, I'm told, about twenty times a month. It may, for example, be the fashion to take soup with a fork, and I'm just as likely as not, you see, to catch up a spoon."

"Oh, you'll be able to manage it very well. Besides, these are not very, *very* aristocratic people."

"I don't know so much about that," said Uncle John—"you can't judge. Sometimes that which is in others deemed the essence of vulgarity, is in them held to be the very acmé of refinement. They do it, I suppose, to show off their independence—to prove that they can do that which, but for them, others would never dare attempt. I recollect that, at our last election dinner, we had Lord George Rattle, who is considered, of course, the very perfection of refinement, and every eye was, in consequence, upon him. Well—he cocked the knife in his mouth, and took the wing of a fowl in his fingers, and placed his elbow upon the table, and picked his teeth violently. Why, such proceedings had been considered by all *rather* unparliamentary, if not indeed vulgar in the extreme: but then, what was the consequence? Why, at the next public dinner we had, there was scarcely a fork used; the flesh of the chickens was gnawed off the bones, and while almost every man placed his elbows upon the table, there was really such a picking of teeth, you would have thought that all the crickets in all the bake-houses in the empire had assembled in honor of the occasion. But I'll go!—of course, that I have made up my mind to." And he commenced at once bustling about, with the view of making himself as tidy as possible.

Well, five o'clock came, and a carriage rattled up to the door. Uncle John ran to the window, and was amazed! It was one of the very gayest he had seen, not excepting even that of the under-sheriff. The widow Smugman was struck almost dumb! she could scarcely announce its arrival.

"Are you ready?" said Valentine, addressing Uncle John, who really felt fidgety himself at the moment.

"Yes, quite ready—quite," was the hasty reply, and they descended, of course with due dignity of aspect, and entered the carriage forthwith.

"I don't think that fellow could look at a man," said Uncle John, as the carriage drove off, "without touching his hat. It comes, however, natural to him, I suppose. A little less of it, perhaps, would be as well. But what will the widow think of a carriage like this, lined with rose-pink satin, driving up to her door! Why, she'll be about as proud of it as if it were her own! Did you see how astonished she looked? Upon my life, she must suppose that we are highly connected."

And it really was an elegant carriage; but then no man could see it without feeling sure that display was the hobby of its owner. The horses, too, were of the most showy character, and, as they seemed to be unable to go at a less rapid rate than that of ten miles an hour, they of course very soon reached the house, before which they stopped almost as instantaneously as if the pole had been absolutely driven against an unyielding stone wall.

"They *must* have gone upon their haunches. I don't myself see how they could——." At this moment Uncle John was interrupted by an unexampled knock at the door, which was instantly opened, when he and Valentine alighted with all the dignity of which they were capable, and were shown at once into a magnificent drawing-room, in which the really-beautiful Louise and her father received them with great cordiality and warmth.

Louise looked more lovely than ever; and as Valentine was comparatively free from embarrassment, he certainly did appear to great advantage himself. This imparted mutual pleasure, and they chatted very freely and with infinite gaiety, while Uncle John was made to feel just as much at home as if he had known Mr. Raven for years.

This was pleasant—they all felt it to be pleasant; and when dinner was announced, Mr. Raven looked at Valentine, as he bowed, and waved his hand towards Louise, and then seizing the arm of Uncle John, observed, "We two old fogies will go down together;" an observation which was certainly remarkable in itself.

Now the first thing which struck Uncle John, as he entered the dining-room, was the plate. It was really of the most massive and gorgeous description, and displayed in such style, and moreover in such extraordinary quantities, that he could not but think that Mr. Raven must possess the wealth of Crœsus.

There was, however, one thing which, in Uncle John's judgment, spoilt all; and that was the restless anxiety of Mr. Raven to inspire him with the belief that he was totally unprepared to receive him. "I beg that you will excuse us to-day," he would observe: then, "You see we are quite in the rough;" then, "I'm afraid you'll not be able to make a dinner"—then, "You see we have only a snack, as, of course, we didn't expect to have the pleasure of your company." And these apologies were so constantly reiterated, that Uncle John—who had never in his life sat down to a more sumptuous dinner—was heartily glad when it was over, for he didn't like to say, "Oh, don't mention it;" or, "I beg that you'll not apologise"—or "Really it will do very well;" or indeed anything of that sort, because he felt that that would not convey quite enough: nor did he like to say, "Upon my life, I never sat down to a more splendid dinner," because he felt that that *might* convey a little too much!—he therefore said nothing, in reply to those apologies; but labored to put down the nuisance, by bowing.

Of course Valentine could not help noticing this; but he was then far too deeply engaged with Louise, to think much about the motive which prompted the annoyance. It was perfectly manifest that *he* was not annoyed. On the contrary, he had never felt so happy before: nor, indeed, had Louise. They were really delighted with each other: and their eyes!—It will probably be useless to say how they looked; but that they met as if the two pair had been under the absolute guidance of one soul, is quite certain.

Mr. Raven, immediately after dinner, commenced drinking with great freedom; and this had the effect of causing him gradually to throw off that sort of restraint, which his wealth and the style in which he lived had imposed. He became very communicative indeed, and very joyous, when Valentine, who had taken special care of his own faculties, discovered the real character of the man.

"Come, come! you don't drink!" cried Mr. Raven, slapping Uncle John heartily upon the shoulder. "Come! never mind the young un's—leave them to themselves, while we two old codgers enjoy ourselves, eh? You're just the sort of fellow I like! None of your stiff, upstart penniless men in buckram, for me! You're just the man after my own heart! so let's both be jolly, eh? let's both be jolly!"

Uncle John had no objection.

"But," continued Mr. Raven, with truly awful solemnity, "I feel that I have one great duty to perform. Louise, my girl, fill up a bumper—a bumper, my girl, for this toast! I rise!" he continued, very slowly and very emphatically, "I rise to propose the health of one to whose brave and noble nature we—I and my girl—owe our present existence. That young man," he added, pointing to Valentine and looking at Uncle John, "saved my life, he saved the life of my child!—God bless him!" Here Valentine rose to take the hand extended towards him, the owner of which was for some time unable to proceed. "I can't," he at length added, "give expression to my feelings, my feelings won't let me; but if ever I forget him, may I be forgotten! If ever I cease to be grateful—God bless you!" He could then say no more, but sank back in his chair, and having wiped away the tears which almost blinded him, emptied his glass and replenished.

The pride of Uncle John at that interesting moment was quite beyond conception. His opinion of Valentine had previously of course been very high; but at that moment really, in his judgment, he was the most splendid fellow that ever lived, and in the warmth of his feelings he expressed himself precisely to this effect, and Mr. Raven entirely agreed with him, when Valentine acknowledged the toast in a highly appropriate speech, and shortly after Louise, though reluctantly, retired.

"There," said Mr. Raven, addressing Uncle John the very moment Louise had left the room, "what do you think of that girl, eh?—what do you think of her for a pawnbroker's daughter?"

"Upon my life," said Uncle John, "you ought to be proud of her."

"Proud, sir, I am proud! Why that girl, when I was in business, kept the whole of my books, sir!—what do you think of that? and never made an error of a penny! Would you believe it? She was worth to me more than fifty clerks put together. She worked like a horse, and now see what she is!"

"She is indeed very elegant," observed Uncle John.

"I believe you!" exclaimed Mr. Raven. "Talk of your aristocracy! I'd back her against the first lady in the land, although she *is* but a pawnbroker's daughter."

"You have of course been out of business some years?"

"Five, sir, five years come Christmas. I'd a long spell at it, a very long spell; but I've done the trick, although I *did* commence as a poor ragged boy!"

"Nothing," said Uncle John, "can be more pleasing than the reflections of a man who has been the architect of his own fortune."

"Of course not!" exclaimed Mr. Raven, who was highly delighted. "Of course not. I glory in it. I feel that there's the more credit due to me, eh? Why when I began life I hadn't, if you'll believe me, such a thing as a penny in my pocket, nor scarcely a rag to my back, yet see now what I am! I began as a boy to run of errands, clean knives, shoes and windows—in short, to make myself generally useful. I did so; and worked my way into the shop, and then married the governor's daughter and had a share in the business; and then I got it all, and now I can buy up one-half of your beggarly aristocracy, and be even then a rich man!"

"It must be a very profitable business," observed Uncle John.

"Yes, it is—it is profitable: there's no denying that. But people make a mistake when they suppose that the profits are chiefly derived from the poor. The little sums tell up, no doubt; but fortunes are made by supplying the wants of our proud peacock beggarly aristocracy! That is how fortunes are realised; when you come to fortunes! Why I've had in one morning in my little room no less than ten ladies of title!—in one single morning, sir?—What do you think of that?"

"You astonish me!" exclaimed Uncle John: and it really is a fact that Uncle John was astonished. He had never before heard of such a thing in his life.

"Some," continued Mr. Raven, who was now fairly warmed upon the subject—"some brought me their cases of jewels; some wore them and took them off before me, while others brought with them the most valuable portion of their plate."

"But did they go into the shop?"

"No!—bless your soul, no; they were somewhat too cunning for that. They would come to the private door, and whenever they came they were sure to be trembling on the very verge of ruin. Of course I understood it! I knew what it meant. I used to tease them sometimes—you know—pretend to be poor—just to hear what they would say. It wouldn't do, however, to carry on long, because they'd go right clean off into hysterics. I have had them, sir, crying and fainting, and begging and praying! 'Now upon my word,' I used to say, 'money is very scarce, but how much will do for you?' 'Oh!' they would almost *scream*—'I must have a hundred pounds, or I'm ruined. I'll leave you my jewels, which cost a thousand—I must have them again to go to Lady Tontino's ball—and I'll give you for the accommodation thirty, forty, fifty, sixty pounds, or anything you like to name. Dear, dear, Mr. Raven, do oblige me!'"

"I wonder," said Uncle John, "they were not ashamed of themselves."

"Ashamed!" cried Mr. Raven; "your beggarly aristocracy ashamed! Catch them at it! Sir, they are ashamed of nothing!—they've got no shame in them. I've seen such scenes, and heard such tales!—they've made my hair stand on end, sir, right up on end!—they have almost made me vow that I'd never again put the smallest faith in woman; and I surely never should, but that I knew these tricks were confined to our beggarly aristocracy. They'll do anything to cheat their husbands—anything in the world; they glory in it—absolutely glory in it! But, really, I couldn't help laughing sometimes. There was old Lady Lumley—she's dead now; she died about the year ——, but that's of no consequence—well, she would come, say on a Tuesday, bustling into the room, in such a fidget and so out of breath, you'd have thought she had not got another moment to live. '*Well*, Mr. Raven,' she would say, 'I've got into another dreadful scrape, and I must have your *dear, kind* assistance; I lost all my money last night. I positively never *saw* cards go so cross. There really *must* have been cheating; but I'm going to meet the same party to-night, and unless I have a hundred pounds now, I shall never be able to recover my loss. I'll leave my suit of brilliants; I am sure not to want them till Friday; but I have no doubt at all of being able to call for them to-morrow.' Well, I'd lend her the hundred, and after calling me a 'dear good creature,' and the rest of it, although if I passed her in the park, or elsewhere, she'd turn up her aristocratic nose and wouldn't know me; she'd trot off delighted to her carriage, which she invariably left at the corner. The next morning she'd call again, not to take away her diamonds, but to beg of me to let her have another hundred pounds. She'd have lost the hundred she had the day before, and perhaps two or three hundred besides, which had been given to her by the earl for some very special purpose. I'd let her have another hundred, for the diamonds were worth three thousand at least; I believe they originally cost five; and the very next morning she'd bustle in again—the earl had missed them! They were *his* first gift, and unless she could have them to wear that night, she would be for ever ruined! She would bring, perhaps, a suit of torquoise, pearls, or anything else she might happen to have worn the night before, to deposit, until she could bring back the diamonds. And thus she went on —and thus they all go on, paying in the long-run at least a thousand per cent. for their money; and I've had in my house at one time, sir, jewels, which couldn't have cost less than five hundred thousand pounds."

"But of course," said Uncle John, "they eventually redeemed them?"

"By no means, sir, is it a matter of course—by no manner of means. They would go on and on, getting deeper and deeper, until they could not pay the money advanced, and then of course would come another jewel robbery."

"Why, I'm utterly amazed!" cried Uncle John.

"Amazed, sir? Why, sir, I have known no less than three most mysterious jewel robberies to be blazing away in the papers in one single week, when the identical jewels have been in my possession. Rewards have been offered for the apprehension of the offenders, the servants have been searched, the houses have been turned upside down, and the track of the villains distinctly chalked out, while the creatures themselves, the very creatures from whose hands I received them, have been running about from place to place, to give color to the thing, apparently in a state of the most absolute distraction. Those lovely brilliants, those beautiful pearls, those amethysts, those rubies, which they would not have lost for the world; their birthday presents and their marriage gifts, were, alas! all gone, the cold-hearted robbers had not left a gem! These are the tricks, sir—these are the tricks; and this is how fortunes are made—when you come to speak of *fortunes*, not by taking in a string of flatirons for twopence, or lending a shilling upon a chemise! But come, let us sink the shop and talk of something else. But you wouldn't have supposed it though, would you?"

"I should not, indeed," said Uncle John. "Upon my life I could scarcely have conceived it to be possible."

At this moment a servant entered with a communication from Louise, which was found to be the prelude to the introduction of coffee. This induced Uncle John at once to look at his watch, and to declare, when he had discovered to his astonishment that it was already past twelve, that he had not an idea of its being so late. He however had coffee, and so had Valentine, who had been throughout an attentive auditor, drawing inferences, and balancing conclusions, as Mr. Raven proceeded, and at length fully made up his mind to this, that he ardently loved Louise, but could not have a very high opinion of her father.

Uncle John now developed strong symptoms of impatience, and a servant was accordingly despatched for a coach, and when its arrival had been announced, he and Valentine took leave of Mr. Raven, who was then, as in fact he had been throughout the evening, on very high terms with himself indeed.

CHAPTER XXXVII.

SHOWS HOW UNCLE JOHN AND VALENTINE MANAGED TO ASCERTAIN THAT GOODMAN WAS CONFINED AS A LUNATIC, AND HOW THEY ALSO MANAGED TO INTRODUCE THEMSELVES BODILY INTO THE ASYLUM.

"Now I say, governor, what's to be done with this old guy?" inquired Horace, alluding to Uncle John, the morning after he and Valentine had dined with Mr. Raven. "He has been here a series of times you know, and I suppose he'll commence a new series to-morrow. Now I think you'd better see him. You can't keep on 'not at home' for ever; besides, it looks rotten, precisely as *if* you were anxious to avoid him, which don't do you know, and never did; therefore my undeniable opinion upon the matter is, that you'd better make a formal appointment, it will look more like business."

"But what am I to say to the man?" cried Walter.

"Say to him! stick to your original text—pecuniary uncomfortables—unexampled shortness of chips—a horrid accumulation of respectable duns striking his monetary system with paralysis. You know how to do it."

"But he's Grimwood's greatest friend," said Walter. "He has come to town, depend upon it, expressly in order to get him out of those pecuniary difficulties in which we have stated he is involved. He will therefore insist upon knowing where he is. He will put it to me whether I would rather see my brother kept in a state of embarrassment or completely disencumbered. That's the way he'll put it. I'm sure of it, and what can I say then? Can I say, No, let him be; don't give him any assistance; all will come right by and by? It strikes me that that wouldn't look *quite* the thing!"

"Then I'll tell you what had better be done. I've just thought of it. Suppose we were to write a lot of letters, you know, dating the first, for example, at Penzance, there, out by the Land's End, signed of course 'Grimwood Goodman,' all regular, inviting the old buffer to run down, and when he gets there let him find another dated Great Yarmouth, with a similar invitation, and when he gets to Great Yarmouth let him find another addressed to him stating that business, which pressed immediately, compelled the undiscoverable to go to York, where he should be inexpressibly delighted to see him, and then when he reaches York let him in a precisely similar fashion be seduced over to Shrewsbury or Welch Pool; and thus keep him cutting about the country until he gives the thing up as a bad job—eh? don't you think that that would be *about* the sort of thing?"

"Horace," said his father, "you are a very ingenious fellow; but you are always making the one little mistake of supposing that every other man is a fool."

"Well, but don't you think it would answer to make him go to the extremes of east, west, north, and south? I don't know what your sentiments may be upon the matter, but my impression is, that there's nothing in life so well calculated to make a man give up a chase of this description."

"And you fancy he'd *go* from place to place in that way?"

"Go!—of course he'd go—can there be two opinions about it?"

"Psha! nonsense! We might get him, no doubt, to any one of the places you have mentioned; but what if we did? Why, he'd find out at once that it was a hoax, and then his suspicions—for that he has suspicions now is quite clear—would be stronger than ever."

"Well, have it your own way—of course you always will. You never *were*, you know, guilty of being influenced by those who were anxious to advise you for your own good. My opinion is, still, that this dodge might be managed; but if you won't do it, why, then the next best thing is to put a bold face upon the matter, and see him at once. It is perfectly certain that he'll never leave London until he has seen you, and he *may* come across you when you are quite unprepared."

"There is certainly something in that," said Walter, "and as of course, I'm never safe, if I leave the house but for a moment, I begin to think that it will perhaps be better to see him here, when I'm perfectly cool and collected."

"There can't be half a doubt about it. You know your old nerves are not worth so much as twopence when you are taken by surprise."

"Well, give me the pen and ink: I'll write to him now: I'll be at home this evening at seven?—say eight."

A note to this effect was therefore written and despatched; and when Uncle John and Valentine, whom Raven and Louise had engaged in conversation that morning for nearly two hours, returned, they found it lying upon the table.

"Well, come," said Uncle John, having read the contents, "I'm to see this man at last. We shall now, perhaps, hear something about Goodman."

"I fear not," said Valentine, looking at the note. "His object, I apprehend, is to tell you the tale he told me, and if it should, there will remain but one way in which it is possible to get at the truth. But then that depends so much upon you."

"Well, my boy! Well! Am I not to be trusted?"

"Scarcely in this matter: I'll explain to you why. This man is very nervous. He conjures up spectres and so on: he actually set fire to his house, with the view of burning out the phantom of his brother, a circumstance which tended, more than anything else, to confirm my suspicions of foul play. Now, if I thought that you could keep your countenance, let what might occur, I'd so frighten that man, that, if there be anything wrong, we should be perfectly certain to have a full confession."

"There's no danger," said Uncle John, "of my being unable to do that. The thing is too serious—far too serious."

"But can you look steadily at the object, and at nothing but the object, however ridiculous may be the circumstances connected with its attainment?"

"In such a case I can: I feel that I can —and will."

"Then," said Valentine, "it shall be tried. We shall see how he will act: we shall hear what explanation he will give; and if that explanation be not satisfactory—and I cannot suppose for a moment that it will be —why then we must work upon his fears, and I have not the smallest doubt of the result. There is only one drawback: Horace, his son, who is perhaps quite as reckless as he is vulgar, will doubtless be with him. It will not be very easy, I apprehend, to alarm him; but our point will be gained, notwithstanding, provided you look at the object alone."

"I'll do it," said Uncle John firmly. "I'll do it! I'll not move a muscle, except indeed it be with the view of expressing surprise."

Very well. This point being thus satisfactorily settled, they sat down to dinner, and at half past seven precisely they started for Walter's residence, where they found him and Horace with a pile of documents before them, with which they appeared to have been deeply engaged.

"Ah! my old tar!" exclaimed Horace, seizing Valentine's hand as he and Uncle John entered the room—"Why what have you been doing with your body for the last half century? We havn't seen so much as a bit of you for an age!"

"You are so seldom at home!" observed Valentine significantly.

"Sir," said Walter, addressing Uncle John, "I'm proud to know you. Take a seat. I am sorry that I should have been so unfortunate as to be out whenever you have done me the honor of calling: but I have been so much engaged with my brother's business that really I've had scarcely a moment to myself."

"Have you heard from him lately?" inquired Uncle John.

"The other day," replied Walter. "Last —what day was it Horace?—Thursday?—Friday?"

"Thursday, you know," said Horace. "Don't you remember?—The day you went to Lincoln's Inn."

"Aye! so it was, of course!—it was Thursday. I had forgotten."

"He was quite well, I hope?"

"Why, yes: as well as you might expect, you know, under the circumstances. His difficulties have been and are still very pressing and very vexatious. When a man once gets back, sir, it's a long time before he gets forward again."

"That is true," said Uncle John; "very true. But what is the nature of those difficulties, may I ask?"

"They are of an exceedingly complicated character: indeed, so complicated are they, that I fear we shall never be able to arrange them with any degree of completeness. These papers which you now see before you all relate to the various speculations in which he has been engaged. My son and I have been working at them constantly, almost night and day for the last month, but we really can make nothing of them."

"Well, I've known him for a number of years," said Uncle John, "but I never before knew that he was a specualting man. I know he used not to be."

"No: it's only within the last year or two that he has been mad enough to engage in them, and some of them are really of the wildest description that can possibly be conceived. It would have been indeed a happy thing could he have been satisfied with that which he had. But he was led into it—blindly led into it."

"But what kind of speculations were they?"

"Speculations, sir; some of them of a description so absurd, that you'd think that the man must have been insane to have anything to do with them."

"But what is their nature?"

"Upon my word they are so various and so mixed up together, that it is perfectly impossible to explain. There is only one thing quite certain, which is this, that he's an utterly ruined man."

"That is indeed most unfortunate; but if such be the case, why does he continue to keep out of the way?—why does he not meet the thing boldly? Is he in town?"

"Oh! dear me, no: he left immediately: he wouldn't stop an hour after he found how things were."

"I suppose," said Uncle John,—"in fact, I believe you have explained to my nephew —that he is anxious for his present place of residence to be kept a profound secret. Now sir, we are friends of long standing: I have known him now nearly forty years; and during the whole of that period, our confidence in each other has been of a character the most implicit and unreserved. I therefore feel that he cannot object to my knowing where he is; my conviction, in fact, is strong, that he cannot be anxious to remain concealed from me."

"My dear sir," said Walter, "if there be one friend whom he respects more than another, it is yourself; but he has enjoined me most strictly to communicate the secret to no one, not even to you."

"'Tis false!" cried Valentine, assuming the voice of Goodman, and making it appear to proceed from the passage.

"Hal-lo!" exclaimed Horace. "Why, what's o'clock, now?"—and seizing one of the candles, he rushed towards the door—while Walter trembled from head to foot.

"What's that?" quickly demanded Uncle John—looking earnestly at the trembling wretch before him. "What's that!"—he repeated in a whisper, which seemed absolutely to strike to the wretch's heart.

Walter started: he was speechless: his eyes glared wildly; and although they were directed stealthily towards the door, he had not the courage to turn his head.

"Who are *you?*" cried Horace, on reaching the passage. "Come in!—don't stand shivering there in the cold!—Oh, there's nobody"—he continued—as he banged the door with violence. "It's nothing but fancy."

"It's a very extraordinary fancy," observed Uncle John, "if fancy it be; and very mysterious in its effects."

"Why governor! governor!" cried Horace, shaking his father—an operation which was perfectly unnecessary—seeing that he was shaking quite sufficiently, without such assistance. "Why, what are you about? are you mad?"

The blood of Walter appeared to be freezing in his veins; his lips became livid; while his eyes seemed glazed with an unearthly film, and he looked altogether very horrible. He did, however, at length, on being roused, manage to articulate indistinctly, what was understood to be a declaration that, since his illness, his nerves had been so weak, that the slightest noise alarmed him.

"Valentine is right," thought Uncle John. "There is, indeed, something very wrong here."

"Walter!" said Valentine, in a tone of great solemnity, throwing his voice as before.

"*Who's there?*" cried Walter, with an expression of terror the most absolute.

"*Governor!*" cried Horace, "don't be a fool! You're enough to make a man jump clean out of his skin. There's *no* one!—of course, there is no one."

"Some one pronounced the name of Walter," observed Uncle John, looking seriously at Horace.

"Oh! it's only somebody having a game!" returned Horace; "I should like to be behind him, whoever he is. I'd make him remember it."

"Walter!" repeated Valentine.

"Oh! this won't do!" cried Horace, darting to the door. "Who's *there?* I'll soon see who it is," he continued, returning for a light. "Now, old fellow, where are you? I only want to see you, that's all. D'ye hear! Susan! Have you any fellow there with you?—because if you have, I'll just break his blessed neck, you know; and no mistake about it."

Susan, on the instant, indignantly flew up, with the view of repudiating the implied imputation.

"Have you let any fellow in, I ask you?" cried Horace.

"Feller! *Me* let a feller in! *Well*, I'm sure!"

"I *only* want to catch one! that's all! If I wouldn't give him *pepper!*—Has *any* one been?"

"No!" cried Susan, "*I* never lets fellers in; I'll not have my character taken away, *I* know."

"Oh! don't bother me with your rubbish," cried Horace, returning to the room, and closing the door again violently. "I should only just like to set eyes on him!—that's all the harm I wish *him*. But, governor!—come! *don't* be a fool!"

Walter tried desperately to shake off his fears, but in vain. He still sat as if utterly paralysed. His mouth was open, his limbs were powerless, and he looked as if he expected every instant to hear the voice again.

"This won't do, you know!" cried Horace. "Here—have a glass of wine." And he rose in order to reach the decanter, which stood on the sideboard; but the moment he had risen, a knock was heard at the door!

Again Walter started, and caught his breath convulsively; but Horace, lifting his hand to enjoin silence, crept softly across the room. Another knock was heard, and in an instant Horace had opened the door, and seized Susan by the throat.

She screamed, of course, violently, and struggled with appropriate desperation; but it was not until Horace—whose face having recently been burnt, was very tender—had been dreadfully scratched, that he became sensible of the error he had committed.

"Good Heavens!" exclaimed Mrs. Goodman from above. "What on earth is the matter?"

"Here's Mr. Horace, ma'am, been throttling at me just for all the world like a polecat, and all 'cause I knocked at the door just to tell him you wanted to see him."

"Well, how did I know?" cried Horace. "Why didn't you speak? How do you think I could tell who it was in the dark?"

"Horace! for Heaven's sake come up!" cried Mrs. Goodman.

"*I'm* coming," muttered Horace; and, as he returned for a candle, it was plain that his personal appearance had not by any means been improved.

At this moment Uncle John felt an almost irresistible inclination to smile; but on turning towards Walter, that inclination was subdued without an effort. There the guilty creature sat, without the power either to move or to speak, writhing under the torturing lash of conscience, and looking as pale as a ghost. He was indeed the very picture of horror, presenting altogether a spectacle which would have excited the powerful commiseration of those who were near him, but that they felt—strongly felt—that he had been guilty of some dreadful crime.

"Brother!" said Valentine, in a deep sepulchral tone.

"Mercy!" cried Walter, whose agony at the moment appeared to be most intense.

"Brother!" repeated Valentine.

Walter again started; and stopping his ears, shrank back appalled.

"Well! how do you bring it in now?" cried Horace, re-entering the room with his face bleeding freely. "What! not got over it yet? Here—take a glass of wine: you'll feel fifty per cent. better after that. Whatever is the *matter* with you, I can't conceive." And he filled a glass, and handed it to his father, who had no sooner raised it to his lips than he dropped it; for at that moment Valentine, throwing his voice as before into the passage, again most solemnly cried, "Walter!"

"It don't signify talking," said Horace, "there *must* be some fellow in the house. I'm sure of it!" And he again went to the door, and listened very attentively, and ground his teeth, and clenched his fists with great desperation. "You'd better look out, my fine fellow," he cried, "because if I *do* happen to catch you, you'll find no mistake about me! Well, how do you find yourself now, after spilling your wine like a senseless old infant? I'll make it out now before I sleep."

"No! Horace, no!" said Walter faintly. "You will find no one there."

"Oh! but I know better! You don't think there *is* any body then, don't you?"

Walter shook his head very mournfully, and heaved a sigh, which amounted almost to a groan.

"Brother, brother!" said Valentine, solemnly throwing his voice just behind the trembling man.

"I will not, I cannot endure it!" cried Walter with startling energy. "It's far worse than death. I must and will explain."

"Don't be an ass!" said Horace. "What have you got to explain?" and he pinched his father's arm very secretly but very severely.

"There is evidently something," observed Uncle John, "that requires explanation, and I certainly do think it had better be done at once."

"Explain!" cried Valentine in a truly awful tone, which really had the effect of startling even Horace, for he looked towards the spot from which it apparently proceeded, with an expression, if not indeed of absolute terror, of something which looked very like it.

"Explain!" repeated Valentine in a tone of still greater solemnity, and Walter, who continued to tremble as if with the palsy, was about to explain, when Horace stopped him, and, with a countenance indicative of no considerable alarm, said, "If it must be known, I'll—pooh I won't have it!" and he looked round as if to defy that influence which a moment before he had conceived to be supernatural.

"Beware!"—cried Valentine—"beware!"

"What is it?" inquired Uncle John.

"Why, the fact of the matter is this," replied Horace, whose firmness the voice had again shaken. "The fact is, the old man went mad, and the governor deemed it prudent, you know, for his own personal safety, to have him taken care of. And that's the long and the short of it."

"Mad!" cried Uncle John.

"Mad, sir! mad as a four-year-old."

"Bless my life and soul! I'd no idea of such a thing. I'd always supposed him to be a remarkably strong-minded man."

"He is mad and no mistake," rejoined Horace, "and I'm sorry to say that madness runs a little in the family. The governor there is frequently mad, but then when the fit's on him he'll no more believe it than nothing. You might just as well try to persuade a brick wall."

"My poor old friend mad! Dear—bless me!" said Uncle John, who believed it, and was really very sorry to hear it. "And what have you done with him? Where is he confined?"

"In a nice quiet private asylum, where he is well taken care of, and treated with the utmost kindness and attention."

"Yes," said Walter, faintly, although he felt quite relieved by the manifest credulity of Uncle John, "it is very expensive to me, certainly, but I really did not feel myself justified in sending him to any one of those horrible public places where poor creatures are treated you don't know how. I therefore went to the expense of placing him in a respectable private establishment, where he has every comfort, and is, I am glad to say, as happy as possible."

"You acted well, sir. It does you great credit, and proves that you possess a good heart," said Uncle John.

"I feel that I have done no more than my duty," said Walter. "He is my brother." And having got thus far, the hypocrite began to breathe freely and to feel very considerably better.

"Right; right; very right," said Uncle John; "that consideration is, indeed, very powerful. And with whom have you placed him?—what establishment is he in?"

"Dr. Holdem's," said Walter, and Horace looked at him as if with the view of conveying his conviction that in stating that fact he had done very wrong; but Walter, who knew the strict rules of the establishment having reference to communications between patients and their friends, also knew that unless suspicion were excited and a public stir made, his brother would be just as secure as before. "Dr. Holdem," he continued, "is a most humane man, and, moreover, a man of extraordinary talent. I therefore feel much more satisfied under the circumstances than I should if he were here."

"Of course! of course!" said Uncle John. "You could do nothing with him, poor fellow! He is better where he is—much better. Then his affairs?"—

"Why, they certainly are somewhat embarrassed," said Walter; "but if even they were not, such a misrepresentation would be, under the circumstances, venial. You are aware—as a man of sense and reflection, you must be aware—that it is very, very painful, to have the fact of a relative being confined as a lunatic generally known. The calamity is sufficiently afflicting of itself, but the torture would be far more exquisite if accompanied by the perpetual inquiries of anxious friends."

"Very true, very true," said Uncle John; "you would be placed in a position very similar to that of a man having multitudes of friends pouring in to console him for the loss of one whom he most dearly loved."

"Precisely," said Walter, who conceived that he had made a most palpable hit; and so he had, indeed, as far as Uncle John was concerned. "You therefore see," he continued, "and properly, I hope, appreciate, my motive in having attributed his absence to the existence of difficulties of a pecuniary character?"

"Oh! you acted very right. Under the circumstances, no doubt I should have done the same myself."

"You will believe that it was out of no disrespect to you that I hesitated to explain the real facts as they stood. I do assure you that I esteem most highly all who take a kind interest in my poor brother's welfare; but had I not known that he and you had been bosom friends so long, I really could not, in justice to my own feelings, have entered into this most afflicting explanation."

"Poor fellow!" said Uncle John, "who'd have thought it! I always fancied that he was *rather* eccentric, but I never for an instant supposed that he was not in reality sane. And yet he certainly would *sometimes* run on very strangely! I should like, although I should, at the the same time, be very sorry, to see him. I wonder whether he'd know me!"

"In a moment," said Walter. "That is, unfortunately, the worst of it. While none but strangers are near he is full of gaiety and happiness; but if he sees an old friend, he becomes so excited, and his subsequent depression is so dreadful, that it is absolutely dangerous to allow a friend to go near him."

"In that case then, certainly," said Uncle John, "I must subdue my anxiety to see him. I would not be the means of exciting him for the world; although, I must confess, that I should like to have had a word—if it were only a word—with him before I left town. However, under the circumstances, I shall return far more satisfied than I came—for even to know the worst is more tolerable than to be tortured with vague suspicions;—and I trust that before long I shall have the happiness to hear that he is perfectly recovered."

Uncle John now rose, with the view of taking his departure; and when Walter, having breathed an apparently fervent prayer for the recovery of his brother, had promised to advise him of the slightest favorable change, he and Valentine, with minds more at ease than when they entered, left, much to the satisfaction of Walter and his son.

"It's very dreadful: is it not?" said Uncle John, as he left the house.

"Do you believe it?" inquired Valentine.

"Why, my boy, I don't see how there can be *much* doubt about the business."

"I believe that they have placed him in a madhouse," said Valentine. "I do go so far as to believe that; but I'll no more believe that he is mad than I'll believe that you are mad."

"But if he's in a madhouse, he *must* be mad! They can't answer to put a man there unless he is; so that the fact of his being there is proof positive of his madness!—don't you see? The thing is as clear as the sun at noonday."

"Uncle," said Valentine, "you have not heard of the system upon which these private lunatic asylums are based; you have not heard that under that villanous system, men—perfectly sane men—can be seized, gagged, chained, and imprisoned for life, to promote the interests or to gratify the malignity of those to whom they are prompted by nature to look for affection; you have not heard that husbands can be incarcerated by wives, wives by husbands, brothers by sisters, sisters by brothers, sons by fathers, and fathers by sons; you have not heard—"

"Now, before you go any farther," said Uncle John, stopping in his usual manner; "have *you?*"

"I have," replied Valentine, "and firmly believe that such things are of constant occurrence."

"I tell you they can't answer to do it."

"To whom need they answer?"

"To the law!—to the law, sir," exclaimed Uncle John—"to the law!"

"What has the law to do with private lunatic asylums? They are virtually placed beyond the pale of the law. The private rules of each establishment absolutely form the constitution under which the inmates live; they are the only laws by which they are governed—the only laws to which they have the power to appeal."

"But their friends, my dear boy!—their friends!"

"How can their friends act in ignorance of the matter? A man is stolen from society—from his home: he is carried away secretly: none but those who have been instrumental, and are interested, perhaps pecuniarily, in his capture, are cognizant of the place of his concealment: how in such a case, then, can his friends appeal to the law, or act at all, not knowing where he is?"

"Clearly, if they don't know where he is, it's quite impossible for them to act; but do you mean to tell me that such monstrous iniquities are in reality practised?"

"Uncle," said Valentine, "I have conversed on this truly dreadful subject with many who have been, like you, incredulous, and they have all asked the self-same question, namely, *Are* these iniquities practised? My answer has been invariably—If I say *yes*, you'll turn away, disbelieve me, and think no more of it: let, therefore, the first question be this—*Can* these monstrous iniquities be practised?—and when you have clearly ascertained that they *can*, you have simply to look at the temptations which exist, and the facilities which are afforded, to feel perfectly sure that they *are*. Suppose I were a villain and wished to enjoy your property, what need I do to secure it?—write to the proprietor of one of these private bastiles, who would at once send doctors to sign the certificate of your insanity, and keepers to manacle and carry you off, without a soul besides knowing a single word about the matter. Suppose I were married and had an abandoned wife, who wished with impunity to enjoy the society of her paramour, what need she do to get rid of me for ever?—The same!—Nay, suppose any case in which the concealment of a man, or even a child is deemed necessary, either to the promotion of the interests, or to the gratification of the malignant spirit of any relative or friend, the same need but be done for the object to be secured! I therefore have not the smallest doubt that in this case those creatures whom we have this night seen, have sent our poor friend to one of these dreadful places, expressly in order to secure whatever property he may have, paying a certain sum weekly, or monthly, with the view of depriving him for ever of the power to reclaim it. This is my conviction—a conviction which every circumstance that has occurred since his absence now tends to confirm."

"You amaze me!" exclaimed Uncle John. "But if it *should* be the case, we'll have him out to-morrow. He shall not be there another day!—We'll have him out to-morrow."

"That, I fear," said Valentine, "is much easier said than accomplished. But we'll first ascertain where this Holdem's asylum is, and in the morning we'll go and see what can be done."

"So we will!—so we will! You're a fine fellow, Val! We will go in the morning, and if he be there!—Well, well: we shall see: we shall see: we shall know better then how to act: shall we not? Poor fellow! Bless my life!—what a world this is to live in! I am really so astonished that I feel quite confused!" And this indeed was a fact. Uncle John was confused! There were so many things entirely new to him pressing upon his mind, that he scarcely knew what he was about: in fact, he felt so bewildered, and so perfectly exhausted, that from eleven that night till eleven the next morning he was utterly lost to the cares of the world.

Valentine, however, rose early. His first object was to learn where the establishment of Dr. Holdem was situated, and having eventually succeeded in this, he returned just as Uncle John came down.

"Well, said Valentine, "I have ascertained where this place is."

"There's a good fellow!" said Uncle John. "Then we'll just have a little bit of breakfast and start off at once. We shall manage it, Val!—I feel sure that we shall do it!—But the existence of such a system as that which you explained to me last night is an absolute disgrace to the country. We'll not, however, say any more about that now: come!—let's make a breakfast."

They did so, and sent for a cab, and in less than an hour they were at the gates of Dr. Holdem's asylum.

"Well, this don't appear to be a very dreadful place," said Uncle John. "It looks quiet and comfortable enough: at all events it has a very fair outside."

Without replying to this observation, which was, however, quite natural under the circumstances, Valentine rang the bell, and in due time a person appeared at the gate.

"I wish to see Dr. Holdem," said Valentine.

"He is out," said the man, "but if it's on business, Mr. Jones, perhaps, will do just as well."

"*It is* on business: let me see Mr. Jones."

They now entered, and when the gate had been secured they were shown into a handsomely built private house, which formed the front of the asylum.

"You have," said Valentine, addressing Mr. Jones, who had immediately made his appearance. "You have a gentleman in your establishment named Goodman."

"How do you know that?" demanded Mr. Jones.

"We have it from good authority," replied Valentine, "and we are anxious to see him if it be but for a moment."

"Oh, is that all you want?"

"That is all," said Valentine.

"Well then, if that's all, of course you can't see him."

"But we are friends," said Uncle John. "I have known him for at least forty years."

"It don't matter if you've known him for at least forty thousand!—I tell you again you can't see him."

"But we only wish to speak one word."

"It can't be done, I tell you!—So that if that's all you want I just wish you a very good morning."

"My good friend," said Uncle John, in a soothing strain, "I have travelled between seventy and eighty miles in order to see him, and—"

"It don't matter a button," interrupted Mr. Jones, "if you have travelled between seventy and eighty millions of miles, it don't make a bit of difference."

"But surely there can be no serious objection to my having one word?"

"It isn't to be done! there, that's all about it!"

"Indeed, I think it very hard that I should not be permitted to see a friend whom—"

"Now the bottom of it is," said Mr. Jones, "that it isn't of any use talking. If you were to stop here till doomsday, and talk all the time, you wouldn't be a single bit nearer the mark."

"But consider, my good friend, what a dreadful thing it is to be thus precluded—"

"It's of no use, I tell you! By stopping here you're only wasting your own time and mine."

"Then I can't see him? Nothing will induce you to let me have a word with him?"

"Nothing! You may safely take your oath of it!"

"*Then*," said Uncle John, who now began to feel particularly indignant, "I see how it is. I see it all! I'll have recourse to other means!—to *other* means! Justice shall be had if it cost ten thousand pounds! —I'll *see* if the law is inoperative here."

"Oh! don't bother me with your law!" cried Jones, who was really impatient for them to go. "Do what you like!—*we* don't care what you do! What do we care?"

"We'll see, sir!—we'll see!" cried Uncle John, who, after looking at Mr. Jones with surpassing fierceness, took Valentine's arm and departed. "I'm satisfied now," he continued as he passed the outer gates; "I'm perfectly satisfied that the practice which you explained to me last night has in this case been put into operation."

"I wish," said Valentine, "that we could but have got inside. But I scarcely expected that we should. You see how impossible it is for the inmates of these dreadful places to hold communication with their friends. But what's to be done now? We have gained one point—that of knowing that he is in reality there."

"Let us go back at once to his brother," said Uncle John, "and tell him plainly our suspicions, and threaten him boldly with exposure, unless he immediately consents to release him."

"Stop," cried Valentine, looking back from the cab window. "Let us go a little out of the road;" and having given the necessary instructions to the driver, he continued, "that seems to be the garden of the asylum. I wish we had a ladder. We might perhaps see him from the top of the wall."

"So we might!" cried Uncle John.—"Stop the cab—so we might. But then you see a ladder is a thing we have not got! However, the wall is not very high, certainly. We'll get out and see what can be done."

They accordingly alighted, and having directed the cabman to wait, went round by the side of the wall. It was higher, much higher than it appeared from the road, but they notwithstanding walked to the back, where Valentine perceived a kind of shed built against it, which had been raised to within four or five feet of the top.

"The very thing," said Valentine. "If we can but get upon that shed, we shall be able to look into the garden." They therefore went round, with the view of ascertaining to whom the shed belonged; and having easily obtained the permission of the owner, Valentine instantly mounted.

He was at first very cautious, and taking off his hat, just peeped over the wall, lest, by being seen, his object should be frustrated. He saw a number of emaciated creatures crawling about; but he could not distinguish poor Goodman amongst them. Some looked idiotic, others seemed to have reached the very depths of despair; but as Valentine's object was not to contemplate the chief characteristics of the scene, every feeling was merged in his anxiety to distinguish his friend.

"Can you see him?" inquired Uncle John from below.

"No!" replied Valentine, "or if he be one of those whom I do see, he must indeed be dreadfully altered."

"Here, let me come up," said Uncle John, "I shall know him from a thousand."

"I'm afraid, sir, it wont bear *you*," observed the owner of the shed.

"Oh! I'm bulky, but not very weighty: I'll try it," returned Uncle John, who, by dint of great exertion, reached the roof.—He looked round: Goodman was *not* amongst them! "Bless my life! I wish they'd come this way," said he. "Val, can't we beckon to one of them? Now, there's a man!—he seems to be no more mad than I am; can't we attract his attention?"

"Keep your head down," cried Valentine; "he sees us—he's coming this way;" and as he spoke, the person alluded to, who happened to be no other than Whitely, approached.

"Do you know Mr. Goodman?" inquired Valentine,

"Alas, yes!" replied Whitely.

"Will you do me the favor to tell him cautiously that Valentine is here?"

"I've heard of you," said Whitely, at once bursting into tears. "But he cannot leave his bed; nor will he ever again, until he ceases to breathe."

"Indeed!" exclaimed Valentine. "What has been the cause?"

"Brutality, sir! absolute brutality! We some time since tried to escape, and succeeded to a certain extent, but were retaken; and, on being brought back, we were subjected to the most horrible cruelties you have the power to conceive. He happened to be the originator of the scheme, and on this becoming known, they inflicted upon him the greatest amount of torture."

"The wretches!" cried Valentine. "But is there no hope of his recovery?"

"None!" replied Whitely. "They have murdered him, sir—cruelly, brutally, murdered him. He is now on the very brink of death."

"What's that? what's that you say?" cried Uncle John, starting up and leaning completely over to the top of the wall.—"Murdered, say you?—murdered him?"

"Hush!" said Mr. Whitely, "for Heaven's sake, hush!" And he instantly walked from the spot; for at that moment Uncle John was seen by the whole of the patients, who raised a shout, and ran towards him with an expression of amazement the most intense.

"But one word!" said Uncle John, addressing Whitely. "But one single word!" Mr. Whitely, however, fearful of being seen by the keepers, did not turn his head. He had but just recovered from the dreadful effects of the treatment he had experienced on being recaptured; he therefore dared not again excite the vengeance of the keepers, well knowing that if another brutal attack were made upon him, it would be utterly impossible for him to survive it; and hence he walked away with a heavy bursting heart, without taking, however, the slightest apparent notice.

"Do *you* also know my friend Goodman?" demanded Uncle John of the poor insane creatures, who were by this time beneath him.

"Hooray!" they cried, dangling their hands and dancing about, and looking altogether as delighted as possible.

"Sir!" cried Uncle John, again shouting after Whitely, and putting one leg over the wall, in order to get as near to him as he could. "Sir! but one word!—*Is he mad?*"

The energy with which Uncle John put this question, and the anxiety which he manifested to receive a reply, were so excessive, that he at once lost his balance, and fell over the wall.

Valentine, who had seized the tail of his coat, and thus split it completely up the back, as he was falling, now saw two brutal looking fellows running fiercely towards the spot. He therefore instantly leaped from the wall to join his uncle, and to protect him, if possible, from the keepers, who appeared to be inspired with the spirit of vengeance.

CHAPTER XXXVIII.

A FORCIBLE EXPULSION, AND A TOTALLY UNEXPECTED ESCAPE.

As Uncle John, in falling, threw his arms round the neck of a poor idiot who, conceiving himself to be the king of the universe, had embellished his cap with a variety of young onions, he alighted without sustaining any very serious injury, although his weight drove his majesty, the monarch of the world, with great violence against a friend who was perfectly clear only upon the one grand point of his having been swindled out of his privileges as the Lord High Chancellor of England ever since a certain antediluvian era, the chief characteristics of which it appeared had been washed from his memory by the Flood.

Before, however, Uncle John could rise, one of the keepers had seized him by the collar, with the laudable view, as he promptly explained, of letting him know the difference; but Valentine, in an instant, sprang at the throat of the ruffian, and compelled him to relinquish his hold. "No violence!" he exclaimed, "It will not do with us."

"No, it won't do with us, sir!" echoed Uncle John, inspiring courage from Valentine, although it must be confessed, that he even then felt rather frightened than not. "There's the law against violence! the law, sir! the law!"

"What's the law to do with us? what right have you in here?" demanded the keeper.

"I overbalanced myself," said Uncle John, "I overbalanced myself. Do you think that I should have tumbled if I could have helped it?"

"But what business had you on the wall?"

"To look for Goodman!" cried Valentine. "Goodman, whom you are murdering!"

"Valentine! Valentine!" faintly exclaimed an emaciated form whom the noise had attracted to the window of his cell.

"It is Goodman!" cried Valentine.

"My friend! my dear friend!" cried Uncle John. "But one word!"

The form sank back, and was seen no more.

"My good man!" said Uncle John, addressing the keeper, "if you are a Christian, you will let me see my friend. Let me have but a word with *him!* and I'll give you all the money I've got."

"What! corruption!" exclaimed the immaculate keeper, alternately looking most virtuously indignant and wistfully glancing at the well-filled purse which Uncle John very promptly held forth. "Do yer want to corrupt me?"

"Let me speak to him but for an instant!"

"Come along!" cried the keeper, "we'll werry soon see what you're made on."

"Now then!" shouted Valentine, making his voice apparently proceed from the other side of the wall. "Let's attack them at once! Now, down with the ruffians!"

"Hal-lo!" cried the principal keeper, looking round with an expression of amazement. "What, more on yer!" he continued; and as at that moment the person to whom the shed belonged peeped over the wall to see how things were going on, he raised an alarm which in an instant brought four additional keepers to the spot.

"Look out! We're attacked! There's a mob on 'em coming!" cried the fellow, as his scowling companions approached.

"Where are they?" demanded a ruffian, who looked as if he had that day returned from transportation.

"Over the wall!" was the reply, and a ladder was procured, while Valentine still in a feigned voice, kept shouting.

"Let's see how many on 'em there is!" cried the creature who looked so much like a returned convict; and he ascended the ladder and looked anxiously round, but the only man whom he could see was the owner of the shed, whose person was perfectly well known.

"Have you seen a mob o' pipple any wheres about here?" he inquired of this person.

"No," was the reply, "there's been nothing of the sort."

"There's none here!" said he who occupied the ladder, looking round.

"I know better!" cried the principal keeper; "I heard 'em!"

"I tell yer there ain't then! can't yer believe me?"

"Well, come let's secure these ere too as we've got!" and while the principal keeper and two of his companions seized Valentine roughly, the other three fastened, like tigers, upon Uncle John.

"Keep off!" cried Valentine, "We'll go where you please, and before whom you please, but we will *not* be dragged!"

In an instant one of the ruffians seized him by the legs, while two others secured his arms and lifted him bodily upon their shoulders, and as Uncle John was favored with a precisely similar lift, they were carried struggling desperately but ineffectually across the garden, while the sovereign of the universe, and those idiotic subjects whom he termed continually, and with all the characteristic regularity of nature, "my people," were dancing and shouting, and performing the most extraordinary antics, apparently with the view of rendering it obvious to all that they were absolutely filled with delight.

The keepers now reached the house with their burden, and as Holdem the proprietor of the Asylum, had just returned from town, they threw Uncle John and Valentine before him.

"Hollo, hollo, hollo! What's all this?" cried Dr. Holdem, whose grateful impression at the moment was, that he had been blessed with two additional patients. "Won't they be quiet? What's the meaning of it, eh?"

"Why these two owdayshus indiwiduals," replied the chief keeper, "is the leaders of a whole mob o' rabble as is come here to let out the patients."

"What!" exclaimed the doctor with an expression of unlimited astonishment. "And how did they get in?"

"Why they shied 'emselves over the wall: the big un come fust, and the tother un follered."

"And what have you to say to this monstrous proceeding?" cried the doctor with a highly appropriate scowl. "Pray what is your object?"

"This:" said Valentine; "you have in confinement a friend of ours whom you have cruelly ill used."

"How dare you talk to me in that fashion?" interrupted the doctor.

"Dare!" said Valentine; "you shall find that we dare do more than talk. Our object was to see that friend whose name is Goodman, and who has been wickedly incarcerated here as an insane man. We applied for permission to see him, and as that was refused us, we mounted the wall."

"I admire your impudence! But are you aware that in trespassing thus upon my premises, you have rendered yourselves liable to be punished most severely?"

"But that was an accident!" cried Uncle John, "I overbalanced myself, and fell into the garden by accident."

"Indeed!" said the doctor sarcastically. "Indeed! And did *you* overbalance yourself, and slip down by accident?"

"No," replied Valentine, "I did not. But we are quite prepared to answer for what we have done before a magistrate at once, or in any other way, for I presume the thing will not be allowed to drop here."

"I have a great mind to give you into custody, and have you both dragged off like felons."

"Do so," said Valentine, "that we may have an opportunity at once of explaining publicly all the circumstances connected with our present position. Let us be taken without delay before a magistrate. It cannot but tend to promote the object we have in view."

"Upon my word, young man, you treat the matter very cooly. But pray how many did you bring with you?"

"None," replied Valentine.

"Oh!" exclaimed the pure and incorruptible keeper, apparently shocked at what he believed to be a falsehood. "What! none? when I heered a whole mob on 'em a-hollerin? *Oh!*"

"We came alone," said Uncle John. "There was no mob with us."

"Well!" said Valentine, "are we to be given into custody, or how do you mean to act?"

"As I please!" replied the doctor. "I shall act as I please. If I thought you were worth powder and shot I should pursue a very different course, but as it is, I shall, simply have you bundled out of the place, believing you to be a couple of characterless vagabonds."

"Vagabonds! characterless vagabonds!" exclaimed Uncle John, whose indignation had gained the ascendancy over his fears. "What do you mean, sir? Here is my card!" But before he had time to produce it, the six keepers seized him and Valentine as before, and having carried them to the entrance, threw them completely into the road.

The moment Valentine recovered himself, he flew at the chief myrmidon and certainly did administer unto him one blow which made him wink and shake his head, and screw up his features, until they portrayed great intellectual confusion. As, however, Uncle John on the one hand dragged Valentine away, and the doctor on the other ordered his men in at once, the gates were closed before the intellects of the fellow were perfectly restored, or doubtless Valentine would have felt the full force of his vengeance.

"Thank Heaven, we are out!" exclaimed Uncle John, when he saw the gates closed. "I really at one time began to feel alarmed."

"Alarmed at what?" inquired Valentine.

"Why, suppose they had kept us in there with the rest?"

"Surely you did not suppose they would do that?"

"Why, my boy, I didn't know what to think. But if they *had* kept us in, it would have been dreadful, seeing that not a single friend would have known that we were there."

"You now see precisely the position in which the victims of this horrible system are placed. Their friends are not suffered to know that they are there! But we were quite safe, for none are kept but those who are paid for. No, all that I was afraid of was, that they would have taken it into their heads to half murder us, for those fellows are very powerful, and we should have been able to do nothing with the six. As for taking us before a magistrate, I felt sure that they would not do that. Their object is secrecy; it would never do for *them* to make a stir."

"Well, well, we ought to be thankful that things are no worse. But poor Goodman! My heart bleeds for him! The vile wretches! But we'll have him out, my boy! We'll never rest till we have him out."

"I fear that it is now too late," said Valentine. "My impression is that on seeing us he sank to rise no more."

"I hope not, my boy," said Uncle John, "I hope not," and as he felt for his handkerchief to wipe the tears from his eyes, he became cognizant of the fact of his coat being split from the waist to the collar. "Why, my boy! why what on earth!—why what's this?" said he, turning round and pulling the tails of the coat before him. "What is it?"

"Why it looks something like a small slit," replied Valentine. "It is by no means bad cloth: if it had been, it certainly would not have had two tails now. It was done when you fell from the wall."

"Well, well," said Uncle John. "Well, never mind that. I don't care a straw about that." And as he spoke they came within sight of the cab which they had ordered to wait their return.

The driver was standing with the door in his hand, and seemed somewhat confused when they appeared, for he hastily closed the door, mounted his box and drove towards them.

"We have kept you a long time," said Uncle John.

"No sconsequence at all, sir; I knowed you was genelmen," replied the man, who looked anxiously inside the cab before he opened the door to allow them to enter. "Beg pardon, sir," he added, as Uncle John was stepping in; "but de yer know, sir, as yer coat's a leetle damaged in the back, sir?"

"Oh yes," said Uncle John, good humoredly. "I met with an accident."

"Beg pardon; I didn't know as you was awares on it, that's all," rejoined the man, who then mounted his box, and made his horse understand that he had not only a whip, but the power to use it.

"We'll go and see that wretch of a brother to night," said Uncle John, after a pause, during which he and Valentine had been completely lost in thought. "That's the first step, my boy: that's the first step: we'll work him!"

"My friend!" said a voice which appeared to proceed from under the seat of the cab.

"Valentine! Valentine!" cried Uncle John, starting up as if some dog had bitten his calf. "My dear boy! you should not! you really should not, particularly at such a time as this!"

"Upon my honor," said Valentine, "it was not I that spoke."

"Not you!" said Uncle John. "Bless my life, it was some one!"

"My friend!" repeated the voice, and Uncle John again started, for at the moment, he felt something touch his legs. Valentine therefore examined the cab, and found crouched beneath the seat poor Whitely.

"Do not be alarmed, my good friends," said he, "it is only the poor creature whom you spoke to in the garden."

"I'm right glad to see you, sir," cried Uncle John; "but come out of that hole, you'll be smothered! There's plenty of room."

"I thank you," said Whitely, "but I am much safer here. They may suddenly pass by and see me."

"Well, sit between our legs," said Uncle John, "and then I'll defy them to see you. You'll be cramped to death there."

"No, indeed I'm very comfortable," said Whitely, although there was scarcely sufficient room for a dog. He was, however, at length prevailed upon, although with great reluctance, to sit at the bottom of the cab.

"And how did you manage to escape?" inquired Valentine.

"I owe it all to you," said Whitely, grasping his hand. "Our poor friend had told me of your power as a Ventriloquist, and therefore when I heard what appeared to be voices in the distance, I felt quite sure that it was you. You will remember that a ladder was brought into the garden immediately after the shouting was heard. It was by that I escaped. The man who ascended it to look over the wall, instead of taking it away with him, simply threw it down to assist his fellows in carrying you into the house, when, taking advantage of the confusion that prevailed, I raised the ladder, and having reached the top of the wall unperceived, drew it over to the other side, and thus alighted in safety. I had not proceeded far before I saw this vehicle, and having ascertained that it was waiting for two gentlemen, I begged of the man to allow me to lie concealed beneath the seat, in order that if it had happened that the cab was not waiting for you, I might still have been safe; but when I heard you mention our friend's wretched brother, and thus knew you were alone, I ventured to speak, feeling perfectly sure that you would not only not betray me, but pardon my intrusion."

"My dear sir!" cried Uncle John, extending his hand, "I'm glad to see you. I only wish that I had found my poor friend here as well. But we'll have him out! we'll have him out before ——"

"*Hush!*" cried Whitely, trembling with great violence, and crouching again beneath the seat. "I hear them coming! they are behind us! For God's sake, don't suffer them to seize me again."

At this moment the sound of horses' hoofs were heard in the distance; and Valentine on looking back perceived two persons on horseback tearing along the road at full gallop. "Don't be alarmed," said he, "dont be alarmed, let what may occur, you are safe." But poor Whitely trembled from head to foot, while the perspiration poured down the face of Uncle John, who was scarcely less frightened then Whitely himself.

The horsemen now gained upon them fast, and their excitement increased in proportion. "These men may be after our poor friend," said Valentine, addressing the cabman; "if it be necessary you will stick to us?"

"And no mistake," replied the man, "I dont stop for nobody. Keep him snug. They shouldn't ketch us at all, ony the wust on it is, I carn't git this ere hold oss along. Phit!—keame up!" he added, as he pulled out of the road. "*Here* they come! fit for to break their blessed necks, good luck to em!"

They were now just behind, and Uncle John perspired more freely. They passed! Two butchers were testing the speed of their horses to decide a bet of some given quantity of beer.

"Thank Heaven!" exclaimed Uncle John, much relieved. "All right, my friend; come forth, all safe."

Mr. Whitely, however, remained where he was; he neither moved nor uttered a word.

"There is no danger now," said Valentine, endeavoring to rouse him. He still, however, continued to be motionless, and silent.

"*Come*, come, my friend!" said Uncle John, who thought it strange.

"Are you not well, my friend? are you not well?"

As Whitely made no answer, Valentine gently drew him forth. He was inanimate!

"Good God!" cried Uncle John, "the man has been frightened to death."

"No, he's not dead," said Valentine; "I feel sure that he's not dead. He has fainted—only fainted. Pull up at the first house you come to," he continued, addressing the cabman.

"All right, sir! there's one close at hand." And in less than three minutes they were before it.

Valentine now darted into the house, and having procured a glass of water, applied it to the temples and palms of poor Whitely; but without any sensible effect. No pulse was perceptible; not a muscle moved; some brandy was brought, and when that had been zealously applied for some time, he inspired as Valentine exclaimed, "He's alive!"

Uncle John now began to breathe with somewhat more freedom. He had been dreadfully apprehensive of Whitely being dead; but when he saw the first symptom of reanimation quickly followed by other signs of returning consciousness, he felt for the moment quite happy.

"My friends!" said Whitely at length, looking up. "Am I still safe? God bless you, my dear friends—God bless you!"

"Will you go with us into the house, till you revive?" inquired Valentine.

"No, my good friends, no; let me remain here, I shall not be out of danger, until I reach town. Pray, proceed, I am quite well now; I am indeed quite—*quite* well now!"

Uncle John and Valentine accordingly readjusted themselves, and having given instructions to the cabman—who drove off as fast as his horse *could* go—they stopped no more, till they reached the house of the Widow Smugman.

The widow was utterly but very naturally astonished, when on answering the knock she saw uncle John and Valentine assisting a poor enfeebled creature, who looked like death in a dressing-gown, out of the cab. She had, however, an extremely high opinion of those gentlemen; and, hence, when Uncle John introduced Whitely as his friend, she expressed herself happy to see him.

"Now then," said Valentine, placing Whitely upon the sofa, "you must banish all your fears; you are quite secure now."

Whitely, however, was unable to rally. He tried with all the power at his command; but sank back in a state of exhaustion, in which Uncle John attended him, while Valentine was rewarding the driver of the cab with a liberality altogether unexpected.

The dinner was now immediately served up, but of this poor Whitely was unable to partake; he was, however, after a time prevailed upon to have some slight refreshment, and was then placed in Uncle John's bed, completely overwhelmed with gratitude.

The attention of Uncle John and Valentine was now turned to the course which they, under the circumstances, ought to pursue. The escape of Whitely was held to be a grand point gained. "We can take him with us," said Valentine, "and convict poor Goodman's unnatural brother at once."

"So we can," said Uncle John; "that's quite right. So we can; and we will! but it can't be done to-night."

"No; but I think that I had better go to-night, and make an appointment, if possible, for to-morrow. Whitely is uninjured; he has only been alarmed, and will therefore be himself again doubtless in the morning. What do you think? Shall I go?"

"By all means, by all means. Tell him I wish to have five minutes' conversation with him before I leave town, which is the fact, you know, of course! I *do* wish to converse with him before I leave town. But I'll leave it to you, my boy; you know how to manage it. Go; go at once. I'll remain at home, and see after our friend. We must have him restored by to-morrow."

Valentine accordingly started, leaving Whitely in the care of Uncle John, who threw himself at once upon the sofa, and went soundly to sleep.

CHAPTER XXXIX.

VALENTINE BECOMES INITIATED INTO THE MYSTERIES OF THE ANTI-LEGAL-MARRIAGE ASSOCIATION.

On reaching Walter's residence, Valentine was informed that he and Horace were out, but were certain to be at home at nine o'clock or half-past at the very latest. It was then but just seven; and as Valentine conceived it to be scarcely worth while to return to Uncle John, he walked leisurely on, without having any object in view, save that of strolling about for two hours.

He had not however proceeded far, when his attention was attracted by a flaming placard, on which was inscribed

THE UNIVERSAL ANTI-LEGAL-MARRIAGE ASSOCIATION!

NOTICE!

A Professor of surpassing eminence will deliver a Lecture on the Natural, Social, and Universal Community Principle this evening, precisely at seven.

"The natural, social, and universal community principle!" thought Valentine. "What do they mean? The universal anti-legal-marriage association! Anti-legal-marriage association! I must look in here." And having paid the admission-fee, he was shown into a room in which a number of persons, of whom the majority were gaily attired females, had assembled.

The professor had not arrived, and therefore Valentine had time to look round before the lecture commenced. He thought it strange,—very strange,—that the persons whom he saw there should patronise or in any way countenance such a thing as an anti-legal-marriage association. What the natural, social, and universal community principle might be, it is true he could not very clearly comprehend; but what was meant by the term, "Anti-legal-marriage," was so plain, that it could not be misunderstood. And yet, was he to infer from the presence of those persons that they were opposed to the institution of marriage? Impossible! They appeared to him to be the very persons by whom marriage would be held to be one of the greatest sublunary blessings. He changed his position, in order to command a full view of the countenance of each. The females, he thought, looked particularly wicked! He really never saw eyes rolling about with such extraordinary restlessness before. Such smiling, such leering, such glancing he beheld! He was perfectly puzzled. He could not understand it! And yet they seemed to understand each other very well! Had any thing like a mutual dead set been made; had one pair of eyes been brought to bear upon another, with the view of being employed with reciprocal firmness—the object would not have been quite so inconceivable; but as it was, as they wandered about with such peculiar inconstancy, as if the design of their owners had been to inspire the souls of all at whom they glanced with affection, Valentine could not tell really what to make of it, although he did think it just possible, that they had assembled for the purpose of quizzing the professor.

The bare possibility of this being their object was, however, repudiated on the entrance of that gentleman, for he was cheered, loudly cheered, and with an enthusiasm which forbade the idea of its being ironical. No, it was plain that they were perfectly sincere, and therefore Valentine became more than ever impatient for an explanation of this natural, social and universal principle, of which it was clear they were deeply enamored.

"My friends," said the professor, after proving to the apparent satisfaction of the ladies that he knew as well how to use his eyes as the best. "My friends! The last lecture I had the pleasure to deliver to the members of this peculiarly wide-spreading association, had reference to the assumed Free Agency of Man, and as I proved to demonstration that man is not a free agent, consequently not a responsible agent, and therefore no agent at all, I propose now to show that human laws in opposition to the laws of nature ought not to be upheld. [*Loud cheers.*] My friends! It is on all hands admitted that nature is perfection, yet the state of society in which we now live is essentially and purely artificial! What is the inference? Why that, being essentially and purely artificial, it is essentially and purely the most imperfect state of society that ever obtained. To be perfect we must be natural. That I hold to be as clear as the proposition of the great Huxley in his *Wonderful Heart or the Liver of Love*, that to be natural, man must be perfect. It hence follows that the nearer we approach to nature, the nearer we are to perfection, and that that state of society is, in reality, the most perfect which is, in reality, the most natural. [*Applause.*] Now look at our present social system! Is there anything natural about it? Have our natural feelings and passions fair-play? Is not their development checked at every point by human laws diametrically opposed to the laws of nature? Look for example at those unnatural laws to which I have so frequently directed attention—I mean the laws relating to marriage! What is marriage? Is it not a most unnatural bond? See with what consummate tightness individuals are tied! It is indeed a Gordian knot: there's no end to it!—nor can they cut it. My friends! just look at its operation for one moment: a man marries—not naturally, but legally marries—well! in a month he becomes tired of his wife, yet is he by law compelled to keep her! She may not at all suit him: they may quarrel perpetually, nay, they may fight!—Still keep her he must till she sinks into the grave! Why, is not this monstrous? But even this is not all. He may see some one whom he likes infinitely better—some one more interesting, amiable, and accomplished, yet he cannot marry *her*, because, and solely because, he is married to another! Surely such an unnatural state of things ought no longer to exist! What, I ask, does a man commonly marry a woman for? The law, it is true, says 'for better for worse.' [*Loud laughter.*] But is it because she is handsome? Well, her beauty fades: she no longer possesses that for which he married her; still must he keep her! Does he marry her because he believes her to be engaging, and sweet tempered? A month after marriage she begins to let out in a style of which he cannot approve, by *any* means—yet must he stick to her still! Is it for her wealth that he marries her? Well; he obtains full possession of that wealth, which he may either spend or lose, but in any case is he compelled to keep *her* even after that for which alone he married her is gone! Why, my friends, this appears to be so truly diabolical, that the only wonder is that a system so repugnant to the perfect laws of nature should not have been blown up centuries ago. But let us take the case of a woman—for women I contend have natural rights as well as men. She marries; and why? Because she believes that the man whom she marries will be kind? Well, she finds that he is not: still must she be his! Does she marry because she believes that she shall be happy? She finds that she is not, but she must be his still! Sickness may overtake him; he may become poor; he may have no other prospect than of starvation! yet let what may happen to him she must stick! Is this just? Is it rational? Does it bear even the semblance of any principle by which men of intelligence should be guided? My friends! legal marriages have cursed every country into which they have been introduced. They are the bane of society. They utterly spoil both women and men. Women would indeed be very different beings were it not for the institution of marriage. It destroys their amiability, poisons their sweetness, and renders them insolent, cross-grained and vicious. When legally married, they know that they are secure, and that very knowledge prompts them at once to show off: whereas, were they as they ought to be, naturally married, the absence of that security would induce them to preserve all their natural sweetness of disposition, all their amiability, in short, all which renders their society charming. Nor would men, were it not for legal marriages, be so tyrannous, haughty, and overbearing. The security which those legal marriages impart, has a precisely corresponding effect upon them. Hence, I say, let none but natural marriages be sanctioned. [*Loud cheers.*] If persons be unable to live happily together, let them part and marry, as nature prescribes, those with whom they are able to live happily. Why should we, as intelligent beings, adhere to social wretchedness when we have the purest social felicity within our reach? We should tolerate natural marriages only!"—

At this interesting point the enthusiastic professor was interrupted by Valentine, who conceiving that he had gone far enough, cried—making his voice apparently proceed from an individual who was deeply engaged with a lady from whom he had just received a card—"And pray what are natural marriages?"

"Natural marriages!" exclaimed the professor with a look of astonishment the most absolute, "What are they?"

"Turn him out! Turn him out!" shouted several gentleman, by whom the natural, social and universal community principle was upheld.

"What are natural marriages?" repeated the professor.

"Aye!" said Valentine, assuming the same voice, "I simply ask you what they are! Do you mean those peculiar broom-stick solemnities?"

"Broom-stick solemnities!" exclaimed the professor with an expression of contempt the most supreme, and again the universal community-principle-mongers expressed their strong disapprobation.

"Well, tell us," said Valentine when the noise had subsided, "what it is you really mean?"

"By natural marriages," said the professor, addressing the person from whom he imagined the voice had proceeded. "By natural marriages I mean those which are in conformity with the law of nature!—marriages by which parties are solemnly bound to live with each other as long as they like."

Loud applause followed this clear explanation. The ladies waved their handkerchiefs and screamed with delight; but as during their enthusiasm, Valentine perceived that the majority of them wore that golden shackle by which they appropriately conceived they had been enslaved, he at once became perfectly disgusted. He now distinctly saw what the social community principle meant!—he saw that it struck at the very root of social virtue and fidelity.

"Is that gentleman satisfied?" inquired the professor.

"Perfectly," said Valentine, "perfectly satisfied that immorality forms the basis of the principle in question."

"Immorality!" exclaimed the professor, who really appeared to be utterly shocked. "Immorality! That principle forms the basis of the new moral world! It is the present corrupt system of legal marriages that is based upon immorality. With natural marriages immorality has nothing to do, seeing that that which is natural cannot be immoral. Is it natural, I would ask, for two persons whose dispositions and feelings and passions are inimical to be bound to each other for life? Is it not, on the contrary, natural for them to part with the view of forming alliances more to their taste? I contend that it is monstrous to bind two rational beings together when their sentiments and views are diametrically opposed. Disagreements should prompt them to separate at once and form other unions in the pure course of nature."

"How often?" inquired Valentine.

"How often! As often as they conceive that their happiness will be thereby enhanced. Why should a man be bound to a woman whom he once might have loved when circumstances have led him to love another better? Why should a woman be tied to a man for whom she might once have had an affection, when her natural passions prompt her to repudiate him, and turn to one upon whom she has set her soft heart? I say that the law which prohibits this indulgence in those passions which are implanted in us by nature is an infamous law, and one of which the existence reflects indelible disgrace upon us as rational and intelligent creatures."

At this point the professor was again enthusiastically cheered, and so perfectly were his sentiments in unison with the views of his amiable satellites, that when Valentine inquired if they really expected that their principles would be adopted by any but the most vicious and depraved, their indignation knew no bounds.

He had certainly heard yelling before—yelling too of a really extraordinary character—in sundry places and on divers occasions; but never—not even in the House of Commons!—had he heard any species of yelling at all comparable with that which proceeded from the members of the anti-legal-marriage association. They were not very numerous it is true, but being extremely energetic they fully made up for the absence of any numerical strength, and as the room in which they were, was comparatively small, their shouts, groans and shrieks were absolutely stunning.

"Who is he? Where is he? Drag him forth!" they exclaimed. The ladies were especially anxious to see him.

"That's the man in the corner!" cried the professor, promptly pointing to the individual to whom the lady had given her card, and the association doubtless would have pulled him to pieces had he not had the presence of mind to declare his perfect innocence; for nothing but the tones of his voice would have convinced them that the professor had made a mistake.

"Wretches!" cried Valentine, throwing his voice immediately behind the professor, who turned with all the velocity of which he was capable, and really appeared to be somewhat alarmed.

"Who's that?" cried the professor. "Who was that?"

None could tell. He looked firmly and with an eye of suspicion at every member, in his immediate vicinity, but no!—they were equally amazed with himself. "Who was it?" he repeated. "Who was it, I ask?"

"One," replied Valentine, in a tone of great solemnity, making his voice appear to proceed from the ceiling. "One who sees that you are faithless, abandoned and profligate—one by whom vice is abhorred."

In an instant every eye was directed towards the ceiling. The gentlemen became very nervous, while the ladies felt dreadfully alarmed, which was not at all wonderful, seeing that superstition and immorality invariably go hand in hand. It was held to be very mysterious! They could not make it out! They were filled with apprehension, and as the ladies clung to their natural protectors, the gentlemen started, and shrank from their touch, so cowardly a slave does vice make the human heart.

The professor, who looked quite as pale as the rest, however, felt himself bound to say something. He therefore rose with the view of addressing his satellites, when Valentine cried, "Down! I denounce you as a villain. But for you and wretches like you, hundreds who are now depraved, would have been reaping those blessings of which virtue is the germ."

The professor seemed utterly paralysed: and his satellites stared with open mouths round the room with an expression of terror.

"Let us go," said one of the females, addressing her friend—"pray, pray let us go, I'm very frightened!"

"Go!" cried Valentine. "Repudiate these proceedings, if you be not quite lost to every sense of female delicacy and virtue. Be not blinded by sophistry: spurn those who, to gratify their own bad passions, would place you on a level with the beasts of the field. Be virtuous and happy in the perfect assurance, that from virtue *alone* real happiness can spring."

The females now tremblingly rushed to the door; and so exceedingly terrified were they, that scarcely one minute had elapsed before they had vanished from the room.—The professor was utterly astounded, and stared at his male disciples, who in return stared at him. Had any man come forward to deliver that address, which had just been delivered by Valentine, he would have contested every point with warmth, eloquence and firmness; but as his opponent was apparently invisible, he could not say a word. He seemed perfectly lost, and so indeed did they all, and as Valentine, who in straining to give effect to his speech, had become very warm, he left them at once in a state of great amazement to solve that which they manifestly felt to be a mystery of no inconsiderable depth.

CHAPTER XL.

UNCLE JOHN HAS ANOTHER IMPORTANT INTERVIEW WITH WALTER, TO WHOM HE DECLARES HIS INTENTIONS WITH FORCE AND EFFECT.

WITH those feelings of satisfaction which commonly spring from the consciousness of having promoted the cause of virtue, Valentine returned to the residence of Walter, and found him and Horace at home.

"Well, my young rattlesnake!" cried Horace, as he entered, "and how do they bring it in now? Come to an anchor! Is there anything extra o'clock? How's the ancient?"

Uncle John was the gentleman to whom he alluded, and Valentine said that he was perfectly well; but was struck with the extremely wretched aspect of Walter. He was the very type of misery. His cheeks were hollow, and his lips were parched, while his eyes swam dimly in their sockets by which they were almost entirely concealed.

"You are not so well this evening?" said Valentine.

"I am not, indeed," said Walter faintly; "I am not, indeed."

"No, the governor, don't look particularly spicy!" cried Horace. "But then, you see it's all his own fault! he won't be ruled! If I've told him once, I have told him five hundred times, that he'll never be well till he gets beastly drunk. I am sure of it!—nothing can alter my opinion upon the point. If he were but to get into a profoundly elaborate state of mops and brooms, he'd be as right as a Roman. But then he won't do it! You may as well talk to a turnip."

"I wish I was dead!" exclaimed Walter.

"Of course! that's a species of donkeyfication you never will get over, if you live a thousand years. You wish you were dead! And what would you do, if you were dead?"

Walter sighed.

"Are you engaged to-morrow evening?" inquired Valentine, taking advantage of a temporary pause.

"Not that I am aware of at this moment," replied Walter.

"My Uncle," said Valentine, "is anxious to have five or ten minutes' conversation with you, before he leaves town."

"What," cried Horace, "is he going to cut it?"

"If you will say," continued Valentine, "at what hour it will be convenient for you to see him, he will be here; he'll not occupy much of your time."

"Will eight o'clock suit him? If not, say nine."

"Eight will suit him well. He will be here at that hour."

"But, I say," cried Horace, "are *you* going to toddle back with him?"

"I am not sure of that; but at all events I shall see you again before I leave. Good evening."

"Well, remember me, you know, to the old tar," said Horace. "He's perhaps about the rummest and roughest old reed that ever *did* come to town. But I don't dislike him. Good night!"

Valentine now left the house, and he was no sooner gone, than Horace put it to his father very pointedly, whether he did not consider himself an idiot. "What did you want to sigh away for," said he, "like an old distressed alligator, right before *him?* And why couldn't you let that old Rufus trot off, without having him boring here again? You know that you have got just as much nerve as nothing!"

"I was anxious to make him think that I was not afraid to see him," replied Walter, "and thus to allay any suspicion that may have been excited."

"Well, but you know that you are not at all fit to be seen. Besides, there is more in the wind than you expect. I know, by that fellow's manner, there's something o'clock. I shouldn't be a bit surprised to hear that he has found it all out."

"How could he?"

"Why you told him all about the place yourself! How do you know that he has not been there?"

"And if he has, is it likely that *they* would give him any information?"

"Well, if you'll take my advice—but you never will, you know, and hence it is that you're invariably wrong—but if you wish to be secure you'll remove him to some other crib, and then no one will know a bit about it."

"But how can that be done?"

"Why, don't you see? Old Neversweat—what's his name? Holdem, has connection with another den a hundred miles off. Well, can't you make arrangements with him to send the old boy there in another name!"

"But, why in another name?"

"Because then they may search all the books in the universe without ascertaining where he is. They may go to Dr. Holdem's—'Is Mr. Goodman here?' 'No, he has left!' 'Where is he?' 'Can't say.' They may apply to the commissioners, and get a sight of the register. They look for the name of Goodman. Goodman *was* at Dr. Holdem's. Discharged such a date. Don't you see? Suppose he is entered as Jonathan Scroggins? Who is Jonathan Scroggins? They may see the name of Scroggins. They know no such a man. He may call himself Goodman down there, it is true; but then they'll call him Scroggins, and if he insists upon it that Goodman is his name, they will rationally conclude that he is laboring under some strong delusion, and hold it to be an invincible proof of his being incurably mad. To be secure, therefore, all you have to do is to send him away under some assumed name, when, if they ever find him out you may safely forgive them, discovery in such a case being an utterly impossible thing."

"There is something in that, certainly," said Walter. "There certainly is something in that. But had we not better, in the first place, see what their object is in coming here to-morrow?"

"Why, as far as that goes, there is no earthly use in doing that which is useless: that's as clear as cream; and his removal will be useless, in the event of their having no doubt about its being all right; but if they have the least suspicion of anything wrong, take my advice, and pack him off at once."

Walter saw in a moment the force of this suggestion, and as security was his object, it was eventually decided, that if anything should transpire to convince him that the secret had in reality become known, Goodman should be removed in the name of Scroggins to some distant asylum, and thus placed for ever beyond the reach of his friends.

By the time these two amiable persons had arrived at this decision, Valentine had reached home, where he found Uncle John still asleep on the sofa, playing loudly upon his nasal organ, that notorious tune of which Morpheus alone can be really enamored.

By dint of great exertion on the part of Valentine, Uncle John awoke, and when he did awake, he said with great presence of mind, "Ah—yes—well;" and yawned, and then added, "What, not off yet? Come, come, you had better start. I'll see after Whitely: I'll take care of him."

"Will you do me the favor to look at your watch?" said Valentine.

Uncle John did him this favor, and then observed, that the thing had stopped ever since eleven that morning.

"You are really a very watchful attendant," said Valentine. "Why, you have been asleep nearly five hours."

"Nonsense," cried Uncle John, "Nonsense! I hav'n't had half-a-dozen winks."

"It was half-past six when I left, and it's now past eleven."

"Tut! bless my life and soul! Why, I couldn't have believed it. Have I been asleep all that time? Dear me, how very neglectful!—Our poor old friend!—Let's go and see how he gets on."

They accordingly went into the bed-room softly, and as, much to their satisfaction, they found Whitely asleep, they returned with equal caution to the room they had just left, when Valentine dwelt upon his interview with Walter.

"He is now extremely ill," said he, after an explanation of all that had occurred. "My firm impression is, that he is on the very brink of the grave. If, therefore, Whitely cannot go with us to-morrow, it will be better for me and Horace to leave the room, while you explain what you know, and how you mean to proceed, if poor Goodman be not immediately released."

"I see—exactly," said Uncle John, "I see precisely what you mean. It will be better—much better." And Uncle John was engaged in rehearsing his part from that time till he retired to bed.

In the morning, Whitely found that his nerves had gained considerable strength: his fears were calmed, and he paced the room firmly. He felt that he was free; and that feeling, however limited may be the space in which he dwells, will prompt a man to be content to remain within it, where the knowledge of his being confined even to *Europe*, would generate within him a wish to go beyond. As however he did not feel equal to the task of meeting Walter, and as moreover his presence on that occasion was not absolutely necessary, Uncle John and Valentine left him, and at the hour appointed found Walter and his son deeply engaged with a pile of dusty documents as before.

When a variety of common-place observations had passed between them, Valentine engaged the attention of Horace, while Uncle John intimated to Walter that he wished to say a few words in private.

"Horace," said Walter, "entertain your young friend. We wish to be by ourselves a short time."

Horace looked at his father with unspeakable significance. He clearly did not think it safe. However, feeling that he could not with any show of politeness remain in the room after that, he rose, and taking the arm of Valentine, said, "Come;

let us leave these old incomprehensibles together."

"Mr. Goodman," said Uncle John, when he found that they were alone, "my object in coming here this evening is to speak upon a subject which concerns you deeply. It has reference, sir, to your brother, whom yesterday I saw!—I perceive," he continued as Walter started and trembled, "I perceive that you did not expect to hear that; but I saw him, sir, yesterday at the asylum you named, and there discovered him to be, sir—*not mad!*—but an enfeebled, emaciated martyr to that foul, that iniquitous system, the existence of which is a national disgrace."

"Not mad!" said Walter hurriedly. "Not mad! I have proofs!" And having opened his desk, he drew forth a printed paper which he placed with an air of triumph before Uncle John. "There, there, sir," he continued, "there you have the certificate of two eminent physicians, Drs. Bowlemout and Dobb. *That* will be perfectly satisfactory, I presume?"

"Not at all," said Uncle John, "Not at all. I am happily not ignorant of the mode in which these things are managed, although I could not till recently have conceived it to be possible that men *could* in a country like ours resort to practices so monstrous."

"Do you mean, sir," said Walter, "to insinuate that *I* have had recourse to monstrous-practices?"

"Mr. Goodman! I have no inclination to have any angry words; but I am not a man to mince a matter of this kind. Your brother is incarcerated in a lunatic bastile as an insane man: he is not insane: never was insane: *you* incarcerated him!—I ask you why?"

"There is my authority!" said Walter, pointing to the certificate.

"Sir!" cried Uncle John, "I am not a child. I know that these things—though potent in depriving men of liberty—are to be purchased with ease; and *you* know that if I were villain enough I could bribe two professional scoundrels to certify to your insanity to-morrow. What proof then is that of the madness of my friend? Under the present iniquitous state of the law of lunacy, it is, it is true, held to be a proof—a legal proof—a proof sufficient to indemnify those into whose hands the victim may be placed, but in reality it is no proof of madness at all. Who are these men, Drs. Bowlemout and Dobb? where are they to be found?"

"They are eminent physicians," replied Walter, "attached to Dr. Holdem's asylum."

"I thought so. But *you* did not apply to these eminent physicians!—you did not engage them! You applied to Dr. Holdem: Dr. Holdem sent them to my friend: they saw him once, and then signed that certificate. That was the process. And why did you apply to Dr. Holdem?"

"Of course, because I believed my brother to be insane."

"But why did you not in the first place apply to two physicians of known respectability? It does *not* follow as a matter of course that you applied to Dr. Holdem, because you believed that your brother was insane. But if even you had that belief, what induced it?—Why did you think that he was mad?"

"Why," said Walter, "because he acted strangely."

"Because he acted strangely! Are we to pronounce every man to be mad who acts strangely? Why every man living acts strangely at times. We have all our eccentricities. We are all apt to deviate from the straight beaten path, and every such deviation is an eccentricity. Eccentricity is the parent of all that is eminent. No man ever yet raised himself into eminence who was not eccentric. But are we to pronounce all such men to be mad? That were in itself indeed madness, and yet you have not only pronounced your own brother to be mad, but have stolen him from society with a view to his perpetual imprisonment, because he acted strangely!"

"Stolen him from society!" exclaimed Walter; "I don't understand you."

"Then let me explain; for I am anxious to make you understand me. Your brother is not mad. Nor is he in the vulgar acceptation of the term eccentric. He is as free from eccentricities as you are, unless, indeed, it be those eccentricities which characterise a benevolent heart. He is a perfectly sane man; and yet you have caused him to be kidnapped—carried away secretly—dragged by brutal ruffians to a lunatic asylum, with a view to his being confined there for life. Now let me be understood. Your brother is my friend. The loss of ten thousand pounds will not ruin me. I am prepared to spend ten thousand pounds to effect his liberation, and to punish those by whom he has been incarcerated, and ten thousand more when that is gone. I am no idle boaster. I am resolved to see him either dead or free; and in order to carry into effect that resolution, I will willingly spend every shilling I have. If, therefore, you wish to avoid being harassed; if you wish to avoid being held up to public scorn; if you wish not to have your life embittered, and your death accelerated by the knowledge of being universally execrated and denounced, you will consent, without delay, to his liberation; for be assured, that if you will not do this, my friendship for him is so pure, and so firm, that all that can be done shall be done; every available means shall be had recourse to, with the view of exposing and punishing the parties to this nefarious transaction; and if once I begin, sir, nothing shall stop me. But let me appeal to your sense of justice—to your feelings—to your conscience. Let me reason with you calmly. Like me, you are an old man—a very old man: we are both sinking fast into the grave: we must both soon appear before Him to whom all hearts are open, and from whom no secrets are hid. Now, assuming that I know your real motive for proceeding against your brother as you have done: assuming that your object was the possession of his property"—

"But that was not my object!" cried Walter; "that was not my object!"

"I simply say, assuming that your object was the possession of his property, how inhuman—how unjust—how unnatural do the means by which you have sought the attainment of that object appear! He is your brother!—your own brother! Nature, therefore, prompts him to look to you for affection. Persecution at your hands is abhorrent to every principle which claims an alliance with nature; and yet have you bitterly persecuted him! You have deprived him, in his old age, of liberty—you have placed every comfort beyond his reach—you have subjected him to a species of brutality the most horrible;—you have banished him from all society, save that of poor idiots and raving maniacs;—and solely with the view of obtaining possession of that which, if it prove not indeed an immediate curse to you, sir, you can never enjoy."

"But I tell you again, that that was not my object. My object was to keep him from harm."

"And in order that that object might be effectually accomplished, you placed him in the power of ruffians by whom he has been nearly murdered."

"Nearly murdered!" exclaimed Walter.

"Sir, if your brother be not already dead, he is dying. He, a short time since, tried to escape, and on being recaptured, was subjected to treatment of so brutal a character, that his recovery is held to be almost impossible. Humanity, therefore, cries aloud for his release. I appeal to you as a brother—as a Christian—as a man—whether his continued incarceration be not now the very acmé of brutality and injustice. Put it to yourself, sir. Suppose that you were placed in the position he occupies, writhing with physical agony on the very verge of death, and morally tortured with the consciousness of having been placed in that position by a brother—a brother, too, whom you had ever treated with the utmost kindness, and who was always at hand in the hour of need. Would you not think it dreadful?—would it not be sufficient to drive you mad indeed? But assuming for a moment that you believed him to be insane, let me ask if you thought that his madness was incurable?"

"I certainly did not."

"Then why send him to such a place as this, when you *knew* it to be directly against the interest of the proprietor to allow him to be cured?"

"I did *not* know that, nor do I know it now."

"You know, I presume, that the proprietor established that asylum for profit: you know that his object is to get as many patients as he can, and to keep them as long as he can;—you know this, and yet you are anxious to induce the belief that you do *not* know it to be directly opposed to his interest to allow them to be cured! His design is not to cure, but to keep them, seeing that in proportion as they are cured, so in proportion do his emoluments decrease; it being from them only that his income is derived. This is no mere assertion, sir, based upon theory; but a straightforward, practical, self-evident truth. Why then, I again ask, if you really were anxious for the restoration of your brother, did you place him in a private asylum?"

"I did all for the best. I was told that he would have every attention."

"But do you not see that the interest of every proprietor of a private asylum runs counter to his duty?"

"It certainly, I must confess, seems feasible."

"Can you then hesitate to release him?"

Walter remained silent.

"I wish you to understand, sir," continued Uncle John, "that I am not in the habit of holding forth threats; but as I have, sir, the means at my command—means of which you little dream, for you cannot for a moment suppose that I derived any part of my information from the proprietor of this asylum; but as I have, sir, the means of proving not only that your brother is not mad, but that the possession of his property was the object—the sole object at which you aimed, those means shall be publicly employed forthwith, unless you consent to restore him to society. I wish it to be an act of yours. I wish to have it appear that you are willing to make all the reparation in your power for the injury you have inflicted, and the agony you have caused him to endure. Again, therefore, I ask, will you release him?"

"But what can I do with him then?" cried Walter.

"I will take care of him. I'll undertake to keep him secure from all harm. If he be insane, let it be fairly and openly proved. What objection can you possibly have? If your object be to see him taken care of, and treated with a view to his restoration, and not the possession of his property, pray tell me what objection you can have to his being released?"

This Walter could not tell, and therefore kept silent.

"Liberate him then," continued Uncle John, firmly, "and I will strive to allay any ill feeling that circumstances may have engendered. But you know his benevolent, charitable disposition; you know that he is of a most forgiving nature. If, however, you will not, his liberation can and shall be accomplished, without your assistance, in which case—I speak to you now as a mere man of the world, looking solely to your own interest and security—I will urge him to banish every feeling consanguinity may have implanted in his breast, and to proceed—as a matter of justice to society—against you with all possible rigor. Your own interest, therefore, if nothing else be sufficiently powerful, the very consideration of your own security must prompt you to consent. Will you do it?"

"I will!" said Walter. "I will. On Monday morning, the first step shall be taken."

"I may rely upon you in this?"

"You may. Go with me yourself. Call early on Monday morning, and we'll proceed to the asylum together."

"Very well. Reflect upon all that I have said. I depend upon you *firmly*."

Uncle John now pushed his chair from the table, and wiped his forehead, for he had been so extremely energetic that he was then in a state of steaming perspiration. "Will you do me the favor to ring for my nephew?" said he, and the bell was accordingly rung, when as Valentine and Horace were summoned, they promptly re-entered the room.

"Why, what in the name of *all* that's incog. have you two unhappy old conspirators been up to?" cried Horace. "Plotting against the jolly old state? Are we to have *another* Guy-Fawkesification?"

"Good night," said Uncle John, as he rose to take leave.

"What, are you off?" cried Horace, with a look of amazement.

"Good night," repeated Uncle John, coolly, as he drew towards the door.

"Well," cried Horace, "you *are* about the rummest old——"

"Horace!" cried Walter.

"Well," continued Horace, "I was only going to say!—because look here!—directly I come down, you cut it—that's all!—But, if you will go, you know, why you will, and no mistake at all about it!" And having thus delivered his sentiments upon this subject, he saw Uncle John and Valentine out with all the politeness which characterised him commonly.

"Well," he continued, on returning to the room, "and what has that old fool been gammoning you about?—the one subject though, I *suppose?*"

"Yes," said Walter. "Heaven only knows where he obtained his information, but he knows all about it, from beginning to end."

"What! has that avaricious old breeches-pocketed crocodile—that what's his name?—Holdem been splitting?"

"Not he! you may take your oath that nothing has been got out of him."

"From whom then did the old fool derive his information?"

"Can't tell; can't guess," said Walter. "He says that he has the means at his command of proving every circumstance connected with the affair; and I believe him, for he stated to me all that I knew to be true."

"Then no time must be lost in removing the old nominal."

"He can't be removed now."

"Why not? What's to prevent it?"

"You may depend upon it, that this information has been derived from the fellows attached to the asylum. It would be therefore quite useless, if even it were possible, for him now to be removed. Besides, I have solemnly promised to release him."

"You have done what?" cried Horace. "Do you mean to tell me—Oh! we are all up the flue!—Do you *mean* to say you have given that promise?"

"I have."

"Then we may as well just go and smother ourselves in the thickest possible mud upon the face of the earth. It's all up! There's no mistake at all about the matter! If you release him, I'd strongly advise you to sell out, and cut away as fast as you can pelt over to Van Dieman's Land or New Zealand, and establish yourself among the blacks."

"But if *I* do not release him, he will be released, and I therefore may as well make a virtue of necessity."

"Well, you know my sentiments. Do as you like: but if you do that, mark my words, you'll make a mull of it! What do you want to release him at all for?

"The thing is done," said Walter, "and can't be helped now!"

"No; the thing is not done! it can be helped now!"

"But he is coming on Monday morning to go with me to the asylum."

"What of that!" cried Horace, "what of that! Can't you go down to-morrow and tell Holdem all about it, and have him removed in the night! It matters not a straw about to-morrow being Sunday; all days are alike to them. They think nothing of Sunday there. All you have to do is to trot down in the morning, and explain to Holdem how the matter stands; and if he don't, before midnight, remove the old nominal to a far distant den, I'll be bound to—to swallow him whole."

"But what am I to say on Monday morning?"

"What are you to say on Monday morning! Why don't you see? When you go the bird has flown! '*Bless* my life! Why, where is Mr. Goodman? He is nowhere to be found! Who saw Mr. Goodman this morning? Here, Figgins, Jenkins, Hoggins! have you seen Mr. Goodman! Go, and search for him again! Search every room in the asylum. I saw him last night, poor man! and he seemed a little better. Well, have you found him? *not* found him? Bless my life! how very extraordinary! He must have *escaped!*' What then can be done? How can you be involved? You went expressly in order to release him. What could a man do more? He has escaped! He's not there! Let his friends find out then where he is if they can."

Walter looked in the fire thoughtfully. His mind was by no means made up. "I'll think of it," said he, at length; "I'll think of it. Say no more now. Go and sit with your wife and mother; go, leave me."

Horace, feeling quite certain of gaining his point, accordingly left Walter musing alone.

CHAPTER XLI.

VALENTINE BECOMES A LITTLE BETTER ACQUAINTED WITH THE CHARACTER OF LOUISE, OF WHOM HE TAKES HIS FIRST LESSON.

THE next morning, Valentine, Uncle John, and Whitely went to church, and nothing could surpass the pure fervor with which Whitely offered up thanks to the throne of Mercy for his deliverance. He had not been at church before for many weary years; and hence, although he had prayed constantly to Him in whom all his hopes were concentered, the sacred place at once awakened the sweetest recollections of his youth. All the miseries he had endured were forgotten. His heart was full of joy, and he wept like a child. Each prayer—each response—brought fresh tears into his eyes; and while the solemn swell of the organ struck awe into his soul, the voices of the children, singing the praises of the Most High, seemed to him so celestial, that he felt, during the service, as if in heaven with the angels, and left inspired with the purest happiness a mortal can know.

He and his friends however had scarcely reached home, when the carriage of Mr. Raven dashed up to the door, and when the widow—who would trust no one to answer double knocks—had communicated some interesting intelligence, having reference to the fact of Valentine and his Uncle being at home, Mr. Raven himself alighted, and, according to instructions, was shown at once into the room.

"Ah! how do, my friends? How do; how do?" cried that gentleman, shaking them both by the hand at once. "I've come, you see, without any aristocratic ceremony: come to press you! *must* go! I want you to spend the whole day with us. Come, you're not engaged?"

"Why the fact is," replied Uncle John, "we have a friend staying with us who"—

"Come, now, none of your aristocracy! can you not bring your friend with you?"

"He is not sufficiently well," said Uncle John, who was about to explain in continuation, when Mr. Raven, addressing Valentine, said, "Well, I must have you, at all events. Louise is in the carriage: you had better get in at once, while I see what I can make of my old friend here."

Of course Valentine did not remain very long in the room after that: on the contrary, he went at once to take leave of Whitely, who had retired on the approach of Mr. Raven, and whom he urged to accept the invitation, if it were pressed, and then without even the slightest unnecessary delay, proceeded to the carriage to join Louise.

Uncle John, to the utter astonishment of

Raven, now briefly explained Whitely's case, and begged of him at the conclusion to believe that he should have been indeed happy to return with him; but that he was anxious not to leave his poor friend so long alone.

"But why *can* he not come with us?" inquired Mr. Raven. "He will be just as well there, you know, as here. We'll doctor him up. We'll take every possible care of him. *Will* you go and try to persuade him to come?"

"By all means," said Uncle John, who went at once for that purpose; but Whitely most earnestly begged to be excused, and at the same time endeavored to prevail upon Uncle John not to remain at home on his account one moment.

"Well," said Mr. Raven, when Uncle John had communicated the result, "then I tell you what I'll do with you. Suppose we split the difference. We dine at six: will you join us then?"

"I will, with pleasure."

"That's all right! Now we'll be off. When your poor friend is well enough to come, I shall be happy to see him. But these are your laws, my friend!—the laws of your beggarly aristocracy!—framed on purpose to swindle their own flesh and blood! But they'll come down! mark my words, they'll come down, and that before many more years roll over their heads! However, six precisely!"

"I'll be punctual," said Uncle John, and he saw Mr. Raven to his carriage, expressly with the view of shaking hands with Louise, who looked so beautiful and so happy, and smiled so sweetly, that really, while her hand was in his, she made him feel that he should have fallen in love with her himself, had he seen her about forty years before.

The carriage of course was not long rolling home; but had it been dragged by a couple of crabs, the time would not have seemed long to Valentine and Louise. They could not keep their eyes off each other one moment. Every instant they met, and then dropped, and met again, and although Mr. Raven tried to fix their attention upon the beggarly characteristics of certain aristocratic equipages which passed them on the way, the attempt was in every case a failure, although *he* was doomed not to know it.

They now reached home, and Valentine assisted Louise out of the carriage with all possible grace, only being unaccustomed to the business, he stood as a mere matter of chance on the wrong side, and thus took the thing entirely out of the hands of the servant. The importance of this was however but slight: it only proved to Mr. Raven, that he did not belong to the "beggarly aristocracy," and as he led Louise into the house very fairly, he thereby recovered his ground.

It was not very long before Louise again joined him, and although Mr. Raven was anxious for him to sit over a biscuit and a glass of wine, and chat about the aristocracy, she very soon had him away. He had *not* seen those beautiful pictures: he had not seen those funny Dutch chairs: he had not even been in the library! Oh! he must come: She had so much to show him, and so much to say, that she robbed Mr. Raven of his society in a short space of time, and they ran about the house like brother and sister. She called him plain Valentine, and taught him to call her Louise; and they seemed to understand each other perfectly; and were both very happy in that understanding; and thus they spent the first three hours, occasionally looking in upon Mr. Raven just to see how he got on with his "beggarly aristocracy," and then starting off again upon some fresh expedition.

As the time flew away, however, Valentine thought this really was an opportunity which ought not to be lost. They were then in the drawing-room, and the beggarly aristocracy's natural enemy was below. He therefore went to the window, while Louise was looking over an annual with the view of finding a piece of poetry, which she held in very high admiration, and began to weigh the importance of the first sentence he wished to utter with as much minuteness as if indeed immortality hung upon every word.

"Why, what *is* the matter?" cried Louise, when he had been standing in this position for some time. "Why on earth are you so serious? I know what you are thinking about," she continued smiling archly, as her laughing eyes sparkled with pleasure. "I *think* that I could guess pretty nearly!"

"Indeed! Tell me what you imagine my thoughts were now, come!"

"Nay, I *will* not tell that: but it strikes me that I could if I felt so disposed." And she ran away to look for the poetry again, with as much anxiety as if *that* really bore upon the point.

"Louise!" said Valentine after a pause, and she flew to the window at which he was standing; but as her hasty approach drove away all his courage, he simply stated it to be his unbiassed conviction that appearances were decidedly in favor of rain.

"Oh!" said Louise. "And is that all you called me for?"

"Why," returned Valentine, recovering himself a little, "I certainly *had* something else to communicate, and have still, but—"

"Anything *very* particular?"

"Very."

"Well, tell me at once what it is. I am impatient to know all about it."

"Louise, I am really so awkward, so stupid, that I wish to become at once a pupil of yours."

"And pray what am I to teach you?"

"How to win your affections."

"Indeed, I know nothing about it," said Louise. "I have had no experience in matters of that sort." And again she ran away, but only *pretended* this time to look for that extremely beautiful piece of poetry.

"But," said Valentine, "I really wish you *would* give me a little instruction!"

"But how can I? How is it possible to teach you that, of which I myself am ignorant?"

"Many begin to learn, only when they begin to teach; and I really think that if anything can justify that practice, it is a case of a precisely similar character to this."

"Well," said Louise, sitting down upon the sofa, "as you seem to be so very, *very* anxious to learn, I will give you a lesson." And Valentine at once left the window, and sat beside her. "In the first place then," she continued playfully, "you must be a *good* boy, and come very, very often. Secondly: Whenever I expect you, and you find it impossible to come, you must send me a note to that effect—"

"Exactly; and how am I to begin it?"

"Why, how would you begin it?"

"My dear Miss Raven? or my dear madam?"

"Neither, sir! Were you to address me as 'my dear madam;' or even as 'my dear Miss Raven,' I would instantly tear off that part, and send it back in a very sharp note. My dear madam, indeed! My dear Louise! or my dearest Louise! or something even stronger than that; and then go on to say that so and so, whatever it may be, you know—precludes the possibility of your having the pleasure or the happiness, and so on, subscribing yourself Yours."

"I see: *et cetera, et cetera.*"

"No, sir! not Yours *et cetera, et cetera;* but Yours—you may say, dear Louise! here again if you please; but at all events, Yours ever faithfully and affectionately; and then sign your own name—your own Christian name at full length. Well! that is in the second place. Thirdly: you must never say a word in my favor, that you are not quite convinced that I shall believe to be true; for, although 'a little flattery sometimes does well,' we cannot bear to *believe* it to be flattery—but in this little particular, you may go to some extent before you fall into any very serious error. Fourthly: you must never—Good gracious!" she continued, suddenly starting from her playfully energetic position, and looking down as pensively as possible.

Valentine slightly turned his head, and saw Uncle John and Raven in the room.

They appeared to be delighted; but Louise and her pupil felt really so confused! What could be done? It is true, there was the Annual lying by her side; but then, what is an Annual in such a case as this?

"Your most obedient," said Uncle John, holding his spectacles to his eyes, and bowing very profoundly.

Louise looked up and smiled: all her courage returned, and she ran to shake hands with Uncle John.

"I thought that we should find them at last!" said Mr. Raven.

"You are two very, very naughty creatures," said Louise; "I have a great mind not to forgive you. How long, pray, have you been behind that screen?"

"I have but just come," said Uncle John.

"But this moment! You have heard nothing, then? You are sure you have heard nothing?—quite sure?"

"We simply heard you giving your pupil a lesson."

"Now that is too bad of you, really! I was simply explaining"—

"Yes, yes! we are aware you were simply explaining," returned Uncle John. "Well, sir! and pray have *you* nothing to say for yourself?"

Valentine smiled and took the hand of Louise, but was silent.

"Well," said Mr. Raven, who had been highly amused, "when you have finished the *fourth* division.—It is, I believe, the fourth?—Yes; well, when the fourth division is finished, we, perhaps, may have the honor of your company below. That's rather aristocratic, I think!" And Mr. Raven really laughed very merrily, and so did Uncle John, whose arm he took, and left the apt pupil and his preceptress together.

"Dear me! how very awkward to be sure!" said Louise. "What tiresome people to come in just then. But, gracious! how odd you did look!"

"I have not the slightest doubt of it; but then, even you *somewhat* changed!"

"Did I? Well, I dare say I did. But we must not remain here. You run down at once, and I'll follow immediately."

"Very well," said Valentine; "but first let me whisper one word in your ear. They may be even now behind the screen."

"Well, what is it? quick!" said Louise,

and as she held her ear towards him, he kissed her!—absolutely kissed her!—which was very extraordinary. Yet what's in a kiss? Really, when people come to reflect upon the matter calmly, what can they see in a kiss? The lips pout slightly and touch the cheek softly, and then they just part, and the job is complete. There's a kiss in the abstract! view it in the abstract!—take it as it stands! look at it philosophically!—what is there in it? Millions upon millions of souls have been made happy, while millions upon millions have been plunged into misery and despair by this kissing; and yet when you look at the character of the thing, it is simply a pouting and parting of the lips. In every grade of society there's kissing. Go where you will, to what country you will, you are perfectly sure to find kissing! There is, however, some mysterious virtue in a kiss after all, and as every one knows what kissing is, it perhaps will be just now sufficient to state, that the peculiarly sweet kind of influence which it has was by no means unfelt by either Valentine or Louise, although they actually, in less than five minutes after, sat at the table, and in the presence of Raven and Uncle John, looking precisely as if nothing of the kind had occurred!

During dinner the "lesson" was a source of great amusement; for both Uncle John and Raven rallied Louise and her pupil at every point.

"In the first place," said Raven, "shall I send you some soup?"

This kept them merry for some time.

"Secondly," said Uncle John, "shall I have the pleasure to take wine with you?"

This also told well, and so indeed did every division of the subject, even up to the nineteenth; but as Valentine and Louise took up the weapons of their assailants, they eventually beat them completely out of the field.

"Well," said Mr. Raven, immediately after dinner, "and what is your opinion of the state of things in general?"

"Do you allude to the state of the country?" inquired Uncle John.

"The country, sir, I blush for the country. I blush, sir, for those who rule the destinies of the country. My firm impression is, sir, that the country is going to pot."

"Indeed! Really I have heard nothing at all of it! I am sorry to hear that."

"Sorry! and so am I, sir, sorry; but how can it be helped? Look at the state of things in general! Every thing is in the hands of our beggarly aristocracy; and when that is the case, sir, what country can prosper?"

"But how long has this country been in the hands of the aristocracy?"

"How long? It always has been in their hands, ever since it was a country."

"That is to say, that they have always had the government of it—the ruling of its destinies?"

"Precisely."

"Then by that I am of course to understand that they have made this country what it is?"

"To be sure they have, they and they alone, sir, have made it what it is."

"The envy of surrounding nations, and the admiration of the world!"

"But we have not to thank the aristocracy for that!"

"If they have made this country what it is, they have made it great and glorious beyond all other nations of the earth; and if they have made it so great and so glorious, they cannot in the long run have mismanaged much."

"But what would this country have been, sir, had it not been for them?"

"It is utterly impossible for me to tell."

"Greater," continued Mr. Raven, "ten thousand times greater and more glorious! But, waiving this subject, just look at the set! Can you *conceive* a more arrogant, haughty, upstart set of wretches? Why, nineteen, sir, out of every twenty are paupers, viewing the country as their parish, and living upon the rates."

"But there is great wealth amongst them!"

"No doubt of it; but what I complain of most is, that they who have it will not even support their own children. They must quarter them upon the public: they must make them national paupers. In their view the provision for one son in each family is sufficient: all the rest—it matters not a single straw, sir, how many there may be—must be provided for out of the public purse. That is what I look at! and I mean to contend that it is monstrous that this country should be taxed for the support of a legion of aristocratic locusts who suck the pucuniary blood of the people, and who, while they suck, tyrannise over and trample them to the earth. Look at them! See with what aristocratic contempt they look down upon a man who, by dint of honest industry, has realised sufficient to buy a thousand of them up! They will prey upon him, borrow of him, gamble with him, cheat him, but they will not associate with him. Oh, no; his veins are untainted by aristocratic blood, the impurity of which is notorious. They will dance with a dustman, drink with a sweep, shake hands with a pugilist, a jockey, or a black-leg; but *he* comes too near them, his wealth cuts them out, he can buy them all up!—they'll do neither with him. The whole system is rotten, sir, rotten at the core. If we have an aristocracy at all, sir, let it be a monied aristocracy: an aristrocacy of wealth. He who has most should stand first: the richest man should be king. That, sir, is the sort of aristocracy to establish; not a beggarly aristocracy, composed of mean, stiff-necked hereditary paupers. What would become of the crew, were it not for the public purse? Why, they'd run about as bare, sir, as unfledged birds: they would not have a rag to their backs—not a rag; but as it is they make John Bull stand Sam, and John Bull is an ass; but when he does kick—and kick he will, mark my words, soon—down comes your beggarly aristocracy."

To Uncle John all this was highly amusing: he, of course, saw in a moment how the matter stood between the aristocracy and Mr. Raven, and felt disposed to humor him, seeing that he cared to converse upon no other topic; but to Louise and her pupil the thing was really tiresome in the extreme, and therefore Valentine no sooner lost his fair preceptress than he resolved upon changing the subject at once.

"You see, sir," continued Mr. Raven, having refilled his glass, "when we speak of an aristocracy as an aristocracy—"

"Ahem!" cried Valentine, throwing his voice near the legs of the speaker.

"Hullo! Who have we here?" cried that gentleman, looking most anxiously under the table. "Who are you?"

"One of the aristocracy," said Valentine.

"One of the aristocracy?" and again Mr. Raven looked under the table, but really could see no one there. "One of the aristocracy?" he repeated looking earnestly in the face of Uncle John.

"I heard some one," said Uncle John, say, 'One of the aristocracy,' and *he* also looked with great apparent anxiety beneath the table, although he perfectly well knew from whom the voice had proceeded.

"Ahem!" repeated Valentine, throwing his voice this time beneath the easy chair in which Raven was sitting.

"Oh you're here, are you?" cried Mr. Raven, starting at once upon his legs, and upsetting the chair in question. "Why, where on earth!—where can he be!" he continued. "He must be somewhere!" And he looked round the room with an anxious eye, and turned the chair upside down with the view of making quite sure that the invisible one of the aristocracy was not in reality perched upon the frame.

"I don't see him," observed Uncle John, with an air of mystery, which did him great credit.

"Nor do I," said Mr. Raven, "but then he must be here!—Again I ask, who are you?"

"Again I say, one of the aristocracy!"

This was indeed held to be very strange. The idea of one of the aristocracy being concealed in his room, struck Raven as being *about* the most extraordinary thing in life. He had heard of nothing—read of nothing in history either ancient or modern—at all to be compared with it, and therefore said, "What do you want?"

"To converse with you upon that great topic," said Valentine.

"What right have you here? But come out and let's have a look at you!" And he quietly winked at Uncle John—which wink seemed to signify that he simply wished to see him—that was all.

"Pray be seated," said Valentine.

"I will *not* be seated till I see who you are."

"Come, come, now be calm."

"Calm! I will not be calm. What business have you here, sir?—who are you?"

"One of the aristocracy!" said Valentine, with an emphasis which implied that he had said so before.

Raven thought this indeed most mysterious, but he cried with great energy, "*Will* you come out?"

"Not till you are perfectly tranquil."

"Tranquil! I'll summon my servants and expel you with the utmost violence!"

"You have not the power. The power is all in the hands of the aristocracy."

"We'll see about that!" and he rang the bell with due desperation, and then paced the room with an air of some considerable dignity and importance.

A servant now entered.

"Bring William and Thomas with you," said Raven. "Tell them to come instantly, with John, and Coachman too, if they are below."

The servant, looking very droll—for he did not understand it—proceeded rather mysteriously to obey orders.

"I'll guard the door," said Uncle John, who enjoyed it very much, but kept his countenance pretty well; "and Val! suffer no one to dart through the window!"

Each now took his station, and Raven still walked about, chuckling at the idea of how he would trounce, when he caught the invisible one of the aristocracy.

The servants entered. They all looked remarkably odd. They had done nothing! Why were they carpeted?

"Now you fellows," cried Raven, who drove them like slaves, and ruled them with a rod of iron, *because* he didn't belong to the aristocracy, "search the room! there's some vagabond here!—find him out!"

A change came over the countenances of the servants. There was nothing to be charged against them, and as they naturally at the moment held that to be a blessing, they commenced a strict search, with unparalleled zeal. They looked under every chair, and into every crevice sufficiently large for a mouse to be concealed, but of course no human being could they see, and they expressed themselves eventually and precisely to that effect.

"You must find him somewhere," said Raven. "I know he's in the room!" And again they looked about with the utmost minuteness, until they positively began to believe that their master must have made a slight mistake!

"Ahem!" cried Valentine, seeing them together in one corner, and throwing his voice dexterously into the corner opposite. "Ahem!"

"Now then!" cried Raven, "Now—now—secure him!" and away flew the servants to the corner of the room from which the voice had apparently proceeded, prepared both to clutch and to torture the very first man whom they saw. But they were able to see no man—no ghost of a man. Their master had evidently made no mistake; but then, where was the vagabond in question? They found it impossible to tell. They could not so much as conceive.

"You'd better come out!" cried Coachman, desirous of conveying an idea of mercy being extended in the event of a voluntary surrender. "It'll be all the worse for you if you don't!"

"Do you think so?" said Valentine, making his voice appear to come from another quarter of the room, and away the servants rushed to that particular quarter, but, of course, with no greater success.

Where, where could he be? He was nowhere *above*—he must be beneath the carpet, and Coachman was proceeding to pull the carpet up, but the rest acutely feeling that they, in that case, should have a most unpleasant job in the morning, put a veto upon the proceeding in the similitude of a hint, that if they heavily trampled over every part of it, it would have a more immediate effect.

They acted upon this suggestion—they did trample over it, and assuredly if any one *had* been beneath, he would have known it: but, no! they met with no lump—no obstruction—the carpet was perfectly smooth.

They now began to feel that *all* must have been mistaken, and they looked at each other with the view of imparting some idea of what they felt, and there really appeared to be a perfect unanimity establishing itself among them, when Raven cried, "Come! look about! look about! I'll have him found!"

The servants obviously had an idea at this moment that it was all very well for Mr. Raven to say, "I'll have him found! I'll have him found!" but where were they to find him! That was the grand point at issue.

They did, however, recommence their search with the most praiseworthy diligence, looking again in every quarter in which they knew that they *had* looked, as well as in every quarter in which they conceived that they had not.

Again they relaxed. They really felt it to be of no use. They were tired and very warm. Their collars and cravats were disarranged; in short, their exertions were upsetting each particular thing which their nature had taught them the expediency of keeping tidy.

"Come, come!" cried Mr. Raven, on noticing this natural disinclination on their part to do more than the existing circumstances really required. "I'll not have you give up. He's about here somewhere. I *will* have him found."

"Ahem!" repeated Valentine, finding that they required some slight additional "spur to prick the sides of their intent," and they were all alive again in a moment. But they now looked angry and desperate; and, doubtless, if they had discovered any one then, they would have handsomely rewarded him for all their trouble. They only wanted to find him. They wanted *nothing* more. They *knew*, at that interesting moment, of no other wish than that! But, unblest souls! even that was denied them. They could not discover the object of their search, although they really did run about the room with an energetic zeal, altogether unexampled.

They stopped again to blow a little after a time. But Raven wouldn't have it. He loudly insisted upon ther keeping up the search, and as Valentine cried "Ahem!" again at this point, they flew across the room with renewed desperation, upsetting every chair which stood in the path of their flight.

"What on earth is the matter?" cried Louise, darting into the room at this moment. "Good gracious, what in the world can it be?"

Raven seized the arm of Valentine, and telling him to take her away, promptly hurried them both out of the room.

The game was up. The real "One of the aristocracy" was no longer present. Still, although they heard no more aheming, they, for a long time, continued to prosecute the search.

Uncle John tried to calm Mr. Raven; but nothing could banish from his mind the conviction that some one was still in the room. He thought it strange—of course, he thought it very strange—but then he felt it to be impossible for them *all* to have been deceived. He wouldn't believe it—he couldn't believe it! But what was to be done? There were the servants panting with unspeakable energy, and really looking greatly fatigued: they had searched every corner—every crevice—every hole—and yet could not find one of the aristocracy! Why, it was marvellous! Raven himself felt it to be marvellous; and, having eventually explained that he felt it to be so with great promptitude and point, he dismissed the sweating servants, who were really quite knocked up, and sat down with a subdued spirit to argue the case with Uncle John.

"Well, what do you think of this?" said he—"what do you think of this? It strikes *me* as being rather of the ratherest!"

"I certainly heard a voice," said Uncle John; "I don't think that I *can* be mistaken in that."

"Mistaken! I'd take my oath of it. I have, it is true, heard of imps and such cattle; and I have also heard that they are in the service of the aristocracy; but I never had faith in the existence of such things; and yet, what in the world could it have been? It is pretty clear now that there is no one in the room but ourselves. What think you?"

"Oh, that has been abundantly proved," said Uncle John, and he looked with an air of mystery again round the room, which was then in a state of the utmost confusion.

"Well, I've seen and heard of many marvellous things in my lifetime, that's clear; but this beats all that I *ever* saw or heard of! Dear me, though, what strange unaccountable things there are in nature to be sure! I have heard of haunted houses; but I never heard noises in this house before!" At this moment, quite a novel idea seemed to strike him, for he at once seized the poker and thrust it up the chimney, which clearly contained his last hope. "No!—no!" he continued, having brandished that instrument with infinite tact and dexterity in vain. "Well! this is extraordinary! I will *not* believe it to have been any supernatural thing; and yet, what on earth *could* it have been? I'd give any money to know what it was."

"You have no parrot in the house, I presume?" said Uncle John.

"Parrot!—bless your life, no!—nothing of the sort! Besides, where is the parrot in nature that could articulate 'one of the aristocracy' with so much distinctness? No, that was no parrot!"

Uncle John, of course, kept the whole thing a profound secret; and as he did so, Mr. Raven could make nothing at all of it. The more he tried to unravel the mystery, the more entangled, in his judgment, it became; and when he had so confused himself with conjectures—some of which were of a very extraordinary character—that he declared that he would puzzle himself no more about the matter, he most appropriately apologised for the way in which the peace of the evening had been disturbed, and, shortly afterwards, Valentine and his Uncle left the house inexpressibly delighted.

CHAPTER XLII.

IN WHICH GOODMAN IS LIBERATED FROM THE LUNATIC ASYLUM.

On the following morning, Horace, who had been quite unsuccessful the previous day in convincing Walter of the perfect soundness of his advice, tried again to make him feel that, if he did not adopt the precise course he had suggested, their prospects would be gathered within the dark pale of ruin.

"I suppose that you have been turning that point *again* over in your nob?" said he, alluding in the first place to the proposition for sending Goodman to a distant asylum in a fictitious name, and in the second to the head of his honored father: "I *suppose* you have deemed the point worth another thought?"

"I have," replied Walter.

"Then of *course* you mean to go the whole quadruped?"

Walter looked as if a slight interpretation were essential to a perfect understanding of that question.

"I say," continued Horace, really marvelling at his father's dense stupidity; "I say, of course you mean to do as I suggest, and have him taken off at once?"

"Most decidedly not," replied Walter, "I have considered the matter in all its bearings; I have looked at it in every conceivable point of view, and having done so, I have arrived at the fixed determination to set him free."

"Then of course," said Horace, "we may just go and groan. We have not half a chance. We must go to the pups. In my view, there's nothing now stares us in the face but lean, leaden-visaged, lantern-jawed starvation."

"And what have we had for months staring us in the face but the most appalling wretchedness?"

"Wretchedness! pooh! Don't talk to me about wretchedness. Have we not had money?—I will not contend that they cannot coexist; but he who is wretched with money is a fool, while he who is not wretched without it must be mad. Look at the wretchedness involved in starvation. Stop till we haven't a dinner and can't get one! then behold how enviable will be our position! What multitudes of friends we shall have pouring in!—what lots of assistance they will be anxious to offer! what mobs of grouse, pheasants and fawns will be sent when they know that our pantry is empty!"

"Aye, aye! that is all very fine; but you look at the dark side of the picture."

"The *dark* side!—Show me, if you can, that that picture has a bright one!—He *must* pursue one of two courses; he must either discard you and prosecute the matter no farther, or proceed at once against you for the recovery of that portion of his property which, of course, you are utterly unable to restore. It matters not a straw, therefore, which he may choose; either must involve us in beggary."

"But suppose we can persuade him that we believed him to be insane?"

"I can't suppose anything half so absurd."

"I've no patience with you, Horace!" exclaimed Walter, pettishly. "A more rash and unreasonable fellow never lived! One can't reason with you at all!"

"Oh! of course not: I knew that last year!—But do you mean to think that you'll make me believe that you fancy yourself that he can be led to suppose that we entertained any such impression?"

"I do!—Can we not say that we were strongly recommended, in the first place, to have the advice of two eminent physicians, and in the second, to place him under the care of Dr. Holdem—understanding that he was a most humane man—when those eminent physicians had pronounced him to be insane?"

"No doubt of it!—Of course we can *say* all this, and just as much more as we please. But that is not the grand point:—the question is, will he believe it?"

"My firm impression is, that he will: for as his friend—Valentine's uncle—has promised to do all in his power to allay whatever ill feeling he may entertain towards us, we have but to play our cards well to win the game."

"Win the game!" echoed Horace. "However any man, in the possession of all his blessed faculties, can cut away and stake his future prospects in life upon an argument so palpably rotten, is a thing which altogether surpasses my weak comprehension. But of course you must have your own way!"

"In this," said Walter, firmly, "I will. I have borne enough already. I'll endure no more. Whatever may be the result of his liberation, liberated he certainly shall be!"

"Oh, well; pursue your own course: I have nothing to do with it."

"Yes, Horace, you have: you have much to do with it. It will be useless for us to oppose each other now; but by acting in concert, we may succeed, at least in averting a great portion of that calamity which you hold to be inevitable."

"Oh! if that's it; if that's what you mean! why of course I shall stick to you as tightly as mortar can stick to a brick. My only object was to show that the speculation was any thing but a safe one; but as you are resolved to enter into it, and nothing can change you, why the oracle must be worked in the best manner possible. Of course I must be as anxious for his liberation as you are?"

"Precisely; nay, more so: you must for months have been doing all you could to persuade me to release him; but while I felt naturally anxious to do so, I reluctantly sacrificed that natural feeling to that which I conceived to be essential, as well to his immediate safety, as to his eventual restoration."

"I see!" cried Horace, "I see. It is not a bad move by any means."

"So that if even he should," continued Walter, "be in the first instance bitter against me, the probability is that he will do something for you, which will at all events be one point gained."

"And a grand one!" cried Horace, "a grand one. I'll work it. He shall be utterly amazed at the constancy and zeal with which I have been in the habit of advocating his cause."

"Here they are," cried Walter, as a coach rattled up to the door, containing Uncle John and Valentine. "Come, you had better go with us."

"Of course!" cried Horace, "I have to play the first fiddle, and in a case of this kind it's no fool of a fiddle to play."

Valentine now entered to ascertain if they were ready to join Uncle John in the coach, and, on being informed that they were, he was about to return, when Horace arrested his progress. "You are just the very fellow I want," said he, unhooking what appeared to be a piece of coarse frieze from a peg in the passage,—"Just help me to get into my new pea. It's a rum un. There's no mistake about it."

Nor was there. It had two sleeves, two gaping pockets, and sundry large horn buttons in front, which comprised its entire shape and make, and so exceedingly convenient was the thing upon the whole, that it might have been put on upside down, and worn with the tail round the throat, and the collar luxuriating about the knees without making any material difference in point of fit.

"Well, how do you like it?" said Horace, when Valentine had succeeded in getting as much of it on as the maker originally designed for that purpose; "What do you think of it?"

"Why its ugly enough," replied Valentine.

"That's the beauty of it," said Horace. "Nine and six! Lined with this blue business all regular. There were only two of them left. I wanted the Governor to have the other, but no, he wouldn't bite: I did all that a man could do to inspire him with a high appreciation of the difference it would make in his personal appearance; but it was no go: the Goth wouldn't have it."

By this time Walter had entered the coach, and as Valentine and Horace immediately followed, they were the next moment whirled from the door. As they proceeded, Walter, Uncle John, and Valentine felt strongly disposed to be silent; but Horace displayed the most restless anxiety to explain to Uncle John how inexpressibly delighted he had been to find that that which he had been so long and so ardently striving in vain to effect had at length been accomplished. "The very moment I heard of his incarceration," said he, whispering very mysteriously in the ear of Uncle John, "I begged of the Governor to have him home again that we might attend to him ourselves, for, although you know he might have been a little far gone, he might not have been dangerous, and if even he had been, we could have engaged a private keeper; but you see——"

"Young man," interrupted Uncle John, "it gives me no pleasure to hear any person speak against his father."

"You mistake," rejoined Horace, "I was about to observe that his argument was, that as uncle would be much better treated in an asylum, he could not in justice to him consent——"

"I see it all; I see it all," said Uncle John. "I see it all.—I require to have nothing explained. You are doubtless an intelligent, and a very amiable young man; but, excuse me, I have something of importance to think of."

This certainly was *not* what Horace expected. He did not anticipate that a communication of so much interest and truth would have been received with so much coldness and apparent incredulity. He, nevertheless, looked out of the window, and having examined the horses which drew them, observed that he would bet any man ten pounds to a tin pot that he would buy a much better pair of trotters for five-and-forty shillings any market-day in Smithfield; and as this observation absolutely fell unheeded to the ground, he declared that he was not going to strike life into a lot of dummies, and, therefore, the whole of the remaining distance was accomplished in silence.

They now reached the hateful bastile, where Uncle John and Valentine anticipated a storm, for which their companions were quite unprepared. The bell was rung; the gates were opened, the coach was ordered to wait and they entered. Walter sent in his card, and they had scarcely reached the receiving room when the Doctor himself made his appearance. To Walter he was particularly obsequious, and to Horace, who nodded knowingly, he was scarcely less polite, but when he recognised Uncle John and Valentine his countenance changed as if by magic, and he stepped back and looked at them with an expression of fierceness which was doubtless designed to be appalling.

"Why these are the very men," said he, "these are the very persons who burglariously entered my asylum, for the purpose of stimulating my patients to break loose!"

"We had *no* such object," said Valentine.

"Silence!" exclaimed Dr. Holdem, in a tone of authoritative thunder.

"Silence!" said Valentine, contemptuously; "you are the keeper of an asylum it is true; but recollect that *I* am not one of your patients!"

The Doctor looked at him scowlingly through his beetle brows as if he *only* wished that he had been! "Do you know these fellows?" said he, addressing Walter.

"Oh yes; they are friends of my brother."

"Friends of your brother! They are enemies to society. They wish to let maniacs loose upon society! They came the other day and got over my wall, and would have set every madman I have in the place free, had my servants not been on the alert to frustrate their impudent design."

"It is false," cried Valentine, "you miserable mass of wickedness, you know it to be false!"

"How dare you," cried the Doctor;—"how dare you talk in this manner to me?"

"I say again and again that it is false! We had no such design and you know it."

"We told you at the time," said Uncle John, "that it was purely accidental."

"Purely accidental! It was purely accidental, I suppose, that you assisted one of my best patients to escape!—a raving maniac!—one whom I had had for a number of years, and who has never been heard of since! that I suppose was also purely accidental?"

"By one of your best patients," said Uncle John with great point, "I presume you mean one of those patients for whom you were best paid!"

"What do you mean, sir? What do you mean by that gross insinuation? I am not to be insulted with impunity, and I will not by any man, sir!—not by any man!" and he struck in an instant an extraordinary attitude, and squared at his antagonist, with grace it must be granted, but with a peculiarly cold-blooded aspect; while Uncle John, whose knowledge of the science of pugilism may be said to have been equal with that of the Doctor, had his eye upon his man, while he held his hat in one hand, and doubled up the other into a striking gladiatorial fist.

"Well done old pigswig!" cried Horace, giving the Doctor a patronising pat upon the shoulder, "you have been taking lessons lately I see! Now keep up your nob, and hit straight from the armpits. You have nothing to do but to go in and win."

The Doctor scowled at the enemy with due darkness, and firmly maintained his appalling position. He would not move a muscle, so perfectly conscious did he feel that his picturesque attitude, being in the abstract terrific, had a tendency to strike an immense amount of awe into the soul of Uncle John.

"We did not come here to fight!" cried Valentine, who had been standing between the belligerents, watching the outstretched arm of the Doctor very sharply. "We came here to liberate our friend Mr. Goodman."

The Doctor dropped his imposing guard, and looked earnestly at Walter: The last words of Valentine had so far unnerved him as to render him for the time being quite indisposed to do battle. "I would speak a word with you," said he to Walter. "Do me the favor to step into this room for one moment."

"If you desire," said Uncle John, "to do justice to your brother; if you desire to keep faith with me; if you desire to have allayed whatever feelings of enmity injustice may have engendered in his breast, you will hold no private communication with that man."

"I desire nothing," said Walter, "but that which is perfectly open and straightforward."

"Then you can have no objection to this matter being arranged in the presence of us all."

"None whatever! None whatever! Decidedly not. Dr. Holdem, I am anxious to remove my brother forthwith."

"Am I to understand that you wish to remove him now?"

"I wish to take him back with me this morning."

"What! as he is!" cried the doctor. "He is not fit to be removed. It will not be by any means safe to remove him."

"Is he so ill?" inquired Walter.

"Ill! In his paroxysms, which have of late been unusually powerful and wild, he has been knocking himself all to pieces."

"Indeed!" said Uncle John, who found it difficult to control his indignation. "Let us see him. We shall then be able to judge of his fitness to be removed."

"I have nothing whatever to do with you," said the Doctor, "I have no knowledge of you in the transaction. With this gentleman only I have to deal."

"Then be pleased to let him be brought," said Walter, "that we may see if we can with safety take him with us."

"Well, well; if you insist, I have but to produce him, and if contrary to my judgment you deem it safe for him to leave, you are of course at perfect liberty to take him."

"Thus," said Valentine privately to Uncle John, as the doctor left the room, "Thus any man whom avarice or malignity may prompt can take the whole of this odious law of lunacy into his own hands! He can liberate, you see, as well as confine: and yet the law, in an enlightened age too, is the instrument with which he works!"

"It is monstrous!" said Uncle John, "truly monstrous. It is amazing that such a law should be suffered to exist."

"If one political faction could incarcerate the other," rejoined Valentine: "if the little band who make up the majority of the House of Commons: if twenty or twenty-three members were to be seized just before a division on some party question, though they were liberated within the hour, a speedy remedy would be found; but I fear that until we can drag faction into it in some way, until we can make faction feel that its interests are either mediately or immediately involved, the glaring evil will not be removed."

"We shall see, my dear boy," said Uncle John. "We shall see. The thing cannot have been properly tried. We shall see."

"What an everlasting length of time this old unhappy pigswig is!" cried Horace. "I wonder whether nature has implanted in him the smallest idea of his being able to fight! I should like to be clear upon that point, because it is one of great public interest, inasmuch as if she has, the fact ought to be exhibited at the British Museum among the rest of the natural phenomena forthwith. I say Val! what wouldn't I give to see him set to in a regular ring with his match! The magistrate who would interfere to put an end to *such* sport ought no longer to be in the commission of the peace. It would be one of the most interesting battles that have come off since knives, pikes, and daggers have been popularly patronised as an improvement upon British bone and muscle."

The door now opened and the doctor reappeared. He was followed by three of his myrmidons, who supported in their arms a pale emaciated creature of frightful aspect, with hollow eyes, which seemed glazed with the film of death. It was Goodman!

"My God!" cried Uncle John, as the tears gushed forth in torrents. "Why—why!" He was unable to articulate another syllable; his utterance was choked.

Goodman feebly pressed his hand and that of Valentine, and having kissed them, held them still, and faintly whispered, "God will bless you, my dear friends!—God will bless you!" but he seemed to be unable to shed a tear.

The ruffians now placed him upon the sofa, and as Valentine naturally imagined that if Walter and Horace approached he might spurn them, which they still had the power to resent, as he was not yet free, he suggested to his uncle the policy of keeping them off if possible until the whole thing had been arranged.

With this view Uncle John on the instant joined Horace, and urged the necessity for an immediate removal.

"Then *you* think he is fit to be removed?" said Dr. Holdem.

"Decidedly," replied Uncle John, "and the sooner the better. It is the only thing that can in my judgment save his life."

"And do *you* think that he ought to be removed in that state?" said the doctor, addressing Walter.

"Why, I really cannot say," replied Walter, displaying a strong disposition to waver. "I wish to be guided. If you think that he had better remain a few days longer where he is, why, perhaps it would be better."

"My firm impression is,"—said the doctor—"and I have had some experience in these matters—my *firm* impression is, that if you take him with you now, he will expire before you reach home."

This settled the irresolution of Walter. It decided the point at once. His death was the very thing he most desired, for the will was in his favor then! He therefore turned to Uncle John with alacrity, and asked him what *he* thought had better be done, when, finding him to be still strongly in favor of a removal, he said, "Well, it shall be so; I am anxious to be guided entirely by you. Dr. Holdem, we have decided on taking him with us."

"Very well," said the doctor. "Very well. Do as you please; but remember you will have killed him, not I!—Here," he continued addressing one of the keepers, "tell Jones to make out Mr. Goodman's bill immediately."

"The amount, without the items, will be sufficient," suggested Uncle John.

"The amount of the balance!" cried the doctor. "Bring it with you. Be quick."

"Will you allow one of your men to tell the coachman to drive into the gates, that he may take up at once at your door?" said Uncle John.

"No, I shall not," replied the doctor, "I shall do no such thing. Nor will I allow the coach to come inside my gates. If you will take him, take him outside, and the sooner you are all gone the better. Now then, here is my bill," he added, taking a slip of paper from the hand of his servant, and passing it on to Walter.

"Bless me!" cried Walter, on looking at this document, "I had no idea of its being so much as this. Why, it was but the other day I paid up. However, I'll send you the amount in the morning—of course that will do?"

"By no means. I trust no man. The account must be setteld before I part with the patient. He is the only security I have for its discharge."

"Horace," said Walter, "what money have you about you?"

"Come, I like that," said Horace. "That's good. It's about the richest thing I have heard for some time. Why, you know I've no money. I never have!—*you* always take special care of that."

"What is the amount of it?" inquired Uncle John.

"Thirty pounds and six-pence," said Horace; "I had no idea of its being more than seven or eight."

"How much did you bring?"

"Just ten pounds."

"We shall be able to manage with that, no doubt. Val, my boy, give me your purse."

"Valentine threw it from the sofa upon which he was sitting with Goodman, when thirty sovereigns and a sixpence were placed upon the table.

"Now," said Uncle John, "we will be off." And he placed one of poor Goodman's arms round his neck, while Valentine placed the other round his, and having joined hands, they lifted him carefully up and carried him slowly to the coach.

The moment they had entered, Horace prepared to follow, which Goodman no sooner perceived, than he shrunk back, and begged that he might not be suffered to come near.

"Your brother wishes to be with us," said Uncle John, as Walter stood upon the step.

"Well," said Walter, "but where am I to ride?—with the coachman?"

"If you do," cried Horace, "where am *I* to ride? That's the point at issue! But I suppose *I* may hang on behind or tie myself to one of the spokes of the wheel, and be twirled round and round to town in that way. Of course I may do what I please with *my* body!" And he went at once to look at the state of things behind, but as he found the foot-board studded with formidable spikes, he returned on the instant and exclaimed, "Now you *must* get inside. It's all spikey behind—so you see if you ride with the jarvey there'll be no room for me, unless I crawl into the boot, and consent to be smothered between two nose-bags."

"Do not detain us," said Uncle John earnestly. "Indeed, sir, you must not detain us. Surely there are plenty of other conveyances by which you can ride to town?"

"There's short stages passes every quarterv a nour," observed the coachman, as he put up the steps and closed the door. "There's vun on em comen along now."

"Dear bless me!" observed Horace, "you don't say so, Mr. Jarvis. Do you mean it?"

The coachman looked at him; but, taking no further notice, mounted his box to obey the orders of Uncle John, to drive back with all possible speed.

"Well, if this isn't gratitude," cried Horace, as the coach dashed away, "I don't know what it is. I did expect—I won't deny it—I did expect to be cocked on the box with the jarvey, but I did *not* expect to be mulled out of it altogether. This is what you get, you see, by doing an act of kindness! But never mind, here is the stage: we shall be in town now as soon as they are. That's one consolation."

Before, however, the coach reached the point at which they stood, it very suddenly struck Walter that he had not a shilling! He had brought but ten sovereigns out with him, and those he had given to Uncle John towards the payment of Holdem's account.

"Don't hail the coach," said he, "don't stop the coach. We can't ride. I've no-money."

"No what!" exclaimed Horace, almost petrified. "No money?—But come, I say, governor! you don't mean that?"

"All that I had went to settle Holdem's bill."

"I wish that Holdem's bill were in Holdem's breeches-pocket, and that his breeches-pocket were dangling just halfway down his throat. Here we have another proof of what men get by acts of kindness!—Well! never mind. We must tramp it. It isn't more than seven miles, or seven and a half, I suppose. Come along. But, I say! are you quite sure you haven't such a thing as a little sixpence, just to get us the ghost of a bait on the road?"

"I haven't a penny!" replied Walter.

"Well, this is a blessing! There can't be two rational opinions about it! It's a pure unadulterated blessing; one of those which peculiarly spring from an act of human benevolence. But, come, let us make a beginning!" And they did make a beginning; and they walked on and on with the most exemplary perseverance for six miles and a half, when they miraculously met with a four-wheeled cab, which took them in triumph to the door.

CHAPTER XLIII.

CONTAINS AN ACCOUNT OF A BREACH OF THE PRIVILEGES OF THE COMMONS' HOUSE OF PARLIAMENT.

Contrary to the expressed conviction of the delicate and disinterested doctor, when Goodman arrived at the house of the widow—who was delighted to see him, for more reasons than one—he was not only alive, but, so powerful is the influence of the mind over the body, much better than when he left the asylum, and that which tended to reanimate him still more, was the sight of his valued friend Whitely, of whose escape he had been, up to that hour, unconscious.

Notwithstanding these favorable symptoms, however, Uncle John at once sent for a celebrated physician, and a general practitioner of some eminence. These gentlemen came promptly. They met at the house. Uncle John unreservedly stated the case, and when they had duly examined the patient, they decided that his frame had been so shattered, and his fine constitution so cruelly undermined, that although there was no immediate danger, his complete restoration would amount almost to a miracle.

The fact of there being no immediate danger, satisfied Uncle John for the time being. For the rest, he hoped!—and he was a man with whom hope had great weight. He begged of them, earnestly, to pay all possible attention to his friend, and to call into action all the talent they possessed, and they in return gave him certain instructions, which he took great delight in having performed to the very letter.

Of course, as the patient was excellently well nursed, having Uncle John, Whitely, the widow, and her two servants constantly attending to him, Valentine was not much required at home. But if even he had been, it is questionable whether Louise would have spared him for two consecutive days, so imperative had she become, and so firmly did she insist upon his visiting her daily. It was therefore, perhaps, fortunate that there was no real necessity for his running counter to her wishes in this respect; and as there was none, no man could have been more constant in his attendance upon her who had obtained full possession of his heart.

Now, it happened at this memorable period of British history, that the majority of the Commons' House of Parliament, being composed chiefly of men of extraordinary sapience, and being, therefore, greenly jealous of their dignity and importance, moral, legal, and political, sought to establish to all eternity—First: That the virtue of their Will was superior to that of the British Constitution; and Secondly: That having elevated themselves above the Law, they had a clear and inalienable right to denounce and to repudiate the decision of any old fool of a judge who, in the due administration of the Law, had nothing whatever but the Law for his guidance. The marvellous wisdom involved in these two eternal principles will be seen by the enlightened at a glance; but the particular species of diablerie which caused the full development of that beautiful spirit, which forms the very essence of those two eternal principles, it will be highly correct to explain here, that the present stiff-necked generation may understand that if anything analogous should occur during their brief existence, they must not presume to set up their dark views in opposition to the bright views of those who compose by prescription the first assembly of the first gentlemen in the world.

In the first place then, at the period in question the libel laws in England were so extremely comprehensive that anything was a foul and malicious libel at which any man chose to take offence. Of course the truth or falsehood contained in that libel had legally a great deal to do with the matter, inasmuch as its truth was adduced in aggravation, and *vice versa*—it being held that "the greater the truth the greater the libel," truth having the greater tendency to provoke a breach of the peace, so that the libel which was most strictly true was the foulest and most malicious, while that which was really the most venial was the libel which contained the most infamous falsehoods.—That such laws were just, may be rationally inferred from their existence; but, independently of this potent and indisputable proof, confirmation may be gathered from the recognised fact that innumerable petitions had been presented to the Commons' House of Parliament, praying for their revision in vain. It is manifest, therefore, that the members of that day, in the fulness of their wisdom, conceived that the existing law of libel was so equitable and sound that it ought to be neither repealed nor revised.

Such being the admirable state of things then, a philanthropic publisher—who, having an eye to the improved morals of the rising generation, was unlike the generality of publishers, inasmuch as he published works which others would have contemptuously rejected—found his celebrated name set forth in a certain report on the state of certain prisons, as the publisher of a certain book found in a certain ward in Newgate, in which certain young gentlemen had been with a view to their edification confined.

As this was most true, it was of course a most foul and malicious libel, and the philanthropist accordingly brought his action thereon, and as this did not succeed to his heart's content, action upon action was brought for the self-same libel, notwithstanding the publishers of the libel were the servants of the House of Commons, and the members of the House of Commons had declared by resolution that they were privileged to authorise the publication of whatever libels they pleased, and upon whomsoever they pleased, and that therefore, he who dared to bring an action for any such authorised libel, and all concerned with the plaintiff in such action, were guilty of a breach of the privileges of the House of Commons, and would be mercifully dealt with accordingly.

Notwithstanding this, however, the plaintiff in this case proceeded. He had at length obtained a comfortable verdict, and absolutely went on to execution. The servants of the House of Commons of course would not pay: their chattels were therefore seized by the sheriff and deliberately and ignominiously sold! What then, under these afflicting circumstances, did the majority of the House of Commons do? Why, stung to the very quick by the contumacious temerity of the wretches, they sent the plaintiff to prison; they sent the plaintiff's attorney to prison; they sent the attorney's son to prison, and the attorney's clerk to prison; they also sent the sheriffs to prison, and here they stopped.. But why? Why did they stop at this point? Why did they not imprison all concerned in this villanous proceeding, from the judge to the broker, including the jury, counsel, officers, and all? This strong disinclination to do more than was absolutely essential to the vindication of their dignity is attributable only to their proverbial forbearance.

But that which made the matter worse, as far as the sheriffs were concerned, was the fact of their setting up a plea of justification! They pleaded, forsooth, that they were compelled to act as they did act by law! which was perfectly monstrous, inasmuch as they were bound by an absolute resolution in direct opposition to the law to act in obedience to the will of those who had set themselves above it. They, moreover, pleaded that they could not have acted in opposition to the law without violating their oaths; which was more monstrous still, for what were their oaths?—what were they when compared with their manifest duty to the majority of the Commons' House of Parliament? They were bound to obey the behest of that majority, as their imprisonment proved. The mere fact of their behest in this case being directly opposed to the law had nothing whatever to do with the matter. They were privileged to trample upon the law if they liked: they were privileged to establish whatever privileges they pleased. Their power to create privileges for themselves, with the view of meeting every conceivable exigency, was unlimited, and the only wonder is that that high-souled majority, when they found themselves vilified and denounced in all quarters, did not start a privileged periodical, wherein to lampoon their opponents right and left, and to choke—if they dared to bring their actions—to choke with the contumacious both Newgate and the Tower. Nearly all who composed that majority would have contributed to such a periodical. They might have got it up without any assistance of a literary character, and brought it out daily; while, being a privileged publication, matters would not have been minced in any sensible degree. This is clearly what they ought to have done under the peculiar circumstances of the case, and the fact of their having abstained from the pursuit of such a course shows the extent of their noble forbearance.

Now this question of privilege as it was termed—although it was in reality no question at all, there being no question about anything being a privilege which the majority chose to designate a privilege—was one which the anti-aristocratic Mr. Raven entered into with infinite spirit. He happened to be on terms of close intimacy with one of the sheriffs, and their incarceration was a source of great comfort to him, seeing that as he viewed it as an act of purely aristocratic tyranny, he entertained a lively hope that its tendency would be to bring the abhorred of his soul, the aristocracy, down. In this, however, Mr. Raven made a slight mistake. The aristocracy had little or nothing to do with it. There were members of the aristocracy in the majority, it was true; but then all their political associations were with the democracy; and although they were joined by certain eminent men who had placed themselves politically in the aristocratic ranks, they were chiefly men of plebeian origin, whom Mr. Raven usually held in high esteem.

The fact, therefore, of its being an essentially democratic movement proved the purity of his character, by affording a strong guarantee that there was nothing in it bearing the semblance of tyranny, it being proverbial that democrats cannot, in the nature of things, be actuated by anything like a tyrannous spirit.

Mr. Raven, however, did not care to look at the matter in this point of view. He contended that all power was in the hands of the aristocracy, and that therefore, every exercise of power was an act of aristocratic tyranny. "I am going to see these victims of your beggarly aristocracy, these martyred incarcerated sheriffs," said he to Valentine, a few mornings after poor Goodman's liberation. "Will you accompany me?"

"Oh yes! I shall feel great pleasure," said Valentine, "I should like to see them much."

The carriage was ordered, and they soon after started, Mr. Raven having put on his most haughty frown and screwed his lips into an expression of contempt the most superb.

"What do you think of this question?" said he on the way—"this unparalleled barbarous question!"

"Why," replied Valentine, "my impression is that while on the one hand the particular publication complained of ought not to be held to be a libel at all, on the other, if the servants of the House of Commons are to be privileged to write and publish what they please of any man with impunity, as we possess no security against the malignity of such servants, they may assail in their reports the reputation of any honorable man and plunge him and his family into inextricable ruin."

As this was an extremely narrow view of the matter, Mr. Raven agreed with every word, and contended, moreover, that the Commons' House of Parliament had no constitutional right to create for themselves just what privileges they pleased, which was in the abstract particularly stupid.

The carriage now stopped, and they alighted, and were ushered with others, by a remarkably thin individual, into the presence of two dark jolly looking gentlemen, who were in fact the martyred sheriffs. They did not appear to be much cut up: on the contrary, they looked rather waggish as if they would not have cared to intimate privately and confidentially that as a whole they rather liked it than not. One of them it is true seemed to want a change of air, for his breath was rather short, and he wheezed sometimes slightly; but with this single exception they appeared to be perfectly easy in their minds, and absolutely induced the belief that they derived from their position a very considerable amount of secret satisfaction. Of course they spoke firmly and boldly on the subject. They declared that they would never give in! They had by some strange perversion of reason deluded themselves into the conviction that in acting in direct opposition to the supreme will of the majority of the House of Commons they had actually done no more than their duty, and such being the case, they gave pointed expression to their fixed and immovable determination to suffer death rather than yield to what they denounced as a most tyrannous exercise of unconstitutional power. They couldn't do it! They wouldn't do it! —their principles wouldn't let them! They felt of course grateful to those affectionate friends who had done them the honor to visit them there in the dark foggy day of tribulation: but as for surrendering to the tyrannous majority of the House of Commons!—they wouldn't.

Of course as these strong and undutiful expressions reached the ears of those who composed the majority against whom they were directed, no merciful consideration could be hoped for from them. They were daring expressions, remarkably daring. The noble and jealous majority, who felt that they ought to be treated with the utmost deference by those whom they had incarcerated for a breach of their privileges, strongly disapproved of those expressions, and hence when, a few days afterwards, a meeting was convened by the contumacious sheriffs to take into consideration the circumstances connected with their imprisonment, and to adopt such proceedings as might be expedient to effect their liberation, a deputation from that noble majority, composed of half a dozen of the most popular statesmen—backed by a legion of individuals, each of whom had been secured by a small retaining fee to advocate privilege for ever!—marched into the hall in which the meeting was to be held, about an hour before the regular proceedings were to commence.

Having thus obtained possession of the place, they determined, instead of waiting for those tardigrade creatures whose province it was to lead the business of the meeting, to commence and carry on the proceedings themselves, and therefore one of the deputation stepped forward to propose that another of the deputation should be requested to take the chair. This produced some slight disapprobation, forasmuch as there were already a few "friends of fair-play" in the room, they protested against the under-sheriffs—whom the sheriffs had deputed to attend—being thus by a dignified manœuvre forestalled.

The Sheriffs Levee.

P. 240.

"Gentlemen!" said the proposer, addressing the retainers, "Is it your wish that our old and tried friend should take the chair?"

In the midst of a slight senatorial yell, the question was nominally seconded and carried with surpassing unanimity, and the old and tried friend vaulted into the chair in the due course of nature.

"We are met here to-day," said that statesman, "to discuss a vital principle of extraordinary vitality."

"You have not been elected to the chair!" cried one of the friends of fair play.

"Haven't I?" said the statesman. "Never mind, I am in it!" and he winked at the senators around him. "I am not going to make a long speech," he continued. "Has any gentleman a resolution to submit to the meeting?"

"I have a resolution!" cried a remarkable senator, who took great delight in beholding dead bodies, and prided himself especially upon the statesmanlike quality of making faces of a character peculiarly grotesque. "I have a resolution to propose."

One of the friends of fair play here protested against the irregularity of the proceedings.

"Why, your honest and straightforward chairman," exclaimed the remarkable senator, "asked if any one had a resolution to propose. I answer, yes, I have one."

"I beg to rise to order," said a gentleman, who was at that time well known in the city.

"Order!" cried the remarkable senator, "why there's no disorder now, except that which you make."

The gentleman, however, insisted upon suggesting, that, in their eagerness to do business, they had forgotten to read the requisition, which, just for the sake of quieting that gentleman, was borrowed and read.

"Now," said the senator, who was still on his legs, "we have every thing regular, and——"

"But," interrupted an enemy to privilege, "we want fair play!"

"Why, the gintleman who calls for fair play," cried one of the deputation, who boasted of having tropically a tail with seven million supple joints, "is ugly enough to be angry. Did ye iver now say sich an ugly baste? Be me soul thin, he's ugly in the extrame."

This sound and unanswerable argument in favor of the privileges of the House of Commons, and consequently in favor of the incarceration of the sheriffs, had an electric effect, and again cleared the way for that remarkable senator, who was still in possession of the chair. "We have to consider," he resumed—"we have to consider, in the first place ——"

"Down! down!" shouted the friends of fair play.

"Indeed!" said the senator with an expression of contempt. "Down! down! Don't you wish you may get it? Down! who's to do it? Who'll put me down? that's what I ask: who'll put me down? Down! It won't do! It's no go! It's been tried on before."

"Are you a freeholder?" demanded one of the friends of fair play.

"Am I a freeholder? there's a pretty fellow! there's a most sensible animal! Why the fellow must be a natural fool to ———"

Here there were loud cries of question.

"Question!" cried the senator. "The question is too much for you. You have too much stupidity to understand the question. I am not at all surprised at a lot of idiots bawling out 'question! question! question!'" And the senator, screwing up his legislatorial mouth, gave interesting imitations of the various tones in which the word question was capable of being uttered.

An elderly gentleman on the hustings here had the unblushing audacity to call "Order."

"I wish," said the senator with infinite propriety, "that I had a straight waistcoat for that old lunatic."

This observation was greatly applauded, but before the applause had died away another gentleman, who was dressed rather better than any member of the deputation, suggested the propriety of the speaker confining his remarks to the object for which the meeting had been called. "What do you mean?" cried the senator. "Who is this man-milliner who dares to interrupt me? What has he done with his band-box?"

At this interesting stage of the proceedings the under-sheriffs entered with their friends, among whom were several highly influential, but grossly deluded magistrates of the county. They proceeded at once to the platform, and one of the under-sheriffs had the daring to request the statesman who occupied the chair to give it up. To this cool, but extremely audacious request of course that great statesman refused to concede. "I am here," said he, "and here I stick, and no mistake about it!"—an appropriate observation which called forth a remark from the under-sheriff, to the effect, that an attempt had been made to corrupt the meeting, which remark had no sooner been uttered than a rush was made from the back of the platform, of which the object was obviously to hurl the under-sheriffs and their influential friends headlong into the body of the meeting.

There were many superficial individuals at this time present, who conceived that this was not precisely the fashion in which a great principle ought to be discussed; but then these individuals really knew nothing at all about the matter: they foolishly imagined that it was the duty of the deputation to allow the sheriff's friends to be heard, whereas it was their duty—a duty which they owed to that majority whom they fairly represented—to silence the sheriff's friends, by all the means at their command.

The under-sheriffs, notwithstanding, kept their ground, with that physical inflexibility by which bold bad men are in the aggregate characterised, and a regular battle ensued. The deputation themselves were particularly active, while the spirit and courage developed by their retainers were admirable in the extreme. They tore down the partition that enclosed the platform, as if it had been touch-wood, and crumbled the chairman's table into one chaotic mass of infinitesimal dust.

"The Riot Act! The Riot Act!" exclaimed one of the dastardly enemies to unlimited privilege, and the under-sheriffs actually did read the Riot Act, and quitted the room with their friends like cowards, leaving the noble deputation of the majority of the Commons' House of Parliament in full possession of the field, after having triumphantly struck the conviction into every British breast, that both in and out of the House they were resolved to reign supreme!

CHAPTER XLIV.

SHOWS WHAT CURIOUS CREATURES LADIES IN LOVE MAY APPEAR.

In the course of their lives, men frequently find their estimate of the character of ladies to be incorrect; and although it may occasionally happen—say once in an age—that a lady will mistake the real character of a man, the striking truth involved in the position loses none of its legitimate force, for it has but to be experienced to inspire the soul with a due appreciation of its purity and importance.

It does not, however, by any means follow of necessity, that when circumstances prompt men to form a second estimate, the second *must* be more correct than the first, for the qualities of ladies, especially if they be loveable, lovely, and young, are so variously developed and concealed, that a man can make sure of being somewhat out, only, when after having added the little items up, he discovers that he has reckoned the amount to be an angel.

It will hence be perceived, that how various and irreconcilable soever may be the estimates of men touching this extremely interesting point, it is perfectly possible for the first to be the true one, albeit the probability inclines to the second. It is, however, strictly within the scope of the imagination to conceive that they may in some cases be equally wrong, and in order to prove this remarkable fact, it will be necessary to explain how Valentine, after having formed his first estimate of the character of Louise, was induced to form a second, and how that was found to be quite as incorrect as the first.

He had for some time observed what he conceived to be an inexplicable change in the general tone and bearing of Louise. She had become in his view more imperative, more haughty, more assuming, and labored apparently to make him understand that she had an inalienable right to insist upon his devoting the whole of his time and attention to her. Whenever he failed to call precisely when she happened to expect him, she would address him in a style which bore the semblance of asperity, and demand to know the reason; when, if he did not explain to her entire satisfaction, she would turn from him at once, and for hours sit sullenly silent alone.

Of course Valentine did not approve of this mode of displaying affection. He felt that she might love him indeed, fondly, passionately: still he conceived that the object she had in view was to make him her slave, to which his spirit would not allow him to submit. His feelings towards her were of the purest and most affectionate caste: he had cherished those feelings from the first, and still fostered them fondly, albeit he had been led to suspect that she was not that sweet-tempered, mild, calm, gentle creature his heart induced him originally to believe her to be; but when he discovered, or thought he had discovered, that she presumed upon the existence of those feelings and appeared to take delight in wounding, playing with, and tyrannising over them, he naturally felt that if the spirit by which she was actuated were not promptly checked, it would eventually acquire too much strength to be subdued.

The more he tried, however, to accomplish the task he had proposed, the more impatient she became. He remonstrated calmly, and delicately pointed out the folly of giving way to a habit which could be productive of nothing but discontent. "My dear Louise!" he would exclaim, "why do you thus strive to make me wretched? Why assume a false character? This is one to which I am sure you have no real claim, and I cannot for the life of me conceive what pleasure you can derive from its assumption, when you know it to be a source of unhappiness to me."

"Sir," she would reply, "understand that I am not to be schooled like a child. I will not be spoken to thus. I cannot bear it. It displays an overbearing disposition to which I will never submit. If I am so odious that my society is the source of pain to you, I do not conceive that you are bound to endure it. There are others more amiable, more calculated doubtless to impart pleasure. I am therefore surprised that you do not prefer their society to mine."

These, and other remarks of a similar character had the effect of inducing Valentine to believe, that while her ostensible aim was to monopolise the whole of his time and attention, her latent object was to tire him out, and thus to force him to do that which she was anxious to avoid doing directly herself. He knew that on the death of her father she would be mistress of some considerable wealth; he knew that Raven belonged to the mere monied aristocracy, and that his purse-proud spirit had been imbibed to some extent by Louise; it was, therefore, but natural for him to imagine that, on its being discovered that his expectations were nothing at all comparable with hers, her father had prompted her to resort to some indirect means of breaking off what he considered an ineligible match.

Of course he no sooner conceived this idea than he resolved to absent himself at least for a time. There had been nothing in Raven's conduct towards him to justify such an impression, while his hopes were in favor of its being utterly false; still he felt himself bound, as a matter of common justice to himself, to have recourse to the only available mode of ascertaining if the notion he had conceived were well founded or not.

He accordingly ceased to visit as usual, and, as he kept away for two entire days without hearing one word from Louise, he began to be particularly wretched in the conviction that what he had imagined was really correct. On the third day, however, his hopes revived, when he saw Raven's carriage drive up to the door. He was, of course, "not at home," but that was perfectly unnecessary, seeing that Louise, who was alone in the carriage, simply inquired after the state of his general health, and, having sent in her father's card, drove off at once.

The lightness and freedom with which Valentine, after this, breathed were remarkable. He actually began to feel himself again, and it really required but little to reassure him that Louise loved him still.

"Why, Val," said Uncle John, who entered the room as the card was brought up. "What is the matter, my boy, between you and your lady love—anything wrong?"

"I am not quite satisfied," said Valentine.

"Not quite satisfied! then you ought to be. That's my impression—you ought to be satisfied. What would you have? She is interesting, amiable, beautiful, intelligent. What more can you desire?"

"Sincerity!" replied Valentine.

"And do you mean to tell me that she is not sincere? Pooh, absurd! I'll not believe it. She is full of sincerity; that girl is all heart. I know it: I am sure of it! Val, you must not have such fancies. You deceive yourself while you trifle with her, and no man has a right to play with the feelings of a woman."

"That, I am sure I have no desire to do; but she appears to take pleasure in trifling with mine."

"Why, of course! They all do it. You ought to know that. It is a thing which every man must expect. It is their province, but their object is simply to see what men are made of."

"That may be very correct," said Valentine, "they may all be coquettes more or less; but I fear that, as I am not rich and they are, the impression of Raven is that Louise, by marrying me, would be to some extent sacrificed."

"Sacrificed!" exclaimed Uncle John, with an appropriate look of indignation. "Why what does he mean by that? What does he mean by his daughter being sacrificed? Does he take you for a pennyless beggar? Never enter the house again, my boy! Show your independence!—sacrificed indeed!"

"Recollect I have no proof of this being his impression."

"But have you any reason to suppose it to be so?"

"I cannot say that I have any strong direct reason to believe it."

"But has he ever hinted such a thing? Has he ever in any shape given you the slightest intimation of anything of the kind?"

"Never."

"Then how came you to entertain the notion?"

"Simply because I have of late observed a change in the manner of Louise."

"Is that all? Why you silly fellow! *Did* you ever expect to find her always the same? do you not know that all women are as variable as the wind? A change in her manner! why, they are always changing. They are continually at it! And so because she has simply done that which is recognised generally as being one of their privileges, poor things! you consider yourself justified in supposing that she is anxious to discard you in consequence of her pecuniary expectations being somewhat more brilliant than your own! Don't be stupid. Go as usual. If, indeed, any hint of the kind be given, you will know how to act; leave the house that very instant and never enter it again. But I don't believe anything of the sort. The girl is passionately fond of you. I am sure of it. Can you imagine that she would have called here this morning if her object were what you suspect it to be? Is it likely? My boy, you do her an injustice. Go to her at once. You are wounding her feelings, which you ought as a man to be anxious to avoid. Depend upon it, Val, she is a good little creature. She is the very sort of girl with whom, if I were again young, I should be likely to fall over head and ears in love."

As the firmness, as well as the birth of affection, in a great degree depends upon our views being backed by the judgment of others, Valentine heard this with pleasure. He felt at the time quite sure that the opinion expressed by Uncle John was correct, and therefore made up his mind to call the following morning. In the evening, however, while engaged in a conversation touching the villany of Goodman's relatives, a note superscribed by Louise and emblazoned with the flaming crest of Raven, was brought into the room, with the information that the servant had been desired to wait.

The note was immediately opened of course, and the following were found to be its affectionate contents:—

"Miss Raven has to apologise for having thus taken the liberty of troubling one so superior in every respect to herself; but as she has the presumption to conceive it to be possible that he may condescend to state whether she may expect him to honor her with a call to-morrow morning, and if not, whether she will be justified in expecting ever to have that high honor again; she humbly begs the favor of some slight information on the subject, albeit, she is fully aware of its being one which to him is extremely displeasing."

Twice Valentine read this affectionate note, being naturally anxious to understand all its peculiar points and bearings, and then smiled as he submitted it to Uncle John, who having laughed very merrily, handed it to Whitely, upon whom it had a totally different effect, for he shed tears the moment he saw it, and on being strongly urged to state the reason, explained that it was in consequence of its being precisely like the handwriting of her, by whom fifteen years before, he had been shamefully dishonored.

"Bless my life and soul!" said Uncle John. "Why, how was that?"

"Some day," replied Whitely, "I will explain. It is a long sad tale—a tale of wretchedness on the one hand, and infamy on the other;" and fresh tears gushed forth as he looked again at the writing, which appeared to call up recollections of a character the most painful.

While Whitely was thus occupied, Valentine was preparing to answer the note. He knew not how to begin, "My dear Louise?"—No, that would not do. "Madam?" no: nor would that. At length, having decided upon sending an answer, in a style corresponding with her own for the time being, he wrote thus:—

"Miss Raven is hereby informed, that he, whose immense superiority has been so happily acknowledged, will have the peculiar condescension to honor Miss Raven with a visit in the morning."

This he thought very fair and highly appropriate, considering; and, having despatched it, he turned to resume the conversation having reference to Goodman's position with his brother. Whitely was, however, then deeply engaged with his own thoughts, while Uncle John seemed quite disposed to commune with himself in silence; and, therefore, as Valentine also had private considerations to entertain him, the subject was not renewed, and they all retired early.

Valentine slept most soundly that night. His rest had, for some time previously, been broken. He had had dreadful dreams: nay, his vivid imagination had actually, on one occasion, placed him in a position from which—although hotly pursued by a mob of individuals whom he wished to avoid—he was utterly unable to stir an inch!—which was very unpleasant. His mind was now, however, comparatively tranquil; and as he, in consequence, made up to some extent for the sleep which he had lost, he rose in the morning very sensibly refreshed, and, having eaten an unusually hearty breakfast, proceeded to keep his appointment with Louise.

"I wonder," thought he on the way—"I wonder how she will receive me? Angrily, perhaps—perhaps coldly—perhaps with a smile." He could scarcely tell which of the three was the most probable conjecture, although it may just as well at once be confessed, that, as his hopes were with the last, he inclined to the belief that the greatest amount of probability rested decidedly upon that.

The thing was, however, soon proved. He reached the house, and was shown into a room, in which Louise sat in state. He approached her: she bowed with that peculiar grace which freezes on the hottest day in June. He took her hand: she withdrew it. He attempted to kiss her!—she would not allow that attempt to succeed, but waved her hand towards a chair in the distance.

"Louise," said he, tranquilly, "may I know your object in wishing me to visit you this morning?"

"Sir, my object was to ascertain why you treat me with contempt. I conceived that if even you had no regard for me, you at least had the feelings of a gentleman. But it appears that even in that, I have been grossly deceived."

"You are inclined to be severe, Miss Raven," said Valentine, good humoredly.

"Not more so than circumstances warrant. If, after having been but too successful in inducing me to believe that your professions were sincere, you discovered in my character, or general conduct, anything calculated to render my society painful, why had you not the manliness to avow it?—why absent yourself from me without a single word of explanation—without uttering a syllable having reference to the cause? Is it gentleman-like? Is it—"

"Miss Raven, shall I call to-morrow morning? The probability is, that you will then be more calm."

"I am sufficiently calm now, sir. I shall never be more calm until you have explained to me that which seems attributable, not to mere caprice, but to something far worse. What have I done? What offence have I committed? Why have you not called here as usual? Give me a single reason for your absence, and then at least I shall know how to act."

"Louise, I will be frank with you," said Valentine, who still preserved his calmness, "I will candidly explain to you the cause of my absence. When I first had the pleasure of seeing you, and for some time after I had discovered your residence, it was not alone your beauty by which I was enthralled, although to that I was never insensible—"

"Sir!" interrupted Louise, "I am aware that we are all sufficiently open to flattery; but allow me to suggest, that there are times at which it becomes too palpable to be pleasing. I demand to know, as briefly as possible, the reason why you have absented yourself from me?"

"Upon my word, Miss Raven, you are somewhat imperious."

"Have I not a right, sir, to demand this, after what has happened? What was the cause?"

"Briefly this: I have noticed, of late, an extraordinary change in your conduct towards me, and, conceiving that my presence had become somewhat irksome, I—"

"How could you possibly imagine anything of the kind, when you know that I have done all in my power to induce you to call more constantly than ever?"

"Nay, nay, hear me out. Having conceived this, I felt that there must be some motive, some secret cause for so sudden a change; and, being utterly unconscious of having done aught to induce it, I naturally attributed the fact to your knowledge of my expectations, in a pecuniary point of view, being greatly inferior to your own."

"What have I to do with pecuniary expectations? Have I ever inquired what they were? Have I ever dropped a syllable, which could be construed into a hint upon the subject? Never! But you conceal the real cause, which lies deeper. You once saved my life; you saved the life of my father, and, therefore, know that I am bound to you in gratitude for ever. You presume upon that, and hence trifle with, and trample upon my feelings; or if not, you have been introduced to some brilliant coquette, some fascinating creature, more accomplished and highly connected than myself, in whose society you experience more pleasure than in mine, and to whom you devote all your happier hours."

"Indeed, Louise, you do me wrong, and I feel that in your calmer moments you will acknowledge, at least to yourself, that your expressed views on both points are baseless and unjust."

"You then wish me to believe that, although you thus shun me, you neither take advantage of the circumstance I have named, nor court the society of another? You wish me to believe this?"

"I wish you to believe, that although my affections are fixed upon you firmly, I never will consent to be a passive, abject slave, to be tyrannised over, and tortured perpetually by the violence of her from whom I ought to expect nothing but gentleness and love."

"You understand, sir, of course," said Louise, with great dignity, "that, at least as far as I am concerned, you are perfectly free."

"It would give me great pleasure to make you understand, that, at least as far as I am concerned, these strong bursts of passion are very painful."

"You would have me then endure all in silence!—though spurned, shunned, contemned, and treated with every other species of contumely, I must be silent! She to whom you have devoted the last three days may do this, but be assured that I will not."

"The last three days I have devoted to those poor old gentlemen, of whom I have so frequently spoken."

"Assuming such to have been the case, even that would not justify your conduct to me. If you derive more pleasure in the society of two old lunatics than in mine, I, of course, feel flattered, and can only, under the circumstances, say that you had better return to it at once."

"I will do so, if you wish it."

"You will?—You will leave me?"

"Most certainly," said Valentine, and he rose on the instant.

"Go," said Louise, who bit her lips violently, and turned pale with passion.—"I have no right, no wish, to detain you. By all means, sir, go. But remember, if you do, if you *do* leave me thus—never, never—my heart will break!—I cannot bear it—"

"Louise!" cried Valentine, who flew to her side instantly, and caught her in his arms, as she was falling. She had fainted. The perspiration stood like dew upon her brows, which were icy cold, and she looked pale as death. For a moment he felt paralysed.—He knew not how to act. He gazed upon, and kissed her; but no sign of reanimation appeared. He reached the bell, still bearing her in his arms, but the rope seemed useless. He tried the other. The shock was far too great for that; it came down as instantaneously as if it had been held by a single thread, but before it descended he had unconsciously made sufficient noise to alarm all the servants, of whom four rushed, at once, into the room, in a state of great excitement.

Of course, they were all stunned on beholding Louise, like a dead individual, in Valentine's arms; but the attitude of the coachman was the most picturesque, although many might have admired the repose of the porter, an extraordinary-looking, sentimental scoundrel, whose comprehensive mind teemed with horrid suspicions, and whom the scene struck physically tranquil.

"My goodness me, what is the matter!" cried the lady's maid, in whose peculiar apron had been established two remarkable pockets, which were always as open as the day. "My dear Miss!—come!—poor thing!—Run and fetch the Eau de Cologne," she continued, addressing one of the servants. "It is lying on the table—a long, narrow bottle, all neck! You will find it—but stay; I'll run myself."

"You had better remain," said Valentine, "you had better not leave."

"Tell Susan to get it then: tell her to make haste! I hope to goodness her papa will not return before she recovers; if he should, there'll be such a to do! My dear young lady!—look up! I never saw her so before. I never did. I cannot think what it could be. I cannot conceive. Susan! Susan! What a time the girl is, to be sure. But there's no getting anything done unless one does it one's self. Coachman, see after Susan. What can she be about?"

Susan entered, and the Eau de Cologne was applied to the nostrils, the temples, and palms of Louise, who eventually sighed, and thus at once dispelled Valentine's fears. That sigh was the prelude to her recovery. Her bosom began to heave with its usual freedom; the blood gradually returned to her cheeks, and she looked round with perfect self-possession.

"Lead me to my room," said she, faintly, to the servants, who carefully raised her from the sofa. "I am better, much better, but I shall there be more quiet and at ease."

Valentine offered his hand, which she pressed and kissed warmly, and as she left him, he fondly conceived that her gaze developed a pure and affectionate heart.

"She still loves me," said he, on being left alone. "She cannot conceal that; but as *her* peace of mind as well as my own is involved in this struggle, I must not yield now. It is lamentable that she thus allows angry passions to disguise the beauty of her natural affections, but more lamentable still would it be if those passions were allowed to gain a permanent mastery. It is clear that my impressions were false. *She* has no wish to break off the connection. Her object is simply to contend for her own supremacy, with a view to the establishment of a species of domestic despotism, which all experience proves to be pernicious; nay, utterly destructive of the happiness both of her who is the ruler, and of him whom she rules. I feel that I am as little inclined as most men, to be a domestic tyrant, but this spirit must be checked; and as I imagine that I possess sufficient influence to check it, I consider myself bound to exert that influence by all the means at my command."

Being unable to ring the bell, he now desired the peculiarly sentimental porter, who was still engaged in turning up the yellows of his eyes in the hall, to make the necessary inquiries, and having at length ascertained that Louise had completely recovered, he at once left the house, with a firm determination to carry the object he had proposed to himself into effect.

CHAPTER XLV.

VALENTINE VISITS THE ZOOLOGICAL GARDENS.

The next morning Valentine called and left his card, having learned that Louise was quite well. It is true, that he was not exactly satisfied with having done this simply. Had his feelings been unfettered, had he consulted them alone, he would have seen her; but as prudence suggested that the better course was that which he had pursued, he started off for a long walk instead. He, notwithstanding, a thousand times wished she had been with him, and as the morning was delightfully clear and calm, he actually turned, on arriving at the gates of the Regent's Park, with a view of retracing his steps. Prudence, however, again interposed, and compelled him to walk on alone.

This was harsh on the part of Prudence, and her dictates are often particularly harsh, although it happens—by mere chance of course—that she is almost invariably right in the long run, seeing that she looks beyond the enjoyment of the passing hour. It is, however, a striking fact, and one which cannot be too extensively known, that that which lexicographers generally call Irresolution, is frequently mistaken for Prudence! It is strange, that so pernicious a mistake should be made—that the one should be taken for the other; yet it is so, yea, even as a bitter bad shilling is frequently taken for a good one. For example; a man is anxious to know himself, and goes to an accomplished phrenologist, who finds an extraordinary bump about the middle of each partietal bone. "You have a deal of caution," observes the professor, as he gropes about in vain for some counteracting organ. "A deal of caution," and assuming the "science" of phrenology, for the nonce to be in this small particular correct, that man would be considered a prudent man, by those who confound prudence with irresolution. But see such a man in the street. He wants something: he wants it very much, but he doesn't know whether to have it or not. He has a very strong desire to enter a house. He goes up to the door, stops to hesitate a little, and then turns away to think it over again. Well, shall he go in? Eh? Yes—and yet—no. But then, let—him—see! and he walks back again. He can't make up his mind. He *wants* to go in!—but, perhaps—no; and again he walks away a few paces; and thus he will amuse you by trotting to and fro, knitting his brows and scratching his head just as long as you like to look at him. Catch such a man taking unto himself a wife, or entering into anything like a speculation. You cannot do it. He is not to be caught. He has not a single spark of the spirit of enterprise in him. He must "see his way clear;" and even *then* he wont move, for "a bird in the hand is worth two in the bush." A perfect specimen of this peculiar species would be a blessing to himself and an honor to his country, for he would never voluntarily stir, because he would never be able to make up his mind to do it. A perfect specimen, however, perhaps never existed. Hypochondriacal individuals approach the nearest to perfection in this respect, their disease being the fruit of irresolution legitimately ripened into rottenness.

Mighty minds must therefore hold it to be marvellous, that prudence should be so generally confounded with irresolution, and although it is perfectly possible that Valentine might not have thought of this as he walked round the park, it is clear that he was guided at the time by real prudence, and was sad only because he then felt it to be harsh.

Having reached a gate, which he found on inquiry to be that of the Zoological Gardens, it struck him that as he never had been in, he might as well spend an hour in viewing the "wonderful" animals, as they are termed, solely because they are in this country rare, which is partial and unjust, seeing that fleas, which are not rare in civilised Europe, are equally wonderful, their physical organization being equally perfect.

Caring, however, but little for this, he

went up to the lodge, and having tendered his shilling, was asked for a ticket.

"I have no ticket," said Valentine.

"You can't be admitted without," said the man.

"Well, where am I to get one?"

"Oh, any where!—at any of the shops. But you can pass with the next party."

At this moment a person approached, and, having tendered a small slip of paper, with a shilling, walked in, when Valentine put down his shilling and followed, which made *all* the difference.

On entering the grounds, the first thing that attracted his attention was a pole, established in the centre of a well, at the bottom of which three melancholy bears were crawling round and round, as pensively as possible. Two of these gentlemen had very decent coats to their backs, but the third was rather ragged, in consequence, probably, of his prospects having in early life been blighted, by circumstances over which he could have no control.

Round the verge of this well stood sundry individuals, of whom the majority had purchased buns, biscuits, and cakes, wherewith to treat the animals generally, and who were having recourse to every species of suasion, with the view of inducing one of the bears to mount the pole. Biscuit after biscuit was thrown into the well, and bun after bun, in little pieces; but, as the bears swallowed all without even looking up to express thanks, the generous donors became disgusted with their ingratitude, and stopped the supplies. This had a very sensible effect, for, almost immediately afterwards, one of the bears climbed the pole, and leaned back, with his mouth wide open, to receive whatever might happen to be put in, which went instantaneously, without mastication, down into the general stock. At this moment, how pure was the delight of those around! They experienced such happiness!—nothing could surpass it! They only, by whom buns to bears have been given, can know the soft pleasure of which it is the source. Every person who *had* a bun gave it to bruin in many little pieces, that the pleasure might be multiplied just as many fold. Sometimes half a dozen would be at it together, in which case the gentlemen below stood a chance, although a poor one; for, as a general thing, the one on the pole caught all, without either trouble or care.

"Now *then!*" said Valentine, throwing his voice into the widely-extended mouth of the animal—"You are not half quick enough: come!"

The feeders started. Upon them the effect was striking. It shook all their nerves, and they looked at each other with an expression of wonder. Was it possible? They turned the matter over in their minds. No, surely they must have been deceived. Pooh! Ridiculous! Absurd! and yet, had they not heard it?—and could they not believe their own ears?

While they were thus trying to solve this mysterious piece of business, the bear, finding that nothing was put into his mouth, thought that he might as well climb to the top of the pole as not; and, having done so, he placed his paws over the ball, and appeared to be exceedingly anxious to ascertain the true cause of the mental confusion of his feeders. He looked at them steadily, and they looked at him; but they did not appear to understand each other, even then, exactly!

"What are the odds?" said Valentine, throwing his voice into the animal's mouth, as before—"What are the odds, that I don't spring right in amongst you?"

No odds were offered. Nothing of the sort. They flew, in an instant, from the spot like uncivilised beings, while bruin stuck firmly to the pole, wondering what on earth could be the matter. The thing appeared to him to be utterly inexplicable. He couldn't make it out. He seemed perfectly puzzled. He looked at the people, as if anxious to induce them to come back; but no!—they continued to keep at a most respectful distance, until he conceived it to be useless to waste any more of his valuable time there, when he descended with the view of communicating the circumstances, as far, at least, as he understood them, to his brother bears below.

The very moment he had descended, the people began to explain to each other their views on the subject, with eloquence and force, starting all sorts of curious conjectures, and bringing old Æsop to illustrate the point, with remarkable tact and erudition. As Valentine, however, like bruin, conceived it to be useless to waste any more of his valuable time there, he left the amazed ones, before even the boldest of the group had reinspired sufficient courage to return to the well, and pursued his way along the most frequented path.

As he proceeded, an infinite variety of ugly animals met his view; but, regarding them, as he did, as creatures formed by *his* Creator, he perceived points of beauty in them all.

"Would you like to have a ride, sir?" inquired a man who had charge of a female elephant, which seemed to stand in awe of a little ragged switch—"she's as tame as a Christian, and goes along as steady as life."

"Does she trot?" inquired Valentine.

"Why, it aint, you see, exactly a trot, 'cause she ony makes a shuffle on it, 'cause she's so big about the pins; but she'll do a good eight mile an hour!"

"Well, mount," said Valentine, "I'll have a ride by proxy."

The keeper simply said to his charge, "Come," when the elephant dropped upon her knees; and, having allowed him to mount, rose, and shuffled along the path, with a gait precisely like that of an exquisite walking upon his toes.

This was a source of great amusement to sundry young ladies, whose presence caused Valentine to wish that Louise had been there; but as—after having rewarded the keeper of the elephant—he went into the place in which the monkeys were exhibited, her absence no longer annoyed him.

There had been, just previously to that period, a remarkable mortality among monkeys. The sharp, easterly winds had swept off the tender creatures by wholesale, and the cages were, in consequence, comparatively empty. The few that remained, however, did not, by any means, fail to excite the admiration of the ladies, who watched them as anxiously as if they had been children, and applauded their playful manœuvres with really affectionate warmth. "Look at that little *dear!*" said one, pointing to a ragged little gentleman, sitting in a singularly graceful position, while two little friends of his were hunting up the fleas about his dear little person, and biting off their heads as they caught them, with infinite dexterity—"Isn't he a love? Pretty creature! Look! Bless him, how patiently he sits!"

"Disgusting," said Valentine, directing his voice behind her whose admiration had thus been so strongly excited. "Are you not ashamed?"

It appeared that she was, for she dared not look round, but dropped her veil hastily, and quitted the place with her friends, when all the other ladies who were present had at once the good sense and propriety to follow their example.

Valentine now went to see the giraffes, and found them exceedingly beautiful creatures; but his attention was soon arrested by what, at first sight, appeared to be a little, emaciated, withered old man, who had recently experienced some appalling domestic calamity, or in consequence of bad debts, or a falling off in business, expected every day to have the docket struck against him, with something like fourpence in the pound flitting scraggily across his diseased imagination. He accordingly approached this diminutive individual—who, as he sat with remarkable gravity in a chair, appeared to have made up his mind to begin life again with a blanket—but as he found the cage in which that individual was confined, duly labelled "*Pithecus Satyrus: Orang Utan,*" all his sympathy vanished. And yet the little animal looked most unhappy. Indeed, it was abundantly manifest, that he had not only caught an extremely severe cold, but had something then pressing upon his mind, with sufficient weight to impart to his whole countenance an expression of sadness.

"Now there's a striking specimen of the animal creation," observed a grave person in spectacles, accompanied by a friend from the country, whom he felt quite determined to astonish. "Do you know now, whenever I look at these creatures, I always feel puzzled! Did you ever see any living thing look so much like a man? Look at his hands, look at his eyes, look at his lips, look at his cheeks, nay, look at his general aspect! Talk to me about instinct and reason! Draw the line!—draw the line, I say; show me the difference—distinctly point out to me where the one ends and the other begins, and I'll then, but not till then, give in. Here we have, without doubt, the connecting link of Nature's extraordinary chain. Just look at him picking his teeth with a straw! Is there any other thing besides man, in the comprehensive scope of creation, that understands how, why, and when to do that? And then see how he folds that blanket around him! Is there any other animal on earth besides man that understands what a blanket is for?"

"As to that," observed the friend of this gentleman, "I suppose he keeps that on because he finds it warm."

"Not a bit of it! Not by any manner of means, because, in a blanket there's no warmth to find. He knows there's no warmth in a blanket. He knows that a blanket would warm him no more than it would a lump of lead. No!—he keeps it on solely because he is cognisant of its virtue being to check the evaporation of perspiration. And does any man mean to tell me, that a creature that can, aye, and does do this, being moreover conscious of what he is doing, is utterly destitute of reason? Will any man contend that the creature before us don't know as well what he's about as we do—or that he ever does anything—for that't the grand point—without having a *reason*—mark, having a *reason*, for doing what he does? Why, the very idea is absurd! Few men who have lived since the ancients have studied this subject more deeply than I have. You may, therefore, with safety depend upon this, that that animal there is a species of man. It is true he is not in every particular precisely like either you or me, but then show me, if you can, in the whole scope of the universe, two men that *are* precisely in every particular alike. Show me two—but two—that look alike, walk alike, think alike, act alike, laugh alike, frown alike, or feel alike, precisely, and then I'll give in."

"Now, if so be as these things here could talk, I'd then say something to you."

"Talk, my dear sir!—they can talk. They can talk in their own language."

"Aye, yaye!—but not in ours!"

"What do you mean by that?" cried Valentine, sharply, making his voice appear to proceed from the animal in question —"Do you wish to insult me?"

The mouth, hands, and eyes of the amazed country gentleman were, in an instant, wide open, while his learned friend started from the rail upon which he was leaning, and established his spectacles more firmly upon his nose; but the creature in the blanket displayed more astonishment than either, for, after having turned his head right and left rapidly, being startled by the sound of a human voice so near him, he muttered, and chattered, and sprang from his chair, and having reached the highest branch of the stump in the cage, sat and grinned with extraordinary fierceness.

"What do you think of that?" said the spectacled individual; but his friend could not tell at all *what* to think of it. He shook his head, and scratched it, but made no reply.

"Why," said Valentine, throwing his voice as before—"why don't you acknowledge your error like a man, instead of standing there scratching your head like a fool? Do you hear me?"

Again the alarmed animal leaped from branch to branch. The thing was altogether new to him. He had never either heard of, or met with, anything like it. The idea of a voice thus hovering about his ears, without being able even to guess where it came from, was really too much for his nerves! He did not approve of it at all, but shook his head, and showed his teeth, and, at length, made such an extraordinary chattering, that the man who had the care of him entered the place, wondering what could be the matter.

"You'd better stand a leetle furder off, marm, please," said the man, as he drew near the animal's cage. "If you don't, the giraffe there'll nibble off the *whole* of them green leaves of yourn, and they does him no good."

In an instant the lady to whom this was addressed placed her hand upon her bonnet, and found her wreath gone.

"Now, what's the matter, Jocko?" said the keeper. "What have they been doing to you, eh?"

"Oh, we've been doing nothing," observed the spectacled individual. "I was merely conversing with my friend, when the animal inquired if we wished to insult him."

"The animal!—what—Jocko—what—insult him!" cried the keeper, who felt quite disposed to laugh loudly—"and so you heard him speak, sir, eh, did you? He talks very well, sir, considering, don't he?"

"It's wonderful!—really I never heard—I'd no idea of that species of creation being able to talk in our language!"

"Lor bless you, sir!—didn't you?"

"Never! I couldn't have conceived it to be possible. If I hadn't with my own ears heard him, no power on earth could have made me believe it."

"No, I dare say not. There aint many that would."

"I'm astonished, absolutely astonished, that the fact is not made more generally known. It ought to be disseminated throughout the whole scope of creation. Nothing but that was required to settle the point of the connecting link for ever."

"That's just my sentiments to a hair."

"And who taught him, my friend?"

"Why, that I can't say, sir, *exactly*."

"He deserves well of his country, be he whomsoever he may."

"Jocko perhaps can tell, sir, if you ask him."

"Dear me, I shouldn't wonder. I never thought of that. My little man," he continued, addressing the animal, as the keeper, who was able no longer to bear it, burst into a loud roar of laughter, of which, however, the querist took no direct notice. "My little man, who taught you the English language?"

"Indeed, I shall not tell you," said Valentine, through Jocko. "I feel most indignant."

"Hullo!" cried the keeper, whose countenance changed as if by magic, as Jocko again jumped about and looked perfectly bewildered. "What't the meaning of all this? Is the creatur bewitched?"

He went round to the door at the side of the cage, and having opened it said, "Why, Jocko!"

"Don't speak to me," cried Valentine; "I've been grossly insulted. Away!—or I'll be revenged on you."

As Jocko flew towards him, in all probability for protection, being alarmed whenever Valentine spoke, the keeper closed the door in an instant, and said, "Well, *this* beats all my acquaintance!" He now no longer addressed the spectacled gentleman in tones of roguish sarcasm, for he felt that however absurd it might have appeared, he could not then dispute the apparent fact of the animal having spoken.

"Why, how in the world is this?" exclaimed the person in spectacles. "How comes it that *you* are so greatly surprised?"

The keeper felt himself compelled to acknowledge, that he had been, as he termed it, "roasting" that gentleman, never having heard the animal in his life speak before; which was all very well, and cleared the way, of course, as far as it went; but the chief point, the grand consideration, the assumed fact of his having then actually spoken the English language, with the accent and the emphasis of an Englishman, remained.

Various were the guesses of the gentleman in spectacles,—his friend from the country was too much amazed to say a word,—and bold were the assertions of the keeper touching Jocko's being victimised by witchcraft; but, although they both displayed great imaginative power, and no inconsiderable amount of ingenuity, the more they labored to unravel the mystery the more entangled it became; and as Valentine now began to feel that he had been sufficiently amused by their ridiculous conjectures, he quitted the gardens and walked home to dine.

CHAPTER XLVI.

WHEREIN WHITELY EXPLAINS THE REAL CAUSE OF ALL HIS MISERY.

From the moment Whitely mentioned the fact of his having been dishonored by her, in whom all his hopes of happiness on earth had been centred, Uncle John had experienced an irrepressible anxiety to know the whole of the circumstances involved from first to last. We may hear of the occurrence of such deep misfortunes daily, pass them over with a word and think of them no more; but when so great a calamity befals either a friend or one of whom we have some knowledge, however slight it may be, our curiosity as well as our sympathy is awakened, and we regard as deeply interesting each minute point.

No idea of the real cause of Whitely's abject wretchedness had theretofore entered the imagination of Uncle John. He had attributed the fact of his being then a forlorn, broken-spirited creature, to the brutal treatment he had experienced in the asylum, but had never thought of inquiring how or by whom he had been placed in that asylum, until, on glancing at the note of Louise, Whitely mentioned the subject in tears. But even then, Uncle John regarded any farther allusion to the matter as a point of extreme delicacy, seeing that his impression was, that Whitely's calamity had driven him to absolute madness, which had, of course, justified his incarceration: still, being extremely anxious to know all, he resolved on giving Whitely the very earliest opportunity of performing the direct promise he had given, that all should be explained.

Accordingly, after dinner, on the day of Valentine's visit to the Zoological Gardens, he started the subject of the character of Louise, with a view of bringing the matter round. "Well," said he, "how was Miss Raven this morning?"

"Quite well," replied Valentine.

"Ah! quite recovered?—And did she let out again, Val?"

"Oh, I simply left my card."

"What! did you not see her? I'll tell you what it is, my boy: you'll play with that poor little girl till you lose her. You ought to have gone in by all means. You ought to have made her—without taking the slightest notice of what had happened—put on her things to go for a walk. That's the way I used to do when I paid my addresses to the girls; and it's the best way too, you may depend upon that. What do you think her state of mind has been to-day, now, to bring the matter close? Why, there she has been, poor thing! sitting alone, sighing, and moping, and fretting her little life out; whereas, had you taken her for a walk, it would have cheered her up, and made her so happy, that nothing could be like it. It's all very fine, and very flattering, to be able to break a girl's spirit, and tame her down to nothing; but what is she fit for, when your object has been accomplished? What is she fit for as a wife? She's fit for nothing! she is not even fit to be trusted! All she can do, is to administer to the despicable vanity of him, by whom the sickening milk-and-watery namby-pambyism of slavish obedience is exacted. It *strikes* me I'm about right there, my friend?" he added, addressing Whitely, who was paying great attention to every word.

"Quite, quite right," replied that gentleman. "Thousands have been plunged into misery and despair, through breaking the spirit of those whom they love, and thus depriving them at once of that shield which is essential—no matter how innately virtuous they may be—to the resistance of powerful temptations."

"So you see, my boy," resumed Uncle John, "that you must not expect to have it *all* your own way. But there's another thing to be thought of: It isn't always that a man can break a woman's spirit, if he tries; and when he fails in the attempt, she either rewards him before marriage, or settles with him afterwards in full of all demands. Besides—and that's another thing to look at—you'll not find every woman fool enough to marry a man who displays a disposition to reign supreme: so you'd better look out, Val, you'd better look out!"

"But I am quite sure," said Whitely, "that Valentine has no disposition to play the tyrant."

"And so am I," said Uncle John, "so am I. But he's such a proud independent dog!—I'm sure he'll lose her: I'm sure of it, if he don't mind what he's about. And she's a beautiful girl, too! a most beautiful girl! You never saw her, I believe?"

"No, I should like to see her much," replied Whitely.

"Well! you have only to say when you'll go!—By the way, it is strange—I have often thought of it since—that you should have been so much struck with her handwriting!"

"It is strange," said Whitely, "and yet it is after all, probably attributable to the fact of my not having seen a lady's writing before for years."

"Very likely. But then, hers is not a common hand by any means. Where is that note, my boy?"

Valentine produced it.

"I should know this hand from a million, there is something so peculiar in the formation of the letters. It is what I should call a remarkable hand. There is nothing, you see," he continued, as he gave the note to Whitely, "there is nothing, you see, formal or stiff about the style: all is perfectly free."

"It is not a common hand, which makes the resemblance the more extraordinary. Fifteen years since, I could have sworn, conscientiously have sworn, to this being the handwriting of her who was my wife. But alas!"—

Whitely paused, and both Uncle John and Valentine watched him intently. In his eye there was no tear, but his heart's wound appeared to have been reopened.

"Had you been married long," said Uncle John at length, "when the unhappy separation took place?"

"Five years, only: five short happy, happy years."

"You will, I am afraid, think me too curious; but ever since you alluded to that lamentable affair, I have felt deeply anxious to have the circumstances connected with it explained. It will, however, be too painful to you, perhaps, to relate them?"

"No, my friend, no; the relation of our woes is sometimes a relief: but I shall weary you. Calamities which strike to the very hearts of those who bear them, have indeed but little effect upon men by whom their force has been happily unfelt."

"You need not, my friend, be at all apprehensive of wearying me. I feel too deep an interest in the subject to be wearied. You are a native of London I believe?"

"Yes; and no man ever had or could have had a fairer prospect of a long life of happiness before him than I had from the period of my marriage, up to the time when every earthly hope was blasted. My father died while I was a minor, leaving me that which I ever regarded as a competence, but I remained single for some years after I had attained my majority. At length, I met her in whom my heart would permit me to see nothing but perfection. She was an orphan, and was living at the time as companion to a lady, who had known me from childhood. A more amiable or a more interesting creature never breathed: I believe her to have had, then, a heart as free from guile as that of an infant. We married; and for nearly five years, lived in the pure and uninterrupted enjoyment of each other's society, when a viper, an illiterate, low, cunning miscreant whom—were he now before me—I could strangle, poisoned the mind of her whom I valued more highly than my life, and eventually induced her to leave me."

"Was he a friend, as the phrase goes? a villain in whom you had confided?"

"A perfect stranger!—whose assumed name was Howard: his real name I never could learn."

"Well, but how did they bring it about? How did she meet with him?"

"I know not. For some months previously to her leaving me, I observed an extraordinary change, not only in her manner, but in her language and style of dress. I not unfrequently saw about her person, jewels, which to me appeared to be of immense value; but having the most implicit confidence in her honor, I took no farther notice than that of expressing my admiration of their beauty; and on being asked whether I did not consider them excellent imitations of the most precious gems, I was satisfied in attributing their display to that species of vanity which, in a woman, is to some extent venial. At length, however, they became so brilliant and so numerous, and were worn with so much ostentation, that I felt myself bound to look into the matter more closely. With that recklessness which impunity generates, even in those who are the most tremblingly apprehensive of detection at the commencement of a career of vice or crime, she would leave these sparkling gems carelessly about, and feeling then quite justified in doing that, which under any other circumstances I should have held to be a pitiful act of meanness, I on one occasion took them to a jeweller, and having learned their real value, my suspicions were aroused. Still I did not, I could not believe her to be false. I felt, indeed, sure that she had been tempted, nay, that she was then on the brink of destruction; but so implicit was the confidence I had been accustomed to repose in her, had she then simply stated that her eyes had been opened, and thenceforth concealed those jewels from my sight, I should have felt quite convinced that she had returned them to the villain, and should have held her to my heart more fondly than ever. She was not, however, sufficiently subtle for this. Instead of striving to allay my suspicions by the invention of falsehoods, the very moment I alluded to the subject—although I did it with all possible calmness and delicacy—she assailed me with a violent burst of passion, of which I never before supposed her to be capable. She would submit to no dictation in a matter of this kind! She would not suffer any such unmanly interference! She would wear what she pleased: she would receive what presents she pleased, and that, too, from whomsoever she pleased!—and, having expressed herself loudly and indignantly to this effect, she bounced with a look of contempt from the room, leaving me in a state of amazement. My friend: that very night she left me!—left me without another word!—taking with her our two dear children—the sweetest innocents that were ever sent as a blessing to man. Had she allowed them to remain, I might have borne the rest in silence. Conscious of her guilt, I might not have pursued her; but, as it was, I made every possible exertion to discover her retreat, with a view to the restoration of my children. For weeks, for months I was unsuccessful. I searched in every place in which I conceived it to be even remotely probable she had concealed herself; but no; every effort was unavailing, every hope of recovering my little ones withered. I became a wretched being; I felt that I had for ever lost all that I cared for on earth; and was then reckless even of life. At length, however, I received information of her having been seen in the neighborhood of Knightsbridge, and to Knightsbridge I went accordingly, day after day, walking through and through the place from morning till night without success, until nearly a month had elapsed, when I saw her one evening at a window, with my children by her side. The recognition was not mutual, and I did not then wonder at it much, for I had become quite careless of my dress and person, and looked, if possible, more wretched than now. I went, however, instantly to the door, and knocked loudly. I knew not for whom to inquire, but the fact of her being in the house was sufficient, and having said, I know not what, to the servant, who seemed satisfied, I made my way at once into the room, at the window of which she had been standing. As I entered, she was drawing down the blinds, and turned instantly to welcome, not me, but the villain whom she expected. On perceiving me, however, she stopped, as if struck with paralysis. She knew me in a moment; but uttered no word. I demanded my children, and she dropped upon her knees, with the view of pressing them more closely to her bosom. It was a sight I could scarcely endure. I could not attempt to tear them forcibly from her, for they clung to her as firmly as she clung to them. Still, still I was resolved to have my children. I demanded them again: she made no reply; she was pale, deadly pale, and trembled violently, but would not give utterance to a word. I spoke to them, to my children, to my own dear little ones; I called them by name:—I was not their papa: their papa would not be home till by and by! Maddened at this, I determined at once to separate them from her; but, before I could accomplish this object, the very miscreant rushed into the room, when I turned to fix upon him. I sprang at his throat, but I had lost my wonted strength. He shook me off, and, having reached a case of pistols that happened to be then upon the table, he seized one, and presented it firmly at my head. In an instant my wretched wife flew to him, in order to induce him not to fire; but, having by this time got the other pistol in my grasp, I called upon her loudly to stand aside. I could have shot him dead, with less remorse than I would a dog; but I could *not* shoot even him through her! Again, therefore, and again, I called upon her to stand aside. She would not. She would cling to him still!—when, taking a deliberate aim over her shoulder, he fired, and I fell. The ball entered my breast, but, though utterly powerless, I was not insensible: I remember all that occurred from first to last, as distinctly as if it had happened but yesterday. It will, however, be sufficient to state, that I was lifted upon a bed, where I remained for nearly three hours bleeding—that I was visited then by two persons, for whom the miscreant had started soon after I had fallen—and that, having dressed my wound, which they had pronounced not dangerous, they removed me at once to a lunatic asylum, as one who had made a desperate attempt upon his own life! While on the way I knew not at all where I was going; and if I had known, it would have been useless, for I had then no power to offer any resistance; but the moment I entered the asylum I saw through the infamous scheme, and considered myself a lost man. With all the strength that remained to me, I demanded to know by whose authority they had acted. The *demand* was regarded with utter contempt. I begged earnestly then, as a favor, to be informed. As a *favor* they showed me the certificate. My friend—it had been signed by my wife!—God forgive her! There was I, stolen for ever, as I imagined, from society, a poor, wretched, broken-hearted creature, writhing, moreover, with physical agony, without a friend with whom to communicate—without a single soul who cared for me knowing where I was; and there I remained for nearly fifteen years, subjected to every conceivable species of brutality, deprived of every thing—even of my name; for, as they insisted from the first upon calling me Whitely instead of Whitbread, I adopted it in order to avoid annoyance, and have ever since answered to the name of Whitely, as if it were really my own."

"To say," said Uncle John, "that I am amazed, were, indeed, but a weak expression of what I feel. But what became of *her*, my friend? what became of her?"

"While there—shut out, as I was, from the world, as completely as if I had been in my grave—it was utterly impossible for me to learn; nor have I, since my escape, been able to ascertain whether she is, at this present moment, dead or alive. I have inquired of the few that remain on earth by whom I was known, but can obtain no information either of her or of the children. It is my children, my friend, for whom I am anxious: I care but little, indeed, about what has become of her; but my soul yearns to hear of my children."

"Well, who knows!" exclaimed Uncle John—"you may hear of them still! You may see them—they may yet be a comfort to you, my friend, and a blessing. Who knows!—But your property: what became of that?"

"Not a vestige remains. It consisted entirely in houses, of which every one, I have ascertained, was immediately sold.—I have claimed them all, and the answer in each case has been the production of the title. He who was my solicitor is dead; but I have learned, from a man who was formerly my servant, that the sales were effected, in every instance, by that wretch whom I hope to meet again, before I sink into the grave. I should know him were I to see him even now. Never shall I forget his scowling, villanous aspect."

"Have you no knowledge at all of who he was, or what he was?"

"Not the slightest. I should say that he was a dealer in diamonds, or a jeweller, or something of that sort. That he was wealthy there can be no doubt; but, although he was dressed in the highest style of the day, he was the vilest, the most vulgar, low-bred scoundrel I ever met with."

"The jewels!—the jewels did it all!" cried Uncle John. "But I am, nevertheless, astonished that so intelligent, so accomplished a creature should have connected herself with a fellow so illiterate."

"My friend," said Whitely, "be astonished at nothing a woman may do, when she yields up her virtue. If once she be guided by the spirit of wickedness, she will elope with a sweep or a satyr. Every quality, which she before highly prized, becomes nothing in her esteem then. The very loveliest will cling to wretches the most shrivelled and withered: the most highly accomplished will connect themselves with boors. Then all considerations of intellect and honor are lost: every feeling is merged in the mere gratification of their infamous passions, for when a woman becomes wicked, she is wicked indeed."

"That is true," said Uncle John—"very true." And this was all he did say; for the circumstances related by Whitely had so amazed him, that he ran them over and over again in his mind, while Valentine, upon whom they had made a deep impression, had no disposition to break that silence which throughout the remainder of the evening prevailed.

CHAPTER XLVII.

SHOWS HOW VALENTINE TRIED AN EXPERIMENT IN THE HOUSE OF LORDS AND FAILED.

If he who was the first to abuse his fellow man, instead of knocking out his brains without a word, laid thereby the basis of civilization, it as naturally as possible follows, that the more highly civilised we become, the more bitterly abusive we must be; and if this bright deduction be perfectly sound, we may infer, without straining the imagination much, that we are now fast approaching the very perfection of civilization, which, of course, is a very great blessing.

Now, in a land of liberty like this, in which every public man, being held to be public property, is abused precisely as the generous public please, it is by no means an unusual thing for public men to be considered queer creatures in the aggregate, by those who have derived their information on the subject from gentlemen who write satires, draw caricatures, and fulminate political philippics, and hence it will not be deemed droll that Valentine—when about to pay a visit to the House of Lords—should have expected to behold some of the oddest individuals, on the one hand, and on the other, some of the basest and most palpably black-hearted villains that ever breathed.

He knew that the artistes in question were worshippers of virtue: he knew that at that particular period they were a peculiarly patriotic species of people in the lump; but although he made a liberal allowance for all this—taking off, perhaps, something like seventy per cent.—he yet thought that if, in their representations, there was a sufficient resemblance to identify the men, the peers of the realm still must be a most remarkable looking lot.

Well!—having been engaged all the morning with the solicitor, into whose hands poor Goodman's affairs had been placed, he happily made sufficient interest to procure a peer's order, and went alone down to the House.

There was an air of what Raven would have designated "beggarly aristocracy" about the various persons in attendance; but, without having recourse to a phrase so harsh, it may be stated with perfect truth, that they were on excellent terms with their own individuals, and seemed to have an amazingly high sense of their position, regarding haughtily as dirt all but peers, to whom their nature compelled them to cringe most servilely.

Of course, Valentine smiled as he passed, at the excessive self-importance of these gentlemen; but the smile had scarcely quitted his lips, when he found himself actually within the House of Lords!—which was very surprising. Instead, however, of being, as he expected to have been, introduced into a gallery, he discovered himself on the floor of the House, and was shown into something which seemed to be a superior sort of witness box in a corner, while behind the bar stood a number of persons, who looked as if they were about to be tried for high treason.

In the body of the House there were three individuals, two sitting at the table in wigs, and one with a dress sword standing beside them. There were no peers then present. It was not five o'clock. But they entered in a body, when that hour arrived, with as much punctuality as if they had been waiting to hear the clock strike. As they entered, Valentine looked at them earnestly, but he really was unable to see many of those oddities, whose appearance he had been led to expect, nor could he discover any creatures whose countenances were indicative of any peculiar blackness of heart. On the contrary, they appeared to be plain, mild, unassuming people; and—with the exception of the Lord Chancellor and the Bishops—were dressed with remarkable simplicity. Their manners, too, were gentle and courteous. There was not even the slightest attempt at display. They conversed in the most familiar strain; and, indeed, looked as much like other men as possible.

About the period at which Valentine arrived at this striking conclusion, the business of the nation commenced. In the first place, a tall and startling person approached the bar, and, addressing the Lord Chancellor, delivered himself precisely to the effect that somebody had got something. He then produced a little gentleman—who singularly enough happened to have some important documents under his arm—and made him bow three times with due distinctness and humility, before he took his oath that all he meant to say was true.

"What have you got there?" inquired the Lord Chancellor.

The gentleman commenced a little speech, that was understood by his lordship before it was delivered, which was fortunate, seeing that had it not been for that, it would not have been understood at all.

"Have you examined them?" demanded the Lord High Chancellor.

"Yes, my lord." This was said boldly.

"Do you find them correct?"

"Yes, my lord," replied the little gentleman, who spoke up again like a man; and, having delivered the documents in question, retired, highly pleased at the fact of the job being done.

The peers now commenced the presentation of petitions, which is beyond all dispute the most interesting portion of the business of the House, although it seems highly rational to suppose, that there would be fewer to present if they, by whom petitions generally are got up and signed, knew the astounding effect they produced when presented.

"My lords," a noble peer will observe, with surpassing tranquillity, "Petition—Norwich—against—destruction—glorious constitution."

"'Tetion," the clerk at the table will then echo—"'Tetion—Norge—'struction—glorse constution."

Such petition—in every section of which there may be an argument sound as a nut—is then crushed together carelessly, and thrown under the table, though heaven and earth may have been moved to obtain signatures thereto.

While the peers were thus engaged in the performance of this solemn duty, there was a movement at the door near which Valentine stood, most strikingly indicative of something. Several persons ran in, apparently in a state of great excitement; and, having glanced round and round, ran out again, for the purpose of bringing in others. The majority of them happened to have papers in their possession, but they all looked as if they had discovered some horrible plot against the State, and were excessively anxious to communicate to the House all they knew about the matter. In this state of feverish anxiety they continued for some time; but, having at length got themselves together, they poured some great secrets into the ear of the person with the sword, who nodded, as if he was not at all surprised at it, and then approached the bar as before.

"My lords!"—said he, "a message from the House of Commons!"

The Lord Chancellor rose and at once waddled towards them, and placed the respectable-looking carpet-bag he had in his hand upon the bar; and when one of the gentlemen of the House of Commons had delivered to him a document, and advised him, as it seemed, not to drop it, he waddled back to his seat as they retired three paces in really admirable order.

As soon as this job had been accomplished, the person with the sword went again to the bar, and said, "My lords!—a message from the House of Commons!"

The Lord Chancellor snatched up his carpet-bag again, and bowled down to the bar as before, and having received another document from another individual, bowled back with that sweet satisfaction, which springs from the consciousness of having faithfully performed a great duty.

"My lords!—a message from the House of Commons!" cried the person with the sword, the very moment his lordship had returned to the table, and again the Lord Chancellor took up his bag—without which he appeared to be unable to stir—and again rolled down to the honorable members.

Valentine thought it a little too bad to make his lordship trot backwards and forwards so often, when they might just as well have put the whole of their documents into his carpet-bag at once. He did not, in fact, like to see a Lord Chancellor played with, and run off his legs in this way, and hence—perceiving that his lordship had too much politeness to say a word about the matter himself, although he evidently felt it very deeply—he threw his voice behind the deputation, as they were bowing, and said, "Why could you not have sent them all in together?"

The members seemed startled as they turned to look round, and the person with the sword cried "Order!"—and looked very fiercely at the strangers behind the bar, of course conceiving that one of them had spoken. The members, however, eventually again reached the bag, and, having placed the third document upon it, Valentine, making his voice apparently proceed from the lips of the Lord Chancellor, whispered intensely, "I say!—have you got any more?"

"One more, my lord—only one more," replied an honorable member, as the Lord High Chancellor looked at the person who stood, embellished with a bob wig, behind him with the mace. His lordship, however, took no farther notice, but bundled back again to his seat.

"My lords!—a message from the House of Commons!" again cried the deputy serjeant, and again the Lord Chancellor snatched up his bag and came down to the bar with due presence of mind.

"Now, *is* this the last?" inquired Valentine, pitching his voice towards the mace-bearer.

"Yes, my lord, this is the last."

"Well, come, that's a comfort."

The Lord High Chancellor again looked gravely at his attendant, and his attendant looked gravely at him. His lordship, however, with striking forbearance, said nothing, but having bowed very profoundly, returned to his sack.

The members of the Commons now left the House, laughing, and the person with the sword distinctly intimated to the strangers, that if they did not keep quiet, they should not remain. Several of the most prominent protested their innocence, and all the rest were very ready to do the same thing; but that was perfectly absurd, he knew better, and therefore advised them most strongly to mind what they were about.

At this moment a noble lord rose, for the purpose of directing the attention of the House to some measure designed expressly for the promotion of the love of religion. He commenced in a quiet, conversational tone, as if anxious to reserve all his power for his points; but, although he spoke fluently for nearly an hour, he ended as coolly as he began, while the only kind of action in which he indulged was that of occasionally tapping the palm of his left hand with two of the fingers of his right.

The very moment his speech had been brought to an end, another noble lord started up to denounce it, and in doing so his violence was so excessive, that at times he was utterly unable to express the indignation with which his bosom swelled. He looked frightfully at the noble lords opposite—showed his teeth, foamed at the mouth, and eventually worked himself up into a passion so terrible, that the noble lords opposite actually smiled! This made him still worse. He became quite hot: and the more indistinct his articulation grew, the more rapidly he rattled away.

"I wonder," thought Valentine, as he listened to this vehement denunciation—"I wonder if it be possible to produce a scene here at all like the one I witnessed in the House of Commons?" On reflection he felt that it was not; but, being anxious to try the effect of an attempt, he cried "Question!—Down!—Down!"—throwing his voice behind the fulminating peer, who turned in an instant and stopped. The thing was really so unusual that the noble lord seemed quite struck! Had it proceeded from noble lords opposite, why then, indeed, he might not have felt so much amazed, although, impious as they all were in his estimation, he had never heard anything so indecent even from them; but the idea of being thus interrupted by noble lords on *his* side of the House—by his own noble friends—his own party—was shocking!—he held it to be, indeed, a heavy blow and a great discouragement, and seemed anxious to move that the journals of the House be searched for a precedent, when the noble lords around him said, "Go on—go on."

"Sit down!" cried Valentine, assuming a totally different voice.

"Order!—order! order!" cried the peers on both sides; for, although they had all had enough of the eloquence of the noble lord then on his legs, not one of them would even by his silence seem to sanction an interruption at once so unusual and inconvenient.

The noble lord then resumed. He seemed to feel a little better, although he obviously could not forget it. "My lords," said he, "in the annals—"

"Monstrous!" cried Valentine—"Why do you hear him?"

"Order, order, order!" cried the peers simultaneously—"Order, order, order!"—and again they looked round, with the view of ascertaining which noble lord it was.

This, in the House of Commons, as Valentine had proved, would have been quite sufficient to produce a little yelling; but—albeit party feeling, at that particular period, ran quite as high there as it did in the House of Commons—he could not get a single peer to join him. He was, on the contrary, opposed by them all. Not one would lend his countenance to any such proceeding. They were absolutely shocked at the interruption, and Valentine at length became convinced that no storm could be raised.

This was the only failure he had ever experienced. In every other place his success had been signal, but there even Faction itself refused to aid him; even Faction!—from which he had ever before derived the most prompt and effectual assistance.

But, although it was impossible to raise an actual storm, was it equally impossible to shake their dense gravity?

Valentine put this great question to himself, and conceiving it to be a point which might as well be ascertained, he resolved at once to bring them to the test.

There were several members of the House of Commons at the bar. They had been running in and out continually, in order to hear what was going forward, but at that particular time there were about a dozen present, when Valentine, assuming the voice of the Deputy Sergeant, cried, "My lords!—a message from the House of Commons!"

The Lord Chancellor left the Woolsack, as a matter of course; and, with characteristic dignity, approached the bar, with the man in the bob-wig behind him. He thought it strange, very strange, that he should have been troubled again, but he thought it stranger still, when, on reaching the bar, he found that the members of the Commons had no message to deliver.

"It is a mistake, my lord," said the Deputy Sergeant, who had been startled by what appeared to be the sound of his own voice. "It must have been one of the strangers."

"Let the strangers withdraw," said the Lord High Chancellor, which settled the business at once, for the strangers were accordingly ordered to withdraw; and as Valentine happened to be one of the strangers, of course he withdrew with the rest.

CHAPTER XLVIII.

RETURNS TO WALTER AND HIS AMIABLE FAMILY, WHOSE POSITION BECOMES QUITE ALARMING.

"What is that, Governor?—what have you got there?" demanded Horace, as he perceived the bright countenance of his honored father fall, while perusing a remarkably legal-looking letter, which had just been delivered by a legal-looking clerk. "A six-and-eightpenny touch?"

Walter made no reply. His heart was full, and he sighed, as he handed the letter to Horace.

"Of course,"—said Horace, with elevated brows, having made himself master of the contents. "I don't know what you may think of it, Governor, but to me it appears to be very much like the beginning of the end!"

"I knew," said Walter, "by my dream last night—"

"Oh, *blister* your dreams!—your dreams have done it all. We should not have been placed in this blessed position, but for your precious hypochondriacal dreams. I knew how it would be, the very moment you took to dreaming. I saw the whole business, and told you all about it, directly I perceived that you were phantomised like a fool. So you can't blame me. You would have your own way. You would be guided by your own morbid nob, and what's the consequence? Why, after having lived in a state of spectralisation, frizzled up to cinder, and reduced to helpless wretchedness, here you are, with palsied nerves and a shattered constitution, without twopence in the world to call your own! Had you listened to reason; had you taken my advice; had you kept the thing dark, or even, after you had thrown a light upon it, had you sent the old man to another den in another name, which you ought to have done—"

"It matters not," said Walter, "what ought to have been done: the question is, what's to be done now?"

"Well, what's to be done now? *I* may just as well sneeze as say a word upon the subject. What is it you *mean* to do? What do you propose?"

"I don't really see how I can help myself."

"Don't you?"

"The property must be given up!"

"Governor!—Oh! but it's just like you. *Do* you want to descend into the region of rags? Do you want to see mother and yourself in the workhouse, and Poll and me bawling duetts in the street? Because if you do, you'll do that."

"Why, what else can I do?"

"What else can you do! Start off to America, Van Dieman's Land, Nova Scotia, or any other place upon earth, and take all you have with you."

"Of what use would it be to me in either of those places?"

"Can you not turn it into money?"

"Not a quarter of it, unless I commit forgery."

"Well!—what is forgery compared with starvation? But without that—turn into cash all you can, and let's start. They can't stop us—they can't do a single thing with us in less than two months."

"But the letter says, that all must be delivered up immediately!"

"I know it: what of that? You will not give it up, and what then? They bring their action: you will defend it, and let it go to trial. Why, before it can be tried, we can be ten thousand miles off, as jolly as possible."

"I will not leave my country," said Walter.

"You will not leave your country! Well, that *is* a start! Why, what need you care for your country? Do you imagine that your country cares about you? I mean to say, that it's a very uncomfortable country to live in, without either money or friends. You'll not leave your country!"

"Besides, Horace, I feel that I cannot be so great a villain."

"That's another go! Thus, little villains are the greatest, because they are villains to themselves. No man should commence a career of villany, without being prepared to go through with it; should he halt, he and his family must suffer. I know you have no wish to be a villain, nor have I; but then you see, if circumstances prescribe acts of villany in spite of ourselves, what *are* we to do? Just look at the thing as it stands. We must either be villains, and live in a style of comfort, or honest men and starve. There is no middle course."

"Yes, Horace, there *is* a middle course, and that course must be pursued. Existing circumstances, you must remember, have been created by ourselves, and can, therefore, afford us no justification. The property *must* be given up!"

"You have made up your mind—I hope to be forgiven for calling it a mind—but such as it is, you have made it up to that?"

"Horace!—Do you know whom you are speaking to?"

"Yes!" replied Horace, with an expression of bitterness—"I am speaking to one who confined his only brother in a lunatic asylum to gain possession of his property, and who is now about to reduce himself and family to beggary, because he has not courage to retain it."

Walter shed tears, and if, to a man who will *do* that of which he cannot bear to be told, a word even from a stranger be sufficiently galling, what must have been the feelings of this father, on being thus reminded by his son that he was a villain!

"It were folly," resumed Horace, "to mince the matter now. You have gone too far to retreat, without involving us all in ruin. I *would* not have said what I have said, Governor, but that I am anxious to bring you to a sense of your position. You restore this property. Well!—what will be the consequence? Rags. What shall we have to live upon? Nothing. You have given up your berth, from which we derived the only means we had of keeping body and soul at all peaceably together, while there isn't a single creature in the world from whom we have any right to claim assistance. As to friends!—they are all very well, and very pleasant, when you are rich, but a man has no friends when he is poor. They are too wide awake: although blind before to his vices and crimes, their eyes become marvellously open. Independently, therefore, of being beggars, we shall have—for this affair is quite sure to be known—we shall have the pleasing consciousness of being regarded as scoundrels and thieves by the world—so completely and so suddenly does poverty change a good fellow into an unrivalled, unsightly rogue. Look at the thing in this light, Governor, and then you'll perceive what madness it would be to give up all with the view of satisfying that time-serving hypocrite, conscience."

"But do you think," said Walter—"do you really think my brother would ever allow us to starve?"

"Why, what else," returned Horace, "have we the smallest conceivable right to expect? *Can* you expect affection from him now? or do you suppose that he can be deluded into the belief that he ought to be grateful to us for having delivered him from the asylum? But even supposing that he would not allow us to starve—that is, supposing he wouldn't mind giving us a pound, if he saw us all shivering on starvation's brink—what if he were suddenly to die—and I don't think he's got a great deal of life in him, which makes me so mad, for in less than a month we should have had to put on mourning, when all would have been secured—but what, I say, if he were to die, where should we be then? Do you think it at all likely that he has allowed his old will to remain as it was? Is it likely at all that he'll leave us a shilling?"

"We cannot know what he may do."

"But is it likely? It isn't as if he were now well affected towards us. See how I —even *I*—am treated when I call, as I have done twice a-day ever since, and that with all the regularity of the clock. He'll not see me. He's 'much the same, thank you,' but never to be seen. If I could only get at him, to tell him how affectionately anxious I have been on his account, and how dreadfully delighted I should be to see him perfectly restored, I should make something of him; but as it is, I may just as well get up that chimney, and smother myself in soot twice a-day, as go there. I meet with no sort of politeness, no ceremony, not a bit. They answer me at once, without quitting the door. I did make the old woman go up this morning, but even then Mr. Goodman could not be seen: he felt obliged by my calling so frequently, but would feel more obliged if I wouldn't call at all. So you see, we are bound, in strict justice to ourselves, to take care of ourselves. *He'll* not leave us anything. It isn't to be expected."

"I think he will," said Walter—"I still think he will. Knowing him so well as I do, I cannot believe that he will allow us to become utterly destitute."

"How ever a man can thus struggle to deceive himself," said Horace, "is to me a perfect mystery. There isn't a shade of probability about it. And if even there were, what madness it would be to run the risk! Look at it in this point of view. Of course, you will admit that he *may* not leave us anything, and if he *should* not, what then can we do?"

Horace paused, for he felt that he had made a deep impression; but Walter, whom conscience had tortured so remorselessly, would not be convinced. He had proved the benevolence of his brother's disposition: he knew well the goodness of his heart; and although he was unable, for an instant, to disguise from himself the fact of his having injured him deeply and most unnaturally, he still felt persuaded that the injury would be forgiven, and hence eventually said, "I will trust him."

"You will?" cried Horace, starting up in a rage—"I am to understand this to be your fixed determination? You are determined, *quite* determined to pursue this course?"

"I am," said Walter, firmly.

"Very well; *very* well! I now know how to act. It is high time now for me to look to myself. I'll *not* be ruined by you! I'll not be dragged down to the lowest pitch of penury. I'll have some of those papers."

"You shall not!" cried Walter.

"But I will!"

"I tell you not one shall be touched!"

"And I tell *you* I'll have them!"

"Why, you insolent scoundrel!—what do you mean, sir?—what do you mean?"

"That all the papers that can be converted into money I'll have?"

"You shall not have one of them, sir!"

"Who will prevent me?"

"I will! Attempt even to touch them, and I'll knock you down, rascal!" cried Walter, who, as Horace smiled contemptuously, rose in an instant.

"Now, keep off," cried Horace; "you had better not come near me! I don't want to hurt you! Keep off!"

Regardless of this warning, Walter rushed at him wildly, when Horace caught his arms, and, having pinioned them, threw him at once upon the sofa.

"What, in the name of goodness, is the matter?" cried Walter's wife, who rushed into the room at this moment—"what is it? —what's the meaning of it?—what's it all about?"

"Why, this old cripple——"

"How dare you?" interrupted Mrs. Walter—"how dare you call your father an old cripple, sir?—are you not ashamed of yourself? Let him get up sir, this moment!"

"Oh, he may get up!—but I'm not, you know, going to be pommelled!"

"But what is the cause of it? What does it all mean?"

"Why," said Horace, "the meaning of it all is simply this: he has taken it into his head to reduce us to beggary, and, because I won't have it, he must try to knock me down."

"But how?—By what means?"

"Why, by stripping us naked of every thing we have, that he may send all back to his brother."

"Well, but surely you can talk this unfortunate matter over without fighting!—Come, my dear, draw to the table, and let us see what can be done."

"I will not be thus treated," cried Walter, "by my own flesh and blood. I will not be insulted by that villain!"

"He who taught me to be a villain—"

"Horace, Horace!" exclaimed Mrs. Walter, "recollect yourself, sir!"

"Well, why can't he be easy? I don't want to quarrel. I'd rather go and have a roll in the mud, ten to one; but it's a hard thing—"

"Well, well, your father didn't mean it, I know.—Come, let us talk the matter over calmly. What is it, my dear, you mean to do? *Have* you made up your mind to restore all to your brother?"

"I have."

"Well then, now, my dear, let us consider how shocking that will be. In the first place, how are we to live?—"

"Of course!—that's the way to put it."

"Be silent, Horace: let us be quite calm and cool, for the thing now begins to assume a serious aspect. If, I ask, this property of your brother be restored to him, how—that being now our only means of support—how are we to live?"

"We must do the best we can," replied Walter.

"Do the best we can! Yes, dear, but what can we do? You have no profession: Horace has no profession; and, therefore, I really cannot see how on earth we shall be able to manage!"

"Then *you* also think that he would do nothing for us?"

"Why, my dear, place yourself in the same position: what would *you* do under similar circumstances?"

"But he's a different man to me altogether. What I would do, therefore, can afford no criterion."

"But, granting that he is a different man, what grounds have we for believing that he will not discard us? We have no grounds for any such belief. On the contrary, since his liberation he has given us every reason to believe that he will. He may be and doubtless is of a generous and forgiving disposition; but you see, my dear, the question is, will he, under the circumstances, feel himself *justified* in doing anything for us? If he should not, Heaven only knows what will become of us, or how shall we manage to exist."

"Depend upon it *he* will never allow us to starve!"

"No, dear, perhaps not; but how dreadful will be our sufferings before we reach the point of starvation!"

"Besides," said Horace, "if I *may* speak—he'll be dead in about a fortnight; and, therefore, as we have it, we may as well keep it as not. What I look at most is, that that fellow—that Valentine—should be enriched by our folly; for, of course, he'll have it all, there's no doubt about that, and, therefore, nothing can be clearer than that by giving it up to the old man we in reality give it up to him."

"Exactly," said Mrs. Walter, "and as I have said again and again, it will, indeed, be a shocking thing if, after having tried all these years to secure it, it should be left to a person who has done nothing for it, and who has, therefore, no right to it whatever."

"But how do we know he will die so soon?—how can we tell?"

"Very true, dear; we cannot exactly tell; but then it appears that the chances are in our favor."

"And do you think that he'd die and leave us nothing?"

"Why, he might not, my dear; but if he *should?* What in the name of goodness should we be able to do then? There should we be starving,—I know we should starve, for we cannot work like those who have been used to it all their lives,—there I say we should be starving, while others who have no earthly right to it are living luxuriously upon that which we clearly ought to have. Why, my dear, it would be terrible! For goodness *sake* look again at the matter before you decide."

"Then you too would have me continue to be a villain?"

"Nay, my dear, that is a most unkind word; and equally unkind is it of you to suppose that I wish you to be anything of the sort. Heaven knows I am sorry—as indeed we must all be—truly sorry that you were induced to go so far; but as it is, I look solely at the circumstances which at present exist, and I really, my dear, cannot see how under those circumstances, you can act as you propose without reducing us to absolute wretchedness."

"I wish that I was dead!" exclaimed Walter; "I heartily wish that I was dead!"

"Nay, that is mere folly."

"Just like him," said Horace; "he never could grapple with a difficulty in order to surmount it. The very moment it appears he must wish himself dead."

"Well, well; wishing that will not at all mend the matter; nor shall we do much good by dwelling upon the point. The question is, will it be better under the present unhappy circumstances to retain what we have at all hazards, or by giving it up at once to run the risk of involving ourselves in utter ruin? For my part—although I should be but too happy to advise the immediate restoration of all if it were possible to do it with safety to ourselves—I do not perceive how it can be done now without the result, as far as we are concerned, being dreadful. We are placed you see, my dear, in so peculiar a position. I would go myself at once to your brother; but then what could I say? I could not ask him to compromise the matter. I could not say to him, 'Indeed, we are truly sorry for what has occurred, and will restore all that belongs to you *if* you will kindly undertake to allow us so much a-year!'—nor can I ask what he intends to do for us when we have made an unconditional surrender. I might indeed say, 'I do hope that you will consider our unfortunate position: I trust that our destitute circumstances will induce you to save us from absolute want;' but, although I might say this and dwell with great feeling upon each point, the very moment he alluded to the cause of my appeal I should be dumb, so that you see, my dear, we cannot act in this case as we might in any other. We must of necessity take one of two courses, that is to say, we must either retain what we have, and defend the possession in the best way we can, or give up all, and be thereby reduced to destitution."

"I tell you," cried Walter, "that it isn't at all likely that we shall be thus reduced."

"But, my dear! what security have we against it? We have none. We can have none. It is a terrible risk, and one which ought not on any account to be incurred. Now, if I might advise, I should say, dear, convert all you can into money at once, restore all that is not available, and retire to some distant part of the country. We could assume another name, and I am sure that we should live very happily: at all events, we should not have starvation before our eyes, which is really very shocking, dear, when you come to think of it! However, I will not tease you any more now; we will leave you to yourself, and I do hope and trust—indeed I feel quite convinced—that, when you have thought the matter over again, you will see how really absolute the necessity is for reversing your expressed determination."

Even when he feels most sincerely anxious to dó so, how exceedingly difficult is it for a man who has quitted the path of honesty to return! Like a liar, whom the first falsehood prompts with a show of necessity to lie on, he creates, by the *first* crime, circumstances which urge him to proceed in his criminal career. Walter, base as he had been, was most anxious to make all the reparation in his power. He would have given up all and trusted solely to his brother's generosity, but the circumstances which his crime had created induced him to pause.

CHAPTER XLIX.

GOODMAN HOLDS A CONSULTATION WITH HIS FRIENDS, AT WHICH UNCLE JOHN FINDS HIS JUDGMENT FETTERED.

While Walter was brooding over the prominent points of the interesting conversation detailed in the preceding chapter, with the view of conceiving, if possible, some medium course, the pursuit of which, while it in some degree satisfied his conscience, might meet at least half-way the views of his amiable family, his deeply injured brother was engaged with Valentine, Uncle John, and Whitely, in a discussion which had reference to the propriety of framing a fresh will. Goodman felt the hand of death upon him. It did not press painfully, nor with sufficient weight to justify the apprehension of an immediate dissolution; but his frame had been so shattered, his constitution so undermined by the brutal treatment he had experienced, that he had become quite convinced, that although human skill might enable him to linger on for weeks or even months, that hand would never more be removed till it had crushed him. This rendered his spirit quite calm. Every harsh, every irritable feeling was subdued. He held it to be peculiarly the time for the forgiveness of injuries, and hence his benevolence reigned in the ascendant. Thus actuated, he could not deal justice to Walter. He felt that it did not, in fact, come then within his province to do so: nor did he desire to leave him to his own conscience, as it is termed, seeing that that would be in effect to desire that he might by his conscience be tortured. He was anxious to express his forgiveness—to make it manifest that he believed him to have been actuated, not by any innate vileness, but by some evil influence, over which he might not at the moment have had entire control. He did all he possibly could to invent excuses for him, with the view of establishing a show of justification; but as this was an object he was utterly unable to accomplish, he began to look, not at what Walter had been, but at what he might become. He conceived that his repentance might be sincere, that he might henceforth be virtuous, and that therefore he who had the power to save him from those temptations to dishonor, with which a state of utter destitution teems, would not perform his duty as a Christian, if he permitted the exercise of that power to be withheld.

It was while in this charitable frame of mind that poor Goodman solicited the advice of his friends, more with the view, as is customary with those who seek advice, of having the satisfaction of inducing them to think as he thought, than of acting upon their suggestions. He could not but feel that they would at first be inclined to be harsh—that they would repudiate the idea of his pursuing the course he had proposed, and hence when he inquired if they did not think that he was bound to let his will remain substantially as it was, he was not at all surprised at their instant reply being, "Certainly not!"

"What!" exclaimed Whitely, "would you reward the wretch, who sought to rob you by means so unnatural, with wealth? Would you give *him* the power of living in luxury, who deprived you not only of liberty but of health, the greatest blessing of life? Reflect upon what you have endured—upon the dreadful position in which you were placed—upon the monstrous brutality to which you have been subjected—and upon the result of that brutality, even up to the present time. Who induced all this? Why he whose unnatural malignity and sordid avarice you now wish to gratify, by leaving him all that you possess!"

"Whatever he may have been," observed Goodman, "however wrong he may have acted, I cannot forget that he is my brother."

"Nor ought you to forget it, for that increases his guilt a thousand-fold. You ought to regard him as a brother, who violated every feeling by which he ought to have been actuated with the view of injuring you, and who thereby sacrificed all claim upon your affections. In a case of this description the admirable precept which urges us to return good for evil may in practice be carried too far. You, for instance, would set a most pernicious example, inasmuch as you would show that, however infamous may be the conduct of a man, however foul and unnatural may be his designs, he may practise his infamies with impunity upon a brother if that brother possess a benevolent heart. Were he a brother of mine I would discard him utterly: if I did not I should consider that I had failed in performing my duty to society as a man."

"But what if I were to discard him?" said Goodman. "What would become of his family? Ought the innocent to suffer for the guilty?"

"You cannot tell that they are innocent. His family may be as guilty as himself, and in this case the probability is that they are. But even supposing that they are not, what would become of justice if men were not to be punished for crimes, lest the punishment should be felt by those with whom they are connected? If, having no proof of their guilt, you could punish him without involving them, you would be bound, of course, to do so; but as this is under the circumstances impossible, justice demands that you should act as if they were not concerned."

"But would not that object be to some extent attained," suggested Valentine, "if, instead of the property being left to Walter, it were secured to his wife, and the wife of Horace?"

"It might," returned Whitely, "it might thus be attained; but it could be so only in the event of the women being unfaithful. If they continue to be virtuous, it will be of slight importance, it will matter not whether it be left to him or them; it is only in the event of their being wicked that he can suffer from such an arrangement; and considering how frequently women, whose principles of virtue are not fixed, feel the fact of their being, in a pecuniary point of view, independent of their husbands, to be an additional spur to an indulgence in vicious practices, I never should, in any case, feel myself justified in advising such an arrangement to be made. No; rather let the property go to him and leave his punishment to Heaven, than secure it so as to operate thus as an additional incentive to vice."

"But do you not think," said Goodman, "that he has been punished sufficiently already?"

"Certainly not," replied Whitely. "He ought to be hanged. I am not vindictive; I hope I am not cruel; but a man like that, sir, deserves to be burnt alive."

"He has endured a far greater amount of torture," rejoined Goodman, "than was ever yet endured at the stake. He *has* been burnt alive! He has been burnt until reduced to a state of insensibility, and then, when death could have given him no additional pang, he has been compelled to suffer those exquisite agonies which must necessarily have accompanied his gradual restoration. And this I attribute entirely to the fact of his having so deeply injured me; for his mind was in consequence so diseased at the time that he fancied he saw me in the room. I therefore cannot—even looking at him only—feel myself justified in inflicting upon him the additional punishment of utter destitution, and when I look at those who must be involved in his ruin, and who may have been innocent even of the knowledge of his offence until the last, I still think that I cannot, consistently with my duty as a Christian, do aught else than that which I propose. But what is your opinion, my friend?" he continued, addressing Uncle John. "You have been silent! Do you think that I shall be justified in reducing my brother and his family to abject wretchedness and want? Is it not your impression that he has been sufficiently punished?"

"Why," said Uncle John, "you see I am placed in a peculiar position. I promised your brother that I would strive to allay whatever ill-feeling recent circumstances might have engendered: I promised this on condition that he would liberate you at once from the asylum. It was a sort of contract between us: but now that he has performed his part, I find it exceedingly difficult to perform mine. I had much rather, therefore, that this affair should be settled without me, for while I cannot conscientiously say any thing in favor of the man, I am bound by my promise to say nothing against him, and even then I am not quite sure that I shall have done in reality all that my promise conveyed."

"Why," said Goodman, "you promised nothing more than that you would strive to allay any ill-feeling that *might* have been engendered: and, most certainly, whatever ill-feeling might have existed has already been allayed. All the difficulty is, therefore, at an end: as I have no ill-feeling whatever towards him now, you can have no ill-feeling to repress: so that all you have to do is to avoid saying anything calculated to excite an ill-feeling, and you will have performed your promise faithfully."

"My promise conveyed more than that,"

said Uncle John. "I don't at this moment recollect what I wished him to understand; but I am sure that it conveyed more than that. I am not quite certain that I did not mean not only that I would do what I could to repress ill-feelings, but that I would do all I could to effect an absolute reconciliation. I should like to be clear upon that point: I should like to know what he imagined I meant at the time."

"But, my friend," said Goodman, "that has nothing to do with your opinion on the point now at issue."

"Why, it may not have anything to do with it, certainly; but, at present, I am inclined to believe that it has, because, you see, if I express an opinion to the effect that he has been already sufficiently punished, I may perhaps be expressing an opinion which I do not conscientiously entertain, while, on the other hand, by stating it to be my opinion that he has not, I may be acting in opposition to the spirit of a contract which, no matter with whom it may have been made, ought of course to be strictly adhered to."

"Well! I certainly should like to have your opinion upon the subject before I decide; because I cannot but feel that it may, and doubtless will be, the last important act of my life. However, as you do not at present feel justified in stating what your real opinion is, my decision had better be deferred."

"Yes: that will be much the better way," said Uncle John, who had really no desire to give an opinion upon the point; for although he felt convinced that in reality Walter did not deserve the slightest consideration, he could not satisfy himself that if he stated that as being his conviction, he should be doing under the circumstances that which was right.

The matter was therefore left open, and Goodman was highly pleased to find that his friend had given that promise to Walter, for he feared that some powerful argument might be adduced to prove that, after what had happened, he ought not to leave the will as it was, in favor of him by whom he had been injured so unnaturally and so deeply. As far as forgiveness went, he forgave him from his heart. The only point upon which he was anxious to be satisfied, was the justice of the course he proposed to pursue. And yet again he conceived that —although if the thing were made public it might perhaps be deemed a bad example— in a private case like this he could not do much wrong in doing that which his benevolent feelings suggested. Besides, he felt that, even if he were justified in taking the administration of justice in this particular case into his own hands, it was not a time at which he ought to administer it harshly, and harshly he could not help feeling it would be administered, if he deprived not only Walter, but his family, of all they had to depend upon in the world. He knew that they had no other means of existence; he knew, that if he left them penniless, they must either starve or plunge into the vortex of infamy; and knowing this, he could not reconcile the act of driving them into temptation, with his duty either as a Christian or as a man. He therefore eventually resolved not to renew the painful subject. He had authorised the recovery of the property, and that authority there was no sufficient reason to withdraw; but he hoped that no act on the part of Walter—that no argument of Uncle John or Whitely—that nothing, in short, might occur to induce him to alter the will.

CHAPTER L.

EXPLAINS THE POSSIBILITY OF MAKING A MAN DIG AN EXTRAORDINARY HOLE.

As Valentine had not seen Louise for five days—as he had called five times and left his card without finding her "at home,"— and as he had received from her no communication whatever—he began to think that Uncle John was right!—that he really had suffered his spirit of independence to carry him a little too far.

And yet, what had he done? It is true he absented himself for two entire days; but then he was calm, quite calm, while she was bursting with passion. He did not retaliate; he simply said, "Well, I will go, if you wish it!" He had said nothing more, and yet, never since then had he been able to see her! He did think that this was not strictly correct. He was not at all satisfied with it: he felt that he had been somewhat ill used! For what could she expect? Could she expect him to submit to every species of indignity? Could she expect that he would ever suffer himself to be her slave? He loved her, fondly loved her, and she knew it; but never would he consent to become the puppet of her caprice. No, he would call once more—but once!—and if she was denied to him, the course which manliness suggested was clear, and he made up his mind to pursue it. He would *not* surrender his spirit as a man! nor would Louise yield her spirit as a woman! They were playing the same game: they had both the same object in view, and they were now equally sure of achieving that object, for although Louise had theretofore felt herself somewhat overmatched, she had a weapon now in store for him, in the shape of a Welshman, whom she meant to use so as to enable her to obtain a signal triumph!

In the warm hearts of lovers whose affections are fixed, and who are really so attached to each other that they seem to be scarcely able to exist but in each other's society, there must be some beautiful feeling in operation while they strive to make it appear that they are perfectly free. The general motive may perhaps be highly laudable; but with the ladies it is sometimes inscrutable, seeing that they will labor to make men believe that it would be a matter of very slight importance indeed, if they were to do that which, if done, would snap their dear heart-strings. This course is, perhaps in many instances, pursued with the view of testing the strength of man's affection; but this was not the object of Louise: she wished to obtain the mastery to begin with; and she played a very dangerous game; for while Valentine's love was of too manly a caste to be inaccessible to reason, he had not had sufficient experience in these delicate matters to know how to make ladies when they are conquered believe that they are really victorious.—It was unfortunate, perhaps, that he did not know this; but that he did not is nevertheless a fact. He was much too serious about the matter. When he called for the last time, in the event of Louise being denied to him, he seriously meant it to be for the last time: he would *not* have called again without a special invitation! It may therefore be held to be on all hands fortunate that when he called Louise was at home.

This he had scarcely expected; but Louise expected him, and had laid her plans accordingly: she had directed him to be shown into the breakfast-room, which overlooked the garden, and the moment he entered this room, he saw her leaning upon the arm of a tall young fellow, with whom she appeared to be on the most affectionate terms!

Valentine looked—of course he looked!—and his aspect was severe. She gazed at the fellow, and smiled, and chatted gaily, and seemed particularly playful! Valentine pulled a piece clean out of his glove. Who was it? What right had he there? He couldn't tell: he could only guess! He paced the room, and knit his brows, and pursed his lips, and breathed hard through his nostrils, and thrust his hands firmly to the very bottom of his pockets. There they were!—oh, yes, there they were!—there could scarcely be two sound opinions about it! He had a great mind to go to them: he had a great mind to ascertain at once what it meant. And yet—well! why did she not come? He rang the bell—with violence he rang it!—he was not in a sweet temper at the time. "Does Miss Raven know that I am here?" he inquired of the servant, as he entered.

"Beg pardon, sir;—quite forgot to tell her, sir:—dear me, beg pardon."

"Why, you thick-headed fool!" exclaimed Valentine—and it certainly was a very harsh exclamation—but before he could get any farther the servant—who only acted up to his instructions—had vanished from the room.

"Now," thought Valentine, "I shall see how the heartless coquette will conduct herself, when she is told that I am here."

He stood firmly in the middle of the room, and kept his eye steadfastly upon her.—The servant entered the garden: he addressed her, and retired. She turned, she did not withdraw her arm: she did not even tremble! She smiled, and looked up at the mortal, and said something to him, and then instead of leaving him there, led him playfully into the house.

Valentine now took his seat upon the sofa, and tried to look as calm and collected as possible. They entered the room, and she absolutely introduced the long wretch to him as Mr. Llewellen.

Valentine *looked* at him!—he was too big to eat—but he was *not* too big to be annihilated!

"Are you not well?" said Louise.

"I am not," replied Valentine.

"What is the matter?"

"Nothing of importance; I shall be able no doubt to *survive* it. Oh I shall *survive* it!"

"Inteet, then look you, these pleak wints plow nopotty coot," observed Mr. Llewellen.

Valentine's tongue itched to mimic the mortal; but, although he felt that it was perfectly impossible to treat him with anything like common civility, he thought that it might perhaps be better not to insult him in any direct manner, then. He therefore bowed very distantly, and looked rather contemptuously at Mr. Llewellen, and then turned abruptly towards the window, at which Louise was engaged in making an effort to suppress a hearty laugh. He knew neither what to say nor how to act. He could not speak before that fellow Llewellen, and as to speaking *to* him!—he would not deign to do it. A pause therefore ensued—a long pause—during which both gentlemen looked particularly stupid, while Louise did not dare to turn her head. At length, however, Llewellen—who had been no more fascinated by Valentine than Valentine had been fascinated by him—happened to think, strangely enough, that he really was not wanted, and no sooner had he conceived this extraordinary idea, than inspired with the spirit of independence he stalked from the room.

This, of course, was precisely what Valentine wanted. The absence of that tall wretch—for as a wretch he most uncharitably looked upon him then—was a thing which he had strongly desired; and yet he did not take immediate advantage of his absence. He wanted Louise to speak first, and she would not speak first. She still kept at the window, and appeared to be lost in admiration of Llewellen, who was then buisily occupied in pulling up the weeds. The very moment, however, Valentine perceived that Llewellen was again in the garden, he felt himself bound to break silence. "I have to apologise," said he, with a bitterness both of emphasis and of aspect, "for having disturbed you. Had I known that you had been thus affectionately engaged, I should certainly not have intruded."

"Why, what *do* you mean?"

"You know what I mean. Who is that fellow—that creature—that Llewellen?"

"Llewellen! oh, he is a very old friend."

"Indeed?"

"Oh yes, I have known him from infancy. We were play-fellows together."

"And are *play*-fellows still, I perceive!"

"Why, we cannot forget the very many happy hours we spent together in childhood. Besides, he is such an affectionate creature, and *so* fond of me!"

"I have not the slightest doubt of it; and you appear to be equally fond of him."

"Why, you surely are not jealous?"

"Jealous!" echoed Valentine, smiling very bitterly. "What, of *him?* He is a nice compactly built, intellectual looking animal for a man to be jealous of, certainly!"

"Why, what is the matter with him? Really, I cannot see much to complain of. He is taller than you and much stouter, and I am sure that he possesses a good kind heart."

"In your eyes, Miss Raven, he is perfection, no doubt. But look you, pless you, the pleak wint is plowing upon his potty. It may, look you, too him no coot. Inteet, his plut may pe chilt: it may set fast his pones!"

"You are satirical," said Louise, "you always were; but your satire has malice in it now, I am afraid. Come why are you so cross with him? What has he done to offend you?"

"Oh, nothing—nothing," replied Valentine, carelessly.

"Why will you not be friendly with him then? you are angry perhaps, because you saw us walking in the garden, but surely there was no harm in that."

"Oh! of course not. There can be no harm in anything Miss Raven does. There can be no harm in clinging to him as if you loved him dearly. There can be no harm in allowing him to play with your hand, your hair, your chin, or your waist!"

"I cannot help his being fond of me!"

"Propriety, Miss Raven, might suggest that you are not exactly bound to encourage his fondness. But that, of course, is nothing to me. I have no voice at all in the matter, although, I must say, that had you dealt somewhat more justly, it might perhaps, on all hands have been quite as well. However, I feel that I am in the way here, now, and shall therefore at once take my leave."

"You are a very cross, unkind creature!" said Louise. "I did intend to press you to dine with us to-day; but I am not quite sure that I shall do so now."

"I beg that you will not trouble yourself. I would not stay if even you were to press me. You have some one else to *press;* therefore my presence cannot be required."

"Of course it must be as you please. I have not the slightest influence over you, I am aware; but I certainly did hope that we might have spent a vary happy day together in mutual forgetfulness of all that has passed. But I perceive that you are of a most unforgiving disposition, and perceiving this, I cannot but observe in my own vindication, that *you* were the cause of all that transpired at our last interview—that your neglect urged me to say what I did."

"Of what passed at our last interview, Miss Raven, I have not since I entered the house even thought."

"Then, why are you so angry? because I walked and chatted with Llewellen in the garden? Do you know who he is?"

"No: nor do I care."

"If you do not care to know, why I do not care to tell you. But I think that you would like to know nevertheless, and I *will* tell you—that is, provided you ask me prettily."

"Miss Raven, you treat me like a child, and as a child I will be played with no longer. I perceive that you are faithless, and unworthy the love of an honorable man; I therefore take leave of you for ever."

"If you are an honorable man," said Louise, who now became somewhat alarmed, "if you possess any one of the feelings of a gentleman, you will sit down at once in that chair and explain to me clearly what you mean by those words. To whom have I been faithless? Why am I unworthy the love of an honorable man?"

"You have been faithless to me!" returned Valentine, "and I have this day proved you to be a coquette."

"I deny it!" cried Louise, "I have been faithless to no one: nor have I ever been a coquette! But are you really serious? Do you really mean to say that I am a coquette —which, if I were, I should despise myself —because I see no impropriety in chatting with my cousin?"

"Is Llewellen your cousin?"

"To be sure he is!"

"Why did you not say so before?"

"You said you did not care to know who he was!"

"But why did you not introduce him as your cousin?"

"I certainly might have done that," said Louise, instead of answering the question, "but, come, for goodness sake don't look so cross, you surely are satisfied now?"

The fact of Llewellen being her cousin somewhat softened him, but he did not feel satisfied exactly. He had heard of ladies' cousins before, and he knew that it frequently happened that constant communication with each other engendered feelings which outstripped those of consanguinity. He therefore felt that he ought to look sharply after the Welshman, especially as Louise had confessed that he was so fond: he also felt, that although they were cousins, those playful familiarities which he had noticed ought not to be sanctioned.

"Well," said Louise, after a pause, "you will dine with us now, I presume?"

"I still beg to be excused. My presence may have a tendency to restrain perhaps the playfulness of your cousin."

"Oh! no; not at all!"

"And if it does not," thought Valentine, "I'll work him!"

At this moment Raven played one of his fifteen-barred stuccatoed knocks at the door, and immediately afterwards marched into the room. "Ah! Valentine, my boy!" he cried, extending his hand, "why, where have you been for the last half century? I tell you what it is you two," he continued, "you conduct yourselves just for all the world as if you belonged to the aristocracy. Why can't you carry on pleasantly together? What's the use of quarrelling, and mumping, and making yourselves miserable? I know you've been at it again. I don't want to be told; I saw it the very moment I entered the room. Now take my advice: quarrel no more; let this be the last, and make it up as soon as possible. You are not like the beggarly aristocracy whose object in matters of this kind is not to secure the affections, but to overreach each other. But what's become of Fred—where is he?"

"In the garden," replied Louise.

"Have you not introduced him?"

"Oh yes; he has been talking about the wints peing pleak."

"He is a droll fellow that; it would do your heart good to see him eat."

"But Valentine will not dine with us to-day," said Louise.

"Not dine with us! Why not? Pooh! nonsense: he must; he has no other engagement. He is here now, and here he must remain. There, run away, and see if you can keep from quarrelling. I have a long letter to write. If you want to be amused, join Fred."

Louise at once took the arm of Valentine, and they went into the garden, where the Welshman was still engaged pulling up weeds.

"It's poiling hot look you to tay," said Llewellen, as he wiped the perspiration from his red round face.

"Do you find many weeds?" inquired Valentine, who now thought it might be as well to be civil.

"Weets! my potty! look you, there's nothing put weets. They tont at all understant how to pluck them here: they preak them off at the pottoms, when they crow acain, pless you, insteet you see of tragging them up py the roots."

Valentine at once perceived the force of this remark, and was able to look at Llewellen with comparative pleasure. He was not quite so ugly as he appeared to be before; he was tall, but quite straight; stout, but symmetrical. The change he had undergone was amazing, and it may seem extraordinary to some, that although he was a finely made, and rather a handsome fellow, Valentine should have thought him at first the ugliest wretch he ever beheld; but they who know the feelings which are generated in the breast of a rival will understand how Llewellen could appear a very ill-conditioned mortal in the eyes of Valentine, when he supposed him to be a lover of Louise, for as love often blinds us to physical defects, so rivalry in matters of love often blinds us to physical beauties. But although Llewellen looked somewhat better than before, Valentine viewed him still as an awkward individual, and resolved to reward him in some way or other for every affectionate word he dared to utter to Louise.

Louise, on the other hand, resolved to reward *him*. She had reason to be satisfied with all that had occurred. She had succeeded in making him jealous, which was to her, as it is indeed to the ladies in general, extremely pleasurable; and although it had been essential to her own security to let him know that Llewellen was her cousin, she still determined to tease him by being as affectionate to the Welshman as one loving cousin could be to another.

"Look you, Louey tear," shouted Llewellen, who was really a very industrious fellow, "shall hur perry these weets at the pottom of the carten, or purn 'em?"

"That I must leave to you," replied Louise.

Llewellen at once pulled off his coat, and chalked out his plans for a hole.

"Louey tear!" thought Valentine, "Why could he not have contented himself with 'Louey?' what did he want to add 'tear' for?" He did not approve of this mode of address; he thought it highly incorrect, notwithstanding they were cousins; and although he said nothing about it then, he made up his mind to punish him even for that.

Coolly and tranquilly therefore did he walk, while Llewellen was digging the hole; and when he fancied that he had got to a sufficient depth for his purpose, he observed that he had had a tough job.

"Yesm," said Llewellen, who looked very hot, "the crount is hart, look you."

"Now is the time to work him," thought Valentine, who accordingly threw his voice into the hole, and groaned in the most piteous manner possible.

Llewellen started. He leaped from the hole in an instant, and turned with an expression of horror, while Louise clung to Valentine, who also looked slightly alarmed, with the laudable view of keeping up the delusion.

"Tit you not hear?" cried Llewellen in a sharp thrilling whisper, "tit you not hear a croan? Potty of me! phot coot it pe look you? Somepotty perried? Hark! pless you, hark!" he continued, as Valentine sent another groan under ground.

"Good gracious!" cried Louise, "what on earth can it be! Had you not better dig deeper?"

Llewellen seemed paralysed. He kept his eyes fixed upon the hole, and imagined he saw the earth move; and yet it struck him at the moment as being impossible for any human being to be there. "Nopotty could preathe!" said he, after having eyed the ground in every conceivable way with great intensity of feeling, "ant nopotty coot live without preath!"

Valentine, who saw the inexpediency of allowing the thing to be reasoned upon, inquired with much earnestness of manner, if he had ever heard of persons being buried in a trance.

"Perried in a trance!" cried Llewellen, quite struck with the novelty of the question, "inteet hur have; put then—no put then never at the pottoms of cartens!"

"Let me out! let me out! oh, do let me out!" cried Valentine, feigning a half smothered voice, which appeared to proceed from about two feet below the bottom of the hole.

"Hur will, look you!" shouted Llewellen, who had then no doubt about the matter at all, "hur will tig till hur fint you!"

"If you do," thought Valentine, "you will *tig* to an extraordinary depth."

Llewellen now set to work in earnest. He used his spade with surpassing dexterity. Had he served an apprenticeship to the first metropolitan grave-digger he could not have been more *au fait* to the work.

"Can I assist you?" said Valentine, as a mere matter of politeness.

"No, look you, the hole is not pig enough for poth."

Nor was it; it was then but about two feet in diameter, and as Llewellen had got about three feet deep, he could not operate with any degree of comfort to himself. Of course Valentine perceived this with pleasure, and being resolved to keep him at it, continued to exert himself so zealously in the cause, that Llewellen soon enlarged his sphere of action.

"A little pit longer!" he cried, "ant you'll then pe releast, look you!"

"Oh!" exclaimed Valentine, "don't tread so heavily upon me."

"Hur wont, my tear poy! hur wont tret upon you any more than hur can help."

"I cannot bear it!" cried Valentine. "Oh!"

"Put pless you, hur must tret a little to tig. Phot part am hur upon you?"

"My back."

"Your pack!" cried Llewellen, when looking up at Valentine, he added, "he's perried upon his pelly!"

So exceedingly natural was this conclusion, and so long was the countenance with which it was drawn and declared, that Valentine could scarcely refrain from laughing. He did, however, by dint of great exertion, succeed in preserving that gravity of aspect which the deep and solemn character of the occasion demanded, and Llewellen again set to work with all the zeal and rapidity of which he was capable. His first object now was to cut out a small standing place for himself, that he might not give pain to the unfortunate person whom he naturally presumed to be beneath; and as he of course soon accomplished that praiseworthy object, he worked away like a sapper, and exhibited the most benevolent anxiety to avoid digging the spade into any part of the body of that unfortunate person; being convinced that if he did so, the wound he should inflict would be neither slight nor pleasant, and might be exceedingly difficult to heal, inasmuch as the dirt would be sure to get in it.

"Now work away!" cried Valentine, in his feigned voice, of course; and Llewellen, who was already working away like a convict, redoubled his exertions, as big drops of sweat left his brow to bedew the hole.

"Come, quick!" cried Valentine; "I only wish you were here instead of me."

This Llewellen conceived to be an ungrateful observation; but as he felt that the life of an unfortunate fellow-creature was at stake, he took no further notice of the matter, but continued to work with all the spirit and strength he had in him.

"Hollo, hollo, hollo!" cried Raven, coming up at this moment, having noticed the extraordinary exertions of Llewellen from the window. "What do you mean by cutting up the garden in this way?—For whom are you digging that grave?"

"Oh, papa!" cried Louise, as Llewellen kept on, for he thought that no time was to be lost, and very properly; "some poor unhappy creature has been buried alive!"

"Buried alive!—What, here? Pooh, nonsense, absurd!"

"But we have heard him!"

"I tell you it's absurd!"

"How too you fint yourself now, my tear poy?" inquired Llewellen of the person assumed to be below.

"Work away!" cried Valentine. "A little to the left!"

"Bless my life and soul!" exclaimed Raven, who heard this. "Why, how could it be?—Run for those fellows, my girl. Tell them all to come instantly!—Val, you will find a lot of spades and a pickaxe in the tool-house; bring them all here—quick, there's a good fellow. Keep at it, Fred!—dig away!" And Fred did dig away!—no Pole on being sent to the Siberian mines ever dug away harder.

"Now then!" cried Raven, as the servants appeared. "Now, off with your coats, and help Mr. Llewellen."

24

The servants looked at the hole in a state of amazement; but stripped, as they were desired, in a moment, although they could not conceive what the object was, exactly.

"Now make this place larger: be quick!" cried Raven; and as two of them caught hold of spades, the other seized the pickaxe, and dropped into the hole.

"Get out!" cried Valentine, "you hurt me!" And he with the pickaxe did get out, and that with remarkable promptitude, for really he felt much alarmed.

"Work round the edge!" cried Raven; "and make the hole larger!—How came you first to hear him?"

"Hur was tigging a hole, look you, to perry the weets," replied Llewellen, who nearly broke his back in standing up to give an answer to the question, "when I hurt a lout croan, pless you, unter the crount."

"How very fortunate you happened to select this spot," observed Raven; and it was held to be a singularly fortunate selection, under the circumstances, by all.

"What do you leave off for!" cried Valentine, as the sweating Llewellen was engaged in readjusting the muscular economy of his back. "Do you hear?"

Llewellen did not exactly like being addressed in so imperative a style by a man to preserve whose life he had been working like a slave. He still, however, felt himself bound, as a Christian, to do all in his power to release him, notwithstanding his manifest ingratitude, and therefore again went to work, but with the full determination to expostulate with him the very moment he got him out.

The servants, under the strict surveillance of Raven, were now digging away like young sextons. They never before had such a job. In less than ten minutes from the time they commenced, the prespiration oozed from every pore. The intense curiosity involved in the hope of digging a man up alive for some short time sustained them; but, as the harder they worked, and the deeper they dug, the more distant the actual realisation of that hope seemed to be, they very soon began to flag, as if unable to stand it. Raven, however, made them stick to it closely; and they felt it to be, under the circumstances, as much as their respective situations were worth, to give in. They felt already nearly exhausted; work was altogether new to them; they puffed, and panted, and groaned; but Raven still kept them at it.

"Let's have some peer!" cried Llewellen, "Hur'm poiling!"

The servants simultaneously looked at their master in the hope of being ordered to run for the beer, seeing that that to either of them would have been a great relief, because neither would have felt himself bound to hurry back; but no, Raven sent Louise to their manifest mortification, and made them keep on, although they declared to each other in strict confidence aside that they felt fit to drop. Their philanthropy had vanished. That beautiful feeling of humanity, which prompted them at first to work with the view of saving the life of a fellow-creature, had died away. They now felt for themselves, and that feeling was at the moment so powerful, that in it all others were merged. It was not, however, thus with Llewellen. He was determined to rescue him whom he believed to be underground, if possible. All considerations having reference to himself were set aside in the pure spirit of benevolence, and therefore when the beer came, he opened his shoulders, and, without even taking his lips from the vehicle, swallowed at least three pints. The servants looked at him while he was drinking, with astonishment, mingled with dismay, forasmuch as they beheld the wide bottom of the can go gradually up into the air, they became most intensely apprehensive of his drawing every drain; for they knew that that can for them alone, would never by the order of their master be replenished. When Llewellen, therefore, left them a pint, it was just a pint more than they expected, and they felt themselves bound in drinking that pint, to be just as long as if it had been half a gallon.

"Come, *come!*" cried Valentine, "work away there!—you don't consider!"

"Yesm, my poy," said Llewellen, whose face glowed like fire. "Are you much teeper town, look you now?"

"How can I tell?" replied Valentine. "Can you not guess from the sound of my voice?"

"Inteet, how the tevil you can speak at all, I can't think, look you!"

"Now then don't chatter, but work!" cried Valentine, and Llewellen more firmly than ever resolved to deliver to the invisible individual a lecture upon his glaring impropriety of speech the very instant he had succeeded in digging him out.

The hole was now about nine feet long by six wide, while its depth was between five and six, and as they had just reached a stratum of brickbats and tiles, the difficulty experienced in digging considerably increased. Llewellen was nothing daunted by this singular circumstance, but the servants who had for some time previously exhibited symptoms of exhaustion, now took upon themselves the responsibility of declaring that they should not be able to stand it much longer.

"Let's have some more peer!" cried Llewellen.

"What, again?" exclaimed Valentine.

"Yesm, can't tig without peer."

Again, then, Louise was despatched with the can, and, on her return, Llewellen did succeed in emptying it at a draught, but sent her to fill it once more for the servants.

"Now are you going to work away, again, or are you not?" inquired Valentine, whose voice now appeared to proceed from about a foot below the bottom of the hole. "You think more of swilling, than of me!"

"Tont be angry, my poy. Flesh and ploot must be sustaint while tigging, in truth."

"If we may judge from the sound," observed Raven, "he don't lie much deeper. You had better dig a trench round, and then you'll be able to pull him up at once, without injury."

"You can't jutch from the sount how teep he is, pless you. Hur jutcht from the sount that he wasn't a foot teep an hour ago; put hur'll try."

He then took the pickaxe, and used it so dexterously that he kept the men fully employed with their spades, until the trench had been established. "Are you pelow this, look you?" he then inquired.

"I think not," replied Valentine.

"All you have to do then," said Raven, "is to raise that earth there in the middle."

"Yesm. Now my poys work away!" cried Llewellen; "he'll soon be out now."

The hopes of the servants revived: their spirits were reanimated to a sensible extent, and they did work away very laudably. They now again firmly believed that they should see that unhappy individual, of whose existence under ground they were satisfied to a man. They, therefore, used their spades with really great ardor, considering: but, as time had cemented the bricks and loam firmly together, the ground was so stiff that, after the first five minutes, they were quite inclined to give the thing up, as being utterly hopeless. The indefatigable zeal of Llewellen, however, again urged them on. He once more seized the pickaxe to loosen the earth, in utter forgetfulness of the fact that he firmly believed the man to be lying in the very spot to which he applied it with all his power. Valentine perceived this, of course, and when Llewellen had picked a deep hole, into which he was driving the implement again and again, with all the strength at his command, he cried, "*Oh!* it has entered my leg! now let me lie in peace."

Llewellen paused, and listened. All was silent beneath. His impression then was that he had unhappily injured the individual very seriously.

"Phot's to pe tone?" he inquired, addressing Raven.

"Why, dig him out, of course," replied that gentleman, "its only his leg! that's not of much importance. We are sure he's there now; therefore, let's have him out at once, dead or alive."

Llewellen abandoned the dangerous pickaxe, and again had recourse to the innocent spade, which, after having called for a "trop more peer," he continued to employ, with unequivocal success, while the servants, who now, as they conceived, had something of a tangible character to work upon, seeing that the victim had really called out about his leg, backed the glorious efforts of Llewellen most manfully, which, duly considering all things, certainly did them great credit.

Upwards of an hour they worked at this solid piece of earth; for, as Llewellen would not use the pickaxe again, their progress was singularly slow. As they proceeded they, of course, thought it strange that they should meet with nothing indicative of the presence of a man. Had they come across a finger, or even a toe, they strongly felt that under the circumstances it would have been something; but, as they dug out nothing but bricks and tiles, it was natural for them to infer therefrom, that there was something about the affair rather mysterious. They, nevertheless, worked away in the hope of picking up anon a loose leg, an odd arm, or the head of an individual, until they had got below the point to which Llewellen had pierced, when the mystery became very dense.

"Nopotty here!" exclaimed Llewellen; "where is the leck that hur injurt? Hur've cot pelow that!"

"And it seems to be impossible for him to have moved in such hard stony earth," added Raven.

"Oh! if he has the apility to move apout the crount, why we may keep on tigging till toomstay. Where are you, my poy, look you, where are you now?"

No answer was returned to this plain, simple question.

"Are you tet?"

There was still no answer.

"Well, this is, beyond all doubt," observed Raven, "the most extraordinary thing I ever met with."

"Extraortinary! hur is thunterstruck, look you!" cried Llewellen, and he really appeared to be so at that moment. "He's tet; there's no tout apout that: hur've kilt him with the pickaxe; ant, therefore, as hur can now too no more coot to-day, hur'll have another tig to-morrow morning for the potty."

"But I don't see how you could have touched him," said Raven.

"Nor can hur, look you; put there's no tout that he's there; ant, as hur can't hear him speak, there's no tout that he's tet; ant as he is tet, hur can't pring him to life again, so that hur hat petter pegin fresh acain tomorrow."

To this series of opinions all promptly subscribed, and Llewellen got out of the hole. The servants followed, not indeed with much alacrity, but with peculiar satisfaction, far as the mere cessation from labor was concerned, but no further. They were unable to stand erect: every attempt they made to reassume that manly position was accompanied by a pain of the most acute character in the back. They were, therefore, content to walk for a time nearly double, as the only available means of avoiding immediate agony. This, however, was not the case with Llewellen—he gave one mighty stretch, and all was over; but his appearance at the time was anything but aristocratical, seeing that his hands, arms, and face were begrimed with dirt, while his clothes were in a most untidy condition. He had done more work in those three hours, than his assistants could have accomplished in a month; not only because he possessed more strength, but because *his* had been purely voluntary labor, while theirs would of necessity be compulsory, inasmuch as, except upon compulsion, they would never work at all.

"Well," said Raven, after having stood over the hole with Llewellen for some time in deep contemplation, "I can't make it out; I shall not be satisfied until we have him up. It certainly is the strangest thing I ever either heard of or met with."

"Oh hur'll have him up to-morrow, never fear. Hur'll tig till hur fint him, if he's town twenty feet."

"Well, come Fred, run away and make yourself decent for dinner."

"Hur wish it was retty look you, now," said Llewellen, "hur shall eat a goot tinner to-tay."

Of this Raven appeared to have no doubt whatever, and when he had given certain instructions to his nearly exhausted servants, who were doubled up still, Louise and Valentine were left in the garden alone.

The fact of a voice having been heard to proceed apparently from the earth, rendered Louise for the time being oblivious of almost everything else: she could speak, she could think, in fact, of nothing but that;

for although the thing in itself must appear extremely stupid to those who know the means by which the effects of ventriloquism are produced, they, who have not even the most remote conception of those means, are not inclined to think so lightly of the effects at the time. To them those effects are invariably astounding, and it may with perfect safety be asserted, that there is scarcely a man who, on hearing a voice proceed apparently from the earth, and being at the same time unconscious of the power of ventriloquy, would not dig a hole, in order to ascertain the cause, as deep as that dug by Llewellen. *He* was as firmly convinced as he was of his own existence, that some unhappy person was alive under ground, and so was Raven, and so was Louise, whose conjectures were certainly of a most extraordinary character. Valentine would willingly have undeceived *her*, but as his object was to make Llewellen anon appear as ridiculous as possible in the event of his continuing to address her in those terms of endearment of which he did not and could not approve, he very naturally kept the thing a secret even from her, and contented himself with subduing her fears.

In a short time Llewellen reappeared in the garden, very warm still, but tidy. His object was to have another glance at the hole before dinner, and he therefore walked up to it thoughtfully and firmly, and stood upon its brink, and shook his head, and looked down, first in the most straightforward manner, and then obliquely. While at his toilet he had conceived the idea that he had not in reality dug below the point the pickaxe had reached; but as after a very minute examination he discovered that he had, the thing appeared to him to be far more mysterious than ever. He could not understand it at all, and he said so, and continued to announce the same fact, with variations, until he sat down to dinner, when, from the time he began till he had finished, he did not appear to have a moment's opportunity for the delivery of any opinion upon any subject whatever. "Hur will trupple you acain,"—"Shall hur have the pleasure?"—"Hur shall pe prout"—"Yesm"—"No"—and "A littel more peer," were the only words he uttered.

Valentine had been led by Raven to expect that Llewellen was able to eat, but he had, he could have had, no idea of the extent of his gormandising powers. Four times he was helped to soup, three times to fish, and three times to beef—although Raven, knowing his customer, took special care to send him upwards of a pound each time—after which he demolished a chicken and a half with a fully proportionate quantity of ham, and then set to work upon the pastry—precisely as if nothing at all had happened—winding up the whole by emptying the bread-basket with a view to the full injoyment of two good half-pound slices of cheese.

It is true that his appetite on this occasion had been very much provoked. As a matter of justice this must be admitted. He had worked very hard, and digging is a species of labor which renders a man liable to eat a great deal. But, allowing for all this, the way in which Llewellen ate proved that it was not for him a very extraordinary quantity, although sufficient to have satisfied a family of twelve, if even they had not had a respectable meal for a month.

"How many meals a-day do you have when you are at home, Fred?" inquired Mr. Raven, as soon as Llewellen was disengaged.

"Only five, look you:—preakfast, lunch, tinner, tea, and supper."

"And do you have animal food at every meal?"

"Yesm. A man in Caermarthen inteet must have foot: he can't live without eating." Which, however extraordinary it may appear, is a positive fact.

Dinner now being at an end, the mystery again formed the topic of conversation.

"That some poor creature," said Raven, "lies buried at the bottom of our garden, there cannot be a rational doubt, and if I were at all superstitious, I should say that the fact of his being there accounts for the singular noises we have frequently heard. If you remember, Valentine, the last time your uncle was here, we heard a strange voice in this very room!—I have never been able to make that out yet.—You recollect?"

"Oh! yes:—'One of the Aristocracy!'"

"Exactly.—Now that was a wonderful circumstance, when you come to think of it!—*We* could find no one in the room, you know!—The voice would answer questions, but nothing could be seen!—Nearly the whole of the following day was I endeavoring to find out what it could possibly have been, and as I could obtain no clue whatever to the mystery, I'd lay my life, if I were at all superstitious, that this affair in the garden is connected with it in some way. I have heard of haunted houses, it is true; but then I never put faith in such absurdities—I have invariably looked upon them either as the morbid imaginings of hypochondriacs, or as the idle fancies of ignorant minds wrought upon by superstitious fear. Thank Heaven I am not superstitious: I never was—I am only saying, that if I were, the chances are that I should attribute the strange noises that I have heard to the fact of some one having been buried in the garden."

"Some of these things," observed Valentine, "are very unaccountable."

"They are indeed. I have heard many persons, strong-minded persons too, declare that they have seen apparitions, and no argument, no reasoning, could ever induce them to believe that they had not. I confess that if there be such things as spectres, I should exceedingly like to see one; but I have no belief in anything of the sort. I can, of course, understand how men can imagine that they behold them. We all see visions in our dreams, and when men see them while, as they fancy, they are awake, they do but dream that they see them, for the process of beholding apparitions is but a morbid species of dreaming after all."

"But both these things to which you have alluded may be mysterious, and yet have no connection with each other," observed Valentine.

"Exactly. With regard to the affair in the garden, I don't know at all what to think about that. The fact of an absolutely dead man being buried in such a place, would lead one to suppose that there had been some foul play, while, if it be any one who has been buried in a trance, it is exceedingly strange that they should have buried him there. Of course, that people have been thus buried we cannot doubt. Many cases have occurred, which prove beyond all dispute, the possibility of persons under those circumstances, being able to exist in the earth."

At this moment, Llewellen commenced snoring most hideously.

"Fred!" cried Raven. "My good fellow, come, come, we can't stand that!"

Poor Llewellen, whom the labor of love in the garden had exhausted, remained quite unconscious of being thus addressed. Raven shook him very manfully, and bawled in his ear, but although the snoring almost instantaneously ceased, it was a long time before he could be persuaded to open his eyes.

"I say Fred!" continued Raven, when he had accomplished this praiseworthy object. "We can't stand snoring!"

"Tear me!—tit hur snore? Hur peck parton, look you, put really—hur—really." Having got to this highly satisfactory point, he dropped off again as soundly as before, when, as the music of his "most miraculous organ" had ceased, no attempt was made again to disturb him. He slept, and slept on, and as Raven soon followed his example, Louise and Valentine passed an extremely pleasant evening, although neither could be said to have absolutely relinquished the object they both had in view.

CHAPTER LI.

IN WHICH VALENTINE ARGUES A POINT IN OPPOSITION TO THE VIEWS OF MANY THOUSANDS.

When Valentine called the following morning, he found poor Llewellen in the hole. He had been digging away ever since six o'clock, but, of course, without any success. When he commenced at that interesting hour, he had firmly resolved to keep at it until he found the "potty," but as the ground, when Valentine arrived, was becoming sufficiently damp to convince him that he could not be very far off water, his ardor was somewhat subdued, and he put it seriously to himself, whether it was worth while, under all the circumstances of the case, to adhere to his original resolution.

"Still at it," cried Valentine, on looking down the hole. "Have you had any sport?"

"Hur have not fount the potty," replied Llewellen, in despair, "ant the pottum is ketting rather tamp, inteet, look you!"

"Well!" said Valentine, who really began to think that he had had enough digging, "if I were you I'd give the thing up."

"Hur tont like to too that, ant yet, if hur tig much teeper hur fint hur shall have inteet to tig in a well."

"Exactly; you have gone deep enough now to satisfy the conscience of any man. Come! give me your hand. The thing has now become hopeless."

Llewellen did not at all like to relinquish his task; but as reason suggested to him at the moment, that he might as well do so as not, he "listened to the voice of the charmer," and leaped at once out of the hole.

"Well," said he, "now there's a jop to fill it up acain, look you."

"Oh, leave that to the servants. Let them do it at their leisure. Don't trouble yourself about that."

In this particular also, Llewellen allowed himself to be guided, and he went to restore the respectability of his appearance, while Valentine was pleasantly engaged with Louise. She had become quite herself again, and chatted so gaily, and seemed to be so happy in his society, that every feeling he had entertained of an unfavorable character towards Llewellen subsided, and he began rather to like him than not. And this happy change of feeling was mutual. Llewellen had become quite partial to him: indeed, when he rejoined him on that occasion, so good an understanding existed between them, that they agreed to spend the evening together "somewhere."

Louise, however, did not approve of this arrangement. She naturally wished that "somewhere" to be there, and would assuredly have put her *veto* at once upon its being anywhere else, if she had not relinquished the imperative mood quite so recently. As it was, she very prudently deemed it expedient to withhold her countenance from the proposed arrangement simply, although she *could* have delivered her opinion upon the subject with no inconsiderable eloquence and warmth! No direct opposition therefore having been offered, the arrangement remained undisturbed, and Valentine, who had promised to dine with his uncle, left with every feeling of jealousy crushed.

He looked upon Llewellen no longer as a rival, so differently do men under different circumstances appear. He knew but little of him—scarcely anything indeed—yet he felt that he possessed qualities the knowledge of which would be pleasing. There are some men whose characters may be seen at a glance; while the characters of others require time to be understood, and there can be as little doubt about which of the two classes succeed best with the superficial as about which are as associates to be preferred; for the difference between them consists simply in this, that whereas the former strive to create a favorable impression by means which are easily seen through, the latter are content to leave all to be discovered.

To this latter class Llewellen belonged, and Valentine, now the film of jealousy had been removed, did not fail to perceive it. It was therefore with pleasure that he called for him in the evening, and, when they had listened to Louise, who had prepared for the occasion a few touching inuendos, which had reference to social influences in general, they set forth in search of some new entertainment.

The first thing which arrested the attention of Llewellen, was a flaming placard, upon which two men were represented in a pugilistic attitude.

"Oh!" he exclaimed, "hur shoot like to co there and see them apove all thinks in life!"

Valentine read the placard, and as he found that a grand pugilistic display was to take place that evening, they started off at once, and soon reached the scene of action. On entering the arena, they found the sport had not yet commenced, and the audience, of whom the majority were respectably attired, while some of them were dressed in the first style of fashion, manifesting symptoms of impatience, it being then past the hour announced in the placard. They were not however kept much longer in suspense, for almost immediately afterwards a person appeared upon the stage, about four or five-and-twenty feet square, and introduced two finely formed athletic fellows to the audience, one as "The Birmingham Bull," and the other as "The Brixton Chicken." They were, notwithstanding this, fairly matched in appearance. They were about the same height, and the same weight; and while the muscles of both were developed with equal beauty, their skin was equally healthy and clear.

As they shook hands as well as they could with their gloves on, they smiled at each other good-homoredly, and then with the utmost coolness set to work. For some considerable time, not a single blow was offered. They looked at each other's eyes firmly, and prepared their defence at every feint; and when they did strike out, for the amusement of the spectators, Valentine was amazed at the rapidity and tact with which each blow was parried. It seemed for some time to be impossible for either to break fairly through his antagonist's guard; and when at length, as if tired of defending themselves simply, they relinquished the defence for the attack, the blows that were given were mutually received with every demonstration of good will.

A shower of sixpences followed this display, which the combatants picked up with infinite alacrity, and looked as if—as far as their own private feelings were concerned—it would have been extremely pleasant to see it rain thus for a month. To them, however, the gods were not quite so propitious: they very soon succeeded in clearing the stage; and when they had left it, two others were introduced by the master of the ceremonies, whose general style was so extraordinary, that Valentine could not resist the temptation to have a word with him *incog.*

"The Bogey and the Pet!—the Pet!—the Bogey!" cried the master of the ceremonies, pointing distinctly to each in his turn.

"Which is the Pet?" inquired Valentine, throwing his voice among the shilling individuals.

"This is the Pet, and this is the Bogey; this is the Bogey and this is the Pet."

"But *which* is the Bogey?"

"Why this is the Bogey!" And as he said so, he looked rather severely towards the spot from which the voice appeared to proceed.

"But the Pet!" cried Valentine, "which is the Pet?"

The master of the ceremonies felt rather ruffled, and left the stage determined to have no more of it.

The Pet and the Bogey then commenced; but Valentine's attention was arrested at the moment by Llewellen, who had discovered a friend by his side, who resided in Caermarthen, and who appeared to be quite shocked at the idea of being caught in *such* a place on *such* an occasion. Llewellen introduced this gentleman as Mr. Jarvis Jones, and subsequently stated, aside, that he was an exceedingly charitable, kind-hearted person, who, by his acts of benevolence, had acquired throughout Wales, the reputation of a philanthropist. Under these peculiar circumstances, Valentine was pleased with the introduction; but although, after what had been stated by Llewellen, he believed him to be a good sort of creature, he could not help thinking that there was something in his general aspect at the time inappropriately severe.

"Are you a patron of the art of self-defence?" inquired Valentine.

"Heaven forbid!" exclaimed Mr. Jarvis Jones.

"Indeed!"

"I came here as a matter of curiosity: but I assure you that I am disgusted with the whole exhibition."

"Upon my word you somewhat surprise me," said Valentine, "for really I am unable to perceive anything in it at all calculated to excite the slightest feeling of disgust!"

"I do not perhaps look so much at the exhibition *per se*, as at its tendency; although it is of itself sufficiently degrading to our nature, that men should come forward thus to knock each other about for gain."

"I fear that the love of gain," rejoined Valentine, "prompts men to acts of a character far more degrading to our nature."

"No doubt of it! that I have no desire to dispute; but it does not follow that one species of degradation should be countenanced because there may happen to be another more vile."

"That of course must be admitted; but if we look at the members of such professions, as are not deemed degrading, but which, on the contrary, are held to be highly honorable, we shall find, I apprehend, human nature in your sense degraded to at least an equal depth."

"You mean of course occasionally?—by individuals?"

"No; in the aggregate: looking at the principle which actuates them all. Take, for instance, the profession of a soldier."

"Surely you do not mean to compare a soldier to a pugilist?"

"Why should I not? Can the love of gain be said to have no influence over him? Take him as he is—as a man; and tell me why, if fighting for gain be indeed degrading, he is not in that respect as degraded as the pugilist."

"But the soldier fights the battles of his country."

"No doubt of it; and were he occasionally to *refuse* to fight what are termed 'the battles of his country,' he would be just as good a patriot; but, apart from this, he fights with a view to his own aggrandisement: with this view he enlisted; for gain he entered the army as one willing to kill whomsoever he might be directed to kill, without remorse, because the country calls it glory, and without the slightest reference to the justice of the cause in which he fights; for that of course he is not supposed to understand. It may be said, indeed, that the leading star of the soldier is fame. Fame is equally the leading star of the pugilist. Its influence is equally felt; it is as dear to the one as to the other. But this is not the point: the question is simply this:—Is the pugilist degraded *because* he fights for gain? If he be, then are all men who fight for gain plunged into the depths of degradation—no matter with what weapon they may fight, whether with swords, fists, pistols, or tongues?"

"Then you would place politicians on a level with pugilists?"

"All of them, of course, who do battle for gain."

"And advocates generally—barristers for example?"

"I would place them considerably lower in the scale of venality, for they—without having ignorance to plead in extenuation—will prostitute their talents in any cause, however unjust to individuals, or pernicious to society. For a fee, they will plunge the most amiable and exemplary into wretchedness and want, by violating every just, every honorable principle, to make the worse appear the better reason; for a fee, they will snatch from justice, and fling upon society again, those whom they *know* to be guilty of crimes the most hideous."

"You will remember," observed Mr. Jones, "I admitted that the love of gain, urged men to acts more degrading to our nature than those even of pugilists, while you in turn, acknowledged that it did not follow that one species of degradation should be countenanced, because another existed of a character more vile. But, as I said, I look more at the *tendency* of such exhibitions as these, than at either the exhibitions themselves, or the characters of those engaged in them."

"And what do you conceive their tendency to be?"

"To generate pugnacity among the lower orders—to render them revengeful—to accustom them to scuffles and drunken brawls —and to lead them into scenes of debauchery and vice."

"This is an awful account, certainly," said Valentine. "But how comes it that, since pugilism as an art has been discountenaced, the lower orders have been as pugnacious, as revengeful, as accustomed to scuffles and braws, and as vicious at least as before?"

"Because the influence of pugilism, in its palmy days, has not yet been effectually suppressed."

"If it has been suppressed at all, these vices—if attributable to that influence—must have decreased in proportion. Years have passed away since the art was discouraged, and that its influence *has* been weakened no man can doubt; for, since its discouragement—I may say its almost total suppression—the cowardly spirit which actuates secret assassins, has supplanted the manly courage it inspired. Knives, daggers, and pikes, are now the popular instruments of revenge. The use of the fist is exploded. Men are murdered outright in lieu of being disfigured. Where they used to have cut lips, black eyes, and swollen noses, they have stabs in the throat, the abdomen, and the back. Wives are made widows, and children orphans, in an instant: where men received blows which simply made their eyes twinkle, they now fall dead upon the spot."

"Deaths sometimes occurred, you are aware, in pugilistic encounters."

"They did: but how rarely! But, independently of all considerations having reference to actual death, the practice of using deadly weapons in silly private quarrels, is repugnant to every British feeling. If the lower orders must quarrel—and quarrel they will—let them not be made to forget the use of their fists: let them rather be prompted to pommel each other till they are tired, than induced to resort to the cowardly, murderous practice of stabbing."

"But how can we ascertain that the increase of stabbing, which all must deplore, is attributable to the suppression of the pugilistic art?"

"By looking at the character of the lower orders of society in conjunction with the promptings of human nature in general: they will quarrel; and when they do, they must have weapons. Teach them to forget the use of those which they have heretofore employed, and they will deem themselves justified in flying to others. They have been taught this: they have been taught to forget the use of their fists, and hence fly to knives, pikes, and daggers."

"But pugilists in general are such abominable characters, so profligate, so dishonorable!"

"All this may be granted, without diminishing the inexpediency of running them down like wild beasts."

"But do you not perceive, that, if they were directly countenanced, we should be in effect countenancing profligacy and dishonor?"

"I do not perceive that; but if even it followed as a necessary consequence, we should attach due weight to the fact that they need not be in any direct manner sanctioned! In all matters of this kind there is a wide difference between direct sanction and active suppression. Let pugilists no longer be hunted from county to county by those elderly ladies who have the honor to be in the commission of the peace, and that manly courage by which the lower orders used to be distinguished will again be inspired; they will again, in the spirit of emulation, use their hands without deadly weapons in them."

"Come, come!" cried Llewellen, "you've pin losing all the sport, look you!—Phot have you been talking apout all this time? —Have you cot any silver?"

This put an end to the conversation: and when Valentine had given Llewellen his purse, he and Jones again turned towards the stage.

Although by no means convinced of the soundness of Valentine's arguments, the philanthropist thought that there must be something in them, for he found that the disgust which he had before felt had vanished. He was able then to witness the exhibition with comparative pleasure, and to smile at the ardor of Llewellen, who was really so delighted that he continued, as he had begun, to throw silver to the combatants after every round.

The more the evening advanced, the more judgment and science were displayed: the best men had been evidently kept in reserve, and their tactics were so various and so clever, that the spirit of the exhibition was kept up till the last.

"Hur can too it!" exclaimed Llewellen, as he left with his friends. "Hur can too it!—Hur'll py a set of cluffs, in the morning, ant kiff you a challench, look you."

"Oh, I'll accept it!" said Valentine, and the thing was agreed upon at once, when the philanthropist insisted upon their having supper with him, at his hotel, where they remained, until Valentine, with a view to his own reputation, deemed it highly expedient to take Llewellen home.

CHAPTER LII.

VALENTINE AT GREENWICH FAIR.

So much had Llewellen and Valentine been together since their reconciliation, that Louise, who had expected all sorts of amusement to spring from the presence of her cousin, began to wish him at Wales again heartily, before he had been in town a week. It was not simply one or two evenings that she had been left alone: no, that she might have endured: they had been out together *every* evening!—which was really very terrible to her feelings. However men could wish to be out so often, she could not conceive. Whatever they could see was a mystery to her. She lectured Llewellen, and insisted upon knowing where he had been, and whom he had seen, and appealed to her father whether she had not a clear and indisputable right to know, and pointedly expostulated with Valentine; but in vain: they agreed with all she said; but continued to go out!—admitted their error, but would not reform.

This was not, however, Valentine's fault. He *would* have spent his evenings with her, had it not been that Llewellen was continually at him. It mattered not whether any appointment had been actually made or not, when Llewellen awoke in the morning Valentine was the very first person whom he thought of, and immediately after breakfast, if no engagement had been made between them, he would call upon him in order to seduce him out somewhere. He could do nothing at all without Valentine. He could not move out without him. Valentine, of course, must go wherever he went, and when Raven insisted upon his dining at home, Valentine, of course, must dine with him.

While this very manifestly tended to raise Valentine in the estimation of Louise, it palpably diminished her regard for Llewellen. Upon his broad shoulders all was laid. Valentine was, in her view, Llewellen's victim. Zealously did she labor to open his eyes to this interesting fact; and constantly did she express her amazement that he should suffer himself to be *so* led away; she declared it to be her unbiassed opinion, that the practice of going out every evening was fraught with pernicious effects, and contended, that if the thing went on much longer thus, she should be justified in believing that he loved Llewellen's society infinitely better than hers.

With Valentine all this had great apparent weight; but he did not conceive it to be strictly just, that all the blame should be attached to Llewellen. He, therefore, with the view of taking some portion of it to himself, did inquire of Llewellen, immediately after Louise had been delivering to him one of her most eloquent lectures—whether he would or would not like to go to Greenwich Fair?

"Apove all things in the worlt!" exclaimed Llewellen, who was invariably ready for anything of the sort. "Phen is it to pe?"

"Greenwich fair!" cried Louise, perfectly astounded—not only at the *idea* of Greenwich fair, but at the fact of that idea having proceeded from him whom she had hitherto believed to be the victim—"Greenwich fair! why surely you would never think of going to such a dreadful place as that!"

"Put phen is it to be? That's the point," said Llewellen—"phen is it to pe?"

"On Monday," replied Valentine, "and the sport I understand is superb."

"That's peautiful, look you; hur'll pe retty, hur'll be retty!"

"Why, Valentine," said Louise, "you amaze me! Do you know, sir, what sort of place Greenwich fair is? Are you aware of its being the resort of the very lowest of the low—a place in which any one would blush to be seen who had the slightest pretensions to respectability."

"If anypotty sees me plush—"

"Hold your tongue, Fred! you cannot know anything about it."

"I have no desire at all to see the fair," said Valentine, "I am anxious only to go into the park, to see the pretty girls roll down the hill."

"Peautiful! Oh! I phootn't miss it for the worlt!"

"I am ashamed of you, Valentine,—perfectly ashamed of you. Ah! you do not mean it; I see by your smiling that you do not mean it—do you?"

"If he ton't mean it, look you, he ought to be smuttert."

"I have nothing at all to say to you, sir! —but, Valentine. you have no real intention of going—now have you?"

"Why, really I cannot see why I should not. Llewellen, you know, will be there to protect me!"

"Oh, hur'll protect every hair of your het!"

"I have no doubt of that, sir. You will so far protect him as to keep him out one half the night."

"No; I mean to be home early, very early. I do not intend to remain after dark."

"Well, if you will promise me that, I shall offer no further opposition, although I cannot bear the thought of your going at all, I have heard so many dreadful accounts of the place."

The thing was, therefore, decided; and when the morning, to which so many thousands, not in England alone, but in every part of Europe, look forward with delight, had arrived, Valentine called for Llewellen, who, of course, was quite ready, and had been for hours.

Having made up their minds to go by water, they proceeded to Hungerford Stairs, where they found a steamer just on the point of starting, and at once got on board. The vessel was crowded in every part to excess. The deck was covered with a mass of human beings, which must have appeared at a distance to be as nearly as possible solid. They had no room at all to shift about: they were fixed in their respective positions as firmly as if they had been nailed to the deck. Their eyes, lips, and tongues were the only things on board which, to human perception, did move, and their motion was certainly perpetual. It is true there were two individuals near the funnel, one of whom was making a peculiarly constructed violin squeak, by some cabalistic means, without moving his elbow, while the other was blowing away like Boreas through a powerful trombone, three parts of which he was of necessity compelled to conceal between a stout licensed victualler's legs—which seemed to have been actually built for the purpose, the knees, although the ancles were close, were so very wide apart—in order to get the notes which he conceived the tune demanded; but, with the exception of these two individuals and the captain, whose arms went up and down as perpetually as if he had been engaged to play the character of a windmill—all on board were firmly fixed.

On passing London Bridge, a scene presented itself of a character the most imposing. This was and still is the grand starting-place for steamers; and thousands were on the various wharfs panting for a chance to get on board of them, and thousands more were already on board, laughing and looking so happy! while the water, as thick as respectable pease-soup, looked at the time as if Vesuvius had been beneath it, so furiously did it boil.

Billingsgate was abandoned; but the beautiful esplanade of the Custom-house was thronged. At the Tower Stairs, which used to be embellished, on these happy occasions, with the stars of the east, the *élite* of Whitechapel and Spitalfields, nothing could be seen save a few grim, withered, old watermen sitting upon the bottoms of their wherries, which they had rowed indeed they knew not how oft; but which were now fast turning into touchwood, and mournfully bringing to each other's recollection the bright characteristics of those truly blessed times when they were able to carry eight at eightpence.

Below these justly celebrated stairs, no striking point presented itself on either side, and the thoughts of the passengers were turned towards their stomachs. It is a beautiful feature in the character of Englishmen, that they are never truly happy but when they are either eating or drinking. The rapid action of their digestive organs seems to be essential to their enjoyment of any scene, however exciting in itself. They must set *them* to work upon something, or their hearts are not at ease; they cannot feel comfortable, their thoughts revert to pecuniary affairs, and their spirits evaporate. It is hence that on this gay occasion the persons upon deck became dull, when they discovered that they could get nothing either to eat or to drink. It is true there was plenty below, but the cabin was so choked up that they could not insinuate themselves by any means down its throat. They were, therefore, compelled—and the idea of being compelled to do anything, is one which a Briton cannot bear—to defer the commencement of their pleasures until they reached Greenwich, which was a pity, inasmuch as a little sour stout, or even a little ginger-beer, would have made them feel joyous and happy.

They, however, made up for the mortification they had endured, the very moment they landed, by pouring into the various public houses in the immediate vicinity of the pier; when, having obtained a supply of the essence of mirth, their features relaxed, and they were all life and spirit.

Valentine and Llewellen made at once for the Park, and, as they entered, it presented a scene of surpassing gaiety. Little indeed of the green sward could be seen, while the hill which rose before them appeared to be one moving mass of hats, bonnets, scarfs, ribbons, and shawls. The effect was striking. Every color that art could produce was displayed, and in the sun all harmonised brilliantly. Such was the appearance of the mass, but, when analysed, its softness and beauty were lost.

As Llewellen was excessively anxious to be active, and as Valentine was not in a contemplative mood, they mounted the hill without delay, and, before they had reached the summit, partook freely of the pleasure with which all around them appeared to be inspired. It was delightful to view their manifestations of happiness, for on such occasions the poorest enjoy themselves the most. Give a poor girl a holiday, place anything like a sweetheart by her side, let her have some pink ribbon—and plenty of it, that the ends may hang well over her shoulders—with a little white handkerchief to carry in her hand, and, when in the Park, princesses might envy her feelings.

"How peautiful all the cirls look!" exclaimed Llewellen. "Can't we have a came with them, look you? Hur want to see more of them roll town the hill."

"I've no doubt we shall see plenty of them do that by and by. They are not yet sufficiently excited. But the people appear to be flocking this way. Let us join them. There is sure to be something worth seeing, or the attraction would not be so strong."

"Hur ton't think we shall too much petter," said Llewellen, "put we'll co."

They went accordingly down the avenue which leads to Blackheath, and which was thronged by persons, of whom the majority were in much better circumstances than others whom they saw, and who appeared to be extremely anxious that those others should know it, they did walk so stately and looked so severe.

The Heath was covered: not alone by human beings, for there were donkeys beyond calculation, and forty-year-old ponies, and marquees, and cockshies, and innumerable other great attractions, which combined to swell out the importance of the scene.

Llewellen felt as if every limb hung upon wires. He could not keep quiet. He ran about like a young lunatic: now getting his hat filled with gingerbread-nuts to pelt the children of the gipsies—who have always swarms of those little articles at command —and then pulling the girls about and kissing—aye, absolutely kissing them, and that too in the face of the sun! He did not know at all what to do with himself, and at length declared that nothing could or should content his soul until he had had a ride on one of the ponies. "Hur'll kiff you," said he, "fifty yarts, look you, out of five huntret, ant peat you, ant you shall have which you please.—There!" he added, pointing to a poor little pony, "he's a Welshman: I know he's a Welshman: hur'll let you take him."

Valentine looked at the little animal; and he might have been a Welshman, but he must have been foaled in the middle ages.

"Phot say you!" cried Llewellen, who was then all impatience. "Will you accept my challench?"

"I will, if you'll ride that nice white one," said Valentine, pointing to a dirty little wretch of a mare that in point of years looked at least a thousand.

"No, no: that's too pat, there's nothing in her: there's no blut in her potty; no pone."

"Why she is all bone!—what would you have?"—Take her; and I'll not have the fifty yards you offered."

"Well: hur'll try her speet!" And he mounted, when Valentine mounted the Welshman; and they made a fair start.

The Welshman went a-head, for there *was* a little stuff still in him; but the other, with all Llewellen's jockeyship, could not be prevailed upon to believe that it was necessary for her to go. The strongly exciting moment of starting indeed did stimulate her into a trot; during which, the active energies of Llewellen caused the saddle to slip off, although he managed, by dint of great dexterity, to stick on; but after that great event the mare would not stir an inch: she would not even make the slightest effort to go along, knowing perhaps that if she did, such effort would be unsuccessful inasmuch as the saddle was dangling between her legs, while her rider sat firmly upon the girth. Of all this Llewellen was utterly unconscious until Valentine pointed it out to him on his return. His firm impression was that he had left the saddle behind him! He could not understand at all the motive of the mare, and wondered that all around him should be roaring with laughter. He very soon however dismounted after that, and acknowledged that Valentine had won.

This calmed him a little for at least ten minutes, during which time he walked very quietly along, but he broke loose again very soon after that, and ran about as much elated as before.

"My little tear, phot shall I treat you to, look you?" he inquired of a smart servant girl, who was rather a shrewed little creature in her way. "Phot will you have for a fairink?"

"That thimble and pincushion, please," replied the girl, as she pointed to the articles stuck upon a stick.

"Which of course you shall have, my little tear," said Llewellen.

"Year, yer har, sir!—Three throws a penny, and six for tuppence!" cried a fellow who approached at this moment with an armful of sticks.

"Hur want these two little things, look you: phot's the price?"

"Can't sell 'em hoff the sticks, sir; it's three throws a penny."

"Oh, nonsense! Hur'll kiff you photever price you ask. Hur shall preak them, if hur throw, look you!"

"Oh, no yer von't, sir! D'yer vornt *them* petickler?"

"Why, of course! ant must have them for this laty."

"Werry well, sir! year's three throws a penny: yer safe to bring 'em down!"

"Oh, hur'll pring them town!—there's no tout apout that!" cried Llewellen, and he at once took three sticks and repaired to the place appointed.

The first he pitched gently, lest he should injure the little articles, but missed them: the next he delivered with a sweep, and down they came in an instant.

"*Hin* the ole, upon me soul!" cried the fellow, who danced to the spot to stick them up again.

Llewellen did not understand this proceeding, and expressed himself exactly to that effect, when the proprietor explained to his own satisfaction that, in order to obtain them, it was absolutely necessary for them to fall out of the hole.

"Very well!" said Llewellen, who threw the third stick which, however, went wide of the mark.

"Ow werry near, sure-*ly!*" exclaimed the active proprietor, who seemed to pride himself especially upon the performance of the most extraordinary antics. "Try again, sir!—safe to get 'em!—no mistake, sir!—Year's three more!"

Llewellen now took a most deliberate aim, holding the stick horizontally in the middle to make sure; and again the little articles fell, but again they dropped into the hole. Conceiving that this was not exactly the way to win them, he seized the next firmly at one end, and with a slashing sweep sent it whizzing at them!—he struck the stick upon which the little articles were perched, but those articles dropped as before into the hole. What could be the meaning of it? Did he not throw with sufficient force? He threw the next more forcibly; but, alas! with the same result.

"Try again, sir!—yer carn't be off gittin 'em!—Ave another shy!"

Llewellen had another "shy," and another, and another!—The little articles *would* fall into the hole.

He therefore changed his tactics *in toto;* for he had begun very calmly to reason upon the matter. "If," thought he, "I roll the stick just over the hole, the little articles will fall upon the stick, and, of course, will not allow them to go in!" which, in the abstract, was a very ingenious idea, and he proceeded to act upon it, but found that the practical part of the business was not quite so easy as he had anticipated. The difficulty was in persuading the sticks to roll "just over the hole." They wouldn't do it. He tried again and again: for he felt, of course, that the theory of the thing was very excellent; but no: it was not to be done—at least it was not to be done by him; and hence he had recourse to the slashing mode again.

"That's your sort!—yer carn't do better, sir; that'll beat the world!" exclaimed the proprietor, who informed his victim *every* time he gave him fresh sticks, that "a faint heart never yet won a fair lady."

Llewellen now threw with desperation—he swept all before him, and at length the little thimble on falling into the hole for about the fiftieth time absolutely leaped out again! Well! that was something. He seized the prize and presented it to the lady, and then wished to purchase the pincushion. Oh! the proprietor would not take any money for it!—it was invaluable to him! Llewellen went, therefore, again to the sticks, which he threw as if he wished to knock a house down.

"Throw them perpendicularly," said a worthy mechanic, who was pained to see so much money wasted upon a thing which was not worth three farthings. "You will never get it fairly down by striking at the stick."

The proprietor looked at this mechanic with an aspect indicative of anything but friendship. He wished him dead and buried; for Llewellen, by acting upon this highly correct suggestion, went alarmingly near the pincushion at every throw, and did eventually knock it off! when the proprietor gave another sweet look at the mechanic; and, conceiving that he had robbed him of a little fortune, felt bound to inform him that, for "two pins," he'd show him the difference between them.

Llewellen of course was delighted. He picked up the cushion in an instant, and the very next instant discovered that the cause of its remarkable tendency towards the hole, was involved in the fact of its being laden with dirt. Considering, however, the various conflicting circumstances of the case, he did not explain to the man his private sentiments upon the point; but presented the prize with great delicacy to the lady, whom he moreover loaded with gingerbread-nuts, of which she appeared to be remarkably fond, and then left her.

"Hur tit pekin to think," said he to Valentine, as they walked from the spot, "that hur never shoult be apel to kit it at all, look you! There's a pair of peautiful plack eyes!" he added, directing attention to a dirty young woman, whose features were certainly of the most handsome caste. "Phot is she?"

"A gipsy," replied Valentine, as she approached them.

"Shall I tell you your *fortune*, good gentleman?" she inquired, addressing Llewellen, whom, at a glance, she perceived to be the greener of the two.

"My fortune, pless you!—my fortune is mate!"

"But I can tell you something much to your advantage. I can tell you the lady you love, and who loves you—the color of of her hair—the first letter of her name, and something besides you'll be much pleased to know."

"Inteet, then: phot is it, look you?"

"Let me see your hand."

Llewellen at once held it forth, and the gipsy proceeded to examine the palm with great intensity of feeling—to trace the cabalistic lines in all their varied ramifications, and to look altogether mysterious.

"There is great fortune here, good gentleman," she observed, after this minute preliminary examination—"great fortune. Just cross your hand with silver."

"That of course is indispensable," said Valentine.

"The charm is in the silver," rejoined the gipsy.

And it is a mysterious fact that therein lies the charm. In all matters of this kind there is infinite virtue in silver.

Of course Llewellen acted quite up to her instructions, when she examined the palm again very minutely, and looked occasionally into his eyes with the view of giving some additional effect to the thing.

"You will be married," she observed, in a low tone of voice, "before the present year is out, to the lady you love."

"Inteet!—that's coot. Put who is she?"

"Her name begins with an L: she is handsome, rather tall, very rich, has dark brown hair, and a delicate complexion."

"Peautiful!—Well! ant how many chiltren look you?"

"I can only count eleven; but you may have more. I can't take upon myself to say to one."

"Oh, that's quite near enough! Eleven will too. Well?"

"I see nothing more but that you will always be prosperous and happy."

"Her name begins with an L!" thought Valentine. "Handsome, rather tall, rich, dark hair, and delicate complexion!—Why, that is Louise!"

"Shall I tell *your* fortune, good gentleman," said the gipsy, who had a splendid eye to business.

"No," said Valentine, abruptly.

"Oh, too!" cried Llewellen. "Too, too have it tolt."

"Not I!—Come!" said Valentine, taking Llewellen's arm.

"I can tell you something which, if it does not please you, good gentleman, will put you on your guard!"

And this was very ingenuous on the part of the gipsy, and reflected great credit upou her powers of perception; for she saw in a moment that what she had said to Llewellen had not imparted much pleasure to Valentine, and felt that, under the circumstances, a warning was the only means available by which he could be caught. "Beware!" she exclaimed, as she followed him. "Beware of false friends!" And this had its effect; but not the effect she desired, for he still kept on.

"It is strange," thought he, as they passed through the gate from the Heath into the Park, "very strange: and yet how is it possible that she can tell?—Pooh!—Absurd!—and even if she could, it would not follow of necessity that it should be Louise. L is the first letter of Laura, Lucy, Lucretia, Lydia, Leonora, and many other names which do not occur to me at the moment; and why should not one of these be handsome, rather tall, and rich, with dark hair, and a delicate complexion? But the idea of her being able to tell is ridiculous!"

And so it was: truly ridiculous; but it was notwithstanding an idea which he could not repudiate. It continued to haunt him, and to make him feel very uncomfortable. In vain he brought reason to bear upon the point: although he tried very hard to persuade himself that he ought to feel ashamed of allowing such an absurdity to vex him, he could not avoid feeling vexed at it still.

"Phot is the matter, look you? Phy are you so tull?" inquired Llewellen, whom Valentine, in spite of himself, again regarded with a feeling of jealousy.

"Dull!—Am I dull?—Well, we shall see more to enliven us presently."

"Oh! too let us mount the other hill!" exclaimed Llewellen, on reaching the Observatory. "Look you! What thousants of people there are!"

"Now then!" cried Valentine, determined to shake off all thought of the gipsy and her prophecy if possible. "Let's have a run."

"Apove all things!—come on!" cried Llewellen, who started off at once very swiftly; Valentine stopped to watch him.—He had had some experience upon Thetford hill, and therefore felt that Llewellen would not loiter long. Nor did he. No man ever made so much haste. His stride gradually increased in length as he descended, until they became amazed. He seemed to fly down. No swallow could have beaten him. He lost his hat, but would not stop to pick even that up, he was in such a hurry, and when he happily arrived at the bottom, he flew over about five hundred yards of level ground before he deemed it expedient to stop.

He then sat down upon the grass and panted freely, while Valentine descended But *he* did not do it half so fast: his was no run at all!—it was, in fact, nothing more than a most disgraceful shuffle. He did, however, get down eventually, and having secured Llewellen's hat, reached the spot from which its owner had no immediate disposition to move.

"Hur tit peat you there," he cried, "look you! Put in truth, hur tit not mean to come town so fast."

"Have you hurt yourself at all?"

"Oh no, not a pit: put hur might just as well have run against a tree, as not, for hur tit not see phere hur was coink. Hur lost sight of everything, look you; put hur thought hur could not too much petter than stretch out my lecks."

"Well, come. Shall we mount the other hill, as you proposed?"

"Oh yes!—hur'm quite retty," said Llewellen, who rose from the ground on the instant, and it may be believed that, profiting by experience, he actually did not run up *that* hill so fast as he ran down the other.

On reaching the top, they at once perceived that as far as life and gaiety were concerned, it was incomparably the more attractive hill of the two. It was less aristocratic than the other. The people were more free and merry. They laughed more loudly, and chatted more cheerfully, giving a more extensive scope to the development of their feelings, and all was in consequence jollity and joy.

The grand point of attraction, however, was the slope of the hill on the other side, where thousands of comfortable creatures were seated enjoying the juvenile revels below. Some had gin in little bottles, to which they applied their lips occasionally; others had somewhat larger bottles of beer; others were eating cakes, gingerbread, and oranges, while others were glancing, and—it must be written—kissing!

It was pleasing to distinguish the lovers from the rest of those who formed this extensive amphitheatre of happiness. They suffered not "concealment like a worm i' the bud, to prey on *their* damask cheeks!" they knew better! They loved; and were not ashamed to let the world know it!—while the warmth with which they loved did develop itself in this, that, whereas the ladies sported the hats of the gentlemen, the gentlemen embellished themselves *pro tem*, with the upper habiliments of the ladies. And, oh! how dearly a lady loves to put on the hat of her lover!—how well it becomes her!—how charmingly she looks!—although, it must be admitted, sometimes a little rakish. Still, she loves it; and there was not a single lady that sported a hat on this memorable occasion, who tried to conceal this fact from either her lover or herself. They all, on the contrary, made the very most of it: they felt that they looked most bewitching; and so they did; which is more than can be said of their lovers, seeing that gentlemen in bonnets, caps, scarfs, shawls, and tippets, do not look bewitching at all.

The great game going forward below, however, commanded the special attention both of Valentine and Llewellen. They saw from four to five hundred lively little youths with their mouths widely extended, giving the very sharpest possible look out for the oranges that were thrown from the brow of the hill. For each orange thrown there were at least a hundred candidates, and the beautiful spirit of emulation it inspired, imparted a high degree of pleasure to all around. If well directed, one orange caused fifty youths to fall, which of course was about one of the purest delights in nature. Scarcely anything, in fact, can be conceived more delightful to a generous and intellectual mind, than the process of a mob of little eager individuals rolling over each other down a hill after an orange which is of course crushed by him who has the joy to fall upon it. It is useless to throw them at the heads of the little mob, for they are caught by the dexterous, and cause no fun: they must be rolled down rapidly to produce the effect desired, and whenever that effect is produced, what a thrilling sensation of delight doth it impart!

Of course Llewellen was at it in a moment, and Valentine very soon joined him. They threw an immense number, and with so much dexterity and tact, that they gave great pleasure to all around, save one, and that one was the lady who had supplied them with ammunition. They had used all her oranges, for which she had had her own price; but as she happened to have a lot more at home, she left the spot with her empty basket, growling gruffly at herself for having been such a fool as not to bring them out with her.

"Well," said Valentine, as soon as he found that no more ammunition could be obtained, "have you anything like an appetite?"

"An appetite! pless you, hur never was so huncry! I coot eat, look you, anything in the worlt!"

"Then we had better return to the town at once, and see after dinner: we shall be able no doubt to get something."

They accordingly descended the hill, and left the park; and after having been stopped by a variety of ladies in long white aprons, who informed them that they could have at their establishments respectively excellent accommodation for tea, with all the fascinating smiles at their command, they sought and found a decent inn in the middle of the town, where they ordered whatever sort of dinner could be immediately placed before them.

In less than ten minutes the table was covered. As they had ordered nothing hot, they had every thing cold; but they nevertheless enjoyed it, and ate like giants.

The window of the room into which they had been shown commanded a fine view, not only of the opposite houses, but of the street in which those houses were situated, together with the people with whom it was thronged. To this window they, therefore, repaired to enjoy their wine, and Valentine felt quite resolved to return to town as soon as it became dark, as he had promised. Llewellen was of course quite opposed to such a proceeding; but as Valentine was firm, his opposition was not urged beyond a certain extent. There, then, they sat, sipping their port and smoking cigars, highly pleased with the scene before them, until twilight arrived.

It may, by some few, have been remarked, that a man's feelings vary. It is strange and mysterious no doubt that they should; but that they do, is a sound philosophical truth which no sophistry can shake. They will vary; and as if with the view of proving to demonstration that they will, Valentine, who had before felt so firmly resolved not to look at the fair, now proposed a walk through it.

Of course Llewellen was delighted with this proposition, and "plest the peautiful wine" that had induced it. "Let's ring the pell for the pill," said he, "ant we'll co off at once my poy, look you."

The bill was, therefore, ordered, and on its being discharged, they started direct for the fair.

The space between the booths was densely crowded. They could scarcely get along, but, being in, they went forward with the struggling stream. The pleasure of being in such a place is doubtless great, although involved to some considerable extent in mystery; but Valentine and Llewellen having resolved to go through it, disdained to retreat, they kept on, and were driven past many great attractions, at which they had not time even to look until they arrived at the top, where a rush was made, and in an instant the crowd was wedged in!

"Now, then, take care of your pockets," said Valentine, who still stuck close to Llewellen, and who understood the movement exactly.

"They must be clever inteet to kit anything out of me," said Llewellen, with a chuckle, which denoted security; and by drawing the tails of his coat forward, he covered all his pockets at once with his hands.

The mass now moved to and fro for some moments very gently: but presently the women began to scream, and, singularly enough, the very instant they left off screaming, the pressure relaxed, and all were able to move.

"Too let us co into that show," said Llewellen, when the mass had given way, "I shoot *so* like to co into one."

"Very well," said Valentine, "I am quite willing. We may as well go up at once."

Up accordingly they went, and on reaching the place at which the money was taken, Llewellen could not find his purse.

"I told you," said Valentine, on being informed of this interesting fact, "to take care of your pockets."

"And so her teet!" cried Llewellen, "until the cirls pecan to scream! There were two little tears just pehind me, nearly smuttert: of course hur teet all hur coot for them!"

"And while you were doing all you could for them, the little dears robbed you of your purse."

"Phot, the cirls?"

"Of course! They are the most successful and dexterous pickpockets we have. Whenever you hear them scream in a crowd like that, look to your pockets. They do do not scream because they are hurt: the fellows whom they are with protect them."

"The little tevils. Oh! hur wish hur hat known it! Put never mind, you are all right, that's a plessing."

The entertainments of the evening were varied and attractive. In the bills—at which they glanced, while a brigand was bawling, "All in! all in!"—it was announced that the performances would commence with a serio-historical tragedy, called *The Speechless Spectre; or, the Sanguinary Stab:* after which, there would be an infinite variety of comic singing: the whole to conclude with the celebrated pantomimic pantomime of *How are you off for Chips?*"

This promised a highly intellectual treat; and on reaching the interior of the theatre—which they did, by diving through a large hole in a blanket, which appeared to have been established expressly for the purpose—they found "the house crowded to the ceiling."

The aristocracy, of course, were duly separated from the democracy. There were both pit and boxes; and, as in theatres of larger dimensions, they convert the worst part of the pit into stalls; so here, as the crowd poured in, they stuck up an additional plank, and called it boxes; which boxes were immediately filled with the *élite*, to the imminent danger of their necks.

When all had been satisfactorily arranged, the curtain rose and the tragedy commenced. An individual who appeared to have, for several months, repudiated the practice of shaving, stole in, and after bouncing about the stage like a maniacal individual, and making a variety of desperate attempts, stabbed a lady who was sleeping upon a plank, placed so as to convey the idea of a couch, and who gave a loud scream, and all was over. This finished the first act; and then came the second. The murderer entered with a number of his associates, dressed in a variety of styles, from that of the duke to that of the dustman—for he evidently kept all sorts of society—and when he had said something which appeared to be highly satisfactory to them all, two sweet ladies entered; but no sooner had he taken the hand of one of them, than the elements let loose their fury!—the thunder roared! and the lightnings flashed! and the rain came down in torrents! Oh! dreadful were the feelings of the murderer then! A gong was heard!—all nature shook!—from a hole in the earth, white smoke arose, and the Speechless Spectre stood before him! The murderer trembled!—of course he trembled!—he must have been in a horrible way. He tried to speak! in vain he tried! but while he was trying, an infinite host of merry devils ran up to him with links, and dragged him down into the bowels of the earth, as the blue fire blazed and the elements crashed!

Thus ended the historical tragedy: the moral of which was, that in Nature there is such a thing as retributive justice. The comic singing came next, and then the pantomime; and as the performances concluded in less than ten minutes from the period at which they commenced, it will be highly correct to state, that the attention of the audience was kept all alive from first to last.

As they came out on one side, hundreds who had assembled on the stage in front, were waiting to go in at the other: which was pleasant to all concerned in the speculation, and tended to show the highly intellectual character of the age.

"Now let us co into that lonk pooth, look you," said Llewellen, "in which they were tancink."

"It is getting rather late," said Valentine; "I think we had better return."

"Well, well! put only just to look!"

Valentine consented; and after struggling back through the crowd for some distance, they reached the entrance of a brilliantly illuminated booth, which at that particular period was called the Crown and Anchor. On the right as they entered, rows of benches, and planks in the similitude of tables were established for the accommodation of those who loved to pick periwinkles and shrimps, while discussing gin-and-water in mugs; while on the left about five hundred couples were engaged in the performance of an extremely picturesque country dance.

To the left, therefore, Valentine and Llewellen went at once, and found the dancers looking all hot and happy. The freedom with which they perspired was perfect, while they seemed to breathe nothing but dust.

As in his innocence Valentine conceived that the place must be ventilated somewhere, they went to the upper end, but there they found it hotter still, and more dusty. They very soon, however, became accustomed to the thing; and while Llewellen was seeking a partner, Valentine sat upon one of the tables to look on.

It may here be remarked that this booth, at that period, was a celebrated place of assignation; and that the ruin of thousands of poor weak girls might be dated from their first introduction therein. It was not a place for the amusement of the lower classes of society—at least not as far as the men were concerned. The clubs of the West End, and the counting-houses of the city poured forth their hundreds on these occasions in search of virtue to corrupt; and as they invariably introduced those whom they meant to destroy, there, it at length became difficult indeed to find a female who wished to preserve her virtue, if even she happened to have any to preserve.

Valentine was not aware of this when he entered, but it soon became manifest that that was not the place for really innocent enjoyment. Llewellen, however, had diametrically opposite ideas on this subject, at that moment. He had managed to get a partner, and she was a flamer: her face was as red as the sun as it declines, and her dress was as red as her face. She was tall and stout, very hot, but very active, and when she laughed she did it fairly from ear to ear. With such a partner, at such a time, of course, Llewellen could not but feel merry, and as he was not a small man, it really was an awful thing for those against whom they came in contact.

While they were thus happily engaged, a large party of gentlemen—each of whom had a nice penny trumpet, which he played in the most engaging manner possible—marched round the booth. Oh, it was such sport, and they looked so interesting, and felt so happy! Some of them had masks on, while others were attired as fresh-water sailors, but the style in which they dressed was of little importance, the thing was so truly delightful: for they not only looked most valiant, but made "most healthful music."

"Now, my tear," said Llewellen, when the dance had concluded. "Phot will you have to trink? Put first allow me, look you, to introduce you to my frient."

The introduction took place with due formality, and Valentine felt himself, of course, highly honored: and as the lady immediately after the introduction, declared that she preferred brandy-and-water to any other thing, of course, brandy-and-water was immediately ordered.

"It is rather warm work I should imagine," observed Valentine, addressing the flame of Llewellen.

"It is indeed warm," said the lady, "but then I don't mind it."

"Have you been dancing much this evening?"

"Ever since they commenced."

"You have friends with you of course?"

"No; I expected to meet some here, but they have not yet arrived."

The waiter now brought the brandy and water, and the lady having taken a very fair sip, politely passed it to Llewellen.

"Too you call this *pranty* and water!" cried Llewellen, after having put his lips to it.

"Yes, sir, brandy and water, sir, you ordered I believe, sir."

"Put this is pranty and water without pranty, look you."

"They never give you anything better here," said the lady. "If you want a glass of good brandy and water you must go to one of the houses out of the fair."

"Well, come then, let's co; hur can't trink this!"

"Oh, with all my heart!" said Valentine, who was really very anxious to get out of the place.

"Now, my tear, are you retty?"

"Don't take her with you," said Valentine, having drawn Llewellen aside.

"Phy not? She's a coot cirl! hur know she's a coot cirl."

"I am quite at your service," said the lady, who at this moment took Llewellen's arm.

"I am afraid that we are taking you from that which you much enjoy," observed Valentine, with great consideration.

"Not at all!" cried the lady, "I can return if I wish it. I should like a breath of air above all things."

Of course there was no help for it then; and as such was the case, why they left the booth together.

The space between the gingerbread stalls was not quite so much crowded as before, and the consequence was that Llewellen was pulled into almost every one of them expressly for the purpose of pressing to buy nuts.

The seductive arts of the ladies who attend these stalls surpass nature. They are so zealous, their importunities are so fascinating, that it is almost impossible to resist them. Llewellen on two occasions felt compelled to make a purchase. They laid violent hands upon him; they would *not* let him pass, and as it was perfectly immaterial to the lady whom he was with, how many nuts he bought for her, for of course she had them all, she with admirable forbearance abstained from pressing him forward when she conceived he was most in danger of being seduced.

They did, however, eventually get out of the fair, and when that important feat had been accomplished, Llewellen's lady led them to an inn, in which the people were singing very loudly. Valentine was not at all anxious to enter, but as Llewellen explained that he could not with any degree of propriety refuse to give the lady some brandy-and-water, after having induced her to leave the booth, expressly in order to point out the place, they went in.

"Oh, do come into one of the rooms to hear them sing!" said the lady.

"Of course!" said Llewellen; and they entered a room in which between two and three hundred persons were sitting. In the mouth of every man there was a pipe, and in the mouth of every woman, a gingerbread nut. And they were all getting tipsy; and they looked upon themselves as being just as good as the best, and cared for no man! Why should they? This question they wished very much to have answered.

"Silence for the next harmony!" was now loudly commanded, and a gentleman volunteered to sing a song for a lady who had been called upon in vain. He commenced. It was a plaintive ditty, and he had an extremely small voice; but at the end of the verse, to his utter amazement, he had a chorus which broke forth like thunder. In vain the little volunteer expostulated with them: in vain he explained that the song had no chorus; a chorus they would have! and they had it throughout, and as it harmonised sweetly, Valentine and Llewellen at once left the room.

"Well," said Valentine, as they walked towards the place from which the coaches started, "what do you think of Greenwich Fair?"

"Phy, I think it very coot, look you, very coot inteet."

"Then, of course, you do not think that it ought to be suppressed?"

"Suppressed! No; do you think it ought to be suppressed?"

"As far as the fair is concerned, I most certainly do."

"Put surely you are not one of those who would take away the innocent pleasures of the poor!"

"On the contrary, I would extend them: but the suppression of this fair would not at all interfere with the innocent pleasures of the poor. Let them assemble on these occasions as usual: let the beautiful park be thrown open to them as now: let them enjoy themselves there; and there the poor do enjoy themselves who seek only pleasures which are innocent."

"Put the shows," said Llewellen, "the shows!"

"If they are fond of dramatic entertainments let them go to the theatres. They can see there far more intellectual and attractive performances than any that can be seen at the fair, and that too at the same price. The fair itself is a mere nursery of immorality and crime, and as its suppression could not in the slightest degree diminish the innocent pleasures of the poor, my firm conviction is that it ought to be suppressed as a glaringly dangerous nuisance."

They now entered a coach, and, as it started immediately, Llewellen immediately dropped off to sleep, and did not wake until they arrived at Charing-cross.

CHAPTER LIII.

IN WHICH A CERTAIN INTERESTING QUESTION IS PROPOSED.

When Valentine called the next morning upon Louise, he found her in the very act of lecturing Llewellen with severity; she had him on the sofa, and nothing could exceed the intensity of feeling with which she insisted upon his making a full confession of all the circumstances connected with their visit to the fair, but more especially those which had direct reference to what they did, whom they saw, and what induced them to keep out so late.

At first Llewellen made an extremely clear and straightforward statement; but as ladies in general conduct matters of this kind in the spirit of the celebrated Spanish Inquisition, so Louise in this particular instance, although professing the discovery of truth to be her object, would not believe truth when it appeared, because its appearance did not meet her views. Llewellen was therefore subjected to a very searching cross-examination, during which she managed so to confuse his faculties, that at length he knew neither what to say, what he meant to say, nor what he had said; and as, under these peculiarly pleasing circumstances, she, with infinite presence of mind, recapitulated the evidence and proved it thereby to be one chaotic mass of contradictions, he started up the very instant Valentine entered, exclaiming, "My tear poy! hur'm so clad you're come; she's pin patchering me apout this pisiness until hur ton't know inteet t' cootness phether hurm'm standing upon my het or my heels."

"What business?" inquired Valentine as he approached Louise.

"Don't come near me, sir, until you have explained your conduct."

Valentine looked at Llewellen as if he

really did not understand it exactly; but Llewellen on the instant threw a light on the subject by exclaiming, "It's apout the fair, pless you! hur never was so patgert in all my porn tays."

"Oh, the fair!" cried Valentine, "just so. Well, let us sit down and explain all about it."

"Hur'll have no more to too with the pisiness," cried Llewellen, approaching the window. "Hur've hat quite enough. Hur'll leave you to it: Cot pless you! hur wish you joy!"

"Now then, Louise, what am I to explain?"

"Your conduct sir, at that wicked fair. I know that it's a wicked place: I'm sure of it!"

"You are quite right: it is a wicked place, and I may say that perhaps Fred and I were two of the most wicked persons that were present."

At this point Llewellen turned and looked quite bewildered.

"His conduct," continued Valentine, "was probably more dreadful than mine; but I confess to you that mine was bad enough."

"Coot!" cried Llewellen, whose countenance relaxed.

"I know," said Louise, "that you are a clever creature, but I am not to be induced to believe that you are better, because you choose to represent yourself ironically as being worse, than you really are."

"Oh," cried Llewellen, "we were poth pat poys."

"Hold your tongue, sir. I was not addressing you."

"If you wish to know seriously," said Valentine, "how we passed our time there, I can assure you that we did so most innocently and pleasantly. We saw thousands of happy people in the park, and thousands more upon the river, upon the heath, and in the town, and as it was on the whole a most enlivening scene, I shall never regret having visited Greenwich."

"Upon my word, said Louise, "your explanation is very lucid and very minute. I ought, I am sure, to feel obliged to you for being so explicit, for I find that I can make nothing of either of you!"

Louise, however, did not despair. She privately made up her mind to subject Llewellen to another severe cross-examination the very first opportunity, feeling certain of being by such means enabled eventually to elicit the truth.

The subject was then dropped, and Llewellen—who did not much like the idea of Valentine being let off so easily, after what he himself had endured—began to whistle, which act being invariably indicative of a desire on his part to go out, Louise well understood, and therefore cried, "Fred, Fred! If you want to go out again, go; for goodness sake, don't annoy us with that dreadful whistling; really, one may just as well be in Smithfield."

"Come, my tear poy!" cried Llewellen. "We've cot leave to co."

"You have sir; but Valentine wishes to remain."

Which was an absolute fact: he did wish to remain; for although he was not inclined to put the smallest faith in the gipsy's prophecy, he found that it had made a deep impression on his mind, and was therefore most anxious to have a little strictly private conversation with Louise, on a subject which bore directly upon the point. Of this, however, Louise was entirely unconscious. When she suggested that Valentine wished to remain, she did so on speculation merely; but albeit, that speculation answered her views as far as the wish of itself was concerned, it signally failed to realise the hope she entertained of getting rid of Llewellen. He was as anxious to go out as any man could be; but then without Valentine nothing could induce him to stir from the house. Where he went, his "tear poy" also must go, which, on that occasion, Valentine as well as Louise thought particularly disagreeable.

"Fred, I wish you would fetch me Poodle's Poems from the library," said Louise, who had conceived a vague notion that Valentine was anxious to communicate something in private.

"Pootle's Poems. Phery coot," said Llewellen, who proceeded to the library in search of them, at once.

"Do you feel at all disposed for a walk?" inquired Valentine.

"Quite: I should enjoy it: but then we shall have that pest with us."

"Oh, we shall be able to get rid of him. You can send him somewhere when we get out; let me see—oh! send him for some ribbon or anything of that sort."

"The only question is, will he go?"

"No doubt of it. If he'll go for Poodle's Poems, he'll go for anything. Let him walk with us, for instance, as far as the Horse Guards, and then we can tell him where to find us in the park."

"Well, what will be the best thing to send him for? Let me consider," said Louise, and while she was engaged with this high consideration, Llewellen re-entered the room. "Inteet hur can't fint Pootle's Poems," said he. "There's Cowper's ant Pyron's, putt tevil of any of Pootle's."

"You are a very stupid creature," said

Louise, who could scarcely keep her countenance.

"Phell! putt there are no Pootle's poems, look you! Is it a pig pook?"

"No matter. It's of no importance now."

"We are going for a walk," said Valentine, "will you join us?"

"Of course: putt just come with me, my poy, while Louey is putting on her ponnet, and see if you can fint this Pootle pook. Inteet hur can't see it, look you!"

"Oh, never mind: the book is not wanted now. You will not be long, Louise?"

"Scarcely a moment."

"I say, Fred," said Valentine, when Louise had left the room, "what was the matter this morning?"

"Oh, Louey was poring and pothering me apout the fair, ant although hur tolt her everything putt apout the cockshy pisiness and the pooth, she questioned me just like a parrister, look you, until hur titn't know inteet phot hur was apout. Putt hur say, my poy, phere shall we go? Hur wish that little tevil, look you, woultn't co with us."

"Oh, we must take her out you know sometimes, poor girl!"

"Yes, yes: putt she is such a pore. Hur say! phill this blue coat too to walk with a latey, look you?"

"Oh, that will do; but run away and put on another if you like."

"Phery coot. Hur'll not pe half a secont."

"You need not hurry yourself. You know how like an hour a lady's moment is, doubtless."

Immediately after Llewellen left the room Louise entered, and Valentine thought that he never saw her look so really beautiful. He took her hands and pressed them, and gazed upon her fervently and exclaimed, "My own Louise!" and—kissed her!

Louise blushed deeply, but was silent.

"Phot too you think of my new pottlecreen?" cried Llewellen, as he bounced into the room, and buttoned his coat, and looked over his left shoulder, and turned round and round with the view of displaying his figure to the best advantage possible. "Ton't you think it looks pherry peautiful and smart?"

"Oh, very," said Valentine, but Louise said nothing, although she wished him at Wales then, more heartily than ever.

Llewellen was amazed that she failed to pronounce upon his bottle-green coat, seeing that generally she took particular interest in those matters, and made him wear just what *she* pleased, and very few articles of dress indeed had he, with which the expression of her pleasure had been unqualified. At any other time she might have given her opinion upon the subject with some freedom, but her thoughts were then engaged on a matter of greater moment, and Llewellen therefore naturally attributed her silence to what he conceived to be a fact, that his new bottle-green was a thing with which no fault whatever could be found.

They now started, and as they walked towards the point they had proposed, Louise and Valentine were both extremely thoughtful—not dull—but in the silent enjoyment of those happy feelings which spring from reciprocal love. Occasionally their eyes met, and then they would smile, but with such an expression!—the soul of each seemed to commune with the other.

"Oh, Fred!" exclaimed Louise, suddenly starting, as they reached the Horse Guards, as if something of importance had just occurred to her, "will you do me a favor?"

"Anything in the worlt!"

"Run, then, there's a good creature, and desire Bull the butcher to send home that beef."

"Phot! is it for tinner?"

"Desire him to send it immediately."

"Phery coot; phere toes he live?"

"At the top of this street you'll see a church, and then inquire of any one. Come back to us. We shall be in the Park: but keep on that, the south side of the water."

Llewellen promised to be back as soon as possible, and started off in search of the undiscoverable butcher.

"Poor Fred!" said Louise, as they entered the Park: "Upon my word it is almost too bad."

And so it was in reality: and, therefore, as he had been directed to keep on the south side of the water, they immediately proceeded to the north.

If any doubt had remained in Valentine's mind having reference to the feelings of Louise with respect to Llewellen, this proceeding would at once have dispelled it: but he spurned the gipsy's prophecy, and utterly repudiated the idea of Llewellen being in any shape his rival; still he felt that he might as well make "assurance doubly sure" by virtue of coming at once to the point.

Louise knew that a crisis was at hand—and the quickness with which ladies generally discover these things is really very surprising—she knew as well as Valentine himself knew that something relating to something which had not before been mentioned was about to be communicated, and, therefore, she clung to him more closely than ever, and waited with breathless impatience for him to speak, for, as the subject was one of deep interest, she conceived it to be entitled to the most profound attention.

For some considerable time not a syllable was breathed: they walked upon the grass very slowly, and felt very oddly; but although the impatience of Louise did prompt her to peep in order to ascertain what was going on next door, not a single word on either side was uttered. Valentine knew that he had to put a question; but how was that question to be put? He felt puzzled. He had conceived it to be a mere matter-of-fact kind of thing which caused simple people only to feel embarrassed; but he now found that if indeed such were the case, he was one of the most simple creatures breathing.

It is not perhaps to be with truth asserted that men who are anxious to marry for wealth or convenience merely, experience these feelings of embarrassment at such a time in any great degree. They in general find no difficulty at all about the matter: they manage the preliminaries like men of business; they put the grand question as a purely commercial matter of course, and come to the point without any unnecessary nonsense. It is however questionable whether any man who sincerely and tenderly loved ever did or ever could do the thing quite so coolly. It is perfectly certain that Valentine could not, for he felt very droll, and thought himself very stupid.

"Louise!" said he at length. "Shall we sit down, Louise?"

Louise looked at him archly, and smiled, and then said, "Why—I have no objection!"

Very well! This was quite satisfactory as far as it went; and they did sit down, but were silent again; which Louise thought particularly tiresome. She wished he would say what he had to say, really, and yet she felt half afraid to hear it: she knew not why she should have this feeling, but this feeling she certainly had, despite her natural anxiety to give him every encouragement to begin. Still in silence they continued to sit—she playing with the fringe of her Lilliputian parasol, and he wringing the necks of the buttons of his waistcoat with his watch-guard—until he began to think this never would do, when he summoned all his courage and spoke!

"Louise," said he, softly. "Upon my word I am very stupid."

"What a number of new and interesting observations you have made this morning!" exclaimed Louise, playfully, conceiving that she might perhaps encourage him in that way. "You have really become more entertaining than ever. One would imagine that you had something on your mind which pressed very, very heavily!"

"I certainly have something on my mind, Louise, which makes me feel very, very awkward. Can you not guess what it is?"

"Now how is that possible? Can you guess—I know you are very clever—but can you guess what is passing at this moment in my mind?"

"I think that I am sufficiently clever for that! You are thinking of precisely the same thing as that which occupies my thoughts!"

"Dear me! what an extraordinary coincidence! But what were you thinking of?"

"The day," replied Valentine, taking her hand.

"Oh! the day! Well, it really is a fine day. The sun, it is true, is rather warm, but then the breeze is extremely refreshing."

"You are a rogue, Louise. You know that I do not mean this day, but that on which we are both to be made happy."

"That on which we are both to be made happy? Are you not happy now?"

"Not nearly so happy as I hope to be then. I expect, Louise, that that will be indeed a happy day."

"Well, I'm sure I hope it may be: but what particular day do you mean?"

"The day," said Valentine, earnestly, "on which we are to be united."

"Oh!" said Louise, between a whisper and a sigh, and she began to pick the fringe of her parasol again; for although she had deemed it incumbent upon her to accelerate Valentine's arrival at that interesting point, conceiving that nothing at all could be done if both were embarrassed at one and the same time, she now found that it was her turn to feel rather droll, and it really was a moment of very deep interest.

"Louise," said Valentine, who now began to feel a little better; "Louise: when is that happy day to be?"

Louise was silent, but she tugged at the fringe with more violence than ever.

"I need not, my dearest," continued Valentine, "explain how sincerely, how fondly I love you: I feel that you already know it all. Tell me, therefore—come! when—when is it to be?"

"Indeed," said Louise, "I know nothing at all about it."

"Do you prefer May to June?"

"Really—I—it is such a curious question!"

"Perhaps it is, but I think it one which might be very easily answered."

"But I don't know how to answer it.—Upon my word, I—I have had no experience in such matters—I never had to answer such a question before."

"Indeed I never for a moment supposed that you had; but what can be in reality more simple? Assuming—I will if you please put it so!—*assuming* that you were about to become a dear little wife, in which month, May or June, would you prefer being married?"

"Why, I don't know—I cannot tell, really; but I think that if I were ever to be placed in that dreadful position, I should perhaps like June rather better than May."

"Louise!—let us come to the point: we have known each other long enough to know each other well. I know you to be a tiresome little creature, upon whom the happiness of my whole life depends, and you know me to be the most handsome—I think the most handsome—and perhaps the most affectionate fellow that ever breathed—who will study to do all in his power to make you wretched. Under these frightful circumstances now, what say you—shall we, my sweet girl, be married in June?"

"Marry?—I marry?—in June?—how ever *could* such a fancy have entered your head?

"I cannot pretend to be able to explain the exact process; but most certainly you introduced it among other strange fancies which I occasionally entertain when inclined to give a party of that description. But Louise, are you conscious of the fact that you have not yet given me an answer?"

"I really—I don't at all know—I—how can I possibly—it is such a question—you have taken me so much by surprise—I don't know how to give an answer, really."

"Let me teach you—say 'yes.' It will save a world of trouble. Say 'yes' and have done with it. Take my advice, and say 'yes.'

"But do you think now, really, that this is a strictly proper question to put to me?"

"Why I think that I thought so, or I don't think I should have proposed it."

"Have you forgotten that I have a father?"

"By no means."

"Have you ever named the subject to him?"

"Never directly. But of course he is prepared to receive the dreadful blow. He has, I have no doubt, been waiting some considerable period for us to inflict it."

"But do you not conceive that he is the first person to whom such a subject as this should be named?"

"Why, Louise, I like you have had but little experience in these matters; but I really thought that he was the second: I did indeed. If however you imagine that in the present afflicting state of things, he ought to be the first, I will first obtain his answer, provided you promise me faithfully now, that if he should say yes—and I shall strongly advise him to do so—your answer will be the same."

"Why I am bound of course to act in obedience to my father's wishes: you would not, I feel sure, in the event of such an answer being returned, have me act in opposition to him!"

"Believe me, not for the world! It is then understood: if he should say 'yes, let it take place in June,' you will also say 'yes, let it take place in June;' that is to say in other words, that you are perfectly willing that it should take place then, if he has no particular objection. That is it I apprehend?"

"You are a very teasing creature; I'll have nothing more to say to you on the subject."

"Until I have obtained the consent of your father?"

"Indeed I'm not going to answer any more questions. You inveigled me here, I perceive, expressly in order to tease me, and now if you please we'll return."

It was natural—perhaps, highly natural—that during this brief, but, to the parties concerned, deeply interesting conversation, Llewellen should have been altogether forgotten, or nothing could have been urged to excuse their oblivion in this particular; for they actually thought of him no more than if he had not been at all in existence, until they rose to return, when they happened to see him on the opposite side deeply engaged in the delightful occupation of feeding the ducks.

There is in all probability no species of pleasure at once so exciting, so generous, and so pure, as that which springs from the strictly philosophical process of feeding these acute and deeply interesting birds. They are so highly intelligent, so sensible; they know as well when they have got a bit of biscuit in their bills as possible! They will swallow it, and enjoy it, and dart after more, and fight and plunder each other like Christians. It is delightful to observe the dignity with which they assert their claim to whatever they can get. It really affords a great social lesson; for although in the Park the majority are foreigners, they insist upon having equal rights with the natives; and as the natives are not sufficiently strong to put them down, they accommodate themselves to those republican principles which have of late years in spite of them obtained.

Under all these circumstances, then, it will not be deemed marvellous that Llewellen's attention could not be drawn to the

The Proposal.

P 290.

opposite side of the water; and as such was the case, Louise and Valentine were compelled to go round, where they surprised him in the very act of playing with a mob of little Muscovites, that by dint of zealous dillying he had seduced upon land.

"Where on earth have you been?" cried Louise, as they approached him.

"Phere have you pin?" retorted Llewellen; "hur've pin pack here a long time! Phell!" he continued, with a mournful expression, "there'll pe no peef for dinner totay! Inteet hur can't fint the putcher, look you!"

"What!" exclaimed Louise.

"Nopotty knows Pull the putcher at all!"

"Did you ever!"

"Phell, hur ton't care; hur tit all her coot to fint him out; hur phent into all the shops; but no,—ephery potty laught phen hur inquirt, put nopotty knew anything apout any putcher named Pull."

"This is always the case," said Louise; "I don't think, Fred, that I shall ever ask you to do me another favor while I live."

"Hur can't help it. Hur knew you't co on; put hur tit all hur coot, ant phith the tirection phich you cave me, the tevil himself cootn't fint Pull the putcher."

"Well, come Louise," said Valentine, "say no more about it. It is not I presume of any very great importance. You had better, perhaps, show Fred at once where Bull lives, and then he will know where to find him."

"Yes too, Louey, come; hur shoot like apove all things in the worl't to know phere he's to be fount, for hur huntit him in ephery tirection. It phill not take you much out of the phay, look you—come!"

"Indeed, sir, I shall not do anything of the sort," said Louise, pinching Valentine's arm very severely; "if people are so extremely stupid as to be actually unable to find out the shop of a butcher, I really don't feel myself bound to take any trouble with them at all. As to you, sir," she added, addressing Valentine, "you ought to be ashamed of having made such a suggestion: I beg that the subject may not be renewed."

Llewellen now conceived that she was indeed very angry, and therefore said nothing more about it; and as Valentine had no desire to induce him to suspect that he had been played with, the propriety of adopting the suggestion he had offered was not urged. They at once proceeded home; and, although the lovers were not quite so silent as before, they were still very thoughtful, and would, to common observers, have appeared very dull.

Of course Valentine felt himself bound under the circumstances to dine there that day. It is true he thought at one time that it might perhaps be better to excuse himself, in order that both he and Louise might reflect upon what had happened, before he took the next step; but having considered the matter for a moment, he felt that this would be quite unnecessary, seeing that while he had firmly made up his mind, he had not the smallest doubt that she had as firmly made up hers; and that therefore the subject might as well be named to Raven without any further delay.

He accordingly consented to remain, and continued to amuse himself in the garden with Llewellen until they were summoned to dinner, when he found that in honor of the occasion Louise had taken pains to look more than usually attractive. Her manner was however much altered; she was far more reserved, spoke but little, and felt in some slight degree embarrassed.

"You are not yourself to-day, my girl," said Raven, on noticing this change, "who has been putting you out?"

"Oh, pless you, she's only pin plowink me up," said Llewellen, "pecause hur cootn't fint, look you, Mr. Pull the putcher!"

"Indeed, sir, you are mistaken," cried Louise, "and I beg that you will be silent."

"What, have you been changing your butcher, my girl?" inquired Raven.

"No, it is only his stupidity—he gets worse and worse."

"Well, but I thought Scraggs supplied us?"

"Of course," replied Louise.

"Putt you said Pull! Titn't she say Pull, my poy? Oh! hur'll take my oath she sait Pull."

"Did you *ever* know any one so stupid?"

"Perhaps," observed Raven, "he was thinking of the bull beef!"

"Oh! as likely as not," cried Louise.

"Putt *too* you mean to say that you titn't say Pull?"

"Good gracious hold your tongue Fred, and don't be so silly!"

"Putt hur say, Louey, look you—too you mean Louey—*too* you mean to say that you titn't tell me Pull?"

"I mean, sir, to say nothing more on the subject. I am ashamed of you."

"Doubtless," observed Raven, "the mistake originated in the remarkable similarity of the names."

"Phot, petween Pull and Scraggs!" cried Llewellen, "phell, cootness knows! —putt is it propaple; is it, look you, at all? —oh!—pesites hur know Scraggs, look you; putt she sait Pull!"

"You had better say no more about the

matter," said Louise, "I'm sorry you expose yourself in this way."

"Never mind, Fred," said Raven, "mistakes will occur; let me send you a little more fish."

Llewellen had no objection to a little more fish, but he had an objection—a very serious objection—to its being supposed that he had mistaken the name of Scraggs for that of Bull. He would not however suffer that circumstance to interfere at all with his dinner: he ate heartily—fiercely; but he made up his mind to have the thing satisfactorily cleared up anon.

The dinner therefore passed off without any further allusions being made to the affair; and when Llewellen began to exhibit strong symptoms of a very deep anxiety to renew it, Valentine happily started a subject which precluded the possibility of its being hedged in.

In due time Louise made her exit, and as she had previously intimated to Llewellen that she had something of importance to communicate to him in the drawing-room, he almost immediately followed, leaving Raven and Valentine alone.

Of course Valentine perfectly understood this arrangement, although he had had nothing whatever to do with it. He knew for what purpose Llewellen had been withdrawn, and he also knew that his absence would in all probability be prolonged, inasmuch as Louise, if she could but get him near the piano after dinner, had the marvellous faculty of playing him to sleep.—He therefore made up his mind to speak to Raven on the subject at once. He felt certainly rather awkward at the moment, and scarcely knew how to begin; but being encouraged by the conviction that the consent which he was about to solicit would not be withheld, he conquered his scruples and commenced.

"Mr. Raven," said he, replenishing his glass as if about to propose a toast, which invariably fixed Raven's attention, it being a practice of which he was particularly fond—"Mr. Raven: the uniform kindness with which you have received me, and for which I shall ever feel deeply indebted, induces me to hope that you will entertain that which I am now most anxious to propose."

"Certainly; by all means," said Raven, who filled his glass, and listened attentively again.

"The affection which exists between Louise and myself," continued Valentine, "I believe to be mutual and firm."

"I have no doubt of it," said Raven, "no doubt of it in the world."

"And as you have never appeared to discountenance the growth of that affection, I am encouraged to believe that you have no desire to check it now."

"None at all, my boy: not the least in life."

"Such being the case, then, my present object is to obtain your consent to our union."

"My dear boy," said Raven, "you have it! I give it freely, and at once. I will not disguise from you how highly I admire your character, and as I feel that as a husband you will be faithful and affectionate, take her, and may every earthly blessing throughout life be yours.—God bless you both!" he added, raising the glass to his lips, as the tears stood and sparkled in his eyes. "But I am sure you will be happy: I am quite sure of that. She is a good girl: I know that she is a good girl, and as a wife will be all that a man can desire."

He then drank off his wine, and having instantly replenished, proposed the health of Louise in a bumper.

"Louise and I," said Valentine, when with heartfelt pleasure he had done honor to the toast, "had some little conversation on the subject this morning, but, as with very great propriety, she suggested that you were the *first* person to whom I ought to speak, she left it in your hands entirely."

"Just like her!" exclaimed Raven, highly pleased with the fact. "She is the best and most amiable girl in the world."

"Now I was thinking," said Valentine, "that June is a very pleasant month."

"So it is: but I must leave all that to be settled between yourselves. Only tell me when it is settled. Let me see—June—oh! yes. I wish you would give my compliments to your uncle, and tell him I shall be happy to see him when convenient. Perhaps he will dine with us to-morrow? Just ask him."

Valentine promised to do so; and, after drinking a few more appropriate toasts, they left the table to join Louise.

"My girl!" said Raven, as he entered the drawing-room, "come here."

Louise approached, and he placed her hand in Valentine's, and blessed them, and then went to pommel Llewellen. That gentleman was soundly asleep on the sofa: but, although it was usually very difficult to rouse him under those peculiar circumstances, Raven, being then in high spirits, soon succeeded in waking him up.

"Now don't you think, Fred, that you are a very pretty fellow!" cried Raven, when his efforts had been crowned with success.

"Intect, cootness knows hur've pin asleep!" said Llewellen, which with him was an occurrence of so extraordinary a character, that he felt quite confused. "Putt," he added, "it phos Louey's fault. She setucet me up here, and phootn't let me co town acain, look you."

Louis, doubtless, at any other time would have given free expression to her opinion on the propriety of this observation; but she was then too much engaged, having coffee to dispense and certain feelings to conceal, to attend to anything so really unimportant. Her reserve was remarkable. She scarcely said a word. She looked, and blushed, and occasionally smiled, but she did not by any means feel self-possessed. Valentine, on the contrary, was buoyant and merry; he chatted with Raven, and rallied Llewellen with unusual spirit, until the evening became far advanced, when he took leave of them, and left the room with Louise, who appeared to be somewhat anxious, on that particular occasion, to see him safely out.

"My dearest love," said he, stopping near the drawing-room door, "I need not perhaps state that your father has freely consented to our union. With me he thinks that June would be a very pleasant month; but as he leaves that entirely to you, pray think of it: I shall see you in the morning. Oh, Louise! I have felt, and still do feel, so happy! My dear girl, good night."

Louise was silent, but she returned his embrace with affectionate warmth, when he once again bade her adieu, and departed.

CHAPTER LIV.

VALENTINE VISITS THE ROYAL ACADEMY, AND RAVEN ASTONISHES THE FACULTIES OF UNCLE JOHN.

On reaching home, Valentine briefly explained the substance of all that had occurred to Uncle John, who was in consequence highly delighted. He had passed a mournful evening; for Whitely, who now despaired of obtaining the slightest clue to the discovery of his children, had been his only companion; but when Valentine arrived with his "glorious news," he at once made up his mind to have an additional glass, and resolved, moreover, that Whitely and Valentine should join him. He found it, however, extremely difficult to prevail upon Whitely to do this, for that gentleman cherished his sad thoughts as if he loved them, and appeared to have a horror of every thing likely to cause them to be even for a moment dispelled: but eventually Uncle John succeeded in inducing him, in honour of the occasion, to yield, when despair by degrees was supplanted by hope, and after an hour's enlivening conversation, he retired comparatively happy.

In the morning—after having held a deep consultation with Uncle John, who felt that he had that day to perform a great duty—Valentine proceeded to call upon Louise, whom he found still embarrassed, but affectionate and gentle. She appeared to have been completely disarmed; and, although she flew to receive him as he entered, she was silent, and subsequently, whenever her eyes met his, which did not unfrequently happen, she blushed, and seemed greatly confused.

"Hur say, my poy," whispered Llewellen, embracing the first opportunity of drawing him aside: "Phot is the matter phith Louey? She hasn't plown me up all the morning!"

"You have not offended her, probably."

"Oh, cootness knows it, that's no rule to co py: there's something pesites in the wint."

"Don't despair," said Valentine, encouragingly. "You will have it no doubt by and by.—Louise!" he added.

"No, no, no!" interrupted Llewellen. "Inteet, hur ton't want it!—No, no! hur ton't want it!—pe still!"

"I was about to ask Louise if she felt inclined to go to the Royal Academy this morning."

"Oh, that's another pisiness! Hur shoot like *that* apove all things in the worlt."

"Well, shall we go, my love?"

"I should enjoy it much," replied Louise, softly.

"Run away, then, and prepare. And Louise!—tell your father that my uncle *will* do himself the pleasure of dinning here today."

Louise left the room; and the moment she was gone, Llewellen said, "My poy, you mate me tremple. Hur was afrait that you were coing to tell Louey phot hur sait, pecause then she woot have pecan, look you, at once. Put her say!—phot's the matter? Pelieve me she titn't say a wort all the time we were at preakfast. Is there anything wrong?"

"Nothing," replied Valentine. "Every thing is perfectly right. You will soon know the cause of this change in Louise."

"Phot! Are you coing to pe marriet!"

"Married: how came you to think of that?"

"Phel, hur titn't know, look you. However, hur ton't care a pit, if there's nothing coing wrong."

As Louise returned shortly after this, they proceeded at once to the exhibition. Llewellen was a great connoisseur: he could tell in a moment if a picture pleased him, and wouldn't pretend to admire what he didn't. To such a connoisseur the exhibition of the Royal Academy did at that particular period present many charms which few others could see, and hence it will not be held to be very extraordinary that Llewellen was highly delighted. He looked at the portraits. Very good! As far as the likenesses were concerned, why of course he knew nothing, and didn't mean to care; they all appeared to be very pleasant people, and that was sufficient for him. The dogs however attracted his particular attention: he was at once almost lost in admiration of them.

"How phery font people are kitting of togs," he observed.

"It would appear so, certainly," said Valentine. "One would imagine that we were a nation of dog fanciers."

"How do you account," inquired Louise, "for so many being painted?"

"Young artists are advised to direct attention to that particular branch," replied Valentine, "it being assumed that all who are anxious to have portraits of their dogs can afford to pay handsomely for them."

"Then if things co on so, phe shall have nothing putt tog painters py ant py, look you!"

"See how highly they are admired," said Valentine, directing the attention of Louise to two ladies and a highly rouged gentleman, who were extolling the sublimity of a portrait of a bloodhound.

"Dear me!" exclaimed one of the ladies, "what a love!—is he not?"

"Foine animal! foine dog! foine creachor?" cried the highly rouged gentleman; but he had no sooner got to the "creachor," than Valentine made an angry growl proceed apparently from the bloodhound, which caused the admirers of the "creachor" to start back amazed.

"Why what!—why!—why!—aloive!" exclaimed the highly rouged gentleman, with an aspect of horror.

"Don't be alarmed, my love," said Valentine, whispering to Louise, "it was I that made the noise."

"You! why it appeared to be the dog!"

"Exactly; I'll explain to you presently. Take no notice now."

In a state of the most intense astonishment did the highly rouged gentleman look at the ladies whom he had accompanied, and then at the bloodhound. He couldn't make it out! He had heard it, surely! Oh! the ladies themselves had borne testimony to that, for while one of them said "Did you ever," the other exclaimed "Well, I never!" which of course was conclusive. But then the "creachor" was not alive! and if the "creachor" was not alive, why —what then? He couldn't tell; he only knew that he had heard the "creachor" growl. He looked again, and approached him gradually, until he was able to make a very minute inspection indeed. It certainly was not alive! He touched the "creachor" —not near the mouth it is true, but he absolutely touched him.

"Keep your hands off the pictchors," said Valentine, throwing his voice behind the offender, "how dare you touch the pictchors!"

The highly rouged gentleman turned, and really felt quite frightened; but as he saw no one behind him that looked like a man who had the courage to speak to him in that style, he naturally felt himself bound to give the ladies a little idea of his valour. Perceiving a very quiet looking elderly gentleman on one of the seats, he therefore marched up to him boldly, and said in a tone which conveyed a great deal of indignation, "Did you speak to me, sor?"

The old gentleman looked at him over his spectacles very inquisitively, and after having carefully examined the animal, replied, "I don't know you, I don't understand you."

"I ask if you spoke to me just now in that abrupt and particularly ungentlemanlike manner?"

"Decidedly not."

"Oh," said the highly rouged gentleman, "oh!" and the ladies becoming alarmed, drew him at once from the spot, but he turned to look again at the "creachor."

"Is it possible," said Louise, "that it was you in reality?"

"Quite. But, Louise, you must keep what I am now about to impart to you a most profound secret."

Louise promised to do so, and to her utter amazement, he proceeded to explain to her his power as a ventriloquist, while Llewellen was particularly engaged with a painting in the subject of which he appeared to take the deepest possible interest. This painting told a plain tale of heartlessness on the one hand, and weakness on the other—a tale of seduction and its wretched results; and while he sympathised deeply with the victim who was there represented sitting in abject misery upon the steps of a mansion, with her infant at her breast, while the tears trickled fast down her cheeks, he shook his fist at her seducer with an energetic action which seemed to intimate that he could, with a great deal of pleasure, knock his head out of the canvass.

"Oh, do," said Louise, when Valentine had explained, "do try the effect upon Fred."

"Well, but you must be cautious; I shall have an opportunity presently. But see how excited he appears."

"What on earth is the matter?" inquired Louise, as they approached him.

"Inteet, now," said Llewellen, addressing Valentine, and pointing to the seducer, "that's a creat scountrel, look you?"

"A what!" cried Valentine, whose voice seemed to proceed from the figure alluded to, "a what!"

"A creat *scountrel!*" repeated Llewellen, nothing daunted, for he was very indignant, and looked at the figure very fiercely. He however recollected himself the next moment, and turned to look alternately at Valentine and Louise.

"Why, what in the name of goodness are you about?" exclaimed Louise.

Llewellen, without immediately replying, examined the painting very closely; but having satisfied himself that it was really a painting, and that no one could possibly be behind it, he thought it better under the circumstances, not to subject himself to the rallying sarcasm of Louise, and therefore, having said "hur only thought somepotty spoke," moved away.

"Dear me," cried Louise, "how excessively natural it seems. For goodness sake don't tell any one about it. We shall have such sport, I'll assist you. But do you not move your lips at all?"

"Can you see them move?" said Valentine, sending his voice behind her.

Louise turned in an instant. "Good gracious!" she exclaimed, "that person overheard us!"

"Of course," said Valentine, throwing his voice as before.

"Let us go," said Louise, "he'll insult us."

"Insult you!"

"Oh, do let us go into the next room!"

"Why, that person has not spoken," said Valentine, in his natural voice, smiling.—"He has not said a word."

"But you don't mean to say that it was you?"

"Why, of course!"

"Well I never!—But you know—you must not frighten *me!*"

"Oh! any one else?"

"Nay, it will not be fair to frighten me! you would not wish to do it, would you?—No, let that be clearly understood."

"Very well. Of course, what you say now amounts to law!"

"No, no, not so. At least," she added playfully, "not yet."

"Is Mr. Llewellen in the room?" cried Valentine, throwing his voice to the opposite corner.

"Cootness," said Llewellen, turning to Valentine, "toes he mean me?"

"Mr. Llewellen of Caermarthen!" cried Valentine as before, and looking at the same time steadily at the victim.

"Yesm!" cried Llewellen, "some frient of mine, no tout. Who t'cootness can it pe?"

As Llewellen walked anxiously towards the spot from which the voice appeared to proceed, every eye was upon him. The thing was so unusual! The *idea* of calling out a gentleman's name in such a manner, and in such a place! It was evidently held by all to be extremely incorrect, and even Louise exclaimed, "what a vulgar person to be sure!"

"Do you really conceive him to be a vulgar person?" inquired Valentine, with a smile, which clearly intimated something.

"Why--gracious Valentine!--surely that was not you then?"

"Why, is it at all likely to have been any one else?"

"Oh! how glorious. Well, I thought it very singular!—Now, let us hear what he'll say. But you should *tell* me! You should let me know beforehand! I should enjoy it so much more if you were to do that.—Here he comes."

"Hur can't fint any potty," said Llewellen, as he approached with a countenance remarkably vacant. "Inteet t'cootness, now hur shoot like to know pho it coot pe!--Phot are you laughing at, Louey?" he added, as Louise covered her face to conceal her convulsions.

"Have you really no idea who it was?" inquired Valentine.

"Pless you! not the least. It was some frient, no tout. Hur shoot like now to fint him apove all things in the worlt." And again he looked round and round the room in the lively hope of seeing some friend from Caermarthen.

"Louise," whispered Valentine, "this

will never do! you'll spoil all if you do not keep your countenance."

"Yes—I know, but I really could not help it. He did look so silly—poor Fred!"

"How do you like that style of painting?" said Valentine, alluding—more with the view of restoring the tranquillity of her countenance than anything else—to a flaming red and blue lightning subject, which appeared to have been done by some eminent artist, while looking through a pair of kaleidoscopic spectacles—"Do you admire it?"

"Why, upon my word I cannot understand it!" replied Louise.

"Nor can I, nor can any one else, I should say, with the exception of the artist himself. But do you admire the style?"

"It is so indistinct and glaring."

"There is an infinite deal of something about it: it may by possibility be very sublime, but I should say its chief merit consists in its being altogether incomprehensible."

"Well, well," said Louise with impatience, "never mind; I've no doubt that it was meant to be very poetic, but do, there's a dear, tease Fred."

The fact is, after Valentine had entrusted her with the secret of his power, Louise took but little interest in the paintings: it had at once so delighted and amazed her, that she looked at them only as a medium through which that power might with effect be developed: and as it was but natural that Valentine should, under existing circumstances, be anxious to please her by all the means at his command, he went up to Llewellen, who had been running about in all directions in search of his undiscoverable friend, and, looking steadily at him, said, in the most cordial manner possible, "Ah! Llewellen!"

The voice apparently proceeded from behind him, and he turned on the instant and scrutinised the features of every man whom he saw. But no! No friend was visible! He could not see a soul of whom he had the slightest knowledge! which in the abstract was very remarkable.

"There's somepotty having a *came* with me," he observed, when he had satisfied his conscience that every creature behind him was unknown to him; "Inteet, t' cootness hur shoot like to fint him out!" And it was not by any means extraordinary that he did wish to do so, more especially as he felt in some slight degree displeased!

"Now, now," said Louise, "make that picture appear to speak to him: do!"

"No, no; it's too bad," said Valentine. "Besides, he will begin to suspect."

"Never mind," said Louise, "he will not suspect us. Do, there's a dear; once more: come, only once!"

"Well, well; you must draw his attention to it."

"Oh, I'll do that.—Fred, I want you to give me your opinion upon this portrait. Now what do you really think of it? Be candid."

"Phell, look you, hur ton't know: hur ton't pretent to pe a jutch; putt her should say it's phery peautiful."

"Do you really," said Valentine, assuming the voice of a female, and making it appear to proceed from the canvass,—"Do you really think me beautiful?"

Llewellen started, and then looked at the portrait in a very steady, straightforward, unflinching manner, and then looked at Louise and then at Valentine, and then at the portrait again. At length, being unable to make any thing at all of it, in the fulness of his heart he exclaimed—"Inteet t' cootness, hur think now the tevil's in the pictures!"

"For shame!" cried Louise. "How dare you make use of that wicked expression?"

"Phell hur ton't care, Louey; he's in the room somephere, look you, that's my pelief. Titn't you hear?"

"I heard you say that the portrait was very beautiful."

"So hur tit!—so hur tit!—ant then it asked if hur *tit* think it peautiful!"

"It! what, the portrait? Why, you do not mean to be so ridiculous as to imagine that the portrait spoke, surely?"

"Hur ton't care a pit about the pisiness, look you, Louey, putt cootness knows hur heart somepotty speak! Titn't you, my poy?—*titn't* you?"

"I heard some one speak, that's quite certain: but it couldn't, by any possibility, be the painting!"

"Absurd!" cried Louise. "Now really, Fred—give me your candid opinion—do you not yourself think that you are getting very stupid?"

"Hur ton't care phot you say: you may call me stupit if you please, putt if hur titn't hear that phery picture ask me plain plank phether hur *tit* think it peautiful, pless me!"

"But how is it possible? How could it?"

"Hur ton't pretent to know how it coot; put it *tit!* Cootness knows, am hur not to pelieve my own ears?"

It does seem hard that a man cannot always with safety have the firmest and the most implicit faith in the evidence of those useful and ornamental organs; but it is notwithstanding a fact, that, in all such cases as those in which ventriloquism is concerned, such evidence is perfectly certain to be false. However direct it may be, however specious, however strong, it is sure to mislead the inquiring mind, so invariable is its perversion of truth—so stubborn its adherence to error.

Of all this Llewellen was utterly ignorant, and hence he stuck firmly to his faith. He of course thought it strange, unaccountably strange; but no reason which he could bring to bear upon the point was sufficiently powerful to shake his conviction; no species of ridicule—nay, not even the manifest impossibility of the thing itself—could induce him to repudiate or even to doubt the evidence of those false witnesses, his ears.

This was a source of great enjoyment to Louise. She rallied him cruelly, not only at the exhibition, but as they returned. He was a martyr; and with the characteristic firmness of a martyr he endured it.

On reaching home, however, Louise became thoughtful again. Knowing that Uncle John was to dine there that day, her thoughts reverted to the cause of his being specially invited, and, although she was as happy as any affectionate little creature under the circumstances could be, she could not but feel in some slight degree embarrassed.

From Valentine this was concealed as much as possible. She naturally did not wish him to know all; she, therefore, left him immediately on their return with the full determination—and it really was a very important determination—not to make her appearance again until Uncle John arrived.

The interim would, doubtless, have been somewhat tedious to Valentine if matters had taken their usual course; but the moment she had left him, Raven entered the room, and, actuated by his characteristic love of display, begged Valentine as a favor to take the carriage for his Uncle. Of course, anything calculated to please the bitter enemy of the aristocracy Valentine had then no inclination to oppose. The carriage was, therefore, immediately ordered, for Raven suggested that, although it was early, his old friend might like to have an airing before he dined: which was very affectionate.

Matters being thus arranged, Raven left the room with dignity, when Llewellen claimed the privilege of going with Valentine, on the ground of his being a great favorite of Uncle John. "Hur too like him," said he, just to strengthen his claim, "pecause hur pelieve him to pe a coot tempert, kint, ant penevolent olt soul, ant hur know he likes me, pecause phenever hur speak to him, look you, he smiles."

This was held to be conclusive, and, as in a very few minutes the carriage was announced, they proceeded to put Uncle John in a fidget. This, strange as it may appear, was the effect which the sight of that carriage invariably had upon him. He was sufficiently feverish when it came to the door on any ordinary occasion, but whenever it was sent expressly for him it threw him at once into a dreadful state of mind, for he held it to be beyond all doubt or dispute entirely out of the regular course.

Fortunately, however, in this particular instance he was sitting with Whitely in poor Goodman's room, when it dashed up to the door, and was, therefore, unconscious of the fact until Valentine announced it.

"But, dear me," said Uncle John, pulling out his watch with great promptitude and tact, "why, it wants a full hour and a half of the time!"

Whitely enjoined silence, for Uncle John's lungs were very powerful, and Goodman was asleep. They, therefore, repaired to the drawing-room in which Valentine had left Llewellen, a fact of which both Uncle John and Whitely were unconscious.

"Ah! Mr. Llewellen!" exclaimed Uncle John, "I hope you're well, sir; I hope you're very well! Allow me to introduce to you my friend Mr. Whitely."

"Hur'm prout to know you," said Llewellen, extending his hand. "Hur've heart of you t' cootness knows how often."

Whitely during the salutation looked at him intensely! He seemed to be struck with Llewellen's appearance, and yet there was nothing in it very extraordinary. Still he inspired on the instant some feeling which caused him to turn pale as death!

Neither Uncle John nor Valentine noticed the agitation into which he had been thrown, but Llewellen did, and, therefore, said,—"You are not well, my frient? Come for a rite. Inteet, t' cootness it will too you all the coot in the worlt!"

Whitely tremulously begged to be excused, and almost immediately after retired from the room.

"Now, then, my tear old frient; come, let us have a clorious rite pefore tinner, ant then you'll pe aple to keep me in countenance, for, look you, nopotty can eat at all here!—hur ton't know t' cootness how it is people manache to live phithout eating."

"But bless my life!" exclaimed Uncle John, "I'm not dressed! You have taken me quite by surprise!"

"Oh, never mint that, look you!—never mint that. We can wait phile you tress! Cootness knows it, our time is not so precious!"

Eventually Uncle John consented: for,

although he thought it hard that he could not be suffered to go quietly, he was pressed so warmly, not only by Llewellen, but by Valentine, who explained how highly Raven would be pleased, that he felt himself bound, as a disagreeable matter of courtesy on this one particular occasion to yield.

He, therefore, left the room to make himself tidy, and Valentine ordered up the tray, it being questionable whether he could by any other means hold Llewellen in a perfect state of happiness. He had not the smallest doubt of being able to effect this great object in that way, and the correctness of his judgment in this particular was abundantly proved by the result. The very moment Llewellen saw a ham and three ribs of beef, that moment did his eyes begin to sparkle with pleasure, and he set to work like a new man.

"I think you will find that a decent glass of sherry," said Valentine, placing the bottle before him.

"My poy," cried Llewellen, "too let's have some peer!"

The beer was ordered on the instant, and when that was produced his views were met to a hair. Nothing could have been better. He slashed away, and ate with so much energy and gusto, that really any stranger would have imagined that he had been experimentalised upon by the poor-law commissioners, from whom he had just escaped. The only thing which at all interfered with his enjoyment was a lively apprehension of Uncle John's return. Every sound made him start; every footstep alarmed him; he trembled whenever he heard a door bang.

His apprehensions, however, were perfectly vain. Uncle John it is true was in a very great hurry, but it is also true that he could not make haste. He had a ten minutes' hunt for a particular stocking, which, as a matter of convenience, he had thrown over his shoulder, and a period of ten minutes more was occupied in looking for a waistcoat he had on.

Under these afflicting circumstances, Llewellen was in no actual danger of being interrupted. But then he did not know that: which was a pity. Had he possessed the slightest cognisance of the real state of things at that period in Uncle John's dressing-room, doubtless he would have been, although equally energetic, more cool; but working away as he was in the dark as to the actual state of the case there, it was but natural that he should have the unpleasant idea that courtesy would compel him prematurely to give in.

It was not, however, until some time after he had said to himself privately, "Now hur ton't care if he toes come," that Uncle John actually made his appearance.

"I have to apologise," said that gentleman, who was in a very great heat, "I have to apologise for keeping you so long."

"Hur peg you'll make no apology at all," cried Llewellen, which was really very good of him considering, "hur've not pin itle, look you! Hur'd recommend you to have a pit! the peef is peautiful!"

Uncle John very gracefully declined, and having miraculously found a pair of gloves, he searched the whole of his pockets at once, with the view of ascertaining if any important little matter had been forgotten, and then declared himself to be quite at Llewellen's service.

"Put hur must pit your olt frient coot py," cried Llewellen.

"He is now in a sound sleep," said Uncle John.

"Tear t' cootness how ott! Toes he alphays co to sleep in the mittle of the tay?"

"Do you mean poor friend Goodman?"

"No, look you, Mr. Phitely!"

"Oh," said Valentine, "he is not asleep; I'll go and tell him."

He did so, and found him in tears, which he hastened, but in vain, to conceal.

"My good friend! come, keep up your spirits!" said Valentine, "Llewellen wants to bid you good day."

"I look at that young man with pleasure," returned Whitely, "but that pleasure is accompanied with a bitter, bitter pang."

"Then do not see him. I'll tell him I have said good day for him."

"Yes, do, please—yet—oh no, I'll bid him good day." And he dashed away a tear which stood trembling in his eye, and went at once to shake hands with Llewellen.

"God bless you!" said he, "I shall see you again?"

"Oh! yes; hur shall alphays pe coming. Putt hur wish you't co phith us for a rite! Inteet it phoot too you a creat teal of coot."

Again Whitely begged to be excused, and after having again shaken Llewellen warmly by the hand, he saw him into the carriage, and they started.

"Home!" cried the servant, as he mounted behind.

"Phot a set of stupit togs to be sure!" cried Llewellen, pulling the check string with violence.

The carriage stopped in an instant.—"What a pity it is," said Uncle John, "that fine horses like those should be pulled upon their haunches like that."

"Titn't hur tell you the park!" cried Llewellen, as the servant reappeared at the door, "co rount the park ant then home."

Correct orders were then conveyed, and they dashed towards the park; and as they proceeded, Uncle John, although he had been put out of his way very seriously, could not help thinking that a carriage was rather a comfortable sort of thing than not! He was cool and collected then, and had the whole of his faculties about him, which was pleasant, and he enjoyed himself exceedingly, and thought, as he rode round the ring, that the Park was in reality very delightful.

"Phoot you like to co rount once more? We have plenty of time," said Llewellen.

"If we have plenty of time I really should," said Uncle John, "for although I have walked in the Park frequently, I had no idea of its being so pleasant a drive."

Llewellen therefore at once gave the necessary orders, and they went round again, and then "home."

It is a singular thing perhaps to place upon record, and yet it is an absolute fact nevertheless, that every time Valentine saw Louise now, he fancied she looked more lovely than before. Especially so was it in this particular instance, for on reaching the drawing-room he really did believe that he had never beheld any creature so beautiful. She was calm, very calm; except indeed when Uncle John held her hand for a moment, and passed a high compliment, to the justice of which her heart cheerfully subscribed; and when Valentine led her to the window to converse with her alone, she really felt that she never was so happy.

Raven's reception of Uncle John was of the most cordial character, and Uncle John did not fail to appreciate it highly; nor did he omit to explain how much he had enjoyed his ride, which pleased Raven perhaps more than anything else.

Llewellen was of course quite shut out; but he was not inactive: he had got the little delicate Neapolitan greyhound—which used to be the very first favorite with Louise—upon the sofa, and while instead of allowing him to bound with delight, he rolled him over and over, as if he had been but a surfeited pug, the little wretch looked at his tormentor, with all the intelligence of which those stupid things are possessed, for he really didn't like it.

Dinner was now announced, and Uncle John took Louise with all the grace he had in him, when, as Raven took Valentine, Llewellen, who couldn't take the dog—and the dog didn't want him!—went down with his appetite alone.

During dinner Raven proved that he was in the highest possible spirits, which Uncle John of course was delighted to perceive; but as nearly the whole of his observations had indirect reference to the coming event, Louise was sadly embarrassed, although Valentine and Uncle John too did all in their power to neutralize the effect of inuendos which opened even the eyes of Llewellen. Still Raven kept on: it was seldom indeed that he was in a happy vein; but when this did occur, no trifle could stop him. It will hence be inferred that Louise was not sorry when dinner was over, having the power to leave when she pleased; but it strangely enough happened that Raven then dropped the subject, much to the mortification of Llewellen, who, having had but little time to attend to it while anything remained on the table to eat, now prepared himself to listen to any observation which might have a tendency to show him a light. It was therefore particularly annoying to him, privately, that no such observation was made; for up to the time Louise rose to retire, they continued to converse exclusively upon matters in which he took really no interest at all.

"Now then," said Raven, when he saw Louise move; "now run away, all you young people: we don't want you here!"

Valentine, of course, started up in an instant; but Llewellen, who really did not understand it, looked round very naturally for a little explanation. The very moment, however, Valentine beckoned him, he rose, and permitted himself to be led from the room in a state of mental darkness.

"Well, my old friend!" exclaimed Raven, when he and Uncle John were alone. "In the first place, we'll drink the health of Val and Louise!—God bless them both: may they be happy!"

Uncle John most heartily responded to this toast, and made an addition directly touching the little consequences of their union. He then gave the health of Llewellen, whom he lauded as one of the best-hearted fellows that ever lived; and when Raven had made a very slight, but a highly eulogistic, addition to that, he said, "Now let us drink our noble selves, and then to business."

"Valentine," he continued, when this toast had been appropriately honored, "has doubtless told you that he has had a little quiet conversation with me on the subject of his marriage with Louise."

Uncle John nodded an affirmative.

"He has also told you that the result was my free and unconditional consent to their union? Very well. Now I admire the character of that boy. Were he my own flesh and blood, I could not love him more. He is a fine fellow, a noble, firm, affectionate, fellow, and Louise is about the best girl that ever breathed. They love each other fondly and firmly: I know it! and they are worthy of each other. And as they are about to be united to each other, now! what can we do for them?"

"What *I* have," said Uncle John, promptly, "I have made up my mind to divide with them. I have been thinking of this matter all the morning, and as I calculate that I cannot be worth, on the whole, more than sixteen thousand pounds, and as I shall have no one then but his mother to provide for, I'll give them eight thousand at once to begin with."

"My friend," said Raven, grasping the hand of Uncle John. "If you have made up your mind to do that, I have made up my mind that you shall not. You shall not, my friend, do anything of the sort!—and if we are to have a quarrel about the matter, we had better at once fight it out. I don't wish to say anything in disparagement of your circumstances, but I will say this, that I can afford to provide for them better than you can. I'll at once give them twenty thousand pounds. I'll not give them a single penny more, because I don't wish to spoil them by tempting them to launch into a sea of aristocratic extravagancies. No: I'll give them that—which is as much as they ought to have, and as much as I will consent to let them have to begin with—and if you will not allow me to do this alone, why the only alternative is, you must fight me!"

"If I were—"

"Stop," said Raven, "stop. Before you speak let us have a glass of wine."

This interruption was indeed a great relief to Uncle John, who had been so startled by Raven's generous proposition, that he scarcely at the moment knew how to reply.

"Now," continued Raven. "What have you to say against it?"

"Why, I hardly know what I have to say, with the exception that I cannot consent to do nothing. I think with you, that they ought not to have more than twenty thousand, but why can you not give twelve and let me give the rest?"

"I'll not have it!"

"Well then—come, I'll meet your views if I can!—you shall put down fifteen and I'll give the odd money."

"I tell you, my friend, I'll do nothing of the sort. I have made up my mind to give the whole, and the whole I will give! I, of course, do not wish to deprive you of the pleasure of doing something!—Make them a present!—I'll let you do that!"

"Well then, I'll give them a house to live in."

"Nonsense!" cried Raven, "young people don't like to be tied. If you give them a house to live in, they'll want to remove the second quarter! Now, I'll tell you what I'll do—I'll conciliate you if possible!—I'll consent to your *furnishing* a house for them, but, to nothing more will I consent, I'm determined."

"Mr. Raven!" said Uncle John, "really your generosity has surprised me."

"I am not a man," said Raven, with dignity and pride—"I am not a man to boast of my wealth and resources; but I may be permitted to state in justification of the tone I have assumed, that as this sum of money is to me a mere flea-bite, I feel that I have a right to insist upon giving it alone. But come, the thing is now settled. I am to have my way and you are to have yours."

"No, no: not exactly!"

"To the stipulated extent!—therefore without saying another single word upon the subject, I'll give you—what?—Health and prosperity to the forthcoming branches, and may they be numerous and strong."

"With all my heart!" cried Uncle John, "with all my soul! and may we live to see the lovely little cherubs playing around us and strewing with flowers our path to the grave."

A pause ensued; but it was not of long duration. The glasses were replenished, and Raven said, "Now sir, I'll give you—oh! of course—their grandmamma!"

"Again, with all my heart!" cried Uncle John, "she is one of the best women in creation—a natural woman! if—"

"Those are the women for me!" exclaimed Raven. "None of your rouged stuck-up beggarly aristocracy!—a natural woman will beat them all into fits."

"If ever there existed a really good woman in the world she is one!"

"We must have her up!" cried Raven. "We must have her up in time. This affair you know must not take place in her absence. *Apropos* we've not drunk our absent friends!"

"Our absent friends!" echoed Uncle John, promptly, "And may," for he *would* make an addition to every toast—"may they always be as firm—as firm—may they always be as firm as the rock of *Gibralter!*"

"Bravo!" cried Raven, "Very good, very good! And now I rise to propose the health of one whom I highly esteem, whom I love, and will cherish—of one to whom I owe my present state of existence—of one—of—of a—brave—of a brave—who—of one who—who—I'll tell you what it is, my old friend—if I go much farther I shall stick in the mud! I am no public speaker; not a bit of it; but I do with sincerity propose, and I know I feel sure—at least, I know you will with equal sincerity, drink the health of Valentine!"

"Let me see, I *think* we drank that before?"

"Did we? Well, I believe we did, now you have mentioned it;—you are right. But never mind!—let us drink it again. And yet, if my memory serves me you know—*if* my memory serves me, we only drank them together! so let's have them separately—Valentine!—he's a fine, noble fellow! I drink his health with all my heart! and success to him!"

Of course, after this Uncle John proposed Louise, and then Llewellen, and then every other toast which had been previously drank, until really he did begin to think that the things around him were getting particularly restless! Happily, however, the real state of the case did not fail to strike him, and he addressed himself to Raven as nearly as possible to that effect, and suggested that albeit they were perfectly right then, the probability was, that if they drank much more they should not be quite so right, and as this correct suggestion accorded precisely with the views as well as the feelings of Raven himself, that gentleman promptly made another suggestion which had immediate reference to coffee. In vain Uncle John made one more suggestion, which touched upon the abstract propriety of having it below: Raven would have him up! and up they went.

At first, Valentine feared from the somewhat studied stateliness of his walk, that Uncle John was not exactly so correct as he had seen him; but he found that he was merry, not tipsy—elated, nothing more. Immediately after coffee, notwithstanding, he conceived it to be proper to send for a coach, and Uncle John, as he gracefully took his leave, declared, openly and warmly, that he never spent so happy an evening in his life.

CHAPTER LV.

THE DAY IS NAMED.—ECHO INSISTS UPON FORMING AN ALLIANCE WITH LLEWELLEN.

"He is a prince, my boy!—nothing less than a prince!" exclaimed Uncle John, while in the coach, and this was all in the shape of explanation that could be obtained from him until they reached home, when he entered at length into the matter.

That Valentine was delighted when he heard, not only of Raven's generosity, but of the high estimation in which he was held, is a fact which it were useless to attempt to conceal. Everything now shone brightly before him: he knew of no joy which he could not possess; with love on the one hand and competence on the other, he felt that he and Louise had but to live and be happy.

"Now, the very first thing," said Uncle John, when he had explained all clearly—"the very first thing, my boy, that you have to do is to get the day fixed, that we may know what we are about. There are many important matters to attend to which cannot be done in a day. There's the house to look after: there's that to prepare: there's your mother to run down for, and a hundred other things which require time and study. Therefore, let the day be fixed, that we may know how much time we have to do it all in."

Valentine promised to prevail upon Louise to name the day if possible in the morning, and, accordingly, when he and Uncle John called together, he remained with that object in view.

Louise was still very gentle, and, although rather timid, very happy; and as Valentine had, the previous evening, imparted the secret to Llewellen, that gentleman correctly felt that his presence was not on all occasions absolutely wanted. He, therefore, left them together on the morning in question the very moment they began to converse, and as this was what Valentine deemed strictly proper and very agreeable, he reverted to the subject at once.

"My dearest Louise," said he, "all is now happily settled with the exception of one point, which rests with you entirely. The *day*, my Louise!—when is it to be? Indeed, it pains me to tease you, appreciating as I do that delicacy of feeling by which you are actuated; but you know, my dear girl, that I must be importunate until I can prevail upon you to give me an answer. Come, settle it at once! Why, you silly girl!—why do you tremble? Smile, my Louise, and be joyous as I am! I know that we shall be happy! Do you not believe that we shall?"

"I do—I do indeed," replied Louise.

"Come, then, why are you so pensive? Look up, my girl, and settle the point at once. Do you think that I would be so teased when I could put an end at once to it, and that with a single word? Well, well, let me manage it for you. Now attend to my instructions. It is to be in June: I will, therefore, commence with the first of the month, and go on until I reach the day on which you would like it to take place, when you must kiss me and say "yes," or to simplify the thing say "yes," and then I will kiss you. Now, then, would you like it to be on the first of June?"

"Yes," said Louise, but in a whisper so soft that, had it not been for the hissing of the s, it might have been mistaken for silence.

The moment Valentine heard it he pressed her to his heart, and paid his debt in the coin above alluded to with the most usurious interest.

"Now, my love," said he, "you must be cheerful and gay! I have to tease you no more: all is settled now; come! banish that melancholy look, Louise, and smile! Where is Fred? I must get him to put you in spirits. I will *not* allow you to be dull. Shall we find him in the garden? Yes, there he is, come."

Into the garden they immediately went, and Valentine, making his voice appear to proceed from various quarters, shouted, "Llewellen!—Llewellen!—Llewellen!—Llewellen!"

Llewellen promptly turned towards every point, and then exclaimed,—"Tear t' cootness now phot an extraortinary echo!"

"Did you ever notice it before?" inquired Valentine.

"Cootness knows it, never."

"You try it: sing."

"Tol, lol, lol, lol!" sang Llewellen, very correctly jumping up an octave.

"Tol, lol, lol, lol!" echoed Valentine, faintly, thereby making it appear to proceed from an immense distance.

"Phunterful! Phell I never tit!—pecause there are no mountains, no hills, look you, here!"

"What is that to me?" said Valentine, assuming a female voice, which appeared to come from the adjoining garden.

"Pho is that?" inquired Llewellen. "Some potty pelonging to next toor!—hur'll see pho it is!" And he instantly ran for a ladder, which he placed against the wall, and then cautiously mounted with the view of peeping over.

"I see you," said Valentine in the same assumed voice.

"Hur ton't care!" cried Llewellen, as he showed himself boldly.

"Get down: don't expose yourself there. If you wish to say anything to me, I'll come over to you. Now," continued Valentine, having drawn his voice cleverly within the garden, "now what have you to say?"

Llewellen stared with an expression of the most intense amazement. There was no one in the garden adjoining! he could not see a soul, and yet he heard the voice as plainly as he ever heard anything in his life! Of course Valentine and Louise stood as if they were astonished, which was perhaps under the circumstances venial.

"*Come* down!" cried the voice, "don't stand there!"

Llewellen was not a man whom a trifle could alarm, but it must be recorded that the blood left his cheeks. He however descended, and feeling secure in the integrity of his intentions, stood firmly again upon the face of the earth.

"Now what have you to say?" inquired the voice.

"Who are you?" demanded Llewellen.

"Dear me, don't be alarmed! I'm only Echo!"

"Echo! putt t'cootness, phere are you? Hur can't see you any phere apout."

"See me! How *can* you expect to see me when you know that there is nothing of me left but my voice?"

Llewellen held this as far as it went to be conclusive. He clearly could not see a voice, and as there was nothing else of Echo, it followed of course that there was nothing to see. But although this sufficiently accounted for the invisibility of the nymph, Llewellen could not understand the exact meaning of her immediate presence; nor had he ever either heard or read of her having the power to converse. "Speak to her," said he to Valentine. "Inteet it's phery ott!"

"I'll have nothing to say to him," observed Echo, "I have this moment taken a regular fancy to you, and to you only will I speak."

"Converse with the lady," said Louise, "she will not harm you."

"Putt, look you, hur ton't unterstant!"

"Freddy," said Echo, "I love you! Speak to me, my dearest! converse with me; do, there's a duck!"

"Oh, speak to her Fred!" said Valentine, "speak to her!"

"Putt pho am hur to speak to?"

"Oh, hear what the lady has to say, and make suitable replies. Shall we retire?"

"Not for the worlt!"

"Well, come then, say something as a matter of courtesy!"

"Put her ton't know phot to say! Inteet hur ton't know phot she wants!"

"I remain here," said Echo, "expressly for the purpose of telling you how dearly I love you."

"Phell! you have tolt me so pefore! Is there anything pesites?"

"Cannot your heart suggest the rest?"

"No; inteet it cannot."

"Oh! Fred; you cruel creature!"

"Oh, hur won't stant pothering here with a thing hur can't see!" cried Llewellen, who was about to bounce into the house, when Louise taking his arm, said, do obtain permission for me to speak to her."

"Phill you allow this laty to speak to you?" said Llewellen, who appeared to be rather pleased with the notion than not.

"By all means," replied Echo.

"Do you really love my cousin?" inquired Louise.

"Oh, most fondly, and he knows it. He'll break my voice, the cruel creature! and when that is gone, I shall be no more; I then shall have nothing left to lose."

"Her ton't care. Let her lose her voice: inteet the sooner it's cone the petter."

"But would you marry him?" inquired Louise.

"Would? I will! I'll unite myself to him at once. He shall carry me about. I'll mock his every word. I'll ride in his pocket. I'm in!"

As the last words were thrown behind Llewellen, he thrust his hands into the pockets of his coat very fiercely, and turned round and round as a cockchafer might under circumstances of a corresponding character, for he couldn't tell at all what to make of it. "Hur'm in a mess!" he cried, "cootness knows it, hur'm in a mess!"

"How marvellous!" exclaimed Louise, with appropriate solemnity, "how excessively strange!"

"Well," said Valentine, "you have a wife that will stick to you at all events."

"Stick to me! Putt I won't have it."

"Well, but how do you mean to get rid of her?"

"How *am* hur to kit rit of her?"

"By smothering her voice! I cannot conceive a better plan. It is sure to be effectual. Sew up your pocket, and smother her voice!"

"Coot!" cried Llewellen, and on the instant he grasped the tails of his coat with surpassing tightness, in the perfect conviction that Echo must be in one of them, he didn't care which.

"Now then," said Valentine, "pull the coat off. But be sure you don't relinquish your hold! If you let go for an instant, she'll be out."

Llewellen was about to act upon this excellent suggestion, but he had no sooner made the attempt than he was struck with an idea, which prompted him to ask how it was possible for him to take off his coat while he kept fast hold of the tails? which was indeed a highly correct question to put.

"Kif me a lift, my poy, look you," he added, "because hur can't kit it off at all now myself."

Valentine wishing to meet his views to some extent, pulled the collar of the coat off his shoulders.

"There, now you catch holt of the tails," said Llewellen, "ant then hur can pull out my arms."

"No; although I suggested the murder, I'll have nothing to do with its execution."

"Phill Louey tear?"

"Not for the world!" cried Louise.

"Cootness knows it now, that is too pat!"

"Let me out!" exclaimed Echo, "let me out!"

"Not a pit of it matam," cried Llewellen, who, grasping his tails yet more firmly, hastened out of the garden with the view of obtaining the assistance of one of the servants, and as he walked with the collar of his coat below his elbows, both Valentine and Louise were convulsed with laughter, he really did look in their view so ungraceful.

"How ridiculous these things appear," observed Valentine. "Without having actually witnessed them, should we not regard it as almost impossible for men possessing any sense at all, to be placed in positions so absurd?"

"It appears to be so natural," said Louise. "Upon my word I am not at all astonished at its effect being to make people look so very silly."

"They are taken by surprise, you see! Were they to reflect for a moment they would doubtless repudiate the notions which alarm them; but they are called upon to act on the instant: they are astounded at once; they have no time for thought. I have seen men—courageous, strong-minded men—men whom nothing on earth visible could appal, so shaken at the moment by sounds for which they could not account, as to appear to be the veriest cowards in existence."

"Oh, I've not the slightest doubt of it!" returned Louise. "Now, this echo: why, I really should have been alarmed myself! —although conscious of its having but a merely mythological existence, and of its being in reality nothing more than a repercussion of sound, upon my word, at the moment I shouldn't know what to make of it: I am sure I should be frightened; I am certain that I should! But poor Fred! Oh do let him carry his wife in his pocket. Don't let her voice be smothered just yet. It will be so glorious!"

This put Louise in high spirits, and her liveliness continued throughout the day. It is true that occasionally the thought of her position would intrude to cast over her beautiful features a slight shade of meditative gloom; but Valentine, whenever he perceived this, dispelled it, and then all was sunshine and happiness again.

CHAPTER LVI.

THE PREPARATIONS FOR THE MARRIAGE.—A SURPRISE.

Business!—business was now the order of the day: and it is a highly popular fact that business must be attended to. Uncle John pronounced himself to be up to his eyes in it! Valentine, Raven, Louise, and all concerned were now plunged into the depths of business. As the day—that day to which lovers in general look forward with joy—had been fixed; all felt that no time was to be lost. The preparations—especially those which had fallen to the lot of Uncle John—were considered immense, for he had made up his mind fully, firmly, and without any supererogatory deliberation, not only to do his duty, but to astonish the nerves of Raven if possible. He felt strongly that he had but a fortnight to do it all in, and it took him a week to look after a house. He never had such a job! At the full expiration of that time, however, he got one, and then he did think he saw his way pretty clearly.

Louise at this period felt dreadfully embarrassed. She had no female friends. The social position of Raven, since he retired from business, had been so peculiar, that they had lived, although in midst of wealth and splendour, almost secluded from the world. He scorned to associate with any below the aristocracy, and the aristocracy looked upon him with contempt. Hence his bitter hatred of them in the aggregate, and hence the embarrassed position of Louise. She had no one to advise with, no one to confide in, but her maid. There were but two ladies in the world with whom she had ever been on anything like terms of intimacy, and they were both absent from town. She was therefore left entirely to her own resources, which she naturally at that period felt to be very distressing.

Valentine—although every effort was made to conceal it from him—was not long understanding the state of the case precisely, and the moment he did understand it he felt himself bound to do all in his power to relieve her.

"Louise," said he, embracing the very first opportunity that presented itself, "Louise, I feel very much hurt."

"Dear Valentine!—at what!"

"Nay, I do not know indeed that I shall ever forgive you."

"My dear boy!—why what on earth is it?"

"My mother," said Valentine. "You have not invited her. You do not know, my love, how happy she would be, if you were to send for her at once to spend a week with you, to advise with you, to relieve you of any little difficulty you may be under, to do, in short, anything for you."

"Dear Valentine!" cried Louise, as the tears sprang into her eyes, for she in an instant perceived his object. "You do not know how much I love you for this. Oh! that would indeed make me happy. I knew not how to mention this, my love; but believe me, my dearest boy, that situated as I am, nothing could delight me so much."

"You are a good girl, Louise: she shall come up at once. I will send her a letter by this night's post, and run down myself for her in the morning."

"There's a dear!—But you will not be long, my love, before you return?"

"I'll be back, my Louise, as soon as possible. She does not at present expect to come up before the thirtieth: but I'll manage that; and as Fred is now only in the way here, I may as well take him down with me."

Most gladly did poor Louise consent to this arrangement; and Valentine, who would not detain her, went at once to communicate with Llewellen.

That gentleman at the time was in the library, reading "Fox's Book of Martyrs," with an aspect of terror, and when Valentine without any ceremony entered, he gave a sudden start, and felt strikingly queer.

"Tear t'cootness!" he exclaimed. "You mate me tremple! Hur've pin reating apout these colt-plootet intivituals, until intect hur pecan to pe *frightent*, look you!"

"Dear me!" said Valentine, gravely. "But I hope it's all over?"

"Oh, it's all over now: putt, upon my wort, phen hur reat apout these tevils purning poor peoples' pellies, ant the like of that, hur plush for their prutality."

"Well, never mind them now: I have something to say to you, Fred.—To-morrow, I am going into the country."

"To-morrow!—Oh! phot for?"

"To bring my mother up.—I start early in the morning."

"Then inteet hur'll lie in pet all tay. Hur wont kit up! It's no use at all, look you! Hur've nopotty to speak to: Louey is pusy, ant ephery potty's pusy: and if hur co out, hur ton't know phere to co to."

"Would you like to go with me?"

"Phoot hur like!—My tear poy!—Apove all things pesites in the worlt!"

"Well then, be it so: we'll go down together; but it is upwards of seventy miles!"

"Hur ton't care a pit apout the miles, if it's seventy millions.—You say hur may co?"

"I shall be glad of your company!"

"That's enough. Hur'll pe retty; if hur sit up all night."

"Oh! we shall not have to start before nine; so that if you call on me about eight, we'll have breakfast together, and be off."

"Hur'll pe there, my poy: oh! hur'll pe there. Hur'll kit lots of cicars, ant we shall have such a peautiful rite. Too you phont any coats?—pecause inteet hur've cot three of the pest in the worlt."

"Well, you had better bring two: you may find them both useful. But I must be off to tell my uncle; for *he* has no idea of it yet."

"Hur mustn't co phith you?"

"Oh, yes: come along."

To the delight of Lewellen, they accordingly started, first to book their places, and then to search for Uncle John, whom they eventually found at the house, in the midst of the workmen, as dusty as any private gentleman need be.

"Ah! Mr. Llewellen," he exclaimed, "here we are you see, up to our eyes in business.—It will be a different place though to look at this day week," he added privately. "I intend to have all this done up, and all this. Before I have done with it, Mr. Llewellen, it shall be fit for any prince!—mark my words."

Valentine, drawing him aside, now explained to him what he proposed to do in the morning.

"I am right glad to hear it, my boy," cried Uncle John. "I was thinking of the same thing myself this very day, for there are many little matters that I find I can't manage: by all means, Val, bring her up!"

"But I want her to be with Louise."

"Well, well; so she can be, my boy; so she can; but she will also be able to give me a little advice if I should want it! You had better run and get my cheque book. The bank will be closed, you know, before I get home."

"I have quite enough money," said Valentine.

"Well, but your mother may want some."

"I have plenty for both."

"If you are quite sure, why be it so. Have you anything more to say?"

"Nothing."

"Very well; then run away with you. Mr. Llewellen, I'm going to turn you out. I shall be home at six. You will dine with us, Mr. Llewellen?"

"Inteet hur shall pe most happy."

"You will not," said Uncle John, taking his hand—"you will not be more happy to be there, Mr. Llewellen, than I shall be to see you. But be off with you—come, you have no business here!"

Being thus fairly turned out of the house, Valentine took Llewellen home with him, and gave him some cold beef and beer to amuse himself with, while he wrote to his mother, when they went for a stroll until six.

At this hour Uncle John returned, and declared himself knocked up as nearly as possible; but as he felt an immense deal better during dinner, everything passed off with unusual spirit. Whitely and Llewellen became great friends; they paid the most marked attention to each other: they seemed to be happy in each other's society, and conversed together with as little restraint as if they had been intimately acquainted for years. The entertainments during the evening were various. Valentine related how Echo had determined on marrying Llewellen, and Llewellen related how the portraits at the exhibition had mysteriously spoken, and how loudly he had been called by some particular friend of his, whom he was utterly unable to find, and as all this was perfectly well understood both by Whitely and Uncle John, they were kept in one continued roar of laughter.

Poor Whitely had not spent so happy an evening for many, many years; he forgot all his cares until Llewellen had left, when the thought of his boy buried gaiety in gloom.

With all the justly celebrated punctuality of the sun, Llewellen reappeared in the morning at eight, and he and Valentine sat down to breakfast; but strange as it may appear—and perhaps it was one of the most extraordinary things that ever occurred to him—Llewellen couldn't eat! He had no appetite! A most substantial breakfast had been provided, a breakfast which was after his own heart, and to which he would at any other time have done the most ample justice; but while he tried hard, and marvelled greatly what on earth could be the matter inside, all he could do was to get down five small cups of coffee, three eggs, and a few extremely delicate slices of ham, which could not altogether have weighed more than a pound. With this, however, he felt himself bound to be content, and as Valentine finished about the same time as he did, they took leave of Uncle John and Whitely, and started.

As the coachman was about to mount his box when they arrived at the inn, they at once took their seats and were off, and no sooner had they got quite clear of the smoke than Llewellen sang every song he could think of. He was in the highest possible spirits, and enjoyed himself exceedingly; he got down every time they changed horses to have a glass of "peautiful peer," and offered his cigar case ever and anon to every creature upon the coach.

In due time—to his unspeakable satisfaction—they reached the house at which the coach stops about seven minutes to enable the passengers to have what is technically termed down there "dinner," which customarily consists of a roast leg of mutton, bread, potatoes, and cabbage. Llewellen was not, however, at that particular period dainty, and therefore at once set to work upon the mutton. He ought to have paid for six. Being resolved to make up for what he deemed his lost breakfast, he made the *look* of the joint vanish as if by magic. The passengers were amazed, but said nothing, which was in all probability much less than the host said when he looked at the remains of the departed.

They now resumed their journey, and mirth and good humour began to flow, and continued to flow on until they arrived at their place of destination, when the passengers—who usually then bless their stars, seemed to think it a pity to part.

It was of course not long after this before Valentine felt that he was in the arms of his mother. In the arms of no other creature breathing could he have had those feelings which he experienced then. The poor lady, it is true, could scarcely speak, but she expressed so much rapture, and smiled through her tears with so much visible joy, that Llewellen, as she welcomed him eloquently and warmly, really felt he possessed a somewhat sensitive heart.

"Well, now, my dear, tea is quite ready," she observed, as soon as this burst of affection was over, "I'm sure you must feel very faint. I hope," she added, addressing Llewellen, "that you will make yourself perfectly at home."

"Inteet t' cootness you have mate me at home alretty," replied Llewellen.

"I'm delighted to hear it; come, draw to the table. Well, and how did you leave Miss Raven, my love? I do so long to see her, you can't think!"

"She is quite well; all are quite well," replied Valentine; "of course you will be able to go up with us to-morrow?"

"To-morrow! impossible! my dearest boy, consider! I have not the least thing ready! I've been preparing ever since I received your letter this morning; but as for going to-morrow! indeed, my dear, the thing is altogether out of the question. Besides it is not proper that you should return to-morrow. I would not have you do it for the world. To come down one day and go up again the next! It would really be sufficient to throw you on a bed of sickness. I am certain, my love, you couldn't bear the fatigue. No; what I was thinking of is this; that if I can arrange things to-morrow, we can go up the next day!—that will be pleasant if we can manage it so."

"You are not then quite sure even of that?"

"Why I think it can be done. At all events I'll try. You have given me no time to prepare! The thing was so unexpected! But I think notwithstanding that I may venture to say that I am sure we shall be able to go then."

During this short colloquy the chickens were fast disappearing. Llewellen was at them, and doing full justice to each particular joint.

"I am glad to see you eat," said the widow, very innocently; "Valentine, my love, pray help Mr. Llewellen to some more ham."

"Mr. Llewellen," returned Valentine, "likes to help himself, mother," which was a fact.

"Cootness knows it, these chickens are peautiful," observed Llewellen.

"I am very glad you like them.

"Inteet hur enjoy them much, look you; ant as for the peer! they don't prew such peer in Caermarthen."

"We are famous for beer here," observed Valentine. "How old is this, mother?"

"Two years, my love."

"Two *years* olt! Tear t' cootness, now,

is it two years olt? Phy town phere hur come from, they prew it on the Saturtay, and trink it on the Montay! Two years! phell, inteet, now, it is very excellent."

And it was very excellent, and he drank a great quantity of it, and he enjoyed himself over it during the whole of the evening, which was spent very happily by all.

The next day was occupied chiefly by Valentine in showing Llewellen the ancient architectural beauties of the town, and by the widow, in making preparations for her journey, which she looked upon as being tremendous, and the following morning they started.

As a pure matter of courtesy to the lady—by whom he felt that he had been most kindly treated, and whom he really admired very much—Llewellen had insisted upon riding inside. This Valentine knew was an ordeal which, as he went through it, he would feel very severely, and for the first forty miles he most certainly did, for he could neither smoke the beautiful cigars he had with him, nor get out *every* time they changed horses for beer; but when they had dined, he felt nothing more of it, for he instantly fell fast asleep, and slept soundly until they reached town.

As Valentine had duly advised Uncle John of their intention to come up that day he considerately met them at the coach and conducted them home. Here everything essential to their immediate comfort was prepared, and they had tea together, and were really very happy. The widow thought that Uncle John looked, if anything, somewhat more pale than he was wont; but as he assured her that he never was better in his life, she was perfectly content.

"But do I look pale?" he inquired. "Do you really now think I look pale?"

"Why, I do not mean to say that it is an unhealthy paleness; but you do not look so ruddy as you did."

Uncle John went to the glass and examined the colour of his countenance most minutely; but he really could not himself perceive any striking alteration. But then, seeing himself as he did every day, he admitted mentally that he was not perhaps quite so well able to judge as one who had not seen him for months. Still he did think that the change was not very alarming, more especially as he remembered that while shaving that morning, it had struck him that he looked extremely well. And yet when he came to recollect himself he had felt for several days rather queer, which might, it was true, be indicative of the gradual decay of nature; but he really, when he reflected upon the matter calmly again, was not by any means willing to believe that it was so. "The fact is, my girl," said he, "I have been of late so flurried, that it wouldn't be surprising if I looked even paler than I do. For the last week, indeed, I have scarcely had a wink; and I'll defy any man, if he's as strong as an elephant, to look so well as he ought to look, if he hasn't his natural rest."

"Oh, you look very well. My remark applied simply to your colour; but mere colour does not always, you know, indicate the existence of health."

Uncle John was, however, not satisfied; if any other friend had then dropped but a hint having reference to his paleness, he would doubtless have fancied himself rather ill.

Immediately after tea, Llewellen and Valentine left them, the one to herald the virtues of the widow to Louise, and the other to assure her of his safe return. Valentine found that he had been anxiously expected, and when she had affectionately welcomed him back, Llewellen commenced a long tale having reference to the admirable characteristics of the widow.

"She is a plain, good, kind, motherly creature," said Valentine, anxious to put an end to Llewellen's warm eulogia. "But Fred is going rather too far."

"Not a pit," cried Llewellen; "she's a tear of a woman, hur atmire her!—ant Louey!—she cave me such peer!—two years olt, Louey!—peer two years olt!"

"Oh, I'm sure I shall love her!" said Louise. "I know I shall, dearly. I must be introduced to her, you know, the first thing in the morning. What time shall I call?"

"Oh! do not call, my love," said Valentine. "There will be no necessity for that, she can come with me here."

"But papa, my dear, insists upon my calling. He says that I ought to call first, in order to prevail upon her to return with me; and I am sure that I am anxious, most anxious to show her every possible respect."

Valentine, in a moment saw how the matter stood, and therefore said no more about it, he simply, at the suggestion of Louise, named the time and there left it.

"And now," said Louise playfully, looking at her watch, "I'll allow you to remain with me ten minutes longer, and then you must go home and have a long night's rest."

"I am not at all fatigued, my dear girl."

"Oh, I am sure that you must be! Poor Fred, you see, is already asleep."

"Well, it certainly is extraordinary that he should be asleep."

"I am aware, of course, that that is no criterion; but ten minutes longer!—I'll allow you no more."

Valentine consented to remain but ten minutes; and they then conversed earnestly upon the subject which almost exclusively occupied their thoughts, until something induced Louise to look again at the watch, when she found that two hours had flown away somehow.

"Good gracious!" she exclaimed; "there, do not remain another moment. Here, have I been keeping you all this time when you ought to have been at rest, poor boy! There, good night. Be sure you give my dearest love at home!"

They embraced each other, and having mutually exclaimed, "God bless you!" with heartfelt sincerity—they parted.

In the morning, at the appointed time, Louise arrived in the carriage. Valentine had quite prepared his mother for this, and had endeavoured to convince her that it was "nothing," which the good old lady. even when she saw it, could scarcely believe. But oh! when Louise entered the room and flew towards her, and kissed her, and hung on her neck, and expressed herself happy, all considerations having reference to style, vanished; she felt that she loved her at once.

Louise, on this occasion, was dressed as plainly as possible, and this tended not only to heighten the effect of her natural charms, but to enhance the good opinion of her friend, who saw in her, not what she would have termed a "fine lady," but a gentle affectionate amiable girl, one whom she could love without any restraint. On the other hand Louise was delighted with her; she felt that she had then indeed a friend in whom she could confide: nay, she felt that she then had a mother.

Under these delightful circumstances—and they were most delightful to both—they sat down side by side upon the sofa, and chatted together, and opened their hearts to each other as unreservedly as if they had really been parent and child. Louise was impatient to take her home. "I will indeed," she exclaimed, "endeavour to make you so happy! and papa will be so highly pleased to see you; and everything will be *so* delightful!"

"Indeed, my dear child, I feel already that I cannot but be happy with you!"

"You are a dear good soul," returned Louise, "and I equally feel that I cannot but love you."

Valentine at this point re-entered the room, and as the widow then retired to "put on her things," Louise began to laud her to the skies. And she did so with most unaffected sincerity; she felt what she expressed: she did love her with the purest affection.

"Now my dear child; I am quite at your service," said the widow, on her return with much gaiety.

The bell was rung and Valentine prepared to go with them, when it was playfully intimated that the honour of his company was not then desired.

"Well, but give me a ride!" cried Valentine. "Let me see you home! I don't want to interfere with your mystic arrangements!"

Nor did he. All he wanted was to be by the side of his mother, lest on getting into the carriage she should feel at all embarrassed; but as he found that they both understood each other perfectly, he just saw her introduced to Raven and left them.

During his absence from town great progress had been made. The carpenters, and the plasterers, and the glaziers, and the paper-hangers, under the active surveillance of Uncle John, had prepared the house for the reception of the furniture which had already been chosen, and which certainly reflected great credit upon his taste. That only had to come in, and when it did come in it was interesting to notice the spirit and pride with which he superintended the whole of the arrangements. In his view Raven must of necessity be astonished. He felt perfectly certain of that; and as that was one of the greatest immediate objects he had in view he was happy.

On the other hand Raven had not been inactive. Jewels, which had not for years seen the light, had been drawn from their obscurity, polished and reset to embellish Louise on the bridal morn.

These Louise in the natural pride of her heart could not conceal from the eyes of her dear kind friend. To her all were displayed, and the widow was amazed at their dazzling beauty; but when Louise placed before her a watch thickly studded with brilliants, which Raven intended to present actually to *her*, she scarcely knew how to express, or what to do with herself, her delight was so intense.

And thus matters proceeded; each taking the greatest pleasure in the task to be performed, and all feeling in the highest degree happy. Louise got on amazingly with the assistance of her friend, whom she considered the most clever creature breathing! Oh, no one could be by possibility comparable with her! The Misses Stevens—who were to be the bridemaids—were nothing equal to her, although at one time she *did* think them clever in the extreme.

The day approached. Louise began to

count the hours, and Valentine's heart beat high. Nothing could exceed in brightness the prospect before them. Not a cloud was visible: all was clear to the horizon, and below it they had not the smallest doubt that all was equally beautiful and fair.

Uncle John was nearly ready. They felt certain, from the delight which his features portrayed, that his views had been met; but not one of them was suffered to enter the house! No: *when* the place was tidy, they might all be admitted: he should indeed be most happy to see them all then: but not before!—Such was the edict.

The task which Raven had proposed to himself had already been performed, with the exception, of course, of that which was not to be accomplished until the very day. He had therefore more time on his hands than the rest: which time he spent chiefly alone. On the evening, however, before the day on which they were all to dine specially with him—which was the day before that on which the ceremony was appointed to take place—he took occasion to intimate to Valentine that he wished to have a word with him in private. Valentine was then on the point of leaving for the night, but he stopped of course then, and as the rest, hearing the intimation given, at once retired, he and Raven were left alone.

"My dear boy," said Raven after a pause, "the day is at hand—the day on which I hope that you and Louise will commence a long and uninterrupted career of happiness—and as I shall not have another opportunity of speaking to you on the subject I wish now to say a few—but a very few words, before you take my girl from me. My boy," he continued, with great intensity of feeling—"All the confidence that man can have in man I have in you. I know you to be affectionate, I know you to be firm: I know that you possess too the spirit of a man, to bear up boldly against difficulties whatever shape they may assume; but I am getting old, and weak, and apprehensive, my boy, and that weakness—in spite of my conviction of its being unnecessary—prompts me to claim of you now a solemn promise, that whatever may occur to me—God knows what may!—but whatever may occur, you will be firm, still firm, to Louise!"

"Most solemnly," said Valentine, "I do promise this; and every feeling of affection, as well as every principle of honour, binds me to the faithful performance of that promise."

"You will never desert her, let what may happen to me?"

"Never!"

"I am content. I never doubted your firmness, I never doubted your sincerity: believe me, my boy, I never did; but I felt it my duty to obtain this promise from you—although it was previously implied—being sure that by any promise *directly* given, you would feel bound for ever. In life, my dear boy, a variety of things occur to us of which we have no previous conception, while things of which we are daily nay hourly in dread never occur to us at all. None of us can tell what may happen. But I am happy in the conviction, that whatever may happen to me, you will still be firm to poor Louise."

"Heaven forbid that anything should happen to you of sufficient importance to bring my firmness to the test."

"To that I say Amen."

"I cannot conceive," continued Valentine, "the possibility of anything occurring to you which could do so much as that, for were you even to be lost to us, the effect upon me would be to make me feel that I was bound to Louise by an additional tie, being the only one—as I should be then—to whom she had to look for protection. Fear not then: under any circumstances I *will* be firm: I cannot be a traitor to my heart!"

"You are a noble boy! I hope nothing may occur; still the brain of an old man teems with strange fears. But away now with all apprehensions. May you be for ever happy! Were anything to happen to that poor girl, I should never survive it. She has been to me all that a child should be to a father, and I feel in my heart that to her I have been all that a father should be to a child. God bless her!—bless you both! You will not mention what I have said to a soul; for others might imagine that I should not have said what I have if I did in reality—as I do in reality—place implicit confidence in your honour!"

Valentine promised that not a syllable on the subject *should* be mentioned, and when Raven had again assured him that he held him in the highest admiration he took his leave. Still he could not but think all this strange. He could well understand how a father, on the eve of the marriage of his child, should feel anxious—deeply anxious—for her welfare; but he could not at all understand why troubles of which no prospect appeared should at such a time as that be, without the slightest reason, apprehended. He would not, however, dwell upon that then. Raven he knew was an eccentric creature, and to that he attributed all.

In the morning Uncle John, having completed his task, gave notice that at one o'clock precisely he should do himself the pleasure of calling at the residence of Mr. Raven, to take him, Louise, Valentine, Llewellen, and the widow to see the house; and accordingly at the hour appointed he did call, and found them all prepared, and very anxious to see it.

"I have the honour to announce to you, ladies and gentlemen," he observed, with all possible pomp, as his little eyes twinkled with pleasure, "I have the honour to announce that the future residence of certain parties—one of whom shall be especially nameless, for her name is now scarcely worth twenty hours' purchase—is perfectly ready for inspection; and I have also the honour to announce that the humble individual who now stands before you will be happy to conduct you thereto without delay!"

This announcement was hailed with delight, and they were all most happy to shake hands with the herald, and to place themselves under his guidance. The carriage—which had been ordered at one on the strength of his reputation for punctuality—was then at the door; and therefore all but Llewellen and Valentine entered it at once—Uncle John having given instructions to the two outcasts to take a cab and keep behind them; and thus in due time they arrived at the theatre of his glory.

What pleasure they all expressed when they entered the house; what raptures they were all in as they passed through the rooms; what delight in short every arrangement inspired, may be conceived. Under less auspicious circumstances probably they would have felt, as a matter of course, bound to express themselves with some considerable warmth; but here was ample reason for their rapture. Uncle John had not realized his sanguine anticipations alone; he had surpassed them!—he had indeed made it "a residence fit for any prince!"

Such being the case then, Valentine, knowing that the cellars had been also well furnished, proposed with great eloquence, Uncle John's health, a proposition to which all responded, and the wine was produced, when his health was drank, and then, "Health to the bride!" and then that of the bridegroom, and then Mr. Raven's, and then the widow's, and then Llewellen's—the whole of which were honoured with the utmost cordiality, and every heart seemed filled with joy.

All but Uncle John then returned. He had to go home to dress for dinner, and to give an impetus to the movements of Whitely—who, on this particular occasion had been especially invited—which he did, and that with so much success, that precisely at half past six, they left home to join the happy people at the house of Mr. Raven.

On their arrival Louise, Valentine, Raven, Llewellen, and the widow, were assembled in the drawing-room, chatting so gaily, and looking so joyous, that they seemed quite resolved that the cares of the world should be shut out at least for the night.

At this happy moment Uncle John and Whitely entered, and Louise ran to meet Mr. Whitely and to give him a smiling welcome, which he gracefully acknowledged; but the instant the eye of Raven met his, he started as if struck with paralysis. In Raven he beheld the seducer of his wife! and he stood for a moment struggling with those feelings which the sight of him had aroused; but as the vivid recollection of his wrongs rushed at once with overwhelming impetuosity upon him, he sprang at Raven's throat with maniacal fury.

"Villain!" he exclaimed fiercely. "Cruel, heartless, monstrous villain! My children! —where, *where* are my children?"

"Stand off!" cried Llewellen.

"Are you mad?" exclaimed Valentine. "Let go your hold!" and he instantly forced him back and held him.

Raven uttered not a word, He sank at once upon the breast of Llewellen, by whom he was borne senseless from the room.

CHAPTER LVII.

EXPLAINING VARIOUS MATTERS TOUCHING THE ILL-TIMED RECOGNITION.

For some time after Raven—who was instantly followed by the fainting Louise, and her dear trembling friend—had left the room, Whitely, Uncle John, and Valentine, stood in mute amazement. The expression of Whitely's countenance, however, amounted almost to that of madness; his eyes rolled frightfully, and he ground his teeth fiercely, while his hands were tightly clenched, as if indeed he had had still Raven's throat in his grasp.

At length a word from Uncle John broke the spell which thus bound him, and he exclaimed, "Why, why do I stand here, when I have him in my power?"

"Hold!" cried Valentine, as Whitely made an attempt to rush from the room. "Would you murder the man?"

"Murder him!"

"This is neither the time nor the place for you to seek redress of wrongs."

"What are time and place to me?" exclaimed Whitely. "What is courtesy to me, when I have that monstrous villain within my reach!"

"By Heaven!" cried Valentine, "you shall not leave this room except with the view of quitting the house. If he *be* the man by whom you have been injured, you know where he is to be found: proceed against him legally as you please; but while *I* have strength to prevent it, you shall touch him no more."

Whitely stood and looked wildly at Valentine; but knowing his resolute character, he made no attempt to force his way.

"My good friend, said Uncle John, soothingly, "pray be advised; pray, pray do not let passion blind you to reason. I know you have cause for being thus; I know that your wrongs have been dreadful; but come, let us talk the matter over; let us see what is best to be done. It is certainly a melancholy thing—a very melancholy thing: but my dear friend, no good can arise from any frantic desire for revenge! Come, let us go together: be guided by me: indeed I would not advise you to pursue any course inconsistent with your duty as a man. There, let us return: there, that's right; I knew that you would be reasonable; I knew you'd be advised."

Whitely was passive as Uncle John took his arm, and permitted himself to be led from the house without uttering another word.

Valentine now was alone; but although the event had come like a thunderbolt upon him, he soon recovered his self-possession. "This, then, is what Raven so much dreaded!" thought he: "this is the discovery which he imagined would so strongly test my firmness. Well, the test has been applied. Has that firmness been shaken? Why should it be? why should I love Louise less than before! Doubtless her father deserves the epithet applied to him by Whitely; doubtless he has been a seducer, a villain; but ought that to undermine my affection for Louise, or to induce me to break my plighted faith to her, solely because she is his child? Are we never to admit the fact when we behold it, that a fair branch may spring from a foul stem? Is every beautiful bud to be blighted, because corruption is to be found in the parent tree? If the child cannot be free from those vices which characterize the parent, honour, innocence, and purity can have no existence but in name. However desperately wicked a father may be, it surely does not follow that he must of necessity contaminate his child. In this case I am sure that it is not so, and hence were he even loaded with iniquities, I could never desert her."

Having paced the room for some time, deeply engaged in suggesting, with the view of repudiating every objection which could by possibility be urged, he rang the bell, for all in the house appeared to be in a most extraordinary state of excitement. No one answered; he rang again; still no one appeared. A third time he rang with some violence, and eventually the sentimental porter came up, and with tears in his eyes, inquired if it were true that he had rung.

"I want Morgan," said Valentine; "tell her to come here."

"She's with Missis, sir: poor dear Missis! which is very ill, sir. I'm afeared that she never *will* get over it."

"Get over what, sir? What do you mean? Desire one of the girls to tell my mother I wish to see her."

The fellow heaved a heavy sigh, and having turned his eyes upwards so dexterously that the pupils became completely invisible, quitted the room with an elaborately lengthened visage.

In a short time the widow appeared, and having thrown her arms round the neck of Valentine, buried her face in his bosom and sobbed aloud.

"Mother, mother!" said he, as he led her to the sofa. "Come, come, come, you must not go on thus."

"Oh, my dear, this is sad, very sad; it is indeed very shocking, and at such a time too!"

"It is unfortunate, most unfortunate; but how is Louise?"

"Poor thing! I don't know how in the world she will ever survive it. She has been twice in the most violent hysterics, and she is now crying fit to break her heart. I much fear that it will prove her death-blow."

"Nonsense, nonsense, mother! The thing is bad enough, it is true; but it is not so dreadful as it at first sight appears."

"Oh, but it is a very terrible shock to the feelings of a poor dear girl at so critical a time as this."

"Well, well: can I see Louise?"

"Bless you, my dear, not on any account. She is in bed, and we have sent for the physician, and I expect him here every instant: I am sure that if she were to see you now, she would go off again and we should never bring her to."

"I am afraid that you are but a poor comforter, mother; but return to her and cheer her, and give her this kiss, and tell her from me that she must bear up against it; that the effects of the shock will very soon pass away; that it really is nothing particularly terrible, and that notwithstanding what has occurred, I shall be ready in the morning at eleven precisely."

"Oh! that, my love, is altogether out of the question; that *must* pe postponed."

"Why should it?"

"Hark! that is the physician; yes, there is his carriage. I'll come again, my poor boy, as soon as I can; but pray keep up your spirits."

"Keep up your's, mother; and be sure you keep up those of Louise."

The widow promised to do so if possible, and darted from the room to receive the physician.

Valentine could not feel surprised at Louise having been shocked at this ill-timed discovery; he thought it, under the circumstances, but natural; and as he did not apprehend that anything serious would ensue, he resolved not to give way at all to dejection. He therefore rang the bell again, and when the same puritanical person, whom Valentine did not suppose to be more virtuous than the rest of his *caste*, reappeared, he desired him to inform Mr. Llewellen, that he was anxious to have a word with him there.

The porter, who appeared to be somewhat more dreadfully afflicted than before, vanished gradually to accomplish the object of his mission, and in a short time Llewellen came into the room.

"My tear poy," said he, "phot's all this treatful pusiness? Inteet hur can make neither het nor tail of it at all, look you!"

"How is your uncle?" inquired Valentine.

"Intect, now, he seems very poorly. Put phot tit Whitely mean by his chiltren?"

"He was enraged," replied Valentine, who perceived that Llewellen had not been much enlightened on the subject. "It appears to be an unhappy affair altogether."

"So it is; put hur tont unterstant it! hur fear there's something treatful at the pottom of it, look you! Inteet t'cootness hur to."

"I wish you would do me a favour," said Valentine, who felt that as Llewellen knew nothing about the matter, he might just as well be kept still in ignorance as not. "I wish you would tell Mr. Raven that I should be happy to speak with him for one moment."

"By all means. Hur wish you coot kit to the pottom of it; for although hur've pin sitting with him all this time, hur havn't pin aple to kit him to explain a single wort."

"Tell him I'll not detain him long."

"Very coot," said Llewellen, who left the room at once; and after a lapse of three minutes, which were occupied by Valentine in rehearsing the part he had to perform, he returned with a communication, the substance of which was, that Raven was so unwell, that he felt quite unequal to the task of conversing with him upon the subject then; but he hoped, that in a few hours he should be sufficiently recovered to do so. "Hur tont at all know phot's the matter," added Llewellen. "Inteet it's all a mysterious tream to me; hur only know, that hur never saw tears in my uncle's eyes pefore. Put hur say, my poy; how apout tinner? Is that to pe totally knocked on the het?"

"Unhappily, the dinner which we were to have had, has been completely set aside by this unfortunate affair."

"Put we must have some sort of a tinner. We can't pe starved to teth! Hur wish t' cootness that Whitely had pin at the pottom of the Tet Sea, insteat of coming here to kick up a preeze before tinner. Put let's see apout it; let's co town at once. Hur know there are some peautiful things, pecause poor Louey tolt me; therefore let's co town and see about the pusiness. We shall all pecome skeletons upon the face of the earth!"

Valentine consented to accompany him, not, indeed, because he had the slightest inclination to eat then; but because, having nothing else to do, it was, at least as far as he was concerned, immaterial whether he sat at the table with him or not. Llewellen, of course, did not suffer much time to elapse before he ordered dinner up, and when in regular course it was produced, he certainly held it to be a lamentable thing that the rest should have been deprived of the enjoyment thereof. He did not, however, consider himself justified in permitting his grief on that account to interfere with his appetite. It would, perhaps, have been unwise if he had; but whether such would in reality have been the case or not, he thought it perfectly unnecessary, and therefore assailed each course with all his wonted zeal. He was, notwithstanding, much annoyed at the fact of Valentine being so delicate on that occasion, and contended that the circumstance of a man's appetite having the faculty of being destroyed by other means than those of eating, was a phenomenon which had never been sufficiently explained. This position was not impugned. Valentine had no disposition at that time to supply the desideratum, for although he had firmly resolved on bearing up against any disappointment of which the ill-timed event might be productive, he was not in good spirits, nor did he feel then the slightest inclination to force them.

It was not until Llewellen had nearly finished his dinner, that the physician left the house, but the moment he had left, the widow came to communicate to Valentine the fact, that poor Louise was in a high state of fever, and that therefore she would have to be kept for several days perfectly quiet. "I explained to the physician," she added, "what was to have taken place in the morning; but although he assured me that the poor dear girl was in no absolute danger, he declared that every idea of that kind must be utterly abandoned."

This point, then, was settled, and Valentine received the intelligence with firmness; and having begged of his mother to return to Louise instantly, and to let him know the moment the slightest change took place, he buried himself in his own thoughts, making his ardent anxiety for Louise, to some extent, counteract the bitterness of that feeling of disappointment, which he found it impossible entirely to suppress.

While he was thus occupied, expecting every moment to be summoned by Raven, Whitely and Uncle John were engaged in a warm conversation, touching the most correct course to be pursued. Whitely, as might have been anticipated, argued the propriety of vengeance. He contended that he was justified in inflicting upon his enemy the utmost terrors of the law: and declared that if he succeeded in doing nothing else, he would have him denounced in a court of justice to the world, and held up to lasting execration. Uncle John, on the contrary, suggested a compromise, and offered to effect it on the most brilliant terms, having resolved, if even Raven would not accede to his proposal, to make up the amount himself. But Whitely spurned the idea at once. "What!" he exclaimed indignantly, "compromise in a case of this description with so consummate, so monstrous a villain! Never! I'll pursue him with the utmost rigour: it shall never be said that I compromised my honour, which in reality I should do, by consenting to compromise with him."

"But let us look at this matter more calmly, my friend." said Uncle John; "let us look at it solely as men of the world. You have been wronged, deeply wronged: of that I cannot entertain the smallest doubt, and you are justified in bringing him who has wronged you to justice, nay, you are in a social sense bound to do so if it be possible; but although I can have no moral doubt whatever of the fact, allow me to ask, what *legal* proof have you that you have been wronged by this man?"

"Oh! I can produce a chain of circumstances, sufficiently strong to bring it home to him legally. I'll fix him! Oh, he shall not escape!"

"Very well, in that case I still say that you are bound to act precisely as you propose; but for your own sake, be sure that ample means are available before you proceed too far."

It was perfectly clear to Uncle John that Whitely had no such means; and being, therefore, more anxious to effect a compromise than ever, he left him to call upon Raven with the view of suggesting to *him* the expediency of some private arrangement.

On arriving at the house, he was immediately shown into the dining room, which was occupied still by Valentine and Llewellen; and although he expected that, as a matter of course, the sudden shock would be sufficient to induce a postponement of the marriage, it affected him deeply when he heard of the serious illness of Louise.

Having expressed his concern very feelingly, and endeavoured to console Valentine by all the means in his power—knowing well that he felt much more than he appeared to feel—he inquired for Raven, and on learning that he was still in his room, he begged Llewellen to inform him that he wished to have five minutes' conversation with him alone. "Tell him," he added, "that it is on a subject of immediate importance, and that although it may be settled in five minutes, there is now not a moment to be lost"

Llewellen accordingly went to deliver this message, and shortly returned with an answer to the effect, that although Raven still felt exceedingly ill, he had consented to see him. Uncle John, therefore, immediately followed his guide, by whom he was ushered at once into the room.

As he entered, Raven was sitting at the table in a state of extreme dejection, but he rose on the instant, and said with a faltering voice, "My friend—for a friend I must still consider you, however much you may loathe the sight of me—this, indeed, is a terrible affair."

Uncle John took his hand, and then sat

down beside him, and then said, "It is a sad business. But," he added, after a pause, "it is a thing which must be met! It is useless now to mourn the event or to dwell upon that which induced it. What has happened has happened. I wish not to refer to it now, but as a thing which having been done cannot be undone. But here is an immediate difficulty, one which must be faced: the only question, therefore is, how is it to be surmounted?"

"That, indeed, is the question. How can it be? What can be proposed? How am I to act?"

"Can it not be in some way *arranged?* Can it not be done privately without having recourse to law?"

"As far as I am concerned, most willingly would I do anything to settle it. I'll give him ten thousand pounds, or if that will not satisfy him, I'll give him fifteen or even twenty, provided he will undertake to annoy me no more."

"It was in order to suggest something of that kind that I came here this evening. I have named the subject to him already, and although he was naturally indignant, and spurned the idea of a compromise, declaring that he would have law and nothing but law, I think that eventually he might be induced to consent to some arrangement, which I am sure would be better for all parties concerned."

"Let him but consent to any arrangement, and I am willing to agree to it at once. I'll give him anything to settle it: any sum he thinks proper to demand: and I *could* suggest something which would render the expediency of such a settlement apparent in his calmer moments, even to him."

"What is it? Let me know that I may urge it, for I am really most anxious to prevail upon him to adopt, as a matter of expediency, the course now proposed."

"My friend," said Raven, with deliberate intensity, "I am perfectly well aware that you abhor the crime of which I at once acknowledge to you that I am guilty, as much as any man can; but as, before me, you have suppressed what you feel, and have come to me in the character of a man of the world to argue the matter upon worldly grounds alone, I will meet you upon those grounds, with the view of stating what I conceive to be sufficient to convince Mr. Whitely—or Whitbread, as I always understood his name to be—of the expediency at least of consenting to settle the matter, as I am anxious it should be settled, and that without delay. In the first place, then, let us look at the course which he proposes to pursue: I would not injure that man more deeply than he has already been injured; I would not have him incur legal expenses, which must, of necessity, fall upon him; nor am I willing to take advantage of his position, as I sufficiently prove, by offering him any sum of money he thinks proper to claim. But he proposes to go to law; and he can do so, doubtless: there is nothing more easy than for a man to go to law; but I am anxious to have him understand, at once, that no law can touch me! He has, of course, told you all. He charges me, in the first place, with the seduction of his wife. How can he, legally, substantiate that charge? How is he to prove it? What witnesses can he produce? He can produce no witnesses; and, if he could, as the thing happened nearly fifteen years ago, he could not bring an action against me now; while, even, if we assume that he could bring his action, the amount of damages he could obtain would be as nothing when compared with the sum I now offer to give him. As far as that is concerned then, it is manifest that he would in any case be a loser by going to law; and when we come to the other charge, which refers to his confinement as a lunatic, it cannot be shown that I had anything to do with that transaction; and, if even it could, he must know it to be perfectly ridiculous to suppose that I am legally responsible for the acts of the two physicians, by whom the certificate was signed, and whose signatures alone would indemnify me if I had even been directly instrumental in obtaining them; but I had nothing whatever to do with the certificate; my name does not in any way appear; so that he can have no possible grounds for proceeding against me as the person who caused him to be confined. If, therefore, he will but reflect upon this; if he can but be brought to understand his position, which is in reality one of utter helplessness, as far as the law is concerned, he cannot fail to perceive the expediency of consenting to some such arrangement as that now proposed. I should not have spoken thus on a subject of this kind, had you not appeared here with the view, not of denouncing the crime of which I have been guilty, but of suggesting the best means of meeting the difficulty which that crime has induced. I should have been, under any other circumstances, ashamed to argue the matter as I have done in this cool calculating strain; for, however hateful I may appear, I still hope that I am not dead to *every* proper feeling; but as you wished to know what I could urge, at all calculated to promote a private settlement of this most unhappy affair, I felt myself justified in stating the case as if the point to be considered were one of a pecuniary character solely."

To every word of this Uncle John listened with deep attention. He weighed every sentence as Raven deliberately proceeded, and could not but feel, that in a worldly point of view, nothing could be more conclusive. He had, indeed, formed an exceedingly bad opinion of his character as a man, but he looked upon him then but as an advocate; and being firmly convinced that the course proposed was the only one which Whitely could pursue with any chance of success, he at once expressed his determination to employ all the means in his power, with the view of inducing him to adopt it.

"Pray, do so," said Raven; "not for me, but for the sake of my child. For her sake I am anxious that this matter should not be exposed in a court of law; for although I know that no law can reach me, the public disgrace of which the fact of its being brought into court, might be productive, would render my poor girl wretched for life. He is justified, of course, in doing all he can against me; but by going to law, he will but injure himself, not me; except, indeed, in so far as the *exposé* may be concerned; and I question much, whether he can bring sufficient evidence to induce even the public to believe him, anxious as they invariably are to believe everything which happens to be charged against a man. Urge him—pray, urge him! to look at the thing in this light. He cannot, in any way, benefit himself: he will, on the contrary, have to pay ruinously for any attempt to obtain legal revenge. Use your utmost influence: prevail upon him, if possible, to consent to an arrangement. I think, that if he can bring himself to look at the case as it stands, with reference solely to his power to injure me, he will eventually yield."

"I think so, too," said Uncle John: "I'll return to him at once, and put each point as strongly as possible."

"But, my friend, independently of this, what is to be done?"

"We had better enter into no other subject at present. Let this be settled first. That to which we have looked forward with so much pleasure, must now, of course, be postponed."

"That," said Raven, "is inevitable. But, Valentine, he has been waiting to see me all the evening, and I know that he bears up against it like a man; but I really have not nerve enough to meet him, my friend!"

"It is unnecessary that you should do so now. I'll take him home with me. He has been waiting, I apprehend, more with the view of being near poor Louise."

"Thank Heaven! she is now much more calm. If anything were to happen to her, the little time I have to live would be passed in constant torture."

"Let us hope for the best. I have not the smallest doubt that with care she will soon be restored. But, good night. This task must, if possible, be accomplished before I sleep."

"I leave it with confidence entirely in your hands. Whatever you propose I will gladly accede to."

Uncle John then left him, and looked in upon Valentine, who, having just heard from his mother that Louise was going on extremely well, and that, moreover, she was then calmly sleeping, consented to accompany him home; and on their way he applauded the anxiety of his uncle to effect a private settlement of the affair; and his uncle, in return applauded his declaration, that, notwithstanding what had occurred, or what might occur hereafter, prejudicial to the character of Raven, he felt, and should continue to feel, bound to keep faith with Louise.

On reaching home, they were informed by Mrs. Smugman, who appeared at the door much perturbed, that Horace was in the house in a state of intoxication, as she strongly suspected; that he had forced his way into Goodman's chamber; and that, after having acted with much violence there, he went into the drawing-room, from which he declared that he never *would* stir till they returned. They were both, of course, highly indignant at this, and proceeded at once to the drawing-room, where they found Horace stretched fast asleep upon the sofa. It was not long before they aroused him, although he slept soundly, for they were not at the moment extremely choice of the means by which persons are, under peculiar circumstances, awakened: they had him up in the shortest possible period of time, and the moment their efforts had been crowned with success, he exclaimed, "Ah! my two trumps! Well, how are you?"

"What is your business with us?" sternly demanded Uncle John.

"Now, is that the way to address an old friend?" returned Horace with an extraordinary look, and in an equally extraordinary tone of remonstrance. "Is it regular? does it sound at all pretty?"

"Whatever you have to say, young man, say at once. We cannot have our time wasted now."

"There you go again—young man! Why do you cut away in that nasty manner? Can't you address me with a little more elegance?"

"Why are you here?"

"That's the point! I am here in the

responsible capacity of plenipo-extraordinary from the governor, and when I produce my credentials, I do expect to be treated with all the courtesy that's regular. I have got a whole lot of dirty documents here, which I am authorized to give up on a certain condition. But come, *don't* be crusty; sit down and look pleasant, and then I'll let you into the whole business."

"I wish," said Uncle John, "that you had come at a more seasonable hour."

"Well, how could I help it? I started off this morning to come early enough, and I should have been here at a more seasonable hour, only I happened on my way to meet with a few out-and-outers, who couldn't at all do without me!"

Conceiving that his object was to restore Goodman's papers, Uncle John then gravely took his seat.

"Now then," said Horace, "here we have, you see, a lot of rummy pieces of parchment, which the governor wished me to deliver into the hands of his brother; but as that old fool, who never was known to listen to reason when it proceeded from my lips, has referred me to you, I have waited here all this time, and would have continued to wait, if you hadn't come home till the week after next."

"Well, sir, what do you propose?"

"Why, assuming that you have full powers to act, I propose to deliver them to you, on condition that, as the governor is not very flush, he is never to be called upon to pay the *little* bill of those dirty scamps of lawyers."

"Are these *all* the papers which belonged to my friend?"

"Why, of course! Do you think that I would bring less than all?"

"Very well, sir; I am willing to receive them."

"And to give me an acknowledgment of your having received them, and to name the condition of course? Then you know it will be all right and regular."

"Well, sir, I'll even take it upon myself to do that," said Uncle John, who accordingly wrote an acknowledgment to the effect that he had received the documents on the condition named, the terms of which he on the part of Mr. Goodman, had agreed to."

"Well," said Horace, on taking the receipt. "And now, what are you going to stand? You never bring out the ghost of a glass of wine to give a fellow."

"We are busy, very busy," said Uncle John; "I beg that you will detain us no longer."

"Oh! very well! Why don't you say at once, 'There's the door; you'd better cut it!' You want to offend me, I suppose, but you won't; although it's enough to make a man go slăp into hysterics, to see the base ingratitude of this blessed world. But never mind. Ta, ta! You don't suppose that I want your eighteen-penny port. It's only the look of the thing that stuns me! But adieu! It'll be all one in the grave. We never know the value of a friend till we've lost him."

Having calmly delivered himself to this effect, he stuck his hat on one side of his head so ingeniously, that his right eye and ear were completely concealed, and walked with an air of magnanimity from the house, when Uncle John at once proceeded to Goodman's chamber with the documents, conceiving that the property of his friend was now secure.

It will, however, be proper to mention here, that these documents were utterly valueless. Walter, yielding to his wife, who was warmly backed by Horace, had disposed of every available species of property, and had sent these worthless pieces of parchment back, in the full conviction that his brother, being then much too weak to examine them, would give instructions for all legal proceedings to be stayed, if indeed he did not undertake to defray the expenses already incurred.

All this had been effectually accomplished; Uncle John had undertaken, in his friend's name, to settle with the attorney, and when the documents were carried to Goodman, he felt so exhausted, that they were at once set aside without even being looked at. The fact of Horace having burst into the room, had thrown him into a state of excitement which nearly proved fatal. It was evident to Uncle John when when he entered, that another such a shock would be the last he would ever experience. He trembled violently even then, and gasped for breath as he pressed his friend's hand, and begged of him not to leave him until he had become more composed.

"Valentine, that good boy," said he, after a pause, in a voice so faint that it verged upon a whisper, "is going to be married in the morning. I pray that he may be happy!"

"The marriage," said Uncle John, "has been postponed. The young lady has been taken very suddenly ill"

"I am very sorry for it. Young or old—young or old, my dear friend—all have their afflictions."

Goodman, with a sigh, relapsed again into silence, which Uncle John did not disturb, but sat patiently with him until he conceived that he had fallen into a slumber, when he stealthily quitted the room. It was then that he ascertained that while he was with Goodman, Whitely, who had been, contrary to his usual custom, from home, the whole of the evening, had returned; and that, having learned that Valentine, by whom he had been spoken to somewhat harshly at Raven's, was in the drawing-room, he had retired at once to his chamber. Uncle John was, therefore, compelled to defer the performance of the task he had proposed, but sat up till midnight conversing with Valentine, who was still sustained by that profound firmness which enables a man to regard difficulties but as evils to be surmounted, no matter what shape they may assume.

CHAPTER LVIII.

THE INTERVIEW OF UNCLE JOHN AND WHITELY WITH MR. WRITALL, AN ATTORNEY-AT-LAW.

IMMEDIATELY after breakfast the following morning, Valentine left with the lively hope of hearing that Louise had made some progress towards restoration; and the moment he had done so, Uncle John very cautiously re-opened the subject of the compromise he so anxiously desired to effect between Whitely and Raven.

"I saw Raven last evening," said he, "and I do not believe that I ever beheld any one so conscience-stricken in the whole course of my life."

"The scoundrel!" exclaimed Whitely, "I wonder he is not ashamed to show his face to you or any other honourable man."

"He is ashamed: he was ashamed to see me last evening. I had the utmost difficulty in obtaining an interview with him, and when I did, I found him frightfully dejected. Of course, our conversation touched solely upon this unhappy subject, and he urged me most earnestly to exert whatever influence I might have, with the view of prevailing upon you to consent to some private arrangement, not for his sake indeed, but for the sake of his child, who is now lying seriously ill.

"For her, poor girl, I am sorry—very sorry; I feel that I could not be more so were she even my own; for Valentine, also, am I sorry; for, although he spoke unkindly to me, I cannot but believe that he did it solely to check a species of perhaps unjustifiable rashness: I am sorry for them both, and would do much to save them from annoyance; but I cannot bring myself to believe that I should be acting, as a man under the circumstances ought to act, if, even for them, I permitted that villain to escape."

"It was for them—only for them, that he pleaded. As far as he was concerned he acknowledged that you were bound as a man to pursue him by all the means in your power."

"And pursue him I will!"

"Of course, knowing him as I do, and being in some degree connected with him through Valentine, as I am, it will be but natural for you to imagine that I lean somewhat towards him without sufficiently considering you."

"Indeed, my dear friend, I do not. Your honesty of purpose, your integrity, the pure principles by which I know you to be guided, tend to strengthen my conviction that you are incapable of advising me to adopt any course which you deem inconsistent with my honour."

"I acknowledge at once, that I lean so far towards him as to be anxious to have this melancholy affair settled, as far as it can be settled, privately: not for him—for his conduct admits of no extenuation—but for his poor child, whose heart any public exposure would go far towards breaking. But if even I had no knowledge whatever of him or of any one with whom he is connected, as your friend, I should advise you for your own sake alone, not to plunge into the uncertain depths of the law, being afraid—as I should be in such a case as this—that although in reputation you might seriously injure him, you would in doing so more seriously injure yourself. You know more of the law which bears upon this point—doubtless, much more than I do: but even in the event of my having no knowledge whatever of the party on the other side, I should argue with you thus: You are anxious to go to law: very well. You cannot proceed criminally: you must bring a civil action; you may even bring two: you bring two actions: you succeed in both: and the punishment awarded is of a pecuniary character. Now, what amount of damages, I ask, would you be likely to get? anything like five thousand pounds?"

"In all probability, not half that amount."

"Well, assuming that there was a prospect of obtaining that amount, what would you say if, instead of the trouble, the anxiety, the *risk* of a trial, you were offered ten thousand pounds down?"

"My answer would be this: I cannot feel justified in entering into anything like a compromise with a villain.'

"Are you justified in utterly ruining yourself to be revenged on a villain? And would you *not* be utterly ruined in the event of a failure?"

"I am poor, very poor: that cannot be disguised."

"Avoid then, going to law with a rich man."

"But if that doctrine were to obtain, the poor would be crushed by the rich with impunity!"

"Not in a case of this description, in which the rich man proposes to pay, perhaps ten times the amount that could be gained by resorting to law. This is not like a case in which a man offers to give a certain sum to escape corporeal punishment: If it were possible to punish him in any other way than that of attacking his purse, there might perhaps be some grounds for hesitation; but he can only be thus punished, and he offers to punish himself ten times more: he offers to pay at once ten thousand pounds, and thus to relieve you from all anxiety about the issue of a trial, and I must say that the issue in this case, to say the least of it, is of an extremely doubtful character."

"I do not think so. From all that I can learn, I am induced to believe that I ought not to entertain the smallest doubt about the matter. Last night I was introduced to an exceedingly clever lawyer—with whom I have an appointment this morning at twelve, who assured me distinctly, when I had explained the chief features, that in such a case as mine, which exhibits so monstrous a combination of wrongs, the law would fall upon the wronger with terrible vengeance. Now, as I am anxious to remove the impression you entertain, that the law is inoperative in a case of this description, I shall be glad if you will accompany me this morning as my friend, that you may hear how the law stands, and judge for yourself."

"I shall indeed be most happy to do so, feeling perfectly assured of your belief, that although I am still in communication with Raven, I shall take no advantage of anything I may hear, which, if known on the other side, might tend to prejudice your case."

"You may be assured that that is my belief. For were it not so, I certainly should not have been so anxious for you to go with me. You can appear in the sole character of my friend; your knowledge of the other party need not at all transpire."

It was at once then arranged that they should wait upon this gentleman together, and accordingly, at the hour appointed, they proceeded to the office of Mr. Writall.

On ringing the office-bell, their ears were addressed by a slight consumptive tick, when, as that caused the door to fly open, they entered, and beheld an emaciated little being, who was then in the act of enjoying a pinch of snuff, which appeared to be the only luxury within his reach, and who, in answer to Whitely's question, which had reference to the fact of Mr. Writall being within, said he didn't know exactly, but he'd see, when, in order to enable himself to see with distinctness, he inquired the name of Whitely, and disappeared. He was not absent long. He soon became enlightened on the subject, and on his return, announced that Mr. Writall *was* within, and immediately ushered them into the sanctum.

As they entered, Mr. Writall, who was a man of immense personal importance, and whose cheeks were peculiarly bloated, was standing with his right thumb in the arm hole of his waistcoat, and his left foot on a chair, looking as pompous as if he had just before swallowed a pot of porter.

"I hope you are well, sir," said he, in a singularly dignified wobble, swelling each word until it became as much as his mouth could hold.

"A friend, I presume?"

Whitely answered by formally introducing Uncle John, and they sat down with business-like views.

"I have been thinking, sir, of this immense case, of which you told me. I have been turning it deliberately over in my mind, and having deeply consulted the best authorities upon the subject, I have no hesitation in saying that the course is quite clear."

"I have," said Whitely, "an absolute hold upon him, then?"

"Undoubtedly; beyond all dispute; an immense hold."

"That is the grand point," returned Whitely, for the satisfaction of Uncle John;—"that is the grand point that I am anxious to have explained."

"Than which explanation, sir, nothing can be more easy. The defendant seduced your wife. He cohabited with her. She was under his protection. Of course an action for *crim. con.* will lie there."

"Notwithstanding it occurred nearly fifteen years since?"

"Notwithstanding it occurred nearly fifteen years since. All we shall have to do will be to show, that by maliciously causing you to be confined in an asylum for lunatics, he placed it completely out of your power to bring your action within the period prescribed by the statute."

"Exactly; I understand; and this of course, can be shown?"

"Of course."

"Will you allow me," said Uncle John, "to ask how?"

"By the production of witnesses."

"But unfortunately my friend Mr. Whitely has no witnesses."

"No witnesses! Where is the proprietor of the asylum?—where are the keepers? Subpœna them all; bring them all up!"

"Can they prove that the defendant, Raven, compassed, or was in any way connected with the incarceration of my friend?"

"That remains to be seen."

"But, like all prudent men, Mr. Whitely is anxious to see his way clearly before he proceeds."

"It is impossible for him not, sir, to see his way clearly."

"Upon my word," observed Whitely, "I confess that I cannot at present."

"Have you, yourself, the slightest doubt that these persons can prove the defendant to have, directly or indirectly, caused you to be confined?"

"I am afraid they know nothing of him. His name did not in any way appear."

"Well, that is a difficulty very soon got over. If *they* cannot prove it, other witnesses can."

"What other witnesses," inquired Whitely.

"Oh, I'll undertake to produce witnesses," replied Mr. Writall, nodding very mysteriously.

"I really cannot see where we shall find them."

"Oh, that is a difficulty soon overcome. I'll stake my reputation on finding sufficient witnesses."

"Then of course," said Uncle John, who looked at Whitely as if he did not understand it, "we may assume that point to be settled?"

"Of course."

"And that the settlement of that point will be sufficient?"

"And that the settlement of that point will be sufficient."

"But, on what authority was my friend here received and detained by the proprietor of the asylum in question? Was not his authority the certificate of the two physicians?"

"Undoubtedly; the certificate of the two physicians."

"How then can we impugn this, their evidence of my friend's insanity at the time?"

"I'll manage it. Leave that to me."

"But," urged Whitely, "how is it to be done?"

"If it cannot be done in one way, it can in another. We can even indict all concerned for a conspiracy."

"But what witnesses have we to sustain such an indictment?"

"Witnesses are to be found: affidavits are to be had. Leave the whole thing to me, and it shall be done. If the worst comes to the worst, we can harass him so, that he will be but too happy to compromise the matter, by coming down handsomely."

"And what, may I ask," said Uncle John, "would you consider a handsome sum in such a case?"

"Why, as he is a rich man, I'd make him come down with a couple of thousand pounds. I'd let him off for very little less."

"But were he to offer to put down at once such a sum as—say ten thousand pounds—"

"Oh, such a sum as that is altogether out of the question. It's a large sum, sir, recollect, is that of ten thousand—a sum which is not to be picked up every day! But whatever sum he might offer, however large, I'd take care to harass him well before I consented to receive it."

"But if, after having discovered that your object was to harass him, he were to defy you, and refuse then to compromise at all, what sort of position would my friend be in then?"

"Money," said Whitely, "is not the primary object. I want to punish him, it is true, and he deserves to be punished severely; but my chief aim is to compel him to produce, or at least to give me some sufficient clue to the discovery of my children."

"Punish him first," said Mr. Writall, "settle that matter first, and *then* make him produce the children."

"But," suggested Uncle John, "were he to propose now not only to put down at once—say ten thousand pounds—but to give, with respect to the children, all the information in his power, would it not, under the circumstances, be advisable to accede at once to such a proposition?"

"Why, as I said before, ten thousand pounds, you know, is an amount which is out of all reason; but if a good round sum were to be offered, together with the required information, I have no hesitation in saying, that it *would* be advisable to do so, but not before proceedings had been commenced, in order that he might know that we are really in earnest."

"I, of course, can compel him to produce my children?"

"Of course. And yet there is some slight difficulty there. I should advise—nay, now I come to reflect on the matter, if he be obstinate, he might be taken on suspicion of having murdered those children!"

"Murdered them!" cried Whitely, with a shudder.

"But," said Uncle John, "how can we prove that he ever saw them?"

"Oh, that could be proved; but as far as the murder is concerned—why, I confess, that it is somewhat difficult to secure witnesses as to murder; but even they are to be had."

"What may you mean by *securing* witnesses?"

"It is a practice, sir, well understood in the profession. At all events, assuming that we should fail in this, the threat alone of charging him with murder would be sufficient to induce him to come down with a little more."

Again, Whitely and Uncle John looked earnestly at each other, and after a pause of some seconds they rose.

"I will reflect, sir," said Whitely, "upon all you have explained, and let you know my decision in the morning.

"Very well, sir," returned Mr. Writall, who was evidently surprised at the fact of the consultation being so abruptly put an end to. "Very well, sir. If the case, sir, be placed in my hands, it shall be properly managed. It is my pride, sir, that I never yet suffered a client of mine to be defeated."

Uncle John and Whitely then took leave of Mr. Writall, with whom they were not highly pleased. He had, indeed, supplied them both with food for reflection; but while one of them looked upon him merely with contempt, the other regarded him with ineffable disgust.

"I cannot say that I am even yet convinced of the incorrectness of my view," said Uncle John, after having walked for some time in silence. "But where could he get all those witnesses from?"

"My friend," replied Whitely, "that is a legal scoundrel. Those witnesses are villains who can be got to swear to anything in any case, to the ruin of any man."

"Is it possible?"

"Quite. They are to be had at all prices, from ten shillings up to ten pounds, either to appear and give evidence, or to make affidavits. Such witnesses he proposed to secure in my case, for clearly none others exist."

Uncle John was amazed. He could scarcely believe it, and thousands, who possess far more knowledge of the profession than he did, would have been quite as incredulous, on being told that the practice of "hard swearing," more especially that branch ycleped "affidavit making," had become quite a trade.

This, however, did not shake the purpose of Whitely; he still was for law; but, as during the consultation with Writall, certain doubts had arisen, he resolved on having the opinion of some eminent counsel, upon whose judgment and integrity he might safely depend.

CHAPTER LIX.

IN WHICH VALENTINE PROVES A GOOD MORAL PHYSICIAN.

That, under any conceivable circumstances, Louise would have felt the postponement of her marriage severely, is a fact which must not be concealed, but under such serious circumstances as those by which the postponement had been induced, she naturally held it to be indeed terrible. It was not, however, the mere disappointment which retarded her recovery from the shock she had received; when the physical effects of that shock had been subdued, its moral effects continued in painful operation; for she could not but feel that the disgrace of her father would inevitably, to some extent, reflect upon her.

For three weary days she had not beheld him whom she had taught herself to adore; but although she had felt this to be of itself very sad, and had panted for the time when she might again see him, when that time arrived her spirit shrank from the interview, as if she feared that he could not be faithful to her then without dishonour.

Eventually, however, at the earnest solicitation of her dear kind friend, whom she regarded as her mother, she tremblingly consented to see him; and when he entered the room in which she was sitting, pale as death, she rose and flew to him, as if all cause for sorrow had vanished; but after having embraced him, and passed her hand fondly over his brow, and gazed upon him with an expression of rapture for an instant, the sudden flash of joy was extinguished, tears gushed from her eyes, and she sobbed like a child.

"My own Louise!" exclaimed Valentine, pressing her fervently to his heart. "Look up, my sweet girl! You see *I* am firm, Louise!—you see *I* am firm!" But, as he spoke, his voice faltered, while the tears were fast rolling down his cheeks. He could not bear to see her thus afflicted. He could firmly endure anything but that; that alone had the power to unman him.

A pause ensued, during which he endeavoured to conceal his emotion, and led Louise to a chair, while his mother, whom the interview had deeply affected, was sobbing as if her heart were about to break.

At length, however, they all became comparatively calm; and while Valentine was standing with the hand of Louise in his, pouring eloquent balm into her deeply wounded heart, the widow sat down beside her, with the view of imparting that solace which she deemed most effectual, and soon after quitted the room.

"My dear girl," said Valentine, the moment they were alone, "come, you must not be so sad; you must not, my love, indeed."

"Valentine," said Louise, with the most impressive earnestness, "I love you—dearly, fondly—you know how I love you; but this unhappy interview *must* be our last!"

"Why, you silly girl: what *do* you mean?"

"That I never will consent to bring dishonour upon you."

"I believe it; I am sure of it: I know you never will."

"But this I should be doing, if, after this hour, I consented to receive you as before."

"Louise, knowing the purity of your mind, and the beautiful delicacy of your feelings, I cannot but be conscious that this lamentable affair appears to you in the darkest colours in which it can appear to innocence: thus let it appear still, my good girl: thus may it ever appear! I would not have those colours brighter in the eyes of one so pure. But, my love, even assuming all we have heard to be true, and looking at it without the most remote reference to any extenuating circumstances, how can my alliance with you bring dishonour upon me? I will not affect, for one moment, to be incapable of perceiving your views; and that they spring from an amiable source is quite manifest. But how can this act affect me? It is not an act of yours: nor is it one over which it is possible for you to have had even the slightest control. It is one of which you possessed no knowledge until now!—How then can you or I be disgraced or dishonoured?"

"Disgrace will attach to the name," said Louise.

"That name will no longer be yours!"

"But will it not be said, and with truth, by the malicious, that you married into a family whose character was tainted?"

"This, indeed, by the malicious might be said; but not with truth. If the character of a family could be said to be tainted, because the acts of any one of its members are impure, few families indeed would be in a position to boast of their characters being without a stain. But let the malicious say what they will: they must be ingenious indeed, if they show that any disgrace that may attach to the name you now bear can reflect in the slightest degree upon me. But, my sweetest girl, no such disgrace will attach even to the name. The thing will not be known. I have the most perfect confidence in the success of those efforts which my uncle is now making, with the view of prevailing upon Whitely to consent to some private arrangement. If it be thus arranged, and I have not the smallest doubt that eventually it will be, unless we ourselves publish the matter to the malicious, their ingenuity cannot be brought to the test."

"Still I fear," urged Louise, "that you may be annoyed; and that such an annoyance as that would interfere with your happiness, and cause you to regret—"

"Louise! if you did not at this moment look so delicately beautiful, I really do think that I should scold you. Why, you little trembling creature!—who is to annoy me if the thing be not known?"

"But we are by no means sure that it will not be known!"

"Well, even if it be: I am sorry to say that the world does not attach so much importance to an affair of this description as you do. But if this be the case, the thing *must* not be known! I'll go and tell Whitely all about it. I will give your compliments to him, and tell him that if he will consent to an arrangement you will have me: but that if he will *not*, it's all over."

Louise slightly, but very slightly, smiled.

"You will think," continued Valentine, "that I view this matter with levity, although indeed, I do not; but it really is useless to grieve and mourn and be miserable about it. Were we to run about the streets, and fill the air with our lamentations, we might astonish the people certainly, and perhaps we might amuse them; but we could not alter the case as it stands. The thing has been done, and we are bound to make the best of it; but I question if even Llewellen himself can instance a case in which any disagreeable position was rendered more pleasant by an indulgence in excessive grief."

"You are a dear good soul," said Louise, arranging his hair as he sat on a stool beside her.

"I'm glad you think so," said Valentine; "I ought to terminate my engagement with *eclat*. I ought to make a decent impression on this my last appearance, as it *must* be the last!"

"I would not lose you for the world!" cried Louise, as she kissed his fine brow and appeared to forget all her troubles; "yet," she added, with intensity of feeling and expression, "I would rather lose you, the world and all, than render you unhappy! But, my love, this sad affair: you say that there is a prospect of its being settled privately?"

"A very fair prospect. In fact I have no doubt whatever of its being thus arranged. Whitely holds out at present it is true; but I'm convinced that we shall eventually induce him to consent."

"Poor man! I had no thought of my dear father having acted as he has. I could not have believed it if he had not himself told me that it was true. Poor Mr. Whitely! how dreadful his feelings must have been! But she must have been a very wicked creature! I am sure that she must have given my father great encouragement, or he never would have forgotten himself so far. Of course that was the cause of Mr. Whitely's insanity?"

By this question Valentine perceived that she did not know all, and, therefore, being most anxious not to throw any additional light upon a subject which would tend to sink Raven in her estimation, he replied that Whitely had never been insane, and that he had been confined in a lunatic asylum by some person, who wished to get him out of the way: which was the fact.

"Then it is not so dreadful," observed Louise, "as it would have been had he been driven to madness by that."

"Of course not," said Valentine; "that would have been a different thing altogether."

"But oh! you gentlemen, you gentlemen! —you are terrible people! But did Mr. Whitely treat her kindly?"

"Upon my word, I don't know."

"Perhaps not: he might have been very unkind to her; perhaps very harsh; and yet nothing could justify her conduct. She must have been bad. I am convinced that if she had not been, she never could have induced my father to bring upon us this dreadful calamity. But what became of her? It is a delicate question perhaps for me to put, but did you ever happen to hear what became of her?"

"Indeed I never did."

"Perhaps she went over to America, taking the poor children with her."

"Perhaps she did: but let us dismiss this painful subject. I have been thinking, Louise, of a certain matter to which it strikes me I never alluded before, but in deciding upon which you can render me very material assistance."

"Indeed! Then, I am sure that I shall be most happy to do so."

"Your politeness is proverbial. Well, then; when do you think—I will put it in that form as being the least unintelligible—when do you think that that ought to be done which was to have been done on the first of the month?"

"The first of the month?—Oh, indeed my dear Valentine, we must not think of that."

"But that happens to be the very thing of which I cannot help thinking!"

"But—I—I don't—really I don't—we must wait till this sad affair is settled."

"Why should we, my dearest? Why should we wait for that? *We* have nothing to do with the settlement of it?"

"My dearest love, pray do me the favour to say no more about it at present. It is useless, I find, to oppose you on any subject. You cheat me of every purpose. I really don't know how it is; but no one else could ever do so!"

The widow at this moment entered the room, and was agreeably surprised to see Valentine smiling.

"I beg pardon, my dears," she observed, "I only came for my bag. Well, come!" she added, gazing with pleasure at Louise. "Dear me, how much better you look! Well, really now, what an extraordinary change!"

And it is a fact well worthy of being placed on record, that the change thus noticed was particularly striking. Louise looked herself again; sadness disappeared; her eyes sparkled with all their wonted brilliancy, and she felt that a heavy load of sorrow had been removed from her heart. And thus for hours she continued to feel cheered by the affectionate eloquence of Valentine, who sat with her until the widow turned him out of the room, deeming it quite inconsistent with her duty as a nurse to allow him to remain with her patient any longer.

CHAPTER LX.

VALENTINE VISITS ASCOT RACES.

VALENTINE was now unremitting in his attention to Louise, whose spirits, by virtue of his enlivening influence, were, in a great degree, restored; but nothing could shake the resolution she had formed, not to fix another day for the celebration of their marriage until her father's unhappy affair had been privately arranged, although, when a fortnight from the day of the discovery had elapsed, Whitely's consent to such an arrangement had not been obtained. Uncle John, day by day, had endeavoured to induce him to adopt the mode proposed, but in vain: he could not be, by any means, prevailed upon to yield: he had made up his mind to take the opinion of a certain distinguished member of the bar, who happened to be then out of town, but had promised, that the moment he had obtained that opinion he would one way or the other decide.

Now it may not perhaps be improper to mention, that Llewellen, during the whole of this time, was a singularly miserable man. He felt wretched. His appetite was falling off frightfully; and although he was utterly unable to explain what was physiologically the matter, his feelings convinced him, that internally there was something uncommonly wrong. He applied to the physician who attended Louise, but the physician, instead of prescribing, looked at him and smiled. He applied again: he drew him aside the very next time he called, and put out his tongue and held out his wrist, and described the diagnosis of his complaint very pointedly, and then indeed he had a prescription; to take a run round his hat fifty times without stopping, and to repeat the dose five times a-day, keeping his fore-finger all the time strictly upon the crown. And an excellent prescription it was. It was, however, one which he thought might be dispensed with, although it did induce him to believe that a little exercise of some sort might not prove pernicious. But then what was he to do? He had no one to go out with! Valentine was constantly engaged with Louise. He could not go out alone! he would not go out alone; and the consequence was, that his case was getting daily worse and worse.

At length Louise, conceiving that a day's relaxation would be of service to Valentine, suggested the propriety of his having a rural stroll; and as it happened, a strange and inscrutable coincidence, to be the Ascot race week, he hinted to Llewellen that he did think it possible that he might go and see the Cup run for, in which case he hoped to have the honour of his company.

For some few seconds Llewellen could not believe that Valentine really meant this; but when, as with a vivid flash of lightning, he was struck with the conviction that the thing in reality was as it was, he was in ecstasies, and ran about the room, and performed a variety of extraordinary evolutions; some of which were of a character strikingly original.

"Is Lucy coing too?" he inquired.

"No, I cannot persuade her to do so."

"Very well," said Llewellen, who was not at all sorry on his account, "phen to we co, my poy, phen are we to start?"

"In the morning; but as we have no conveyance of our own, we must be off rather early."

"As early as you please! Well now t' cootness knows it, look you, this will pe peautiful! Put how apout preakfast? Shall hur come as hur tit pefore?"

"That will be the better way."

"Very well. And phot coat shall hur put on? Must hur co in sporting style? Hur've cot top poots and preeches."

"No, no; go as you are."

"Very coot," said Llewellen, to whom Valentine's every word was law. "Very coot, hur'll pe retty. Inteet t'cootness now this is a plessing." And he absolutely felt it to be one, and that feeling prompted him to run about so much, that he ate that day a respectable dinner.

In the morning he awoke about four, and fearing that he might over-sleep himself somewhat, as he had to be with Valentine at half past eight, if he suffered his head to remain upon the pillow, he rose, and embellished himself deliberately, and whistled like a lark, and sung several new songs, and then wended his way into the pantry, to see if any little article therein had the power to tempt him; and having discovered a variety of things rather delicious, he had a substantial foundation for a breakfast, and took his departure for the day.

It was then nearly six; and as he walked from street to street, he really couldn't tell exactly what to make of the silence that prevailed. It struck him as being rather awful. He looked acutely up and down: not a soul could be seen: there he was walking about with his hands in his coat pockets, a solitary individual in a wilderness of houses. He didn't like it. His intellects were, in some degree, confused. Was it a dream? Had all the people emigrated during the night? Was he in some deserted city? It all at once struck him that the people were not up yet; and when he looked round, he really didn't wonder at it. Presently he heard a few human beings singing, and the chorus he discovered to be strictly to this effect.

"For we're all jolly good fellows,
For we're all jolly good fellows,
For we're all jolly good fellows!—
And so say all of us."

But although he could hear them with a distinctness, which to him, at that time, was peculiarly refreshing, he was unable to see them until he arrived at the corner of the next street, when he beheld four gentlemen coming towards him, arm in arm, with a striking irregularity of step, appearing to be very happy, but looking indeed very pale.

"Ah! old fellow!" exclaimed one of these gentlemen. "How are you!"

"How to you too," said Llewellen in return.

"Come tip us your fin, old fellow! you're one of the right sort!" Hereupon the whole party shook him cordially by the hand, which was very affectionate. "I say, is there any house open about here?"

"Well, inteet now, I think all the people are in pet, look you!"

A loud burst of laughter immediately followed the announcement of this thought, which was very remarkable; but, as Llewellen inferred, from sundry vague observations, which had reference to leeks and toasted cheese, and other purely unintelligible matters, that the gentlemen were, to some extent, tipsy, he passed on, and the last he heard of them was an exceedingly loud declaration in song, that they wouldn't go home till morning.

The fact of his having met with this interesting party, notwithstanding, relieved his mind a little; and as he walked on, a few sober persons appeared, some with baskets of tools, some with hods, rules, and spades; but the whole of them carried cotton handkerchiefs, containing something destined for the stomach; still time seemed to move as if engaged in some political conversation, while walking arm in arm with a tortoise.

At length Llewellen,—which is really very singular,—found himself standing before the house in which Valentine dwelt; but the blinds were all down, no sign of life appeared: the house could not have been in less of a bustle, had all the occupants been dead. He would not, however, then leave the street; he walked up and down whistling, until he saw the girl open the parlour shutters, when he knocked at the door, got into the house, went at once up to Valentine's room, was admitted, and was happy.

Valentine was not long dressing; nor was it long when he had dressed, before they had breakfast; and when that had been disposed of satisfactorily, they started for the Railway terminus at Paddington, with the view of going by one of the early trains. On reaching this place, a train was just about to start, and immediately after they had entered one of the carriages, they were off at the rate of some considerable number of miles an hour.

"Time," observed Llewellen, "must put his best foot forward, to keep up with us now."

"He'll not allow himself to be beaten," returned Valentine. "Let us go at whatever rate we may, he'll be there as soon as we are."

"T'cootness knows now that's very extraortinary inteet, phen you come to reflect upon it, look you."

"It is extraordinary, that while he goes at all paces, he should preserve, with perfect steadiness, his own pace still."

"Ant will wait for nopotty."

"Nor will he be hurried!"

Llewellen was done. He tried very hard to come again, but failed, although he did not entirely give the thing up until they had arrived at Slough. Here they alighted; but they had no sooner done so, than down came a pelting shower of rain.

"Hascot, sir!—course, yer honour!—take yer there in no time!—slap wehicle!—hex'lent 'oss!—ride, sir—ride!"—exclaimed a number of extremely anxious persons, placing themselves before each other alternately, as if among them no question of precedence had been settled.

"What's the fare?" inquired Valentine, of one of the most forward.

"A guinea an edd, sir; *ad* no bistake at all about the haddibal."

Valentine looked to windward; and as he saw at a glance the black cloud coming up, leaving all fair behind, he decided upon standing under shelter for a time, during which the individual, whom he had addressed, came up and stated, confidentially, that he would take them both for a pound. This offer was not accepted. The cloud passed over and the sun again shone brightly, when the fellow again approached and offered to take them for half-a-crown a head! conceiving, however, that the walk would do them much more good, they declined even this, and passed on.

In due time they reached Windsor, where they stopped to have some slight refreshment, and then started again; and having enjoyed their walk exceedingly, up that delightful avenue, called Queen Anne's Drive, the course opened before them, and a brilliant scene it was. Llewellen's rapture was unbounded when he beheld it; while Valentine had never seen anything to equal it in splendour.

Having sufficiently dwelt upon the spectacle at a distance, they drew near the course and viewed each attractive feature with admiration. For some time Llewellen was dumb with enthusiasm, but when they approached the Grand Stand, he let his tongue loose at once, and it rattled away in Welsh with amazing rapidity. It did, however, after the first eloquent burst, happen to strike him, that although the Welsh language was beautifully flowing, and, moreover, comprehensively expressive, it was rather unintelligible to those who knew nothing at all about it; and this idea had the effect of inducing him to descend into that which he was unable to speak with equal force and purity.

For some considerable time they promenaded the course, studying; and it was, indeed, amusing, as well as instructive, to study—the distinguishing points which mark those who move in each social sphere, from the highest to the lowest—from that of royalty to that of beggary.

"Well, inteet," observed Llewellen, "phot a horse-racing nation this is, look you?"

"It is the first in the world, certainly; but we must not suppose that the whole of these persons are here with the view of seeing the races solely."

"No, inteet? Phot pesites too they come for?"

"The great majority to see and to be seen by each other. They themselves form the principal attraction."

"Then, look you, it must pe py their own attraction they are attracted!"

"Very good, I don't know that we shall make any thing better of it."

"All the worlt comes pecause all the worlt comes," added Llewellen, who then really did think that he had done very well.

The horses entered for the first race now appeared, and Valentine and Llewellen at once made their way towards them, for the purpose of seeing them saddled. They experienced, however, some slight difficulty here, for hundreds were rushing at the same moment with the view of seeing the same ceremony performed. They did, however, eventually, by dint of perseverance, manage to get to the point proposed; and the sight of the highly-trained beautiful creatures, that seemed to be anxious to exhibit their symmetry and action to the best possible advantage, well repaid them for the temporary inconvenience of a rush.

At various points groups of sharp-featured, hard-mouthed, sporting individuals, were engaged in giving and taking the odds, with as much profound earnestness as if, indeed, betting not only formed the principal business of their lives, but the only great object for which they had been born. It was pleasant to behold the sensation created by the appearance of a rich and inexperienced young fellow, as he approached these acute old characters. They eyed him, and wriggled round and round him, apparently bent upon searching his very soul to ascertain in what way it was possible to take him fairly in. It was evident that they viewed it as a general commercial matter, and as they all seemed most anxious to do business, Valentine, making his voice appear to proceed from the lips of a likely looking personage, cried "fifty to one against the saint!"

"Done, my lord, in thousands!" cried one of the sharpest, producing his book on the instant.

"*I'll* take you, my lord," said another.

"I'll take you over again," cried a third; and his lordship, on being thus suddenly beset, looked at them as mysteriously as possible.

"Is it to be in thousands, my lord?" inquired the person who had first addressed him, and who had already half entered the bet.

"Is what to be in thousands?" demanded his lordship.

"Why the fifty to one your lordship offered."

"I never offered fifty to one."

"Beg pardon, my lord, but really I fancied—indeed I—*some* gentleman offered that bet!" when, as they certainly were, under the circumstances, wonderful odds, he looked round with extraordinary sharpness for him who had offered to give them.

By this time one horse only remained to be saddled for the Castle stakes, and he was indeed a noble animal, and seemed actually to know it. His owner was standing by his side, apparently lost in admiration of his beauty, while the little old jockey, who had adjusted the saddle upon his own back, as if he intended to mount himself, was twisting about, and looking knowingly at every point, as if powerfully struck with an idea that he should win.

"I'll bet a hundred to one against that horse," cried Valentine. "He's sure to be last."

"What, my oss! I'll take you!" cried the little old jockey, turning round with astonishing promptitude and spirit, while the owner of the animal looked at him from whom the voice seemed to proceed with an expression of ineffable contempt.

This person was a farmer, and one who would not have offered any such odds; and he said so distinctly, and with consummate point, as the jockey observed, that if he meant anything, he had better then put his money down. This threw the innocent farmer into a state of perspiration, which poured upon a gentleman who sat under the rail, bobbing at a cherry, with unspeakable delight.

The horse was now saddled; and when the jockey had mounted, they all repaired to the starting post at once. Although it was not the grand race, great anxiety prevailed: it was manifest that thousands upon thousands of pounds had been staked upon the issue even of that.

"Hur say, my poy, every potty's petting," said Llewellen; "can't we have a pet?"

"Why, I think we might manage even that," replied Valentine.

"Well, phot shall it pe?"

"Oh, anything you please; I am not at all particular."

"Very coot. Hur'll pet you the pest tinner to pe hat, that the horse that was last sattled wins."

"Very well," returned Valentine, "let it be so. He *ought* to win; that seems quite clear: but a race is not invariably won by the best horse."

"Phot, tont you think the jockeys will win, if they can?"

"Undoubtedly they will, if they can get more by winning than by losing."

"Tear now, t'cootness, are they not to pe trusted?"

"There are but few of them whom *I* should feel at all inclined to trust. Human nature, as we find it developed in jockeyism, certainly is not quite perfect.

"Put, look you, if one of those fellows were to keep a horse pack, wouldn't he therepy lose his character?"

"Oh, not at all; he may struggle with desperation; he may apparently do his utmost to urge the horse on, and get applauded for doing his utmost, without allowing him to win."

"Phy then it all depends upon the jockey?"

"Entirely, if he be on the best horse; he has the power in his own hands; and prizes are sometimes afloat, too brilliant to be resisted by even the honour of a jockey."

"Then look you, when we pet upon a race, we in reality pet upon the honour of the fellow who happens to rite the pest horse!"

"Precisely. It amounts but to that."

All was now ready; the course was clear; the signal was given, and the horses were off. "*Here* they come; *here* they come!" shouted the mass. "Hats off there, hats *off!*—Hurrah!—*Go* along!—*Cut* away!—Now! now! now! Blue for a million!—Stripe!—Fly!—There's a pace!—*Now* then!—Beautiful!—*In* to him!—Out and out!—BRAVO!"

The race was decided, and the next moment all on the course knew which had won. The excitement was no sooner raised than subdued. The thing was over in a minute. No species of pleasure can be of itself more fleeting, than that of a race. The horses are off; they pass, they are in!—the eye can scarcely rest upon them before the issue is known.

"Well, my poy," said Llewellen, "Hur've cot to stand the tinner. To you think that little wretch tit his pest?"

"He appeared to do all in his power."

"Well, perhaps he tit, look you; put t'cootness knows it now—hur tit think that he titn't. But come along; shall we have tinner now, or phen?

"Oh, not yet! Let us wait until after the Cup race, and then we can take our own time."

"Very coot: yes, that will pe petter. But hur say, my poy, let's co into one of those pooths, and win some money."

"Let us go in and lose some, you mean, of course."

"Phot, don't they play fair?"

"Upon my word, I'd not undertake to prove that they do; but if you do play, you had better, at once, make up your mind to lose."

"Well, it won't matter much if hur too lose a little."

"But why do you want to play at all? You have plenty of money; quite as much as you want: you have no use for more. But you are certain to lose."

"Well, never mind: Hur'll only lose a sovereign; a sovereign is nothing!"

"Fred," said Valentine, pointing to a poor withered heartbroken creature, who seemed to have travelled far to beg, but knew scarcely how to do it, for she had evidently seen more prosperous days, "would a sovereign be considered nothing there?"

Llewellen drew his purse, and having taken out a sovereign, placed it in the hand of the poor old creature, who looked at it, and then looked at him, and then burst into tears. From her soul she seemed to bless

Valentine at Ascot.

P. 326.

him, but she had not the power of utterance then.

"Will not that do more good than if you had given it to those swindlers?" said Valentine.

"Hur feel it will," replied Llewellen, "hur feel it will. Put hur say, my poy, let's co in only to look."

"Oh, by all means! All I object to is the encouragement given to such pernicious scoundrels!"

"Phot, are they all scountrels, look you?"

"There's not a commonly honest man amongst them. They have no honour to keep them honest: in fact, they know nothing of the feeling of honour!"

"Then they must pe pat fellows, pecause they want put to pe poor, to pe retty for plunter."

"They profess to be as honest as they can afford to be, Fred, which has a most comprehensive meaning. Well, it matters not, I suppose, which we go into: let us go into this."

They accordingly entered, and found everything arranged in brilliant style: the place was elegantly festooned; the ground was carpeted; there was a table on either side, and one at the top, while a temporary sideboard stood near the entrance, on which there were sherry, champagne, soda-water, and brandy, for those players who might descend to call for a glass of either gratis. On each table an immense amount of money appeared: piles of notes, heaps of gold, and imperial pecks of silver: but as the upper appeared to be the principal table, they made their way to it at once.

The person who presided at this table was one of those excessively amiable creatures who appear to have no real enemy but the law. His countenance was screwed into an inflexible grin; every muscle appeared to be at its utmost stretch. Men laughed when they looked at him—laughed when they lost: he defied them to help it—he would make them laugh. Had he picked their pockets in the most literal manner, they could scarcely have felt offended with the man; while, if even they had given him in charge, he would have made the police laugh too heartily to hold him.

Valentine watched him for a time with some interest, for he found him to possess —although he did grin perpetually—the keenest eye to business he ever beheld; and as he could not help wishing to ascertain if it were possible to make him look serious, he made up his mind, having no great respect for the profession, to try.

"*Now*, my leetle roley-poley," cried the presiding genius—his custom always when he sent round the ball—"off again, my little hinnocent!—there's a leetle beauty!—make yer game, genelmen's sons!—make yer game!"

"Hush!" cried Valentine, with a desperate hiss, which he dexterously sent beneath the table.

"Hul-lo!" in a sweet tone, exclaimed the laughing creature. "Bless yer leetle heart! Are you *ony* there?—*nothink* more? Vell, come now, that's werry reasonable at the price. I say, Bill, my affectionate!—here's *ony* a hindiwidual which is anxious for you to take him by the scruff *off* the neck, and to shy him bang out off the booth."

"Vare?" cried the affectionate Bill, whose general aspect was not quite so amiable as that of his friend. "Vare his e?"

"Oh, *ony* under the table here! *and* nothink less."

"Hunder the table!" cried the affectionate, darting round with something like ferocity.

"Don't go for to wring the blessed neck of the genelman: don't mercycree him, not by no manner *off* means."

"Hullo, I say!" cried the affectionate, peering beneath the table with remarkable acuteness: "now hout o' that will yer?—vot d'yer vornt there?"

"Hush!" whispered Valentine, "Hush!"

"*Ony* a kipple!" exclaimed the laughing genius, "and *no* more!"

"Vort d'yer mean!" cried the affectionate Bill, who now got completely under the table, and looked about him with praiseworthy zeal. "Vy, there's no coves here!" he added, addressing his friend.

"*Aint* there! I des say there aint. No, *praps* I didn't hear 'em! No, it aint a bit likely I did! How *unfort'nate* I'm deaf!"

"I tell yer, it's pickles!" cried the affectionate Bill. "There aint nobody here. Can't yer believe me? Look yerself."

"*Not* if I know it. What, don't you see the dodge? Don't you see, if I was for to take my leetle eyes off the tin, their pals wouldn't p'raps borrow a trifle? *Oh*, no! I *don't* s'pose they would."

"Carnt yer kiver it up?" cried the affectionate.

"Keep close!—keep close!" whispered Valentine.

"There aint no one there, you think, don't you?" cried the genius, and in an instant his affectionate friend resumed his search, while he himself kept rather a keen eye upon the specie, expecting every moment an attack upon the bank. But the affectionate certainly could see no one there! —not a soul!—which was indeed somewhat striking, and he said so pointedly, and without the slightest fear of contradiction, and he felt himself in consequence justified in declaring that there *was* no one there, which, however, failed to shake the conviction of his friend, who intimated boldly that he wouldn't believe him if even he were to swear till he sweat.

"*Do* you think," he added, with an ironical grin, "that you'll go for to gammon me into that air! I'm hinnocent, I know, but I wasn't born yesterday exactly."

Valentine now introduced a remarkably slight chuckle, which, slight as it was, caused the laughing genius to come at once to a decision. "*I'll* see after you now, my leetle darlings!" said he, as he gathered up the cloth with which the table was covered, to render the bank more secure. "*I'll* see what you're made on, and no mistake in any indiwidual pint. Now," he added, after having made all safe, "let's see the colour *off* your complection."

He stooped, and looked round the interior, with one fist duly prepared for the delivery of an extraordinary blow, and one foot just as ready for the prompt administration of an equally extraordinary kick. But where were they for whom these favours were designed? He really couldn't see them!—he could'nt see one of them,—not even one! He wished he could; and if he had, the immediate consequences to that one—let him have been whomsoever he might—would in all probability have been unpleasant.

"Where are you, my darlings?" he enquired, in the most insinuating manner. "Ony say! I shall, indeed, be werry happy to see you! I'm sorry you should cut your little interesting sticks."

"Vale, can *you* see 'em?" spitefully demanded the affectionate.

"*Not* exact. *Praps* I wouldn't give a small trifle if I could. How they managed their luckies though, cert'ny gets over me a leetle above a bit."

"They couldn't do it!" cried the affectionate. "How could they go for to get out if they was in?"

"That's the particular dodge as walks over me, rayther. Howsoever the hinnocents aint here now!—that's about as clear *as* mud!—still the go's oncommon. But never mind: I've *ony* lost the pleasure off letting 'em know that I would'nt have given 'em nothink by no means. *But*, to business," he added, readjusting the cloth. "Now, genelmen's sons, make yer game! —make yer game! Here's fortun at yer feet, and you've ony got *for* to pick it up—make yer game!"

During the whole of this time, the shining countenance of the genius presented one immutable grin. A frown never came over it for an instant: not a cloud even approached it—a fact which went far to induce Valentine to suppose that his face was incapable of any other expression than that of unadulterated glee. He was not, however, quite convinced of this, and therefore, in order that he might not, on a point of much importance, entertain a false impression, he resolved to bring the matter once more to the test.

The genius was still actively engaged with the ball, lavishing upon it the most endearing eulogia, and making it abundantly clear to all around that he appreciated highly its innocence and beauty. Nor was this unnatural. He was winning very fast, and the stakes were rather heavy, and as it, strangely enough, happened that the more he won, the more rapturous he became, he had just attained the highest pitch of ecstasy, when Valentine sent beneath the table an extraordinary laugh.

"*Hullo!*" cried the genius, who kicked out furiously, and by virtue of doing so injured his shin. "Bill, *come* here! Here they are again! *Ony* let me jist ketch 'em, the warmint!"

His countenance fell!—This was not to be borne. He was reaping a harvest of plunder, and his time might be valued at ten pounds per minute. It was cutting. He couldn't bear it; and as the laughter still continued, his rage rose to a high pitch of frenzy. No endearing terms were applied to the invisibles then: they were no longer darlings—no longer little innocents: he no longer blessed their little hearts; but on the contrary, his epithets proved to all around that, like the rest of his patronized caste, he was a most depraved ruffian; when as Valentine was more especially satisfied of this, he and Llewellen left the booth, duly impressed with the conviction of its being monstrous that the practices of these degraded wretches should be so extensively encouraged.

During the time they were in this den of "honourable" thieves, the second race had been run; they therefore established themselves in a commanding position to see the grand race of the day. In this all the interest appeared to be centered. Thousands were waiting the issue with an anxiety the most intense; and although thousands more cared but little about which might be the winner, it was the grand race, and that was sufficient to rivet the attention of all.

"Well, my poy!" said Llewellen, "let us have another pet: come, hur'll pet you a pottle of wine."

"About what?"

"Oh, anything you please. Hur tont

know one of the horses. Come, how is it to pe?"

"Why one of us had better take the two first horses against the field."

"Very well! Which shall have the first?"

"Oh, it matters not! You take them."

"Very coot! Now look out: the two first are mine."

The horses started. It was an excellent start. They were all off together, and seemed to fly. It was a long and most beautiful race, and being on all hands admirably contested, the excitement was well kept up till the last. The favourite won by half a length, and when the result became known, it was interesting to discriminate between the winners and the losers. Sunshine on the one hand, and clouds on the other, marked those of each class with unerring distinctness. It seemed to be impossible to make a mistake. No man could suppose that they who sported heavy overhanging brows and compressed lips, were the winners; or that they were the losers who looked round and smiled. Some it is true can bear to lose better than others; for there are men who cannot lose to the extent even of a pound without feeling remarkably wretched; but although there are many who make a point of kindling up their countenances, in order to make it appear when they lose that they feel just as joyful as if they had won; the amiable hypocrisy is perceptible at a glance, so sure are they to overdo the thing with a smile which is truly expressive of nothing but pain.

Valentine lost of course, but his loss was so inconsiderable that he scarcely gave it a thought; yet even he did not appear to be so highly pleased quite as Llewellen: for although it is possible for a man to avoid the expression of pain when he loses, he cannot avoid expressing pleasure when he wins.

As soon as the excitement produced by the race had subsided, Llewellen became impatient for dinner, and as his importunities increased in earnestness every moment, they entered a booth in which various kinds of provisions were displayed in the most tempting manner possible.

"Now, my poy," said Llewellen, "pefore we pekin, too let's have a pottle of peer, for inteet cootness knows it, hur feel fit to trop."

A bottle of stout was therefore obtained, and while Llewellen was whetting his appetite with that, Valentine ordered the dinner of an extremely fat fussy attendant, who obviously prided himself much upon his agility. It appeared that he had never learned to walk; run he could with any man in England of his size; but he was clearly afraid to trust himself out of a trot. His pace was about eight miles an hour, and out of that pace, when in motion, it was manifestly impossible for him to get. When called, he seemed startled: his legs were shocked: they could no more have kept still when a man shouted "Waiter!" than they could if they had been at that moment powerfully galvanized. He was, in short, one of the most perfect pieces of mechanism ever produced in the shape of a man; while the state of excitement in which he revelled was, in the abstract, distressing.

While dining, Valentine watched the extraordinary movements of this automaton with a high degree of pleasure. It was the first of the species he had ever seen, for a regular waiter is a different thing altogether. There is little about *him* to excite admiration. He is all starch and method. When sober he seems to know exactly what he is about. Nothing can get *him* into a run: he wouldn't do it to save the soul of any man upon earth. But here was one of the "occasional" hands, whose assiduity is at all times striking. They can no more be got to walk than the "regulars" can be got to run, wherein lies the difference between the two classes.

No sooner had Valentine brought his mind to bear upon this highly impressive distinction, than an over-dressed personage marched into the booth with a rather remarkable degree of pomposity, and having looked very severely upon all around, took his seat with an immense air, removed his hat, of which the shape was rather *recherché*, adjusted his curls, raised his stock, and called "Waitor!"

The occasional on the instant flew to him, as if a flash of forked lightning had been pricking him behind, and rather trembled to behold the immense one who, as he frowned, said with much regal dignity, "Waitor! or—er, bring me some lunch."

"Weal an am sir chicken sir beef roast an biled?"

"Well-or-m! bring me a dish of ham an beef. And-or—" he added with great deliberation, waving his hand with theatrical elegance—"You may-or—" He was about to say more, but the occasional was out of sight, and had they both kept on, by the time the one had finished, the other might with ease have got a mile or two below the horizon. As the occasional however had not so far to go, he soon shot back with the dish of ham and beef that had been ordered, and when the great man had given another order for some stout, he set to work with considerable spirit.

It was then five o'clock—a fact which would not, perhaps, have been placed upon record, but for the circumstance of the individual in question having called for a "lunch"—and as Valentine thought that he did not look much like a man who had been in the habit of dining at eight, he felt curious to know whether that dish of ham and beef was or was not to be in reality his dinner.

But then the question was, how could this knowledge be got at: how could the interesting fact be ascertained? Valentine considered for a moment, and having conceived a scheme which he imagined would be effectual, he resolved to embrace the first opportunity for carrying it into execution.

By this time the immense one had about half emptied the dish, and as the occasional was assiduously hovering near him, Valentine imitating the voice of the pompous personage, who at the moment was raising a glass of stout to his lips, cried, "Waitor! take away waitor!—cheese!"

In an instant the occasional seized the dish and plate, and before the immense one, who was drinking, could speak, he had reached the other end of the booth, and shot the contents of both into a bucket of kitchen-stuff.

"Waitor! waitor!" shouted the immense one, half choked, for the last gulp of stout had been excessively violent.—"Waitor!"

"Comin, sir!—comin, sir!" cried the occasional, who shot back at once with a small slice of cheese.

"What do you mean, waitor, by taking away my dinner before I'm half done?"

"I beg pardon, sir, reely sir, I thought sir, you told me."

"Told you!—Not a bit of it!—Bring it back instantly!—What do you mean?"

Bring it back! The utterance of these awful words made the occasional look unspeakably blue. Bring it back! It was all very well; but how was he to get it? He wasn't going to pay out of his own pocket for half a dish of fresh! A thought struck him!—He glided like a sound substantial sylph towards the bucket, and fished the pieces out, and having scraped them into cleanliness, he placed them picturesquely upon the dish, and then did "bring it back" with great presence of mind.

"Another time, waitor," said the immense one, "remove not a gentleman's plate till he is done;" and having delivered himself with some striking dramatic action to this effect, he recommenced operations, and appeared to enjoy it much.

Valentine was now of course satisfied on the particular point proposed; but the actor—for an actor he evidently was—continued to behave in so ridiculous a fashion, that had Valentine met with him in any other place, he would doubtless have worked him into a high state of frothy excitement.

"Garshong!" cried the great one, when the ham and beef had wholly disappeared. "Garshong!" he repeated, being anxious to make a hit, as there were several persons near him—"*Garshong!*"

The occasional heard him, but conceiving very naturally that some other gentleman had been called, he of course did not feel it to be his duty to interfere.

"WAITOR!" at length shouted the immense one, disgusted with the fellow's profound ignorance of the French language—"Some frummidge here!—cheese!"

"Yes, sir, beg pardon, sir; cheese, sir, and what else?"

"Nothing, you unintellectual individual," replied the great man, who looked round for some applause, but to his horror he "hadn't a hand." When therefore the cheese had been produced, he set to work upon it at once in a somewhat savage manner, which Valentine no sooner perceived than assuming his voice, and making it appear to proceed from his lips, he cried "Waitor! a bottle of the best champagne!"

The occasional started off at a rate which rather exceeded his usual eight miles an hour to execute this order, and on his return very naturally placed it before the great one, who seemed somewhat struck.

"Waitor, what's this?" he demanded.

"Champagne, sir."

"I want it not; why bring it here?"

"You ordered it, sir."

"Fellow! what do you mean? I ordered it not."

"I'd be sorry to say, sir, you did, if you didn't."

"Am I to inform your master of your insolence? Away with it. Do you hear?"

"Beg pardon, sir, but I've paid for it. I'm obleeged to pay for everything as I has 'em."

"And what's that to me? Let me have no more of it, I desire."

"Very well, sir; only you ordered it, sir, that's all. I shouldn't have brought it if you hadn't."

"Waiter!" cried Valentine in his natural voice.

"Yes, sir," said the occasional, who approached rather gloomily.

"What have you there?—gooseberry wine?"

"Champagne, sir; the best in the world."

"It *is* good?"

"Excellent, sir; the finest ever made."

"Then open it."

With all the alacrity in life, the occasional drew the cork, and as he evidently felt much better, he was off for another glass like a shot.

The immense one now prepared to make his exit. He did not appear to feel happy. The production of the champagne had unsettled him somewhat, but having made up his noble mind to leave with *éclat*, he cried, "Waitor! now then, what's the damage?"

"Am an beef sir cheese sir bread, bottle stout—seven an six."

"What!" exclaimed the great one, inspired with amazement.

"Seven an six, sir," repeated the occasional, coolly.

"Seven and sixpence! *Seven* and six! What, for a lunch?"

"That's the charge for what you've had."

"Why, they never charged me seven and sixpence for a lunch at the Clarendon!"

"Werry like, sir, some stablishments cuts werry low; but, sir, we gives the best of everythink here."

"Extortionate! seven shillings and sixpence for a lunch! Why I never in my life heard of so gross an imposition."

"It aint a imposition, sir. It's nothink but the reg'lar charge."

"Silence, sir! don't talk to me! I say it is an imposition—a vile imposition! The idea of seven and sixpence for a lunch! There's the money. I'll post you all over the course."

The waiter took up the silver which had been thrown down with great indignation, and having counted it slowly three times, looked with singular significance at the victim.

"Well, why look at me? Is it right?"

"Seven an six, sir. Waiter, sir, please."

"Not the ghost of a copper, if I know it."

"We has nothink sir ony what we gets," urged the occasional; but the immense one contemning this powerful argument in favour of a gratuity, frowned darkly, and marched from the booth.

"He is some creat man, I suppose," said Llewellen, who had been watching his movements for some time with interest.

"No doubt," returned Valentine, "in his own estimation he is the greatest man of the age."

"Putt he is no potty inteet? Tont you think he's a gentleman, look you?"

"Did you ever see a gentleman act like him?—But come, let us be off, or we shall lose the last race."

"Very coot, hur'm quite ready."

The waiter was called, and when they had settled with him to his entire satisfaction, they returned to the course full of spirit. All but the last race had been decided, and Valentine began to amuse himself again by offering the most extraordinary odds upon record. The betting men were perfectly amazed. They perspired with anxiety to take the odds offered, but their utter inability to discover him whom they so eagerly panted to victimize, was a thing which they could not at all understand, and which therefore created a singular sensation.

To Llewellen all this was uninteresting of course. Had he been in possession of Valentine's secret, his rapture would doubtless have been rather alarming; but being in a state of utter ignorance on the subject, he naturally held it to be extremely dull work, and therefore endeavoured to prevail upon him to mingle with those who seemed somewhat more lively. Valentine consented, and as there were yet no symptoms of an immediate start, he proceeded to initiate him into the various systems of swindling which characterize race-courses in the aggregate. Llewellen was absolutely astounded when practices, of which he had never had the most remote conception, were explained, and when Valentine had pointed out to him divers illustrations of the truth of what he had stated, he began to look upon all those who thus permitted themselves to be victimized as fools, although on many occasions he found it difficult to abstain from becoming a victim himself. This was made more particularly manifest while they were standing at a "prick in the garter" table, at which a gentleman had a long piece of list, which he wound round and offered any money that no man could prick in the middle. This seemed to be simple, very simple, very simple, indeed, and the gentleman who presided laboured zealously all around that although he would bet all he had that none could do it, his private impression was that nothing on earth could more easily be done. Several gentlemen—who were perfectly unknown to him of course!—tried and won divers sovereigns off hand, which had the effect of inducing Llewellen to believe that the conductor was most intensely stupid, and ought not to have been trusted out alone, and so firmly did he entertain this belief, that he pitied the man, and was about to stake a sovereign himself solely in order to convince him, that as he had not the most remote chance of winning, he had better shut up shop and go quietly home to his wife and family; but Valentine, the moment he perceived Llewellen's object, did without the slightest ceremony drag him away.

The next respectable group they met with, had been attracted by a thimble-rigging gentleman, who seemed to have set his soul upon losing every sovereign he had—and he displayed about forty—so bungling and awkward he appeared. In Lewellen's view he didn't half understand his business. It was perfectly ridiculous to suppose a man incapable of discovering the pea; an infant might have told where it was; the only thing which seemed to him to be extraordinary was that a man with eyes in his head should be sufficiently blind to make any mistake at all about it. The thing was so palpable, so singularly clear; the impossibility of being deceived was manifest even to the meanest capacity.

"Why, my poy!" said Llewellen, "can't you tell phere it is every time?"

"Yes," replied Valentine, "*I* can tell, but you can't."

"Pless your soul ant potty! Hur'll pe pount to tell ninety-nine times out of a huntret."

"Where do you suppose it to be now?"

"Why, under the mittle thimple, of course."

"It is not under either of the thimbles; depend upon it, Fred, the fellow has it in his hand."

"Putt, my dear poy, hur saw him place the thimple right over it."

"He appeared to do so; but as he placed the thimble down he took the pea up: he has it now between his fingers, and were he to raise the one nearest to us, he could make it appear to have been under that."

Llewellen held this to be impossible, and began to argue the matter aside with great spirit. He contended for the absurdity of the idea of a fellow like that being able to deceive *him*, and expressed himself anxious to have one trial for the sole purpose of convincing Valentine of his error.

"How strange it is," said Valentine, "that men will not be guided by the experience of others."

"Putt, my coot fellow, in such a case as this, it is only my own experience that *can* satisfy me that what you conceive to be correct really is so. Shall hur try?—Just to convince you?"

Valentine smiled, and Llewellen took a sovereign out of his purse and went close to the table. It was in an instant perceived that he had been caught, and the thimbles were adjusted, when with the most perfect confidence he threw down his sovereign, but on raising the thimble beneath which he felt quite sure the pea was, he discovered, as a mere matter of course, that beneath that thimble the pea really was not.

On this highly important discovery being made, the respectable individuals who were standing round the table began to laugh very loudly, as if indeed they looked upon it as an extremely good joke, but Llewellen, after having made a series of mysterious faces, while he yet held the thimble between his finger and thumb, made no sort of remark upon this general manifestation of merriment, but left the spot with Valentine, wiser than before.

"You are right, my poy, quite right," said he, "t' cootness knows it! Putt phy tit they laugh so particularly phen hur lost? Phen the others lost they titn't laugh at all!"

"No, the others were confederates; each has a share of the profits of the speculation; they have nothing to laugh at when *they* win or lose among themselves; they laugh only when they happen to catch a gudgeon like you, Fred, and that they *should* laugh at such a time is not amazing."

"Well, inteet, now hur never was pefore so much teceived. Hur was as sure that that little fool of a thing was there, as hur ever was of anything in my life. Put, however, they will have to kit up very early in the morning inteet to kit anything like another sovereign out of me."

"You have made up your mind then not to patronize them regularly?"

"Never more, my poy—never more," said Llewellen, who after having shaken his head with sufficient solemnity to convey an idea of the firmness of his resolution, became as merry on the subject as if he had merely seen the process performed upon some other victim.

The horses were now about to start for the last race, and the friends took their station. They had another bet of course; Llewellen *would* have a bet, for as they had made up their minds to walk back to the railway, he suggested the propriety of stopping to have one more bottle of champagne at Windsor, and coffee at Slough, which suggestion was unopposed, and the race commenced, and it singularly enough happened to be as much like all other races as possible. The horses started; they ran the distance, and on reaching the winning post one was a-head. It is inscrutable perhaps, that this should be invariably so; but that it is so invariably, is a fact which no man may dispute.

Immediately after the termination of this race all around became one scene of bustle and confusion. Thousands of horses were put to simultaneously, and every creature seemed anxious to quit the scene as soon as possible. Had a hostile army appeared in the distance they could not have been in more eager haste to retreat, while each charioteer seemed to have made up his mind to break the necks of all under his immediate protection.

Valentine and Llewellen walked coolly from the course, noticing everything worthy of notice, and, accompanied by thousands, reached Windsor, where they stopped as they had previously proposed. They then went on to Slough, and after having had coffee, returned to town by one of the trains highly delighted with their day's recreation.

CHAPTER LXI.

DESCRIBES SEVERAL INTERVIEWS, BUT MORE PARTICULARLY ONE BETWEEN WRITALL AND RAVEN.

Another week elapsed, and nothing had been decided. Whitely, who had resolved not to act in any way until he had taken the opinion of Serjeant Talbot, was waiting for the serjeant's arrival in town, although Uncle John urged him again and again to delay the thing no longer, but to take the best advice he could immediately procure. In the mean time Raven confined himself almost exclusively to his room. His spirits continued to be dreadfully depressed, and he had become so excessively peevish, that the servants absolutely trembled to go near him. He had never been a very affectionate master, and they knew it, but the way in which he treated them then was in their view insufferable beyond all precedent!—and it was very harsh.

There was, however, one of them to whom he was particularly mild, and that was Joseph, the sentimental porter, whose comprehensive faculties, Valentine, who viewed him as a most superb hypocrite in his way, had ever gloried in distressing. Raven's conspicuous kindness to this fellow had always appeared to be inexplicable. No one in the house could at all understand why *he* should be petted—for petted he had ever been, albeit he was a most decided wretch in appearance, and remarkably insolent if he happened to be put at all out of his way. His fellow-servants hated him heartily, forasmuch as they did very strongly suspect him of having on sundry occasions told divers abominable tales about them, with the view of depreciating their value as confidential individuals in their master's estimation; but they never did hate him so intensely as then, for while Raven's special behaviour to him was rendered by contrast more striking, he had become a great man, and boasted not only of the money he possessed, but of the fact of his having a certain person under his thumb! which they held to be very mysterious, particularly as he often condescended to explain to them, that he might if he chose, have the best place in the house, and *would*, but that the one he then occupied afforded him more leisure for reflection. All this was intended exclusively for the kitchen, but it soon reached the ears of Louise through her maid, who conceived it to be her duty on all occasions to be as communicative as possible, and the moment she heard of it, it became known to Valentine of course, for he and Louise were now as one: they lived in each other's hearts: they seemed to have but one soul, and while in him she found a perfect realization of her dearest hopes, he loved her so fondly that

> "If heaven had made him such another world
> Of one entire and perfect chrysolite,
> He'd not have sold her for it."

"It is very extraordinary," she observed, after explaining the whole matter, "is it not? What on earth can he mean by his boast of having a certain person under his thumb?"

"Oh, servants will talk," said Valentine, who was anxious for Louise to think nothing more of it. "We ought not to examine such matters too closely; it were indeed a most unprofitable task to analyze everything *they* say."

"But whom can he mean by a *certain* person? Surely he cannot mean papa? And yet the way in which papa behaves usually to him, has frequently struck me as being most strange. I cannot endure the creature myself; I never by any chance speak to him; but papa is continually making the man presents. Upon my life I think there is something very mysterious about it."

"Do not distress yourself, my love," said Valentine. "The probability is that the man knew the secret which has just been disclosed, and presumed upon it as such fellows will; but now that the thing is no longer a secret, his power is of course at an end."

"That was it!—no doubt of it. Well,

now it never struck me. I have always thought it singular that he should have been treated with so much consideration; but this accounts for it at once."

"If I were your father I'd kick him out of the house. I'd not have such a fellow about the premises."

"Nor would I; for he is a very idle person, and moves like a sloth, except indeed it be to promote any species of mischief. I'll speak to papa about him. I should like to have the matter cleared up."

"You had better not mention the subject to him at present. It will but annoy him. Let us wait till things are settled."

"Well, perhaps under the circumstances it will be as well to do that. But I do think it very bad conduct, and I am sure it ought not to be concealed from papa."

Valentine now changed the subject, for although he affected to treat the thing lightly before Louise, he felt that the mystery had not yet been solved, and that therefore it was a matter upon which she ought not to be permitted to dwell.

A few days after this, Serjeant Talbot returned to town, and Whitely lost no time in going to consult him. He explained to him how the case stood precisely; every circumstance was mentioned; he kept nothing back, and the result was, that the serjeant, after due consideration, declared that there was no law in existence by which Raven could be reached.

"He is in fact," said he, "shielded by the law. It is his panoply; it affords him the most complete protection. It is of course disgraceful that it should be so; but the law as it at present stands *allows* a man to incarcerate another, however sane, under the plea of insanity. It protects him in the act; no malice can be shown, and if even it could, the signatures of the medical men exonerate him; their certificate is his indemnity, and they are indemnified in turn by the law, which assumes that at the time such certificate was signed, the victim was, in their judgment, insane. For this then you have no redress, and as far as regards the collateral villanies—the seduction of your wife, the disposition of your property, and so on—you are not in a position to adduce a single particle of proof; you have not the slightest evidence to bring forward; not a witness; not a document of any kind to show. My advice to you, therefore, under the circumstances, is to come to an arrangement with this person, and make the best terms you can."

"But is it not," said Whitely, "a duty I owe to society to expose such a villain?"

"It may be; but have you the power to do it? And if you have, can you afford to do it? These are two highly important questions to be considered. An attempt to expose him effectually would in all probability cost five hundred pounds, and if you failed in that attempt, and fail you most assuredly would, you would subject yourself to an action for slander, which would cost you at least five hundred pounds more."

"But can I not compel him to restore, or at least to give me some information respecting my children?"

"No. What if he were to say that he knows nothing of them: how can you prove that he does? Nay, how can you prove that he ever saw those children? You have no such proof: in law, his word of course, would be held to be equal in value with your own."

"But do you not think that if I were to threaten a public exposure in the event of his withholding this information from me, it would have some effect?"

"As a man of the world he would despise such a threat. No; as he appears not to be quite lost to every sense of justice—for clearly if he were he would not have offered the compromise as a sort of reparation—you can stipulate for such information being given: that is to say, you can promise, *provided* it be given, to consent to a private arrangement. But let me, sir, strongly recommend you to avoid mistaking perhaps a natural desire for revenge, for any sense of public duty. They are perfectly distinct, but often confounded, so specious an excuse does the idea of such public duty afford for indulging our most vindictive passions. Men frequently inflict upon themselves irreparable injury by falling into this very error; in your unhappy case this mistake would amount to utter ruin."

Whitely was convinced. He now plainly perceived that Raven was beyond the reach of law, and therefore immediately after his consultation with Serjeant Talbot, he decided upon giving his answer to Uncle John, who had been anxiously waiting his return.

"Well, my friend," said Uncle John, as Whitely entered the room; "have you seen him?"

"Yes," replied Whitely, who appeared to be unusually depressed.

"And what is his opinion?"

"He has proved to me, my friend, that you were right—that I cannot with any degree of safety proceed. I have therefore no alternative: I must consent to an arrangement, provided I receive from him such information as may lead to the recovery of my children."

"All the information he *can* give respecting them you may make up your mind, my friend, to have. I'm quite sure he'll do it. He can now have no motive for withholding it from you. What then shall I propose? Shall I say that in the event of his giving you this information, you will accept the sum he offered?"

"No," replied Whitely; "I will receive nothing from him but that which is my own. I cannot of course tell what my property realized; but as *he* can—for I have not the smallest doubt that he sold it and took the proceeds—let him return to me that which it produced: I require nothing more."

"If he did sell it, as you imagine, he must be a very bad man indeed, and one with whom I should not like to have any dealings. However, as I *have* gone so far I'll not retreat. I'll go to him at once, and depend upon it all that I *can* do to promote your views and interests shall be done."

"Of that I feel convinced, my dear friend," replied Whitely; "I leave the whole matter with the most perfect confidence in your hands."

Uncle John then started; and at about the same time a person called at Raven's house, and having ascertained that he was within, sent up his card with an intimation that he wished to speak privately with him on business of immediate importance.

"Mr. Writall!" said Raven, on looking at the card; "I don't know him. Writall? —Well—let him walk up."

When the servant had departed to fetch Mr. Writall, Raven endeavoured not only to remember the name, but to conceive what this business of importance could be. In both points, however, he failed, and Mr. Writall was formally ushered into the room.

"Mr. Raven, I presume," said Mr. Writall, with all his characteristic pomposity, "I hope, sir, you are well."

"Be seated, sir," said Raven, without replying to this affectionate interrogatory, and Mr. Writall accordingly took a seat, and coughed three times in order that his throat might be clear, and drew out his handkerchief gracefully and wiped his noble brow, and then said,

"Mr. Raven, my object in calling upon you, requires perhaps some little preliminary explanation in order to its being distinctly understood. I am a solicitor, sir, and among my clients I have the honour to number Mr. Whitely, of whom I believe you have some slight knowledge."

Mr. Writall here paused to watch the effect of Whitely's name being mentioned; but Raven, who was reposing in an easy chair, said, "Well, sir?" without displaying the slightest emotion.

"My client, sir," continued Mr. Writall, "having of course entered into that unfortunate affair, to which I need not perhaps more particularly allude, has placed the matter entirely in my hands; but as I find him resolutely bent upon vengeance, and as I make it a point never to promote the purely vindictive views of any of my clients, I have called upon you, conceiving you to be a man of the world, to ascertain whether the thing cannot be arranged, you know, privately between us."

"Has Mr. Whitely authorized you to call?" inquired Raven.

"Decidedly not. No, he has not the most remote idea of my calling."

"Then in plain terms," said Raven, "your object is to sell him?"

"Why—er—not exactly," replied Mr. Writall, who at the moment felt somewhat confused by the prompt way in which this matter-of-fact question was put. "Most decidedly, not exactly."

"Am I to understand," said Raven, pointedly, "that you regard me as a mere man of the world?"

"Most decidedly," replied Mr. Writall.

"Very well, then; the plainer you speak to me the better. Let there be no disguise; no beating about the bush; let everything be perfectly plain and straightforward. What is it you propose?"

"Mr. Raven, you have saved me a world of trouble. I'd rather do business with one man like you, than with fifty who have no idea of the nature of things, and who are laden with scruples, and doubts, and apprehensions. It is pleasurable in the extreme to transact—"

"Well, sir," said Raven, impatiently, "let us come to the point. You have, you say, the management of this affair for Whitely?"

"I have; and he certainly has been—"

"No matter what he has been; that has nothing whatever to do with it. The question is, what proposition have you now to make to me?"

"In a word, then, to be plain, for I find that we perfectly understand each other, I am prepared to undertake—of course for a consideration—either to put him upon the wrong scent, by bringing actions which cannot be maintained, or to induce him to agree to whatever proposition for a private arrangement you may feel disposed to make."

"Is it your impression that any action which may be brought against me *can* be maintained?"

"Why," said Writall, with an air of

mystery, "that is a question which you cannot at present expect me to answer. It would hardly be honest to—"

"In this business," interrupted Raven, "we had better not speak about honesty."

"Well, I agree with you; perhaps it would be better to put that altogether out of view; but you see, as far as I am alone concerned, it would not be quite prudent to explain just at present my own private feelings upon that point."

"I understand you. Nor is it essential that you should. Your disinclination to answer the question is a sufficient proof to me that you do *not* think that any action can succeed."

"Why, I don't know that."

"As a lawyer, you *must* know that no law can touch me!"

"Well, even assuming it to be so, of course you are aware that you are in a position to be seriously annoyed."

"Now you speak! I am quite aware of that, and am anxious to avoid it. I wish to take no advantage of your client; on the contrary, I am willing to give him the sum I proposed, provided he will give me an undertaking that he will let the unhappy affair drop for ever. If you can induce him to do this, you and I may come to terms; if not, why he must take his own course, and the matter as between you and me will be at an end."

"I will undertake at once to induce him to do this."

"You of course have the power?"

"Beyond all dispute."

"Very well. As his legal adviser you *ought* to possess the power to do it; and in the event of its being done, what would you consider a fair remuneration?"

"Why—you see—I can scarcely tell. I'd much rather leave it to your liberality."

"Leave nothing to my liberality. Let us come to terms at once."

"Well, should you—as it's rather an irregular thing—should you consider now, a hundred pounds too much?"

"No; I'll give you a hundred pounds, and the sooner you earn it the better."

"Depend upon it, sir, it shall be done."

"Very well; then set to work immediately, and let me either see you or hear from you as soon as his consent has been obtained."

"That I'll do," said Mr. Writall, and a pause ensued, during which he looked mysteriously at Raven, who at length inquired if anything more need be said?

"Why," replied Mr. Writall, with great deliberation, "of course you are aware that in cases of this kind—I can speak to you because you are quite a man of business, a man of the world, and perfectly understand the nature of things—I therefore say, that of course, you are aware that in all such cases it is usual, you understand, to pay in advance."

"Oh! it *is* usual? Well, I'll not dispute the matter with you. I take it for granted that it is so, for I should say that few men know better than you whether in all *such* cases it be usual or not! But if you imagine that *I* shall pay you in advance for this service, I may as well tell you at once that you are mistaken. You give me credit for being a man of business, a man of the world, and yet you would deal with me as with a natural fool. Were I to pay you in advance, what security should I have that this service will be performed?"

"Oh! I'll undertake to do it!—I pledge you my honour it shall be done!"

"Your honour, Mr. Writall, is a thing to which I should never dream of trusting. You are a great rogue, Writall; you know it, and you evidently hold me to be almost as great a rogue as yourself." Mr. Writall smiled at this, and would have laughed heartily, had not Raven continued: "Let us, therefore, in this business, deal with each other as rogue deals with rogue. When the thing has been done, I'll pay, but not before."

"Well, sir, I like every man to be candid; I admire him who tells me at once what he means; but when you speak of security, what security have *I*, that when I have effected the object the money will be paid?"

"I am always to be found!"

"And so am I! I am always to be found, and you object to trust *me!* Besides, what if you are always to be found? You well know that I could not attempt to recover, were you inclined to be dishonourable, without compromising my reputation as a professional man. No; I'll tell you what, as one of us must trust the other, we had better split the difference thus: you pay me now half the money down, and I'll trust to your honour to pay me the rest when the work has been accomplished. You understand?"

"Oh, perfectly! I *understand!* But it will not do, Writall. I should be sorry to mislead you on any point, and therefore I tell you at once, that it will not do. You are as honest, I have no doubt, as you appear to be: I am quite disposed to go so far as that, although I am bound to admit that that is no great distance. It is, however, as well that you should know this, in order that you may be well assured I shall not pay you until you have accomplished the object proposed."

"Well, sir; that is certainly as it should

be—plain, and much to the purpose. But as you see, I am entirely in your hands, or as it were, at your mercy, what say you to advancing five-and-twenty pounds or so, just to go on with, or rather as an earnest of what you intend to do when I have performed my part of the contract? Surely you cannot with any show of reason object to that?"

"Bring me in writing your client's consent to my proposal, and I'll instantly give you a cheque for the amount; but before that is brought to me I'll not advance a shilling."

"But," urged Writall, who seemed determined not to give the thing up, "do you conceive that to be under the circumstances *quite* fair? You will not trust me to the extent of one quarter of the amount; yet I must trust you to the extent of the whole?"

"Why, surely I am safe for a paltry hundred pounds!"

"Safe, my dear sir! You are safe, I have no doubt, for a hundred thousand! But that has nothing whatever to do with it! I would trust you in the regular way to any amount, because I perfectly well know that I should in that case be able to recover. But you see, this is an altogether different thing! It is not like a regular transaction. It cannot even appear in my books. It depends entirely upon your honour, and if you should—mark, I only say *if* you should—when I have done what is necessary, be indisposed to pay me, I should be utterly unable to compel you to do so, without exposing myself, and thus destroying my reputation, which of course I would not do for a hundred times the amount. So that you see I have no security at all!"

At this moment Uncle John knocked loudly at the door, when Raven, who knew his knock, exclaimed, "That's fortunate!" and rang the bell to desire the servant to show him up. "Here is a friend," he continued, "to whom the whole affair is known. He will be my surety."

"Is he a man upon whom you can depend?" inquired Writall. "You must remember, my character is at stake in this business, and that the most profound secrecy must be observed."

"Fear nothing from him," replied Raven; "I would trust him with my life. Your character is as secure in his hands as it is in mine."

Mr. Writall did not much approve of the idea of introducing a friend; he felt fidgety for the moment, but on being reassured that his secret would be safe, he had just succeeded in calming his apprehensions as Uncle John entered. The very moment, however, he saw him, the expression of his face was at all points peculiar. He recognised in him Whitely's friend at a glance; but as there was no possibility of escape, he bridled himself up, and facing the enemy like a rat in a corner, made up his mind to the worst.

Uncle John bowed distantly as Raven introduced him, and wondered very naturally what had brought him there. He had scarcely however, taken his seat when Raven proceeded to enlighten him on the subject with all possible gravity and effect.

"This gentleman," said he, "who is Mr. Whitely's legal adviser, has called to make a proposition to which I am inclined to accede: not because I am desirous of taking the slightest advantage of Mr. Whitely, but because I consider that man to be his friend who will induce him to consent to a private arrangement instead of foolishly having recourse to law. Mr. Writall has offered to do this, and I am disposed to accept his offer, conceiving it to be the best possible course he can recommend his client to pursue."

Uncle John was surprised. He scarcely knew what to make of it. He looked at Writall and Raven alternately for some few moments, and then exclaimed, "Why, what a shameless man he must be who, while acting as the solicitor for one party, betrays him by offering to meet the views of the other!"

"We are aware," said Mr. Writall, "that this is not a regular transaction."

"A regular transaction! Why you ought to be struck off the rolls!"

"Strike me off! Who's to do it? What can you prove?"

"Are you not rather hasty, my friend?" observed Raven, addressing Uncle John. "This proceeding is dishonourable; Writall knows it to be dishonourable, and were it calculated to injure Mr. Whitely, it should not have my countenance; but as it must tend to his good, don't you think that it would be better to sanction it rather than induce him to resort to law, in which he must of necessity fail?"

"You don't know that man," said Uncle John, "you don't know what he is. Of course you are to pay him for this service?"

"He has offered to do it for a hundred pounds, which sum I have consented to give him."

"You have not yet done so, I hope?"

"No, I have told him that I decidedly object to pay in advance."

"Then he did want the hundred pounds down? Of course!—just what I expected."

"Did you indeed!" said Writall, with a sneer. "Dear me, how very wonderful!

So it was what you expected—eh?—was it?"

"Why what a disreputable man you must be!" said Uncle John. "How disgraceful is your conduct! You have had the audacity to come here for the purpose of robbing this gentleman, when—"

"Rob, sir!—rob! What do you mean?" cried Writall, who finding that it was now all over with him there, felt that the best thing he could do was to brazen it out; "Do you mean to say that *I* wish to rob any man?"

"I do, distinctly," returned Uncle John; "you came here for the express purpose of getting a hundred pounds of Mr. Raven under the pretence of being Whitely's solicitor, when you perfectly well know that you are not."

"You are ——" (this was a very bad expression).

"You infamous man!" cried Uncle John, very indignantly, "how dare you apply such an epithet to me, when I never, to my knowledge, told a falsehood in my life! I say again that you are not his solicitor. He never called upon you but once, and that was when he was accompanied by me, and when you disgusted him by offering to procure false witnesses to prop up the case!"

Again the gross epithet was applied by Mr. Writall, which made Uncle John look remarkably red.

"Did you go with Mr. Whitely to the house of this man?" inquired Raven.

"I did; at his request, he being anxious to prove to me that his intentions were perfectly honourable and straightforward."

"Leave the house!" said Raven, pointing to the door.

"Leave the house!" echoed Writall. "That is rather a cool way of addressing a man."

"Do you wish me to have you thrown into the street?"

"That is still more cool! Thrown into the street! *Very* rich! I should like to see the fellow that could do it!"

"You bad man," said Uncle John, rising. "Do you mean, sir, to leave the house quietly?"

"What if I don't?"

"Why in that case, you impudent person, I must make you."

"Make me! *You* make me! Why that's about the most spicy thing I've heard yet!"

"You would soon be glad to retreat, sir, if my Valentine were here."

"Your Valentine! Who's she? Did she send you anything *very* inflaming on the fourteenth of February, eh?"

"My friend, ring the bell.—Now, sir, do you mean to leave the room?"

Writall placed himself firmly upon the edge of the table and cried "No!—not until I think proper. What do you mean by telling lies about me, you abominable old slanderer?"

Uncle John was now excessively ruffled, and approached him more nearly.

"Touch me!" cried Writall, "only touch me!—lay so much as a finger upon me, and I'll give you a little law. Do it!—now here I am!—do it!—you can't well miss me!—I'm big enough and near enough!—why don't you do it? I only wish you would."

"Now, sir, am I to summon the whole of my servants!" said Raven, as one of them entered.

"Don't distress yourself," said Writall, "I beg. I should be sorry to give a gentleman of your refined feelings the slightest unnecessary trouble; but if you think to intimidate me, sir, you are mistaken. I go, because and solely because I have no wish to remain, but I am not, sir, a man to be intimidated!—of that you may take your oath. Good morning to you, *gentlemen!* Privacy is your object! Oh, everything shall be kept strictly private! The time will come, sir, when you will curse the day on which you insulted *me!*"

Mr. Writall then screwed his thick lips into the best expression of superb contempt of which they were capable, and having frowned at them both with inimitable darkness, stuck his thumbs into the armholes of his waistcoat, and marched with a series of swings from the room.

Uncle John now proceeded to describe the interview which he and Whitely had had with this "limb" of the law, and concluded by stating that he did not feel justified in entering before into this explanation, nor should he have felt justified then, had not Whitely at length consented to a private arrangement.

"Is that a fact?" exclaimed Raven, on hearing this. "Is it a fact?"

"It is. I have just left him. He came to a decision this morning."

"I am very glad to hear it! My friend, I owe you much.—Well how is it to be? What does he propose? What will he consent to?"

"He has authorized me to say that he will consent to receive the sum his property realized, provided you will give him all such information as may lead to the recovery of his children."

Raven paused, but as it immediately struck him that he might betray the feeling by which that pause had been induced, he said, "Well, my friend, and what did his property realize?"

"He cannot tell! He says that of course you know, as the sales were effected by you."

"Effected by me!—Why who could have told him this monstrous falsehood?"

"He received his information from a man who was formerly his servant."

"And where is that scoundrel? Where is he to be found?"

"That Whitely is unable to tell. He saw him but once and desired him to call, but he has not yet done so. He told him distinctly that you—that is to say, he with whom his wife eloped—sold the property and took the proceeds."

"I should like to see that villain. Believe me, my friend, it is a most groundless falsehood. I had nothing whatever to do with it: I knew nothing of it, as I hope for mercy! No, no; I'm bad enough, it is true, but not quite so bad as that."

"Well, I thought that it was *rather*——"

"Rather, sir!—But where were the title deeds at the time?"

"In the hands of his solicitor."

"And where is that solicitor?"

"He is dead."

"He was some such solicitor, I apprehend, as the one who has just left us. Besides, look at the absurdity of the thing! Is it likely that he or any other solicitor would have given those title deeds to me?"

"Why, when I come to look at it, I certainly must say that it does not appear to be probable. It never struck me before, and I am sure that it never struck Whitely. I'll name the point to him: I have no doubt he'll see it at once."

"I hope that he will, for I declare most solemnly that what I have stated is true. But, to the point. What does he consider this property to have been worth?"

"About six thousand pounds."

"Very well. The sum I proposed then will cover the whole. I will give him that sum."

"He will not consent to receive more than the value of his property, I know."

"Then let it be thus settled. He shall have what he considers its value to have been."

"Well, then, the thing is arranged *so* far!—Now about the children."

"On that subject," said Raven, "he must not expect that I can give him the slightest information."

"Ah! That's the grand point. That is the very thing about which he is most anxious. Can you give him *no* clue? The man whom he saw hinted that *he* could obtain information which might lead to their recovery! If he can do so, what a pity it is he has not called, is it not?—Although I must say that after what you have told me, I am inclined to believe that he knows nothing of them."

"What sort of man *was* this? Have you any idea?"

"Not the slightest. Whitely never described him; but I'll get him to do so."

"I wish you would. I should like to know much."

"Then," said Uncle John, "the thing amounts to this: that you will send him a cheque for this sum on his giving you an undertaking that he will trouble you on the subject no more, and that unhappily with respect to the children, you cannot give him the slightest information."

"You see, my friend," said Raven, "it may be supposed that I ought to know all about them; but you are aware that the woman who proves unfaithful to her husband, seldom prides herself much upon her fidelity to another."

"Very true," said Uncle John. "Very true."

"The subject, of course, is painful for me to enter into; but I have stated enough for you to understand all."

"I see, I see! Well! You cannot do impossibilities, and therefore this must be no bar to an arrangement. I should have been far more pleased if you could have given this information, but as you cannot, why you cannot, and nothing more can be said. I'll go back to him at once and explain all you have stated, for the sooner the thing is settled now the better, and as he is not an unreasonable man, I hope to be able to bring you his written undertaking in the course of the day."

"Do so, my friend, and he shall at once have the cheque. I cannot sufficiently express to you how much I feel obliged—"

"Not a word, not a word," said Uncle John, who then left in the full conviction that Raven's answers had been ingenuous, although a man more prone to suspicion would have perceived that, as far as the children were concerned, those answers evinced studied prevarication.

CHAPTER LXII.

EXPLAINS A VARIETY OF MATTERS OF IMPORTANCE TO THE PARTIES CONCERNED.

Llewellen, a few days after he accompanied Valentine to Ascot, relapsed into wretchedness; and as his appetite again most signally failed, he began to suspect that he was somewhat consumptive—a suspicion which was to a lamentable extent confirmed, on reading a highly popular work upon consumption, which induced him to feel the very symptoms described.

Under these unhappy circumstances he took to writing poetry, and in the short space of two days did really succeed in composing the burden of a song, which he sang aloud from morning till night for inspiration, thus—

Peautiful peer,
Peautiful peer,
There's no trink in Nature like peautiful peer!

But having miraculously accomplished the burden, he was utterly unable to do any more. The rhymes puzzled him frightfully. They wouldn't come. Let him drink what he might, or pull his shirt collar down ever so low, he couldn't get them; and hence, having gone through a whole quire of paper without any, even the most remote prospect of success, he gave the thing up in a fit of despair, and took to beauing out Valentine's mother.

Nor was this at all amazing. He had no one else to go out with!—and certain it is that no one else could have appreciated his politeness more highly; for he had always been a most especial favourite of the widow: she had always esteemed him a well-behaved good-hearted creature, and therefore did not at all disapprove of his practice of taking her about: in point of fact she rather liked it than not! And so did Valentine; and so did Louise; for although Louise loved the widow dearly, while Valentine possessed a strong feeling of friendship for Llewellen, in the view of the lovers their presence was not at all times agreeable, and more particularly now that Valentine, in order to raise the spirits of Louise, walked out with her daily.

Now it happened that on the morning on which Writall had an interview with Raven Llewellen and the widow went to see the industrious fleas, and they had no sooner started than Louise and Valentine left the house with the view of having their customary walk in the Park. On their way, however, the attention of Louise was attracted to the window of a linen draper's shop, in which was displayed a peculiar style of shawl which she admired very much.

"Dear me," she exclaimed, "how exceedingly elegant! I should so like to look at it! Would you mind going in with me?"

"Oh! not at all," replied Valentine, and they accordingly entered, and were instantly addressed in the most obsequious style by an extraordinary individual, the business of whose valuable life seemed to consist in walking up and down the shop, with great presence of mind, placing chairs for those who entered, with infinite grace, and calling "Forward!" in a highly authoritative tone, and with an expression which obviously signified something.

"What can we have the pleasure?" said this remarkable being, addressing Louise with a most winning smile.

Louise briefly explained, and when the elegant creature had placed her a chair with all the tranquil fascination at his command, he cried "Forward!" as if he had been addressing some dog that had had the unhappiness to introduce himself clandestinely among the silks.

In an instant an exquisitely dressed young man—who had clearly been used to this style of address, for he did not throw anything at the head of the individual, nor did he appear to think a very great deal about it—approached Louise with characteristic politeness, and having ascertained what it was she wished to see, he produced it with all imaginable alacrity, and displayed it to the best advantage possible.

While Louise was listening to the voice of the charmer, who spake eloquently, blandly, and with much poetic feeling of the innumerable beauties which peculiarly characterized this unparalleled article, Valentine was watching the conduct of the individual who walked the shop, with some interest, for he had never before seen the tyrant and the slave by any one man so conspicuously developed. To those who entered he was the cringing, smirking eel-backed creature; but to all over whom he presided, he was the tyrannous, scowling despotic bully: he would crawl and lick the dust from the feet of the former, and the next moment frown down and trample upon the latter.

"Allow me," said he, addressing a customer who was leaving, "allow me to

Mr. Todd attracts Valentines attention.

P. 341.

have the happiness of sending that small parcel? I beg that you will. I will do so with infinite pleasure!"

The customer declined, and was bowed out with the utmost humility by the creature, who immediately walked up to him by whom she had been attended, and demanded to know why he had not sold her a dress.

"The lady didn't want one," replied the young man, and Valentine thought this a very good reason, substantial, conclusive, and perfectly sound, but diametrically opposed to this view was the creature. "Not want one!" he cried, as if no reason could have been more dead and rotten. "Do I keep you to sell merely what people want! Any fool, any idiot, can do that! I expect you to serve them with what they don't want, sir!—that, sir, is what I keep you for!" and he scowled with great ferocity at the delinquent, who never raised his eyes, but having rolled up some material that was before him, walked silently away.

"Why," what kind of men can these be," thought Valentine, "who thus endure the degrading tyranny of so pitiful a slave? Have they neither soul nor sense? What can they be made of? They seem to have been decently educated; they talk very well, although they dress very absurdly, and have some of the most remarkable heads of hair tonsorial art ever designed; but they cannot possess a particle of manly spirit, they cannot have the independent feelings of honest men, or they never could bear to be thus tyrannized over and treated like convicts!"

"Why don't you show the six quarters, sir, do you hear?" cried the creature, addressing one of his slaves, for he clearly conceived it to be much to his own interest to degrade his young men in the eyes of those whom they were serving.

"It strikes me that I must have a word with you," thought Valentine, who was really disgusted with the fellow's behaviour; and he had no sooner satisfied himself that the pursuit of such a course would not be at all incorrect, than throwing his voice behind him some distance, he said, "Who is that ridiculous person in the middle of the shop?"

The person alluded to turned with great promptitude and frowned. *Ridiculous* person above all things in the world! He didn't like it. In the spot from which the voice appeared to proceed there happened not to be a soul, which puzzled him a little, but he notwithstanding walked up the shop with great dignity, and glanced at each customer as he passed with suspicion.

"Is that the proprietor?" inquired Valentine of the young man who was waiting upon Louise.

"Yes, sir, one of them: that is Mr. Todd."

Valentine waited the return of Mr. Todd, whose nerves seemed seriously unsettled, and when he did return, he occupied his mind with the adjustment of his neckerchief and hair, during the progress of his fingers through which latter ornament Valentine shouted "Here, Todd!"

"Mr. Todd looked contemptuously round. The idea of being addressed as "Todd" struck him as being extremely vulgar. "*Mr.* Todd" would have commanded his immediate attention, but it appeared to be a settled principle with him that plain "Todd" should not.

"I say, Toddy, my boy! how are you?" cried Valentine; and Mr. Todd looked round again with an aspect of intense magnanimity. Whom could it possibly be! There were but two gentlemen in the shop!—Valentine, whom of course he could not suspect, seeing that he was close to his side, and another, who was perched upon a stool at the end. He therefore concluded that it must have been the gentleman on the stool, and conceiving that he might be some person of importance, he approached him. But no: that gentleman took not the slightest notice of his approach: nor did he appear to be a person at all likely to address any man with any undue familarity. Besides, his voice was so strikingly different!—it could not have been him; and as such was the case, Mr. Todd at once conceived the horrid notion that it must have been one of the young men.

"Who was that?" he demanded, with a withering glance, and the young man addressed declared promptly, upon his honour, he didn't know.

"Don't tell me you don't know," said Mr. Todd, "you must know—it was one of you!"

Again the young man, with considerable earnestness, protested his ignorance of the matter, but Mr. Todd would not believe him, he was sure that he did know, and having announced that be the delinquent whomsoever he might, he should "start" on conviction, he returned to his station near the door.

Valentine, assuming the voice of a female, now made a dead set at one of the slaves. "How dare you!" he exclaimed, "you insolent fellow! I'll tell Mr. Todd, sir, I'll tell Mr. Todd!" and the voice was so loud and so shrill, that every eye was directed at once towards the spot from which it appeared to proceed.

Mr. Todd was there in an instant, and looked right and left with indefatigable zeal, and perspired at the idea of being able to make nothing of it. He could perceive no lady in a rage! They all appeared to be perfectly tranquil. What could be the meaning of it! It was quite clear to him that one of them *had* been insulted. Could she have been pacified on his approach? In his view nothing could be more probable, and he therefore went round and inquired of them if anything unpleasant had occurred, but as they all declared that nothing of the kind had, he could not but deem it remarkably strange.

"Did you not hear some lady complain of insolence?" he inquired of one of the slaves, who having nothing else to do, was endeavouring to ascertain how long it was possible for a man to be smoothing a piece of coloured muslin.

"Why," replied the individual who was engaged in this experiment, "it struck me that I did."

"Just give a look out then: there's something wrong somewhere."

"Mr. Todd," said Valentine, in an assumed voice, of course.

"Well, sir!" cried Todd, with great sharpness.

"Mr. Todd," repeated Valentine.

"Well! what do you want?"

"Have the goodness to step here for one moment."

Mr. Todd marched to the point to which the voice had been thrown, and said, "Now, sir! what is it?" to the first whom he approached, but as this person intimated boldly that *he* had not called, Mr. Todd very naturally wished to know who had.

"Mr. Todd!—Mr. Todd!—Mr. Todd!" cried Valentine, in three distinct voices, and making them apparently proceed from three different points.

"What is the meaning of this?" cried Todd, on looking round, for he began to feel very indignant. "Who called me?"

"Mr. Todd," repeated Valentine, in a very calm tone.

"Come here, sir, if you want me! come here, I desire!"

Valentine now introduced a very highly effective laugh; indeed, so effective was it, that he was joined by almost every person present, to the utter annihilation of Mr. Todd's tranquillity of spirit.

"What are you laughing at, sir?" he demanded of the slave who stood near him.

"Nothing, sir, nothing," was the prompt reply.

"Do you always laugh at nothing? I desire to know instantly why you were laughing?"

"I don't know, sir. I laughed because the rest laughed—for no other cause."

"If you cannot conduct yourself properly, sir, you had better make out your account."

Here Valentine burst forth again, and was again joined with spirit. The customers gave full swing to their mirth, having nothing whatever to fear, but the people behind the counter laughed only at intervals: when the awful eye of Todd was upon them, each seemed to have his mouth quite full of a laugh, which was struggling to burst his lips asunder.

In the midst of this general joy, Todd stood with a dignified frown. Why they were laughing he could not pretend to tell, but as every eye seemed to be upon him, he was suddenly struck with an idea that they were actually laughing at him, and as in his judgment this could be possible only in the event of something being very wrong in his dress, he put it plainly to Mr. Jubbins, his partner, whether such were the fact, and although Mr. Jubbins declared solemnly that *he* could see nothing, so firmly had the idea taken possession of Todd's soul that there must be of necessity something incorrect, that he quitted the shop with the air of a man quite resolved on having prompt satisfaction.

Mr. Jubbins now performed Todd's duty of looking as fascinating as possible in the middle of the shop. He was a better looking fellow altogether than Todd, and if possible more highly dressed, but his manners were precisely the same.

"You seem to be merry here," said Valentine, as Jubbins approached him.

"Yes, very, very, very!" replied Mr. Jubbins. "It's a mystery to me: it passes my comprehension altogether. I cannot make it out. It's excessively odd. By the by, sir, we have just received fifty thousand pounds worth of superb cambric handkerchiefs, the immense superiority of which over the French is universally acknowledged, and which we are now selling at a sacrifice truly alarming. Allow me to have the pleasure of introducing them to your notice.—Mr. Higginbottom, where are those handkerchiefs?"

"Which, sir?"

"Which? Have you lived all these years and ask me which? Why the P'ses Q's of course, sir!—Which should I mean?"

This seemed to be conclusive, for Mr. Higginbottom immediately produced the P'ses Q's, which Jubbins submitted to Valentine's inspection.

"This, sir," said he, "is the most elegant lot imaginable, and dirt cheap, sir!—two and eleven pence three farthings."

"They appear to be cheap," said Valentine, "but I am ignorant of the value of these things."

"The value, sir, is seven and nine. Had they been purchased in the regular way, sir, I couldn't have sold one for less, but having picked the whole from a bankrupt's stock, we are enabled to put them in frightfully low. The size, sir, is alarming for the price, while the texture is magnificently delicate!—Allow me to say a dozen?"

"I have plenty at present," said Valentine.

"Were you to purchase them to put by, sir, they would pay you good interest for your money."

"I have not a doubt of its being a splendid investment," said Valentine, "but unhappily at present my capital is tied up."

Mr. Jubbins smiled sweetly, and said, "But, upon honour, I hold this to be an opportunity which seldom presents itself: in point of fact I don't know that we are not running counter to our interest in pushing them; but let me say a dozen? *Half* a dozen? I assure you they are an article seldom to be met with. It is a sacrifice of upwards of seventy per cent., which is very distressing."

"So it is: so it is:" said Valentine. "Did the person of whom you bought them fail for much?"

"About forty thousand pounds."

"That is rather a large sum for a man to fail for, especially as he had about fifty thousand pounds worth of cambric handkerchiefs in stock. What do you suppose the value of the *entire* stock to have been when he failed?"

"Why," replied Mr. Jubbins, who did feel a *little* confused, for he happened to remember that he had purchased the fifty thousand pounds worth, "I scarcely can tell. It is difficult to form a judgment, very difficult, very."

"Of course he will be able to pay a very decent dividend?"

"Yes, a very fair dividend, I should say, I've no doubt of it, very.—Then you'll not allow me to tempt you with a dozen?"

"No, I think not to-day."

"Anything in Irish linens or gloves of any kind?"

"No, they never allow me to purchase those things: they imagine I am not to be trusted."

Again Jubbins smiled; but as he understood the state of the case precisely, he said nothing more about the matter.

"Well, now I have indeed tried your patience," said Louise. "Dear me, what a quantity of things I have purchased! There now," she added, addressing the clever creature by whom she had been tempted to spend twenty pounds, although she had no idea of purchasing anything but the shawl, "you must show me nothing more: you really must not, indeed."

"Has the lady seen those satins, sir?" inquired Mr. Jubbins, with a scowl.

"I connot look at anything else," said Louise; "no! let me have my bill as soon as possible, or you can send it with the parcel, any time after four."

Louise then presented her card; and after observing to Valentine, that she was sure that he had lost all patience, they were bowed out of the shop most gracefully by Mr. Jubbins, who, notwithstanding all the young man had done, was exceedingly angry with him, because he had not introduced "those satins."

"What singular creatures they are!" observed Valentine, on leaving the shop.

"They are, indeed," returned Louise; "and their politeness is so excessive, that you positively feel yourself in a measure bound to purchase the things they introduce to you, whether you really want them or not."

"But while admiring their politeness, did you notice the brutal conduct of those tyrannous, slave-driving dogs, their employers?"

"Oh yes! that is generally conspicuous. But what I object to most is, their interference with him who is serving me. That is very annoying, and whenever it occurs, I have done: no matter how many articles I may want, I take those which I have purchased, but will have nothing more."

They now proceeded to the park, and had a most delightful walk; and while sitting beneath their favourite tree, Llewellen and the widow unexpectedly approached them.

"Hur knew we shoot fint them," cried Llewellen; "titn't hur tell you they were sure to pe here? Oh, Louey! such peautiful fleas! Trest, ant armt, ant mountet on horse-pack like Christians. Oh! too co ant see 'em apove all things in the worlt!"

"What sort of horses are they?" inquired Valentine. "Fine cattle, Fred?"

"Horses? Fleas!—every horse is a flea, look you, pritled ant sattled ant all!"

"We must go and see these warriors on flea-back!" said Valentine to Louise.

"Do, by all means, my love," said the widow; "they are wonderful creatures!—such active, intelligent little dears. I'm quite in love with them really! Do go there this evening: I should so like to see them again."

"This evening!" said Llewellen, looking archly at the widow; "have you forgotten your engagement this evening?"

"The promenade concerts!" cried the widow; "dear me, how very stupid! Oh! is not that kind of Mr. Llewellen? He is going to take me to the promenade concerts!"

"Upon my life! Master Fred," observed Valentine, "if you continue to go on in this way winning the heart of my mother, I shall feel myself bound to demand an explanation of your intentions!"

The widow blushed, and patted Valentine playfully on the cheek, and Llewellen informed him that all had been settled, and that he was therefore quite ready to explain, which was very agreeable and highly enjoyed.

"At all events," said Valentine, addressing Louise, "it will be our duty to accompany them to the concert this evening."

"Too co, py all means!" said Llewellen, and as this invitation was backed by the widow strongly, it was decided that they should all go together.

While they were thus happily engaged, Uncle John was endeavouring to prevail upon Whitely to allow the assumed impossibility of Raven giving the required information about the children, to form no barrier to an immediate settlement. He had already succeeded in convincing him that Raven had had nothing to do with his property; but he found it extremely difficult to induce him to believe that he knew nothing whatever of his children.

"The only thing," urged Whitely, "which tends to justify such a belief is the assumed fact, that she became so abandoned as to leave even him for another: but even in that case it seems scarcely probable that being lost, as she must have been, to every sense of decency, as well as to every proper feeling, that she would have taken the children with her."

"Why, I don't know that," said Uncle John. "It is very clear to me that her affection for those children was very strong: my firm impression is, that had it not been, she would not have clung to them so tenaciously when she left you; and as it is but natural to suppose that, as they grew older and more engaging, the strength of that affection increased, I am inclined to believe it to be extremely probable that she did take them with her; for clearly if her affection for them *did* thus increase, she would have been less disposed to part with them then than before."

"Very true; very true: but this is merely assumption."

"I grant it: but it is a very natural assumption. Besides, what motive could he possibly have in withholding this information, if he really possessed the power to give it? Upon my life! I cannot conceive what motive he could have. He can scarcely be supposed to have cared much about them, and if he had provided for them, he would surely be proud to let you know it, in order that you might not deem him quite so depraved as you do. But even assuming that he could give you such information as might lead to their recovery, his refusal to do so, ought not to prevent an immediate arrangement, at least in so far as pecuniary matters are concerned; but feeling as I do, quite convinced that he is utterly unable to do so, I cannot see why you should hesitate for a moment."

"Well, my friend, if I give him an undertaking to annoy him, as he terms it, no more, it must be with this proviso, that if I should at any time discover that he absolutely does know where they are to be found, I am not to be precluded from demanding of him such information as may be essential to their being restored."

"Most decidedly. You will still have the right to do so. I look at the spirit of this arrangement. You agree to it on the assumption that he does not know where the children are: should you at any time discover that he *does*, your right, with reference to them will, of course, stand the same as if no such arrangement had been made."

"Very well. Let this be, on all hands, distinctly understood, and I am ready to sign the undertaking."

Uncle John now opened his desk, and they began to draw out an agreement, but how to introduce the proviso, without leading Raven to suppose that they believed him to have told a direct falsehood, was a task which puzzled them exceedingly. In the first place they drew up a "sketch"—which of itself would have done very well—and then their labour commenced; but they stuck to it zealously, amending and erasing, until their interlineations stood perfectly unincumbered by a single word of the original, when, on being summoned to dinner, they left it thus, to be tackled again when they had done.

Whitely was by no means scrupulous about the matter: he was an advocate for its being done as plainly as possible; but Uncle John, judging from the sensitive character of his own feelings, contended for the correctness of its being done with so much delicacy, that while it had the force of a law, not a word should be introduced at all calculated to inflict the slightest wound upon the feelings of him whom it bound.

On this, as on all other occasions, Whitely wished to meet the views of Uncle John, and immediately after dinner they again set to work, and did eventually succeed in accomplishing their task in every point to their entire satisfaction. Two fair copies were then drawn up, and when both had been signed by Whitely, Uncle John left in order to obtain the signature of Raven.

The party which had been formed in the morning for the concert, prepared to start soon after dinner, and Uncle John happened to arrive in great spirits at the moment they were about to leave the house.

"Any news?" inquired Valentine.

"Yes, my boy; good news; come here," said Uncle John, taking his arm and leading him into the parlour.

"Please let me come, too?" said Louise.

"May she come, Val? Well! yes you may. But I mean to set a price upon the information I have to impart. I intend to have a kiss for it."

"Oh! that you shall. I will pay you with pleasure! What is it?"

"All's settled!" exclaimed Uncle John; "All's settled."

"Bless you!" cried Louise. "You deserve two for that. But are you sure?—quite?"

"I have the agreement now in my pocket, with Whitely's signature attached."

"Well this is indeed great news. Oh! I feel *so* delighted!"

"Of course," said Valentine, "Mr. Ravan knows nothing of it yet."

"He expects it, and I have come as soon as possible to put an end to his suspense. But where are you all going?"

"To the promenade concert."

"Very well, let your minds be at ease. Now, be happy both of you: there, run away. I must be detained no longer."

Valentine and Louise shook him warmly by the hand, and having kissed each other fervently, they rejoined the widow and Llewellen, and proceeded to the theatre in which the concerts were held.

As they entered one of the boxes the first piece was being performed, and the action of the conductor was so extremely striking, that he riveted their attention at once. He was a small man and singularly thin: his cheeks were hollow, but his eyes were full, and while at certain forte passages they appeared to be anxious to start from their sockets, he closed them at each piano phrase, with the view of conveying to the performers an idea of how mild were the moon beams contrasted with thunder. The performers, however, seemed not to take the slightest notice of his eloquent gestures, for they worked away like blacksmiths, with their eyes fixed firmly upon the music, with the single exception of the individual who did the drums; and even he, having thirty or forty bars' rest, seemed to be counting his *one* two three four, *two* two three four, *three* two three four, up, with extreme depth of thought.

Having sufficiently admired the poetic action of the conductor—who, had the whole of the instruments been mute, could have rendered the thing, by virtue of his pantomime, effective, so distinctly and so delicately was each phrase expressed—the happy party left their box for the promenade.

The place was crowded, but to the majority the music was but a secondary consideration, which indeed is invariably the case in England, and speculators generally would do well to understand that patronage here is extended, not in proportion to the excellence of an entertainment, but precisely in proportion to the facilities which it affords for the display of wealth, fashion, and beauty.

On this occasion the display of these three attractive articles was in a measure magnificent, but if any one could be said to surpass the others, it was fashion. The dresses both of the ladies and of the gentlemen had been made in conformity with the most extraordinary conceptions, while the hair was so arranged—if an arrangement, as far as the gentlemen were concerned, it could be called—that it covered the ears as completely as if, at that particular period of British history, it had been no uncommon thing for those useful and ornamental organs to be nailed, for political offences, to posts.

As the space behind the orchestra was the only spot which could be promenaded with comfort, thither Valentine and Louise repaired, and walked for some time in silence, but with feelings of pleasure, listening attentively to the various pieces which were admirably performed, and which seemed to inspire general delight.

"Valentine," said Louise, at length, "why are you so silent?"

"I apprehend it is because I am so happy!"

"Are you happy? Well so am I: very, very happy: I could cry I am so happy. And I shall cry, I am sure of it, unless you make me laugh. Now do, there's a dear, put some poor unfortunate person in a fever. You will, to please me; will you not?"

"Oh! I had better astonish the whole house at once!"

"But you must not startle me! You know that is a thing which is perfectly understood."

"Of course! I am sure you will be an excellent wife, Louise: you are so fond of looking at home! But listen."

At this moment the band was playing a set of quadrilles, in which an echo was introduced by dint of establishing an individual in the one shilling gallery to do the refrain out of sight. This had a good effect, and on its being repeated, Valentine sent an echo into the slips, and then one into the upper boxes, and then one into the dress circle near the proscenium, and then another, most dexterously, into the chandelier! This of course produced several rounds of applause, and the demand for an encore was universal; but the conductor stood struck with amazement: he could not even guess what it could mean, and his first impulse was to send round to the various parts of the house from which the sounds had apparently proceeded, with the view of setting his face against every echo save the one which he himself had established. On turning the matter again over in his mind, however, he could not—as the thing was effective and had brought down thunders of applause—see why it should not be repeated. He therefore gave the usual signal, and the band recommenced, and when he came to the echo, he listened with a peculiar expression for the invisible auxiliaries; but what was his dismay when Valentine, instead of following the established orthodox echo, introduced, in various parts of the house, snatches of popular tunes, and thus produced fits of laughter! "Ha!" said he gutturally, grinning like a griffin in great anguish, and holding his ears as if a couple of wasps had introduced themselves clandestiuely therein—"*Perdu!*" whereupon the whole house was in a roar.

"Bravo! bravo!" shouted the audience. "Encore! encore! encore!"

"Not if I knew it," the conductor seemed to say confidentially to himself, for he looked very droll, and almost buried his head between his shoulders; but although his indisposition to repeat the thing was manifest; although it was evident generally that he wished to intimate that he had had no hand in the matter, the enlightened audience still continued to demand an encore, which, to his own private feelings, was very afflicting. He sent an emissary up to the slips, and another into the upper tier of boxes; and while he planted sundry confidential fiddlers as spies upon the dress circle, he himself strained his eyes with the bright and lovely hope of discovering one of the individuals among the multitude of promenaders. In this he was, however, unsuccessful; and as the audience still remorselessly demanded an encore, he did, in his extremity, shake his head with much significance, and having given the signal, the band made a dash at the next piece.

This silenced the majority at once, and they would with due patience have waited for a repetition of the novel echo, had not the minority, who, having somewhat more refined and experienced ears, on perceiving that this was not the same piece, shouted "No, no!—Encore! encore—No, no, no, no!" which had the effect of inducing the whole house to join them.

The band notwithstanding kept on. The conductor was firm. He would have no more *ad libitum* echoes: he had already had quite enough of *them*, and hence resolved within his own mind that, come what might, he would go through the piece then in hand as completely as if nothing whatever had happened.

The audience, fortunately for him, were in an excellent humour: they had enjoyed the echoes much, and that they did wish to have them again is a fact which ought not to be disputed, but when they saw the distress of the conductor, who was an accomplished, and withal a very amiable man, they pitied him as an individual, and soon became calm.

"Dear me!" said Louise, when the storm had subsided, "how very, very cleverly that was done, to be sure! Poor man!—what odd faces he made!"

"They were rather droll," said Valentine. "I wonder what he thinks of it. I should like to know his strictly secret feelings upon the point."

The band ceased: the first part was concluded, and shortly after, a small thin man, in an old hat, came close to the spot with several persons whom he knew. He seemed powerfully excited, and looked very fierce, and said in answer to a question which touched upon the echo, "Sare, I sall give you five pounce with great pleasir for to *dis*covare sem tam peple."

"They ought," said one of his friends, "to have their instruments taken from them and broken about their heads."

"Instrumence!—say vas ton wisout instrumence! Say teed him wis sare mouse, and pe tam!"

This caused Louise to laugh so immoderately, that Valentine was compelled to remove her from the spot, and when the conductor had given sufficient vent to those feelings of indignation which were plainly effervescing within him, he gave one desperate shrug, which seemed perfectly conclusive, and then left the inquiring group to cool himself with an ice.

"My poy," said Llewellen, on coming up with the widow, after a very long absence, "Teet you hear that wonterful echo?"

"The whole house heard it, I apprehend," replied Valentine. "There is a numerous family of the Echoes it appears. They are all relatives, you will remember, of your invisible wife."

"His invisible wife!" cried the widow; "has Mr. Llewellen an invisible wife?"

"Yes, the mother of the whole family. She became enamoured of him in the garden, and would have him."

The widow, who now saw it all, exclaimed, "Gracious, my dear, and was that really you?"

Louise instantly placed her finger upon her lips to enjoin silence; but Llewellen, who was struck with the singularity of the question, had a very strong desire to know what it meant.

"There is some creat secret apout this,—some extraortinary secret.--Too tell me phot it is?—Pless your soul, too?—Inteet hur shoot like to pe tolt, cootness knows it!"

"What secret do you allude to?" inquired the widow.

"Hur ton't know inteet then; putt ——"

"This is not a place for telling secrets," said Valentine. "Come, come, let us go in and have some refreshment."

"Apove all things in the worlt!" cried Llewellen. "Oh! that is the pusiness.—Phot have they cot?"

"We shall see by the carte," said Valentine.

"Well, my poy, you order all: hur'm font, you know, of anything in the worlt."

"Order ices," whispered Louise, "and let us see how Fred will like them. We have had none at home since he came up, and I dont't think they ever gave him any in Wales."

Ices were accordingly ordered: and when Llewellen took his, he looked at it for some time studiously.

"It's a mighty little trifle," said he, at length. "Cootness knows it." And having taken the whole of it up with the spoon, he put it bodily into his mouth. It was, however, no sooner in than out. He shuddered, and dropped it without a second thought.

"Is it too hot for you?" said Valentine, gravely, although Louise and the widow were convulsed.

"Hot!" cried Llewellen. "It makes me shiver to think of it!—*Cruel* cold!—My whole potty's freezing, look you!—*Ant* my teeth!—Oh!"

"Did you never have an ice before?"

"No, never,—cootness knows: ant hur never wish to have one again."

"Well, what will you have?"

"Any thing in the whole worlt putt that."

"Well, as I have been so unfortunate, I must leave you now to order for yourself.—There is the *garçon*."

"*Phot's* his name?" inquired Llewellen.

"Upon my word I don't know.—You had better call 'Waiter.'"

Llewellen did so; and a foreign individual, whose mind seemed to be intently fixed upon something, approached him.

"Waiter," said Llewellen, in a confidential tone, "have you cot any peer?"

The foreign individual dropped his head upon his right shoulder, and shrugged up his left, but said nothing.

"Not coot?" said Llewellen, who misunderstood altogether what the action of the Frenchman was designed to convey. "Is it not coot in pottles?"

The Frenchman employed the same gesture as before, with this addition: he extended his chin, which was naturally a long one, and looked most intensely mysterious.

"This is a very honest fellow," thought Llewellen. "It isn't often one meets with a man who will refuse to sell an article which is not quite the thing to a stranger.—Well," said he, "never mint.—You're a coot fellow to tell me, for hur hate pat peer apove all things in the worlt; putt let me have some pranty-and-water, look you; warm."

The Frenchman again gave a national shrug.

"Phot!" said Llewellen, "is that pat too?—Cootness knows it!"

"Ve sal vas, monsieur," said the waiter, who prided himself especially upon the purity of his English. "Ve sal nevere is eau de vie non monsieur."

"Phot to you say?" inquired Llewellen, as Valentine, Louise and the widow were laughing convulsively. "Come, let's have it at once."

"Mais I sal vos non comprendre a tall vous."

"Yes," said Llewellen, "hur'll pe pount it's all right, olt poy, so you'd petter run away, now, ant fetch it." And as he waved his hand precisely as if he wished him to be off, the puzzled Frenchman took the hint at once, and started.

"Well," said Llewellen, addressing Valentine, "I shall pe all right at last."

"What have you ordered?"

"Some peautiful pranty-ant-water, look you! ant cootness knows it!"

"He'll bring you no brandy-and-water."

"Inteet then hur'll wring his plesset neck, if he ton't."

"If he brings you anything, he'll bring you an ice."

"An ice!—Oh! it freezes my plut!"

"If he don't bring you that, he'll bring nothing."

"Phy, hur ortert it, look you!"

"And he told you, as plainly as he could,

that they hadn't got it; and you sent him away."

"Oh, hur'll see apout that," said Llewellen. "Here, waiter!"

"Garçon!" cried Valentine, throwing his voice a short distance from him."

"Oui, monsieur."

"Garçon!—Garçon!—Garçon!" cried Valentine, at appropriate intervals, and in three distinct tones.

"Oui, monsieur, oui!" cried the Frenchman, who seemed in some measure perplexed.

"If hur ton't make an effort, my poy," said Llewellen, "hur shall not, hur see, pe aple to get anything, look you!—Phot am hur to orter?"

"Why, as you want something warm, ask him why he has not brought the *glace*. Tell him you want a *glace*, distinctly, and then he'll understand you."

"There's a coot fellow," said Llewellen. "Now! waiter!"

"Oui, monsieur?"

"Come, come, you have not brought my glass!—There, never mind making those faces:—hur prefer pranty-ant-water; put pring me a glass of anything, no matter what, if it's putt a coot *glass*."

The Frenchman bowed, and looked as if he saw his way now pretty clearly, which rather delighted Llewellen, who, when he had left, said: "Well, hur *have* mate him understant me at last."

"I'm glad of it," said Valentine. "But if he should make a mistake, you had better tell him what you mean in Welsh."

The Frenchman now returned with a strawberry ice, which he presented with characteristic grace to Llewellen. Llewellen looked at it!—he knew what it was in a moment!—and then he looked at the Frenchman. His blood was a little up: he felt indeed very angry, and proceeded to explain, with due severity of aspect, the precise state of his feelings in Welsh to the Frenchman, who was perfectly amazed, and on perceiving that Llewellen was very indignant, he let loose in French, and thus made a duet of it, which was interesting, because highly calculated to bring about a good understanding between them.

Valentine, however, when he fancied that the thing had gone quite far enough—for Llewellen was turning very red, while the Frenchman was grinning and gnashing his teeth fiercely—shouted "Garçon!—garçon!—garçon!" when the Frenchman, hearing himself thus imperatively called, screwed up his lips, and with a ferocious look of scorn, left the spot much excited.

"Tit you ever in all your porn tays," said Llewellen, "hear anypotty chatter like that little wretch?"

"I was afraid you would come to blows," said Valentine.

"Plows! hur coot eat him, cootness knows it."

"You are always getting into some scrape," said Louise.

"Well, Louey, it wasn't my fault. Phen a fellow prings an ice for warm pranty-and-water, it's enough to make a man's plut poil."

"It's too bad," said the widow, who sympathized with Llewellen; "it is indeed," and she looked at the carte, and then consulted a female attendant, and in a short time some *ponch à la Romaine* was produced, which she presented to Llewellen, who, having tasted it, was in ecstasies, and called her an angel.

"Now," said Valentine, when Llewellen had finished his punch, which he indeed highly relished, "a little more music, and then we'll return."

Llewellen, who was blessed with a most happy disposition, had now forgotten all his troubles, and on their return to the body of the theatre, he chatted and laughed in the merriest mood, and enjoyed the scene perhaps much more than any other person present. The pleasure which Louise felt was probably of itself not less pure, but its brightness was occasionally dimmed by thought, which was perfectly absent from the mind of Llewellen. Could she hope to be always as happy? Should she always experience in Valentine's society the same degree of pleasure? Would he always be the same kind, good, dear creature—always as anxious to inspire her with delight? These were questions which would suggest themselves constantly; for although she had no reason to suppose that he would ever change; although she tried on all occasions to repudiate the notion; she was still apprehensive, because, and solely because, she neither knew nor could conceive more perfect pleasure than that which she invariably experienced when with him. Her fears on this subject, however, were vain. Valentine was always himself. He never thought of assuming another character: he never desired to make himself appear to be that which he really was not. This, of course, it was impossible for her to know; and as she thought on the subject most, when she felt most happy, she, on this occasion, while clinging fondly to him, gazed occasionally upon him with an aspect of sadness.

"My poor girl," said he, "are you fatigued?"

"Oh, no; not at all."

"You look so sad!"

"I am so happy," said Louise, and as she spoke, a tear glistened in her eye.

They now went in search of Llewellen and the widow, who were perfectly certain to go astray the very moment the attention of Valentine happened to be directed to some other quarter, and having eventually discovered them engaged in a close examination of certain plants which were placed round a fountain, Valentine gave them the word of command, and they followed him and Louise out with all due obedience.

They then entered a coach, and at once proceeded home, and it may be said, that no party was ever more happy. They were on the highest possible terms with themselves and each other, and it is not quite certain that both Louise and the widow did not, on their way home, shed tears of joy.

The very moment they arrived at the house, Louise, as usual, inquired for her father, and on being informed that he was still where she had left him, and that it was supposed that he was asleep, as they had heard nothing of him for more than two hours, she ran up at once to his room, and as on reaching the door she heard Joseph, the porter say, in a loud and threatning voice, "I'll not go for a shilling less: and if you don't give me that, I'll blow up the whole affair!"—she, without the slightest ceremony, entered the room, and was struck with amazement on finding him seated at the table with her father.

"Hush!" whispered Raven, the moment she appeared.

"How dare you, sir, thus address your master!" cried Louise.

"Mind your own business, Miss!" said the fellow; "Master 'll mind hisn, and I'll mind mine."

"You insolent man! how dare you speak to me? Leave the room, sir, I desire!"

The fellow did leave the room; but with a sneer, which, to Raven, was one of great significance. —

"Why, papa, why do you allow yourself to be thus insulted by one of your own servants?" cried Louise.

"My dear child!" said Raven, "do not distress yourself. I shall soon, very, very soon get rid of him now!"

"But how dare he presume even to sit in your presence! Father! have you anything to fear from that man?"

"Anything to fear from him, my child?"

"If not, why keep him in the house? If he knew of that, which is now no longer a secret and kept it faithfully, reward him; but do not allow him to remain."

"My child, have I not said that I am about to get rid of him! But why do you imagine that he knew of that secret?"

"Because he was continually boasting of the power he had over you: nay, he boasts that you are in his power now!"

"Indeed! to whom does he make that boast?"

"To the servants. He is constantly telling them that he could command the best place in the house; that he could force you to do anything for him he pleased, and that, to use his own expression, he has you under his thumb."

Raven pressed his lips and breathed very hard, and having drawn Louise closely to him, kissed her with much warmth.

"Dear papa," she continued, "tell me, pray tell me, what mystery is this?"

"Mystery? What *mystery*, my child?"

"I fear that there is more than has yet transpired, and if so, do disclose it; but if there be not, I do beg of you, father, to discharge that man, for there is in him something which, while I look at him, I feel that I have reason to fear."

"Fear nothing, my child. You are correct in supposing that he knew my secret; he did know it; he knew it from the first; had it not been so, I never should have kept about the house so pernicious a scoundrel. But you have nothing to fear from him now."

"Have you, papa? You will not object to answer me the question. Is there no other secret? Has all been explained? Has that man the power to make known any circumstance you are anxious to keep unknown?"

"My good child," said Raven, "you shall know all anon. He shall quit the house to-morrow. Go, my girl: go, there leave me. But, Louise, not a word of this to Valentine! You will promise me that?"

Louise did so and kissed him; but she left with a heavy heart, and a mind teeming with fresh apprehensions.

CHAPTER LXIII.

GOODMAN QUITS THE SCENE FOREVER.

UNCONSCIOUS of all that had occurred between Louise and her father during their interview, Valentine in due time left for the night. He did indeed perceive, on her return to him, that she was agitated; nay, he perceived that she had been in tears; but as she frequently wept for joy, and as, since her father's secret had been proclaimed, her smile had always been seen through a soft veil of sadness, her appearance failed to make a deep impression; and, therefore, after having playfully delivered a lecture on the physical operation of tears upon beauty, he gave his sweet pupil the preliminary kiss, when as usual, at lingering intervals, they twenty times reiterated—as if they had really become enamoured of the words—"Good night!"

As in the early part of the evening Uncle John had explained to him that Whitely had consented to a private arrangement, Valentine hastened home, being anxious to ascertain if that which formed the only bar to his immediate union with Louise had been entirely removed.

A mournful scene, however, awaited his arrival: poor Goodman was dying.

He had been tempted by that fallacious strength which declining nature, struggling to the last, seldom indeed fails to summon on the near approach of death, to make an effort to walk across the chamber; but no sooner had that effort been made, than he sank upon the floor in a state of absolute exhaustion. This occurred about an hour before Valentine arrived; and as, immediately on his arrival, he was informed of the fact, he proceeded at once to his good old friend's room, in which, besides the attendants, were Uncle John and the physician.

As he entered Goodman smiled; his appearance seemed to cheer him. He took his hand, and pressed it feebly, but with earnestness, and kissed it.

There is before the eyes of men on the brink of dissolution, a glassy film which death imparts, that they may have a brief prospect of eternity, when some behold the angels of light, while others have the demons of darkness before them. This film *then* glazed the eyes of Goodman; but his spirit was calm, and his look serene; resignation was seated on his brow; death had no terrors for him.

Having gazed for a few moments at Valentine with an expression of pleasure, a slight cloud seemed suddenly to pass over his countenance, and he looked round the chamber, and then gently drew Valentine nearer, when whispering in his ear, he said, "My brother: I should like to see my brother: do you not think that he would come to me now?"

"He would be but too happy," said Valentine. "I will go to him instantly."

"Do, my dear boy; Heaven bless you! Tell him I am anxious to say farewell; but haste, for I feel that my hour is come."

Valentine again pressed his hand, and left the room, and then proceeded without delay to Walter's residence, in the full conviction that fraternal affection would overcome shame, and that the summons would be instantly obeyed. He reached the house: light was to be seen. It was late, certainly, but earlier than Walter was wont to retire. He knocked; no answer was returned: he knocked again and again; still no one appeared. At length, however, after knocking and ringing with sufficient violence to have aroused the seven sleepers, he heard one of the upper windows open, and on looking up, saw the head of a female, who half screamed, "*Who's there?*"

"I must see Mr. Goodman immediately," cried Valentine. "Open the door."

"Go away, tipsy man!" cried the female; "there's no one of that name lives here."

"My good woman," said Valentine, having satisfied himself that he had not mistaken the house, "He *did* live here; can you tell me where he is to be found?"

"I know nothing about him. I'm only in the house to take care of it. The family that left last week are gone a long way in the country; I don't know where—but they're gone."

The female then disappeared and closed the window, when Valentine went to the public-house opposite—to which he knew that Horace had been in the habit of going—and there learned that Walter and his family, after having sold everything off, had indeed left town; but how they went, or where they were gone, he could not ascertain.

He therefore immediately retraced his steps, and being anxious of course to keep everything from Goodman at all calculated to give him the slightest uneasiness, he made up his mind on the way to conceal from him all but the naked fact of Walter being absent.

As he cautiously returned to the chamber, the eyes of Goodman were closed as if in death; but they were re-opened the very moment he entered, and turned inquiringly towards him as he drew near the bed.

"He will come?" said Goodman, feebly, for he was sinking very fast—"He will come?"

"He would," returned Valentine, "I am sure that he would with pleasure; but unhappily he is at present out of town."

"Well, well. The meeting might have been painful to him—yes, it might have given him pain. You will not fail to let him know that all—all has been forgiven? I should have been pleased—much pleased —but for his peace—for his peace—it is perhaps—as well."

Valentine now sat beside him with one hand in his; and while the physician, who expected his death every moment, was watching his countenance with the utmost anxiety, Uncle John was in an easy chair blinded with tears, though his sorrow was silent. Goodman was his oldest friend: he had been his companion in infancy; and while his name was associated with his earliest recollections, their friendship in manhood had been cemented by the knowledge of each other's integrity and goodness of heart. He was therefore much affected, and wept bitterly, albeit still in silence.

Philosophy at such a time as this has no effect; nor can religion and philosophy conjoined check, when over the bed of death, the tears which gush from the reservoir of Nature. We must weep. But why? The dying do not weep!—they may be calm, serene, free from pain, happy—most happy in the enjoyment of the prospect of celestial bliss—still we weep! Is it to lose them?—They lose us! But in their view then they lose us but for a time, while in ours we lose them for ever. We therefore weep: we weep to be left in the world without them, while the fountain of their tears is dried up with the sweet hope of meeting us "where the wicked cease from troubling, and the weary are at rest," in the realms of peace, to part no more.

"Hush!—hush!" exclaimed the dying man, in a thrilling, startling whisper, after having gazed on vacancy for some time in silence—"Hark!—do you not hear?"

The physician raised his hand to enjoin silence.

"Hark!—hark!" he continued, with an expression of rapture, raising his feeble hands and straining his eyes upwards.

A sigh escaped—a heavy lingering sigh: it was his last—he breathed no more! His eyes were still fixed, but his spirit had fled!

* * * * * *

Thus died the benevolent, amiable Goodman, the victim of a monstrous, a barbarous system, which has long been a foul and pernicious blot upon civilization, and of which the existence in full force still, reflects the deepest *disgrace* upon us as Christians and as men.

CHAPTER LXIV.

HORACE ANNOUNCES THE FACT TO WALTER.

Nearly a fortnight elapsed after the mournful occurrence detailed in the preceding chapter, before Valentine was relieved in any sensible degree of the sadness that scene had induced. His knowledge of poor Goodman had been in reality but slight—the seizure having been effected so soon after his arrival—but his death still had made a deep impression upon his mind, for he had seen sufficient of him to feel well convinced that no man ever did or could possess a more purely benevolent heart.

Louise, too—albeit, under the then existing circumstances, it was but natural for her to partake of any feeling which gave him pain—was affected more deeply than might have been anticipated, considering that Goodman was a man whom she had never even seen. She, however, knew his history: she knew of his cruel incarceration, and of the brutal means by which his death had been induced, and that knowledge was accompanied by the ever constant thought that the self-same means had been employed by her father. She therefore felt it very acutely, as indeed they did all; for while Uncle John mourned the loss of his friend as if, indeed, he had been a brother, Whitely became still more inveterate against Raven, and Raven himself appeared to have lost his own esteem.

There was, however, one who felt it more deeply still: and that was Walter!

Horace had been left by him in town to

watch the progress of events, and to report from time to time; and as he was in constant communication with the servant by whom Goodman was attended, and whom he had promised to marry "when the old man was dead," he of course was informed of that event as soon as possible, and no sooner did he hear of his death than he called to inquire particularly after his health.

Of course, on receiving the only answer he could receive on that occasion, he was perfectly struck with amazement! He had made up his mind to be suddenly struck: it was part of the plan he had deliberately laid down,—and after having, in his own peculiar style, expressed his concern to the widow Smugman, whose grief was excessive, he thanked her for feeling so much for his uncle, and begged of her to prevail upon Valentine to see him, that he might know if there was anything in the world that he could do.

The affected widow—who began to look upon Horace as an individual who had been scandalously libelled—of course consented, and proceeded to the drawing-room, in which Valentine was sitting with Uncle John, with the view of inducing him by her eloquence to see *him* whom she termed "the poor afflicted young gentleman."

Valentine, however, needed no such inducement: the very moment he heard that Horace was below he came down, and was by no means displeased to perceive that he was not dead to every proper feeling, for he had made up his face for the occasion, while the tones in which he spoke resembled those which are subdued by real grief.

The interview was but short. Valentine explained to him all that had occurred, but dwelt emphatically upon Goodman's earnest wish to see his brother before he died; and when Horace had ingeniously got at the fact that the will had not been altered—which, indeed, was the only thing he cared to know—he promised to communicate immediately with his father, and with that view at once took his leave.

The country is beyond doubt the most unpleasant place to which a man with a stinging conscience can retire. Such a man must keep in town if he expects even partially to drown his thoughts: the country cannot calm *his* troubled breast: its tranquillity affords no peace for him.

This Walter felt strongly. The peace which he there saw around him so strikingly contrasted with the perpetual agitation within him, that it drove him almost mad. Drink was the only means of excitement which *he* found available there. Whether he walked abroad or remained at home, to him it was still the same: everything appeared to be tranquil but his conscience, and by that he was tortured so perpetually that the very day on which Goodman died he made up his mind to return to town; not only with the view of escaping the torture which the peaceful character of a rural life induced, but in order to see his brother, and to solicit his forgiveness. Upon this he had fully and firmly resolved, and was on the point of explaining that resolution to his wife, and to urge her to prepare immediately for their departure, when Horace arrived to announce his brother's death.

"What has happened?" inquired Walter, as he entered.

"There, now, sit down," said Horace, "and don't be in a fever. Take a drop of brandy, and give me ditto, and then as soon as I've got off my benjamin, I'll tell you all the news. I can't before."

Walter trembled. He had no conception of his brother's death, but he felt that something might have occurred that would plunge them at once into ruin.

"Well," said Horace, having adjusted himself to his entire satisfaction, "we seem to have made a bit of a mull of this business, after all."

"What business?" cried Walter, impatiently.

"Why, the old buffer's gone, and—"

"Gone?—dead?"

"Why, of course!" replied Horace. "Come, come," he continued, on perceiving the strong effect the announcement had upon Walter; "there, that's quite enough; you do it on the whole pretty fairly; but now,—come,—cut it. It's all very natural to be struck all of a heap when you've got your game to play, but here there's no necessity for it.—Well, *may* I be swindled! I say, governor!—do you mean it?"

"*Silence!*" shouted Walter, with an expression of rage.

"Well, that's very pleasant and very pretty, and would sound very correct if set to music; but the tone doesn't harmonize exactly with my feelings, I must say. Haven't I done all I could do?—didn't I swindle the buffers into the belief that the papers I returned were *the* papers, and nothing but?—didn't I get a written acknowledgment for the lot?—and didn't I get hold of the slavey, and make her believe that I was single and was going to marry her, in order to get at the bottom of every move? and yet it's '*Silence!*' This is the reward of virtue!"

"Horace!—Horace!" exclaimed the mother, "don't for goodness sake go on so!"

"Go on, how? This you know is what I call gratitude, this is!"

"We know that you have done a great

deal; we know that; and we appreciate it."

"Yes, so it seems! it bears a striking resemblance to that!"

"But do, for Heaven's sake, talk more like a Christian."

"Talk more like a Christian! Well, that's rather rich—rich enough to disagree with any stomach, that is. How am I to talk?"

"With less vulgarity, Horace! It is really quite shocking."

"Well, I shouldn't be surprised. But what's the governor dreaming about now? He hasn't heard a quarter of what I have to tell him."

"Tell me all," said Walter, "and at once."

"Now don't speak in such an uncomfortable tone. It would be much more mild if it wasn't so strong. I should before have pulled it all out at once if you hadn't stopped me. But to whom do you think he has left all his property now?—guess."

"Perhaps to that Valentine," exclaimed Mrs. Walter, "I shouldn't be surprised."

"I care not if he has," said Walter, despondingly, "I am reckless of everything now."

"What!" exclaimed Horace, "what would you say now if he had left the lot to you?—made you his sole executor, notwithstanding what has occurred?—forgiven and forgotten all, like a good Christian."

"*Is* that the fact?" inquired Walter, with the most intense earnestness. "Has he really done that?"

"He has. He has left no one else the value of twopence."

"Thank Heaven!" exclaimed Mrs. Walter; but Walter himself became motionless and silent. Had his brother displayed the slightest feeling of enmity or revenge; had he, as a punishment for his unnatural conduct, left him destitute, it would have affected him but slightly; he would have regarded it but as a punishment, and all his energies would at once have been directed to the means of avoiding it by retaining illegally that which he had; but as, notwithstanding the injuries he had received at his hands,—notwithstanding he had been treated by him with the most unnatural cruelty, he had acted precisely the same as if he had experienced nothing but kindness and brotherly affection; it cut him to the quick: for hearts are wounded far more deeply by kindness undeserved, than by the barbed shafts of malice or revenge.

"Why," said Horace, who expected fully that his father would, of course, be elated, "you don't appear to be particularly up in the stirrups even now."

Walter rose and left the room, and as he left, his eyes seemed to be starting from their sockets, while he groaned and ground his teeth, and with his clenched fists struck his head with violence.

"Well," said Horace, "did you *ever* see anything to come up to that? I tell him the very best news that could possibly be told, and instead of being in regular ecstasies, he cuts away, and knocks his old head about, just like a man without hope."

"The news of his brother's death," said Mrs. Walter, "has affected him, and very naturally."

"Well, that may be regular, as far as it goes; but it won't go very far, you know, when he has been expecting his death daily for months!"

"Very true; still, however long it may have been expected, when it does come we cannot but feel it."

"Well, I shouldn't be surprised. But it wasn't the death that affected him most; it was the property that put him in that state of mind. But I say though, what donkeys we have been in this business! That's what I look at. Here have we been muddling away the money like mad individuals, in the first instance sacrificing one-half in order to keep the other, and then cutting away with that as if we hadn't above six months to live, when if we had but kept quiet we should have had the whole in the regular course of nature, and that too in a lump, which of course would have enabled us to live like fighting-cocks, in a state of the most pleasant independence for the rest of our days."

"Very true; very true; we have indeed been extravagant."

"Extravagant, yes; but that which hurts my feelings most is the fact of our having seen nothing at all for it! The money has been regularly slobbered away. It is true we havn't had much luck: that must be admitted by universal nature. That fool of a fire was the first go—that cost a little above a trifle. Then there was the buying of that Spanish, only just as it was *on* the point of dropping down to nothing. Had we waited but half an hour longer, we shouldn't have been in time for that. Then the loss of the governor's mysterious pocket-book containing those notes—that was another nice blessing. I never saw such a sweet run of luck; it beats all my acquaintance. And then again you see, buying that house full of furniture at the very highest price, and then selling it at about the very lowest to come down here, and now we shall have to buy another house-full, at the very highest. You see all these things tell!"

"They do indeed. We have had neither a moment's peace of mind nor anything but misfortune since your uncle was taken to that place."

"It was a badly managed business; nay, the whole thing has been most miserably muffed, and I don't care who knows it. However, we must make the best we can of it now."

"I am very sorry we disposed of that furniture. Had we delayed the sale but a few days, you see there would have been no necessity for selling it at all."

"That's the beauty of it!—That's the very thing I look at! We are always *just* in time!"

"But then who could have supposed it? Who could have supposed that your uncle after all would have been so considerate, so good? I am sure, for my own part, *I* never expected it. I never supposed it to be at all probable. I fully made up my mind when you mentioned the property that the whole had been left to that young man, to whose arrival in town I attribute all our misfortunes, and that we should have been in consequence compelled either to quit the country or to remain here concealed, to avoid being ruined by actions at law. But say what you will, Horace, your uncle must have been a good man."

"Oh! he was a decent old fellow enough, I dare say. I should have liked him perhaps better had he liked me better, for there is always a great deal in that; but as he didn't much care about me, why I didn't care much about him. But where's the governor? It will never do, you know, to allow him to get into a state of confirmed uncomfortables. I must say I don't like the look of him sometimes."

"I fear that he never will be himself again."

"Well, you'd better see after him, you know. He may give us a little more of his hanky-panky business, and set us all in a blaze as he did before. There's no accounting for buffers that see apparitions."

Mrs. Walter took the hint and left the room, when on entering the little back parlour, she found Walter seated at the table, with his eyes fixed on vacancy, and groaning with intense mental anguish. She spoke to him—he started, but returned no answer. She tried to rouse him from his reverie, but in vain.

From that hour his misery became appalling.

CHAPTER LXV.

IN WHICH THE DAY IS FIXED AGAIN.

When a month from the period of poor Goodman's death had passed without a single syllable on the subject of the marriage having been mentioned, Valentine very naturally felt, that as every thing which might have been considered a bar to its immediate celebration had been effectually removed, it would be absurd to defer the renewal of that subject any longer, particularly as he began to be very impatient. He saw Louise daily; he dined and conversed with her daily; and he could not but feel that they might as well be married as not; nay, he thought it would be better, inasmuch as their minds would be more at ease, and they would feel far more settled, and so on.

Accordingly, having satisfied himself that nothing *could* be more correct, he resolved to revert to the subject at once, and as at the time this unimpeachable resolution was formed, he and Louise were in the drawing-room alone, he closed the book he had in his hand, and drew up to the table at which she had been working for some time in silence.

It is a curious fact in natural philosophy, that ladies in almost every case of interest, clearly understand the designs of their lovers. The process by which they arrive at this clear understanding is inscrutable of course, but that they do possess the faculty of perceiving it at once when an interesting proposition is about to be made to them, is a fact which experience has placed beyond dispute. It is hence that at such a time as this they are never off their guard, for let a man go round and round, and beat about as his apprehensions or his natural diffidence may prompt, they well know that his design is to come to the point, and that sooner or later to the point he will come; and hence it was that in this particular instance Louise no sooner perceived Valentine draw mysteriously up to the table, than she began to work away at an extraordinary rate, and to feel her cheeks glowing with "ineffectual fire."

"Louise," said he, "I mean to be merry again. I have been solemn already too long; for although the mournful scene which caused me to be sad, made an impression which I sincerely hope may never be obliterated, still I hold it to be the very reverse of wisdom to cherish gloomy thoughts until they obtain so great an influence over the mind as to tinge every feeling of pleasure with sadness."

At this point he paused; but Louise kept on working with great intensity and zeal without offering the slightest remark, or even raising her eyes for an instant.

"Louise," he continued, "you are very industrious to-day!"

"That is rather an equivocal compliment," said Louise. "Am I not always industrious?"

"Your mind is always active, I admit; but I never saw you work quite so fast, I think, before! Shall you be long about that business?"

"What business, dear?"

"Why that muslin affair.—What is it?—Oh! by no means!—I have no wish to know!—But you'll not be long about it, I presume?"

"Oh! no. But why do you ask?"

"Because, when you have completed it—whatever it may be—I should like to have a little conversation with you on a subject of some interest."

"Can we not converse while I am working quite as well?"

"No, my Louise, not quite, for your eyes are then fixed upon the work when I am anxious to have them fixed upon me."

Louisa bowed, and having set the work aside, was all attention.

"You heard me say just now," he continued, "that I mean to be merry again. Louise, we must both be merry."

"I fear," said Louise, "that I shall never again be habitually cheerful."

"That, my dear girl, is the effect of the very influence to which I alluded, and against which we must take care to guard. I am glad, however, to find that you *fear* you never shall, because as that implies a wish that you may, I have no doubt you will. Cherish that fear until you prove it to be groundless. Entertain it till then, and you are safe. But *I* have no fear of the kind; I have not even a doubt that you will be, and that soon, the same light-hearted, animated, merry little tyrant you were three months ago."

Louise shook her head, and sighed.

"*You* do not think so, of course," he continued; "I don't see how you can! But, my good girl, we must not hug sorrow to our hearts as if we loved it. We shall have enough of it, without courting its society. It will come often enough, without any invitation, and stop long enough, without being either welcomed or fostered. We must give it no encouragement; if we do, it will stick to us, and make itself so perfectly at home, that after a time we shall not be able to get rid of it at all. They are the wisest people who turn sorrow out at once, for it really has no engaging qualities; it is always looking wretched, and groaning about something. How ever rational beings can love such a companion I cannot conceive."

"Its visits," said Louise, "are, unfortunately, not confined to those by whom it is beloved."

"Of course not. It will force itself anywhere; it is externally trying to extend the circle of its acquaintance; but having gained an introduction, the length of its visit depends entirely upon the treatment it receives. If you meet it with spirit, it will be too much shocked to remain long; but if once you fall into its views, it will love you too dearly to leave you. Now I perceive, my dear girl, that it is getting rather fond of you; its affection for you, indeed, is becoming very conspicuous, and as such is the case, would it not be wise to make it understand that on your part there is no reciprocity of feeling? What is your opinion upon the point?"

"Upon my word," said Louise, "I cannot say."

"Are you enamoured of sorrow?"

"No."

"You have no desire to be wedded to it for life?"

"Certainly not."

"If you knew how to remove the heavy burden from your heart, you would do so willingly?"

"I would."

"Then the thing shall be done. I will undertake to show you how to do it. But let us have a clear and distinct understanding. You engage to be guided by me? You promise to act upon my instructions to the very letter?"

Louise paused, but at length said, "I do."

"Very well. In the first place then—(now I expect the most implicit obedience)—in the first place, let me see, this is the sixth: yes; well then, decide upon what day, between this and the twentieth, we shall take full possession of our house."

"Oh! that's an entirely different thing!" exclaimed Louise. "We were speaking on the subject of sorrow!"

"We were; and as I have made up my mind to entertain no sorrow at that house, the sooner we take possession of it the better. Remember, you have promised obedience!—between this and the twentieth."

"Nay, but this is a snare! You can

hardly expect me to feel myself bound by a promise into which I have been entrapped! But seriously, my love, pray let us defer it a little longer."

"Well, my dear girl, I will consent to defer it—provided you can prove to me that it ought to be deferred."

"Would not the mere expression of my wish on the subject be sufficient?"

"Why that depends entirely upon what form of government we are under. If it be an absolute despotism, of course the wish would have but to be expressed to be obeyed; but if it be but a limited monarchy the consent of others must be obtained before it can have the force of law. But I thought you were my pupil—my subject for the time being. I thought you promised to obey *me*. Was it not so?"

"I certainly did promise; but —"

"That is sufficient! Your will then of course is quite out of the question: *my* will is the law to which you have promised obedience; nevertheless, if you can show me any just cause or impediment why we should not take possession of that house before the twentieth, I am pérfectly willing to yield; at the same time I think that I am quite safe in making that promise, believing that no sufficient reason can be adduced. But what have you to urge?"

"I know of nothing which you would consider a sufficient reason; but I don't, my love, feel—exactly—prepared."

"Well, sure you will have plenty of time for preparation before the twentieth! Consider, an immense deal can be done in fourteen days. Besides, look at that furniture! Now, I should be very sorry indeed to see that fall into decay; and is it likely that it will not all be spoiled if we drive this affair off much longer?"

"Oh! but I hope it is well taken care of."

"It may be; I say it *may* be; but you know what servants are when they have no one to see after them. But independently of that, I don't like to see the house as it is now. We should feel more at home there,—much more at home. I admire the house. And shall we not be happy in it, my love? Yes, I feel that we shall, and you feel that we shall, too. Let us then be happy at once. I am not at all particular as to the day; any day between this and the twentieth. The earlier, the better, of course. Come, my Louise, we must have no more gloom, no more melancholy thoughts or afflicting apprehensions. To-morrow—I will not press you too closely now—but tomorrow let me know the day on which our happiness is really to commence, and then we'll make sorrow *fly* before the prospect!"

Louise was silent. Valentine had drawn his chair quite close to hers; and had both her hands in his; and although she endeavoured to fix her eyes firmly upon her dress, they would almost every moment meet his, which of course she couldn't help.

"Louise," said he, after a pause, during which he gazed with the highest and purest feelings of admiration upon her, "what say you; shall we go this morning and look at our house, and see how the furniture stands, and so on?"

"Oh, yes! I should like it indeed."

"Then we'll go, my dear girl, run away and prepare."

Louise now raised her eyes, and before she left the room fixed them firmly upon him, and said that he was a dear good creature, and that she loved him more and more; for which, of course, Valentine appropriately rewarded her, and a heavy burden seemed to have been removed from the hearts of both.

"*Oh*, Louey!" exclaimed Llewellen, who happened to enter unperceived at the very moment their lips accidentally met,—"*Oh!*"

Louise blushed, and darted from the room with all possible speed.

"Well, Fred!" said Valentine, precisely as if nothing at all had happened, "What's the news?"

"Well, cootness knows it, now, that's the first time I ever frightened Louey! Hur'm so clat! Won't hur tease her now, look you!"

"Tease her?" said Valentine, "What about?"

Llewellen made a very droll face, and gave five or six very deliberate nods as if he quite understood it.

"Why, you don't suppose, Fred, that it is very extraordinary for a lady to receive a kiss from him to whom she is just on the point of being married?"

"No," said Llewellen, "no! It isn't extraordinary, *that;* but look you; there's a tifference between kissing phen nopotty's apout, ant kissing phen somepotty's hanty; and cootness knows Louey wouldn't have hat me seen her for the worlt; so hur'll roast her to teath apout it, look you! Putt hur say, my poy, wouldn't you like to have a walk? Hur've pin reating those plesset books pelow till hur'm plind."

"Louise and I are going to look at the house."

"Oh! apove all things in the worlt! Hur may co, hur suppose?"

"Of course!—that is to say, if Louise has no objection; but I know she will put her veto upon it at once if you say another word about the kiss."

"Oh, very well; hur ton't care so long as

hur can co, only hur shoot like to tease her a pit apout that."

"But her spirits, poor girl, have of late been depressed, and you ought not, you know, to take any advantage—"

"Not for the worlt!" cried Llewellen, with much feeling, "Not for the worlt! For hur love Louey, look you; were she my sister, hur coultn't love her more."

Valentine grasped his hand, and shook it warmly; and, having said that he was a good fellow, strongly recommended him to go and brush his hair, not because it was at all disarranged, but in order that Louise, when she returned, might not feel at all embarrassed.

"Hur ton't think hur can make it look *much* petter, look you," said Llewellen, after having surveyed it in the glass. "Phot's the matter with it, my poy? Ton't you like the *co* of it?"

"Oh, go and give it a brush; it will look all the smoother, especially behind."

Very coot: hur'll make it co petter if hur can."

"That's right; but be quick; don't keep us waiting long. Run away, Louise is coming."

Llewellen was off like a shot to arrange his hair, and Louise the next moment returned.

"Oh! where is Fred?" she inquired, having looked stealthily round. "Gracious!—what *did* he say?"

"What did he say! Why, he *said* that he should like to go with us."

"Yes, yes; but about—you know what I mean. Did he make any remark?"

"I believe that he said 'Oh!' or something of that kind playfully, before you left the room."

"Dear me, what a fidget I was in."

Llewellen now entered, with his hair in the best trim. He had altered the "go," and it looked rather tidy.

"Will it too?" he inquired, addressing Valentine.

"Aye! now it looks more like the thing."

"Hur wish, Louey tear, you woult puy me some pears' grease, will you, Louey?—there's a coot cirl!"

Louise promised to do so, and they left the house, and at the suggestion of Valentine called for Uncle John, whom they found alone, and in rather low spirits. He was, however, pleased to see them, for their appearance was cheering; more especially that of Louise.

"We are come," said Louise, after a most cordial greeting, "to steal from you those gloomy thoughts which Valentine thinks we have all entertained long enough."

"And I believe that he is right, my dear," returned uncle John, "I believe that he is right."

"I am glad that you think so too," said Louise. "You will accompany us? We are going to look at the house."

"Tou come," urged Llewellen; "it's a plesset deal petter than peing here, and cootness knows it."

"Oh! I'll go with you with pleasure."

"But I thought," said Louise, "that my dear friend was here?"

"She has been here; but we shall find her there: I have just sent her to see that everything is going on right."

"Well, that *is* fortunate. I hope she will not have left."

"Shall hur co pefore," said Llewellen, "and tell her you are coming?"

"Yes, do," replied Louise, "there's a dear fellow, do."

Llewellen started off, and they followed him leisurely, and on the way Valentine hinted to Uncle John that between that day and the twentieth they should be in possession, which pleased Uncle John, although it slightly, but very slightly, embarrassed Louise.

"I do not see," said the old gentleman, "the slightest necessity now for delaying the thing any longer; on the contrary, I think that as every obstacle has been removed, any further delay would be folly; for of course we shall all feel unsettled until it takes place."

Valentine was delighted to hear his uncle speak out on the subject, and Louise was by no means unhappy about it, albeit she was silent.

On arriving at the house, they were received by the widow, who with Louise at once proceeded to make a most minute inspection, while Valentine, his uncle, and Llewellen, were having a glass of wine. This inspection, however, did not occupy the whole of the time the ladies were absent, for Louise, embracing the earliest opportunity, opened her heart to her affectionate friend, and having explained the substance of all that passed between her and Valentine that morning, it was decided then that the fifteenth should be fixed, and the widow was deputed to announce the fact to Valentine, in order that he might immediately communicate with Raven.

Accordingly, on entering the drawing-room in which the gentlemen were enjoying themselves, the widow drew Valentine aside, and to his great satisfaction, imparted to him the result of their private conference; but Louise at the time felt so excessively awkward, and trembled with so much violence, that she dared not attempt to raise the glass of wine presented by Uncle John to her lips; nor was it until Valentine, on rejoining them with a smile, began to converse on general topics with the highest consideration for her feelings, which he on all occasions studied, that she was able to reassume her self-possession. On recovering herself, however, she began to explain how much delighted she was with the whole of the arrangements, and soon made it manifest that she really did feel that the sooner matters were settled the better.

The object proposed having been thus accomplished, Valentine, Louise, and Llewellen, left the house in the occupation of Uncle John and the widow, who remained to give additional instructions; and as Valentine was resolved that Louise should be gay, that she might feel as little embarrassed under the circumstances as possible, he suggested that they should go to a certain scientific exhibition, which he had seen advertised in the papers that morning. Louise —always peculiarly happy to visit exhibitions with her Valentine, who had the power to render them all sources of infinite amusement—applauded the suggestion, and they proceeded to act upon it at once.

On passing Langham Church, however, Valentine's attention was attracted by two persons who were in earnest conversation at the corner. He saw at a glance that one of these persons was Whitely; but being anxious that the thoughts of Louise should not revert to the affair with which his name was associated, he of course took no notice, and they were about to pass on, when at the moment Llewellen exclaimed, "Look you!—Is not that Mr. Phitely?"

Louise in an instant turned her eyes, and saw not only Whitely, but Joseph, her father's late porter.

"Too you know the other, Louey?" added Llewellen. "Apove all other people in the worlt it's that lazy scountrel Joe, ant cootness knows it!"

"Don't appear to notice them," said Valentine. "The fellow is, perhaps, merely trying to get another situation."

"Phitely ton't live with you now, I pelieve?"

"No, he left about a fortnight ago."

They passed on, and Llewellen again expressed his wonder that Whitely should converse with a fellow like that; but Louise neither said a single word upon the subject, nor felt at all surprised; indeed, as she knew that Raven's secret had been known to the man, she viewed it as a thing to be expected that whenever he and Whitely happened to meet, they would speak on the subject as a matter of course.

To Valentine this was unknown, and hence he thought far more of the matter; but he appeared to be as gay as before, and conversed in as lively a strain, and kept Louise constantly smiling until they reached the exhibition, being anxious for her to think as little as possible about that which they had seen, and which on his mind had made a deep impression.

On entering the exhibition, the first thing which attracted their notice was the process of spinning glass by steam, which Llewellen pronounced to be "wonterful beyont all things in the worlt," and when informed that the glass thus spun could with silk or thread be manufactured into various articles of dress, he declared in a confidential whisper to Valentine, that he would have a pair of "peautiful preeches" made of it, but that, if he "*tit* happen to tumple town, then they would certainly preak into pits."

They then proceeded to the principal room, which was crowded with models, and scientific apparatus, which Llewellen minutely examined, and upon which he made divers extraordinary remarks.

"Valentine," whispered Louise, "I don't think that Fred has ever been galvanized. I wonder how he would like it!"

"We'll see," said Valentine, "there's a wire in that basin: drop something in, and ask him, as a favour, to get it out."

"Oh that will be glorious; but what shall it be?—my purse?"

"Anything: a ring will be better; he'll be some time getting at that."

Louise drew off a ring, and let it fall into the basin, and when Llewellen, who had been looking at the model of a steamboat, approached, she cried, "Oh, Fred, I've just dropped my ring into the water; can you see it?"

"Yes," replied Llewellen, "there it is at the pottom. Wait a minute; *I'll* get it!"

He drew off his glove, and put his hand into the water, but it was out again, of course, in an instant!—the shock, being perfectly unexpected, astonished every nerve he possessed.

"Why, Fred, what's the matter?" inquired Valentine.

Llewellen couldn't tell. He stood and looked at the water with great intensity of feeling, and with a very remarkable aspect; but what it was that had thus travelled through his system with the velocity of light, he was not in a position to say.

"My poy," said he, at length, "do you see anything there in that pasin?"

"I see a ring at the bottom."

"Putt nothing alive, look you?—nothing alive?"

"No," replied Valentine, gravely.

"Nor can I—ant yet there was something which made my plut curtle, and shook every pone in my potty."

"Come, Fred," said Louise, who had been convulsed from the first, "you said you would get me my ring."

"So hur tit, Louey—yes, ant so hur *will* —putt cootness knows it!"

Hereupon he put his hand into the water again, and as it was out in an instant, as before, he demanded to know what it was.

"Phot *is* it?" he cried—"Phot in the name of Saint Tavit *can* it pe? Hur never saw water alive pefore! Just try it, my poy: just try it."

"Is it hot?"

"Oh no, cootness knows it's not hot, putt *so* queer!—*too* try it."

"Nonsense," said Louise, affecting to be serious. "I suppose that I must get it out myself."

"Not for the worlt!" exclaimed Llewellen—"not for the worlt! it will shake you to pits! No, hur'll get it out presently, putt inteet her ton't know phot to make of it at all."

He now tried very cautiously with one of his fingers, and the result caused him to feel a deep interest in the thing, and he became less alarmed, still he could make nothing of it.

"Now," said Louise, "did you ever see so silly a creature! There has he been for the last ten minutes dipping for my ring, and hasn't got it up yet!"

"Hur ton't care phot you say, Louey: there's a mystery in this pusiness, cootness knows, ant hur'll get to the pottom of it, look you!"

"Well, I wish you would, for at the bottom lies the ring."

"Hur ton't mean that: but hur say, my poy, try it: *too* try it!"

"Oh! I've no objection," said Valentine, who quietly removed the wire, and drew out the ring, without the smallest inconvenience.

"Well," said Llewellen, "how very extraortinary! Put titn't you feel something that mate you tremple?"

"No," replied Valentine, as he slipped the wire in again.

"Well, hur can't pear to pe peat!—hur'll try it again, look you!"

He did so, and on finding that, as a matter of course, the effect upon him was the same, he became quite distressed. "How *very* remarkable," he cried; "how very *troll!*"

"Oh! Fred, Fred!" cried Louise.

"Hur ton't care, Louey, the water's pewitched. *You* try it; only try one finger! If Valentine can stant it hur can't, and hur'm sure it will shake you to pieces."

"I've no particular desire to wet my fingers," said Louise, as Valentine again removed the wire, unperceived, "but in order to show what a very silly creature you are, Fred, I will."

She then at once introduced her little hand into the water, and held it there, of course, with perfect steadiness, which so amazed Llewellen, that he scarcely knew how to express what he felt.

"Now," said Louise, "I do hope you are satisfied." But Llewellen was *not* by any means; and he was about to explain, with great force, that he was not, when Louise playfully told him to say no more about it, and with gentle force led him away.

At that moment a man in a diving dress was about to enter a basin at the upper end of the room, about twelve feet in diameter and eight feet deep. They therefore drew as near as possible at once, in order to have a good view of the operations, and when he had got beneath the surface, he appeared to walk about with very great deliberation and safety, his movements being marked by the water which continually boiled above his head. Having been down for some time, he ascended, and when a box had been handed to him with the view of giving a practical illustration of the power of voltaic electricity, he went down again, but he had no sooner done so, than Valentine, having whispered to Louise, threw his voice towards the diver, and cried "Pull me out!"

In an instant the men who were in attendance, threw ropes to the diver and held a life-preserver above his head, and would doubtless have proceeded to great extremities in order to save him, had he not, on perceiving through the glass in his helmet, a very unusual bustle above, reascended the rope ladder to see what it was all about, in the perfect conviction that *something* was decidedly wrong. He had scarcely, however, got above the surface, when he was seized by the attendants, who exhibited the most laudable anxiety to render him every assistance in their power, which astonished the diver more and more, and he shook his head at them and seemed by his gestures to be demanding an explanation; but it had no effect; they led him with great humanity to the edge of the basin and made him sit down, and having carefully removed his helmet, they anxiously asked him how he felt himself then.

Of course, the diver didn't know what to make of this display of affectionate zeal, and very naturally begged to know what it meant, for being totally unaccustomed to such considerate attention, it rather confused him than not.

"What's the matter?" said he, "any thing broke?"

"What was the matter with *you?*" inquired one of the men.

"The matter with me!—nothing."

"What did you call out for then?"

"*I* call out! How came you to think of that? *I* didn't call out!"

Here the spirit of incredulity seized them all, and they asked him distinctly if he really *meant* to say that he had not uttered the words "Pull me out."

"Of course I do," he replied. "Why should I want to be *pulled* out? If I'd felt queer, couldn't I have come out of my own accord in about the space of an instant?"

The men said no more; but they looked at each other as if they felt something very acutely.

The helmet was now readjusted, and when the submarine explosion had taken place, the diver again went down for a short time, and having completed his task, reascended.

"Any lady or gentlemen for the diving-bell?" shouted one of the attendants. "The diving-bell!"

"Have you courage enough to go down, Louise?" said Valentine, hardly expecting that she had.

"I have courage enough to go anywhere with you," replied Louise. "I fear nothing when you are with me."

Valentine smiled, and pressed her hand. "Would you like," said he, "to go down with us, Fred?"

"Apove all things in the worlt!" replied Llewellen. "Hur should like it, if only to say that hur *hat* pin town, look you!"

The necessary tickets were therefore procured, and they entered the bell, which would have held five persons, but they were alone, and the moment they were seated they were launched into the middle of the basin, and began to descend. The pumping then commenced, and they began to experience a singular sensation, which gradually increased as they descended, until it became one of absolute pain. Their ears seemed to be completely stopped up one moment, and the next to have a passage directly through them, while their heads felt as if they were quite prepared to split.

"Oh! I shall tie!" cried Llewellen, "ant cootness knows it."

"Nonsense!" said Valentine.

"Oh! put hur can't preathe!"

Valentine knocked for more air, and they immediately felt more oppressed; he then knocked for less, and although they felt in some degree relieved, the sensation was still very painful.

"Oh my poor het!—it will pust!" cried Llewellen.

"We are ascending now, my love," said Valentine, who regretted exceedingly that he had brought Louise down; for although she exhibited no signs of fear, he well knew that she must be in pain.

"Oh! my potty's as empty as a putt!" cried Llewellen; "*ant* my het! Oh! my het!"

"We are very near the surface now," said Valentine.

"Only let me once more get apove it!" cried Llewellen—"hur'll never get pelow it in a tiving pell acain." And he shook his head, and gave some extraordinary winks; and appeared to be altogether very uncomfortable.

The next moment they got above the surface, and began to breathe freely again; and the instant the bell had been landed, Llewellen rushed out, holding his ears, and looking very mysterious. The persons who stood round smiled, of course, but the knowledge of that fact did not hurt his private feelings: he thought of his head—he then cared about nothing in nature but that.

"You are in pain, my poor girl," said Valentine, having handed Louise from the bell.

"No, I don't feel much now," replied Louise; "I have a tingling sensation in my ears; but it isn't very painful."

"I am indeed very sorry that I induced you to go down; but I had no idea of its having this effect."

"Oh it will very soon go off! Do *you* feel much of it?"

"Very little. But look at poor Fred!"

Llewellen was at that time standing with his hands to his ears, and his elbows on the frame, looking very severely at the water. His expression was that of a deaf individual, and the whole of his intellectual faculties appeared to be in a most distressing state of confusion.

"How do you feel now, Fred?" said Valentine, "Better?"

"Petter!" cried Llewellen, "my het's in a roar! Its tangerous, look you!—very tangerous indeed!"

Valentine admitted that it was dangerous; and that ladies especially ought never to go down; for although in the bell there were instructions to knock once for more air, twice for less, and so on, nine persons out of ten, when they experience a difficulty in breathing, suppose that they have too little air when they have too much, and knock for more: independently of which, his decided impression was, that its tendency in many cases of weakness was to produce instant death.

An announcement was now made, to the effect that something was going forward in the Theatre of the Institution; and as Valentine and Louise had nearly recovered from the effects of their diving experiment, they playfully rallied Llewellen, and having insisted npon his keeping his fingers out of his ears, proceeded with him in the direction pointed out.

As they entered the theatre, it was perfectly dark, which rather alarmed Fred, who displayed an inclination to retire. "Is this another scientific experimental pusiness?" he inquired; "pecause if it be, hur can't stant it, my poy, hur can't inteet."

"It is only the microscope," said Valentine, and the next moment the disc appeared before them, exhibiting a mass of unhappy little wretches, that appeared to be in a frightful state of excitement. They darted about, and drove against each other, and lashed their tails, and kicked as if conscious that they had not another minute to live, and were therefore resolved to make the most of the time allowed them.

Llewellen was delighted. He at once forgot his head, and took the deepest possible interest in the evolutions of the little animals, which were somewhere about a million times less than they appeared.

"Phot are they?" he inquired; "phot are they all about? They appear to have pins in their tails, look you!"

"Listen," said Valentine, and at the moment an individual began to explain that what they saw was merely a drop of Thames water, and that the animals therein were so minute, that the idea of being able to see them with the naked eye was about the most ridiculous that could be conceived.

"Oh!" exclaimed Valentine, sending his voice some distance from him. "How then can they see each other? Are *their* eyes stronger than ours?"

This was done of course merely to create a sensation, and that object was in an instant achieved; and the lecturer paused, but disdained to reply to so strikingly irregular a question.

"Well!" said Valentine. "But I *suppose* you cannot tell."

The lecturer scientifically struggled for some time with his feelings; but at length said with very great solemnity, "What is it the gentleman wishes to know?"

"Whether," replied Valentine, "their eyes are more powerful than ours?"

"Beyond doubt," said the lecturer, in a very severe tone—"infinitely more powerful in their sphere. Eyes are not powerful in proportion to their size. If they were, the eagle would be able to see a far less distance than the elephant, and assuming that the elephant has the power to distinguish objects at a distance of twenty miles, the ant would be able to see nothing beyond half a millionth part of a quarter of an inch."

Here the lecturer was applauded, and by the light of the lamp beside him, it was perceptible that he felt a little better.

"What a very silly person he must be," observed Louise, to ask so ridiculous a question!"

"Very, returned Valentine; when, assuming the same voice as before, he added, "Who is it that says I am a very silly person?"

"Good gracious!" cried Louise, "I had no idea of his having overheard me."

"Who is it?" again demanded Valentine, when many began to laugh, and many more cried "I!—I!—I!—We all say that you are a very silly person."

"How dare you laugh at me!" cried Valentine, and the laughter recommenced. "I know," he continued, "I well know the laugh of one excited individual; it is that of Fred Llewellen, who has just been down in the diving-bell."

"Oh!" cried Louise, "it is you!"

"Hush!" said Valentine.

"Tit you hear?" cried Llewellen; "tit you hear? Co phere hur will, hur am sure to pe known."

"I know you," cried Valentine.

"Silence!—silence!—Order! order," shouted several persons, who began to feel indignant.

"Am I to be insulted by a Welshman?" cried Valentine, in a very scornful tone, "Is it likely?"

"Phot to you mean, sir?" pointedly demanded Llewellen, for his blood began to boil. "Phot to you mean?—Who are you?"

"Gentlemen," said the lecturer, soothingly, "it will be perfectly impossible for us to proceed unless you are silent."

"Do not be brow-beaten, Fred," said Louise, in a very wicked whisper.

"Too you think to prow-peat me?" shouted Llewellen, whom Louise had thus inspired with unlimited courage. "If you too, you are mistaken. "You're no gentleman, sir!"

"What!" shouted Valentine, at the same time patting him encouragingly on the shoulder.

"Hur say you're no gentleman!" repeated Llewellen, under the influence of the liveliest indignation.

"Gentlemen!" said the lecturer—"Gentlemen! I would put it to your own good sense whether this ought to be. Is it decent? —Is it correct?—Is it a thing which ought to be tolerated for one moment? You really must be silent, or we cannot proceed."

"He may be silent," cried Valentine, "but I will not: "I'll have satisfaction!"

"It is to you, sir, I more particularly address myself," said the lecturer. "You are the aggressor."

"Do you tell me that to my teeth," said Valentine. "I'll have satisfaction of you."

Loud cries of "Turn him out!—turn him out!—Turn him out!" now proceeded from every quarter, and when the noise and excitement had reached the highest pitch, the shutter of the skylight was suddenly removed, and about three hundred persons were discovered in a state of great anxiety.

This unexpected and instantaneous introduction of light had a striking effect. The noise ceased on the instant, but all appeared to be panting to catch a glimpse of him who had created the unseemly disturbance.

"Which is the gentleman," inquired the lecturer, "who is so anxious to have satisfaction?"

No one answered. The question was repeated more emphatically; still no one answered.

"As he thought proper to insult me personally," said Llewellen, "hur shall be clat if he'll make his appearance, that hur may invite him to walk quietly out."

"He durst not show himself," cried several voices.

"Who says that?" demanded Valentine, promptly, making his voice appear to proceed from the other side of the theatre.

"I!" cried Llewellen, looking towards the quarter from which the sound apparently proceeded. "I say that you tare not show yourself."

Another pause ensued, and every eye was directed towards the spot; but although a low muttering was heard distinctly, no one appeared, with the view of asserting his dignity as a man.

"My impression is, that he's a plackcart!" cried Llewellen, "a tirty plackcart!"

"That's enough!" said Valentine, throwing his voice as before, "that's enough! I'll be with you!"

The effect which this had upon those who were in the quarter from which the voice seemed to come was extraordinary. They looked at each other in a state of amazement, and marvelled not only that they were unable to see him there, but that they could not discover him while he was speaking.

"Now then!" shouted Valentine, throwing his voice towards the door, "are you coming?"

This puzzled the audience still more. They had seen no one making his way out, and they felt sure that if any one had, they *must* have seen him. It was a mystery to them; they couldn't understand it. Llewellen, however, without waiting to see what effect this had upon the audience generally, started out the very moment he heard the summons with all the alacrity at his command. Valentine and Louise followed, and the majority of the audience, who seemed to take particular interest in the matter, followed them, and found Llewellen very naturally looking about the entrance for the person by whom he had been challenged.

"Well, have you seen him?" inquired Valentine.

"No, cootness knows it; hur'm afrait he knows petter than to let me."

"Now then!—Here I am!" cried Valentine, throwing his voice among the crowd.

Llewellen again looked about with great acuteness, and the crowd, who sympathized with him, assisted him in his efforts to discover the individual, but in vain; he was there, there could be no doubt of that, but he evidently hadn't the courage to stand forth.

"Now, phot can you too with such a fellow?" said Llewellen, appealing to Valentine. "Phot can you too with him? If hur coult see him, hur shoult know petter apout it; put as he won't pe seen, phy cootness knows, hur ton't know phot's to pe tone!"

"Treat him with contempt," said Valentine, in his natural voice, "He is quite beneath your notice. I thought from the first, you'd be unable to discover him. Now, let us be off."

"Put we had petter not co just tirectly, my poy! He will say that hur was afrait, and run away!"

"Not he," returned Valentine; "but we shall walk out leisurely, and if his courage should come up, he can follow us to the door."

They then proceeded towards the entrance, and on the way Llewellen—the thought of whose head had gone out of that head altogether—turned to see if the invisible individual had plucked up sufficient courage to follow; but no one did so—no one approached to announce himself boldly like a man, which Llewellen could not but think strange; but still more strange did he consider the fact of his invisible enemy having addressed him by name.

Of course Louise was delighted with this little adventure. She thought it, indeed, too bad that poor Fred should have been teased to so great an extent; but he was soon made perfectly happy by her and Valentine, who felt themselves bound to applaud the invincible courage he had displayed.

CHAPTER LXVI.

IN WHICH ANOTHER IMPORTANT SECRET IS REVEALED.

On the following morning, when Valentine called at the usual hour, he just presented himself to Louise, and then proceeded to the library, having ascertained that Raven was there alone, with the view of communicating with him on the subject, which then almost exclusively occupied his mind.

It was the first time that he had sought a private interview with him since the unhappy recognition took place. He had seen him—he had dined with him indeed almost daily since then, but as he had on all occasions appeared to be anxious to avoid being with him alone, Valentine had, of course, never thrust himself upon him.

The time, however, had now arrived when it was absolutely necessary for him to do so; and as he entered the library, Raven appeared to know his object, for he threw aside the paper he was reading, and having shaken his hand warmly, pointed to a seat.

"Well, Valentine," said he, "so you have come to have a little private talk with me at last. Of course I know upon what subject; at least I presume that it is on that of your marriage?"

"Exactly," returned Valentine. "It is thought that, if it meet your views, the fifteenth will be a very correct day."

"The fifteenth, my dear boy, then let it be, by all means; and the sooner the fifteenth comes, why the sooner I shall be happy. I hope that *this* time nothing may occur to cause the slightest disappointment."

"I hope so too. I have no fear of that."

"Nor had you before, and yet you see—"

"Nay, nay," said Valentine, gently interrupting him, "don't let us revert to that subject; let us shun it; let us forget it. The thing is over now—settled—let it rest."

"There is one consideration, and only one," rejoined Raven, "which enables me to recur to it with pleasure, and that consideration has reference directly and solely to you. When I intimated to you ambiguously, that that which did occur might happen, you promised that come what might, you would be faithful and firm to Louise. You have kept that promise nobly: you *have* been firm: I am convinced that you never wavered for an instant, but felt as a man ought to feel, that whatever might be my errors, she was pure, poor girl! and I admire you for it."

"I apprehend," said Valentine, "that in that instance far less credit is due to me than you are inclined to award; for I much question whether, if even my head had made an effort to shake my firmness, my heart would have allowed it to succeed. But let me suggest that we bury this matter for ever—that we never, in any shape, or on any occasion, allude to it again. Come, let us change the scene. We have been looking already too long at the dark side of things; let us turn to the bright one, for a bright one there is! The day of our marriage must *not* be one of gloom."

"You are a fine fellow, Valentine—a noble fellow: there is none of that sickly, sentimental aristocracy about you. You see things at a glance, as they are. I have the highest opinion of your judgment."

"The fifteenth, then," said Valentine, "is to be the day?"

"The fifteenth. Exactly. And as your wish is to avoid all allusion to that affair, I had better not enter into any explanation."

"That will be by far the better way. I should like things to go on now, precisely as if nothing of the kind had occurred."

"Well it's useless to make ourselves miserable eternally about that, which, being done, can't be helped. It was a sad affair, certainly. However, it's passed, and we'll say no more about it. Will your uncle be here to-day?"

"It's very likely he'll call."

"If he should, let me see him. We have not to go over the same ground again, exactly; but—don't let him go away without looking in upon me."

Valentine promised that he would not; and as the object for which he had sought the interview had been accomplished, he was about to leave the room, when Raven, as if a thought had just occurred to him, said, "Valentine!—Mr. Whitely has left you, has he not?"

"Yes," returned Valentine.

"Have you seen him lately?"

"Not to speak to him."

"I am not very anxious to know, of course; but you *have* seen him?"

"Why, I just *saw* him, yesterday."

"Yesterday! Oh! indeed, so recently as that? Then he intends to remain in town, I suppose?"

"Upon my word, I am unable to say."

"Oh! it's a matter of no importance. I merely thought that he intended to go into the country: that's all."

Valentine looked at him intently. He was half inclined to mention the fact of his having seen Whitely with Joseph; but as it struck him that its tendency could only be to reproduce unpleasant feelings, he abstained, and left the room.

Louise and the widow now began to be excessively busy again; for although it is true that everything from the most important even to the most minute had been previously prepared to their entire satisfaction, it is equally true that when they came to look again calmly over everything, everything required to be slightly altered. They therefore became as full of business as before; nay, their minds were more constantly occupied, seeing that whereas in the making of matters a great deal had been left to the judgment of other persons, the alterations were effected under their immediate superintendence, it being absolutely necessary for those alterations to be in accordance with their mutually improved taste.

In this business, of course, Valentine was shut entirely out of all confidence. Generally he stood in the position of family counsel, for his opinion was solicited in cases of emergency, and acted upon without another thought; but in this particular case he was not applied to at all!—a fact which did not however disturb him.

Uncle John, having been deeply engaged about the house—the appearance of which in every point may be said to have been the subject of his "thoughts by day, and his dreams by night"—did not, as was expected, call the day on which Valentine had his interview with Raven. On the following morning, however, having been informed that Raven had expressed a wish to see him, he did call, and found him in unusually high spirits. He had just received a letter, it appeared, dated from a vessel which had that morning sailed. He did not, however, enter into the subject of this letter; but he seemed to feel that the whole of his troubles were at an end, and shook the hand of Uncle John with extraordinary warmth.

"My friend," he exclaimed, "we shall not sink beneath this blow now."

"I hope not," said Uncle John—"I hope not."

"It must all be forgotten, my friend, it must all be forgotten. We have had these aristocratic miserables too long. We must now turn and dwell upon the prospect before us."

"I am glad to perceive," said Uncle John, "that you have come to that wise determination."

"A weight," cried Raven, striking his breast with violence; "a dead weight has been removed, and I feel myself again. Oh, my friend, you don't know what I have suffered; you can't know: but as Valentine says the marriage-day must not be one of gloom, it shall not be; it shall be a joyous day. I have not felt so happy for years!"

"I am right glad to hear it!" said Uncle John, "I hope sincerely that that happiness will be lasting."

"It's sure to be now," said Raven; "quite sure to be now! But to business," he added, and he proceeded to open a secret drawer in his desk, and to deposit the letter therein.

It was perfectly evident to Uncle John that something had happened more than Raven cared to explain. He felt sure that the fact of the marriage-day having been fixed again, had not alone elated him thus. Since the day of the recognition, he had been a wretched being; he had kept himself almost entirely secluded, and had worn the aspect of a miserable man: yet now he was in raptures; his eyes sparkled with pleasure, and he spoke of happiness, as if he had then felt it for the first time. In the judgment of Uncle John there was far more in this than appeared, seeing that Raven had not dined, and therefore could not be supposed to have been under the influence of wine. However, he felt that he had no right to pry into the matter, and that as no explanation was offered, it was a thing which Raven had no desire to explain.

"Valentine," said Raven, having settled himself down, "has informed you, of course, that his marriage has been fixed for the fifteenth?"

"Yes; that is to say, this day week."

"Precisely. Well then, my friend, this day week must be a day of perfect happiness; and as happiness *must* be the prominent feature, what can be done to secure it?"

"I have done nothing. I want to do much more towards the accomplishment of that object, than we have done already!"

"Why," replied Uncle John, deliberately, "I don't exactly see that we can do much more."

"I must do something. *What* can I do?"

"I really don't know what you *can* do! I know of nothing that requires to be done. There is everything prepared for them—everything! As far as their own personal happiness is concerned, it of course depends now upon themselves; we have at least the satisfaction of knowing that we have done all we could to promote it."

"You have that satisfaction; but I have not. I have as yet done absolutely nothing. I wish you would suggest something. What can I do?"

"Well now, do you know," said Uncle John, "you couldn't possibly have asked me a more puzzling question!"

"Of course the transfer of the sum we before fixed upon has been arranged, and the little marriage presents have been prepared, and so on. It strikes me, however, still, that I ought to do something more!"

"Well, I am sorry I am unable to assist you in deciding upon what that something is; for upon my honour, I can't conceive what it can be! No, my friend, be assured, that nothing more can be done. We start them fairly, and I should say that few, indeed, ever had a brighter prospect of happiness before them."

"That I feel," rejoined Raven; "nor have I the smallest doubt of that prospect being realized. Still I should like, you see, to bring the affair off, as the beggarly aristocracy say, with *éclat!* Now let us put our heads together. How is this to be done?"

"For my own part," said Uncle John, "I am inclined to believe the less *display* we make the better."

"Well, what would you suggest? Some arrangement must be made. How do you think we ought to proceed?—on the day—I mean the day of the marriage."

"Why," said Uncle John, "I don't know what your views on the subject may be, nor what arrangements you have in contemplation, but I would suggest, that on returning from church, we should have some slight refreshment, and that the young people then should start off to spend the honeymoon, leaving us happy in viewing the prospect of their happiness, and in the conviction of having done our duty."

"What, then, are we two old fogies to be left dreaming at home?"

"I dare say that they would rather be without us than with us!"

"Well now, do you know, I don't think so! I think that they would enjoy themselves more if we were all to be actively happy together. The consciousness of having performed one's duty is all very well, and very pleasing; but that is not exactly the thing: it doesn't meet my views of what a wedding-day ought to be at all. My impression is, and always has been, that on such a day as that, we ought not to be becalmed! It ought to be a joyous day; a merry day—a day upon which we can all dine, drink, and be jolly together!"

"Well, what do you propose?"

"Why, to act upon your suggestion in all but one point. Let them leave by all means to pass the honeymoon at Brighton, or wherever else they may please: they shall have my carriage and four, or six if they like: immediately after the ceremony let them be off! But let us go with them. Let us start immediately after them: let us race them down; let us have a joyous, glorious day of it; and a glorious night too!"

"Well, of course," said Uncle John, "I can have no objection. I should like to be with them."

"Of course you would! I know you would! Why should they go moping down there alone?"

"They would not be exactly alone; they would have the bridesmaids and the old lady, and——"

"What are they? What can they do? How can they of themselves form a really happy party? They have all the elements of happiness in them, but they want a couple of young fellows like us to inspire them with spirit. Just imagine the party down there. There they are, after a fifty miles' ride, say, at dinner. There's only one man amongst the lot, and that man's the bridegroom. Why, what can he do with them? How can he keep them from sighing themselves down into a state of sentimental misery? He can't do it! I'll defy him to do it. But even if he could, look at him, mark his position. Give him the best of it; say that the dinner passed off well, and that they were all full of gaiety and joy, which of course they wouldn't be, but say that they were. Well, an hour after dinner the women retire—of course they retire, and when they do, look at him! There's a lively position for a bridegroom to be placed in!—there's jollity!—there's joy! He sits there, silently sipping his wine; not a creature to speak to; perfectly alone. Why such a position is monstrous for a man to be placed in at such a time as that. Come, let us go with them."

"Oh! with all my heart!" said Uncle John, "I should enjoy it; but I didn't know how far such a course might be correct."

"Why, you see, our arrangements

wouldn't interfere with theirs. Besides, why should we follow the beggarly aristocratic fashion of dividing families at the very time they ought especially to be together? Let us accompany them. I am sure that they will be much more happy with us than without us. They are sure to be merry then; but if we let them go alone, my friend, mark my words, neither for them nor for us, will it be a joyous day."

"Well, then, let it be so; let us all go together. There can be no doubt about our being more merry in that case."

"None, whatever. You see I'm not one of your beggarly aristocracy; I haven't fifty thousand dowagers, and toadies, and hangers-on to give a sumptuous dinner to on such an occasion; with the exception of yourself, there's scarcely a man whom I'd care to break bread with in any place, much less at my own table; and although I have no doubt that you and I should enjoy ourselves, and be in a measure jolly, it wouldn't, it couldn't come up within a mile of my notions of what ought to be the glorious characteristics of a wedding-day. As, therefore, you are willing to fall into my views, I would suggest that it be proposed to the young people—who will agree, I know, to anything of the kind—that immediately after the ceremony—which ought to be over early, say ten—they take my carriage and four horses, and start, say for Brighton, in the lively expectation of being passed by us on the road; that we drive there all together, and then stop a week or a month, or in fact, just as long as we think proper."

"Very good," said Uncle John. "And if the bride and bridegroom wish to leave us after a few days, why they can start off and go where they please."

"Exactly! They may start the next day if they like. All I am anxious for is, that we may have the wedding dinner together."

Very well. It was decided that this plan should be proposed forthwith both to Valentine and Louise, and Uncle John was deputed to make the proposition, before he left the house, which he did, and they were both much delighted.

Valentine, however, was not exactly at ease; he had nothing to do; all were busy but him, and they would not allow him to assist them. He could scarcely be said to be uncomfortable, or annoyed, but he felt fidgety and impatient, and looked at his watch very often, and walked about without an object—in a word, he was unsettled.

Such being the case, having plenty of time for thought, he conceived the idea of getting up a dinner at *the* house, that Louise might officiate as mistress before her time. He thought that under the circumstances it would tell extremely well, more particularly as they should not be able to give a dinner there for some considerable time, and therefore as all kind of restraint had worn away—for the party to be invited felt as if they were already one family—he named the subject to Uncle John immediately after he had communicated the result of his interview with Raven, and that gentleman not only had no objection to the course proposed, but applauded the notion highly, as one calculated to be a source of great amusement and delight. The next step was to obtain the consent of Louise, and with that view Valentine returned to her at once.

"My love!" said he, "I want you to be my wife before we are married!"

"Oh! of course," said Louise, with a playful expression, "by all means. What have you got for me to do? I have not much time you know to spare; but I'll do it if I can. What is it?"

"Why, I am anxious that we should give a party at our house to-morrow, in which case you, of course, must be there to receive our guests."

"*We?* Of course you mean that you and your uncle will give a party?"

"No; I mean that you and I should give the party, Louise."

"What, already?"

"Aye! a sort of preliminary party, just to let them know what we can do."

"But will it be correct?"

"I should say that there will be nothing at all incorrect about it."

"Oh, well, if you think that, I should enjoy it amazingly. Oh! it will be glorious!—the idea is so new. I am sure that it is yours. I need not ask you that. Did you ever hear of such a thing before?"

"I confess that I never did; but I don't see why that should prevent us from doing it!"

"By no means. On the contrary, it will be all the better. I shall enjoy it the more. The novelty of the thing will be delightful! But understand, sir, I must not be teased too much. Oh! my Valentine, do not suppose that I am inclined to treat the great subject of our marriage with levity. Indeed, indeed, I am not; but I am so happy! oh, *so* happy! I feel that the time is past for it to be necessary to conceal my feelings from you."

"My own Louise!" exclaimed Valentine, with fervour, "I know that the native purity of your heart is to be equalled only by the correctness of your mind. Fear not, my love, that I can entertain a thought which can tend to diminish my estimation of either. My object in proposing this is to render you, if possible, more happy still!"

"I know it; I feel it, oh, believe me I am quite sure of that. Well—well!" she added, playfully, "and whom shall we invite?"

"Why, it must, of course, under the circumstances, be confined to ourselves."

"Why, of course!—What a silly thing I am! Well, then, let me see, there'll be papa, and—oh! six altogether. Well, have you any invitation cards? If not, I have some—beauties!—they have been printed—perhaps more than a thousand years—I can't say: at all events we have had them ever since we came here, and not one of them has ever been, by any chance, used. I'll go and hunt them up immediately. Get the envelopes ready, and we'll despatch them at once."

Louise then ran for the cards, and on her return they were prepared and enclosed; and when Valentine went to the house with the view of giving the necessary instructions for the dinner, he despatched them with all due formality, by one of his own servants.

This, as Valentine expected, delighted them all; but not one of them was so much delighted as Raven. He was in ecstasies! He declared to Uncle John confidently—for he spoke to no one else on the subject—that it was, beyond every species of doubt, the best thing he ever heard of.

"We must go full dressed," said he. "What can we wear to astonish them? Let me see. That, perhaps, doesn't much matter; but we must go full dressed. We must keep the thing up. We must do it in style. I'll call for you in the carriage at a quarter to six."

The thing being thus arranged, he did call with the Widow and Llewellen, and when Uncle John had joined them, they proceeded full of life and spirits to the house, where Valentine and Louise, with due dignity, received them.

Valentine had ordered the best dinner that could be, on so short a notice—prepared; leaving the thing, of course, entirely to the cook. But although it was really excellent, the dinner itself was quite a secondary consideration with them: it was the fact of their having been thus invited which rendered their enjoyment so rich, for they really were in raptures the whole of the evening, and left inspired with the highest and purest delight.

On the following morning, however, as Valentine and Louise were in the drawing-room, conversing in a most happy strain, each pointing out to the other the various bright little features of the prospect in view, which had before been overlooked or indistinctly perceived, a coach drove up to the door, and Whitely, with an expression of mingled pleasure and indignation, alighted.

"Good gracious!" exclaimed Louise, as her heart sank within her. "What can be about to happen now!"

"Be calm, my sweetest girl; be composed," said Valentine.

"Look!" she exclaimed, starting, and bursting into tears, as Joseph also alighted. "Valentine! Valentine!—my dearest love! Some dreadful mystery is about to be revealed!"

"My Louise!—Come, come, my sweetest!—Courage! Why inspire these fears on speculation, my love?"

"What can they want here?"

"Oh! Whitely may be dissatisfied; he may wish to have the terms of his engagement slightly altered—a thousand things may have occurred to induce him to call."

"But why bring that man with him? Oh, my Valentine! I cannot but anticipate the disclosure of some dreadful secret."

"Well, my Louise, let it be disclosed; and let us meet it boldly, whatever it may be; not tremblingly sink beneath it, as if a consciousness of guilt made us imbecile. Be firm, my Louise; I know that you can be firm; let it come! Let it be even the worst that can befall us, my love, it shall not subdue us without a struggle. But, my girl, it may be nothing of importance after all! Come, let us wait the result of this interview with patience."

By this time Whitely and his companion had been shown into the parlour. The latter was unknown to his successor, who therefore made no distinction between them, but bowed to both as he left to take Whitely's card to Raven, who was at the time in a pleasing reverie, almost buried in an easy chair.

The very moment, however, Raven saw the card, he started, and turned pale as death, and then fixed his eyes wildly upon the carpet, until after a time he seemed to become again conscious of the presence of the servant, when he made a strong effort to rally.

"This person," said he, waving his hand, and affecting an air of supreme indifference, "may walk up.—Be a *man!*" he continued, muttering to himself, when the servant had left him. "Display the spirit of a man! What have I now to fear? What danger is there now?"

He rose, and struck his breast, and breathed deeply, and tried to subdue every feeling of fear, and succeeded at least in recovering his apparent firmness by the time Whitely was ushered into the room.

"Well, sir!" said Raven, with marked

deliberation, "and what is your business with me?"

Whitely stood and looked at him fiercely for a moment, and then said with a sarcastic smile, "Are you at all astonished to see me?"

"I am," replied Raven. "I am astonished. I thought that you were to annoy me no more?"

"I did undertake to annoy you no more; but with this proviso, that if at any time I discovered that you had not dealt fairly and openly with me, the undertaking should be cancelled. I have discovered this; I have discovered——"

"*Well*, sir! *what* have you discovered?"

"That you are a more consummate villain than I even supposed you to be before."

"*Sir!*" shouted Raven, as he rose from his seat fiercely, "I can endure much: I have endured much; but if you suppose that I am to be *trampled* upon, you are deceived. Have you come here expressly to insult me? Is that your *only* object in coming?"

"No!" replied Whitely; "my object in coming here is to claim my children!—*my* children!—villain!"

At this moment Valentine, Llewellen, and Louise, rushed into the room.

"What in the name of Heaven is all this?" demanded Valentine, as Louise flew to Raven, and tried to calm him. "What does it mean?"

"He is a madman!" cried Raven,—"A madman!"

"What *is* this?" said Valentine, addressing Whitely. "Why, why are you here? Is it fair—is it just—when the thing was understood to have been for ever at an end?"

"Valentine," said Whitely, looking at him with a most intense expression, "I respect you: I always have respected you highly!—do not destroy that respect by interfering hotly in this matter while in ignorance of its merits. I have come to claim my children! They are here!—These are my children!"

The effect produced by this announcement was electric. A thrill ran through the veins of them all; but Louise clung still more closely to Raven, who again and again declared that Whitely was mad.

"No!" cried Whitely, "I am not mad. They are my children. They know me not; of course they do not know me, although there was a time—but that is passed."

"Mr. Whitely," said Valentine, "are you acting advisedly in this matter—What proof have you?"

"Aye!" cried Raven, "what proof has he? Let him produce his proof!"

"I *have* proof—ample proof; and *will* produce it!" cried Whitely, who instantly rushed from the room.

During his absence not a syllable was spoken. They were dumb with amazement, and remained in a state of breathless suspense until he returned with his witness.

The very instant Raven saw this man, he started, and looked at him as if he had been a spectre.

"Don't you know me?" said the fellow, with a sneer.

"Devil!" cried Raven, "is it you?"

"It's nobody else! What, you're caught then at last! You thought I was off to America, didn't you? I hope you received my affectionate epistle, because—"

"Silence, fellow!" cried Valentine.

"Fellow!"

"Aye, fellow!—State what you know of this matter, and no more."

"I shall have my revenge on every one of you, before I've done with you, it strikes me. I owe you all a grudge,—the whole set of you!"

"Now," said Whitely, "suppress whatever feeling of enmity or anger you may have, and answer me distinctly, and with truth. There stands 'Miss Raven,'—there 'Mr. Llewellen;' whose children are they?"

"Yours!"

Here Raven rose suddenly, as if about to seize the witness, who placing his foot against the door, cried, "Come, keep off! keep off! I know what you're up to; I won't be turned out!"

"No one wishes to turn you out," said Valentine.

"Don't they! I don't want nothing from you. I speak nothing but the truth, and he knows it! and that's what cuts him to the quick."

"Now, sir," said Whitely, "attend to me: you say that these are my children?"

"Of course they are, and he knows it."

"State how *you* know them to be mine."

"Why, wasn't I with 'em when they were infants, and haven't I been with 'em all along? Whose should they be? *He* never had no children. He never had no wife, but your wife which died of a broken heart; and didn't she take 'em with her when she left home? I can't be mistaken in 'em, it strikes me!"

"Have you no other proof than this man's word?" inquired Valentine. "Are you yourself sure that he has not invented this tale for the gratification of some malicious feeling?"

"Certain," replied Whitely.

"Of course, he is certain!" cried the man. "And if he wasn't, I could make him. It don't depend upon me; if it did, he'd stand me out in it. I can produce both documents and witnesses; but look at him! That 'll tell you whether what I say is truth or not. Only look at him! That's quite enough! He hasn't got so much as the face to say they're his. He knows that what I say is right. He don't deny it; he hasn't denied it yet. Let him deny it, that's all! Let him deny it!"

"Father!" exclaimed Louise, in agony. "Father!—I feel that you are my father still; you have always been like a father to me; is it—*no!*—I'll not believe it."

"Let him deny it! Let him deny it!"

"Say but one word," cried Louise; "but one word to silence for ever this slanderous man. Is it true?"

Raven sank into his chair, exclaiming, "My dear child, it is!"

CHAPTER LXVII.

IN WHICH A VARIETY OF MATTERS ARE EXPLAINED.

As this confession at once sealed the lips of incredulity—albeit Louise clung to Raven still as if she felt it even then to be impossible—Valentine, whom nothing could deprive of self-possession, on the instant begged of Whitely to retire with him, in order that the effects of the sudden disclosure might in some degree subside before any other decisive steps were taken. To this Whitely consented, and they quitted the room, leaving Louise with her face buried in her hands by the side of Raven, who appeared to have reached the very depths of despair, while Llewellen stood at his back, as motionless as if he had been absolutely petrified.

On reaching the drawing-room, Valentine and Whitely, with the view of considering what course would be the best to pursue under the circumstances, drew to the table, while the sentimental Joseph, in order to listen without being suspected, went to one of the windows, where, having drawn a hymn-book from his pocket, he seemed to be lost in religious contemplation.

"Well," said Valentine, "of course there can be no doubt now about the correctness of that which this man has disclosed, Raven himself having admitted it to be true: the only question therefore is, what is best to be done?"

"That is the only question," said Whitely; "I wish to do nothing with rashness—nothing without due consideration."

"I am sure of it: I am also sure that, however great may be your contempt for the feelings of Raven, you will avoid doing anything which may inflict an additional wound upon those of poor Louise."

"I am of course anxious, most anxious, to act with strict regard to the feelings of my own dear child," said Whitely.

"Being quite certain of that," rejoined Valentine, "it is with confidence I suggest that the immediate departure of Louise from this house ought not to be insisted upon."

"What!" exclaimed Whitely, "leave her here, and that with the wretch who would have kept her for ever from me?"

"For the present!—until she becomes more calm!—until matters can be arranged! You would not surely insist upon her leaving at once, without having time allowed to make the slightest preparation? But I wish you would speak with my uncle on the subject. Will you remain here till he comes? I will send for him instantly."

"I'll wait for him with pleasure. Before I act in this matter I'd rather, much rather see him."

Valentine therefore rang the bell, and having written a hasty note to his uncle, requesting him to come without a moment's delay, he desired the servant to take it with all possible speed, it being a matter of the highest importance.

While the servant was waiting for this note he caught sight of the sentimental Joseph—notwithstanding that pious individual was so deep in the beautiful spirit of his hymns that he kept the book strictly up to his eyes, that those organs might not vainly wander—and having become assured of its being *the* Joseph and no one but the Joseph, he took the note, and promised to make all possible haste; but before he left the house, he communicated what he had seen to the rest of the servants, who undertook to keep a remarkably sharp look-out till he returned.

Valentine, as soon as the note had been despatched, begged Whitely to excuse him, and returned to Louise, whom he found in tears on the sofa with Llewellen, while

Raven, with his hand over his eyes, still sat in his easy chair motionless.

"This," said Louise, extending her hand to Valentine as he entered, "Oh! this is a heavy blow indeed!"

"It is," returned Valentine, as he approached and sat beside her; "it is a heavy blow, my dearest girl; but we must not sink beneath even this."

Louise moved her head mournfully, and sighed.

"Courage, my own Louise, courage!" continued Valentine. "Retire for the present; come, let us seek my mother: with her you will be more calm: come!—come!"

He raised her from the sofa, and led her gently to the door, but they had no sooner reached it than Raven cried, "Louise!"—when on the instant she turned and flew into the arms extended to receive her, exclaiming, "My father!—Oh, be my father still!"

For some time she remained clasped in Raven's arms, but neither uttered, nor attempted to utter, another word: she sobbed aloud, while the tears gushed down his furrowed cheeks, and they both seemed to endure the most intense mental anguish.

At length Valentine approached with the view of prevailing upon them to separate until they had become more tranquil, and eventually succeeded in inducing them to do so, having declared again and again that he would not allow Louise to be taken abruptly from the house.

"I rely with the utmost confidence upon you," said Raven. "I feel that whatever I may be, or may appear—for I appear in this case, to be worse than I am—you will not suffer her to be torn from me yet."

Valentine repeated his assurance, and left the room with Louise.

The widow had heard nothing of this revelation. She had indeed been informed by one of the servants that there had been something of a stir; but of the cause she continued to be in the most perfect ignorance until Valentine explained it on bringing up Louise. How great her surprise was then may be imagined. She confessed that she in reality knew neither what to think nor what to say, and when Valentine had intimated to her that, until the whole matter had been explained, the less she thought and said about it the better, he left her and Louise, to rejoin Whitely and his pseudo-sentimental companion.

On the stairs, however, he encountered Llewellen, who was in a truly wretched state. The whole of his intellectual faculties appeared to be deranged: he looked like a morally disorganized man.

"My tear poy," said he, "here's a plesset pusiness!—here's *tooings* and cootness knows it! Putt phot's to pe tun, my poy, phot's to be tun? Too step here, ant just tell me phot hur'm to too."

Here he took the arm of Valentine, and having led him into an apartment with an expression of vacant wonder, resumed:—

"Now phot's to pe tun? How am hur to act? Phot can hur too, look you? I never tit!—oh! my tear poy, too tell me how hur'm to proceet."

"Have patience for a short time, Fred, and I shall know how to advise you. At present there is but one thing I feel myself justified in recommending you to do, and that is to keep silent."

"Putt it is such a pusiness! Am hur pount to pelieve that Mr. Phitely is really my father?"

"Why, I think there can be but little doubt about it now."

"Well, putt inteet, now, look you, cootness knows, it will pe so very ott to call him father, inteet!"

"I have no doubt it will seem rather strange at first; but you will soon get accustomed to that."

"Very coot, my poy; putt hur'll not pelieve it! Have'nt hur another father town at Caermarthen?"

"I should say that the chances are, if Mr. Whitely be your father, that you have not."

"Putt hur ton't pelieve that he is my father. Hur'll write town to Caermarthen by this plesset tay's post, and ask my own father—that is, my father Llewellen—phether he is my father or not. If he says that he is, hur shall know phot to too; hur'll not pelieve Phitely, nor ten thousant Phitelys pesites! Hur'll write town this plesset tay, look you!"

"Wait, my dear fellow; have patience," said Valentine; "at least for a day or two wait."

"Well, well! if you think it will pe petter to wait, phy hur'll too so."

"Before the day is at an end, we shall doubtless know more, much more than we do now."

"Very well; then hur'll tefer writing, look you; putt hur ton't inteet like to pe pount to pelieve that any potty's my father that chooses to say so without any particle of proof, ant cootness knows it. Put hur say, my poy," he added, with a singular expression, "phot a very troll co it will pe if Louey *shoot* pe my sister!—hur say, if she shoot! If that phere all, look you, hur shootn't care a pit apout that, for hur always tit love Louey tearly; putt hur won't pelieve Phitely's my father pecause hur shootn't mint if Louey phere my sister."

"No, that would be scarcely worth while. I confess to you that at present I have very little doubt about it myself; but we shall see. In a few hours the thing will be placed beyond dispute."

A coach at this moment drew up to the door, with the servant who had been sent for Uncle John upon the box. "Now," cried Valentine, "we shall soon know all. Here is my uncle. I must go and explain to him before he sees Whitely; but immediately after our interview I'll let you know, Fred, precisely how the matter stands."

He then ran down, and met Uncle John in the hall, and having led him into the parlour, related what had occurred with all possible brevity. Uncle John was astounded at the intelligence.

"Is it possible!" he exclaimed, "is it possible! Is it—can it be possible! Whitely's children—not his! He has not kept faith with me; I've been deceived! He led me to believe—What could be his motive? Not his, but Whitely's children, after all! Are they together?"

"No. Whitely is in the drawing-room with the man whom he brought as a witness. He is waiting to see you. I begged of him to do so, being anxious for you to prevail upon him not to insist upon the immediate removal of Louise, because, as that *must not* be, his refusal to consent may create a disturbance which it would be of course better to avoid."

"Of course, my boy; of course: yes, I'll go to him at once. Come with me. Bad conduct; bad, very bad conduct."

They now reached the drawing-room, and Whitely rose to meet Uncle John as he entered, and they shook hands with all their wonted warmth.

"Why, my friend," said Uncle John, wiping his brow with great energy, the perspiration the intelligence had caused being very profuse, "I have been amazed!—absolutely amazed!"

"And well you may be," cried Whitely, "well you may be amazed; but not at the falsehood of a villain!—no, that is not amazing!"

"I couldn't have believed it!" rejoined Uncle John; "I really couldn't have believed it!"

"I don't see that we had any right to expect that what he stated was the truth. It is now, however, useless to dwell upon that. The question is, having (thank Heaven!) discovered my children, how am I to proceed? As I explained to Valentine, I wish to do nothing rashly. Before I act, I am, therefore, anxious to have your advice."

"Upon my word," said Uncle John, "I scarcely feel competent to give any advice at all; I seem bewildered; the thing appears like a dream. Did Raven himself enter into any explanation?"

"Not the slightest; nor was any explanation demanded. It was sufficient for me that he confessed that the children were mine."

"But I cannot conceive what induced him to wish to keep them from you! What object could he have!—what motive! Until I have some explanation from him, I shall not feel myself justified in advising you how to act. You are not I hope in haste; let me go to him at once and hear what he has to say upon the subject. I shall then be better able to judge. Shall I do so?"

"By all means if you wish it," replied Whitely, "I am in no sort of haste, I can wait."

"I'll detain you but a very short time," said Uncle John; "I'll be back as soon as possible. Valentine, remain with Mr. Whitely till I return."

He then left them, and after having sent to Raven to request an immediate interview, which was granted, he proceeded to the room in which the secret had been revealed, and in which he found Raven apparently half dead.

Their meeting was awkward. Raven himself seemed ashamed to advance, while Uncle John felt that if he offered his hand as a friend he should be a hypocrite. They therefore regarded each other with coldness; but Uncle John, the very moment he had taken a chair, said, "My good friend, how came you to mislead, to deceive me? While conducting the arrangement which it gave me great pleasure to conduct, I did expect, I had a right to expect, that acting as I was in the capacity of friend to both parties, both parties would treat me with fairness and candour. I am however sorry to find that you were not candid with me—that you induced me to believe that which has been proved to be false."

"It is true," said Raven, "that although I was guilty of no direct falsehood, I led you to believe, when I said that I *would* not, that I meant that I *could* not give any information on the subject of the children: that I admit, and I was prompted to this species of prevarication by a most powerful motive; but as I have ever regarded you as one who would scorn to press heavily upon a fallen man, harshness from you is what I did not expect: it is, sir, a thing which I will not endure."

"I have no desire to be harsh," said Uncle John; "I have no right to be harsh; but I have a right, when a man misleads me, to let him know that I feel myself aggrieved."

"Even assuming that you have this right," rejoined Raven, "is it correct, is it generous to exercise it just as you see a man's spirit broken down?"

"Heaven forbid that I should augment any man's affliction, but—"

"Had I been lost," resumed Raven, "to every sense of generosity and of justice, or dead to every virtuous feeling, viewing the world as it is, and like a man of the world holding its opinion in contempt; all this would have been avoided. I should not have been placed in so humiliating a position; but as—by virtue of endeavouring to conciliate those who never could be conciliated, instead of putting at once a bold face upon the matter, and setting them at defiance—I *am* in this position, unkindness at the hands of those from whom I expected friendly advice and assistance, has a tendency to make me callous and to incline me to treat the world as the world treats me, with disdain."

"Mr. Raven," said Uncle John gravely, "I do not think that you will feel yourself justified in saying that I ever behaved in an unfriendly manner towards you."

"It is unfriendly to speak with harshness to me at such a time as this. At any other time I could have borne it. It is only when a man is in an extremity that he needs a friend, and that is precisely the time when he finds himself deserted. All that I have done since the first false step was taken the whole world may know; with that single exception there is no act of mine of which I need be ashamed, having been prompted by generosity on the one hand, and on the other by the purest affection. However I have no wish to explain; I find that all are against me."

"I am not against you; none who were previously for you are against you. I spoke to you on the subject rather sternly, I admit; but why? not because I wished to be against you, but solely because I conceived it to be a pity that you were not more ingenuous, more candid."

"I was as candid as under the circumstances I could be, or at least could feel myself justified in being. The fact of those children being Whitely's I wished from my heart to conceal. I promised *her* who was their mother—I promised her on her deathbed that I would keep from them all knowledge of her shame, and for ever would it have been kept from them, had it not been for that atrocious hypocritical villain whom I have pampered for years, and who of course sold the secret after having sworn solemnly to preserve it in consideration of my having given him a sum sufficient to keep him independent for life."

"Then," said Uncle John, "their mother is dead?"

"Yes, she died soon, very soon after she left her husband; for although she had every possible comfort, and was treated by me with the utmost tenderness and affection, the step she had taken weighed so heavily upon her heart, that it was not long before that heart was broken. Her children I loved as dearly as if they had been my own, and had they been my own they could not have displayed a greater affection for me. That dear girl, Louise, was especially fond of me: I need not add that I doted upon her, I dote upon her still; I love her with all the fond intensity of an affectionate father, and must continue thus to love her till I sink into the grave. She has been more than a child to me; she has been an angel!—May the angels hover round and protect her for ever! Oh, my friend, it may have been thought that my commerce with the world would have destroyed the best feelings of my nature; but if you knew how purely, how devotedly I love that affectionate girl, you would not be surprised at my having descended to prevarication in order that she might still be, in her view, as well as in the view of the world in general, my own dear child. As my own I have cherished her fondly, tenderly: she was my comfort, the fountain of my joy: it was my delight, and the highest delight I ever experienced—to promote her happiness; and yet on the very eve of my pleasurable task being perfected—just as that happiness was about to be permanently secured, she is proclaimed to be not my own child, and torn from me for ever! It is this which afflicts me beyond the power of expression. Nothing could have afflicted me more; no calamity which could have befallen me could have struck so deeply into my heart, for I now feel completely alone in the world, deprived for ever of her who was my solace—my child!"

Here Raven was much affected, and so indeed was Uncle John, who, scarcely knowing what to say, remained silent. At length Raven, with considerable emotion, resumed:—

"It may have been wrong," said he, "nay, I cannot but feel it to have been wrong, very wrong, even to wish to conceal those children from their father. I cannot justify myself, nor can I on any grounds be justified; still, in extenuation, it may be said that I did not conceal them wantonly, or with any cruel aim, my object for such concealment—besides that of fostering that fond devoted girl as my own—

being the performance of my promise to her broken-hearted mother, that her children should if possible be kept for ever in utter ignorance of her disgrace. This was the great object I had in view, and that object would assuredly have been attained, had it not been for the treachery of that pernicious miscreant. But the die is cast—I am alone!"

Raven again paused, but Uncle John still knew not what to say. He could not tell what Raven really was. He could not believe him to be an absolutely heartless villain; for, notwithstanding his conduct towards Whitely himself had been villanous in the extreme, he, in the view of Uncle John, had certain redeeming points, to which he was not indisposed to attach due weight. He therefore did not feel justified in saying anything which could be construed into an opinion upon the subject; but, at length, finding that Raven was not about to proceed, he, conceiving that he ought to say something on the occasion, inquired why Fred had in infancy been separated from Louise.

"I parted them," said Raven, "I brought them up, not as brother and sister, but as cousins, in order that the secret might be the more effectually preserved. I regarded it as being highly probable that when Fred became a man his curiosity would prompt him to go back, with the view of ascertaining certain matters having reference to their origin, which Louise would not think of herself, or if she did, she would not have those facilities which would be at his command. I therefore sent him into Wales, and placed him under the care of a kind, quiet creature, who brought him up as his own son, and a good fellow he has made of him; a better hearted boy never breathed: still the loss of him, my friend, I could endure: I have not, of course, those feelings for him that I have for Louise; she has ever been with me,—she has ever been my joy, my sweet companion, my pride; I cannot bear to part with her: I feel that I shall not long survive it; but at all events she must not be torn from me yet."

"We shall be able to arrange that, I have no doubt," said Uncle John. "Valentine has already spoken to Whitely on the subject. I'll return to him, and urge it still further. I think that I may say you may be sure that that at least will be arranged."

"Now that I am in your hands again," observed Raven, "my mind is more at ease. You will do the best you can for me, I know."

"All that can be done shall be done, be assured of that. I will go at once, and make the best arrangement I can."

Uncle John then returned to the drawing-room, where Valentine and Whitely were still engaged in earnest conversation, while the sly sentimentalist, with the utmost attention, was listening at the window with the hymn-book in his hand.

It was abundantly evident to Uncle John, as he entered, that Valentine had been applying the balm of reason to Whitely's inflamed passions with success, for he was perfectly calm, and spoke with the utmost composure.

"Well, my friend," said he, when Uncle John had taken a seat beside him, "are you now in a position to give me advice?"

"I now feel that I am," replied Uncle John. "But in the first place, in order that you may judge for yourself, I'll not only relate the substance of what passed between us, but will repeat it word for word, as nearly at least as I can remember."

He did so: he went through it faithfully: he made no effort to colour any fact: the points which related to Raven's great affection for Louise were extremely effective; but that effect was produced without design.

Whitely was throughout most attentive. He weighed every word. Sitting in a studious attitude, his head resting upon his hand, not a single muscle moved, nor did he utter a syllable until Uncle John had concluded, when he exclaimed aloud, "Had he not been the seducer of my wife, I could have honoured him!—had he taken the children of a fallen woman, not being himself the cause of her fall, and thus cherished them until the feelings of a father had been engendered, I would have worshipped—aye, *worshipped* that man!—but being the seducer, the *murderer* of my wife, his love for them prompts me to hate him the more! But I will be calm—I will still be calm!—he has robbed me of their affection—the dear love of my own children—still I will be calm."

During this burst of passion, brief as it was, the sentimentalist at the window placed the hymn-book upon his knees, and rubbed his hands in a state of ecstasy. He was in raptures, and would have gloried in it had Whitely, in a paroxysm of rage, rushed into Raven's room, and either strangled him or stabbed him to the heart. Whitely, however, as if to cut the sentimentalist to the soul, resumed his former attitude, and after a pause, said, tranquilly, "Well, my friend, what do you advise?"

"Why," replied Uncle John, "I should say that for the sake of poor Louise, and for her sake alone, things ought to remain for the present as they are. You of course would not think of compelling her to quit the house at an hour's notice. Under the circumstances, that would be on your part impolitic, seeing that it might tend to shock her feelings, and thus to create an unfavourable first impression. No, let what is to be done be done gently. For a day or two, say, let no stir be made in the matter; in the interim, you know, something may strike us: at all events, nothing can be gained either by harshness or precipitation."

"In that I quite agree with you," said Whitely. "Well, my friend, well!—I will be advised by you: for the sake of my child, I'll allow her to remain for a day or so, in order—"

"You're a fool, sir, if you do, sir!" exclaimed the sentimentalist.

"Come here, sir," said Valentine.

"D'yer think I'm afeared, then, to come?" cried the fellow, closing his hymn-book, and bouncing up to the table with great ferocity of aspect.

"Now, sir," said Valentine, "why will Mr. Whitely be a 'fool' for allowing his daughter to remain here for the present?"

"Why will he!" cried the sentimentalist —"why will he! What! d'yer think *I'd* let her stop with him? No, not another hour! I'd drag her away at once! I'd break his heart! That would do it! I know it! I'm sure of it! Oh! I'd let her remain with that son of Satan! not—"

"Joseph," said Whitely, with much coolness, "I don't think that I shall want you again to-day; you can go now, but let me see you early in the morning."

"*Very* well, sir! Oh! very well; but you take my advice, sir; don't you let her stop; if you do, you only study the comfortabilities of a man which has a soul as never can and never ought to be saved."

"At ten in the morning," said Whitely, "I shall expect you."

This quiet way of repudiating the advice of the sentimentalist did not exactly meet his approbation; he, notwithstanding, on the instant prepared to depart, and having delivered himself finely of "Oh! very well!" he raised his extensive cravat, and left the room with the air of an individual slightly offended.

"Is that the man who was formerly in your service?" inquired Uncle John.

"Yes," replied Whitely, and I believe him to be one of the vilest and most contemptible scoundrels that ever had existence, although in this case I have been of course compelled to employ him. However, to revert to the great subject—for to me it is great, indeed all in all—I am willing to follow your advice, that is to say, I'll consent to allow my children to remain here a day or two longer, or until they shall have recovered from the sudden effects of the disclosure, provided, my friend, you feel sure, quite sure, that there will be nothing like concealment."

"I do feel sure," said Uncle John, "*so* sure, that I would willingly stake my life that nothing of the sort will be attempted."

"And so would I," cried Valentine; "indeed, I might perhaps be justified in declaring, in the name of Louise, that if under the circumstances such a proposition were made, it would be spurned."

"I am satisfied," said Whitely. "Thus, then, let it be. I shall probably see you in the course of to-morrow?"

"At any time," replied Uncle John; "but if you are not engaged, let us dine together to-day. Walk home with me, and then we can talk matters quietly over. It will be much better; come, what say you?"

Whitely consented, and they almost immediately afterwards left the house, much to the gratification of Valentine, with whom Whitely shook hands with unusual warmth on being accompanied by him to the door.

While descending the stairs with them, Valentine heard a most singular uproar below; but the moment they were gone, his ears were assailed with half-stifled cries of "Murder!—murder!—Fire!—fire!—Help!—help!—Fire!" mingled with certain shouts of indignation and of derision.

As all this was extremely irregular, Valentine, without the slightest ceremony, hastened below, and on arriving at the door of the kitchen beheld a strikingly effective and deeply interesting scene.

Joseph, the sanctimonious and sentimental Joseph—who, on being dismissed by Whitely, had been silently seized by the servants, who were anxious to settle certain matters with him privately—was at that particular period before the fire, between the reflector and the dripping utensil, in the central pool of which his devoted smalls had been immersed; and while the coachman held him tightly by the collar, and looked at him very fiercely indeed, the cook shook him with great ability with one hand, while with the other she held to his noble breast a sacrificial spit, which rendered it impossible for him, without being pierced, to move forward, and as for stepping back!—why, the fire was very large, and very clear at the bottom, while at the top the flames ascended with a roar. It was an affecting sight. In the Martyrology of the middle ages, there is nothing at all like it described. The idea of an individual, a tidy individual—an individual, moreover, of sentiment and feeling, being pinned in this position—the tails of his respectable coat being scorched, even after his smalls had been saturated with hot mutton fat, is ap-

The Roasting of Joseph.

P.374.

palling; and if the idea, the bare idea, is appalling, what must the reality have been!

And yet there stood Valentine coolly at the door, while the victim was being thus roasted behind and assaulted in front by two creatures, neither of whom had the slightest respect for his feelings, and who were stimulated by the applause of the butler, the footman, and two housemaids, who were absolutely base enough to glory in the scene! Why, it was monstrous!—almost as monstrous as the outrage itself! And why was that outrage committed? Why simply because this individual had, in the plenitude of his politeness, undertaken to pay into a certain Savings' Bank certain sums of money, belonging to those two creatures, which money, while lost in the contemplation of the world's unrighteousness, he had altogether forgotten to pay in, albeit every sum, without a single exception, had been entered in their books with the utmost regularity! It was for this, forsooth—this omission, this oversight—that *he*, a respectable person, was pummelled—that *he* was made to sit with white kerseymere smalls, first in a dripping-pan's well-supplied pool, and then in an adjacent scuttle of coals—that he was throttled, half strangled, and shaken, by the coachman, and scarified, nay, almost sacrificed by the cook, while the perspiration starting in a state of alarm from every pore, he was being roasted behind into actual crackling! Again, it may be said to have been an affecting sight. It was touching in the extreme to hear him implore them to desist. He spoke to them with all the ardour of a righteous man upon the subject. He besought them for their own dear sakes to give in; he assured them, with a beautiful expression, that if they did not, they could never be saved; but he couldn't reach their hearts—he could make no impression; they still kept on, until he caught a glimpse of Valentine, to whom he on the instant cried aloud for aid.

"Oh! save me, sir!—save me!" he exclaimed, in the most touching tones, and with a heart-rending aspect, "save me, or I drop!"

"What is all this?" cried Valentine, coming forward. "Why are you here?"

"They dragged me down here, sir; I didn't come down o' my own accord."

"Well! why do you make so much noise?"

"Oh! they've been a-murdering of me, sir: they've been a-using me shameful! They have indeed!"

Hereupon the ill-used individual burst very correctly into tears.

"What is the meaning of all this?" inquired Valentine of the coachman. "What is it all about?"

The coachman and the cook on the instant set to work, and explained it all with amazing clearness, considering they made a duet of it throughout.

"You are a scoundrel!" said Valentine, addressing the sentimentalist, which was highly reprehensible; but he said, "You are a scoundrel!" and then added, "Do you mean to return this money?"

"You haven't heered the merits of the case," cried the grossly ill-used man, while with a knife he was endeavouring to scrape the grease off his clothes, and thereby to restore the respectability of his appearance.

"You received this money to pay in, did you not?"

"I certingly did."

"And you did not pay it in."

"Why, that's where it is—that's the point!"

"Exactly!" said Valentine, "that *is* the point. Instead of putting it into the bank you put it into your pocket. There's no mistaking the *point!* Now, villain, I mean to take this matter entirely into my own hands. The sum you have thus *stolen* is twenty-five pounds."

"I didn't steal it!—nor it aint twenty-five pounds! But I'll give 'em the twenty-five pounds! Lor bless us! I aint destitute of twenty-five pounds!"

"I know that you are not," said Valentine; "but we shall want a hundred pounds of you to settle this affair."

"A hundred pounds! You won't get a hundred pounds out of me I can tell you."

"Oh, yes, we shall!" said Valentine. "Coachman! I want you to run to Mr. Whitely—"

"Mr. Whitely has nothing to do with my private affairs."

"Oh! but in this case he will have a little to do with them. You have a cheque of his now in your possession. That cheque shall be stopped."

"But it shall not be stopped! And if it is, I can recover: I can recover, sir, by law."

"Law! That is well thought of!—an excellent suggestion. It will be the shorter way. Oh! never mind the money. Coachman! fetch me an officer."

"An officer! What for?"

"Merely to take you into custody."

"But I've committed no crime! It's only a debt—it aint a robbery!"

"We shall see what it is, when we get before the magistrate; and since I have taken the matter in hand, be assured that if it be a transportable offence, you *shall* be transported. Fetch me an officer."

"Oh! for the love of grace, sir, don't send for no officers! I don't like officers; I don't, sir, indeed, sir! I'll give cook and coachman the money back with pleasure."

"You shall give, sir, fifty pounds to each of them. By doing so only can you induce me not to proceed according to law."

"But fifty pounds a-piece, that is to say, a hundred pounds, sir—consider, sir, what an enormity!"

"Well! it is not of much importance. It will be better that you should pay in person, perhaps, after all."

"But I'd rather not, sir! much rather not."

"What is the amount of that cheque?"

"It's only a hundred and fifty, sir: only a hundred and fifty."

"Very well. Mr. Raven had provided amply for you when you betrayed him: you will therefore take your choice: either give one hundred pounds out of that cheque, to those two persons whom you have robbed, or take the consequence of being pursued, as I will pursue you with the utmost rigour of the law."

"But fifty, sir! fifty between 'em!—surely that will content 'em! they wouldn't like to press upon me *too* hard!"

"Nothing less than the sum I named shall they receive. Decide at once: if you hesitate—"

"No, no, no; I don't hesitate, only it is *very* hard; I'll send them the money tomorrow."

"You are not to be trusted. No, that will not do."

"Well, as soon as I get the cheque cashed, sir, I'll come back, upon my word and honour."

"I have no faith in either your word or your honour. Besides, I am inclined to take the responsibility entirely off your hands. Give coachman the cheque. It will save you a deal of trouble. Let him get it cashed, and then the thing will be settled."

"I'll not give the cheque! I'd rather die than be thus plundered of my money. I won't do it."

"Very well. We now see the value of your word and honour. You have taken your choice. We'll have no further parley. An officer shall be sent for at once, and I'd have you understand, that if once you get into an officer's hands, the thing must go on;—a compromise then, will be out of the question."

The cruelly ill-used individual did not like this by any means. He wept bitterly and sobbed like a child, but having a natural horror of being brought to justice, and being ignorant of the amount of punishment that would be inflicted upon him, in the event of his being unable to convince the court that, in keeping the money he had no dishonest motive, he eventually drew forth the cheque, and gave it to the coachman to get cashed, and while doing so it was really heart-rending to see him. The coachman was, of course, in the highest possible spirits, and so was the cook, but the rest of the servants were not, perhaps, in such ecstasies as they would have been, had it happened that they had been plundered as well. They were not, however, displeased; on the contrary, they enjoyed the thing much; and endeavoured in their way to solace the victim, who was at that time a most intensely miserable man.

As the coachman had been ordered to take a cab to the banker's and back, he soon returned with three fifty pound notes, which he placed in the hands of Valentine, who, in the name of the victim, gave one to cook, another to coachman, and the third to the victim himself, at the same time intimating to him that he was then at perfect liberty to go.

Of course, the state of the sentimentalist's mind at that period was extremely afflicting: his heart was wounded to an unfathomable depth, while the feelings which reigned in the ascendant were those of agony. He, notwithstanding, without delay, took the hint that he might leave, for, having deposited his note in a bag, he looked at his enemies with unspeakable ferocity, and stepped into the area, from which he declared with great solemnity that they should suffer for what they had done, and that he would have his revenge upon them all, and having delivered himself freely to this effect, he rushed up the steps in a state bordering upon madness.

Valentine—who felt that although the settlement of this matter had taken up some time, that time had not been altogether wasted—now returned to Louise, whom he found with the widow still in tears.

"Come, my dear girl," said he, taking her hand, "this, indeed, must not be; I must not have you trembling as if you were on the very brink of despair!"

"Oh! my dear Valentine!" exclaimed Louise, again bursting into tears, "you are the only one on earth now to whom I can with confidence look for protection!"

"I know it," said Valentine, assuming a gaiety, with the view of relieving her, to some extent, of her sadness. "I know it, my Louise, and I shall presume upon it accordingly. I have you now in my power, and shall therefore, of course, make you act precisely as I may command."

"I am not afraid of you, my dearest,"

said Louise, with much emotion. "The more I might feel myself in your power, the less I should fear your tyranny, my love."

"Have you so much confidence in me? Well, I believe it. You are a dear good girl, but you want more courage."

"But consider, my dearest boy!" said the widow, "consider what an awful thing it is! It is not like one of those common occurrences which may be borne without a pang, because their character is ephemeral. It is a permanent thing, my love, you must remember, and a dreadful thing it is to be permanent, when you come to think of it!"

"That is a very correct observation of yours, mother. You are perfectly right. But I can't see very distinctly why we should either cover ourselves with sackcloth and ashes, or lie down and die, because a circumstance occurs over which we had and could have no control! Resignation, mother,—your own fovourite resignation,—is a great Christian virtue, I admit; but I hold that it does not become us as Christians to sink under every trouble which may assail us, seeing that we are morally and physically formed to oppose them with success. It is our duty to grapple with troubles as they rise: if we do so boldly and at once, they are perfectly sure to be overcome."

"Yes, my dear boy, that is all very well; but we cannot help feeling: when troubles like these come so suddenly upon us, we cannot but be shocked: it is natural."

"I admit it; but it is not natural for a shock to continue. It soon ceases to be a shock. We have no control over it: we cannot grapple with it. But we have control over, and therefore ought to grapple with the effects of that shock. A shock no sooner comes than it goes, leaving its effects for us to manage, which effects can be managed and ought to be managed: he who allows them in any case to obtain the mastery over him, must never presume to boast his moral strength."

"Yes, my dear, this mode of bidding defiance to Fate, by standing erect and with a bold front exclaiming, 'No circumstance shall ever bow me down to the earth; no series of troubles shall ever break my spirit; nothing shall ever prevent me from grappling with an enemy who will be sure to conquer me if I fail to conquer him!'—this, I say, is all very correct, and very laudable in you men, and nothing more than we have a right to expect; but with us it is totally different, my dear; we haven't the strength, we haven't the nerve to bear up against these things: we are more sensitive: our feelings are more acute; our hearts are more easily wounded, more delicate, more tender, more susceptible of sad impressions; this boldness is not to be expected from us."

"I have often," said Valentine, as the widow took the hand of Louise, and pressed it and held it in her lap, "I have often thought it a pity that it should be the fashion to cultivate female weakness."

"The fashion to cultivate female weakness! The fashion, my love!—the idea!"

"Doubtless in your view it seems very absurd; but if you examine the morally enervating tendency of the present system of female education, you will find that weakness in every point is cultivated studiously, and that therefore the application of the term 'fashion' is correct. But we will not dwell upon this. Whatever your physical weakness may be, your moral strength—although enervated by education—is naturally equal with ours. You have the power to meet troubles—for troubles form our text—with equal firmness. If you repudiate the exercise of that power, of course weakness will prevail."

"But this of ours," said Louise, "can scarcely be called one of the ordinary troubles of life—a mere casualty!"

"Granted. If it were, its importance would be diminished. If such things were to happen every day, we should think but little of them; but troubles, my love, are the emblems of cowardice: you no sooner oppose them than they take to their heels; but if you fear them, or try to run from them, or sink before them, or exhibit the slightest irresolution, they will tyrannize over, trample upon, and torture you. Meet them boldly, my Louise, and behold how they fly!"

"But how is this to be met? How am I to meet this?"

"I can tell you, and will, if you promise to act upon my advice."

"Well, I *never* saw any one take things so coolly in my life!" exclaimed the widow. "Whatever may occur, however serious, however momentous, you look at it as calmly as if you had expected it: nothing seems to disturb you—nothing seems to put you out."

"Many things disturb me, mother; but I look at whatever difficulty may occur as a thing which ought promptly to be met, and I accordingly make up my mind at once to meet it."

"What, then, in this instance, would you propose?" inquired Louise.

"You promise to be guided by me?"

"I have so much confidence in you, my love, that I do, without a moment's hesitation. I place myself entirely in your hands.

I will go by your directions; whatever you direct me to do shall be done."

"You are a dear, good, confiding little creature, my Louise; but I believe you know that I knew that before. Now attend: Mr. Whitely is your father—there can, of course, be no doubt of that now—and as a father, you are called upon to regard and to love him. Very well. Now although we have frequently heard of such things, and have frequently seen them represented on the stage, I hold it to be impossible for you at once to inspire those feelings of affection for him which a child ought to feel for a father, and which, although they may be indeed engendered in infancy, time and constant communication alone can establish. But your position is one of even greater difficulty than that: your affections as a child having been engrossed, cherished, and ripened by the love and fostering care of another, you are called upon suddenly to transfer those affections from him whom you have ever believed to be your father to one of whom you had previously no absolute knowledge."

"Precisely so," interposed Louise. "It is that which I feel most acutely. It is, indeed, the very difficulty which I fear is insurmountable."

"A moment's patience," said Valentine. "That is the point to which we are coming. It is abundantly clear, that, if under these circumstances you were to leave this house—in other words, that if you were to leave Mr. Raven, to live with Mr. Whitely, you would feel, to say the least of it, excessively awkward."

"Oh! I should be wretched!—perfectly miserable!"

"Exactly. However highly you might esteem Mr. Whitely; however sincerely you might respect him, or however anxious you might be to love him; you would be conscious that you possessed not those feelings towards him, which a child ought to have towards a parent—for those feelings *must* be established by degrees—and that very consciousness would render you unhappy."

"It would indeed; I might perhaps, in time, teach my heart how to love him; but to love him at once, as I feel that as his child I ought to love him, would be impossible, and the impossibility of doing so, to me, would be dreadful."

"This, then, is the difficulty which we have now to meet. It is manifest that you will not be permitted to remain here much longer. It is scarcely to be expected, that Mr. Whitely will consent to that: I confess to you, that if I were he, I would not myself. The question, then, resolves itself to this. I'll put it plainly, because I conceive that, in all such cases, plainness is much to be preferred. Will it be better, under the circumstances, for you to live with Mr. Whitely, or—with me?"

Louise blushed, and dropped her head.

"Nay," continued Valentine, "I do not expect you to answer this question. I have undertaken to answer it for you; *I* have to decide, and really, to give expression to that which I most sincerely feel, I do think that, all things considered, it will be infinitely better for us to marry at once, when, without the slightest annoyance, you will be able to imbibe and to cherish by degrees, those feelings for Mr. Whitely, which, of course, you will be anxious to entertain."

Valentine paused; but Louise was still silent.

"What think you, mother?" he at length continued. "Do you not think that that will be the better course to pursue?"

"Why, my dear," returned the widow, "that you know, is an extremely delicate question for me to answer. It would certainly, at once, do away with that which we conceived to be the greatest difficulty to be encountered."

"Of course," rejoined Valentine. "What I propose then, is this: that the fifteenth be still the happy day—that we, Louise, be as we had previously settled, on the fifteenth, united. This is what I *propose*, and as I can see no objection at all to it, I hereby direct you—seeing, that you have promised to go by my directions—to prepare for our union on the fifteenth instant, not only that you may escape that position of embarrassment which we have just been considering, but that we may no longer be subjected to those disappointments and delays which we have found so particularly disagreeable."

Still, with downcast eyes, Louise was silent; her heart beat an approval, which her tongue, however, refused to express.

"Having thus," resumed Valentine, with a smile—"Having thus, then, given my directions, my task is for the present at an end; unless, indeed—for I have no desire to be despotic—you can give me a single reason why those directions should not be implicitly obeyed. Am I," he added, after a pause, "to understand by your silence, that you know of no such reason?"

"My dearest Valentine!" exclaimed Louise, fervently, "I am at your disposal. I *said* that I would be guided by you, Valentine; I will! But do not, pray do not wish me to take this step before the consent of Mr. Whitely—I mean, of my father—has been obtained."

"Of course, my love, he must be consulted: I would not, on any account, proceed without first consulting him."

"There's a dear!"

"Although I, on one occasion, did speak harshly to him in order to protect Mr. Raven, I believe that he has ceased to think of that; and I feel quite convinced, that when I point out to him the peculiar position in which you will otherwise be placed, his consent to our immediate union will not be withheld. He dines to-day with my uncle. It may, perhaps, appear too precipitate if I name it to him to-day; but when I join them in the evening—they will, no doubt, have been conversing on the subject—I will invite him to dine with me tomorrow, at our house, when I will lay the whole matter before him, and I have not the smallest doubt that, for the sake of your feelings, which, I am sure, he is anxious to study, he will readily give his consent. Do not, therefore, for a moment, anticipate an unfavourable answer from him; feel certain, as I do, that we shall have to encounter no opposition, and act precisely as if he had consented already."

"I will do so," said Louise, "you have made me comparatively happy: you have, indeed, proved to me that difficulties, when promptly met, vanish, and have thereby taught me a lesson which, if acted upon, must smooth the path of life."

"It is the grand secret, my love," returned Valentine. "But I wish it were a secret no longer: if it were but universally known, the happiness of mankind in the aggregate would be very materially enhanced, for it would then be apparent to all, that although men are 'born to troubles,' they are also born to surmount them."

"Well, now, really!" exclaimed the widow, "upon my word, this appears to be comparatively nothing, my love, now!"

"The difficulty," said Louise, "does seem to be, in a measure, overcome. I shall not, at all events, be placed in that distressing position, if, indeed, we are not opposed."

"Expect no opposition from Mr. Whitely," said Valentine, "I am convinced that he will gladly agree to anything calculated to promote your happiness."

"Do you think so?"

"I am sure of it! he has proved it already."

"He is a good creature: I feel that I almost love him now."

"Proceed with your preparations," said Valentine, rising from his seat; "you have nothing to fear, nor have you any time to lose. You will remember this is the tenth! The fifteenth will soon be here Louise, and then, my love!—and then!" he added, embracing her, and gazing upon her with the fondest affection—"But you know the rest! I'll now detain you no longer: for the present, adieu!" And again he embraced her, and having given the widow, who was more than ever proud of him, a filial kiss, he left them in tears, but they were not tears of sadness.

During the whole of this interview, Fred was in the library, waiting with the utmost impatience for Valentine to communicate to him the result of his conference with Whitely and Uncle John. He was very, very wretched; for although his case differed from that of Louise, inasmuch as he had never regarded Raven as his father, he had the feelings of a son for Mr. Llewellen of Caermarthen, whom he believed of course to be his *bonâ fide* father still.

When, therefore, Valentine, on leaving Louise, related to him all that had passed, as well between him and Whitely as between Raven and Uncle John, he felt and looked more bewildered than before.

"Phot!" he cried, "tit my uncle—that is, Mr. Raven—tit he confess it himself inteet? Tit he say my father—I mean Mr. Llewellen, cootness knows it, hur ton't know phot hur'm apout; hur ton't know phether hur'm stanting upon my het or my heels; it's like a tream!—putt tit he say that my father was not my father, ant that my name was Whitely, ant not Llewellen, look you? Now *tit* he say that?"

"He did," replied Valentine; "and it is of course perfectly certain that he would not have said it had it not been true."

"Oh! there's not a pit of tout at all about it if he said so: it's evitent he woot have teniet it if he coot: putt t'cootness, now, phot am hur to too? It is such an extraortinary pusiness!"

"It is an extraordinary affair; but we must manage to get over it, Fred, in some way!"

"Well, how am hur to act, look you? Only tell me phot hur'm to too, ant hur'll too it!"

"Well, we shall see. Shall we go and have a dinner together somewhere?"

"Apove all other things in the worlt! You are not then coing to tine here to-tay?"

"Why, I think it will be as well for me not to see Raven under the circumstances: you understand?"

"Oh, perfectly!—ant hur tecitetly acree with you. Phere shall we co?"

"Why, as we have just time to run down to Greenwich, I'll give you some white bait. It will be a change of scene. We'll have a quiet dinner, and then immediately return. I wish to go home early to join my uncle."

Fred was highly pleased with this proposition, and as they started at once, he seemed at once to forget all his troubles. It is true that on the way the fact of Whitely being his father did occasionally occur to him; but the thought seldom occupied his mind more than a moment: forasmuch as he was not a deep thinker, the appearance of almost every new object was sufficient for the time being to engross his attention, while Valentine, being himself in high spirits, made him as gay as if nothing of an extraordinary character had occurred.

On arriving at Greenwich they proceeded without loss of time to that which is decidedly the best house in the town, and ordered dinner, and until it was produced, Fred amused himself at the window by throwing sixpences into the depths of the mud—it being happily low water—that sundry particularly interesting and ragged young gentlemen might dexterously dive after them, and then turn ingenious somersets, to show that they did themselves a pleasure thereby. And it was extremely glorious to behold the development of pure joy which accompanied their agreeable evolutions—evolutions by which less gifted individuals would have been smothered, but which seemed to be the principal business of their uninsured lives. They were in raptures as they picked up the sixpences, and translated them freely from the mud to their mouths, as well to cleanse as to secure them, while —actuated by one of the purest and most beautiful feelings of our nature—they plunged with surpassing grace for more. Fred enjoyed it exceedingly. It was the very thing for him; indeed, he entered so fully into the spirit of the scene, and was so much delighted with its chief characteristics, that when dinner was produced, he rather regretted it than not, a thing which never did happen to him by any mistake before.

Once at the table, however, he quite forgot the mud larks, having transferred the whole of his attention from them to the scene before him. He ate, and, ate, and praised everything he ate; but when he came to the "phite pait," oh!—and goodness knew it—he never did in all the world taste anything so delicious. Were they "titlebats?" He made this inquiry, but to him it was a matter of the slightest importance, as he shovelled them into his mouth with the fork with at least as much spirit as grace.

When he had quite given in, when he felt and expressed himself perfectly sure that he was done, Valentine recalled his attention to the subject of the position in which he then stood, and after having briefly touched upon various points connected therewith, he explained to him that Whitely was then dining with Uncle John, and that it would, in his judgment, have an excellent effect if they were both unexpectedly to join them. To this proposition Fred was at first most unwilling to accede: "Hur shall pe so very awkwart," said he; "hur shan't know how to act, nor phot to too, nor phot to say."

"Why," said Valentine, "you have but to act as you would under any other circumstances. There will be no necessity for you to allude to the matter: I question, indeed, whether the subject will be mentioned this evening at all."

"Putt it's unpleasant, look you. Hur'd rather not, inteet."

"Well, I'll not press it; but I am quite sure that nothing would delight him more; and as you are his son, while I am his son-in-law, nearly, I think that we ought to begin now to do all in our power to please him."

"Phy, my poy!" exclaimed Fred, suddenly throwing himself back in the chair, with his eyes, mouth, and arms, very widely extended,—"Phy!" Here the idea stopped his breath again. "Phy!" he resumed, at length, "phy, phen you marry Louey, you and I shall pe *prothers*-in-law, look you! Well, I never heard of anything to come up to that!"

"Did it never strike you before?"

"*Ne*-ver!—cootness knows it, now, that will pe peautiful, inteet! Well, apove all other things in the worlt! Oh! hur ton't care now a pit apout it!"

"Then shall we go this evening?"

"Oh, yes! hur'll co, my poy, hur'll co; hur shall feel very awkwart, putt hur'll co."

"I think it will be better. Besides, it will break the ice. In a few days you will have to live with him, you know."

"Hur unterstant. Very coot. Yes, hur think it will pe petter. Putt, my poy!—the idea of our peing prothers-in-law!"

He dwelt upon this idea for some considerable time, and carried it out to a great extent, and viewed it in every shape with pleasure; in fact the subject in all its varied ramifications at intervals lasted him until they returned to town, indeed, it may be said, until they entered the room in which Whitely and Uncle John were sitting.

To Whitely their appearance was happiness. He rose the moment they entered, and grasped them both by the hand, and stood and looked at them alternately, as the tears gushed from his eyes, scarcely knowing which gave him the greater pleasure, the presence of Fred, or the fact of Valentine having brought him. Uncle John, too, was delighted to see them come in: indeed, the introduction made them all very happy, and they spent the remainder of the evening together in the most pleasant manner possible.

On the following day—Valentine having, in the course of the previous evening, invited Whitely and Fred to dine with him and his uncle at *the* house—they all met at the time appointed, and had a very agreeable dinner; shortly after which, Fred—as had been previously arranged—was sent for poste-haste by Louise; and as soon as he had left with the promise to return as soon as possible, Valentine opened the subject which was nearest his heart.

"Well," said he gaily, "you have not told me yet how you like the house?"

"I like it much," replied Whitely: "it is an elegant house, and the way in which it is furnished reflects great credit upon *somebody's* judgment and taste."

Uncle John bowed and smiled: he felt that remark to be particularly agreeable.

"Mr. Whitely," said Valentine, with some deliberation, "this house, as you are aware, was taken and furnished for one special purpose."

"I *am* aware of it," returned Whitely, "and as I guess your object in introducing the subject now, I will say at once that I hope that the purpose will be eventually fulfilled."

"As I view this," said Valentine, "as a consent on your part as the father of Louise, to our union, I am anxious, in connection with this subject, to appeal at once to your feelings as a father, and to your judgment as a man. Of course, Mr. Whitely, I need not explain to you the position of that good girl, Louise; you understand her feelings as well as I do: of that I am quite certain. But first allow me to ask you what you intend to do with her when you take her from Raven's house?"

"I mean to give her to you:—to enjoy for a few months her sweet society alone, that our affections as parent and child may be developed and cherished, and then to give her to you."

"*Give* her to me now," said Valentine, with great fervour of expression; "forego the pleasure which you anticipate from her society before marriage, and give her to me now."

Whitely was for some time silent; but after weighing the matter deliberately in his mind, he said, "If I should oppose your immediate marriage—I do not know that I shall, but if I should—you must not attribute that opposition to any objection on my part to you as a son-in-law; for I candidly confess to you that I have none: you must ascribe it solely to my desire to cultivate previously those feelings of affection which I am, of course, anxious should exist between me and my child."

"Precisely," said Uncle John, "I understand your motive, and I appreciate it highly. Although not a father myself, I can enter into your feelings as a father, and I must say that the anxiety you have expressed is very natural, very."

"You see, my friend," said Whitely, "I have been deprived of the affections of my children from their infancy. They have been unconscious even of my existence. Others have taken that place in their hearts which I ought to have occupied, and hence my desire to resume my natural position with regard to them must by all be understood and respected."

"Of course," said Uncle John, "and I am sure that Valentine sees the matter in precisely the same light."

"I do," said Valentine, "I do understand that desire, and I respect it. Heaven forbid that I should wish it to be in the smallest degree diminished. But why are you anxious to cultivate those feelings of affection previously to our marriage?"

"Because," replied Whitely, "after marriage I apprehend her affections will be devoted to you."

"I hope they will: I am sure that they will: but not exclusively! That kind of affection to which I as her husband may be supposed to be entitled, will not, I submit, interfere with her affection for you. Women, I apprehend, do not love their parents less for loving their husbands more. If that were the case, marriage would be destructive of the love which exists between parents and children, and he who gave his daughter in marriage to the man whom she loved would be thereby surrendering the affections of his child,—a thing of which he never dreams."

"I see that," said Whitely, "I clearly see that."

"Take it in another point of view," continued Valentine: "assume that Louise loves me—which I believe from my very soul—is it to be expected that, in the event of her remaining for some time single, her love for me will be diminished in proportion as her affection for you shall increase, or that, foster her affections for you as you may, she will love me in consequence less?"

"Decidedly not."

"If, then, her affection for her father would not interfere with her affection for her lover, why should her love for me after marriage interfere with her love for you? But waiving that point—for under the circumstances it is not the grand one—let us look at her feelings in the matter without reference to our own. She leaves Raven, whom from infancy she had looked upon as her father, to live with you, who have been, up to this time, a stranger. Conceive what her feelings must be in such a position, while striving to transfer her affections from one to the other! Must it not be one of great embarrassment? Must she not feel awkward in the extreme? If so, why should she be placed in that position at all? I am perfectly sure that whatever feeling you may have of a selfish character—if I may in its mildest sense use the term—is so natural, that you cannot repudiate its entertainment; but I am also sure that you are inclined to study her feelings in preference to your own."

"In that you do me but justice," said Whitely.

"Do you not conceive, then," said Valentine, "that she would rather escape the position to which I have alluded than embrace it?—that she would rather—to speak plainly—be married, and then imbibe and fondly foster those feelings of affection for you gradually, than be compelled to wait until you have become satisfied that her affection as a child has been firmly established? Which do you think she would prefer?"

"Why, I must confess," replied Whitely, "that I think she would prefer entering into the marriage state at once. I must say that under the circumstances it would be but natural for her to give that the preference."

"But independently of that," continued Valentine, "as a matter of expediency, I would urge the adoption of this course, without the fear of being regarded as an advocate pleading for myself. Your great immediate object is of course to gain the affections of Louise. Very well. How would you proceed to accomplish this object? Is it easier or more effectually to be done by opposing *in limine* that step in which she believes that her happiness is involved, than by allowing that step to be taken, and thereby proving not only that you have her happiness at heart, but that you are willing to sacrifice your own strictly personal feelings with a view to promote it? Will you not, by giving your consent, be laying the foundation of her love?—in other words, will she not rather love you for giving that consent than for withholding it? I do not mean to say that I believe for one moment that your opposition would have the effect of engendering in her mind any species of dislike, but I do think that, as matters now stand, the surest and the speediest way to win her affections is by giving your consent. It will strike her at once as being an act of kindness: it will prove to her that your great object is to see her happy: it will force the conviction that you fondly love her, and will thereby inspire her with fond love for you."

"I am inclined to agree with you," said Whitely; "I am quite inclined to agree with you. You have put it very forcibly and very correctly. I did not see it in that light before. Having set her mind upon marriage, certainly my consent would be more pleasurable than my opposition, however mildly, or with whatever arguments it might be urged. There is no absolute necessity for any farther delay: that is quite clear; and as by withholding my consent I now perceive that I should be studying my own feelings alone, it shall not be withheld. I give it freely. I have so much confidence in you that I will willingly accede to whatever you may propose. She has had, poor girl, sufficient trouble already. I feel now that I ought not to disappoint her in this matter again. Let the day be named—no matter how early—you will meet with no opposition from me."

"I felt certain," said Valentine, "that I should induce you to take this view of the matter, but I am not on that account less happy in having succeeded."

"Upon my life, though," observed Uncle John, "I didn't see it in that point of view: much as I desired the settlement of this affair, I thought that another delay of a few months must have taken place, as a matter of course."

"That was certainly my impression," rejoined Whitely, "but I perceive the force and justice of Valentine's observations, and I therefore need not ask if Louise is—I will not say anxious, but willing for the marriage to take place immediately."

"Oh!" cried Uncle John, playfully, "they have settled it between them, there is no doubt of that. It was all arranged, my friend, before we knew a word about the matter."

"As far as the consent of Louise is concerned," said Valentine, "it certainly was: after much persuasion on my part—for I had far more difficulty with her than I have had with you; Louise did consent, but only on the condition that I succeeded in obtaining the consent of her father."

"*Did* she make that a *sine qua non?*" inquired Whitely, with much feeling.

"Indeed she did; and urged it with great earnestness."

"God bless her! God bless her!" exclaimed Whitely, with a broken voice, as the tears sparkled in his eyes, "God bless her!"

"She is a jewel," said Uncle John, "a jewel! you are a happy fellow, Val—a happy fellow."

"I believe him to be worthy of her," said Whitely; "I am sure of it. Well," he continued, addressing Valentine, "and when is the day to be?"

"Why, as the fifteenth was fixed before the secret was revealed, I thought it would be as well not to alter the day. I therefore propose that the ceremony take place on the fifteenth."

"Well, be it so, I have no objection to urge. The fifteenth will soon be here, but the sooner the better, perhaps. Let it be the fifteenth. I have, however, one stipulation to make: she must not marry from the house of that man."

"Of course not," said Valentine, "I anticipated that, and have arranged it in my own mind thus: that on the morning of the fourteenth, she leaves Raven's house with my mother to take up her abode here; that we dine here together on that day, and that the next morning you accompany her from here to church."

"That will do!" said Whitely, "that will do. I quite approve of that arrangement; it will do very well."

It was accordingly thus settled, and immediately after the settlement had taken place, Fred returned in high glee. Louise had introduced him to Miss Lovelace, a young lady who was to be one of the bridesmaids, and of all the most peautiful cirls he had ever seen in the worlt, with the single exception of little sister Louey, she was the most peautiful, and cootness knew it!

This, of course, was quite sufficient for Valentine to go on with. He seized it with avidity, and rallied poor Fred in a style which produced roars of laughter. He assailed him at every point, and Fred met him in a manner too droll to be resisted. He again and again declared that he felt himself in love, and didn't care if the whole world knew it! Thus the remainder of the evening was spent very merrily, and at eleven they all left the house much delighted.

Valentine, however, was determined to communicate to Louise the pleasing result of his consultation with Whitely, without delay. He had therefore no sooner seen Whitely and Uncle John home, than he walked with Fred to Raven's, and found that Louise had been expecting his arrival, her heart having told her that, however late it might be, when the party broke up he would call. When, therefore, he entered the drawing-room, she flew to meet him, and with a look of intense anxiety, read the expression of success in his countenance, and was happy.

"Why do you look so intently at me?" inquired Valentine. "Is it to see if I have been taking too much wine?"

"No," replied Louise, with a playful movement of her head. "It is not that. You know why I look at you so earnestly. You know that it is to read that which I feel that I do read, the fact of my father having given his consent. It is so, is it not?"

"My dearest girl, it is," said Valentine, who then sat beside her and explained to her all he deemed it necessary for her to know, and having impressed upon her how worthy Whitely was of her affection, he drew one picture of happiness, and left another behind him.

It was then past twelve; but as the night was calm though dark, he decided on walking home, notwithstanding he knew that Uncle John would not retire till he returned. He had scarcely, however, left the house, when an emaciated form with an aspect of madness, hurried past him muttering incoherently to himself, and then suddenly stopped, and then hurried on again, and then again stopped, and turned, and then again hurried on, alternately laughing and groaning.

Valentine, when the form turned, felt a sudden thrill. He had certainly seen that figure before! who could it possibly be! Resolved on being satisfied, he quickened his pace. Again the figure stopped. He passed it, and on reaching the next lamp, turned, that the light by falling upon the face of the man, might aid him in discovering who he was. The form came on, groaning and gnashing his teeth as before, and on reaching the lamp stopped again, as if struck. The light fell full upon him; it was Walter!—mad; obviously mad! His sunken eyes glared, and he looked like a fiend.

"Just Heaven!" thought Valentine. "This, indeed, is a dreadful retribution!—Do you not know me?" said he, addressing Walter, and taking his arm.

"You can't prove it!" cried Walter, fixing his eyes upon Valentine, wildly. "You have no proof. I must be acquitted. I did *not* murder him!—let me go."

"Do you not remember Valentine?"

"Yes! he was the cause! the only cause!—I know him: I know him."

"He is here: he stands before you: I am he."

Walter again glared upon him, and seized his arm, and having passed his hand over his eyes several times, shook his head, and said, "No—no—no. You are not! Let me go home!—home."

"I'll go with you," said Valentine. "Tell me where you live."

"I told you before. Let me go. I must not be detained. You have no proof, I tell you! Ha, ha! No proof!—no proof! Do your worst! No proof!—I'll *not* be detained!"

Having suddenly disengaged his arm from Valentine's grasp, he hurried on, still muttering wildly to himself, and occasionally giving a maniacal chuckle.

Valentine now scarcely knew how to act; should he give him in charge of the police, or follow him? He had spoken of home. He might then be going home. Valentine knew not at all where he lived, but eventually decided on allowing him to proceed without interruption, resolved, however, not to lose sight of him until he should enter some house. He accordingly kept a few paces behind him, but in order to do so, he was compelled to walk as fast as he possibly could, and sometimes, indeed, to run, for Walter's pace could not have been much less than six miles an hour.

On reaching Bloomsbury Square, Walter suddenly stopped, but as on turning sharply round, he saw Valentine approaching, he kept on, and got into Holborn, where he increased his speed, being evidently anxious to avoid all pursuit. Valentine, however, kept up with him, marvelling at the extraordinary strength he displayed, and expecting every moment, of course, that he would either turn or stop at some house; but he still kept on and on, until he reached the bottom of Holborn-Hill, when he turned up Farringdon Street, muttering and laughing, and clenching his fists, and striking out with increased energy.

"Well," thought Valentine, who began to feel fatigued, "it is impossible for him to keep on at this rate much longer," when, conceiving that the fact of his keeping behind him, might accelerate his pace, and perhaps, deter him from going in even when he reached home, he crossed the street and walked on the opposite side.

Still Walter kept on. He passed Fleet Street, and when he had done so, he looked sharply round, and as he could perceive no one behind him he slackened his pace, but stopped not until he had arrived at Chatham Place, where he made a dead stand, fixing his eyes upon the ground, dropping his hands listlessly, and muttering aloud. Having stood in this position for some few moments without raising his eyes, he suddenly started off again, and proceeded over the bridge at a rapid rate, apparently most anxious to get home. Just, however, as he had reached the centre arch of the bridge, he turned into one of the recesses and leaped upon the seat. In an instant Valentine flew towards him, and called to him by name! The wretched maniac heard him, but uttering a dreadful yell of defiance, sprang over the balustrade, and Valentine but reached the spot in time to hear the water opening to receive him with a roar.

How was it possible to aid him? How could he be saved? "Police! Police! Help! help!" shouted Valentine, darting to the stairs, and a person on the instant ran towards him.

"A gentleman has thrown himself from the bridge," cried Valentine. "How can we save him?"

"I fear we can render him no assistance," said the stranger. "There's no waterman near."

Valentine rushed down the steps, and the stranger followed. The tide was running down; it was nearly low water: every boat was aground, and nothing could be seen moving upon the river within hail.

"What—what can we do?" exclaimed Valentine.

"Nothing!" replied the stranger. "Nothing: nothing can be done! He's lost."

The tide glided smoothly on. Scarcely a ripple could be seen. Once Valentine saw, or imagined he saw, the head of a man rise above the surface, but in an instant it disappeared, and was seen no more.

Still he lingered at the water's edge, his eyes fixed upon the stream, while dwelling upon the frightful catastrophe, almost in a state of unconsciousness, until the stranger aroused him, when, with a heavy heart he proceeded home, and by relating the sad event filled the mind of his uncle with horror.

CHAPTER LXVIII.

IN WHICH THE HISTORY DRAWS TO A CONCLUSION.

NEARLY the whole of the following day, Valentine was endeavouring to ascertain if the body of Walter had been found; but his efforts were unsuccessful. He took a boat at the Tower Stairs, and was rowed a considerable distance down the river, stopping to make inquiries at every point, but could hear nothing of him; nor could he communicate with his family, not knowing where they resided. He could, therefore, do nothing; and although he strongly felt that it would have been better had he arrested Walter's progress on perceiving his madness, and placed him at once under restraint, he could not reproach himself under the circumstances, seeing that he had done that which at the time appeared to him to be most advisable; still the dreadful event made a deep impression on his mind.

From Louise, of course, this was concealed. Whitely was informed of it, but it went no farther: the preparations for the marriage, therefore, proceeded as if nothing of the kind had occurred, and Valentine, in the presence of Louise, appeared to be as gay as before.

As Raven had been informed of its having been decided that Louise should leave his house the day previously to that of her marriage, his spirits now became more than ever depressed. He was indeed a wretched being. He felt that, although in the midst of wealth and splendour, he should be thenceforth alone in the world without a child to love him,—without a friend to esteem him,—without a single creature near him with whom he cared to associate; excluded from all society—an outcast.

Sometimes he would shut himself up in his room for hours, and seek relief in tears; sometimes he would bitterly rail at the world; at others he would sit and gaze upon Louise with all the fondness of a father, for that he loved her dearly no doubt could exist. To him this parting was a heavy blow indeed. It blasted every prospect, withered every earthly hope; not a flower could he perceive in his path from thence to the grave.

As the day of parting approached, his wretchedness increased, and when the thirteenth arrived, he sent to beg of Uncle John to look in upon him if even it were but for a quarter of an hour.

Uncle John went accordingly the moment he received the message, and found him dreadfully dejected. His eyes were dim and half closed; his cheeks were hollow, and his lips livid; he was spiritless, nerveless: Despair seemed to have marked him for her own.

"My friend," said he, "if I may still call you so, I am a miserable man. I cannot bear to part for ever with her whom from infancy I have reared, loved, and cherished as my own. I am childless, friendless, helpless. I have been actively battling for more than half a century with the world, but my spirits never deserted me, my strength never failed me, till now. *What* am I to do, my friend? Give me your advice."

"Why, upon my life," said Uncle John, "I don't see what advice I can give you, unless, indeed, it be to raise your spirits, and to bear up against the calamity."

"Which is precisely what I feel that I can't do. I seem to have no moral strength, no courage, no nerve, as if I were the only man in the world by whom a wrong had been inflicted. Other men can commit crimes, and think comparatively nothing of it. The fact does not afflict them; they are not bowed to the earth by the reflection; they can stand erect, and bid the world defiance: yet I, who in a moment of passion, folly, phrenzy—call it what you will—committed an act of which thousands upon thousands around me have been guilty, am thus struck down and tortured."

"It must not be imagined," observed Uncle John, "that he who, having committed a criminal act, braves the world, is not afflicted. He may feel it the more, for that feeling is usually most acute which a man takes most pains to conceal. I hold it to be impossible for any man capable of reflection in its popular sense, to inflict any serious injury upon another, or to commit any crime, which in his heart he acknowledges to be a crime, without being afflicted. Some men may show it more than others, but that is *no* proof that others feel it less."

"Well, but my friend—now—do you—Oh! I remember the time when my pride would have swelled, when my heart would have revolted at the idea of asking any man's forgiveness; but my spirit is now so subdued, I am now so humble, that if you think that he whom I have injured would forgive me, I would solicit his forgiveness—aye, even on my knees."

"Why, as far as his forgiveness is concerned," said Uncle John, pausing—"But what do you mean by forgiveness? As Christians, we are taught to pray for forgiveness of our trespasses '*as* we forgive them that trespass against us;' but the forgiveness which we pray for is so perfect that it comprehends reception and reconciliation. Do you mean by forgiveness, in this case, reception and reconciliation?"

"I would willingly give all I possess in the world to be thus forgiven by that man!"

"You mean, of course, for him to be reconciled to you, to associate with you, to receive you as a friend?"

"I do."

Uncle John shook his head with a very, very doubtful expression.

"You think it impossible?" said Raven.

"Most certainly I do. I have heard of men, who, actuated by the vilest and most sordid motives, have received and associated with the seducers of their wives, but I never heard of a virtuous man becoming reconciled to, or receiving him, by whom the wife of his bosom had been corrupted. Inasmuch, therefore, as I feel that Whitely loved his wife, fondly, passionately loved her, and as I know him to be a strictly honourable man, I do think it impossible, utterly impossible, to prevail upon him to receive you now as a friend."

"I am satisfied," said Raven, "quite satisfied now. But without such a reconciliation on his part, might I not be allowed occasionally to visit his children?"

"Why, that may be managed. It may be managed without any formal consent on his part. He will not be always with them."

"You see, my friend, I know that you see and understand the position in which I am placed. I have studiously kept aloof from all society: I am a man of no family: I have not, to my knowledge, a single relative in the world. I have formed no connections, no friendships: I have not a single creature to care for me with the exception of yourself, Valentine, Fred, and Louise: there is, it is true, one besides whose favour I would conciliate—I mean Valentine's mother, but I feel that I must not think of that. If therefore you desert me, if I am henceforth deprived of your society, and that of those with whom you are connected, the world will be to me a perfect wilderness; I shall indeed be alone."

"You speak like a man without hope," said Uncle John. "You will not be deserted. I will not desert you: Valentine will not desert you: nor is it at all likely that you will be deserted by Louise, whom you have treated with so much kindness and affection."

"My friend—and you have proved yourself to be a friend indeed—we are all fallible: not that I wish to shield myself under this general proposition; but we are all of us occasionally led into temptations, which we feel at the time to be too strong to be resisted. This was my case, at the period from which the birth of all my troubles may be dated; I yielded to the temptation into which I had been led; but although I cannot expect, that he whom, by thus yielding, I wronged, will so perfectly forgive me as to receive me as a friend, I do think that—having proved that I am not only sorry for having acted as I have done, but anxious to make all possible reparation—others may without dishonour."

"I would rather," said Uncle John, "associate with a man, who, like you, not only feels, but acknowledges that he is sorry for having committed an offence, than with one who treats that offence with levity, and affects to hold the opinion of the world in contempt."

"Then will you come often and see me, notwithstanding what has occurred?"

"I will," replied Uncle John.

"You will come and dine with me?"

"Frequently. I think of living entirely in town now."

"I am very glad to hear it. I think I need not say that I shall be at all times most happy to see you. When my poor girl is gone, I shall feel, I well know that I shall feel very wretched."

"Come, come, you must bear up against it."

"I will as well as I possibly can, but this is a dreadful position for an old man like me to be placed in."

"Well, well: we must make the best we can of it. These things always seem to be greater in anticipation. You will feel it no doubt; but we must endeavour to let you feel it as little as possible."

"My dear friend; I have no right to expect this kindness from you."

"Yes you have: you have a right to expect kindness from every man, who professes to be your friend. But let us say no more about it. Although we cannot do all, something may be done, and you may rest assured of this, that all I can do I will."

Raven, whose spirit was indeed subdued, again and again thanked him, and the gratitude which he warmly expressed was unfeigned. He did feel grateful to him, very, very grateful, for the loneliness of his position pressed heavily upon his heart, and none appreciate kindness so highly as those whom society in general spurns. An act of friendship then, shines forth as an act of friendship indeed. The veriest wretch feels it: it strikes to his heart's core: he would fly through fire and water to protect or to serve him who treats him with common kindness, when he feels that he is treated by all but him with scorn, or who extends the hand of friendship when all other friends are gone.

The conduct of Uncle John may, in this particular instance, be by some rigid moralists condemned; but let those who would condemn him point out what save penitence can be offered for injuries which cannot be redressed: and if, on discovering their inability to do this, they still condemn him, they must deny that that Heavenly attribute, Charity, ought ever to enter the soul of a just man.

He viewed the crime of which Raven had

been guilty—and none could have had a greater horror of that crime than he had *per se*—with due reference to the proverbial fallibility of man's nature: nothing could have induced him to palliate that crime; but, although he regarded it not alone as a personal offence, but also as an offence against society in the aggregate—when he saw Raven spiritless, bowed to the very earth, and broken-hearted, he would not *trample* upon him: no!—prompted by the voice of nature, he extended his hand to raise him, with those charitable feelings which he felt that he could not repudiate either as a Christian or as a man.

But notwithstanding he thus benevolently sought to inspire him with sufficient strength to bear the pang of parting with Louise, Raven was still much dejected. He felt indeed, greatly relieved while Uncle John was with him, but when he had left, he sank again beneath the dread of the morrow, and when the morrow came, it found him as wretched as before.

Having passed a restless, miserable night, he rose early, and tried to raise his spirits, but in vain: on being summoned to breakfast he burst into tears.

Louise, who as usual presided at the table, rose to meet him as he entered the room, when he took her hands and pressed them, and gazed upon her mournfully, and kissed her pale brow, and gazed upon her again; but neither uttered a word: their hearts were too full to speak; they sat down in silence, and scarcely, during the time they were at breakfast, was that silence broken.

Fred, who like the rest, felt miserable, was the first to leave the table, and soon after him Louise and the widow retired, leaving Raven in sadness alone.

"With whom shall I breakfast to-morrow," thought he, "and to-morrow, and to-morrow? Henceforth I shall be desolate. What comfort, what joy can I hope for now? This, twenty years since, or even ten, I might have borne: I had energy then—spirit—nerve: I could have struggled with it then; but to be left thus now in the vale of years, when I most need the comfort which those whom I have cherished alone can impart, when my faculties, both moral and physical, are withering, when I am sinking, fast sinking into the grave, is—just, just; I admit it to be just, but—dreadful."

Pursuing this sad train of thought, he sat weeping like a child—for all his manhood seemed to have left him—until the clock struck twelve, when he started up, and paced the room, trembling with violence.

It was the hour appointed for the departure of Louise, and soon afterwards she entered the room to take leave, accompanied by Fred and the widow.

"I know, my dear child," said he, with a tremulous voice, as she approached him in tears, "I know—your object—in coming to me now. It is—it is—yes—I am getting, my dear child, a feeble old man—bowed down—bowed down by affliction—Well, well—the grave—the cold grave—God forgive me!—God forgive me!"

"Father!" exclaimed Louise, passionately, "if you are not my father, I feel that you have been to me all that a father should be—for mercy's sake, do not—do not—father!" she added, falling upon his neck, "my heart will break."

"My child!" exclaimed Raven, whose utterance was half-choked, while tears of agony gushed from his eyes—"my sweetest, loveliest child, *you* must not be unhappy! Wretchedness is mine—I alone must be wretched! The only comfort, the *only* comfort I can hope for now is to see *you* happy—to see you happy! You will not deprive me of that!—No, you will not—*Bless* you! Come—come," he continued, albeit scarcely able to articulate a word, "come: to-morrow, you know, to-morrow! You only leave this for a happier home! But you will not forget me? You will think of me sometimes? You will not forget him who loved you from childhood so fondly, so dearly?—You will not despise me? No, *you* will not despise me?"

"Never!" exclaimed Louise, fixing her eyes earnestly upon him, although they swam in tears; "my heart tells me that, whatever may have happened, whatever may occur, I can never despise, I can never forget, I can never cease to love him by whom from my infancy I have been treated with so much affection."

Again Raven blessed her, and pressed her to his heart, and endeavoured to cheer her, although tears were trickling fast down his cheeks, and he continued to sob bitterly.

"I'll no longer afflict you, my loveliest girl," said he.—"No! I'll no longer afflict you. This parting is sad, *very* sad. You would say farewell to me: yes, farewell you would say: it may be the last—the last time. I am sinking, I know I am sinking; my strength has deserted me; I am getting very feeble; I shall not survive it long: no, I feel that I can't survive it long—*But*," he added emphatically, raising his eyes with great fervour of expression, "in the midst of my affliction I have one comfort, one consolation, which is, that whatever I may have been, whatever I am now, I have done towards her of whom I am now to be deprived all that a parent could conceive to be his duty to a child, and that she leaves me now with a heart as guileless and a mind as pure as when in infancy I fondly adopted her as my own."

At this moment a coach drew up to the door, and Fred—who had been standing at the window, apparently firm as a rock, while engaged in closing his eyelids as his eyes became full, that the tears might fall straight upon the carpet unseen—announced Valentine's arrival. Raven took Fred's hand, and pressed it warmly, and then drew Louise aside.

"My dear girl," said he, producing a small pocket-book, and placing it in her hand, "before you leave me, my love, take this: give it to Valentine. He will take care of it for you; but promise me—it may be my last request, Louise—yes, my dear, it may be my last—promise me that you will not name it to your father. I know that you will not refuse to take it—for my sake—I know you will not; but it need not be mentioned to him, my dear: it *need* not. You promise?"

"I do," replied Louise, "I do."

"God bless you, my child!—God bless you! And now," he added in broken accents, as Valentine entered, "farewell!—farewell! Be happy! May Heaven protect you all!"—when, placing Louise in the arms of Valentine, he turned and sobbing aloud left the room.

His utter prostration of spirit touched them nearly. Even Valentine was deeply affected; but as upon him devolved the task of restoring them all, his feelings were studiously concealed. He assumed an air not of gaiety, but of calmness; and as he felt that the sooner they left then the better, he hastened their departure as much as strict delicacy could sanction, and soon succeeded in getting them into the coach. Here he allowed their feelings to have free vent. He did not attempt to check them; but on arriving at the house, he soon subdued them by explaining how ill they would accord with the feelings of Whitely, and how calculated to induce him to believe that Raven still held that place in their affections which ought to be occupied by him.

Louise saw at a glance the justice, as well as the expediency of acting upon this suggestion, which Valentine no sooner perceived than he began to talk in a livelier strain, and thus by degrees raised her spirits.

Having partaken of some refreshment, Louise and the widow, who were inseparable, left Valentine and Fred, playfully intimating that they hoped to have the honour of their company at six. Before, however, Louise left the room, she grave Valentine the pocket-book which Raven had presented to her, and having explained to him the promise she had given, told him to see when she was gone what it contained. He did so: it was the cover of a pocket-book merely; but he found therein twenty one-thousand pound-notes, and a packet, apparently of parchment, sealed and addressed to him, with instructions that the seal was not to be broken until after Raven's death.

"I scarcely know," thought Valentine, "that we ought to receive this; and yet, were we to return it, it would perhaps break his heart! Well, well, we shall see."

"Hur never tit!" cried Fred, as if he had that moment awakened from a dream. "As true as cootness!—Well, now, inteet, look you, really, ant, in truth, now: hur never—cootness knows it!"

"Did you speak?" inquired Valentine, as if he had not been quite positive about the matter.

"Hur was only thinking apout the treatful scene petween my uncle—that is, Mr. Raven—ant Louey. Hur titn't like to let them see me, although cootness knows it. Putt hur say, my poy, how tull he must pe now, without anypotty apout him! Hur wish he was coing to tine with us to-day, after all; hur too intect."

"Fred," said Valentine, "to-day you must on no account suffer his name to escape your lips."

"No, hur know, hur know!—it's only to you. Putt as true as hur'm alive, hur wish he was coing to tine with us."

"You would rather that he should dine with us than Miss Lovelace?"

"No, cootness, no: hur'd rather have her than five thousand Mr. Ravens. Putt is she coming, my poy?—is she coming?"

"She will dine with us, of course."

"Hur titn't know that, now. Inteet, then, hur titn't. Hur'm very clat you tolt me."

"Are you really in love with that girl, Fred?"

"Over het ant ears! Putt isn't she a peautiful creature?"

"She appears to be a very sweet girl. But I shall know more about her in the morning. I shall have to kiss her to-morrow, you know: all day long I shall be at it."

"Phot! kiss Miss Lovelace?"

"As the bridesmaid, of course."

"Is that the etiquette of the pusiness? If it is—oh! hur wish hur was you! Ant yet hur tont, pecause then hur shoot pe marriet to Louey, and shoot have to love nopotty pesites. Putt hur ton't think hur *coot* kiss Miss Lovelace! Hur think hur shoot plush too much, ant tremple. However, hur'm very clat you tolt me she was coming, pecause hur must co ant tress a little for tinner."

"Of course! That is indispensable. But will you first go with me?"

"Anyphere in the worlt!" replied Fred.

"Let us start, then," said Valentine; and they left the house at once, and proceeded to a jeweller's, where Valentine purchased several rings, but especially one which he was anxious for Louise to present to Whitely. They then called upon Uncle John, and while he was dressing, Valentine summoned the widow Smugman, and commissioned her to purchase a bride cake—the richest she could meet with—and an extraordinary quantity of white kid gloves, which were to be sent to the house forthwith; and when Uncle John considered himself sufficiently beautified to accompany them, they entered a coach, and drove round for Whitely, who was delighted with the idea of their calling for him under the circumstances, and joined them without delay.

On arriving at the house, they were received with much elegance by Louise, who introduced them to Miss Lovelace, the only stranger present; and then addressed herself almost exclusively to her father, whom she thereby made perfectly happy. Fred managed—he would have been indeed puzzled to tell how—but he did manage, to get to one of the windows with Miss Lovelace, and while Uncle John and the widow were on the sofa conversing about sundry domestic arrangements, Valentine was giving various instructions to the servants, but more especially for the cake to be produced in the event of its arriving in time for the dessert. He was however but a short time absent, and soon after his return to the drawing-room dinner was announced, when Whitely of course took Louise, and Valentine Miss Lovelace, which Fred thought particularly hard. He sat however next to her at table, which was a great consolation; but then he couldn't eat! He managed the soup very fairly; the wine too he managed: he also disposed of a little fish, but after that he had no more appetite than an infant. He could not tell at all what to make of it. He was more than half inclined to become alarmed. He did fancy at one time the breast of a chicken; but as it happened that on its being placed before him he caught the eyes of Miss Lovelace, the breast of the chicken remained untouched. He held *this* to be somewhere about the oddest thing in life; but that which he considered more particularly odd, was the fact that Miss Lovelace arranged it so that her eyes met his every moment. He had no idea that her immediate object was to give him every scope to take wine with her. No: that indeed was the very thing he was anxious to do, and he tried to do it several times; but the very moment her eyes were turned towards him with an encouraging expression, he *averted* his and looked extremely stupid. To his purely private feelings this was very distressing, while it was not very pleasant to Miss Lovelace, for she certainly did try very hard to give him courage, and thought it very odd that it should be without success. At length being quite out of patience, she gave the thing up, when he became more composed; still he never in his life made so frightful a dinner!—the quantity he consumed was really out of all character trifling: indeed so trifling, that when his appetite returned with the tranquillity of his mind, he cherished serious thoughts of temporary starvation until the cake was produced with the dessert—according to the instructions of Valentine, who conceived that while its production could not be very incorrect, as they were by themselves, it would at least have novelty to recommend it—when he fully made up for lost time by setting to work upon it with unexampled zest.

There was, however, one at the table whose enjoyment was superior to that of any other person present, and that was Whitely. His pleasure was of a peculiar character. He felt intensely happy: his felicity was tranquil, but his heart was filled with the truest, the purest delight. He addressed himself chiefly to Louise, with whom he felt more than ever charmed, and when she had retired, his burden was his child, whose name he appeared to be unable to pronounce without shedding tears of joy.

As they had all to be up early in the morning—ten being the hour appointed for the ceremony to take place—they sat but a short time over their wine. Nor did they remain long on rejoining the ladies. They all, indeed, seemed most unwilling to leave, for they all felt most happy; but certain considerations which had reference to the repose more especially of Louise, induced them to take their departure early, when Uncle John—suddenly recollecting that although the health of the bride and the bridegroom had been drunk, it had not been drunk properly—would have them all home with him, and with him they remained till past midnight.

In the morning at nine precisely, as had been previously arranged, Valentine and Uncle John—who had risen at half past five with the view of being in time—

called for Whitely and Fred, and then proceeded in the highest possible spirits to the house which contained the fair bride.

It has been said by some philosopher either ancient or modern, that a woman never looks so beautiful as on the morning of her marriage with him whom she loves; but as it seems perfectly unnecessary to say that which has been said perhaps several times before, it will in all probability, be sufficient to state that on this happy occasion Louise looked more lovely than ever. She was dressed with extreme neatness, and that very neatness imparted to her appearance an additional charm, while from her eye softly beamed fond affection, and she smiled with surpassing sweetness upon him by whom she knew that she was tenderly beloved.

"Well, now inteet," said Fred addressing Miss Lovelace, as Valentine and Louise were exchanging such terms of endearment as those which lovers in general under the same sweet circumstances are prone to exchange; "phot am hur to too, look you, phen hur'm in church? Hur've peen looking over the pusiness, but cootness knows hur can fint no instructions inteet neither for you nor for me, look you!—phot have we poth cot to too?"

"Why unfortunately," replied Miss Lovelace, as her merry eyes twinkled "we have to do nothing but to stand and look on."

"Tit you say unfortunately?" inquired Fred with much emphasis.

"Why—I think—yes—I'm quite inclined to believe that I did. But do you wish to have something to do?"

"Tecititly!—ant something to say."

"And so do I. What a remarkable coincidence! Suppose we insist upon having something to say!—suppose we are married at the same time!"

"Oh! apove all other—putt too you mean —cootness knows—*too* you really mean *that?*"

"Why"—said Miss Lovelace, archly hesitating—"not—exactly."

"Now that is too pat!—pecause if you tecititly tit, inteet the pusiness shoot pe tone!"

"Your politeness is conspicuous. I appreciate it, believe me. But I am strongly disposed to think, do you know, that if we defer *our* marriage it will perhaps—taking all things into consideration—be as well!"

"You are a very creat tease to me," said Fred, "ant cootness knows it. You first raise my hopes, ant then tash them to the crount."

Had Fred studied for a month to make a formal declaration, he could not more effectually have imparted to Miss Lovelace the knowledge of how matters stood. She however disdained, of course! to make it appear that she knew aught about it, and continued to address him in the most playful style, without apparently giving it a single thought that with her playfulness, she was dealing destruction to his peace.

The time for starting now arrived, and the carriages dashed up to the door, when Whitely took the hand of Louise, and having fondly embraced her, he blessed her with fervour and led her forth with pride.

On arriving at the church, Valentine saw a figure anxiously hurrying into one of the curtained pews near the altar. He merely caught a glimpse of that figure, but he knew it in an instant to be Raven. He was, however, silent on the subject, for as he alone had seen him, he was anxious of course, that to all besides, the fact of his presence should remain unknown.

Having been courteously received by the officiating minister, they proceeded to the altar, and the ceremony commenced, and during its progress the firmness of Louise never deserted her for an instant. Whitely shed tears, and so did the Widow and Uncle John: the eyes of Fred sparkled, and so did those of Miss Lovelace: but Louise was as firm as Valentine himself: her hand never trembled, her voice never faltered: the purity of her heart and mind sustained her, and both were as calm as they were pure.

The ceremony ended, they repaired to the vestry, but while at the altar Valentine frequently heard a deeply drawn sigh and a fervent response proceed from the pew which the broken-hearted Raven had entered. He would have gone to him willingly, had it been only to shake hands with him in silence, but as this was impossible without being observed, he tried to forget him and the agony which he knew he would that day especially have to endure, and so far he succeeded, that on leaving the church all his thoughts were fixed on his beautiful bride.

On their return they sat down to a sumptuous breakfast, and all felt inspired with gaiety and joy. Each dwelt upon how the others looked during the ceremony, but nothing was lauded so generally or so highly as the firmness and graceful deportment of Louise.

As the carriage had been ordered at twelve, to convey the bride and bridegroom, Miss Lovelace and the Widow, to Brighton —where, as originally proposed, the honeymoon was to be passed—the ladies immediately after breakfast retired to prepare for their journey, and thus occupied themselves in a transport of happiness until the hour appointed for their departure had arrived, when, after a most warm and affectionate adieu, they started with the understanding that Whitely, Uncle John, and Fred, should join them at Brighton on the morrow.

CHAPTER LXIX.

BRINGS THE HISTORY TO A CLOSE.

The life and adventures of Valentine as a ventriloquist may be said to have ended with his marriage. He did—for the pure gratification of Louise, whom he continued to love with the most affectionate warmth—indulge occasionally in the development of his power; but as he found that in proportion as the strength of his assumed voice increased, that of his natural voice diminished, he on all other occasions contented himself with a relation of the various scenes which his peculiar faculty had enabled him to produce, and never failed to excite by such relation the most uproarious mirth.

As a wife Louise was most devoted and most happy. Before marriage, words had passed between her and her Valentine indicative of the possession of a fiery disposition; but that fire—which is commonly kindled in those who have been petted and spoiled, who have been the kings or the queens of their immediate sphere, and who have neither known society beyond their own circle nor tasted affliction—was extinguished. She seemed to live upon his smiles: her highest aim was to make him happy. No frown ever gathered upon *her* fair brow; no word of reproof ever passed her lips. He gave her indeed but little cause for reproof; for while in him no vicious habits had been engendered, he had seen far too much of the world to be drawn by its dazzling ephemeral follies from the sphere of honour and permanent peace; but, independently of everything which might have been supposed to be a cause, she felt disinclined at all times to notice any slight accidental irregularity, which morbid minds are too prone to construe into neglect, and this disinclination was based upon the knowledge of that all-important matrimonial secret, that wives, to be happy, must study at all times the happiness of their husbands.

"Dear Valentine," she would say, "I know not whether all married people enjoy the felicity which we enjoy; but if, my love, they do, marriage in general must indeed be a delightful state of existence."

"It *is* in general a delightful state of existence," Valentine would reply; "but the felicity which we enjoy is experienced only by those who, like us, strive to promote each other's happiness. It is not every man, my Louise, that has a wife so devoted, so affectionate, as I have; but with all that affection, with all that devotion, I should not, I could not be happy, did I not believe that you were. Amiability, if even it be without fond affection, is a greater promoter of happiness, my love, than the fondest affection without amiability; but where a man has, as I have, a dear little wife, who developes, as you do, both, he must be—if, indeed, he can appreciate both—he must be as I am, happy indeed."

And thus they lived, devotedly attached to each other, cherishing reciprocal confidence and love.

Raven did not long survive the blow inflicted upon him by the loss of Louise. On the morning of her marriage, he returned home after the ceremony in a state of extreme wretchedness, and was in consequence, for several days, confined to his bed; but by virtue of great care and skilful treatment on the part of his physician, he rallied, and was no sooner enabled to get about again, than—in a letter, in which his whole history was condensed, and in which he again and again expressed his contrition for what had occurred between him and the wife of Whitely—he sent a formal proposition of marriage to Valentine's mother; declaring, in terms the most eloquent, that the remainder of his life should be proudly devoted to the pleasurable task of rendering her happiness complete.

The widow, on the receipt of this proposal, scarcely knew how to act. She consulted Uncle John; she consulted Valentine; she consulted Louise; but as from neither could she extort a single word of advice, she was compelled to fall back upon her own judgment, and the result of the deliberate exercise of that judgment was that she gracefully declined, on the sole specific ground of her having resolved not to marry again.

This refusal—although couched in the most delicate and elegant terms—was a death-blow to Raven. He never left the house alive after that. He considered his fate to be thereby sealed, and, as he ascribed it to the assumed fact of his being despised, he gave himself up to despair. While on his death-bed, he was frequently visited by Uncle John. Valentine, too, often saw him, and when on the point of dissolution, his spirit was cheered by the presence of Louise, whom he caressed with all the rapture he had strength to display. The delight, however, which her visit excited had the effect of accelerating his death. Almost immediately after her departure, he ceased to breathe, while in the act of praying that she might be blessed and protected for ever.

To Valentine he bequeathed the whole of his wealth, and although he had lived for many years in the most splendid affluence, so strictly had he kept aloof from all society, that had it not been for the mere sake of appearance, Valentine and his uncle were the only two persons by whom he would have been followed to the grave.

Nor did Whitely long survive him. The cruel treatment he had experienced while confined in the Asylum had so effectually undermined his constitution, that when the excitement which gave him an unnatural strength had subsided, he calmly and gradually sank. In his last moments, however, he had the joy of being attended by his children: he was happy in viewing their prospect of happiness, and thus he tranquilly died.

Soon after his death, Fred married Miss Lovelace, and goodness knew it. It was a long time before she would give her consent—although the affair had been to all intents and purposes settled at Brighton—but at length she really could not any longer withhold it: he was such an extremely good-natured soul!—he had so happy a disposition!—he was so attentive, so kind, so affectionate—so excessively affectionate!—so devoted! And they lived very happily together, and in the due course of time had a very fair family of children; but if the truth must be told—and the necessity for telling it may be fairly admitted—she most certainly did—albeit not much enamoured of equestrian exercises in general—ride the high horse in reality rough-shod over the proud pre-eminence of his position as a man. Sometimes he would attempt to reason with her on this special point; but in the vocal department she could beat him out of the field. He stood no chance at all with her there: competition was quite out of the question. He, notwithstanding, often thought that if she could only understand a little Welsh—that being the tongue in which he was able to express his sentiments with most eloquence—he should have a better prospect of success, and with this view he tried on various occasions, by divers strong arguments, to prevail upon her to learn that peculiarly euphonious and liquid language, but in vain; she had a horror of the "buzz" of it; she could not endure it: she pointedly declared that it set her teeth on edge, and he was therefore compelled to give it up. Still Fred was not unhappy—far, very far from it. He loved his little Caroline, and she loved him: neither would have been separated from the other for the world; but she would go occasionally to rather alarming lengths, with the view of establishing her ascendancy upon a sound substantial basis.

"Toes Louey," he inquired of Valentine, with a singular expression, in the early part of his matrimonial career, "toes Louey ever pounce apout, my poy, ant plow up, look you?"

"Never!" replied Valentine.

"Not phen you are with her alone?"

"Never! She is always the same gentle creature, always amiable, always calm."

"Well, inteet, then, cootness knows, Cary's not a pit like her. Hur ton't mean to say that she's anything pat, look you!—No, she's a coot cirl; at heart a very coot cirl inteet; putt hur must say that if she were a little more like Louey hur shoot like it all the petter."

"Why Caroline always appears to be very amiable and kind; and I am sure she is fond of you, Fred."

"So she is, my poy; yes, so she is! Ant she pehaves herself like a princess phen aproat; it's quite peautiful to pe with her; putt phen she gets home it is *not* inteet so peautiful!"

"What! does she scold, Fred?"

"Scolt! Hur pelieve you. Hur ton't wish to say a single wort against Cary, nor woot hur say a wort to any other creature preathing; putt if hur coot putt make her unterstant that it woot pe most tecitetly petter if she were always as milt as Louey, hur shoot like it, look you, apove all other things in the worlt!"

Fred however never did succeed in prevailing upon Caroline to understand *this.* His very inability to pronounce his b's formed an insuperable bar to his perfect success, although this was not so great a thing as might have been expected, for notwithstanding the existence of this bar she was very well considering, when she had her own way; but whenever he wished to have his, or offered the slightest opposition to her will, it beoame strictly necessary for him to look out.

They visited Valentine constantly. He

was poor Fred's adviser although he never interfered: Caroline needed no adviser; she found that she could manage matters very well without; but although they dined with Valentine, Louise, and Uncle John, twice and frequently three times a week, she never by any accident exhibited there the pre-eminence she had acquired, which made things pleasant to all, and thus year after year their social intercourse continued to be uninterrupted.

One morning, as Valentine and Louise, having sent the carriage on, were pursuing their way towards Pall Mall, their attention was attracted by an extraordinary looking cabman, who while bowing to them and smiling, and raising his hat, seemed to be in a state of general ecstasy. Valentine shook his head with a view of intimating to him that his services were not required; but the fellow—about whom there was a great deal of style, for his cravat was tied in the newest knot, and while he sported an imperial beneath his nether lip, an eye-glass appeared by the side of his badge—was not satisfied with this, but continued to smile and to raise his hat with unexampled grace, and at length drove up to them, when Valentine recognised him at once—it was Horace.

"What, Horace!" he cried, smiling with an expression of amazement.

"This is the dodge, sir: this is the dodge," observed Horace, "I hope you are in a state of salubrity. Haven't seen you for *several* generations."

"Why, how long have you been at this work?"

"A blessed six months come the seven-and-twentieth."

"Well, call upon me," said Valentine, giving his card, "we'll talk things over and see what can be done."

"*Let* me drive you home," said Horace. "*Do* let me drive you. I want a bit of felicity just at this time, and that will be about the thing. It's much better than pedestrianising over the stones. Besides it will make me happy."

"Well!" said Valentine, "be it so;" and when he and Louise had entered the cab, the horse dashed away in the highest style of which he was capable.

On arriving at the house—and they were not long doing the distance—Horace leaped from his seat with amazing alacrity, and performed one of the most *récherché* knocks upon record.

"Come in," said Valentine, on alighting; "the servant shall hold your horse."

"You are very polite," returned Horace, "but he never stirs without me, except upon the stand. But you may," he added, addressing the servant, and waving his hand with an air, "you may give an eye to the animal!"

"Now, then," said Valentine, when he and Horace had entered the parlour, "let us have a glass of wine. How are they all at home?"

"Polly is pretty salubrious," replied Horace, "but the old lady's no great things. She has never been able to get over the fact of the governor having walked into the water. You heard of that affair, I suppose?"

"Unhappily, I saw it."

"You did!"

"I happened to be on the bridge at the very time."

"What, did he leap off the bridge? How was it? Do tell me; we never could learn. All we know is, that he was picked up at Limehouse Hole, dead as—but how did it happen?"

Valentine explained, and with so much feeling, that he even drew tears from the eyes of Horace.

"After all," said Horace, when Valentine paused; "it's of no use for a man to go crooked in this world. Things are sure to come round; it's sure to come home to him; he's sure to be served out in some way. That property of uncle's—you know all about it?—What good did it do us? Why it flew like blessed chaff before the hurricane! Twenty shares in this dodge, fifty shares in that, and a hundred shares in the other: safe to turn up something out and out: safe! And so they did: they all turned up swindles, the dirtiest swindles, and thus the money was dodged away. The day on which we missed the old governor, an execution was in the house, and there were we without the money even to buy a leg of mutton. Of course every stick was walked off with the utmost regularity: we hadn't a bed to lie upon, nor a gridiron to cook a mutton chop. The governor was buried by the parish, because as we didn't happen to hear of it in time, we couldn't own him, so that expense was spared; but starvation looked us right full in the face, and starved we must have been beyond all dispute, had it not been that the old lady luckily had a whole mob of pawnbroker's tickets—for everything portable had been pledged—which tickets we gradually sold, and for a week or two managed to get a bellyfull of victuals with the proceeds. I endeavoured, of course, to obtain employment, but the fools to whom I applied made a point of setting up a loud laugh, as if they derived the most exalted satisfaction from the *idea!* I knocked several of them down, and got fined for the assault, but that was a luxury I was soon obliged to cut, for the fines walked into the tickets most amazingly! I was willing to do anything in the world, but was able to get nothing in the world to do. I tried it on at the wharfs: it was no go there: stronger men were standing about unemployed. I answered a lot of advertisements for clerks: no character, no recommendation. I tried to get a birth as a groom. 'How long did you live in your last place?' That settled it. I told them all as plainly as a man could speak that I'd do my very utmost and try all I knew. But no, the fools would not have me! What then was I to do? I would not come any felonification. I made up my mind to that, come what might; although it certainly was a very rotten position for a fellow to be placed in without twopence halfpenny in his pocket, and without a friend whom he could borrow twopence halfpenny of: for all those trumps whom I used to meet and treat with brandy-and-water cut me dead when I became a little seedy: it was wonderful how suddenly they became short-sighted: they could not see a bit beyond their noses: it was quite an epidemic amongst them, and I had some thoughts of applying to the opticians for employment, conceiving that the spectacle trade must of necessity be looking up; but then what did I know about the spectacle trade or any other trade? what did I know about anything? Nothing. Look at the way in which I was brought up! Train up a child in the way he should toddle—you know the rest, but what was I fit for? That's where I felt it! What could I do? I should not have cared if I alone had had to grub my way through it: I shouldn't have cared if I'd had no one to look to but myself. I'd have trotted into the Army if that had been all, or gone on board a man-of-war, or walked over to Australia or New Zealand, or any other uncultivated feature on the face of the earth. I'd have got a crust somewhere for myself; but there were the women!—what were they to do? That was the pull! I couldn't leave them! They suffered enough as it was, for I couldn't earn a penny, nor they couldn't earn a penny. They had strong thoughts at one time of taking in mangling, but we hadn't enough money to get a machine. We hadn't sufficient even to buy a board—'Mangling done here'—although that might have been advertised in chalk upon the shutter; but the machine was the thing; let them have tried all they knew, they couldn't have mangled without a machine. Nor would the washing dodge do, for they hadn't a tub, while there was not a creature under the canopy of heaven who would give them credit for a ha'porth of soap. I tried to raise money on my own personal security; but that was no go, they wouldn't have it, although I offered them anything per cent. And thus we went muddling on week after week and month after month,—I out from morning till night to get sufficient for a meal, and they at home more than half naked, praying for my success. Sometimes I took home a sixpence, but more frequently nothing. They knew the moment I entered whether I had anything for them or not. If I had, their eyes brightened up like brilliants as they kissed me; if not, they kissed me all the same, and I heard no complaint but that involved in a sigh, which they would have suppressed if they could."

"That was very sad, very sad, indeed," observed Valentine.

"Sad!" echoed Horace, "there, if you'll believe me, I was sometimes ready to go and crib a mutton-chop!—I was, indeed! And I should have done it frequently, when I saw them at home starving; I know I should; but that I had firmly resolved that as an act of dishonesty had brought us to that, I would never, while I lived, be engaged in another."

"And to that resolution you adhered?"

"I did, and ever will. I cannot have greater temptations than I have had, and I know now that I can resist them."

"But why did you not apply to me?"

"Pride was the first cause, inability the second. I was too proud to do so till everything was gone, and by that time you had left the house in which you used to live, and I suppose they thought you didn't want to be troubled with me at all, for I couldn't persuade them to give me your address."

"That was wrong of them; very, very wrong."

"Fortunately, however, soon after I called, which was not till every other hope was withered to a stalk, I managed to pick up a few sixpences by assisting the grooms to rub their horses down, and so on, which carried me for a long time over the ground, indeed until one of the grooms turned livery-stable keeper, when, fancying that I knew, perhaps, something about a horse,—and I flatter myself I do,—he did the handsome, and put me on a cab, which suits me very well, and I have been at it ever since, and the women are of course gathering together a little flesh again, although I don't suppose that the old lady will ever get over the governor's death. How ever he could dream of cutting out of the world in that way I can't for the life of me imagine."

"But of course you believe him to have been insane at the time?"

" Why, to tell you the truth, and its useless now to disguise it,—he was never in his right senses after that unblest kidnapping affair. His mind was always diseased, always wandering. His imagination was always on the rack. He was continually conjuring up some spectral nonsense, continually fancying that his brother stood before him. But that which hurt him more than all was the fact of the brother having left him the whole of his property precisely as if nothing had occurred. That was the thing; that was his real death-blow. After that he took to brandy, of which he drank enormous quantities, sufficient, I should say, in a week, to sew up a whole regiment of soldiers. But it never made him drunk! That was the most remarkable point of the compass. It made him mad, doubtless, and desperate in his speculations, for of all the extraordinary—there, I do firmly believe that if a company had been started for the restoration of rotten eggs, he would have taken a hundred shares at a premium. However, he is gone, and perhaps the less that is said of errors the better."

" Well," said Valentine, " touching your present position: you must be doing something better for yourself than driving a cab. Turn the thing over in your mind, and let me in a day or two see you again. If there be any kind of business into which you would like to enter, let me know, and if I see the slightest prospect of your being successful, I'll lend you sufficient money to commence with, and you shall undertake to return it to me when you grow rich. In the mean time," he continued, writing a cheque for a hundred pounds, " give this to your wife, and tell her to hope for better days."

For some time Horace looked as if unable to believe what he heard; but when Valentine shook hands with him, and gave him the cheque at the same time, his feelings of gratitude overcame him, and he burst into tears.

" I don't know what to say!" he cried at length.

" Say nothing," returned Valentine. " Let me see you again soon."

Horace wiped his eyes with the bow of his cravat, and prepared to depart; but before he left the room, he grasped Valentine's hand, and with the most intense earnestness and feeling, said, " In the names of my poor wife and mother I thank you."

Valentine frequently saw him after this. He assisted him in every possible way, and Horace lost no opportunity of evincing his gratitude. He purchased for him the lease of some livery-stables, which were a source of considerable emolument, and had the gratification of seeing him prosper by virtue of indefatigable zeal. And to Valentine—who gloried in acts of benevolence—it was a high gratification indeed. Being exceedingly wealthy, he had the power at his command to do an immense amount of good, and he never permitted an opportunity for the exercise of that power to escape him. The more happiness he imparted to others, the more happy he felt. He was esteemed by all who knew him: he was honoured, beloved. With his beautiful, devoted Louise, his sweet children, his good mother, and Uncle John—who was always in a state of rapture, and seldom, indeed, whether at home or abroad, without a child upon his knee—he continued to live in the purest enjoyment of health, wealth, honour, and peace.

THE END.

Lightning Source UK Ltd.
Milton Keynes UK
UKOW05f1954300417
300225UK00012B/228/P

9 781290 497565